WRITING WOMEN'S HISTORY

Writing Women's History
International Perspectives

Edited by Karen Offen, Ruth Roach Pierson and Jane Rendall
on behalf of
The International Federation for Research in Women's History

Indiana University Press
Bloomington and Indianapolis

Manufactured in Hong Kong

Library of Congress Cataloguing-in-Publication Data
Writing women's history: international perspectives / edited by Karen
Offen, Ruth Roach Pierson, and Jane Rendall on behalf of the
International Federation for Research in Women's History.
    p.   cm.
  Papers presented at the First Meeting of the International Federation
for Research in Women's History in July 1989 at Bellagio, Italy
    ISBN 0–253–34160–4. — ISBN 0–253–20651–0 (pbk.)
    1. Women—Historiography—Congresses.   I. Offen, Karen M.
II. Pierson, Ruth Roach.   III. Rendall, Jane.
IV. International Federation for Research in Women's History.
Meeting (1st : 1989 : Bellagio, Italy)
HQ1121.W96   1991
305.4'0722—dc20   90–49155

1 2 3 4 5   95 94 93 92 91

Any royalties generated by the sale of this book
will go toward supporting the future work of the
International Federation for Research in Women's History/
Fédération internationale pour la recherche de l'histoire des femmes

CONTENTS

Contents

ix

Acknowledgements

We wish, first of all, to acknowledge the financial support of the Rockefeller Foundation for the launching of the International Federation for Research in Women's History/Fédération internationale pour la recherche de l'histoire des femmes and for helping to defray, in part, the production costs of this book. We are particularly grateful to Alberta Arthurs, vice-president for the arts and humanities, and Susan Garfield, head of the Bellagio Conference Centre programmes, for their assistance and encouragement. We also thank the American Historical Association for its support and for expediting financial arrangements.

As editors of this volume, we are enormously indebted to the Ontario Institute for Studies in Education for giving considerable financial support to this project and to OISE's Department of History and Philosophy of Education for hosting preparation of the manuscript and production of the camera-ready copy. We especially wish to thank Margaret Brennan, Administrative Officer of the OISE Department of History and Philosophy, for her expert computerising of the entire text and management of its final formatting. We are awed that she accomplished all this while continuing to smile as the deadline approached, receded and approached again. Without her, the project would not have been possible. We are also grateful to Beth McAuley for her eagle-eyed proofreading and fine indexing skills.

Karen Offen extends her thanks to Mary Beth Norton, co-organiser of the Bellagio Conference, and to Natalie Zemon Davis and Carl Degler, past presidents of the American Historical Association, for crucial support at critical times as well as for their ongoing commitment to promoting women's history at the international level. She is grateful to the Marilyn Yalom Research Fund, of the Institute for Research on Women and Gender, Stanford University, for a timely grant-in-aid in support of California-based production expenses for this book. She also wishes to acknowledge the gracious assistance of staff members at the Institute, especially Dee Gustavson, Lorraine Macchello, and Sally Schroeder, for help with taking phone calls, handling the voluminous mail, and keeping the photocopy machine in good repair. She also thanks Christine Muelsch for her skillful translation from the German, Annette Lawson for making the telefax machine available, Catherine Offen for typing help, and George Offen for innumerable kindnesses and contributions above and beyond the call of duty.

Ruth Roach Pierson wishes to express her deep personal gratitude to Margaret Brennan for the many ways in which she facilitated the massive international communications, by mail, fax, and telephone, that this project entailed as well as for her unfailing commitment to the book's completion. She also wishes to thank Ria Bleumer for her speedy translations from the German, Dieter Misgeld for his patient answering of German translation questions, Jacinthe Michaud for her patient answering of French translation questions, Kathryn Morgan for help with clarifying philosophical distinctions, and Mary Nyquist for help with clarifying literary distinctions. Dwight Boyd also deserves thanks for his tolerance of the book's intrusions into Ruth's and his shared life.

Jane Rendall wishes to thank the University of York's switchboard operators, who have introduced her to the possibilities of the fax machine, and dealt so swiftly with so many communications. She would also like to thank Margaret Fraser for her informed translation from the Italian, Susan Mendus for philosophical information, Steve Paxton for his invaluable technical assistance, and Adam Middleton for his generous and continuing support, both technical and domestic, throughout the demands of this international project.

Finally, as co-editors, we wish to acknowledge the stimulation and pleasure of working with one another and with our many colleagues around the world to produce this book.

Karen Offen
Ruth Roach Pierson
Jane Rendall

December 1990

Foreword

Ida Blom

According to a Kenyan myth, at the beginning of time women founded the tribe system and acted as heads of tribes. These matriarchs ruled over men in a harsh and ruthless way; therefore, all the men got together to discuss how they could put an end to matriarchal tyranny. They decided that they had to make the women – all of them – unable to wield their authority just long enough for the men to carry out a successful revolt. They managed to do so by making the women pregnant all at the same time. While women were creating new life, men took over power in society; thus, it remained until the present day.

It is interesting to compare this myth to the legend within christianity of the origin of human life. According to this legend, God created man – Adam – in his own image. Later he created woman – Eve – from one of Adam's ribs. But Eve let herself be tempted to break one of the important rules in Paradise: she ate from the fruit of the tree of knowledge, and offered it also to Adam. Burdened with knowledge, guilty of breaking one of God's rules, Eve and Adam were driven out of Paradise. Adam was punished by having to earn his living by endless toil, Eve by being condemned to painful childbearing. In addition she would have to obey Adam in all things. 'He shall rule over you' was a formula read out to marrying couples in western cultures at least until around 1900.

Nothwithstanding their differences, these two myths have something in common. Women are seen as strong, but dangerous beings, responsible for continuing the tribe or humankind. In the Kenyan myth this responsibility becomes also women's weakness. In the christian legend, painful childbearing is part of a punishment for having wanted to obtain forbidden knowledge – and for sharing this knowledge with man. The other part of the punishment is that men are given the power over women.

Ida Blom

Myths and legends may mirror people's self-perceptions and their perceptions of others, and offer explanations of important structures in society. If our history was as simple as these myths, we might have saved ourselves many hours of wrestling with complicated theoretical problems of how to explain the importance and perseverance of gender differences. But we might also have reduced real life and the functioning of societies as well as of the historical sciences to very plain dimensions.

Fortunately, myths and legends also have the important effect of stimulating our desire to investigate the truth of their contents. Historians find that describing and explaining the realities of gender relations and of how societies function require complex research strategies and more sophisticated theories than stories of outright confrontation between women and men.

But some of the contents of the myths we may be wise to accept: women are resourceful, their reproductive capacities are important and they want knowledge; not least, knowledge of their own history. Following the example of Eve, we do not attempt to keep this knowledge to ourselves. We want to share it with each other and with other historians as well.

A five-day conference at the Rockefeller Foundation in Bellagio, Italy, in July 1989 was an important occasion for historians of women's history to do just that.

Most of the contributions to this volume were first presented at the Bellagio Conference. They illustrate that research in women's history is gradually entering a new phase. Based on solid knowledge acquired through studies at the local and national level, cross-cultural comparative studies have begun to appear, focusing on similarities and differences in women's past. The search for theories explaining gender hierarchies across cultural boundaries has led to critical questioning of western theories and awareness of the need to pay attention also to theories that may develop outside western academe.

The internationalisation of research on women's history has made it increasingly important to keep track of the latest developments all over the globe. Early knowledge of new research is stimulating research elsewhere, facilitating comparative cross-cultural studies.

The conference contributed vastly to the sharing of knowledge and building of cross-cultural networks between historians of women's history. Participants came from nineteen countries: Australia, Austria, Brazil, Canada, Denmark, the German Democratic Republic, the Federal Republic of Germany, Great Britain, India, Ireland, Japan, the Netherlands, Nigeria, Norway, Spain, Sweden, Switzerland, the United States of

America and Yugoslavia, and included also representatives of The International Commission on Historical Demography and the Société de Démographie Historique. They came to discuss theoretical and methodological problems pertaining to women's and gender history, and to analyse the state of historiography on women in each of the nineteen countries.

These historians represented the national committees and two demographic history organisations affiliated to the International Federation for Research in Women's History/Fédération International pour la Recherche de l'Histoire des Femmes, (IFRWH/FIRHF). Founded in April 1987, IFRWH/FIRHF was accepted in September 1987 as an Internal Commission of the International Committee of the Historical Sciences. This achievement was the result of long and tenacious efforts to build a network uniting historians of women's history worldwide. The aim of the IFRWH/FIRHF is to encourage and co-ordinate research in all aspects of women's history at the international level, by promoting exchange of information and publications, and by organising and assisting in arranging large-scale international conferences as well as more specialised meetings. The Bellagio Conference stimulated lively discussions lasting well into the night, and represents the first of what we intend as a series of conferences.

As will be seen from these contributions, and those that supplement them, approaches to and results of research into women's history around the world are rich and varied. They range from reports of pioneering excavations in the recovery of women's past to sophisticated theoretical analyses. They emphasise common ground as well as differences in perceptions of theory and methodology and illuminate the possibilities for feminist scholarship in history.

And above all, this initial gathering served to build and strengthen cross-cultural networks among historians of women's history, to open avenues for mutually inspiring exchanges of experiences and for cross-cultural learning processes. A solid foundation has been laid for future common efforts to foster and refine theoretical as well as empirical research on women's history in the spirit of truly cross-cultural understandings.

The IFRWH/FIRHF network, which encompasses all continents, will be maintained and extended by subsequent conferences. The first large-scale, conference has just taken place during the 17th International Congress of the Historical Sciences in Madrid, Spain, in August/ September 1990. On a smaller scale, several cross-cultural research projects have already been started, bringing together scholars working on common areas of interest within women's history. It is our hope that future

IFRWH/FIRHF publications will make the results of these conferences and projects known to a wider public.

We are proud and happy to launch this volume, a testament to the exciting possibilities for cross-cultural scholarship that lie ahead for the International Federation for Research in Women's History/Fédération Internationale pour la Recherche de l'Histoire des Femmes.

Ida Blom

Editorial Note

Each of these essays has been written from a particular national perspective (though in some cases also from a varied international experience); at the same time, each of them, though coming out of a national viewpoint, represents the point of view of the author(s) alone.

Some of these essays have been translated. Others have been written in English by contributors who are not native speakers. As editors, we acknowledge the peculiar imperialism of selecting one word rather than another, of imposing certain forms of punctuation over others, and of offering a particular rendering in English in an attempt to clarify the complexities (and sometimes the obscurities) of other authors' thoughts. We hope we have done justice to the insights of the writers; this has been our only intention. In the same spirit, we recognise our annoyance with the necessities of systematisation, of imposing an arbitrarily selected version of spelling and punctuation, though we believe the book reads better for the attention paid to consistency. The editors wish to thank the contributors for their patience with and tolerance of these impositions.

When the initial conference of IFRWH/FIRHF was held in July 1989, and during most of the period we were preparing this volume, there were two German states in existence, as indeed there had been for the past forty years. For this reason, two separate papers are included here. Throughout this book when we are referring to East Germany of the period 1949 to October 1990, we continue to speak of the German Democratic Republic. But because the two Germanys are now united within the Federal Republic of Germany, to avoid confusion we refer, except in titles, to the Federal Republic of pre-1990 as West Germany.

As the final contribution to the volume we have included an important and useful bibliography of books and articles, to some large extent published in the west, on east European and Slavic women's history. Since the development of women's history by historians within these countries is in its initial stages, and since the countries from this part of the world, with the exception of Yugoslavia, are not as yet represented in the Federation, this bibliography may serve to acquaint readers with the possibilities and prospects for future work.

An effort has been made in the footnotes to provide English translations of titles for all cited materials that have been published in languages other than English and French (the official languages of the International Federation for Research in Women's History/Fédération internationale pour la recherche de l'histoire des femmes). We have also provided, to the extent possible, full publication data on books.

Introduction

Karen Offen
Ruth Roach Pierson
Jane Rendall

The founding in 1987 of the International Federation for Research in Women's History/Fédération internationale pour la recherche de l'histoire des femmes (IFRWH/FIRHF) has made it possible to assess, cross-culturally and internationally, the state of the art of writing women's history. Once suppressed or simply ignored, the study of women's history has emerged during the last twenty years as an exciting, indeed ebullient, scholarly endeavour in many parts of the world. In this book, we have brought together essays by scholars from twenty-two countries to consider the achievements and trace the future trajectories of women's history from different national and cultural perspectives. Most of these contributions were first presented at the initial conference of IFRWH/FIRHF held in early July 1989 at the Rockefeller Foundation Conference Center in Bellagio, Italy.[1] Several others have been solicited especially for this volume.

Any consideration of the state of the art in such a new scholarly field cannot be separated from questions of differing national historiographical contexts and institutional infrastructures.[2] What has been the development of women's history in the various countries represented here? What have been the points of connection between the contemporary women's movement and the emergence of women's history as an academic discipline? Given the variations in infrastructure and funding possibilities for historical research, can generalisations be made about sociopolitical contexts across countries and cultures? What, for instance, is the relationship of this growing area of scholarship to established university programmes? to alternative teaching opportunities and curricular development in women's and feminist studies? Are there common theoretical concerns and issues? common methodological approaches or tools? How are women's historians in various settings responding to the call to recover women's history and to the challenges posed and opportunities opened up by postmodern theories for achieving new understandings of the complexity of women's pasts? In short, what can we learn from one another about the strategies and the practices of women's historians around the world – the scope of their enterprises, the depth and detail of their analyses, and the social meanings they are contesting or seeking to constitute through their historical writing?

Historiographical Contexts

The range of contexts in which research in women's history has emerged is wide indeed. Within that range, however, one feature surfaces as common to many contexts: the tremendous influence of the contemporary women's movement on kindling an interest in the history of women. Efi Avdela of Greece directly links the development of women's history, internationally, 'to the growth of the feminist movement'. Yvonne Hirdman writing on Sweden, Phyllis Stock-Morton on the USA, Jane Rendall on Great Britain and Ruth Roach Pierson on Canada all contend that the impetus behind the recent proliferation of women's history in their countries can be traced to the so-called 'second wave' of feminism. Aparna Basu cites 'the growth of an active women's movement' in India and the publication in 1974 of *Towards Equality*, the Report of the Committee on the Status of Women in India, as crucial factors in stimulating the development of women's history in her country. According to Cécile Dauphin et al., 'the explosion of the feminist movement' contributed to the real take-off of women's history in France in 1970. In Norway, Ingeborg Fløystad informs us, the first feminist groups that organised in the autumn of 1970 'created a demand for more knowledge of women's past lives'. In West Germany, too, 'the history of women arose in the context of the new, autonomous women's movement' of the 1970s. Even in Japan in the 1970s, according to Noriyo Hayakawa, 'women's history began to blossom' in the wake of women's 'increasing desire to analyse the roots of sexual discrimination'. Although somewhat later in coming and consequently as yet more limited in impact, the feminist impulse behind the emergence of women's history is also apparent in Andrea Feldman's Yugoslavia, Brigitte Mazohl-Wallnig's Austria, and Regina Wecker's Switzerland. Mary Cullen laments the fact, however, that, in Ireland, many historians are coming into the field of women's history with 'little understanding of the feminist origins' of the new field.

Introduction

In Australia, we learn from Patricia Grimshaw, it was only after feminists *outside* the academy began 'a massive revision of Australian history in the light of feminist theory' that writing women's history was taken up by academic historians. For Italy also, Paola Di Cori points to the extra-academic location of the initial production of women's history, 'within the feminist structures that typified the first half of the 1970s'. And Nanna Damsholt writes of the changing interest in women's history with regard to the maturing of the women's movement in Denmark. By now, in various parts of the world, the association between women's history and feminism is such that many researchers and writers of women's history refer to themselves as feminist historians.

In many countries, the contemporary history of women's history is inseparable from the history of the emergence of the multi-disciplinary field of women's studies, one of the most visible signs of the impact of feminism on the academy. In both the USA and Canada, women's history has frequently benefitted from its ties to women's studies, and the benefits have been reciprocal. In Austria, women's history is located within and nurtured by women's studies, not formally organised as an academic programme but informally embracing a whole range of scholarly activities focusing on women. In Spain, women's history has effectively spearheaded the development of women's studies, as the Centre d'Investigació Històrica de la Dona [Centre for Research on Women's History] has done in Barcelona; and among women's studies scholars in Sweden, too, 'women historians interested in women's history turned out to be in the majority'. In Brazil, in contrast, women's history has not been in the vanguard of the development of women's studies.

While the influence of contemporary feminism has rarely been negligible, the paths to women's history have been multiple. Some practitioners have come to it through explorations in social, economic, or labour history. Anne-Lise Head-König demonstrates the impossibility of arriving at 'a clear understanding of the position of women in European societies' without 'a close study of structural and cyclical economic and demographic situations'. In Brazil, where 'history' as a discipline exists in tension with a hegemonic (and male-dominated) historical sociology, the push for women's history has come through demographic history. Clearly marxism has exercised a strong influence not only in countries formerly within the 'eastern bloc' but also in a number of western countries, among them Sweden, Italy, and the Netherlands. In Great Britain, the key socialist journal *History Workshop* became, in 1982, in name as well as in practice, a journal of socialist *and* feminist historians. But socialist-feminist historians have also been critical of marxist theoretical traditions, pointing to the inadequacy, in the words of Yvonne Hirdman, 'of marxist ideology to explain and interpret the experiences of women's lives'.

As Paola Di Cori argues, 'the legacy and use of, as well as conflict with, different national historiographical traditions' and differing patterns of political development have also played a major part in shaping the specific concerns of women's history scholarship.[3] In the case of Spain, the tremendous upsurge of women's history is closely tied to and influenced by the renaissance in national historiography since the end of what Mary Nash has called the 'collective amnesia' fostered by the Franco regime. Within this monumental task of historical recuperation, the focus has been on 'public' or 'political' issues, impelling historians of women in Spain to search for feminist precursors in the labour and suffrage movements. In India many historians of women found their starting-point in the work of an earlier nationalist generation of historians. In France, the development of women's history has inescapably been in dialogue with cultural anthropology, the history of 'mentalités', and the history of social, cultural, and political representations. Women's historians in Nigeria, Bolanle Awe states, face the 'uphill task' confronting historians of Africa in general, namely that of 'eradicating the prejudices and misconceptions about the African past that have been perpetrated by many western writers'. In the former German Democratic Republic, the Communist Party line left no room for a women's movement and little space for women's history. Nevertheless, a few women and men in research institutes were able to investigate topics on women's history, though no university teaching was possible: this situation is now, in 1990, changing. In West Germany, women's history was strongly shaped by the impact of the student movement and the new left of the 1960s. Equally important have been attempts to deal with the burden of the National Socialist past in gender terms, including growing awareness of many women's consent to the Nazi government, and of the complicity of some with its crimes. The study of the female victims of such crimes – and particularly of Jewish women in the Holocaust – is only now beginning to attract the attention of women's historians.

Institutional Constraints and Ingenious Initiatives

Women's history in the USA is exceptional in the degree to which it has secured an institutional base in university and college curricula. The relative autonomy and flexibility enjoyed by institutions of higher education in the USA, as well as national prosperity and the strength women's historians have gained from numbers, have all contributed to this development. The Berkshire Conference on the History of Women, begun by women historians in 1973 and held every two years from 1974 to 1978 and every three years thereafter, now attracts hundreds of paper presenters and thousands of participants, rivalling in size the annual meetings of the American Historical Association and attesting to the extraordinary growth, energy, and following of the field. The Conference Group in Women's History regularly publishes a newsletter and provides a network for women's historians (while the Coordinating Committee on Women in the Historical Profession serves the broader constituency of women historians). The rapid growth of women's history in the United States, its powerful organisational base, and its sheer volume of publication have had an impact on the practice of women's history in almost every other nation represented in this book.

While largely positive, as many contributors to this volume attest, the overwhelming character of the US impact also poses problems for women's historians located elsewhere in the world. At the international level, the greater affluence and securer institutional base of women's historians from the USA, together with the hegemony of the English language, often threaten to overshadow other perspectives. Women's historians in Canada, for instance, sometimes feel caught between assimilation to theoretical models imported from the former mother country, Great Britain, and the unwitting cultural imperialism of their strong neighbour to the south. A recent Canadian-Nigerian workshop, Awe tells us, concluded in general that 'existing theories and methodologies from western experiences are extremely limited in accounting for the historical and cultural peculiarities of Nigerian societies'.

Although far thinner on the ground than women's historians in the USA, Canadian women's historians have also secured a foothold within the academic establishment. According to a 1989 survey, almost every department of history in Canada offers at least one women's history course.[4] A founding member of IFRWH/FIRHF, the Canadian Committee on Women's History, which was itself founded in 1975 and became an affiliated committee of the Canadian Historical Association in 1977, today boasts over 200 members. In 1984/85, a federal Liberal government allocated funds for five university chairs in women's studies in Canada but these have rarely been held by women's historians.

Far more formidable difficulties exist in other nations, both in terms of developing women's history within existing institutions and in terms of the political problems associated with centralised governmental control over educational institutions, whether administrative, financial, or both.

In several countries (such as West Germany, the Netherlands, Austria, and Japan) significant grass-roots efforts in women's history co-exist in a state of tension, and sometimes conflict, with the efforts of university-based researchers, who are suspected of elitism and co-optation to the establishment. In Austria, some women historians continue to organise outside existing academic and research institutions, even as others gain a foothold within. Austrian academic historians of women only recently founded a Society for Historical Women's Studies and in 1990 established a journal for feminist history entitled, not without intentional irony, *L'Homme: Zeitschrift für Feministische Geschichtswissenschaften* [Man: A Journal for Feminist Historical Sciences]. In West Germany some women historians distanced themselves from the academic establishment at an early stage, attempting to establish their own institutions, such as the Summer University in Berlin. But they are now reentering the universities as professors and assistants. Dutch women historians organised initially as students, and now have a national association of their own, working not only to influence university scholarship, but to develop popular interest in women's history through exhibitions, public lectures, and broad-based publications as well as through their own research. They have organised walking tours focused on women's history (as have the Austrians, and as the Swiss are about to do).

State centralisation can promote swift change, but can also throw up severe obstacles to curricular reform. Feminist historians in Denmark take pride in having helped to make the study of women's history a compulsory part of the curriculum in upper-secondary schools. In contrast, the centralisation of undergraduate university curricula in Spain and France has made the introduction of women's history extremely difficult. Consequently, in these countries, historians of women who do hold professorships have placed emphasis on developing women's history in the graduate research programmes, at the Master's or Third Cycle doctoral levels. In Nigeria as well, it has seemed more practicable to develop academic women's history at the graduate research level rather than for undergraduates. In Brazil, where women professors outnumber men in history departments, no curriculum decisions whatsoever are made at a departmental level. Centralised control of the national university curriculum has prevented women's history from being taught as such, even where interested women historians are clustered in teaching positions. In Greece, the university establishment has been so resistant to women's history that younger scholars have gone abroad to pursue advanced degrees with a women's history emphasis.

Introduction

A key issue in most countries is the presence (or absence) of women historians in senior university positions. In Great Britain, many of the leading practitioners of women's history find academic employment not in the major universities but in polytechnics and adult education programmes. In Ireland there are as yet no women in chairs in any university history department. In Yugoslavia, a combination of state ideology and centralisation have created problems. There women's history is just emerging as a focus among younger researchers, and until recently, as the late Lydia Sklevicky, a pioneer Yugoslav historian of women, remarked, there were 'more horses than women' in accounts of Yugoslav history.[5] Unfortunately, the women who currently occupy senior academic positions are uninterested in women's history.

In West Germany, there have been promising developments, but it is not yet all smooth sailing for women's history. There are three chairs with a specialisation in women's history or gender history, each occupied by a woman professor – Gisela Bock at the University of Bielefeld, Annette Kuhn at the University of Bonn, and Ute Frevert at the Free University of Berlin. Two other women professors work in women's and gender history, Karin Hausen at the Technical University of Berlin and Heide Wunder at the University of Kassel. An organised group of university-based German women's historians, including the five above, have been working for some time to effect a greater acceptance of women's history and of women historians by the profession. Bock returned to Germany in 1989 after four years in the Chair of Nineteenth and Twentieth Century European History at the European University Institute in Florence where she promoted women's studies in general and women's history in particular.[6]

In Austria, the first, and as yet only, chair in women's studies, established in 1988 at the University of Innsbruck, is a chair in 'political science with particular reference to women's studies'. In Switzerland, only four women hold chairs in history (out of a total of 45 chairs), but one of these, Beatrix Mesmer, actively supports other researchers in women's history and has herself contributed importantly to the field.

Women's history in Scandinavia has to date enjoyed considerable governmental support, including significant appropriations for research. Both the Swedish and Norwegian governments have established permanent university chairs in women's history, currently held by Ida Blom at Bergen and by Yvonne Hirdman at Gothenburg. In Denmark and in Sweden, however, women historians express concern about the 'greying' of the practitioners and about problems in recruiting the next generation of university-based women's historians.

In the Netherlands, no chairs exist in women's history, but historians of women have succeeded in obtaining appointments to non-permanent positions in every Dutch university except one. There women's history is part of both the secondary school and the university curriculum. And halfway around the world in India, although there are as yet no courses dedicated to women's history, there are women historians interested in women's history who hold senior positions. These women professors smuggle women's history into the curriculum by incorporating it into existing courses on the social history of India and the history of national movements. They also insert women's history into topics for papers and into examination questions.

The above survey of conditions raises the issue of the difficulties - and also the necessity - of sustaining a vision of women's history's importance in the face of institutional exclusion (or resistance) and complex political logistics. To those who argue that women's history is just another narrow specialty, we must reply that we are talking about the rich and varied past of over half the human race. Paradoxically, it has sometimes been precisely these difficulties - and this felt necessity - that have stimulated creative grass-roots initiatives for bringing women's history to a broader audience beyond the universities.

Women's historians, like all other historians, are inescapably dependent on their sources. Thus, a development of particular significance is the growth of archival and library collections in women's history in a variety of countries. Important collections include the women's history archives at the University of Gothenberg, Sweden; the Fawcett Library in London, England; the Bibliothèque Marguerite Durand in Paris, France; the Gosteli Foundation Archives for the history of the Swiss women's movement in Worblaufen, Switzerland; and the Archives of the International Women's Movement in Amsterdam, the Netherlands.[7] Denmark has also initiated efforts to establish collections, and, in Spain, plans are underway to survey and catalogue extant women's history materials in library collections in several major cities.

Microfilmed collections of older books, pamphlets, and periodicals,[8] as well as on-line computer access to new publications in women's history,[9] add to the reservoir of sources available for future research in women's history. Published collections of documents, especially those by little-known women,[10] as well as carefully-edited bibliographical studies,[11] help to provide access to women's impressively varied pasts in many cultural settings. Similar collections of source materials should be encouraged and funding found for such enterprises in other countries as well as for the development of new types of sources, such as oral histories, for more recent times.

In most countries, funding possibilities for women's history - or for academic research in general - from the private sector and foundations seem to be minimal. A notable exception exists in Brazil, where the Carlos Chagas Foundation has been a particularly important supporter of the development of women's history, underwriting both conferences and publications. Support for our own new federation from the Rockefeller Foundation has proved decisive in its infancy, but there is a real need to insist on the necessity of support from other private sources as we attempt to put the Federation and its activities on a solid footing.

With respect to public sector support, of course, the situation varies greatly. In some parts of the world, women's history initiatives, for research and for conferences, have received state support - from the Norwegian Research Council, for example. Women's history efforts in Sweden also enjoy sustained governmental support. In India, money began to flow to women's history research when a sympathetic woman professor who was vice-chancellor of the largest women's university became head of the university grants committee for all Indian universities; as a result, seven universities have now government-funded women's studies centres. However, the project of women's history in many of the countries represented in this book, among them Great Britain, Australia, Denmark, and Canada, suffers from state financial retrenchment policies, including varying degrees of cutbacks in funding to higher education. In Nigeria, Brazil and Yugoslavia, women's history efforts are inevitably adversely affected by the chronic economic problems plaguing these countries, as are scholarly endeavours in the arts, humanities, and social sciences more generally.

Scholars in women's history are acutely aware of the importance of international scholarly exchanges for stimulating the development of women's history in their own countries. The importance of obtaining funding for such exchanges in women's history is a matter that the Federation would like to be able to address. Historians of women may be no more disadvantaged than other historians in this respect, but this fact does not diminish the need actively to seek such support in order that we can learn from one another in this rapidly growing new field of knowledge.

Parameters of Scholarship in Women's History

What can be said of the range and scope of current research in women's history worldwide? How can we assess its comparative development? Here we will first remark on the territorial and chronological patterns, followed by a consideration of emerging thematic and theoretical issues.

In general, most historians of women are researching and writing about the experiences of women and the construction of gender in their own countries or territories. Edited collections with a national base, along with special issues of scholarly journals with such a national focus, have often provided the first scholarly publication opportunities in women's history as this area of research begins to be developed. Such collections, along with journals dedicated to women's history, provide access to the latest research, and their importance cannot be overestimated.[12] International or multinational collections based on a theme, with an international or multinational authorship, or international or multinational surveys are still rare.[13] Yet sizeable numbers of scholars do work on women's history outside their own national boundaries; in the United States, for instance, historians routinely investigate European, Latin American, Asian, African, and Middle Eastern women's history, as well as women's history in antiquity.[14] The range of such scholarship is illustrated in the bibliography on Eastern European women's history in this volume, compiled by Mary Zirin. Such scholars can also be found in many other countries. Their contributions are unfortunately underrepresented in these essays, which for the most part present a decidedly nation-based historiography. More must be done to render such cross-national and comparative work visible.

As concerns periodisation and chronological foci, in most countries one finds a heavy concentration of research effort on recent history, that is, since ca. 1800, but there are some important exceptions, as well as wide variations in coverage. We will discuss these in terms of the four periods which derive from European historiography: ancient, medieval, early modern (which continental European historians refer to as modern), and modern (since roughly 1800, which Europeanists call contemporary).

In India considerable work has been accomplished on the ancient period, but very little on medieval (except for some new work on land-holding patterns and women ascetics in the devotional tradition). By contrast, the medieval period has received considerable attention from Swedish, Norwegian, Danish, Icelandic, and Finnish scholars, who have been working together across national boundaries for some time.[15] The Swiss and the Japanese also are paying increasing attention to this period, and Spanish historians of women have already produced a distinguished body of work on medieval Spain.

In the former German Democratic Republic, 'historical research on women' also includes important contributions in the medieval period, but as in Scandinavia hardly any research has been undertaken on the early modern period, that is, between 1500 and 1800/1850. Issues in early modern women's history, especially as concerns the development of a sexual division of labour in early capitalism, are attracting increasing attention from historians in Italy, France, West Germany, and Anglo-Americans who work in European history. In Brazil, by contrast, access to ecclesiastical archives has opened up a whole range of new demographically-based research in the 1750-1850 period; problems of women's continuing illiteracy and a dearth of written self-expression makes more conventional work in the modern period difficult, although oral history techniques are beginning to be employed. In Nigeria, to study women in the non-literate societies of the past, oral traditions have to be recaptured through the study of mythologies, folktales and proverbs, and through the disciplinary techniques of anthropology and sociology. Such methods and procedures raise important questions about the applicability of conventional - and largely Eurocentric - periodisation.

There is clearly much scope for comparative work in the examination of the historical experiences of women during the process of colonisation and the emergence of new cultural/national identities. In this volume this theme links nations marked both by the British colonial experience (which variously affected the USA prior to national independence, Australia, Canada, India, Nigeria and Ireland) and by the Portuguese, from the perspective of Brazil. The study of colonisation raises serious questions concerning the intersection of gender and ethnicity as components in the formation of national identities. These questions are also particularly important for historically multi-ethnic and/or multi-racial societies, such as Brazil, Yugoslavia, and Canada, where they are vital to the understanding of issues of identity. In Yugoslavia, a multi-cultural, multi-ethnic nation of relatively recent creation, scholarship with regard to women as well as men must necessarily proceed by taking regional and local differences into account. As Pierson argues, it is not only a question of diversity and conflict, but of historically dominant cultures, and historically oppressed racial, ethnic or linguistic minorities. As Grimshaw bluntly states, 'the Australian' is identified as male, and 'he' only emerges once the aborigines are conquered. This is a common theme in the essays in this volume, taken up in relation to the subordinated cultures of, for instance, aboriginal peoples, Blacks, Asians and other non-white and non-

Northern European immigrants in Canada and the United States, Black and Asian communities in Britain, and the Lapps in Norway.

The problems of writing about other people's cultures and cultural practices, and the challenge of overcoming a Eurocentric bias, are issues Ida Blom addresses in her essay in this volume in connection with the bold initiative of ten Scandinavian women's historians to produce, under Blom's editorship, an interpretative world history of women for a Scandinavian audience. The ten collaborators engaged in this monumental undertaking began their work by considering whether a single united theoretical approach to the study of women's history worldwide could be adopted. Their difficulty in resolving this question is indicative of the many differences in perspective represented in the essays in this volume.

Theoretical Dimensions

The discipline of history, as Pierson points out, is both 'intrinsically empirical' and yet also 'a site of political struggle'.[16] In women's history, this struggle may take many forms, from the thrusting of women into the visible historical record, to the introduction of new theoretical frameworks that question the subjectivity of the historian herself. Most essays in this volume refer, if only by allusion, to the challenge to the discipline, experienced worldwide over the last ten years, from forms of deconstructionist and postmodern analysis, which offer new routes towards uncovering the hidden agenda of texts both historical and contemporary. The approaches to the history of women incorporated into this volume all share a tension, between the drive towards the empirical recovery of the lives of women, and the changing and fragmenting possibilities of new explanatory models. It is only through a commitment to continue such an enterprise on these multiple fronts that women's history will retain both its political and its intellectual vitality.

In a key article published in 1975, Gerda Lerner wrote of the early stages of women's history as 'compensatory history', the history of notable women, and as 'contribution history', describing women's contribution to, and subjection in, a male-defined world.[17] She referred to such developments as transitional, a stage in the growth of new conceptual frameworks. Yet it is important to remember that in international and intra-national contexts such a process of recovery may take place alongside further theoretical developments and co-exist with them. Indeed, the very process of recovery can yield important theoretical insights.

Historical demography might appear to be one area in which attention to sexual difference was intrinsic: yet only in the last decade has full account been taken of, for instance, the differentials between women and men in birth, marriage and death. Head-König's essay in this volume charts the shift in perspective within this important historical field. In examining the demographic history of western European women between the seventeenth and nineteenth centuries, she demonstrates how the recovery of such sexual differentials can inform our understanding of the social and economic situation of women in a particular society. The differential mortality rates of male and female infants, of young children and of adults, can be shown, where the sources exist, to have a profound effect on the marriage market and the conditions of marriage for women and men. And equally demographers need to pay attention to the social and cultural influences upon such mortality rates – were boys weaned earlier? were more girls than boys abandoned? The interplay of economic and demographic variables can be critical to the development of different patterns in the sexual division of labour: the evidence from western Europe suggests that charting the relationship between the surplus of adult women in the towns and changing economic conditions could significantly clarify the process of occupational segregation. The recovery of such a perspective promises a more comprehensive understanding of the history of the sexual division of labour, and perhaps even of a history of sexual difference, as opposed to gender difference.

Equally, it has seemed important not only to gain insight into prescriptive patterns, but also into the experience of women themselves, to recover not only the record of women's past, but their own 'voice', their perceptions of their lives, wherever these can be recovered. As many of the essays in this volume remark, late twentieth-century historians have come to place a singular emphasis upon subjectivity, upon the question of women's consciousness: and they have therefore come to stress the importance of such written sources as diaries, autobiographies, and correspondence, where these exist. In recovering these 'voices' historians have been drawn, in different degrees, to make use of literary and psychoanalytic theoretical approaches.

As Bock notes in this volume, over the last twenty years an enormous and growing body of work on women's history has focused directly on the lives of women, placing them in the centre of the picture, finding explanatory frameworks for the relations between the sexes. That framework incorporates both women's subjection – and their subjectivity. An approach to women's history that stressed simply subjection and common oppression by men – a simplistic appropriation of the term 'patriarchy' – was soon considered unhelpful and ahistorical, unless placed in a specific context.[18]

Bock shows that this expanding body of scholarship has employed a binary vision, incorporating sets of apparently inescapable dichotomies that seemed to shape the roles and separate spheres of women and of men. The hierarchical and contrasting dualism between 'nature', defining women's world, and 'culture', shaped by men, was seen by many historians, and continues to be seen, as a persuasive, and, it has been sometimes claimed, universally valid, prescriptive version of the inequality between women and men.[19] Many saw it as their task to decode the prescriptions of 'nature' that ordained the patterns of women's lives. The division between the worlds of 'work' and 'family', on the other hand, though a starting-point as an approximating framework of sexual difference, has been rapidly recast into the hierarchy of male and female work, paid and unpaid. Again, a fundamental though shifting dualism of European political theory, the contrasts between public and private worlds, between the political arena and the domestic sphere, have provided other and parallel frameworks for understanding the unequal worlds of women and men. Each of these dualisms overlaps the others. Their power and their impact on historiography can be traced in a number of the essays in this volume.

Stock-Morton has commented on the extent to which public/private distinctions shaped the early years of writing women's history in the United States: social history, in particular, was understood as providing a route to the recovery of the private sphere, whether in the history of the family, the history of consumption, or in that 'female culture' which functioned within different class and ethnic groups in such a way as sometimes to allow women to exercise informal power within private life. She has pointed to the importance of the adoption of interdisciplinary methods here, especially those derived from anthropological and sociological approaches.

Similarly, Dauphin et al. locate the development in France in the 1980s of new approaches to the history of women's culture: the successes of insights drawn from anthropology and ethnology, and the new history of social and cultural representations, have brought the recovery of women's worlds in societies hitherto inaccessible, especially those of western Europe in the early modern and modern periods. These approaches have permitted new understandings of the working of sexual difference in such societies: patterns of female sociability, of ritual and of the symbolic meanings of such difference have been recaptured, and the history of private life enriched. Our understanding of the history of sexuality, including both heterosexual relations and lesbian and 'romantic' relationships between women, has been enhanced. It has been possible to begin writing a history of women's reproductive roles: pregnancy, childbirth, nursing and the care of children. The notion of complementarity between women and men in their use of space and in daily working activities, then, has been an effective one for allowing the historian to recover traces of women's informal powers, but it has also, these French historians argue, sometimes erased the formal structures of male authority and the hierarchical relations between the sexes.

While at one time helpful, each of the dualisms considered above has more recently come under attack. The distinction between 'nature' and 'culture', for instance, it is now argued, is *not* a universal one: in the sense used here, it arose out of a particular moment in western European history, and quickly became a politicised distinction *used* to devalue women's lives and activities. The term 'nature' or its equivalent has everywhere a specific meaning in its own historical and linguistic context. The worlds of 'work' and 'family' have only in a few times and places been described as separated and distinct: the distinction, drawn here from the experience of some industrial societies, is a false one even with respect to them. Women's life-cycles and family lives structured the jobs they did, their levels of wages, and their training. Occupational patterns could, as suggested above, influence demographic patterns in significant ways. The public/private distinction similarly has been shown to misrepresent entirely the interdependence and interconnectedness of the public and private domains. As Rendall has indicated in her essay, the formation of the nineteenth-century English middle classes rested on a specific form of gendered familial relationships as well as on political and economic dominance. Bock points out below that the National Socialist state of Germany asserted the primacy of the state over private life, and in the end over life and death.

Once crucial to the development of women's history, such conceptual dualisms have been demonstrated to be inadequate. As in the case of the public/private divide, they fail effectively to explain the histories of the societies out of which they emerged. Much more fundamentally, too many of these conceptual categories universalise from what are specifically western and European traditions, mainly modern ones, of discussing sexual difference: they do not offer adequate routes towards understanding societies with different economic bases, cultural patterns, and political languages, either in the past or in the present. They contain intrinsic dangers: the first is that of universalising a particular pattern of experience. The second is that of essentialising, of implicitly acquiescing in the separation of spheres in writing the history of women's worlds. The third is that of the depoliticising of women's history, of forgetting that women's history is not merely the history of the 'social', the 'private', the 'natural': it is also the history of inequality, of subordination, and dominance.

New directions can be and have been found, themselves subject to continuing debate and criticism. Bock has drawn together three new and rather different sets of dichotomies, which emerge in other papers in this volume also. The term 'gender', as distinct from 'sex', is now widely used: where 'sex' is seen as biologically differentiating women and men, 'gender' refers to the social and cultural constructions of female and male roles in different times and places. Such an approach has considerable strengths, and attractions for historians: the debate on Joan Scott's key work *Gender and the Politics of History* (1988), which has had a worldwide impact, has shown how relevant are the questions raised here.[20] Insights drawn from postmodernism have also been used to develop analyses of discourses of gender. So Basu shows in her paper how Indian historians have considered the discourses engaged in the nineteenth-century and early twentieth-century debates around *sati* and child marriage between British officials, Hindu reformers and orthodox Hindus: for the politics of imperial/colonial relationships were also the politics of gender.

Secondly, the contrast between 'equality' and 'difference', diversely expressed in different languages, has been of particular interest to those engaged in writing the history of feminism, but is of much broader relevance. It suggests the tension which existed in the past between those who advocated equality between women and men, on grounds of their similarities or common humanity, and those who, like the Swedish Ellen Key in the 1890s, argued that sexual difference might provide a more equitable basis for a just society. Yvonne Hirdman has written of the way in which the debate in Sweden in the 1980s seemed to revive the tension between 'sameness' and 'difference' in nineteenth-century Swedish feminism. In the 1980s it has also been argued that sexual difference may be the starting-point for a redefinition of equality that does not rest on masculine norms.

Finally, the third contrast is that between 'integration' and 'autonomy'. This is both an institutional and theoretical dilemma. Women's history, feminist history and gender history, as we have remarked earlier, are all still far from accepted by the academic establishments of most countries represented in this volume, with the exception of the United States. Their impact on the rewriting of the historical record of humanity is still very limited: women's history may win some slight recognition, in the occasional incorporation, for instance, of the importance of the history of the family, of women's work, of women's suffrage movements, into a more general treatment. But a fuller understanding of the past, one which incorporates the history of sexual difference, still awaits its historians. Writers of women's history, or gender history, today have still to choose their own priorities: the development of an autonomous field of research, or the ambitious possibility of rereading not women's worlds or women's past, but the fundamental turning-points, and continuities, in human history. Yet to pose such alternatives as if there was a self-evident hierarchy, an evolution from 'autonomy' to 'integration', is already to make a political judgment: in the Netherlands, as Francisca de Haan has described in her essay in this volume, the 1980s have witnessed fierce debates on this issue. Women's history, it has been argued, needs to become a strong and autonomous field in its own right.

Bock suggests that these dualities too are subject to criticism. But, as the debate moves on, it becomes possible to see the directions of future developments. Some historians are beginning to confront and to deconstruct the earlier representations of their past, recognising the basis of these dualities to lie in a masculinist epistemology. They argue that dichotomies, opposites, contradictions, the whole inheritance of a binary vision, may be unnecessarily confining: the temptations of dualism should be constantly analysed and where appropriate discarded. New scholarship may begin to incorporate a different epistemology: self-reflexive, self-critical, and self-conscious, in employing the methodology of the historian, and in its political purposes. Such changes should, however, incorporate past insights, since 'to develop a historically grounded feminist theory we must transcend its philosophic past, not obliterate it'.[21]

One way forward lies not only in the recognition of sexual difference and masculine domination, but in the issue of 'difference' between and among women. A number of papers in this volume note the range of differences that exist within a national experience, whose historical record may be dominated by that of the elite or privileged ethnic group. Moreover, women's history cannot be written without recognition of the imperial/colonial relationships of past and present, creating relationships of dominance and difference between women. De Haan's essay in this volume explicitly traces the history of recognition of 'difference' in the Netherlands, as, after the International Conference on Women's History of 1986 in Amsterdam, the ethnocentric character of so much women's history was challenged.

The need to rethink the concept of 'experience' in the light of such challenge has been recognised in a Canadian context by Ruth Roach Pierson, in her essay in this volume. In discussing Sylvia Van Kirk's history of Native Canadian women in the Canadian fur trade, Pierson notes that it was possible for Van Kirk to contextualise, and to reconstruct, from existing records, the 'discursive' world in which Native Canadian women involved in the fur trade lived. But is it possible for the historian from a different and dominant culture to recover and reclaim the 'interior experience' of those oppressed by that dominant culture? Pierson suggests the need for the historian implicated in such dominance to exercise self-reflexivity and self-knowledge, an 'epistemic humility': that the marginalised may themselves recover their experience of oppression.

In her essay on women's history in the Netherlands in this volume, de Haan has shown how the approach of the 1970s and early 1980s to the study of women's culture, which focused on the nineteenth-century United States, recapturing 'a female world of love and ritual', has been transformed. The Dutch historian Mineke Bosch, de Haan informs us, has contrasted such a specific historical culture, rooted in time and place, with an historian's vision, which could challenge heterosexual orthodoxy, based on a new epistemological foundation. The choice of whether or not to write lesbian history was the choice of the historian, again exercising self-reflexivity in a political act, 'as part of our attempt to build a new symbolic universe'. These 'differences', between the dominance of heterosexuality and those oppressed by it, have also to be recognised.

Dauphin et al. argue for the reintroduction of a political perspective into analyses of women's history, redressing what might seem to be the false neutrality of approaches rooted in 'women's culture' and 'women's worlds'. The authors call for the study of the causes and effects of some of the 'watersheds' of history, juridical, economic, or political, and the ways in which both sexes represent and redefine themselves. So the introduction of the dowry in the late middle ages, or of divorce legislation in France in 1792, or the French Revolution itself, might yield contrasting and contradictory male and female perspectives on the redistribution of power. So too approaches to the study of gender may increasingly 'bring the concept of power back into women's history', as Stock-Morton has remarked of US historiography in the 1980s. Deconstructive approaches may help to dismantle ideological systems claiming universalism in the interests of male and ethnocentric dominance.

Ida Blom's essay addresses the attempt by ten Scandinavian scholars to write a worldwide women's history, for a Scandinavian audience. The writers had hoped to find a common theoretical framework but failed to do so, though all contributors were obliged to address the question of women's oppression. Writers did find that an analysis rooted in gender difference yielded some striking examples of similarities in different cultures: limitations, for instance, on women's mobility. But qualifications needed to be made: class, caste, and state powers cut across such similarities. Nevertheless, the analysis of different 'gender systems' as defined by Yvonne Hirdman provided one way to proceed. Though the Scandinavian authors set out to learn as much as possible from historians of women writing of their own cultures, Blom now admits to finding the exercise especially problematic when examining cultural practices western women find objectionable, such as clitoridectomy, *sati*, and child marriages. As she notes, such practices raise serious ethical problems for the feminist historian from a different culture, who must first attempt to understand what happened, and why, from those who have written from within that cultural tradition. Having so informed herself, she may nevertheless make her own personal judgment. A Eurocentric perspective may be rooted in an individualist culture with goals of individual self-fulfilment and self-determination: other cultures value forms of collective solidarity and collective realisation of goals.

Blom acknowledges in her essay the importance of a reflexive, self-critical approach by the historian, that she should, as Pierson enjoined, always 'recognise the position from which she speaks'. Blom's conclusion pointed not towards any possibility of overarching theory, but towards dialogue between those of different cultural backgrounds as a route towards cross-cultural understanding. Awe writes in this volume of the recognition by Nigerian historians of the need to construct a different theoretical framework, appropriate to the experience of African and specifically of Nigerian women. Such recognition may point to alternative paths to writing women's history in the future.

The continuing process of analysing, deconstructing, and challenging the categories of women's history will continue. The conceptual tools of the 1980s have already proved their value even as they have been subjected to criticism. The tension between the recovery of women's past worldwide and its changing theoretical framework will continue. But in its theory and in its practice, women's history has achieved international importance. This volume begins to address and to celebrate the multiplicity of international perspectives on writing women's history.

Karen Offen, Ruth Roach Pierson, and Jane Rendall

NOTES

1. The founding meeting of IFRWH/FIRFH was preceded by over ten years of earlier efforts, sparked by women's historians' protests over the absence of women scholars and women's history at the XIVe International Congress on the Historical Sciences, held in San Francisco in August 1975. For a brief review of these developments, see Karen Offen, 'Notes on the Prehistory of the International Federation for Research in Women's History', *Newsletter of the Conference Group on Women's History (CGWH)*, 19, no. 2 (April/May 1988), pp. 3-5.

To this account should be added that the 1975 protests were followed up in the USA by the calling of an international women's history conference, 'Women and Power: Dimensions of Women's Historical Experience', organised by Hilda Smith, for the Conference Group on Women's History, in consultation with a London-based women's research group, and held at the University of Maryland in November 1977. A number of the papers from that conference appeared in *Feminist Studies*, 5, no. 1 (Spring 1979). See the CGWH *Newsletter*, 3, no. 1 (December 1977), pp. 5-10, for the programme and addresses of European participants. See also the bibliographical articles in subsequent issues (April 1978 and January 1979) on the status of women's history in Italy, Latin America, the Middle East, Canada, and South Asia. A subsequent international women's history conference was organised in Amsterdam by Dutch historians in March 1986; see Arina Angerman et al. (eds.), *Current Issues in Women's History* (London: Routledge, 1989), which includes selected papers from that conference.

2. Information incorporated in this section was compiled primarily from questionnaires completed by national group representatives in preparation for the 1989 Bellagio Conference.

3. Selma Leydesdorff similarly underscores differences in historiography as products of national traditions of historical writing. See 'Politics, Identification, and the Writing of Women's History', in Angerman et al. (eds.), *Current Issues*, pp. 9-20.

4. Linda Kealey, 'The Status of Women in the Historical Profession in Canada: 1989 Survey', paper presented at the Annual Meeting of the Canadian Historical Association, University of Victoria, May 1990.

5. Lydia Sklevicky, 'More Horses Than Women: On the Difficulties of Founding Women's History in Yugoslavia', *Gender & History*, 1, no. 1 (Spring 1989), pp. 68-75.

6. From late 1991, this chair will be occupied by Professor Olwen Hufton.

7. The most important US archives for women's history are the Arthur and Elizabeth Schlesinger Library on the History of Women in America, at Radcliffe College, Cambridge, Massachusetts, and the Sophia Smith Collection Women's History Archive, at Smith College, Northampton, Massachusetts, which contains many European materials. Both these archives published multi-volume catalogues in the 1970s. A guide to women's history materials in other US repositories, now

somewhat out of date but still exceedingly valuable, is Andrea Hinding (ed.), *Women's History Sources* (Ann Arbor: R. R. Bowker Co., 1979).

On the women's history archives at the University of Gothenburg, Sweden, see Beata Losman and Louise Rönnroth (eds.), *Bibliotheca Feminarum: Om de kvinnohistoriska samlingarna i göteborg, kvinnoliv och kvinnotanke under 300 ar* [Women's Library: the Women's History Collection at Gothenburg, Women's Lives and Women's Ideas during 300 Years] (Gothenburg: Kvinnohistorist Arkiv, 21, 1984). On the Fawcett Library in London, see the special issue of *Women's Studies International Forum*, 10, no. 3 (1987). On the German collections, see Karin Schatzberg, *Frauenarchiv und Frauenbibliotheken* [Women's Archives and Women's Libraries] (Göttingen: Herodot, 1985). On the Archives of the International Women's Movement in Amsterdam, see Ineke Jungschleger, *Bluestockings in Mothballs* (Amsterdam: Internationaal Archief voor de Vrouwenbeweging, 1987). The Bibliothèque Marguerite Durand (Paris) publishes yearly lists of acquisitions and periodicals received. Further information on these and other European archives and libraries specialising in women's history and women's studies can be found in Stephen Lehmann and Eva Sartori (eds.), *Women's Studies in Western Europe: A Resource Guide* (Chicago: American Library Association, Western European Specialists Section, 1986).

8. Microfilm collections provide a vital means of making women's history sources available to researchers. Two particularly important collections of published works, including periodicals, are the *Gerritsen Collection in Women's History* (Glen Rock, N. J.: Microfilming Corporation of America) and *History of Women* (Woodbridge, Conn.: Research Publications, Inc.). The Gerritsen Collection contains materials in a number of languages besides English.

9. For the use of computerised data-bases, see Joyce Duncan Falk, 'The New Technology for Research in European Women's History: "Online Bibliographies"', *Signs: Journal of Women in Culture and Society*, 9, no. 1 (1983), pp. 120-33.

10. New document collections published in English include Margot Badran and Miriam Cooke (eds.), *Opening the Gates: A Century of Arab Feminist Writing* (Bloomington: Indiana University Press, 1990), and Alison Prentice (series ed.), *Women in Canadian History Documentary Series*, 3 vols. (Toronto: New Hogtown Press, 1980-1990) (see Ruth Roach Pierson's essay below for the specific volume titles). See also the massive Swiss collection, Elisabeth Joris and Heidi Witzig (eds.), *Frauengeschichte(n)* [Women's History(ies)], 2nd ed. (Zurich: Limmat Verlag, 1987).

11. See, for example, Barbara Kanner (ed.), *Women in English Social History, 1800-1914: A Guide to Research in 3 Volumes* (New York: Garland Press, 1987 - 1990), and *Restoring Women to History: Teaching Packets for Integrating Women's History into Courses on Africa, Asia, Latin America, the Caribbean, and the Middle East* (Bloomington: The Organization of American Historians, 1988).

12. Earlier newsletters of the International Federation for Research in Women's History/Fédération internationale pour la recherche de l'histoire des femmes have published lists of such edited collections and special issues. A sampling of recent ones would include Mary Nash (ed.), *Més Enllà del silenci: les dones a la*

història de Catalunya [Beyond Silence: Women in the History of Catalonia] (Barcelona: Comissio Interdepartamental de Promocio de la Dona, 1988); Albertina de Oliveira Costa and Cristina Bruschini (eds.), *Rebeldia e submissão: Estudos sobre Condição Feminina* [Rebellion and Submission: Studies of the Feminine Condition] (São Paulo: Vertice, 1989); Raewyn Dalziel (ed.), special issue of women's history, *New Zealand Journal of History*, 23, no. 1 (April 1989); special issue 'Feminism and History', *Australian Feminist Studies*, nos. 7 & 8 (Summer 1989); Kumkum Sangari and Sudesh Vaid (eds.), *Recasting Women: Essays in Colonial History* (New Delhi: Kali for Women, 1989); Cherryl Walker (ed.), *Women and Gender in Southern Africa to 1945* (Capetown: David Phillip, 1990); Maria Luddy and Cliona Murphy (eds.), *Women Surviving: Studies in Irish Women's History in the Nineteenth and Twentieth Centuries* (Dublin: Poolbeg, 1990); two special issues on women's history in Africa, Asia, Latin America and the Middle East, *Journal of Women's History*, 1, no. 2 (Fall 1989) and 2, no. 1 (Spring 1990); and the most recent issues of the *Jaarboek voor Vrouwengeschiedenis* [Yearbook for Women's History] (Amsterdam).

      13. Two notable exceptions are Renate Bridenthal, Atina Grossmann and Marion Kaplan (eds.), *When Biology Became Destiny: Women in Weimar and Nazi Germany* (New York: Monthly Review Press, 1984), with contributors from Germany and the USA, and Judith Friedlander et al. (eds.), *Women in Culture and Politics: A Century of Change* (Bloomington: Indiana University Press, 1986). See also the collective surveys of European women's history by Bridenthal, Claudia Koonz and Susan Stuard (eds.), *Becoming Visible: Women in European History* (Boston: Houghton Mifflin, 1987, 2nd ed.); and Marilyn J. Boxer and Jean H. Quataert (eds.), *Connecting Spheres: Women in the Western World* (New York: Oxford University Press, 1987). Another historical collection with an international list of contributors is Gisela Bock and Pat Thane (eds.), *Maternity: Visions of Gender and the Rise of the European Welfare States* (London: Routledge, 1991). A multi-volume series is being prepared by Georges Duby and Michelle Perrot (eds.), *Storia delle donne in occidente* [The History of Women in the Western World] (Bari: Editori Laterza). Two volumes have appeared in 1990: vol. 1, Pauline Schmitt Pantel (ed.), *L'Antichità* [Antiquity]; and vol. 2, Christiane Klapisch-Zuber (ed.), *Il Medioevo* [The Middle Ages]. Three further volumes are in press: Arlette Farge and Natalie Zemon Davis (eds.), *Dal Rinascimento all'età moderna* [From the Renaissance to the Modern Era]; Geneviève Fraisse and Michelle Perrot (eds.), *L'Ottocento* [The Nineteenth Century]; and Françoise Thébaud (ed.), *Il Novecento* [The Twentieth Century]. French and English-language editions of this series are underway.

      14. See, for example, Lois Beck and Nikki Keddie (eds.), *Women in the Muslim World* (Cambridge, Mass.: Harvard University Press, 1978); Asunción Lavrin (ed.), *Latin American Women: A Historical Perspective* (Westport, Conn.: Greenwood Press, 1978) and *Sexuality and Marriage in Colonial Latin America* (Lincoln: University of Nebraska Press, 1989); Sherrin Marshall (ed.), *Women in Reformation and Counter-Reformation Europe* (Bloomington: Indiana University Press, 1989); and Barbara S. Lesko (ed.), *Women's Earliest Records from Ancient Egypt and Western Asia: Proceedings of the Conference on Women in the Ancient Near East* (Atlanta: Scholars Press, 1989).

15. They have published five volumes of consolidated work; see Yvonne Hirdman's essay (below) for references.

16. See Pierson's essay below.

17. Gerda Lerner has defined 'compensatory history' and 'contribution history' in her essay, 'Placing Women in History: Definitions and Challenges' (1975), in *The Majority Finds its Past* (New York: Oxford University Press, 1981 edition), pp. 145-153.

18. Criticism of the use made of this term in the 1970s may be found, for instance, in the essay, first published in 1979, by Sheila Rowbotham, 'The Trouble with Patriarchy', reprinted in her *Dreams and Dilemmas: Collected Writings* (London: Virago, 1983).

19. One of the most influential essays expounding this view was that by the late Michelle Zimbalist Rosaldo, 'Woman, Culture, and Society: A Theoretical Overview', in Rosaldo and Louise Lamphere (eds.), *Woman, Culture and Society* (Stanford: Stanford University Press, 1974); see also her later article, 'The Use and Abuse of Anthropology: Reflections on Feminism and Cross-Cultural Understanding', *Signs: Journal of Women in Culture and Society*, 5, no. 3 (Spring 1980), pp. 389-417. For historical contributions to this discussion, see Maurice Bloch and Jean H. Bloch, 'Women and the Dialectics of Nature in Eighteenth-Century French Thought', in Carol MacCormack and Marilyn Strathern (eds.), *Nature, Culture, and Gender* (Cambridge: Cambridge University Press, 1980), pp. 25-41; and Penelope Brown and Ludmilla J. Jordanova, 'Oppressive Dichotomies: The Nature/Culture Debate', in The Cambridge Women's Studies Group (eds.), *Women in Society: Interdisciplinary Essays* (London: Virago Press, 1981), pp. 224-41.

20. Joan Wallach Scott, *Gender and the Politics of History* (New York: Columbia University Press, 1988). For discussion of the impact of this work, see, for instance the essays by de Haan, Rendall, and Stock-Morton in this volume.

21. Janet Afary, 'Some Reflections on Third World Feminist Historiography', *Journal of Women's History*, 1, no. 2 (1989), p. 151, quoted in Phyllis Stock-Morton's essay in this volume. Janet Afary, who is based in the United States, works on the history of the women's movement in Iran.

PART ONE

CONCEPTUAL AND METHODOLOGICAL ISSUES

1

Challenging Dichotomies:
Perspectives on Women's History

Gisela Bock

Women's history has come a long way. Some twenty years ago, Gerda Lerner wrote that 'the striking fact about the historiography of women is the general neglect of the subject by historians'.[1] Historical scholarship was far from 'objective' or 'universal', because it was based on male experience, placed men at the centre and as a measure of all things human, thereby leaving out half of humankind. In the past two decades, the situation has changed considerably. In an enormous (and enormously growing) body of scholarship women have been rendered visible. They have been placed at the centre, and what women do, have to do, and want to do has been re-evaluated in view of social, political and cultural change, of an improvement in women's situations and, more generally, in terms of a change towards more freedom and justice. More precisely, what has been rendered historically visible by making women a subject of research was, in the first place, their subjection. In the second place, however, it was their subjectivity – because women are not only victims, but also actively shape their own lives, society and history.

Much of this research was carried out in the context of three conceptual or theoretical frameworks that have been used by many feminist scholars, particularly historians, in the past two decades and which will be outlined in the first section of this paper. These frameworks point to three dichotomies in traditional thought on gender relations, and all of them have been not only used, but also profoundly challenged. The second section will illustrate three further dichotomies which, in the development of modern women's history, have emerged more recently and which presently seem to dominate and direct women's studies. All of these dichotomies have been discussed, to a greater or lesser degree, internationally, but there are some interesting national differences in the debates themselves

1

as well as in their sequence over time. Particularly noteworthy are certain changes in language brought about in this context. These are, of course, nationally different, but they also indicate to what extent women's history and women's studies have succeeded in crossing national boundaries.

Women as subject, the subjection of women and women's subjectivity

1. Nature versus culture. It was mainly in the United States in the early 1970s that the relation of the sexes was discussed in terms of the relation, or rather dichotomy, between 'nature and nurture' or 'nature and culture'. Men and their activities had been seen as culture and of cultural value, whereas women and their activities had been seen as natural, outside of history and society, always the same and therefore not worthy of scholarly, political or theoretical interest and inquiry. Moreover, it was the relations between the sexes, and most particularly their relations of power and subjection, that had been attributed to nature. 'Nature', in this context, most often meant sexuality between men and women, women's bodies and their capacity for pregnancy and motherhood. Fatherhood, however, was usually seen not as natural but as 'social'. Female scholars challenged this traditional dichotomy. They argued that what 'nature' really meant in this discourse was a devaluation of everything that women stood for, that '"nature" always has a social meaning',[2] that both 'nature' and 'culture' meant different things at different times, in different places and to the different sexes, and that women's bodies and bodily capacities were not always and everywhere seen as disabilities, but also as a basis for certain kinds of informal power and public activities.[3] The nature/culture dichotomy was recognised as a specific and perhaps specifically Western way of expressing the hierarchies between the sexes. The binary terms of this dichotomy only apparently refer to antagonistic and independent terms; but in fact, they refer to a hierarchy of social realities and cultural meanings, between strongly interdependent terms. In other words: no such nature without such culture, and no such culture without such nature. One of the linguistic results of such insights in women's history is that the term 'nature' is now almost always placed in quotation marks.

The study of women's identification with nature, of their embodiment and their body-related activities, such as motherhood, nursing and caring, has resulted in a number of important works which deal with these distinctively female domains. Early works on the history of motherhood were written by French scholars. More recently, research on the female body has shown to what degree it is historically conditioned and dependent on the cultural context.[4] Feminist philosophers, particularly in France, are building theoretical frameworks precisely around the distinctive female experience, and this approach is currently arousing great and controversial interest in the United States.[5] On the other hand, French and other historians argue that this focus on women's 'nature' may be politically counterproductive because it seems to confirm traditional stereotypes according to which women seem to be exclusively defined by their body, by motherhood and by their sex, and to overlook the more important political dimensions of women's history.[6]

2. Work versus family. A second theoretical framework for rendering women visible, and for dismantling their identification with the merely natural, unchanging and therefore uninteresting, was the issue of their distinctive patterns of work. The discussion around it had its origins more in the European than in the American context, particularly in Italy, Britain, Germany and France. What had been seen as nature was now seen as work: bearing, rearing and caring for children, looking after the breadwinner-husband and after other family members. To call this activity 'work' meant to challenge the dichotomy 'work and family' (because the family may mean work to women), but also 'work and leisure' (because men's leisure may be women's work), and 'working men and supported wives' (because wives support men through their work). It meant questioning the view that work is only that which is done for pay. Women have always worked, and unpaid work was and is women's work. Obviously, men's work is valued more highly than women's work. In theoretical and economic terms, it has been demonstrated that women's work was overlooked by male theoreticians of work and the economy and why this happened; accordingly the value or 'productivity' of domestic work came to be discussed.[7] In historical terms, it has been shown how strongly this work changed over time and cross-culturally. For example, in Britain and Australia, housewives were counted among the 'occupied' categories in the census up to the end of the nineteenth century, when they were excluded from them; around the same time, radical feminists in Germany and elsewhere were demanding that their work be included in the measurement of the Gross National Product.[8]

The sexual division of labour was found to be not just a division, but a hierarchy of labour; and not just one of labour but, primarily, a sexual division of value and rewards. The lower value of women's work continues – through economic and cultural mediation – in employment outside the home. Here, where women have always worked, they earned only 50 per cent to 80 per cent of men's earnings in the nineteenth and twentieth centuries in western countries, with variations over time and space.[9] Women's employment in the caring and nursing professions, where they are the overwhelming majority, usually does not guarantee them a decent survival income,[10] the 1989 nurses' strike in West Germany being just one example. The recent international increase in the

Gisela Bock

number of single mothers has led to a 'feminisation of poverty', even beyond the traditionally high level of female poverty.[11]

The apparent dichotomy between 'work and family', between men as workers and women as 'non-workers', turns out to be one between paid and unpaid work, between underpaid and decently paid work, between the superior and inferior value of men's and women's work respectively. The underlying assumption of mutually exclusive superiority and inferiority seems to be another common feature of such gender-linked dichotomies. The challenge posed by women's studies to this opposition is obviously linked to political and economic challenges to pay women's as yet unpaid work, to raise their earnings in low-pay jobs, and to admit more women to well-paid professions. It has also led to some linguistic changes. Even though, in the English language, the terms 'working women' and 'working mothers' are still reserved for employed women only, and non-employed women are still often called 'non-working', the terms 'work and family' are now often replaced by 'paid and unpaid work'. In German, women's historians distinguish consistently between 'work' and 'employment', *Arbeit* [work] and *Erwerbstätigkeit* [income-earning], and *Arbeitslosigkeit* [unemployment, literally 'worklessness'] has been replaced by *Erwerbslosigkeit* ['incomelessness'].

3. Public versus private. A third conceptual framework of women's history has been the relation between the public and the private, or the political and the personal, or the sphere of power and the domestic sphere. Traditional political theory has seen them, again, as a dichotomy of mutually exclusive terms, identified with women's 'sphere' and men's 'world'. Women's studies have profoundly challenged this view, pointing out its inadequacy for understanding politics and society. The slogan 'the personal is political' indicated that the issue of power is not confined to 'high politics', but also appears in sexual relations. Men inhabit, and rule within both spheres, whereas women's proper place was seen to be only in the domestic sphere and in her subjection to father or husband. This means, on the one hand, the dichotomy is not one between two autonomous, symmetrical and equivalent spheres, but rather a complex relation between domination and subordination, between power and powerlessness.[12] On the other hand, women's studies have shown that the public 'world' was essentially based on the domestic 'sphere'. Male workers, male politicians and male scholars perform their tasks only because they are born, reared and cared for by women's labour. The boundaries between public and private shift significantly over time and cross-culturally, as in the historical transition between private charity and public assistance, in both of which women played important roles.[13] State policy has not left women out, but has shaped their personal circumstances by public intervention in, for instance, legislation on rape and abortion, and by the absence of legislation. The modern welfare states have discriminated against women in old age pensions and unemployment benefits; they have introduced maternity leave for employed women without replacing their loss of income – in Europe, this was changed mainly through the struggles of the women's movements since around 1900 – and income tax reforms have supported husbands and fathers, but not wives and mothers.[14] The welfare state has not excluded women's sphere but included it as private, implying that it is under the rule of the husband. The Nazi regime went much beyond this, because its intervention tended to destroy the private sphere; not however, as is often said, by promoting motherhood, but by promoting precisely the opposite: a policy of mass compulsory sterilisation for women and men who were considered 'racially inferior'. This antinatalist policy was explicitly based on the doctrine that 'the private is political' and that the definition of the boundaries between the political and the private is a political act;[15] according to the National Socialists, it was the sterilisation policy which established and asserted 'the primacy of the state in the field of life, marriage and the family'.

Women's history has also discovered that what is perceived as 'private' by some may be seen as 'public' by others. The domestic tasks of bearing and rearing children, for instance, were proclaimed as being of public importance by many women in the early women's movement. They requested that it be re-evaluated, and many of them based their demand for equal political citizenship precisely on this vision of the 'separate sphere', understood not as a dichotomy of mutually exclusive and hierarchical terms, but as a source of equal rights and responsibilities of the female sex in respect to civil society.[16] On this basis, they did not so much challenge the sexual division of labour, as the sexual division of power. In this sense, the late anthropologist Michelle Zimbalist Rosaldo argued that women could, and did, challenge male rule either by seeking to enter the distinctively male sphere, or by stressing the value of their own sphere; sometimes they attempted to combine both. Women's historians have also pointed out that the traditional nineteenth-century or Victorian version of the female separate sphere was not oppressive in a simple way, but left considerable space for female bonding and the development of a women's culture as an expression of women's subjectivity. [17]

* * * * *

These three dichotomies seem to have some important characteristics in common. They are eminently gender-linked, and as such they have distant roots in European and western traditions of gender perception. They have been taken up and used as crucial conceptual frameworks in the newly emerging women's history of the past decades, and simultaneously their long-standing apparent validity for the perception of gender relations has been thoroughly challenged. This challenge concerned the analysis, historicisation and deconstruction of the character and meaning of these three dual categories, as well as the links between them, and it questioned the traditional assumption that these dichotomies were expressions – natural and necessary expressions – of sexual difference.

The question has been raised as to whether these dichotomies are just a few examples among many similar binary oppositions and dualistic modes of western thought in general, or whether their gender-linked character makes them very special. (Of course, other classic dichotomies, such as 'subjective/objective', 'rational/emotional', have also assumed gender-linked meanings, even though not all of them have been equally central to historical analytical frameworks; on the other hand, the dichotomies discussed above have also been studied in contexts which were not primarily gender-linked.)[18] But it seems that, whenever they are used for describing gender relations, they do not refer so much to separate, autonomous, independent, equivalent dual spheres, as to relations of hierarchy: hierarchies of spheres, meanings, values, of inferiority and superiority, of subordination and power; in other words, to relations where 'culture' subjects 'nature', the world of 'work' reigns over that of the 'family', the 'political' dominates the 'private'.

In terms of logical rules, these apparent dichotomies are not mutually exclusive contradictories, as in A is not B, B is not A (woman is not man and vice versa). Rather these apparent dichotomies are (really) contraries, for they may coexist freely, and/or coexist with C (as alternatives to the dichotomous attributions) and all of them may have a positive reality. Patriarchal theorists have constituted these dualisms on the model of logically contradictory opposites, as in the impossible combination of A and Not-A, in which what defines Not-A is its privation with respect to A, that is, its lack of A. These contradictory opposites in their rigidity, allow for neither alternatives (*tertium non datur*) [no third value is given]; nor reversals, as in Not-A being attributed to men and A to women. When, for instance, gender is constructed on a model of mutually exclusive, binary opposites, if men are defined as rational, then women are defined by an absence of rationality. In this construction, for the woman to take on rationality is for her to begin to assimilate to the male norm and thus to begin to cease to be a woman. Contraries, in contrast, allow for a multiplicity of alternatives. Feminists have argued that 'mere contrary distinctions are not eternally tied to dichotomous structure, and as dichotomies they are limited in scope'.[19] Therefore, it might be useful to distinguish more clearly between dichotomies of mutual exclusion and hierarchy on one side, and contraries, distinctions or differences, on the other, which are neither hierarchical nor mutually exclusive. Above all, sensitivity to the prevalence of binary oppositions of a dichotomous kind in discourses of gender has taught us to beware of their historical and political pitfalls.

Gender equality, sexuality difference and women's autonomy

Somehow, ironically, the same process by which women became historically (and not only historically) visible through the critique of these contradictories has also led to a number of new dichotomies of which little or nothing was heard during the first phase of women's studies, and which later came to the fore within the context of feminist scholarship itself. In part, they are the result of past attempts to resolve the earlier binary modes with the help of new concepts and theoretical frameworks. It seems that future strategies for women's history lie precisely, and once more, in the possibility and necessity of challenging these newer dichotomies.

1. Sex versus gender. The concept 'gender' has been introduced into women's history and women's studies in the 1970s as a social, cultural, political and historical category, in order to express the insight that women's subordination, inferiority and powerlessness are not dictated by nature, but are social, cultural, political and historical constructions. Whereas 'gender' had previously referred mainly to linguistic-grammatical constructions, it now became a major theoretical framework.[20] One of the reasons for its success in replacing the word 'sex' has been the insistence that the study of women does not only deal with sexuality, wifehood and motherhood, but with women in all walks of life. Women's studies do not only concern half of humankind, but all of it, because it is not only women who are gendered beings, but also men who are therefore far from representing universal humanity. Consequently, 'men's history' and 'men's studies' which analyse men as 'men' have emerged. The concept of 'gender' radicalised and universalised the efforts to make women visible, and the insight that gender is a basic, though flexible structure of society meant that women's and gender studies concern, in principle, any field or object of historical (and non-historical) scholarship.[21]

But the new terminology has also brought to the fore major problems. They result from the fact that the concept of gender has been introduced in the form of a dichotomy. It distinguishes categorically between gender and sex, 'sex' to be understood as 'biological' and 'gender' as 'social' or cultural, and both are seen as combined in a 'sex/gender system' where 'raw biological sex' is somehow transformed into 'social gender'. The dichotomous structure of the pair had been evident since the late 1950s when, even before being taken up by feminist scholarship, it came to be theorised by male scholars who studied intersexuals and transsexuals.[22] But this dichotomy between the 'biological' and the 'social' does not resolve but only restates the old nature versus culture quarrel. Again, it relegates the dimension of women's body, sexuality, motherhood and physiological sexual difference to a supposedly pre-social sphere, and it resolves even less the question of precisely what part of women's experience and activity is 'biological' and what part 'social' or 'cultural'.

Furthermore, the new dichotomy differs in one important respect from the traditional one. It reduces women's embodiment no longer to a traditional nature, but to a modern 'biology'. Today 'biology' is in surprisingly current use by feminist scholars, and it refers almost always to women's body and especially to maternity. The term nature is now regularly placed in quotation marks, but not 'biology', which seems to be self-evident. Yet it is far from being self-evident because historically and culturally 'biology' has itself been a socio-cultural category, a discourse and a strategy for intervention. It came into circulation only since around 1900, was soon taken up by the right and the left and it meant, first of all, 'inferiority'.[23] Modern 'biology' is as little self-evident as 'nature' in traditional language, but it has probably more threatening consequences for women's studies and women's liberation, particularly in view of current heavy attacks on nature in the natural (and especially biological) sciences.

The new feminist use of 'biology' as distinct from, and opposed to, gender as a social category has made it possible for gender to be used not only as a radicalising weapon in the intellectual debate, but also as an instrument for rendering women again invisible. Gender has sometimes lent itself to a gender-neutral discourse which implies that women and men are members not of a sex but of a 'gender', in the sense that they are in reality nothing else than essentially identical 'individuals' and that sex doesn't matter, because it is 'biology' and therefore socially irrelevant.[24] Here again, the dichotomy expresses a hierarchy: 'gender' seems to be more important than 'sex'. On the other hand, there are feminist attempts to reverse this hierarchy and to view the female body as a female resource against overpowering male culture (but usually referring less to 'biology' than to old-fashioned 'nature'). Both views tend to attribute such 'biology' to women only and to leave unquestioned and unanalysed male 'biology', and they fail fully to historicise not only gender, but also sex.

Feminist scholars who insist on the dichotomy 'sex versus gender' or 'biology versus culture', even though they are aware of these problems, usually do so because this seems to be politically useful or tactically wise, in view of the ever-recurring attempts at confining women to their 'biological' sphere, mostly put forward by antifeminists adhering to 'biological determinism'. But this is merely a defensive position, not an advance. Rather, it seems that as long as intellectual and historical insights are rejected for reasons which are dictated by antifeminists and not by feminists' and women's experience, they will not lead to intellectually, historically and politically better results. In fact, it has been argued that what is called 'biological determinism' is 'not more of an attack on freedom than the social or economic determinism which is accepted . . . throughout social sciences', and what is really injurious is 'fatalism, the pretence that problems which are in our control lie outside it and are uncurable'.[25]

Finally, the dichotomous distinction between sex and gender is largely specific to the English language. Attempts have been made to introduce it into other languages – *sesso v. genere* in Italian, *sexe v. genre* in French – but their linguistic dynamics and connotations are very different (also, the traditional controversy of 'nature versus nurture' had much less historical impact in Italy and other countries of Romance languages than in the English- and German-speaking and the Scandinavian countries); for instance, the English 'gendered being' will continue to be an *essere sessuato* in Italian.[26] There are Turkish feminist scholars who must simply use both terms in English because their own language has different ways of expressing sexual relations. In German, there is only one concept for both, the old term *Geschlecht* which refers to grammatical gender, to sexual physiology, to the sexes, to families and generations, and to race such as in 'human race', *Menschengeschlecht*. German-speaking scholars are therefore in the position, both difficult and promising, of not being able to distinguish neatly, even though problematically, between physiology and culture with this terminology.

In this situation, it is not the concept of gender that should be challenged – as some feminist historians seem to prefer at present – but the linguistic and theoretical dichotomy of sex and gender. Particularly in history, the humanities and social sciences, it might be challenged through a procedure that has already been used fruitfully in historical research: doing away with the term 'biology' in the sense of the female body, its perception and activities (other and better terms are readily at hand), using 'gender' in a comprehensive sense which may include both the physiological and the cultural dimension, and using 'sex' in the same sense as 'gender', thus leaving space for continuities instead of polarities of meaning.[27]

2. Equality versus difference. The problems of the sex/gender dichotomy are closely related to those of another dichotomy with which we are faced today in a new way and in an international debate which has taken on different shapes and phases in different countries: that of 'equality versus difference'. Women's studies have largely relied on the concept of 'sexual' or 'gender equality' as an analytical tool, and physiological 'difference' has been played down as insignificant because it has so often been used to justify discriminatory treatment of women. In this perspective, it has been demanded that women be treated in the same way as men, as if they were men, and that new laws and reforms be formulated in gender-neutral terms (for instance, in recent debates in the women's rights commission of the European Parliament), thus eliminating sexual difference and rendering masculinity and femininity politically irrelevant. Other feminist scholars, however, argue that burning issues such as rape, abortion or wife-battering cannot be dealt with adequately in gender-neutral terms; that female 'difference', physiological as well as social, should not be erased but recognised, in historical, philosophical and legal terms; that it has never had a chance to develop autonomous political and cultural forms other than in social niches and in opposition to dominant cultures; that emphasis should be laid on a critical evaluation of men's distinctive needs and activities and that women's distinctive needs and activities should be valued, thus opening alternatives both to female inferiority and to women's assimilation to men.

The best known work using the first approach is Shulamith Firestone's *The Dialectics of Sex*, written at a time when the term 'gender' was not yet in widespread use. It proposed to abolish 'female biology' and sexual difference, pregnancy and motherhood with the means offered by modern technology such as *in vitro* fertilisation and childrearing by others than the 'biological' mother.[28] On the other side, and equally well-known, there is Carol Gilligan's important psychological work of the 1980s on women's 'different voice'. It avoids 'biological' reductionism and argues that women's distinctive development of moral judgment emphasises less the values of individual rights and properties than those of care, responsibility and connectedness; and that these values should not be seen as inferior to those of justice and rights, but of equal importance in the development of both sexes, and that they should be respected and practised also by men.[29]

The shift of public and scholarly interest from an emphasis on 'equality' to an emphasis on 'difference' is particularly visible and controversial in the United States.[30] But it is by no means entirely new. In the 1960s, the issue had been raised by the women's movement and the women's studies movement. They challenged the then prevailing assumption that equal rights alone can bring about women's liberation. This assumption has sometimes also been seen as specific to white culture. In 1968, African-American feminist Margaret Wright put it this way: 'In black women's liberation we don't want to be equal with men, just like in black liberation we're not fighting to be equal with the white man. We're fighting for the right to be different and not be punished for it'.[31] In Italy, feminist history, philosophy and feminism *tout court* are called, by feminists as well as in other people's daily language, *il pensiero della differenza sessuale*: thinking and acting in terms of sexual difference, affirming a female subjectivity which refuses to be assimilated ('homologised') to male versions of subjectivity such as the values and rights to compete, to possess, to dominate. They maintain that the affirmation of 'difference' in no way indicates weakness and resignation, but that it is a powerful weapon of women's liberation, and they distinguish this type of feminism from 'emancipationism' (*emancipazionismo*), which demands only the same rights and the same treatment with men – and therefore too little.[32] An Australian feminist philosopher has pointed out that 'odd things happen to women when the assumption is made that the only alternative to the patriarchal construction of sexual difference is the ostensibly sex-neutral individual'.[33] Among such odd things there is the argument, used by the United States Supreme Court in the 1970s, that the discrimination against pregnant women and young mothers who are refused maternity leaves and benefits, cannot be considered a discrimination on the basis of sex, because many women are neither pregnant nor mothers: in other words, that motherhood has nothing to do with womanhood. Other examples are the European welfare policies which do indeed grant maternity benefits with fewer problems than those prevailing in the United States, but do so on the grounds that pregnancy and childbirth are a disease.[34] These arguments and practices originate in the efforts of male paternalist politicians to homologise women's experience of maternity to the male-centred policy and experience of sickness insurance, which did not recognise women and mothers in their own right (and from female and feminist efforts to secure financial help for employed mothers within the established insurance system).

Some scholars tend to believe that the dichotomy 'equality versus difference' is simply a false dichotomy, more the result of misunderstandings than of insight. But others insist on the mutually exclusive character of the relation between 'equality' and 'difference', and therefore on the necessity of an either/or choice. The historian Joan Hoff-Wilson urges that a decision be made, particularly by feminist leaders, between either 'equality between the sexes based on prevailing masculine societal norms' or 'justice between the sexes based on a recognition of equal, but different socialised patterns of behavior'.[35] On the other hand, the historian Joan Scott considers this to be 'an impossible choice', and she questions precisely the dichotomy itself.[36] I also believe that it is unacceptable, among other reasons because both the 'difference dilemma' ('difference' being used, overtly or implicitly, to confirm women's inferiority in relation to men) and the 'equality dilemma' ('equality' being used, overtly or implicitly, to erase gender difference in view of women's assimilation to male societal norms) are far from being sufficiently explored.[37] Such an exploration should be put on the agenda for future women's history. Why is it, for instance, that 'equality' and 'justice' seem to complement each other in the case of men, but be opposed to each other in the case of women? Why is it that 'difference' is only attributed to one half of humankind and not to the other? Why is it that 'equality' is so intimately bound up with 'fraternity', but not with sisterhood, since the French Revolution but also in earlier political thought?[38]

Again, the only way forward seems to be to challenge the dichotomy itself, and to do so by analysing and dismantling the sexist construction of difference as well as of equality: of an equality that may merely be 'based on prevailing masculine societal norms' and of a (female) difference which is merely understood as 'socialized patterns of behaviour'. An Italian philosopher of the *differenza sessuale* maintains that 'different *and* equal is possible', if equality is not understood as 'eliminating one of the two different entities in the other', if 'each of the two different sides is free, and if the concept of equality radically abandons its logical foundation in the abstract, serialising universalisation of the male one'. Carole Pateman has explored and challenged this dichotomy through a critique of the traditional construction of equality as a relation between 'individuals' who are essentially of the same, masculine, sex and which excludes difference, namely women. She has also interrogated this dichotomy through a critique of the traditional construction of difference which is defined not in natural terms, but in political terms as subordination, inferiority and powerlessness.[39]

The debate seems to be of particular significance to women's and gender history, not the least because of the fact that studying women and the sexes is important not only in situations where women and men have been treated differently in the past, but also where they have been treated identically – as in the case of the victims of National Socialist anti-Semitism and racism who became victims regardless of their sex.[40] But history may also be useful for today's attempts at challenging the dichotomy, and three historical issues show that we are by no means the first generation to struggle with it. Karen Offen has recently pointed out that the earlier western women's movements of the nineteenth and early twentieth century dealt with it in theory and practice, and they searched to establish a new relationship between the hierarchical and apparently exclusive terms. These movements demanded equal political citizenship, equal access to well-paid positions as well as equal recognition of the value of women's distinctive ('different') contributions where a sexual division of labour exists. They did so in the United States and in Europe, on the part of radical and of moderate feminists. Concepts that were equally important to this approach include equality, equivalence, equity, and 'equality in difference' and also, perhaps, 'difference in equality'.[41] The discussion of the relationship between equality and difference has some of its roots in the early modern European 'querelle des femmes', at the time when the concept 'equality' came to be used explicitly in efforts to improve women's condition, in place of the earlier controversy around the superiority or 'pre-excellence' of the female or the male sex respectively; it was carried on mostly in France, Italy and England.[42] New, and sometimes dichotomous, formulations of their relationship emerged during the nineteenth and the early twentieth centuries, often linked to new feminist ideas and policies for the improvement of the situation of mothers, particularly those living in poverty, and especially with respect to the issues of the endowment of motherhood by the state and protective labour legislation. Since the 1920s, most conspicuously in the United States and Britain, women's movements have split along the lines of emphasis on 'difference' and on 'equality'.[43] The terms of this historical debate have not yet been sufficiently explored, but it seems clear that we are dealing here with a female and feminist heritage which needs to be both accepted and overcome since we cannot afford to remain trapped in an impossible choice.

Another historical example concerns the questions raised above by Margaret Wright: whom do we want to be equal to? what is the relation between the right to be equal and the right to be different? what is legitimate 'equality' and legitimate 'difference'? In recent years, the gender-based assumptions and uses of the concept of equality have been studied extensively, particularly in the context of the French Revolution. Women's progress towards the great goal of equal political rights during the past century has often been compared to the earlier extension of suffrage from the male propertied class to the male working class. But another comparison seems to be yet more illuminating: the comparison with the emancipation of groups which have been excluded from equal political and social rights in ways similar to women's exclusion, but different from the exclusion of the male working class, namely the emancipation of ethnic minorities, the male and female victims of racism.

For instance, the concept of Jewish emancipation in nineteenth-century Germany, as it was formulated mostly by non-Jewish German men, was based on an equality which explicitly excluded difference. Male Jews were accepted as German citizens on equal terms if they gave up, at least ostensibly, their Jewishness, if they accepted assimilation to German non-Jews. Among Jews themselves, this situation was expressed in a phrase which characteristically refers to one of the dichotomies outlined in the first section: 'Be a human being (or rather: a man) in the public world, a Jew in the private home' [*sei draußen ein Mensch und zu Hause ein Jude*]. Jewish men had to become equal (to German men) in order to be accepted as equals. Among others (for instance the various currents for Jewish cultural and political revival), it was the German Jewish women's movement in the first third of our century that questioned this view of equality. Often pointing to the parallels between Jewish and female emancipation, Jewish women insisted in both respects on the right to be equal as well as on the right to be different, as women from men and as Jews from non-Jews.[44] Later, National Socialist racism, and particularly anti-Semitism, excluded Jews not only from the right to be equal to German non-Jews, but also from the right to be different as Jews.

A third historical example refers to our specifically European heritage of political thought. There is one reason why the emphasis on sexual equality so often seems to be the only powerful weapon of and strategy for women's liberation and women's studies, despite the awareness that it may imply an assimilation to prevailing androcentric and unquestioned societal norms which not all women (and men) may want to share, and that is the fact that, since the time of the Greek polis, democratic and socialist movements have pursued their goals under the banner of equality (and reactionary movements have attacked them on these grounds). This concept is therefore not only a most precious heritage of western political thought, but also one of its most well-established and accepted concepts. There is, however, another and equally precious heritage: the idea of tolerance as it emerged from the bloody religious wars in early modern Europe. Tolerance emphasised, at least in its early and radical formulations, liberty, justice and mutual respect, understood as a recognition of both difference and equality. Of course, tolerance and liberty, just like equality, were reserved for male or male-dominated groups and should be analysed and historicised in this perspective. But perhaps one challenge to the gender-linked dichotomy 'equality versus difference' could and should be the idea and reality of a reconceptualised tolerance instead of mutual exclusiveness.[45] In other words, the task might be to recognise *and* deconstruct 'equality' as well as to deconstruct *and* recognise 'difference'.

The idea and practice of tolerance of 'difference' has had manifold meanings and important implications for women and women's studies at scholarly institutions. In Germany around 1900, when women's admission to the universities on equal terms with men was debated, an inquiry among about one hundred professors brought to the fore many voices which insisted that academic scholarship was 'men's work' [*Männerwerk*] and that women were not welcome. Others agreed to their admission on the condition that women were proved to possess capacities equal to those of men. Only one of them, a Jewish scholar, welcomed women precisely because they might have not only equal, but also different capacities; he hoped they would contribute to 'the revival of rigidified institutions' by 'dealing with obsolete methods and authorities in a different way than the men who have been educated, from early youth on, towards iron-hard discipline'.[46]

3. Integration versus autonomy. An analogous argument may be appropriate in regard to the problems of the 'integration' or 'autonomy' of women's studies in respect to scholarship at large, and of women in respect to academic institutions. Despite the expansion of women's studies, and even though it is now occasionally admitted as a 'sub-disciplinary specialisation',[47] its impact on and integration in the academic disciplines have remained minimal, and what has been called 'mainstreaming' is still far from being implemented, even though there are important differences here as to countries and disciplines. For example, the German author of an essay on Edith Stein, a Catholic philosopher of Jewish descent who was killed by the National Socialists, justified his interest in her by writing that 'Edith Stein was not only an outstanding woman, but also a great human being' [*ein großer Mensch*].[48] Women, it seems, are still not worthy of interest in themselves, are not even necessarily *Menschen* unless they may be placed alongside 'great men'. On the other hand, women's history is able to change the study of other historical fields, too, even though slowly and in paradoxical ways. For instance, historians still write of 'universal suffrage' for the period when women were excluded from it.[49] Many others are now also using the term 'universal male suffrage' – but this does no more than illuminate explicitly the assumption that male activities are considered 'universal'. When instead the correct term 'male adult suffrage' is used, it shows that a broadening awareness of women's history leads also to an awareness of men as men.[50] But this does not yet, by itself, lead to the integration of the struggle for women's suffrage into books on political history at large; it is still dealt with as a separate and segregated field of research.

Clearly, women's studies need to be recognised as an integral part of scholarship at large. But such 'mainstreaming' may also risk being drawn into a dynamic that makes women invisible again. There are now a number of cases where 'gender history' is being opposed, in a dichotomous way, to 'women's history', and where chairs in 'women's history' are strongly opposed, but chairs in 'gender history' are welcome.[51] As an institutional problem, the latter situation may be dealt with according to institutional circumstances, but the theoretical problem remains, largely due to a specific definition of 'gender' which excludes sexual 'difference', meaning women, by classifying it as 'biological' and therefore as socially and historically irrelevant. In such a view, the radical promise of gender history as an extension of women's history risks being subverted by the reduction of the history of women, once again, to a mere appendix of an allegedly more 'generic' gender history. Again, women are not considered to be an equally universal subject as are other, and male-centred subjects.

Therefore, women's history also requires autonomy from male-dominated scholarship, in institutional and particularly in intellectual terms, in order to develop its full potential. But 'autonomy', another virtue central to the heritage of the Renaissance and the Enlightenment, also needs to be redefined.[52] In practice, the difficult question is to recognize the fine line, which is also a profound divide, between autonomy and segregation, the ghetto in which women's studies often find themselves. It seems that the problem 'autonomy versus integration' cannot be adequately dealt with through terminological distinctions, between women's history, feminist history, and gender history, or, in the terminology of the French debates, between *histoire des femmes, histoire féminine, histoire féministe,* and *histoire des sexes*, or between all these and history *tout court*; nor does the problem coincide with the debate for and against 'institutionalisation' which has been the main theoretical political issue in the West German debate on women's studies for over a decade. Important women-centred and gender-conscious research has been done under all these labels, even outside these labels,[53] in universities, in feminist institutions and outside male-dominated or female institutions.

* * * * *

Challenging dichotomies seems to be a major issue on the scholarly as well as the political agenda of women's and gender history, and of women's studies more broadly. The act of challenging requires, of course, further study of the precise character of the opposing categories, of the particularities and dynamics of the dichotomous relationship, and of the form and character of the challenge itself.

As to the nature of gender-based dichotomies, there is obviously a significant difference between the first set of three which have been mentioned in the earlier section of this paper, and the latter set of three. This difference reflects, among other things, the increasingly complex character of the categories under which gender relations are being considered and studied. The dichotomies nature/culture, paid/unpaid work, public/private were constructed in alignment with a fixed divide between women and men, the ostensibly internally homogeneous categories on each side of which pointing either to women or to men. In the case of sex/gender, equality/difference, integration/autonomy, however, both (apparently) opposing terms refer to both sexes. We are therefore not dealing just with relations between the sexes, but with relations between relational categories; and not just with (apparent) contradictories between women and men, but with opposing or apparently opposing conceptualisations and practices of gender relations. Hence, women's studies and the search for new visions of gender has led us – despite, or rather because of sometimes profoundly different approaches – to at least one common ground: gender issues are issues which concern complex human relations, relations both between the sexes and within the sexes.

And what could or should be the character of the challenge? It requires continuous work on the dismantling, historicisation, and deconstruction of the apparently given meanings of the various categories. I believe that it also implies the rejection of mutually exclusive hierarchies, and especially of either/or solutions, in favour of as-well-as solutions; it also implies the rejection of the principle *tertium non datur*. In the case of the two latter dilemmas, we may particularly need to challenge their mutual exclusiveness and claim 'equality in difference' and 'difference in equality', 'autonomy in integration' and 'integration in autonomy'. For both of them one might object, and it has been objected, that women cannot have their cake and eat it too. But for too long, women have baked the cake and taken only the smallest slice to eat for themselves.

NOTES

1. Gerda Lerner, 'New Approaches to the Study of Women in History' (1969), in *The Majority Finds its Past* (New York: Oxford University Press, 1979), p. 3. My paper is a revision of one that was first presented at the conference of the Nordic Research Councils on 'Strategies for Women's Studies in the Humanities' (Helsinki, May 1989) and was published as Working Paper no. 89/396 of the European University Institute (Florence, 1989). I wish to thank particularly Ida Blom, Mineke Bosch, Rosi Braidotti, Annarita Buttafuoco, Sara Matthews Grieco, Karen Offen, Ruth Roach Pierson, Marjan Schwegmann and Heide Wunder for their helpful comments.

2. Sherry Ortner, 'Is Female to Male as Nature is to Culture?', in Michelle Z. Rosaldo and Louise Lamphere (eds.), *Woman, Culture and Society* (Stanford: Stanford University Press, 1974), p. 72; the quote is from Carole Pateman, 'Feminist Critiques of the Public/Private Dichotomy', in Anne Phillips (ed.), *Feminism and Equality* (New York: New York University Press, 1987), p. 110.

3. See Gianna Pomata, 'La storia delle donne: una questione di confine [The History of Women: A Question of Boundaries]', in Giovanni de Luna et al. (eds.), *Il mondo contemporaneo: Gli strumenti della ricerca*, II (Florence: La Nuova Italia, 1983), pp. 1434-69; Marilyn Strathern (ed.), *Dealing with Inequality: Analysing Gender Relations in Melanesia and Beyond* (Cambridge: Cambridge University Press, 1987).

4. Yvonne Knibiehler, *L'histoire des mères du moyen-âge à nos jours* (Paris: Edition Montalba, 1980); Mireille Laget, *Naissances: L'accouchement avant l'âge de la clinique* (Paris: Seuil, 1982); Francoise Thébaud, *Quand nos grand-mères donnaient la vie* (Lyon: Presses Universitaires de Lyon, 1986); Susan R. Suleiman (ed.), *The Female Body in Western Culture* (Cambridge: Harvard University Press, 1986).

5. See, for example, the special issues of *Signs. Journal of Women in Culture and Society*, 6, no. 1 (1980), and 7, no. 1 (1981); cf. Elizabeth Grosz, 'Philosophy, Subjectivity and the Body: Kristeva and Irigaray', in Carole Pateman and Elizabeth Grosz (eds.), *Feminist Challenges: Social and Political Theory* (Sydney: Allen and Unwin, 1986), pp. 125-43.

6. Michelle Perrot (ed.), *Une histoire des femmes est-elle possible?* (Paris: Édition Rivages, 1984); Cécile Dauphin et al., 'Culture et pouvoir des femmes: essai d'historiographie', *Annales: E.S.C.*, 41 (1986), pp. 271-93, reprinted in translation in this volume.

7. Mariarosa Dalla Costa and Selma James, *The Power of Women and the Subversion of the Community* (London: Falling Wall Press, 1975); Ellen Malos (ed.), *The Politics of Housework* (London: Allison and Busby, 1980); Luisella Goldschmidt-Clermont, *Unpaid Work in the Household: A Review of Economic Evaluation Methods* (Geneva: International Labour Office, 1982); Bettina Cass, 'Rewards for Women's Work', in Jacqueline Goodnow and Carole Pateman (eds.), *Women, Social Science and Public Policy* (Sydney: Allen and Unwin, 1985), pp. 67-94. The analysis of women's domestic work has also been a way of questioning the dichotomous use of the multi-faceted categories 'production' and 'reproduction'.

8. Desley Deacon, 'Political Arithmetic: The 19th-Century Australian Census and the Construction of the Dependent Woman', *Signs*, 11, no. 1 (1985), pp. 27-47; Edwards Higgs, 'Women, Occupations and Work in the 19th Century Censuses', *History Workshop*, 23 (Spring 1987), pp. 59-80; for the French census see Martine Martin, 'Ménagère: une profession? Les dilemmes de l'entre-deux-guerres', *Le Mouvement social*, 140 (1987), pp. 89-106; for the German feminists' demand see their memorandum to the Imperial Statistical Office, *Die Frauenbewegung*, 3 (1 February 1901). For the history of housework see, for example, Gisela Bock and Barbara Duden, 'Arbeit aus Liebe – Liebe als Arbeit: Zur Geschichte der Hausarbeit im Kapitalismus [Work as Love, Love as Work: On the History of Housework under Capitalism]', in Gruppe Berliner Dozentinnen (ed.), *Frauen und Wissenschaft* (Berlin: Courage Verlag, 1977), pp. 188-99; Karin Hausen, 'Große Wäsche. Technischer Fortschritt und sozialer Wandel in Deutschland vom 18. bis ins 20. Jahrhundert [Large Washes: Technical Progress and Social Change in Germany from the 18th to the 20th Century]', *Geschichte und Gesellschaft*, 13 (1987), pp. 273-303; Sibylle Meyer, *Das Theater mit der Hausarbeit. Bürgerliche Repräsentation in der Familie der wilhelminischen Zeit* [Housework as Theatre: Bourgeois Representations in the Family in Imperial Germany] (Frankfurt: Campus, 1982); Caroline Davidson, *Woman's work is never done: A History of Housework in the British Isles 1650-1950* (London: Chatto, 1982); Susan Strasser, *Never Done: A History of American Housework* (New York: Pantheon, 1982); Ruth Schwartz Cowan, *More Work for Mother: The Ironies of Household Technology from the Open Hearth to the Microwave* (New York: Basic Books, 1986); Glenna Matthews, *'Just*

a Housewife': The Rise and Fall of Domesticity in America (New York: Oxford University Press, 1987).

9. Alice Kessler-Harris, *Out to Work: A History of Wage-Earning Women in the United States* (Oxford: Oxford University Press, 1982); Julie A. Matthaei, *An Economic History of Women in America* (New York: Schocken, 1982); Angela V. John, *Unequal Opportunities: Women's Employment in England 1800-1918* (Oxford: Basil Blackwell, 1986); Ann Curthoys, 'Equal pay, a family wage or both: women workers, feminists and unionists in Australia since 1945', in Barbara Caine et al., *Crossing Boundaries: Feminisms and the Critique of Knowledge* (Sydney: Allen and Unwin, 1988), pp. 129-40.

10. See the review of recent publications on Britain and the United States by Regina Morantz-Sanchez, 'Nurses and their History', *Women's Review of Books*, 6, no. 4 (1989), pp. 12-14. Shortly after the West German nurses' strike, there was also a considerable number of nurses among those who left East Germany, often because of low pay.

11. Hilda Scott, *Working Your Way to the Bottom: The Feminization of Poverty* (London: Pandora, 1984); Wolfram Fischer, *Armut in der Geschichte* [Poverty in History] (Göttingen: Vandenhoeck and Ruprecht, 1982); Bettina Cass, 'The Feminisation of Poverty', in *Crossing Boundaries*, pp. 110-28.

12. Carole Pateman, *The Sexual Contract* (Cambridge: Polity Press, 1988), especially, ch. 1.

13. Leonore Davidoff and Catherine Hall, *Family Fortunes: Men and Women of the English Middle Class, 1780-1850* (London: Hutchinson, 1987); Frank Prochaska, *Women and Philanthropy in 19th-Century England* (Oxford: Clarendon, 1980); Christoph Sachße, *Mütterlichkeit als Beruf: Sozialarbeit, Sozialreform und Frauenbewegung 1871-1929* Maternalism as a Profession: Social Work, Social Reform and the Women's Movement 1871-1929] (Frankfurt: Suhrkamp, 1986).

14. Carole Pateman, 'The Patriarchal Welfare State', in Amy Gutman (ed.), *Democracy and the Welfare State* (Princeton: Princeton University Press, 1987), pp. 231-60. See also Jane Lewis (ed.), *Women's Welfare, Women's Rights* (London: Croom Helm, 1983); Cora V. Baldock and Bettina Cass (eds.), *Women, Social Welfare and the State in Australia* (Sydney: Allen and Unwin, 1983); Harriet Holter (ed.), *Patriarchy in a Welfare Society* (Oslo: Univerfsitetsforlaget, 1984); Jennifer Dale and Peggy Foster (eds.), *Feminists and State Welfare* (London: Routledge and Kegan Paul, 1986); Helga Maria Hernes, *Welfare State and Women Power* (Oslo: Oslo University Press, 1987); Anne Showstack Sassoon (ed.), *Women and the State* (London: Unwin Hyman, 1987); Seth Koven and Sonya Michel, 'Gender and the Origins of the Welfare State', *Radical History Review*, 43 (1989), pp. 112-19.

15. For this political theory, the authors of the National Socialist sterilisation law of 1933 referred to the philosopher Carl Schmitt: Gisela Bock, *Zwangssterilisation im Nationalsozialismus: Studien zur Rassenpolitik und Frauenpolitik* [Coercive Sterilisation under the National Socialist Regime: Studies in Racism and Sexism] (Opladen: Westdeutscher Verlag, 1986), p. 87; see also pp. 369-465.

16. Karen Offen, 'Depopulation, Nationalism, and Feminism in Fin-de-Siècle France', *American Historical Review*, 89 (1984), pp. 648-76; and 'Liberty, Equality, and Justice for Women: The Theory and Practice of Feminism in

Nineteenth-Century Europe', in Renate Bridenthal et al. (eds.), *Becoming Visible: Women in European History*, 2nd ed. (Boston: Houghton-Mifflin, 1987), pp. 335-73; Karen J. Blair, *The Clubwoman as Feminist* (New York: Holmes and Meier, 1980); Barbara Leslie Epstein, *The Politics of Domesticity* (Middletown: Wesleyan University Press, 1981); Paula Baker, 'The Domestication of Politics', *American Historical Review*, 89, no. 3 (1984), pp. 620-47, especially p. 646. Mary Madeleine Ladd-Taylor, 'Mother-Work: Ideology, Public Policy, and the Mothers' Movement, 1890-1930', Ph.D. thesis, Yale University, 1986.

    17. Lamphere and Rosaldo (eds.), *Woman, Culture and Society*, pp. 37-38; Carroll Smith-Rosenberg, *Disorderly Conduct: Visions of Gender in Victorian America* (New York: Knopf, 1985); Linda Kerber, 'Separate Spheres, Female Worlds, Women's Place: The Rhetoric of Women's History', *Journal of American History*, 75, no. 1 (1988), pp. 9-39; Lois W. Banner, 'Women's History in the United States: Recent Theory and Practice', in Esther Katz (ed.), *Recent Work in Women's History: East and West*, special issue of *Trends in History*, 4, no. 1 (1985), pp. 93-122.

    18. For example, Jürgen Habermas, *Strukturwandel der Öffentlichkeit: Untersuchungen zu einer Kategorie der bürgerlichen Gesellschaft* [The Structural Transformmation of the Public Sphere: An Inquiry into a Category of Bourgeois Society] (Neuwied: Luchterhand, 1962).

    19. Nancy Jay, 'Gender and Dichotomy', *Feminist Studies*, 7, no. 1 (1981), p. 44.

    20. Ann Oakley, *Sex, Gender and Society* (London: Temple Smith, 1972); Gayle Rubin, 'The Traffic in Women: Notes on the Political Economy of Sex', in Rayna Reiter (ed.), *Toward an Anthropology of Women* (New York: Monthly Review Press, 1975), pp. 157-210; Joan W. Scott, 'Gender: A Useful Category of Historical Analysis', *American Historical Review*, 91 (1986), pp. 1053-75, reprinted in her *Gender and the Politics of History* (New York: Columbia University Press, 1988).

    21. See, for example, Elizabeth Grosz, 'What is Feminist Theory?', *Feminist Challenges*, p. 194. For 'men's history' see David Morgan, 'Men Made Manifest: Histories and Masculinities', *Gender and History*, 1 (1989), pp. 87-91; Lois W. Banner, 'Women's History', pp. 119-20; 'Book Review', *Signs*, 14, no. 3 (1989), pp. 703-8; Marilyn Lake, 'The Politics of Respectability: Identifying the Masculinist Context', *Historical Studies*, 22, no. 86 (1986), pp. 116-31.

    22. Robert Stoller, 'A Contribution to the Study of Gender Identity', *International Journal of Psychoanalysis*, 45 (1964), pp. 220-26; see especially Donna Haraway, 'Gender for a Marxist Dictionary: The Sexual Politics of a Word', unpublished paper, pp. 6-8.

    23. See my *Zwangssterilisation*, pp. 33-34, 76, 326, and 'Women's History and Gender History', *Gender & History*, 1 (1988), pp. 11-15.

    24. See Pateman, *Sexual Contract*, p. 225.

    25. Mary Midgley, 'On Not Being Afraid of Natural Sex Difference', in Morwenna Griffiths and Margaret Whitford (eds.), *Feminist Perspectives in Philosophy* (London: Macmillan, 1988), pp. 38-39.

    26. See Paola Di Cori, 'Dalla storia delle donne a una storia di genere [From Women's History to Gender History]', *Rivista di storia contemporanea*, 16 (1987), pp. 548-9; *Les Cahiers du Grif*, 37-38 (1988), special issue on 'Le genre de l'histoire [The Gender of History]'.

27. In such a non-dichotomous way, gender has also been used, at least occasionally, at earlier periods; for examples, see Scott, 'Gender', pp. 1053; French examples, to which Karen Offen has kindly drawn my attention, are the *Requête des dames à l'Assemblée nationale* (1789), in Amedée Lefaure, *Le Socialisme pendant la Révolution Française* (Paris: Dentu, 1863), p. 139 ('2. Le sexe féminin jouira toujours de la même liberté, des mêmes avantages, des mêmes droits et des mêmes honneurs que le sexe masculin. 3. Le genre masculin ne sera plus regardé, même dans la grammaire, comme le genre le plus noble, attendu que tous les genres, tous les sexes et tous les êtres doivent être et sont également nobles'), and Mme d'Epinay, *Les Conversations d'Emilie* (Paris: 1776), p. 11. See also Marilyn Strathern, Introduction to *Dealing with Inequality*, pp. 6 and 31, note 4.

28. Shulamith Firestone, *The Dialectic of Sex. The Case for Feminist Revolution* (New Haven: Yale University Press, 1970).

29. Carol Gilligan, *In a Different Voice: Psychological Theory and Women's Development* (Cambridge: Harvard University Press, 1982).

30. Controversial particularly in the context of the defeat of the Equal Rights Amendment, the case of the U.S. Equal Employment Opportunity Commission v. Sears and Roebuck (cf. *Signs*, 11 (1986), pp. 751-79, (1988), pp. 897-903), and the litigation around maternity leave and maternity benefit for employed women; see Joan Hoff-Wilson, 'The Unfinished Revolution: Changing the Legal Status of U.S. Women', *Signs*, 13, no. 1 (1987), pp. 7-36.

31. Margaret Wright, 'I Want the Right to Be Black and Me', in Gerda Lerner (ed.), *Black Women in White America* (New York: Random House, 1972), p. 608.

32. See, for example, Adriana Cavarero et al., *Diotima. Il pensiero della differenza sessuale* [Diotima: Philosophy of Sexual Difference] (Milano: Tartaruga Edizioni, 1987).

33. Pateman, *Sexual Contract*, p. 187.

34. See the references in note 14 above; for the history of and the juridical and feminist debate on the United States Supreme court decisions and on their change in the 1980s, see Wendy Williams, 'The Equality Crisis: Some Reflections on Culture, Courts, and Feminism', *Women's Rights Law Reporter*, 7, no. 3 (1982), pp. 175-200 and 'Equality's Riddle: Pregnancy and the Equal Treatment/Special Treatment Debate', *New York University Review of Law and Social Change*, 13 (1984/85), pp. 325-80; Sylvia A. Law, 'Rethinking Sex and the Constitution', *University of Pennsylvania Law Review*, 132 (1984), pp. 955-1040; Herma Hill Kay, 'Models of Equality', *University of Illinois Law Review*, 1 (1985), pp. 39-88; Lucinda M. Finley, 'Transcending Equality Theory: A Way Out of the Maternity and the Workplace Debate', *Columbia Law Review*, 86 (1986), pp. 1118-83.

35. Hoff-Wilson, 'Unfinished Revolution', p. 36.

36. Joan W. Scott, 'Deconstructing Equality-versus-Difference: or, The Uses of Poststructuralist Theory of Feminism', *Feminist Studies*, 14, no. 1 (1988), p. 43.

37. For discussion of the 'Difference dilemma' see Scott, 'Equality-versus-Difference', p. 48; cf. p. 39. On 'Wollstonecraft's dilemma', see Pateman, 'Welfare State', p. 252.

38. See Pateman, *Sexual Contract*, especially p. 3 and ch. 4.

39. Adriana Cavarero, 'Eguaglianza e differenza sessuale: le amnesie del pensiero politico [Equality and Sexual Difference: On the Amnesia of Political Thought]', in her paper presented at the conference on 'Equality and Difference: Gender Dimensions in Political Thought, Justice and Morality' at the European University Institute (Florence), December 1988; Carole Pateman, 'Women's Citizenship: Equality, Difference, Subordination', paper presented at the same conference, and also *Sexual Contract*; see also Jean Bethke Elshtain, 'The Feminist Movement and the Question of Equality', in *Polity*, 2, no. 4 (1975), pp. 452-77; Douglas Rae et al., *Equalities* (Cambridge: Harvard University Press, 1981).

40. Gisela Bock, 'Equality and Difference: Gender Dimensions of National Socialist Racism and Genocide', paper presented at the conference mentioned in the previous note.

41. Karen Offen, 'Defining Feminism: A Comparative Historical Approach', *Signs*, 14, no. 1 (1988), pp. 119-57; see also her 'Depopulation', and 'Ernest Legouvé and the Doctrine of "Equality in Difference" for Women: A Case Study of Male Feminism in Nineteenth-Century French Thought', *The Journal of Modern History*, 58 (1986), pp. 452-84; Annarita Buttafuoco, *Cronache femminili. Temi e momenti della stampa emancipazionista in Italia dall'Unità al fascismo* [Women's Time: Themes and Events in the Emancipationist Press from Unification to Fascism] (Siena: Università di Siena, 1988); Jane Rendall (ed.), *Equal or Different. Women's Politics 1800-1914* (Oxford: Basil Blackwell, 1987).

42. Joan Kelly, 'Early Feminist Theory and the Querelle des Femmes, 1400-1780', *Signs*, 8 (1982), pp. 4-28. Marie de Gournay, *Egalité des hommes et des femmes* (1622), was the first to employ 'equality' as a key and title concept. For the texts of the earlier 'querelle' see Marina Zancan (ed.), *Nel cerchio della luna. Figure di donna in alcuni testi del XVI secolo* [In the Lunar Cycle: Images of Women in Some 16th-Century Texts] (Venice: Marsilio, 1983), pp. 236-64; Maria Luisa Doglio (ed.), *Galeazzo Flavio Capra, della eccellenza e dignità delle donne* [On the Excellence and Dignity of Women] (Rome: Bulzoni, 1988), pp. 113-25; Maité Albistur and Daniel Armogathe, *Histoire du féminisme français*, vol. 1 (Paris: Édition des femmes, 1977), ch. 4 and 5; Madeleine Lazard, *Images littéraires de la femme à la Renaissance* (Paris: Presses Universitaires, 1985), ch. 1; Moira Ferguson, 'Feminist Polemic: British Women's Writings in English from the Late Renaissance to the French Revolution', *Women's Studies International Forum*, 9, no. 5 (1986), pp. 451-64.

43. Jane Lewis, *Models of Equality for Women: The Case of State Support for Children in 19th-Century Britain* (Florence: Working Paper No. 87/314 of the European University Institute, 1987); Suzy Fleming, Introduction to: Eleanor Rathbone, *The Disinherited Family* (1st ed. 1924) (Bristol: Falling Wall Press, 1986), pp. 9-120; Nancy F. Cott, *The Grounding of Modern Feminism* (New Haven, London: Yale University Press, 1987); Ladd-Taylor, *Mother-Work*; Jennifer Friesen and Ronald K. L. Collins, 'Looking Back on Muller v. Oregon', *American Bar Association Journal*, 69 (1983), pp. 294-98, 472-77; Susan Kingsley Kent, 'The Politics of Sexual Difference. World War I and the Demise of British Feminism', *Journal of British Studies*, 27 (1988), pp. 232-53; Gisela Bock and Pat Thane (eds.), *Maternity, Visions of Gender and the Rise of the European Welfare States* (London: Routledge, forthcoming).

44. Shulamit Volkov, 'Jüdische Assimilation und jüdische Eigenart im Deutschen Kaiserreich [Jewish Assimilation and Jewish Distinctness in the German Empire]', *Geschichte und Gesellschaft*, 9 (1983), pp. 331-48, p. 339; Marion A. Kaplan, 'Tradition and Transition. The Acculturation, Assimilation and Integration of Jews in Imperial Germany: A Gender Analysis', *Year Book of the Leo Baeck Institute*, 27 (1982), pp. 3-35 and *The Jewish Feminist Movement in Germany. The Campaigns of the Jüdischer Frauenbund, 1904-1938* (Westport: Greenwood Press, 1979).

45. See Hans R. Guggisberg, *Religiöse Toleranz. Dokumente zur Geschichte einer Forderung* [Religious Tolerance: Documents on the History of a Demand] (Stuttgart-Bad Cannstatt: Frommannholzboog, 1984), especially pp. 9-11; and 'The Defence of Religious Toleration and Religious Liberty in Early Modern Europe: Arguments, Pressures, and Some Consequences', *History of European Ideas*, 4, no. 1 (1983), pp. 35-50; John Horton and Susan Mendus (ed.), *Aspects of Toleration: Philosophical Studies* (London and New York: Methuen, 1985); W. J. Sheils (eds.), *Persecution and Toleration* (Basil Blackwell, 1984); Jay, 'Gender and Dichotomy', p. 54.

46. Quoted in Karin Hausen, 'Warum Männer Frauen zur Wissenschaft nicht zulassen wollten [Why Men Won't Let Women Do Science]', in Hausen and Helga Nowotny (eds.), *Wie männlich ist die Wissenschaft?* [How Masculine is Science?] (Frankfurt: Suhrkamp, 1986), pp. 38-39.

47. Anna Yeatman, 'Women, Domestic Life and Sociology', in *Feminist Challenges*, p. 177; for an illuminating discussion about the relation between autonomy, integration and 'mainstreaming' of women's history, see Louise A. Tilly, 'Gender, Women's History, and Social History', *Social Science History*, 13, no. 4 (1989), pp. 439-62, and the responses by Gay L. Gullickson and Judith M. Bennett, pp. 463-77; see also Gerda Lerner, 'Priorities and Challenges in U. S. Women's History Research', *Perspectives* (April 1988), pp. 17-20.

48. 'Allein das rechtfertigt schon unser Interesse [That alone justifies our interest]': Ulrich von Hehl, 'Edith Stein und die Deportation der katholischen Juden aus den Niederlanden [Edith Stein and the Deportation of Catholic Jews from the Netherlands]', *Frankfurter Allgemeine Zeitung*, 30 March 1987.

49. Klaus Erich Pollmann, 'Arbeiterwahl im Norddeutschen Bund 1867-70 [Workers' Suffrage in the North German Confederation 1867-70]', *Geschichte und Gesellschaft*, 15, no. 2 (1989), p. 165.

50. Hans-Ulrich Wehler, *Deutsche Gesellschaftsgeschichte* [German Social History], vol. 2: *1815-1845/49* (München: Beck, 1987), pp. 716, 733; 'male suffrage' in Peter Flora, *State, Economy and Society in Western Europe 1815-1975*, vol. 1 (Frankfurt, a.m.: Campus, 1983), p. 91.

51. One of these cases is described in Susan Magaray, 'Australian Women's History in 1986', *Australian Historical Association Bulletin* (October 1987), pp. 5-12; there are similar examples in European countries, for instance, in West Germany.

52. For attempts at redefinition see Midgley, p. 39, and Pateman, *Sexual Contract*.

53. One example is Jill Stephenson, *The Nazi Organisation of Women* (London: Croom Helm, 1981), who underlies that this book is not 'intended to be of the "women's history" genre' (p. 11).

2

Demographic History and Its Perception of Women from the Seventeenth to the Nineteenth Century

Anne-Lise Head-König

Historical demographers are especially concerned with changes observed in respect to nuptiality, fertility and mortality, which are interwoven with socio-economic evolution. These factors are, of course, never static and have to be examined with respect to a specific time and context.[1] It should be pointed out that demographic history is a field of research that can develop only in the presence of appropriate and abundant data. In European (and North American) history this data has existed for many centuries, thanks to systematic efforts by churches and states to record (however sporadically) baptisms (which permit deductions in respect to births), deaths or marriages.

Until the late 1970s demographic history did not invariably take account of differences in the experiences of women and men. This can partly be explained by the fact that, being a young discipline, it was necessary first to define the relevant field of research and the necessary methodology. Since an integral element of the discipline in its early stages was the reconstitution of the family data, logically there was a need for a global approach involving the study of the two sexes simultaneously. However, as the discipline developed, it became clear that the study of both similarities and differences within the interrelationship would provide new and fruitful insights. Such work allows us to argue that both physiological and social factors are of prime importance when considering women's role in society. So, sex and gender are certainly central categories for collecting and analyzing demographic data.

The evolution of the 'condition of women', which can be defined as women's status in respect to work, the family and society in general, has been governed for many centuries by factors closely related to birth, marriage and death. It is only possible to arrive at a full appreciation of the changes that have taken place in women's lot after a detailed study of such elements as the differential death rates of the two sexes in the relevant age groups and the subsequent inequality that results in respect of marriage opportunities. Similarly, one must also consider the increase or decrease of the population as a whole, involving, as it does, the equilibrium or disequilibrium between the sexes, which in turn has had serious repercussions on women's place in society and the nature of women's involvement in the world of work.

Nevertheless the condition of women cannot be described solely in terms of demographic factors. There is always an interplay between demographic and economic variables and, clearly, the long-term fluctuations in the economy, and notably those relating to the labour market, are fundamental to an understanding of the way in which women are integrated both into society and into the economy as a whole.[2] Historical evidence from Europe suggests that a significant surplus of women of working age can easily be absorbed by an expanding economy,[3] whereas, when the economy begins to slow down, women are the first to suffer from the exclusion mechanisms in the labour market or, at the very least, in certain segments of it. Thus, changing economic conditions related to demographic variables are crucial in explaining the appearance of a sexual division of labour and, in the end, the existence of segregated areas of occupation and production.[4]

It is from such a standpoint that we must endeavour to appreciate the fundamental differences existing between the condition of European women in the Middle Ages and their condition in later centuries as far as most countries are concerned. The sixteenth century witnessed an enormous rise in population without a corresponding increase in employment possibilities which could have absorbed those of the younger generation coming onto the labour market. This resulted in the introduction of a series of discriminatory measures with respect to certain social groups, in contrast to the situation existing previously.

In medieval times, the growth of towns and the considerable increase in demand and production which ensued made it imperative that all the available human resources within the family, including women, should be involved in all production processes.[5] Women's extensive involvement in urban activities, from production to wholesale and retail trade, banking or money-lending, demonstrates in exemplary fashion the effects of an expanding economy, which characteristically necessitates a rise in the number of workers to satisfy the increasing demand. This development enabled women in certain urban settings to attain virtual social and economic independence.[6] Some German towns can similarly serve to illustrate the status and economic role of urban women with particular reference to their capacity to contribute economically.[7]

Such a picture of relative economic and social independence contrasts starkly with the developments in some countries from the sixteenth century, when restrictions on women's activities were introduced, it appears, to resolve the problems of a population that was growing too rapidly with regard to the inadequate resources available. A first stage is the limitation of women's rights, not only in the sphere of work,[8] but in respect of the totality of their rights.[9] When such measures failed to produce the desired result, similar restrictions were applied to additional social groups, such as the poor. As their number increased, so the impediments to marriage were multiplied and the access to communal property restricted.

In these instances, the crux of the problem is to be found in the relationship between demographic and economic factors and, in a world where continuous employment was unknown, in the ever-present discrepancy between population growth and economic expansion. It is only possible to arrive at a clear understanding of the position of women in European societies after a close study of structural and cyclical economic and demographic situations such as those indicated above.

In the following pages we shall focus on what can be learned from studying the relevant demographic evolution (such as can be observed in respect of the inequality of the sexes at death, for example), and demonstrate how a lack of fundamental equilibrium between the sexes can in turn induce changes in behaviour in relation to nuptiality and fertility that lead ultimately to significant historical repercussions in the medium and the long term for both the social and economic development of all women.

Birth and Death: the frailty of the 'stronger' sex

It is common knowledge that people live longer nowadays than in the past. Demographic evidence shows the life expectancy has increased from twenty-eight years in France and thirty-seven in England around 1750, to more than seventy at present. Paradoxically, though, the two sexes have not benefitted in equal measure from this improvement. Despite the constant rise in the standard of living and progress in medicine, the disparity between the two sexes in respect of life expectancy at birth has increased, and in France a difference of scarcely two years at the middle of the nineteenth century rose to 3.4 years at the beginning of the present century and as recently as 1987 exceeded eight years.[10]

In fact, it can be said that, during the period under review, there is a wide variation in the chances of survival not only according to sex but also in respect of locality, with considerable variations being registered in individual regions and countries. Yet it cannot be said that one sex profits at the expense of the other since, depending on the period, a decrease or an increase in life expectancy may provoke a reversal in the respective chances of survival for men and for women.

The exact development of male mortality in comparison to female mortality and the reasons for death that influenced this difference are still largely unknown for all periods before the nineteenth century. Our ignorance results from a lack of documentation and research that might reveal the individual characteristics of the relevant population group. In order to compare and determine the mortality typical of each sex at different ages, three conditions must be fulfilled: (1) there must be a detailed but extensive reconstitution of a specific population group, which is a very slow process if one works on pre-industrial sources, where the variable quality of the data poses numerous problems; (2) the population group under examination must be relatively stable so that mortality figures are not rendered unreliable by emigration; (3) finally, if one intends to go beyond the mere statement of the excess mortality of one sex in comparison to the other at certain ages, it is necessary to elucidate detailed information relative to the cause of death, which few documents from earlier periods provide.[11]

Evidence gathered to date does, however, support some generalisations about inequalities in the survival chances of girl and boy babies. The newly-born's risk of early death results both from physiological factors and from factors linked to each sex depending on the characteristics of the socio-economic environment in which its parents live (place of residence, way of life and economic activities, as well as social class), factors which in turn conditioned the relative roles of women and men in pre-industrial society.

The analysis of differential mortality according to sex requires the ability to differentiate and evaluate these various types of causes and, in addition, to determine the influence of endogenous factors on mortality, a difficult task under the best of conditions. The characteristic which has become best known so far is biological morbidity ('vital inferiority' in the language of nineteenth-century authors), which affects male embryos in particular.[12] The statistics of all countries in recent times show that the fragility of males in the womb, at birth and in the early stages of life is far greater than that of females. The true extent of that phenomenon only becomes apparent, however, when one is able to obtain details of the still-born and the prematurely born. If we consider only live births, the usual sex ratio at birth is 105/100 males to females; in contrast, in Switzerland (1876-1885) the stillborn sex ratio of male to female was 132/100.[13] Prenatal, perinatal, neonatal and infant mortality until the fifteenth or sixteenth month are all higher for male babies than for female babies. But the evolution in time of this excess mortality figure for males shows that even the physiological handicap and the lower survival potential of small boys are only partly a result of physiological influences and that the socio-economic environment plays an important role. This can be seen all the more clearly in the twentieth century.

When we move on to the infant stage, the preponderance of male infant mortality continues to be a dominant factor. If one compares male with female infant mortality during the early months of life, it is evident that the females also have a considerable advantage. The study of the statistics available for a dozen European countries demonstrates that from the eighteenth to the end of the nineteenth century infant girls had a 7-15 per cent better chance of surviving the first year as compared with boys.[14] This phenomenon would seem at first to preclude the possibility that the boys received better treatment or that they were otherwise protected more than their sisters during the first year of life in view of their perceived future role as heirs of the family possessions.[15] This excess mortality of male infants exists irrespective of class[16] and equally when the child is cared for by its own mother.[17] It must be stated that the risks run by children separated from their mothers are not the same. Amongst children put out to wet nurses, there is a slight excess mortality among baby girls dying before the age of one (at Rouen in the eighteenth century, 457 per thousand as against 431 per thousand for boys).[18]

The results of abandoning children, which concerns both sexes (with the exception of Italy, where this practice was more frequent with respect to baby girls),[19] are still relatively unknown as far as the differential mortality of female and male infants is concerned.

Few analyses have been made of possible explanations for the difference in survival chances apart from the often quoted weakness of male infants. One may wonder, though, if one is not justified in assuming that parents treated female and male children in distinctly different ways,

Table 1   The ratio of male mortality to female mortality in infancy (1‰)

Parishes	Generations Born In			
	1741/1760	1761/1790	1791/1820	1821/1850
Matt	181	154	129	120
Naefels	135	128	28	132

and that preferential treatment in order to assure a male heir might not in the end have succeeded only in producing the opposite of the intended result. Two examples illustrate the enormous disparity between the sexes among infants dying before the age of one. The infant death rate according to sex in a population group of the Swiss Pre-Alps (not far from Zurich) in the eighteenth and at the beginning of the nineteenth centuries demonstrates the unequal chances of survival during the first year of life in different generations of children resulting in a very high ratio of male to female mortality in the first year of life (Table 1).[20]

In another research project in progress in a small town in Switzerland (Zofingen) and its surrounding countryside, the analysis of the death rate according to sex reveals a similar phenomenon, with a death ratio of male to female mortality of 169/100 for the town, whereas the ratio is only 103/100 for the inhabitants of the surrounding countryside.[21]

Such a discrepancy leads us to reflect on the reasons for the origin of the preponderance of male infant deaths in places where infant girls and infant boys are theoretically embedded in the same environment. Can it be attributed to different habits with respect to breastfeeding or the general nourishment of infant females and males? Might it have been presumed advantageous to wean the boys earlier and to replace mother's milk with gruel? Might there not have been a family option aimed not at preserving life in all cases but perhaps at treating boys less carefully when two or three male children had already survived in a family? This attitude might perfectly well be the result of differing economic preoccupations in town and country, both of which could nevertheless be characterised by the problems of transmitting an inheritance to the following generation. In rural districts the concern would be the retention of a smallholding as long as mountain farming remained the principal source of revenue, followed by a change of behaviour when agriculture was no longer an adequate means of satisfying the needs of the family and the inheritance in the shape of land has already been partly eroded. In towns, the concern would be the unfavourable economic situation in which artisans found themselves subjected to guild rules strict enough to make the prospect of a limited number of heirs appear attractive.

The medical approach to infant mortality based on an analysis of the causes of death is doubtless inadequate to explain satisfactorily the reasons for such a significant structural inequality in the death rate of males and females in early infancy. Only a micro-economic study of individual families would allow us to determine whether the decisive factors in this preponderance of male deaths in early infancy were related to family choices and, perhaps, a function of the birth order of boys.

A related issue is the survival rate of children in their early years. In fact, the probabilities of survival for children appear to vary greatly according to sex, geographical location, and the chronological period under consideration. It would appear that a higher death rate of young females from the age of 15-16 months and increasingly up to the age of 19 years as compared with that of young males became a fairly widespread phenomenon in nineteenth-century Europe, but the causal factors for this state of affairs have yet to be determined.[22] One characteristic of this development is its late appearance, in the eighteenth century,[23] at least in urban environments, which favoured the spread of infectious illnesses that particularly affect female adolescents, such as tuberculosis and smallpox. Before that time we can only cite such evidence as is available: the preponderance of male mortality seems to be the norm in this age group until the eighteenth century, even though it seems to have declined somewhat during the seventeenth century. Indeed, the demographic upsurge experienced by certain regions of Europe is due largely to a decline in the mortality rate, which manifested itself in terms of extended life expectancy and a higher survival rate. The principal factor seems to have been a diminution of the male mortality rate. A comparison of two generations born in the seventeenth century in the region of Glaris (Switzerland) shows clearly that it was the boys who benefitted most from the increase in life expectancy. The ratio of males to females surviving at the age of sixteen was as low as 88 males per 100 females for young males born in the second third of the seventeenth century and 100 males for those born at the end of that century, all else being equal, since the number of girls surviving during the period in question did not change.[24] It goes without saying that in the long term this massive reduction in male mortality produced important structural changes in the population which, in turn, would determine the levels of nuptiality and celibacy of the relevant generations.

We turn now to the issue of female excess mortality in the adult age group, beginning with the question of maternal mortality. First, it is necessary to note some methodological difficulties that complicate the possibilities for comparative study. One of these is the variation in definitions of maternal mortality from country to country. For the United Nations, maternal mortality is currently defined as 'the decease of a woman occurring during pregnancy or in a period of forty-two days after its conclusion, whatever this duration or situation, for any reason . . . except by accident or chance'. The sources available to historians do not allow us to determine after the event and for periods distant from us in time the 'accidental' or 'fortuitous' influences that may have been responsible for death. Concerning the period in question, forty-two days after birth, it would appear to have little medical justification. Indeed, even at the present day the length of time necessary for the cicatrisation of the post-partum uterus is a matter of some dispute, with varying figures being quoted in the United States and in Europe, which would seem to hint at different underlying cultural traditions. It recalls Judaic tradition and corresponds to the period of purification which, according to Leviticus, is required of a woman who has born a male child, a point of view adopted by the Christian Church in certain countries since the reference to the death of mothers occurring 'within six weeks' is to be found also in German parish registers.[25] It is the accepted procedure among contemporary demographers, however, to take into account only those deaths that occur within thirty days following birth, in order to calculate the accompanying risks. But it is clear that a longer period (say, sixty days, in order to take account of the increased risk of infection run by women in the past) seems preferable for calculating the mortality of women when giving birth or dying as a result of doing so. German data deal with deaths occurring less than forty-two days after giving birth. In England and France, however, historians take into account a period of sixty days, whilst in Switzerland the norm is either thirty days[26] or sixty days. Thus, in order to arrive at mutually comparable figures with respect to the length of the period under observation, certain adjustments of available figures are necessary.

A second major methodological problem is the following: the diversity of rules that govern the registration of births and deaths in different countries leads to significant distortions, and in certain regions the existing documents do not allow us to gain a clear overall view of maternal mortality. Thus, in England[27] and in France the calculations that have been made are based on the number of women whose children were baptised in church or baptised in emergency. This means that in these countries, as also in Germany,[28] only a partial number of stillbirths has been covered by the relevant statistics. Consequently, the possible subsequent death of the mother eludes us. To this number of deaths of mothers already 'delivered of child'[29] must be added such deaths occurring as a result of a pregnancy that did not end in a birth,[30] that is to say deaths that resulted from abortions and miscarriages, which the registers do not always mention, as well as pregnancies that ended tragically when the foetus could not be successfully expelled. The mortality rates have therefore been readjusted for the population groups in which such details were missing in accordance with the Swedish data calculated by Roger Schofield.[31]

A comparison of data from France, England, Germany and Switzerland (which unfortunately do not use the same time periods) reveals the many different risks run by a mother when giving birth to a child.

(1) The death of the mother may be directly related to her religious background. In Germany and Switzerland, for example, maternal deaths were more numerous in Catholic regions than in Protestant ones.

In Switzerland, for the period 1761-1820, we may observe 19 per thousand deaths for the period 1761-1820 amongst Catholic mothers, whereas there are only 11 per thousand in Protestant parishes.

(2) There seem to be differential mortality rates for mothers depending on their economic status.[32] In Rouen, the proportion of workers' wives dying in giving birth was higher than that of shopkeepers' and craftmen's wives. This discrepancy was even significantly higher when we compare the workers' wives with the wives of the local worthies.[33]

(3) The proportion of deaths after giving birth is higher in rural than in urban populations, in Germany as well as in France.[34] Nevertheless, it must be added that in French towns giving birth in a hospital doubled the risks of deaths (19.6 per thousand confinements in Rouen hospitals in the period 1750-1800 as against only 9.3 for women confined at home).[35]

(4) Significant variations appear in maternal mortality and in its relation to age according to country. These variations appear to be largely a result of exogenous causes such as cultural practices and socio-economic levels of development. The mortality of women giving birth (in France and Germany) is always lower than that in England, except in older age groups. For example, female mortality in France for the 25-29 age group was 7.7-9.3 per thousand for the period 1740-1789[36] compared with 11.4 per thousand in England for the period 1550-1849.[37]

(5) Variations in maternal mortality also reflect the risks incurred with the increase of age at the time of giving birth. Research done up to the present shows that maternal mortality has always been higher for the later childbearing ages. Maternal death in the above-mentioned Swiss parishes was more than fifty per cent higher when the mothers gave birth at the age of 35 and above than in the 20-34 age group (calculated for the period 1761-1850).[38] When there is no fertility control, an increase of age at marriage – when the economic situation deteriorates, for instance – can be an explanation for more mothers dying when giving birth. Thus, the greater number of births at higher ages due to the later age at marriage exposes the mothers to increased mortality.

(6) There is a clear correlation between the mortality of mothers and the size of the family. One can observe a slow decrease in deaths relative to maternal deaths at childbirth which seems linked to a reduction in fertility. As the risks increase with the number of confinements, the fewer children born in a family, the better are the mother's chances of surviving. In Geneva, for example, 8.5 per cent of women died in confinement in the seventeenth century compared with 6.9 per cent in the eighteenth century.[39] A reduction in the risks inherent in bearing children among women over 35 can be seen in two Swiss parishes, where there was a reduction of 29 per cent of mothers' deaths between 1761-1820 and

1821-1850; there was at the same time a significant reduction in the number of children being born to women after the age of thirty-five. Thus, it appears to be the lowering of age at childbirth in consequence of a smaller number of children, which accounts for this decrease.

The mortality among adult women in the absence of death due to childbirth offers another field of inquiry. A question which has frequently been discussed is whether there may be a preponderance of mortality among adult females in any case, this being inherent and quite independent of the risks involved in bearing children. Louis Henry, in a study of recent French data, concluded that 'in the 25-44 age group male mortality would have exceeded female mortality if maternal mortality had not existed or if it had been negligible as in our day'.[40] For Alfred Perrenoud, on the other hand, the excess of female mortality among women of working age, which can be observed in Geneva, doubtless resulted from a decline in their living standard, which must be seen as concomitant with an extension in the demand for female labour during the expansion of industry between 1750 and 1785.[41] This point of view is shared by Arthur Imhof, who sees in the combination of work in the home and work in the fields in Germany one of the reasons for the worsening of women's lives that manifested itself in a higher ratio of female to male mortality (in the 15-49 age group it was of the order of 124/100 for the period 1780-1840 and 109/100 for 1841-1899). This decline in the preponderance of women's deaths may, however, also be attributable to the worsening of men's way of life due to industrialisation.[42]

We must, however, also seek to explain why, in France, the mortality rate of men should be on a par with that of women whilst there was an excess of female mortality elsewhere. Would it not, in this case, be reasonable to assume a different type of economic growth dependent on its own distinct parameters? Could the low growth in the agricultural sector in France explain the absence of excess female mortality? It appears that in certain parts of Germany, and especially in the south of the country, economic development and agricultural innovations substantially increased the peasants' work in many different ways. The peasant women in particular were obliged to cope with the extra work resulting from the new activities connected with development of near-by markets and the more intensive forms of agriculture this necessitated.[43] Such reasons would also explain the absence of a higher mortality rate among adult women in the mountainous regions of Switzerland. In regions situated on the north flank of the Alps women were probably less overworked because of the fragmented land holdings and the type of agriculture practised: pasture and cattle demanded a much smaller contribution in terms of female labour.

Thus, we have seen that the position of women in society does not depend only on socio-economic factors, such as are concomitant with an expanding or declining economy or with an increasing or decreasing demand for labour. Women's position is also closely related to the unequal chances of survival of the members of each sex. These unequal chances depend in turn partly on physiological factors, which seem to determine the higher male infant mortality, and partly on environmental influences characteristic of a specific historical period and the relevant society.

The Sexual Imbalance: differential effects of mortality on the demographic structure of the population

Differential mortality between girls and boys is of fundamental importance for both economic and social structures. The significant disequilibrium in the sex ratio it produces in certain periods provokes a certain number of typical strategies concerning marriage and family formation. It is obvious, for example, that medieval Italy with its very high rate of nuptiality ('almost all women marry, many at a very early age')[44] reflects a fundamental numerical imbalance between the sexes resulting from factors that produce a shortage of women of marriageable age.

Fifteenth-century Tuscany was characterised by a sexual imbalance that extended from childhood to old age, with the exception of the 15-20 age group. Two factors contributed to the massive surplus of males (110 males for 100 females). The first is the practice of abandonment of children, especially of small girls (twice as high as for boys), which occurred more in towns than in the countryside, resulting in an even greater shortage of urban women of all ages (with a female ratio of 89 for 100 males in towns as against 92 females for 100 males in the countryside).[45] The second factor is provided by the great epidemics which were responsible for the deaths of far more women than men. Similarly, in Geneva, during the plague years 1636-1640, 66 per cent of the victims were women. This selective death rate created a pronounced underrepresentation of women in certain age groups, which in turn had a marked effect on the marriage rate. This structural element in the population provides the basis for a demographic system, like that in Europe before the sixteenth century, where the norm was for most women to be married young and to older husbands.[46]

In contrast, as we saw when analysing mortality figures, the seventeenth, eighteenth and nineteenth centuries are often characterised by the survival of a surplus of female babies. This differential mortality affected the marriage market in all age groups. The resulting tensions are particularly striking wherever it is possible to calculate the numbers of individuals involved at the age of marriage (table 2). The surplus of women increases with the increase in age between the women and their potential husbands for two reasons. (1) The more the choice of husband is limited to men of an older age group, the fewer potential husbands are available, since death takes its toll with advancing age. (2) In a period of demographic growth, and even when this growth is fairly weak, the

Table 2   Natural female surplus on the marriage market in the Catholic parish of Naefels, Switzerland: generations born between 1761 and 1790

Age groups				
Women		Men		
20-24		25-29	30-34	35-39
20-24 years	6.4	11.1	17.0	22.7
25-29 years	2.8	7.4	13.0	18.5
30-34 years	- 3.0	1.3	6.0	11.8

generations of men who marry younger women are already less numerous at birth. Generally speaking, a yearly growth rate of 1.2 per cent – which can be observed in England in the second half of the eighteenth century as well as in certain parts of Switzerland – and an age difference between marriage partners of five years brings with it a deficit of 6 per cent of males for the women who wish to marry. It must be noted, though, that in this example mobility was not taken into account. In reality, the numerical discrepancy between the two sexes on attaining adulthood is exacerbated by the departure of a large number of males for foreign countries (for instance, with the army) which accounts for a further deficit of 10 to 15 per cent for the generation under observation.

Obviously, the number of males and females reaching marriageable age does not alone determine the number of men and women who will eventually marry during their lifetimes. The marriage market is also affected by the death rate of the already married and the resulting dissolution of marriages. Thus, depending on their age at the time of dissolution, single women and men may marry widowers and widows respectively. In countries with a high mortality rate among young women and where men remarry frequently, the majority of women of marriageable age were able to find a husband. The remarriage of widowers, from the point of view of nuptiality, has the same effect as

Süssmilch's 'successive' polygamy.[47] Similarly, when there is a shortage of young women, the remarriage of bachelors with older widows can also be an integral part of the matrimonial system.[48] So it can be said that any significant change in mortality with respect to either sex has a profound effect on the marriage market and hence on the economy in general, assuming, of course, that migration does not provide a compensatory function.

Migration and the Marriage Market: Non-structural factors affecting the demography of a population and their particular impact on women

Most societies do not exist in isolation and compensatory developments arise when it is not possible to match supply and demand in respect of potential marriage partners on a local basis. So far we have focused on the so-called 'natural' factors affecting a population and their particular impact on women. But other variables can also have a considerable effect on the development of a specific population and we shall now turn our attention to two such phenomena: migrations and the marriage market.

Migratory movements can produce significant variations in the composition of a population, the results being particularly striking in respect of emigrations from European countries to their colonies. The position of women in the home marriage market worsens, resulting in a rising level of celibacy and a rising marriage age for women.[49] In the colonies, by contrast, one finds a marriage squeeze for men due to the shortage of women, resulting in a very high frequency of marriage among women at a very low age and a high age for men at first marriage.[50]

Migratory movements towards the towns similarly accentuate the disequilibrium of females to males. In the case of a significant immigration of males, as was the case in towns such as Geneva (before 1585 with the arrival of Huguenot refugees) and Amsterdam (until about 1650),[51] the surplus of men affected the marriage market in several ways. In addition to low frequencies of female celibacy and a low age for women at marriage, we find a different structure in the choice of marriage partner with a different age distribution of those marrying for the first time. The ratio of single men is extremely favourable for single women wishing to marry (in Amsterdam from 1601 until 1650, 95 brides for 100 grooms).[52] This is clearly an indication that the abundance of men favoured a type of marriage where the shortfall of single women offered the opportunity to a large number of widows to remarry with previously unmarried men.

With the decline of economic expansion and a certain stagnation in some Dutch, German and Swiss towns during the seventeenth and eighteenth centuries, male migratory movements are reversed, with a reduction in the number of men moving into the towns and at the same time an increased number of women migrating into them. We see as a result the development of domestic work which provided employment for between 7 and 15 per cent of the total population and in places such as late eighteenth-century Zurich, almost 20 per cent.[53] Indeed, this appears to be one of the predominant characteristics of urban history. It contributes to a surprising surplus of adult women in towns, which may even exceed the corresponding adult male population by as much as 50 per cent, that is more than 150 women for 100 men in the eighteenth century.[54]

The migratory factor is not, however, the only element that conditions the marriage market. Clearly, the 'natural' marriage market – which is already affected by the differential mortality of women and men – may also be seriously impeded as a result of a certain number of external variables. These are mostly of a religious, economic or social character.

(1) The marriage market was limited by a set of religious rules and hindrances relating to the Judeo-Christian tradition, which prohibited marriage within certain degrees of kinship and affinity (generally speaking, the Protestant rules were stricter than the Catholic ones), the result being a restricted choice of partners in small and medium-sized communities

(2) An economic stagnation could prevent the formation of new couples. Although this phenomenon can be observed wherever resources became scarce, it was, perhaps, most evident in mountainous and Alpine regions. A representative example is that of the Swiss Alpine village of Törbel, where the average age at first marriage is 27.1 for females and 31.1 for males from 1750 to 1799, rising to 29.1 and 33.4 respectively between 1850 and 1899, with a celibacy rate rising from 20 to 30 per cent in the same period.[55]

(3) Restrictive legislation prevented the marriage of the destitute, and could result in high rates of births out-of-wedlock.

(4) Social conventions could make the choice of a marriage partner more difficult, as for example, assumptions with respect to age discrepancy, restrictions on social mobility, and the necessity of remaining within one's own social class when choosing a marriage partner.[56]

(5) Specific strategies linked to questions of property, aiming at the conservation of a holding large enough to support a family, could also affect marriage choices. For instance, more or less egalitarian partible inheritance practice, with its evident effect on the size of holding, made it ultimately necessary in regions without industry for households to find ways and means to limit the number of children marrying. This mode of inheritance was often accompanied by a high level of female celibacy which acted as a sort of compensatory factor that enabled society to survive. On the other hand, the transmission of the whole of an inheritance to one individual – usually a male – created inequality, affected the possibilities of marriage and implied a complex organisation of the family

so that female and male offspring who were not able to marry continued to live and work in the family home.[57]

(6) Finally, in rural areas the marriage rate depended on additional considerations, such as the extent to which a local society was 'open' or 'closed', with rules favouring or preventing migration and the possibility of finding a spouse outside the resident population.

In conclusion, we can say that from the above discussion we have seen how the examination of some fundamental mechanisms of historical demography helps in understanding the underlying options open to women in a society at a given time. We have also seen that the variation in mortality according to sex has had a profound influence on nuptiality. In fact, as yet, we still know comparatively little as to the differences in survival rates, either for a given society or within the family, since historical demographers have rarely focused on the specificities of each sex. Most researchers use a global approach that emphasises statistical analysis, but in the event often obscures rather than illuminates the case in point. Because the study of mortality according to gender has often been regarded as peripheral, demographers have all too often ignored important questions such as socio-cultural influences on mortality at early ages and their repercussions on the status of women and indeed even on women's value in purely material terms on reaching adulthood.

In addition to mortality, one must underline the central role of nuptiality and fertility in the functioning of a given society. Clearly, the variability of these demographic determinants and in particular the importance of changes in the age at marriage – as well as the proportion of those never marrying – are influenced both by the economic and demographic context. Firstly, one must be aware that, historically, marriage created the foundations of an economic unit of production primarily based on family members, a phenomenon well documented in regions with important proto-industrialisation, as this existed in the seventeenth and eighteenth centuries. The number of people having access to the marriage market was closely related to an adequate or inadequate expansion of the economy, and in such a production system the death of one of the partners wreaked havoc on the surviving members of the family. This was especially the case with the loss of the husband, as he was mostly the principal breadwinner, and when his widow did not manage to remarry – as frequently occurred – effectively deprived herself of the necessary economic basis for survival. Research reveals all too many widows with young children caught in the cycle of poverty. Secondly, changing conditions of nuptiality must also be seen as interwoven with changing patterns of mortality and migration. In this context, the marriage market has had a prevailing influence on women's position overall. I have stressed that in some areas (mostly towns, but sometimes also rural districts that suffered from considerable out-migration) there was an enormous surplus of women in the adult groups compared with the available male population. Demographic historical evidence, coupled with socio-economic historical evidence, gives us every reason to believe that only when there is a large surplus of women combined with an expanding labour market can any significant degree of female economic and social independence be achieved.

NOTES

1. Martine Segalen, 'Quelques réflexions pour l'étude de la condition féminine [Some Reflections on the Study of the Feminine Condition]', *Annales de démographie historique* (1981), p. 10.
2. See, for example, Louise A. Tilly and Joan W. Scott, *Women, Work, and Family* (New York-Chicago: Holt, Rinehart and Winston, 1978).
3. A case in point is England in the seventeenth and eighteenth centuries. This can be illustrated by the fact that while the economy is expanding no need is felt to restrict the occupations to which girls are apprenticed and which they later practise. See K. D. M. Snell, 'The Apprenticeship of Women', *Annals of the Labouring Poor: Social Change and Agrarian England, 1660-1900* (Cambridge: Cambridge University Press, 1987), p. 298. *(Cambridge Studies in Population, Economy and Society in Past Time,* vol. 2).
4. See Yvonne Verdier, *Façons de dire, façons de faire. La laveuse, la couturière, la cuisinière* (Paris: Gallimard, 1979); Martine Segalen, *Mari et femme dans la société paysanne* (Paris: Flammarion, 1980); Pierre Goubert and Daniel Roche, *Les Français et l'Ancien Régime. Culture et Société,* 2 (Paris: Armand Colin, 1984), pp. 150-1.
5. Erika Uitz, *Die Frau in der mittelalterlichen Stadt* [Women in the Medieval City], (Leipzig-Stuttgart: Fischer Verlag, 1988); Peter Ketsch, *Frauen im Mittelalter, Part I: Frauenarbeit im Mittelalter. Quellen und Materialen* [Women in the Middle Ages I: Women's Work in the Middle Ages. Sources and Materials], (Düsseldorf: Schwann-Basel, 1983), *(Geschichtsdidaktik: Studien, Materialen,* ed. Annette Kuhn, vol. 14).
6. G. Jehel, 'Le rôle des femmes et du milieu familial à Gênes dans les activités commerciales au cours de la première moitié du XIIIe siècle', *Revue d'histoire économique et sociale,* 53, no.2/3 (1975), pp. 193-215.
7. Between 16-33 per cent of the declared fortune was owned by women (See Erika Uitz, 'Zu den auf eine Verbesserung ihrer gesellschaftlichen Stellung hinzielenden Aktivitäten der Frauen in den deutschen Städten des Spätmittelalters [On the Activities of Women Aiming to Improve their Social Position in German Cities in the Late Middle Ages]', *Untersuchungen zur gesellschaftlichen Stellung der Frau in Feodalismus. Magdebürger Beiträge zur Stadtgeschichte,* 3 (1981), p. 49, quoting H. Wachendorf, *Die wirtschaftliche Stellung der Frau in den deutschen Städten des späteren Mittelalters* [The Economic Position of Women in German Cities of the Later Middle Ages]) (Quakenbrück, 1934).

8. See, for example, Merry E. Wiesner, 'Spinning Out Capital: Women's Work in the Early Modern Economy', in Renate Bridenthal, Claudia Koonz and Susan Stuard (eds.), *Becoming Visible: Women in European History*, 2nd ed. (Boston: Houghton Mifflin Company, 1987), p. 233.

9. This can be seen, among other things, in the fact that women were no longer allowed to apply for admission to the status of 'burger' in their own right at the end of the fifteenth and beginning of the sixteenth century (E. Uitz, 'Verbesserung', p. 62 ff.).

10. Jacques Vallin and France Meslé, *Les causes de décès en France de 1925 à 1978* (Paris: INED, 1988), p. 467 (*Travaux et documents*, vol. 115). See also Jacques Vallin, 'La mortalité en Europe de 1720 à 1940: Tendances à long terme et changements de structure par sexe et par âge', *Annales de démographie historique* (1989), p. 49 ff. The difference between male and female life expectancy can vary considerably even under the Ancien Régime: in Geneva, the difference is only 0.8 year for the generation born between 1625 and 1684 [according to Alfred Perrenoud, 'L'inégalité sociale devant la mort à Genève au XVIIIe siècle', *Population*, special issue (November 1975), p. 231], but 3.5 years for the generation born in Sweden between 1751 and 1755 [according to Dominique Tabutin, 'La surmortalité féminine en Europe avant 1940', *Population*, 33, no. 1 (1978), p. 139].

11. Alfred Perrenoud, *La population de Genève du seizième au début du dix-neuvième siècle. Etude démographique. Vol. 1: Structures et Mouvements* (Genève: Société d'histoire et d'archéologie, 1979), p. 413 (M.D.G., vol. 47).

12. Leon Tabah and Jean Sutter, 'Influence respective de l'âge maternel et du rang de naissance sur la mortinatalité. La notion de létalité', *Population*, 3 (1948), p. 89.

13. Louis Crevoisier, 'Etude de statistique sur la mortalité enfantine en Suisse pendant les dix années 1876 à 1885', *Journal de statistique suisse*, 25 (1889), p. 111.

14. Louis Henry, 'Mortalité des hommes et des femmes dans le passé', *Annales de démographie historique* (1987), p. 89 (Article translated into English: *Population*, 44 (1989): English Selection, no. 1).

15. Antoinette Fauve-Chamoux, 'Innovation et comportement parental en milieu urbain (XVe - XIXe siècles)', *Annales: Economies, Sociétés, Civilisations*, 40 (1985), p. 1026.

16. Alfred Perrenoud, 'Surmortalité féminine et condition de la femme (XVIIe-XIXe siècles). Une vérification empirique', *Annales de démographie historique* (1981), p. 96.

17. For German results, see John E. Knodel, *Demographic Behaviour in the Past: A Study of Fourteen German Village Populations in the Eighteenth and Nineteenth Centuries* (Cambridge: Cambridge University Press, 1988), pp. 80-1. (*Cambridge Studies in Population, Economy and Society in Past Time*, vol. 6).

18. Jean-Pierre Bardet, *Rouen aux XVIIe et XVIIIe siècles. Les mutations d'un espace social* 1, (Paris: SEDES, 1983), p. 369.

19. Giovanna Da Molin, 'Les enfants abandonnés dans les villes italiennes aux XVIIIe et XIXe siècles', *Annales de démographie historique* (1983), p. 112.

20. Anne-Lise Head, 'Population, société et économie alpestre. Le pays glaronais de la fin du XVIe siècle au milieu du XIXe siècle', (Geneva, 1986 [typescript]), vol. 1, pp. 455-62.

21. My research project deals with the generation born between 1826 and 1830 in Switzerland.

22. Michel Poulain and Dominique Tabutin, 'La surmortalité des petites filles en Belgique au XIXe et début du XXe siècle', *Annales de démographie historique* (1981), p. 105. See also Henry, 'Mortalité', p. 93.

23. Perrenoud, 'Surmortalité', p. 94.

24. Head, 'Population, société et économie alpestre', p. 442.

25. Arthur Imhof, *Die gewonnenen Jahre: von der Zunahme unserer Lebensspanne seit dreihundert Jahren oder von der Notwendigkeit einer neuen Einstellung zu Leben und Sterben: ein historischer Essai* [The Years We've Gained: On the Increase in our Lifespans in the Last Three Hundred Years or On the Need for a New Stance toward Life and Death: An Historical Essay] (München: C. H. Beck, 1981), p. 145.

26. Perrenoud, 'Surmortalité', p. 99.

27. Roger Schofield, 'Did mothers really die? Three centuries of maternal mortality in the World We Have Lost', in Lloyd Bonfield, Richard M. Smith and Keith Wrightson (eds.), *The World We Have Gained: Histories of Population and Social Structures* (Oxford: Basil Blackwell, 1986), p. 248.

28. Arthur E. Imhof, 'Die Ueabersterblichkeit verheirateter Frauen im fruchtbaren Alter. Eine Illustration der 'condition féminine' im 19. Jahrhundert [The Excess Mortality of Married Women in their Childbearing Years. An Illustration of the 'feminine condition' in the 19th Century]', *Zeitschrift für Bevölkerungswissenschaft*, no. 4 (1979), p. 505.

29. Bardet, *Rouen*, p. 364.

30. Henry, 'Mortalité', p. 98.

31. Schofield, 'Did mothers really die?', p. 256.

32. Imhof, 'Die Ueabersterblichkeit verheirateter Frauen', p. 506.

33. Bardet, *Rouen*, p. 366. See also Mireille Laget, 'La naissance aux siècles classiques. Pratique des accouchements et attitudes collectives en France aux XVlle et XVllle siècle', *Annales: Economie, Société, Civilisation*, 32 (1977), p. 972; Perrenoud, 'Surmortalité', p. 101 gives a more nuanced view and observes a reversal of the trend to the advantage of lower-class mothers towards the end of the eighteenth century.

34. For Germany, see Imhof, *Die gewonnenen Jahre*, p. 155. For France, see Alain Bideau, 'Accouchement "naturel" et accouchement à haut risque', *Annales de démographie historique* (1981), pp. 65-6.

35. Bardet, *Rouen*, p. 366.

36. Henry, 'Mortalité', p. 116.

37. Schofield, 'Did mothers really die?', p. 256.

38. Head, 'Population, société et économie', p. 471. For Germany, see Knodel, *Demographic behaviour*, p. 111, and for France, Hector Gutierrez and Jacques Houdaille, 'La mortalité maternelle en France au XVllle siècle', *Population* (1983), p. 982.

39. Perrenoud, 'Surmortalité', p. 99.

40. Henry, 'Mortalité', p. 99.

41. Perrenoud, 'Surmortalité', p. 95.

42. A. Imhof, 'Ueabersterblichkeit', p. 498.

43. Arthur Imhof, 'Säuglingssterblichkeitim europäischen Kontext, 17.-20. Jahrhundert. Ueberlegungen zu einem Buch von Anders Brändström [The Mortality of Nurslings in the European Context, from the 17th to the 20th Century. Reflections on a Book by Anders Brändström]', in Egil Johansson (ed.), Demographic Data Base. Umea University, *Newsletter*, no. 2 (1984), pp. 22-3.

44. By the age of twenty-five, 97 per cent of women in medieval Tuscany were married or widowed, according to David Herlihy and Christiane Klapisch-Zuber, *Les Toscans et leurs familles* (Paris: Editions de l'École des Hautes Etudes en Sciences Sociales, 1978), p. 404.

45. Herlihy and Klapisch-Zuber, *Toscans*, p. 348.

46. In Italy, we find a difference in age between husband and wife of nearly eleven years in the town of Florence (in 1480) compared with seven years for the surrounding countryside (in 1470), the mean age of women at marriage being practically the same for both (about 20.8 years for the town and 21.0 for the countryside). See Herlihy and Klapisch-Zuber, *Toscans*, p. 207.

47. John Hajnal, 'European marriage patterns in perspective', in David V. Glass and David E. C. Eversley (eds.), *Population in History. Essays in Historical Demography* (London: Edward Arnold, 1969), p. 128.

48. Needless to say this system is hardly the norm since social convention and economic considerations are rarely on the side of a widow desirous of remarrying. See Martine Segalen, 'Mentalité populaire et remariage en Europe occidentale', in Jacques Dupâquier, Etienne Hélin, Peter Laslett, Massimo Livi-Bacci, and Sølvi Sogner (eds.), *Marriage and Remarriage in Populations of the Past* (London-New York: Academic Press, 1981), p. 468 ff. (*Population and Social Structure: Advances in Historical Demography*).

49. There could also be repercussions on the structure of the labour market with the women remaining behind obliged to take on the type of employment usually reserved for men in more 'normal' times, as in the town of Seville, where in the sixteenth century some unmarried women had to earn their living by performing heavy manual work due to the emigration of a large proportion of the male population to the Spanish colonies in Central and South America. See Richard Konetze, *Süd- und Mittelamerika. Die Indianerkulturen Altamerikas und die spanisch-portugiesische Kolonialherrschaft* [South and Central America: The Indian Cultures of Old America and Spanish-Portuguese Colonial Rule] (Frankfurt a.M.: Fischer, 1965), p. 65 (*Fischer Weltgeschichte*, vol. 22).

50. Seventeenth-century Canada offers a case in point: 97 per cent of women aged twenty-five and more are married or widowed; whereas more than 25 per cent of men aged thirty and above are bachelors. See Hubert Charbonneau and R. Roy, 'La nuptialité en situation de déséquilibre des sexes: le Canada du XVIIe siècle', *Annales de démographie historique* (1978), p. 288.

51. Adrian M. Van der Woude, 'Population developments in the northern Netherlands (1500-1800) and the validity of the "urban graveyard effect"', *Annales de démographie historique* (1982), p. 73.

52. Van der Woude, 'Population developments', p. 62. Obviously men marrying for the first time were obliged to marry widows, due to a shortage of women.

53. Anne-Lise Head, 'Contrastes ruraux et urbains en Suisse de 1600 au début du XIXe siècle: la croissance démographique des villes et des campagnes et ses variables, in Liliane Mottu, Dominique Zumkeller (eds.), *Mélanges d'histoire économique et sociale offerts au professeur Anne-Marie Piuz* (Genève: Département d'Histoire Economique, 1989), p. 138.

54. Head, 'Contrastes', p. 138.

55. According to Robert McC. Netting, *Balancing on an Alp: Ecological Change and Continuity in a Swiss Mountain Community* (Cambridge: Cambridge University Press, 1981), p. 132. See also Pier Paolo Viazzo and Dionigi Albera, 'Population, resources, and homeostatic regulations in the Alps: The role of nuptiality', *Itinera*, 5/6 (1986), p. 186. The same pattern can be discerned in towns without any economic expansion. In Olten, a small town in Switzerland, we can observe a rate of celibacy at age fifty which is even higher than in Törbel. For the generations born at the end of the eighteenth and beginning of the nineteenth centuries, the celibacy rate for females was 36 per cent, whilst the male rate was 20 per cent. See Head, 'Contrastes ruraux', p. 12.

56. Rudolf Braun, 'Historische Demographie im Rahmen einer integrierten Geschichtsbetrachtung: Jüngere Forschungsansätze und ihre Verwendung [Historical Demography in the Framework of an Integrated Conception of History: Recent Approaches to Research and their Application]', *Geschichte und Gesellschaft*, 3, no. 4 (1977), p. 529.

57. Antoinette Fauve-Chamoux, 'Les structures familiales en France aux XVIIe et XVIIIe siècles', in Jacques Dûpaquier (ed.), *Histoire de la population française*, vol. 2: *De la Renaissance à 1789* (Paris: Presses Universitaires de France, 1988), p. 317-47.

3

'Uneven Developments': Women's History, Feminist History and Gender History in Great Britain

Jane Rendall

The development of women's history over the last twenty years has been uneven, marked by significant differences in the pace of change and in national experience, yet also simultaneously inspired by outstanding and creative growth, notably in the United States. The title of this article has been most recently used in a study of contested and unevenly growing ideologies of gender in nineteenth century England; but its original coiner, Marx, offered it as a means of analysing differential rates of international economic change, which incorporated the specific historical context of each nation's economic growth, yet also explained the interaction between different national patterns of development.[1] By analogy – however imperfect – we may reflect upon the dilemmas which now face those who write and read women's history within national contexts, contexts which themselves contain great variations, yet are also within an international framework.

My understanding of the massive developments in this field in the English language in this period is clearly rooted in a personal viewpoint, from Great Britain. It has been possible for me at an English university not only to be involved in the women's movement, but also to teach women's history and to collaborate with others in teaching women's studies. I have been conscious of the relative privilege of such a position, yet also of provincialism in an international context. For here women's history in almost all institutions of higher education, remains, despite prolific publication, a marginal area, lacking academic respectability, outside the mainstream, an academic extra occasionally demanded by troublesome women students and subversive temporary staff. The course of women's history has been marked by the strength and importance of approaches to history that lie outside academic establishments: in this has lain an outlook which is radical but also marginalised.[2] It is from this perspective that I would like to look at the relationship between women's history, feminist history, and the history of gender, and to consider the implications of the relationship now being forged between history and other disciplines. We should welcome the richness and liveliness of current theoretical debates: though at the same time we should be conscious of their relationship to political practice.

There is of course nothing new in the relationship between women's history and feminist history, which overlap yet are by no means identical. There is clearly no easy equation between the two. Social historians, economic historians, and historians of political movements have in certain periods located women's history as a branch of their own discipline: we as feminists have sought strength and support in the reconstruction of our own past. So successive generations of women and men have linked intellectual and political concerns. In the same way the social science of the eighteenth century might be echoed in the work of the Glasgow historian John Millar who wrote his powerful essay 'Of the Rank and Condition of Women in Different Ages' in 1771. But it was also echoed in Catharine Macaulay's *Letters on Education* in 1790 and in the writing of Mary Hays, the radical friend of Mary Wollstonecraft who turned from the advocacy of women's rights in the 1790s to the safer territory of female biography in the next decade.[3] And the generation of women who became social and economic historians at the end of the nineteenth and beginning of the twentieth centuries – women like Eileen Power, Alice Clark and Ivy Pinchbeck – reflected in their work at once the new insights of their discipline of social and economic history, the novelty of their own situation as working women, and the continuing debate over women's role in the public world.[4]

Today there is also a marked contrast between a women's history that has emerged from the new approaches to social history, and the work of feminist historians. In Great Britain there is particular awareness of such a distinction. Empirical traditions, aspirations towards objectivity, and rejection of theory are all still deeply rooted within a conservative profession. At the same time, from the 1970s onwards the close co-operation and interaction of British and American scholars working on British women's history have proved to be particularly fruitful in generating new perspectives.

It is now commonplace to acknowledge the dual origins of the growth of women's history in the political impetus of the women's movement, coupled with new approaches to social history. Social historians have seized upon the possibilities of extending their historical range, in dealing with, for instance, demography and the history of the family, or with the histories, differentiated by sex, of literacy and

education, or of witchcraft and criminality. They have accepted the
necessity of a social history which incorporates or even at times focuses
upon the lives of women. The journal *Social History* illustrates the strength
of this approach in Great Britain. Important studies have been published
– to name but a few examples – on family structures and attitudes, on
women's work from the medieval period onwards, and on deviance and
criminality in the early modern period.[5] So it could be said, for instance,
that much of the most substantial historical work relevant to women's
history in medieval and early modern Britain has been done in Britain by
social historians, whose interest is not specifically in women's history and
who would disclaim any political purpose: there are, however, exceptions
to this.[6] Regrettably, the same can be said of the writing of the history of
European women's lives. Few British feminist historians have ventured
into such territories, even in comparative terms.

　　　One reason for this may be the attractions of investigating the
nineteenth century paradigm, and its twentieth century legacy. I would
want to suggest, tentatively, that a second reason may be more pragmatic,
not unrelated to the condition of women in the historical profession. Work
on the history of earlier periods or different national experiences requires
some technical ability, access to specialised libraries, and time spent in
other countries. In 1986-7 women, though one third of higher degree
graduates, were still, at around 18 per cent, grossly underrepresented
among the academic staff in the history departments of our universities.[7]
Their absence from such institutions has undoubtedly influenced the kind
of history that has been written. Many feminist historians working in
modern British history have found their institutional base in the social
sciences rather than within history departments.[8]

　　　For the writing of women's history from a feminist perspective has
drawn much of its impetus from outside our universities, from an
alternative and critical viewpoint which has taken its energy from less
well-funded, under-resourced institutions, from polytechnics and from
adult and community education. Informal feminist history groups, and
autonomous, if struggling, resource centres – for instance, the Women's
Research and Resource Centre, later renamed the Feminist Library, in
London – offered support and encouragement.[9] The Fawcett Library,
originally the library of the London and National Society for Women's
Suffrage, based in the City of London Polytechnic since 1977, provided
a welcoming base for those interested in the history of the women's
movement.[10] And much was owed to feminists working in both
mainstream and alternative publishing, who stimulated and made possible
the publication of work in women's history: the availability of such work
brought the very notion of subverting the historical record to a far greater
audience.

Feminist historians inspired by the concerns of the women's movement began in the 1970s to recover their own past. One way was to return to earlier models, to the lives of great women, such as Mary Wollstonecraft, Alexandra Kollontai, or Eleanor Marx. Another was to consider the constraints upon women's lives – to ask how much could be learned from prescriptions that appeared to justify secondary and inferior roles for women, from the ideologies of separate spheres? At this stage it seemed a question of recovery, of rescuing women invisible because of their class and sex, even when they could be found in familiar public settings. One important work characterising the concerns of the 1970s was Jill Liddington and Jill Norris' *One Hand Tied Behind Us* (1978),[11] which brought to light the wholly new world of the political activities of Lancashire working women neglected by previous generations of both suffrage and labour historians. Equally in evidence was a prevailing concern with the understanding of the nineteenth century form of the separate spheres of women and men, which remains for capitalist societies today such a dominating legacy. In all these illustrations of the concerns of the 1970s I think one can see the relationship between the women's movement in Britain and the politics of the left – the constant renegotiation of the relationship between socialism and feminism, the dominance of the concerns of labour history. While radical feminism existed within the women's movement it remained a minority voice among feminist historians.[12]

This then is the context from which I come to the emergence of gender as a primary category of historical analysis, and to the contrasts I want to point out. In the mid 1970s the American historians Natalie Zemon Davis and Joan Kelly, among others, wrote of the need to understand not merely a history of subjection, but the significance of gender groups in the past, of the construction of sex roles, their meaning and functions. It is interesting that both these scholars, as early modern European historians, had been exposed to those new developments in social history – the history of mentalities, of material life, and new anthropological perspectives – stressed above. Joan Kelly wrote of the displacing of separate spheres, 'the earlier split vision of bourgeois patriarchal society' by a social theory that united different sets of social relations, work and sex, or class and race, and sex/gender.[13] While these formulations were imprecise, the weight of variables – particularly that of race – still unclear, nevertheless such a programme was welcomed by those working within the marginal and radical framework I have outlined.

A most important focus for women's history in Britain until recently has been the key journal *History Workshop*. Founded in 1976 as a socialist journal, *History Workshop* stood apart from academic establishments. Its first editorial argued that history is too important to be left to professional historians. It has remained at the forefront of our thinking about women's history, and about the relationship between history and theory. By 1982 the journal had become a journal of socialist and feminist historians, in recognition, as the editorial suggested, that it was involved not only in 'contributing to the sexual enlightenment of socialist history' but in participating 'in the construction of a new *autonomous* feminist history'. The relations of production had to be supplemented by those of reproduction. In more general terms *History Workshop* explicitly rejected the philistinism of British empiricism and called for the recognition of the importance of theoretical work drawing upon structuralist and poststructuralist debates.[14] One influential study undertaken in the 1970s by a US-based historian demonstrated how an analysis of gender relations, drawing upon both empirical research and theoretical insights, might throw new light on nineteenth-century British political history. Judith Walkowitz' work, on the regulation of prostitution in Victorian Britain and the resistances to such regulation, illuminated our understanding of sexuality and political structures alike. Its impact on feminists, teachers and students alike, cannot be overestimated.[15] In *Eve and the New Jerusalem*, an equally influential work published in 1983, Barbara Taylor pointed to the possibility of reconstructing the history of socialism in a way that took not only class but also sexual difference into account.[16]

By 1985 our index of change, *History Workshop*, had suggested that 'while rediscovering the worlds that women have inhabited is important . . . it can lead to a ghettoisation of women's history and to its presentation in forms which historians working in different fields find easy to ignore'. It called not only for the writing of women's history but for 'a feminist commitment to reconstructing the history of men as social group and gender category' as a part of the re-reading of the whole historical record.[17]

The possibilities of writing the history of gender have since been indicated in a work whose reverberations are still being absorbed. In the most ambitious attempt to write a history uniting the variables of class and gender, the major work by Leonore Davidoff and Catherine Hall, *Family Fortunes*, deployed the categories of gender and of class in a study of the middle classes of early nineteenth-century England, uniting feminist theory and a form of marxist analysis. They place gender at the centre of that analysis, starting 'from the premise that identity is gendered and that the organization of sexual difference is central to the social world. Distinctions between men and women are ever present, shaping experience, influencing behaviour, structuring explanations'.[18] Class is their second variable: but the very process of class formation is itself given a new dimension, because it is gendered. The modes of production, distribution and exchange are, in *this* study, integrally related to the consumption and reproduction of the household. Central to the emergence of class consciousness was its gendered identity: and only through analysis of domestic and private discourses, as well as of market and public worlds, can the creation of that powerful bourgeois culture be understood. In consequence this is a history which has as much to say of masculinity and of capitalist structures, as it does of femininity and of domesticity, in a survey as rich in cultural analysis as in discussion of material life.

So a term once purely grammatical has taken on a new meaning, a meaning which many historians have yet to discover. We should not underestimate the importance of this linguistic achievement. Those who as feminist historians have come to use the term 'gender' have done so by many routes, and not only in English.[19] And from all directions the possibilities for the future are exciting ones. The new journal, *Gender & History*, founded in 1989 and edited by Leonore Davidoff, is the first academic journal devoted to these issues.

We now have the means by which to examine all historical social relationships from a feminist perspective: this includes the study of male institutions and the construction of masculinity. The male domination of the historical record has made that construction invisible: it should now be possible to unmask it. Those who have seen only activity in the public sphere as historically worthy of study should now be challenged, as it becomes possible to explore all aspects of gender relations – political structures, cultural representations, symbolic systems. And those relations must be considered at all levels, where the most powerful are found – in parliaments, and cabinets, in international relations and in academies – and among the least powerful – in work and in play, in armies, communities, and private relationships. Those whose concern has been the descriptive, the recovery of the 'social' lives of men and women, should equally be challenged, for such descriptive work obscures the political structures inseparable from the construction of gender. We can now examine the varieties of masculinities and femininities that have been created, contested and negotiated over time: and we have to relate those varieties in their specific locations to those other variables of race, and class, ethnicity and sexual orientation. In some societies gender will provide a separation of the worlds of men and women overriding all other affiliations: in others the distinctions and boundaries of race or class may have the most fundamental effects in shaping lives.

Awareness of gender has already offered us the benefit of an interdisciplinary perspective: we are committed to the study of gendered divisions as a totality and to do that we need to draw upon the methods developed in other disciplines. The focus of the 1980s has been on the meaning of sexual difference rather than its cause, on literature and psychoanalysis rather than on social science or political theory, though the latter have had their place also.

To understand the creation of gender identity historians have begun to look at language, symbol, form, and at the challenge of the subjective. They have, for instance, begun to examine the way women construct their own lives in the differing narratives of autobiographical writing, life histories and oral histories. They have reconstructed the gendered symbolic order of revolution and republic in France. Following the work of Michel Foucault in particular, they have taken further the understanding of gendered political structures through arguments shaped by structuralism and poststructuralism. Joan Scott has persuasively argued that the radical potential of women's history 'comes in the writing of histories that focus on women's experiences *and* analyze the ways in which politics construct gender and gender constructs politics': we are offered 'multiple and mobile power relations'.[20]

And we do have work now, mainly but not only from the United States, which exemplifies the benefits of such approaches in subtle and original ways. In her work on sixteenth-century Augsburg, Lyndal Roper has studied the impact of the Reformation on shifting patterns of gender, and the construction of heterosexuality through the close reading of criminal records.[21] A recent history of involvement with spiritualism in Victorian England becomes a reading of the subversion of existing power relationships, of the celebration of female spiritual authority, a hidden element in a female ministry.[22] Like Davidoff and Hall, Mary Poovey has addressed the middle-class world of nineteenth-century England and in analysis of the discourses of law, literature and medicine, has drawn out the significance of its dualities and contradictions, of how the masculine identity of the middle classes has depended on its construction of the Other and the subordinate, the feminine.[23] Joan Scott's critique of E. P. Thompson's *Making of the English Working Class* has been paralleled by more specific scrutiny – which still awaits much further research – of the gendering of working-class culture in nineteenth-century England.[24]

More speculative work has been published in recent years. Denise Riley has expanded discussion of the construction of gender to that of the construction of 'women' as a volatile and inconstant category of discourse. She has suggested that an increasing degree of sexualisation and stress on gender boundaries in western Europe from the seventeenth to the nineteenth centuries constructed the collective category of womanhood. From that category grew both the strength and the ambiguities of nineteenth-century western feminism, torn as it notoriously seemed to be between equality and difference.[25]

But as feminists we may still have reservations about focusing upon the history of gender, diversely conceived. I should like to restate two, both of which have implications for the relationship between theory and practice.

First there are the implications of the recent stress on writing the history of gender through the analysis of discourse. Much of the work already completed in this area has drawn on the texts and symbols of the literate, reading their interesting complexities, noting those male discourses – ideologies of the public sphere, of political economy, of medicine – that explain the relations of power. These are the texts to which the attention of historians has been especially drawn. In themselves, that is admirable. Yet to study the history of gender does not and should not mean that we forget to explore the worlds of the less literate, the less powerful, of the ways ordinary men and women lived their lives. Did they absorb or ignore the public written discourse of elites, did they respect or reject the symbolic forms of power? How far should we read the culture of a society not only in terms of its public writings but of its material culture also? As one literary critic has suggested, an interdisciplinary project may have two purposes: to locate and pursue the common ground between disciplines, and to illuminate by difference and comparison.[26]

Historians need to ask questions about the location, and extent, of those constructions of masculinity and femininity as they change over time and place. They must still supplement the new skills of the reading of meaning with older historical practice. We have not only to learn from literary and psychoanalytic paradigms, but to meld those with our own. There are the archival sources historians need to demonstrate the extent and effectiveness of prevailing patterns of gender-determined authority and subordination, whether in terms of property ownership, of structures of employment or relations of marriage: so we may be talking of church courts or business records, of census materials or freemen's rolls. There is the material culture to which we should also turn our attention: the exploitation of new sources such as artefacts, the building and spatial arrangements of town and countryside, of household, neighbourhood and community, the technology of labour and the commodities of consumption. I do not suggest that one kind of source material has greater weight than others, but simply that we remind ourselves of the range that needs to be used. The history of gender should not be regarded as narrowly conceived in a single mould: engagement and debate, with marxist theory as with the historicisation of the concept of patriarchy must enlarge our understanding.

To the best historical work cited above these points are entirely superfluous. Yet an earlier point is relevant here. In Britain what is particularly noticeable is the absence of feminist historians from so much historical territory beyond certain well-mapped paths: it has been, for instance, social historians, rooted in empiricist traditions, who appear, with one or two obvious exceptions, as the most distinguished exponents of women's history of the medieval and early modern period. That ground should be challenged by feminist historians who combine a theoretical and political perspective which deploys the insights of other disciplines, with a sufficient grounding in their craft. That is the only way in which the excitement of the theoretical insights currently being generated will successfully confront the dominant myth of objectivity. And there is still so much that remains to be done, if we have to consider the interaction of gender, race or class in those contexts of which as yet we have little or no knowledge.

My second point is related to the first, to the central political importance of continuing to write women's history. This can again be illustrated simply from one national perspective, though the point is more generally relevant. Almost all the work I have mentioned so far arises out of the characteristic concerns of a dominant white and English culture. But Britain is a multicultural society. No one has yet written the history of women in the black and Asian communities in Britain, though there is material to do so; relatively few have used the sources that exist for the history of British imperial relations, to undertake that analysis of gender, race and class for which there is such need.[27] Nor should the history of gender relations in Britain focus only on England. To give one instance only: as one distinguished Scottish social historian has acknowledged, the neglect of women's history in Scotland is 'a historiographical disgrace'.[28] Very rich source materials exist from which the history of women in Scotland might be written: yet the conservatism of academic establishments has meant that such materials are in the main left to be exploited by those with few resources, outside the institutions of higher education. For those working in such areas, the process of recovery, of making visible, is still of vital political importance in all attempts to challenge a masculine establishment.

The new feminist history, and the history of gender are developing with a remarkable velocity. They need to retain a respect for a process that must remain at the heart of feminist concerns. There is very great unevenness, both across periods and between those within and outside dominant cultures. The idea of moving on from the recovery of women's history to the history of gender may seem a dangerous one, giving hostages to an already hostile establishment. As the Australian historian Marilyn Lake has written, the significance of women's history is greater than merely illuminating how men may grab and hold on to power. Our analysis of political structures, of the construction of masculinity, must not simply re-legitimate such subjects and perpetuate the absence of women from the historical record. Perhaps as yet there is little chance of that: compared to the wealth of publications on women's history there is as yet relatively little in print which has accepted the challenge of defining and constructing the history of masculinity. Lake suggests that our task is 'to transform the disciplinary paradigm by challenging the masculine model of social reality which underpins it'.[29] We may know increasingly more of the fluidity of the categories of masculinity and femininity: but let us not forget, in such knowledge, that the challenge of an alternative practice and an alternative history remains to be forged.

NOTES

I am very grateful for the comments of Karen Offen and Leonore Davidoff, though they are in no way responsible for the finished product.

   1. T. B. Bottomore, *Dictionary of Marxist Thought* (Oxford: Basil Blackwell, 1983), pp. 502-3; Mary Poovey, *Uneven Developments: The Ideological Work of Gender in Mid-Victorian England* (Chicago: University of Chicago Press, 1988).

   2. See, for discussions of the situation in Britain: Jane Lewis, 'Women Lost and Found: the Impact of Feminism on History', in Dale Spender (ed.), *Men's Studies Modified: The Impact of Feminism on the Academic Disciplines* (Oxford and New York: Pergamon Press, 1981); Anna Davin, 'Redressing the Balance or Transforming the Art? the British Experience', in S. Jay Kleinberg (ed.), *Retrieving Women's History: Changing Perceptions of the Role of Women in Politics and Society* (Oxford and New York: Berg/UNESCO, 1988).

   3. John Millar, *The Origin and Distinction of Ranks* (Edinburgh, 1776); Catharine Macaulay, *Letters on Education, with Observations on Religious and Metaphysical Subjects* (London, 1790); Mary Hays, *Female Biography, or, Memoirs of Illustrious and Celebrated Women, of all Ages and Countries* (London, 1802).

   4. On this generation, see Joan Thirsk, 'Foreword', in Mary Prior (ed.), *Women in English Society, 1500-1800* (London: Methuen, 1985).

   5. The works of distinguished social historians in this category might include, for example: Alan Macfarlane, *Marriage and Love in England: Modes of Reproduction, 1300-1840* (Oxford: Basil Blackwell, 1986); Ralph Houlbooke, *The English Family, 1450-1700* (London and New York: Longman, 1984); Martin Ingram, *Church Courts, Sex and Marriage in England*, 1570-1640 (Cambridge: Cambridge University Press, 1987); J. A. Sharpe, *Defamation and Sexual Slander in Early Modern England: the Church Courts at York*, Borthwick Papers, 58 (York: St Anthony's Press, 1980); Keith D. M. Snell, *Annals of the Labouring Poor: Social Change and Agrarian England, 1660-1900* (Cambridge: Cambridge University Press, 1985); David Levine, *Reproducing Families: The Political Economy of English Population History* (Cambridge: Cambridge University Press, 1987).

   6. See, for instance: Lindsey Charles and Lorna Duffin (eds.), *Women and Work in Pre-Industrial England* (London: Croom Helm, 1985); Mary Prior (ed.), *Women in English Society, 1500-1800* (London and New York: Methuen, 1985); Bridget Hill, *Women, Work and Sexual Politics in Eighteenth-Century England* (Oxford and New York: Basil Blackwell, 1989).

Substantial recent monographs in this area by American scholars include: Barbara Hanawalt, *The Ties that Bound: Peasant Families in Medieval England* (New York: Oxford University Press, 1986); Judith M. Bennett, *Women in the Medieval English Countryside: Gender and Household in Brigstock before the Plague* (New York: Oxford University Press, 1988); Hilda Smith, *Reason's Disciples: Seventeenth-Century English Feminists* (Urbana, Illinois: University of Illinois Press, 1982); Susan Dwyer Amussen, *An Ordered Society: Gender and Class in Early Modern England* (Oxford and New York: Basil Blackwell, 1988).

7. These figures are for the humanities cost-centre of the Universities Funding Council. This information was received from the Association of University Teachers, LA/3716 April 1989.

8. For instance: Leonore Davidoff, Department of Sociology, University of Essex; Carol Dyhouse, Department of Education, University of Sussex; Jane Lewis, Department of Social Science and Administration, London School of Economics; Penelope Summerfield, Department of Education, University of Lancaster; Patricia Thane, Department of Social Policy, Goldsmiths College.

9. See Davin, 'Redressing the Balance'.

10. See 'The Fawcett Library: Britain's Major Research Resources on Women Past and Present', a Special Issue of *Women's Studies International Forum*, 10, no. 3 (1987).

11. *One Hand Tied Behind Us: The Rise of the Women's Suffrage Movement* (London: Virago, 1978).

12. The work of Sheila Jeffreys has been particularly influential. See Jeffreys, *The Spinster and her Enemies: Feminism and Sexuality, 1880–1930* (London: Pandora, 1985), and Lesbian History Group (ed.), *Not a Passing Phase: Reclaiming Lesbians in History 1840–1945* (London: Women's Press, 1989).

13. Natalie Zemon Davis, 'Women's History in Transition: the European Case', *Feminist Studies*, 3, nos. 3-4 (1976), pp. 83-103; Joan Kelly, 'The Doubled Vision of Feminist Theory', in *Women, History and Theory: The Essays of Joan Kelly* (Chicago: University of Chicago Press, 1984), especially pp. 59-62.

14. Editorial, *'History Workshop Journal* and Feminism', *History Workshop Journal*, 13 (1982); Editorial, 'History and Theory', *History Workshop Journal*, 6 (1978), pp. 1-6.

15. Judith Walkowitz, *Prostitution and Victorian Society: Women, Class and the State* (Cambridge: Cambridge University Press, 1980).

16. Barbara Taylor, *Eve and the New Jerusalem: Socialism and Feminism in the Nineteenth Century* (London: Virago, 1983). Taylor does not use the term 'gender': her work 'is an examination of how a vision – the vision of women's emancipation as an integral feature of a general social emancipation – arose, became part of the ideological armoury of a popular social movement, and inspired attempts to construct a new sexual culture in a society riven with sex- and class-based conflicts' (p. xi).

17. Editorial, 'Women's History and Men's History', *History Workshop*, 19, (1985), pp. 1-2.

18. Leonore Davidoff and Catherine Hall, *Family Fortunes: Men and Women of the English Middle Class, 1780-1850* (London: Hutchinson, 1987), p. 29.

19. Gisela Bock, 'Women's History and Gender History: Aspects of an International Debate', *Gender & History*, 1, no. 1 (1989), p.10.

20. Joan Wallach Scott, *Gender and the Politics of History* (New York: Columbia University Press, 1988), pp. 25-6.

21. Lyndal Roper, *The Holy Household: Women and Morals in Reformation Augsburg* (Oxford: Oxford University Press, 1989); 'Discipline and Respectability: Prostitution and the Reformation in Augsburg', *History Workshop*, 19 (1985), pp. 3-28; 'Will and Honor: Sex, Words and Power in Augsburg Criminal Trials', *Radical History Review*, 43 (1989), pp. 45-71.

22. Alex Owen, *The Darkened Room: Women, Power and Spiritualism in Late Victorian England* (London: Virago, 1989).

23. Poovey, *Uneven Developments*.

24. Scott, 'Women in *The Making of the English Working Class*', in *Gender and the Politics of History*; Catherine Hall, 'The Tale of Samuel and Jemima: Gender and Working-Class Culture in Nineteenth-Century England', in Harvey J. Kaye and Keith C. McClelland (eds.), *E. P. Thompson: Critical Perspectives* (Oxford: Polity Press, 1990); also relevant is the work of Anna Clark, *Women's Silence, Men's Violence: Sexual Assault in England 1770-1845* (London: Pandora, 1987), and 'Whores and Gossips: Sexual Reputation in London 1770-1825', in Arina Angerman et al. (eds.), *Current Issues in Women's History* (London and New York: Routledge, 1989); and John Gillis, *For Better, For Worse: British Marriages, 1600 to the Present* (New York: Oxford University Press, 1985).

25. Denise Riley, *'Am I That Name?': Feminism and the Category of 'Women' in History* (Basingstoke: Macmillan, 1988).

26. Judith Walkowitz, Myra Jehlen, and Bell Chevigny, 'Patrolling the Borders: Feminist Historiography and the New Historicism', *Radical History Review*, 43 (1989), pp. 23-44.

27. This 'absence of a black British historiography' is charted in Ziggy Alexander, 'Let It Lie Upon the Table: The Status of Black Women's Biography in the UK', *Gender & History*, 2, no. 1 (1990), pp. 22-33: the history of Asian communities in Britain is discussed in Rozina Visram, *Ayahs, Lascars and Princes: Indians in Britain 1700-1947* (London: Pluto Press, 1986). There is an important recent work on black women in the West Indies: Barbara Bush, *Slave Women in Caribbean Society 1650-1832* (Bloomington: Indiana University Press, 1989). Other approaches to the study of imperialism are discussed in: Catherine Hall, 'The Economy of Intellectual Prestige: Thomas Carlyle, John Stuart Mill and the Case of Governor Eyre', *Cultural Critique*, 12 (1989), pp. 167-96; Joanna de Groot, '"Sex" and "Race": The Construction of Language and Image in the Nineteenth Century', in Susan Mendus and Jane Rendall (eds.), *Sexuality and Subordination: Interdisciplinary Studies of Gender in the Nineteenth Century* (London: Routledge, 1989).

28. T.C. Smout, *A Century of the Scottish People 1830-1950* (London: Collins, 1986), p. 292: this disgrace is just beginning to be remedied. See R. A. Houston, 'Women in the Economy and Society of Scotland, 1500-1800' in R. A. Houston and I. D. Whyte, (eds.), *Scottish Society 1500-1800* (Cambridge: Cambridge University Press, 1988); Linda Mahood, *The Magdalenes: Prostitution in the Nineteenth Century* (London: Routledge, 1990); Esther Breitenbach and Eleanor Gordon (eds.), *The World is Ill-Divided: Women's Work in Scotland in the 19th and Early 20th centuries*, 2 vols. (Edinburgh: Edinburgh University Press, 1990). For the history of women in Wales, see Deidre Beddoe, 'Images of Welsh

Women', in Tony Curtis (ed.), *Wales: the Imagined Nation – Essays in Cultural and National Identity* (Bridgend: Poetry Wales Press, 1986); Angela John (ed.), *Our Mothers' Land: Essays in Welsh Women's History, 1830-1930* (Cardiff: University of Wales Press, forthcoming 1991). *Llafur*, the journal of the Welsh Labour History Society, also carries important material on Welsh women's history.

    29. Marilyn Lake, 'Women, Gender and History', *Australian Feminist Studies*, 7-8 (1988), pp. 8-9.

4

Finding Our Own Ways: Different Paths to Women's History in the United States

Phyllis Stock-Morton

Women's history is an area of scholarly endeavour still in its first full and variegated bloom. Historians of women have properly adopted no single methodological approach, but have instead developed a multiplicity of perspectives on how it should be practised. This is probably more true in the United States than elsewhere, for a number of reasons. In the American setting, ideology is suspect, and eclecticism accepted. This would be true even if, as in many countries, women's history had been concentrated on the experiences of its own women. But this is not the case. While historians of women in the US have been mining the vast field of material on women readily to hand those US-based historians who study women in other parts of the world, more restricted in access to research materials, have had more time to concentrate on theory.[1] Another reason for the variety of approaches in the field is the concept of women's studies, which brings together scholars across disciplines to work on the topic of 'women in society'.[2] Historians of women differ on whether, or to what degree, they should utilise anthropological methods, for instance. There are serious differences between historians and students of literature on the uses of autobiography; yet the recent discussions on deconstruction by historians have been provoked by interchanges with practitioners of literary theory.

Even within strictly historical scholarship there are great differences. Much of women's history is done by women working in particular fields of history, such as labour history, or ethnic history. First they try to fit women into the framework of what has been done by previous scholars, using the same methodology. When they find it difficult to fit women in, they may challenge the framework and perhaps the methodology as well. There are women in every field in different stages of that process.

The practice of women's history, like culture itself, is subject to lag and uneven development. Practitioners in the United States are to be found at all levels; and there is no consensus on the goal toward which development is heading. Different historians, or groups of historians, move on to another stage at different points; no one can say that women's history reached a certain stage at a certain time.

As a result, any attempt to sum up the 'stages' in women's history will not only be artificial; it will also reflect the vantage point of the individual historian, who – as in my own case – may not be an expert in United States history. Thus there will inevitably be lacunae in a presentation that attempts to draw upon works in that field. It will be idiosyncratic, moving swiftly through early debates that seem to be ended, and lingering on those that seem to be still alive at present. It will use the arguments, and often the very language of practitioners in the area, in an effort to portray the varied discourses that reflect growth towards maturity.

*   *   *   *   *

Historians in the United States have been engaged for nearly twenty years in the effort to situate women in their rightful place in history.[3] During this time we have engaged in a continuing process of self-criticism that has both broadened and refined the theoretical bases of the field. Growing out of the feminist movement of the sixties and seventies, women's history tended at first toward the recording of women's oppression. Unfortunately this brand of history, although a logical beginning, made women seem passive victims rather than active agents in history. The re-evaluation of the lives of 'women worthies' seemed a more positive approach; however, although certainly necessary, it was soon recognised as limited, and failing to represent the experience of women in general.[4] A more rewarding kind of 'compensatory history' outlined the contributions of women to great historical movements, such as temperance reform, the abolition of slavery, pacifism, and progressive social reform. But these movements had been defined and usually led by men. Soon not only the traditional categories (such as the Progressive movement), but also the very periodisation of traditional history (including terms such as the Renaissance) were recognised as male-determined and inapplicable to women.[5]

In this dialectical process (women were dependent victims/women were strong heroines) many scholars became increasingly convinced that the most fruitful approach to the history of women would be that of social history, which concentrated on groups of women who shared common experiences.[6] But before it could transcend the traditional historical emphasis on power in the public sphere, where women appeared only when they went out to work, joined organisations, fought for property rights or suffrage, women's social history had to become interdisciplinary. It was only through use of the tools of anthropology and sociology,[7] as well as of our own discipline, that it was possible to demonstrate how women in the past acted in ways that affected the structure, function and development of their societies. In the process we have challenged the dominant myths about the nature and roles of women. However, many theoretical problems remain. I should like to point to a few of them, and to some of the debates they have raised.

For instance, there has been much discussion about the value of family history, which has many practitioners of both sexes in the United States.[8] The advantage of the family as a field of concentration is that it is historically a prime locus of a female culture in which women clearly wield power in a variety of significant ways. Here anthropology has contributed the concepts of kinship ties and 'networking' as crucial factors in shaping women's lives. Joan Scott and Louise Tilly analysed variations of the 'family economy', as an illustration of how families developed strategies to meet the challenge of developing capitalism in different industrial environments in Britain and France.[9] The idea of family strategies was also used to show how immigrant families in the United States integrated themselves into the culture and economy of their new homeland.

In this kind of analysis the family is usually viewed as a unit. Yet the impact of any family policy was different on women than on men, on the younger generation than on the older, on daughters than on mothers. Clearly the family can no longer be viewed simply as an organic unit, in which decisions are made in the best interests of all its members. Instead, it must be viewed as a field of conflict as well as harmony.[10]

For some years the public sphere (male)/ private sphere (female) dichotomy served as a basis for research on industrialising societies. In North American women's history the concept of 'separate spheres' began to take on new meaning, as historians elaborated on the 'woman's sphere'[11] that bound women together in close ties completely separate from the male world. This concept was deepened by the discovery that, for some nineteenth-century women, their bonds of friendship with other women were more meaningful than those with their husbands.[12] The existence of a separate women's culture among middle-class women in the nineteenth century was soon accepted as demonstrated.

Yet there remained a tendency to assume that working-class women shared the values and interests of their men. In working-class and immigration history women often remained undifferentiated, subject to 'the presumption that male experience and points of view are universal and exhaustive'.[13] Historians have discovered that working-class women, because of the different impact of immigration and urbanisation on the lives of women and men, had other perspectives than those of their male relatives. As feminist scholars have investigated the informal influence exerted by women within the family, and in kinship and neighbourhood networks, they have laid new emphasis on how working-class women socialised children, created neighborhood life, formed their own women's values.[14]

Historians have demonstrated that women also affect the economy in other ways than by working for wages and through the economic value of their housework and childrearing. They make choices as consumers, even initiate boycotts of food and other products.[15] Considerable work remains to be done in exploring the influence of women on male decision-making in the economy. Research has also revealed that, in both immigrant and black communities, it has been women who have maintained the structure and culture of the ethnic community, as well as the extended family ties.[16] Any study of how ethnic culture is maintained and/or adapted, any study of intergenerational differences, must see the role of women as crucial.

Thus, by exploring the subjects of reproduction and childbirth, of female social relations within and across class and ethnic divisions, of a separate female culture and the dialectic between it and the male culture, we began to 'restore half of humanity to the pages of history'.[17] However, we must admit that what we celebrate as female culture has usually developed as a protective, reactive mechanism utilised by women to gain some control over their situation in a 'man's world'. We recognise that in investigating woman's sphere, we are dealing with an area whose parameters are limited by male power. Even though the status of mothers within the family may be high in a particular culture, this indicates nothing about women's status in the society at large. 'The decisive historical fact about women', Gerda Lerner warned in 1976, 'is that the *areas* of their functioning, not only their status within those areas, has been determined by men'.[18]

The most serious criticism of family history is that, by concentrating on the nuclear or extended patriarchal family, it tends to reinforce the view of one particular relationship of the sexes as natural, whereas actual family patterns, including the sex of the child nurturer, are socially, rather than biologically determined. Family history risks reinforcing patriarchy, as the social sciences have done for so long. To quote Hilda Smith: 'We cannot uncover the realities of women's past if we look on them as adjuncts to, or minor participants in, the male power structure'.[19] We now recognise that even 'separate spheres', useful as the concept was in focusing our thoughts during the early development of women's history, is a social construct whose boundaries, Linda Kerber notes, have required constant maintenance and repair throughout the past.[20]

Concentration on family history also leaves out large numbers of women. For instance, for any cohort of women born in Europe after the fifteenth century, 10-20 per cent remained single; and at any time one-quarter to one-half of all women under thirty were unmarried.[21] This recognition leads naturally to the study of those women who do not fit into the typical family pattern – single women living alone, widows, prostitutes, lesbians. In the United States women's history pioneered lesbian history, which was crucial to developing the field of gay history for both sexes.[22]

Practising social history with women at the centre also brings into question the methodology that stresses establishing class origins and judging status by power, both political and economic. Since women stand in a different relation to society at large than men do, and since women do not necessarily partake of the attitudes of their male relatives, the importance of class in social history seems to be different in their case. When one has established the class origin of a young woman, one has said something about her father, which may also be applicable to her brother. But it does not describe her own true position in the social and political hierarchy.

If one were to create a social pyramid of any particular past society, inserting the women in their true place in that structure by assessing their actual political and economic status, one would find that the wives of the bourgeoisie would rank below many male artisans, and in some cases, unless those wives had independent incomes, even below many female workers. In general, the women would be clustered somewhere near the bottom of the pyramid. If, as Gerda Lerner insisted, 'women's status cannot simply be defined in legal or economic terms',[23] then fixing class origin is less useful in women's history than in men's.

Fortunately there are different approaches to social history. As studies of popular culture have shown, power may be informal, and exercised only on certain occasions, such as family celebrations or public holidays.[24] In any case, social structure is more complex than a social history which concentrates on status relationships has allowed for. Not only do women not fit into the traditional class structure, women are not a class; and while elements of class analysis can be applied to them, these do not yield complete explanations.

However, class certainly cannot be ignored altogether. In trying to capture women's own understanding of their experience, Elizabeth Fox-Genovese urges us to listen, not only to their own narratives, but to the discourse of the group to which they belonged, or by which they were, in a sense, 'colonised'. Patriarchy and misogyny, she insists, can be understood only through 'precise references to historical relations of genders and classes'.[25]

'Colonisation' has been common to all women in societies dominated by males; the experience of being colonised has been exacerbated for Afro-American women, who share this particular burden with their men. For instance, when black women, in their efforts to raise the status of their race, preached the manners and morals of the dominant white society, particularly in the club movement and religious organisations, one result was to add the gender limitations of that society to the racial ones they already suffered.[26] Once it is recognised that 'the oppression peculiar to women is experienced differently by women of a subject caste than it is by women of the dominant race',[27] the question arises, whether black women's history lends itself to the same treatment as that of white women.

Ideally, the historian ought to compare the lot of black women in the past, not only to that of their men, but to that of white women.[28] For instance, we know that in the sexual division of labour during the nineteenth century, occupations opening up to white women were not extended to black women.[29] Black women's history has often suffered by being subsumed under that of blacks in general, or women in general. Often black women receive treatment in separate chapters of general works, or are treated separately in works devoted to them.[30]

Some good comparative work has been produced. In 1979 Elizabeth Pleck contrasted the maternal values of black women with mothers of poor Italian immigrant families.[31] Recent efforts to integrate the study of black and white women in the south have analysed their relations to each other and to the white male society that dominated both. Suzanne Lebsock compared the family and socio-economic patterns of free black and white women before the Civil War in a southern town.[32] Fox-Genovese showed that race and class divided southern women who might have had interests in common.[33]   According to Dolores Janiewski, gender, by prescribing domestic work as female, kept black women serving white women; race, by separating black and white women in the workplace, prevented the recognition of their common problems.[34] It is only in the 1930s that there is clear evidence of black and white women banding together in the south to oppose male patriarchy in the anti-lynching movement; and even then, banding was not bonding.[35]

In recent years historians of women have been much concerned with the concept of *gender*. This interest grew out of Joan Kelly's discussion of the 'social relations of the sexes',[36] which involved viewing sex as a necessary category for social analysis, and relations between the sexes as integrally related to historical change. Incorporating these relations into theories of social development required consideration of the dialectical relationship of changes in social production and reproduction – in the case of industrialisation, for instance, where the effects of changes within the family and in the society were reciprocal. The work of Tilly and Scott provides one example among many.[37]

At the second Berkshire Conference in 1974 Natalie Zemon Davis urged the necessity of understanding the significance of 'gender groups' in the historical past, of discovering the meaning of various sex roles and symbols and how they functioned to maintain or change societies.[38] It is generally agreed that, while biology produces sex, society produces gender. But how is gender related to anatomical differences, to sex, class and race, to individual identity? Are there distinctly male and female modes of thought and social relations, and if so, are they innate or socially constituted? Are gender distinctions socially useful and/or necessary? Do gender relations change over time; that is, does gender have a history? How many genders are there?[39] Luckily, historians are not alone in addressing these questions, which are being studied by psychologists, sociologists and anthropologists as well.

The discussion of gender has given rise to men's studies,[40] at a point where there is still much confusion over the various definitions of women's culture. Some fear that, with all that we have accomplished so far, we have managed to document the existence and activities of women in the past, but have not necessarily changed the importance, or lack of it, attributed to what women do. 'Indeed', Scott points out, 'the separate treatment of women could serve to confirm their marginal and particularised relationship to those [male] subjects already established as dominant and universal'. In concentrating on gender, and the social functions of symbols connected with male and female behaviour in society, we have not, she points out, dealt adequately with the question: Who controls these meanings, and in whose interests are they constructed? In determining the experience of women in society these symbols determine the understanding of gender, thereby creating a vicious circle.[41]

This problem is one of many that haunts writers of women's biography. There is still no agreement on how to write the story of an individual woman's life, except that it is essential to modify the traditional 'objective' methodology, particularly by taking into account the gender structure of the subject's society. Much of the discussion revolves around how to interpret autobiographical texts.[42] There are also the problems of discontinuity in the female life and of the struggle for identity.[43] We have been more successful with groups of women who are able to identify with one another, particularly if we can establish this identification. One may also use cohorts, such as the women who travelled west with their husbands across the continent in the mid-nineteenth century and experienced similar hardships.[44] Group experience is particularly useful in writing black women's history, where the experience of slavery and sexual exploitation was common to a large number of women.[45] In their attempts to reconstruct women's lives, historians of women usually try to find means of depicting their subjects as agents, moulding their lives rather than enduring them.

Many historians believe that women's history cannot be practised apart from men's history. This would be one way to go about answering the question, how many genders? Some historians have recently advocated the literary methodology of 'deconstruction' to break through binary female/male discourse, revealing it as a purely rhetorical opposition of concepts that are mutually dependent, and that have considerable heterogeneity within them. Scott points out that only by deconstructing the absolute categories of gender difference can we attack the normative rules attached to gender and the power attached to gender discourse.[46]

This method would bring the concept of power back into women's history, revealing it as the base for the ideological construction of gender concepts. Deconstructive techniques would also solve, to some extent, the problem of integrating the history of women with that of all the powerless. The economic and political discourses of a society have been expressed in terms of gender to indicate the presence or absence of power; for instance, the equation of unskilled work with female, skilled work with male space.[47] Similar discursive practices relate to other groups without status, whether on economic, racial, religious, or sexual grounds. It is probable that the construction of gender concepts can be related to the attitudes of male elites toward all non-elite members of any particular society – whether economic, racial, religious, female, or gay.

There is an important advantage in deconstructive approaches, particularly in the dismantling of 'universal' concepts such as liberty, reason, and science. The ideological systems which control modern liberal discourse, and therefore gender definitions, are presented by traditional male scholarship as rational, scientific, universal, and therefore just. It is in the interest of feminist historians to subject these systems to criticism that reveals their contradictions and omissions. Scott points to the abstraction 'man' as a crucial part of these systems. Deconstruction would go a long way toward eliminating woman's difficulty of trying to secure status 'as an abstract individual in the face of its masculine embodiment', by breaking down abstract essences into historical realities.[48]

'Family', another universal term often accepted as a given by historians, has already been subjected to such criticism, particularly through the addition of the adjective 'patriarchal'. Gerda Lerner has sought the origins of male dominance in the family by attempting to trace the conditions of patriarchy back to their origins in ancient times. One important by-product of her research is the suggestion that subordination of women within the family provided the paradigm on which slavery was instituted.[49]

Deconstruction might also lead to the elimination of the ethnocentric tendencies in women's history, where western values are often treated as universals in the assessment of women's lives in non-western cultures. The problem of ethnocentrism has arisen in an argument among practitioners of women's history over the definition of feminism. If feminism is defined in purely Anglo-American terms, it involves demands for equal rights, suffrage, and female autonomy. Does using these standards when discussing other cultures assume that feminism is basically a western experience transferred to other cultures? It certainly does not take into account some prevalent types of continental European 'feminism'.[50] Recent efforts to bifurcate the concept of feminism to provide for a 'relational feminism' structured around the complementarity of the sexes,[51] which might be more useful in dealing with European and Third World women, have given rise to debate. Fuel for this debate came from the Sears case of 1986,[52] in which two 'feminist' historians testified on opposite sides in a court of law. Rosalind Rosenberg,[53] testifying to women's 'difference', supported the Sears Roebuck company in an affirmative action case against it for not successfully placing women in certain highly paid sales jobs. Women had historically not wanted such positions, the argument ran, because they interfered with home life and did not provide a guaranteed remuneration. Alice Kessler-Harris[54] opposed this position, pointing out that women had in the past accepted all kinds of jobs when genuinely open to them, and noting the social pressures on women that had to be taken into account. Sears won its case. This raised the serious question of whether emphasis on women's difference from men did not in fact provide a basis for discrimination against them in public life.

Women historians had already discussed this question in a symposium on 'Politics and Culture in Women's History'.[55] In examining the question of 'domestic feminism' versus 'egalitarian feminism' in the United States during the late nineteenth century, it was agreed that women moved domestic values into campaigns for moral reform, sustained by the loyalties developed in a women's culture. Women went on to claim more control within the family, over property and over reproduction. They also brought about legal protection for women and children in the workplace. But none of these gains brought political power to women. In fact, as Suzanne Lebsock has shown for the women of Petersburg, gains in the field of property, divorce, and wage labour could take place at the same time as a loss of public power.[56]

In another forum in 1986 Linda Kerber cautioned historians concerning the dualism inherent in the concept of 'difference'. She asked what forms difference between the sexes had taken historically, and how we should weigh these differences in relation to racial, class, lifecycle, and sexual differences among women themselves.[57] Jacqueline Jones has concluded that black women paid a high price for their acceptance of a patriarchal family structure.[58] It is also disturbing that what Kessler-Harris called 'the ideology of domesticity' helped to solidify the segmentation of the labour market by gender.[59] It seems difficult to speak of feminism in the context of a 'difference' in which separate cannot be equal, and women cannot be autonomous.

Is feminism perhaps an ahistorical term, which should be reserved for situations when it includes demands for women's autonomy? From this point of view, it is unnecessary to broaden the concept of feminism to bring in more women in the past, when we can study them without labelling them feminists.[60] However, it is true that women have called themselves feminists while merely engaging in what Nancy Cott would call a 'woman movement',[61] not demanding autonomy, and including men.[62]

If we use Margot Badran's recent definition of feminism, as the growing awareness of women's oppression, plus an analysis of that oppression and some active opposition to it,[63] we may end up by including certain males in the category of feminist. Some historians have accepted advocates of power for women, even if that power is limited to the domestic sphere, as feminists in some sense.[64] This might lead us down a slippery slope, however; the predominant power of the oldest woman in a family can, for example, be detrimental to the lives of other women in the same family, just as confining women's power to the private sphere can be detrimental to all women.

What is at issue in these debates might be seen as an attempt to deconstruct the term *feminist* in order to show that there is great variety within the term, as within the terms *masculine* or *feminine*. The question is, can one do this and still use feminism as an 'historically powerful concept'?[65] As Mary Poovey has noted, deconstruction is a useful feminist tool, but one that must be subjected to historical scrutiny.[66]

One of the problems may be a lack of clarity between the areas of women's history and the history of feminism. Women's history contains the history of feminism, which contains the history of feminist theory. But each asks different questions. An independent history of feminism, undertaken on a comparative basis, is necessary to establish whether there is anything universal in feminist experience, and also to counter the tendency to 'read the discourse of feminism too narrowly'.[67] However, we may not have to discard concepts that originate in the west, if they are grounded in history and development. 'To develop a historically grounded feminist theory we must transcend its philosophic past, not obliterate it', Janet Afary points out, particularly as third world feminism is usually linked to Marxist theory.[68]

At present there is a growing trend in US historiography to deny the validity, not only of the traditional binary, dialectical approach, but even of historians' attempts to find a logic in history. First anthropologists and literary critics, and now some historians have questioned the structures erected by scholars to explain texts, societies, or events in the past. Feminist scholars have often seen these structures (such as feudalism and modernisation) as inherently anti-woman, since women have consistently suffered by being treated as minor elements in them. Therefore partisans of deconstruction such as Scott suggest that, rather than trying to insert women into the past as it is currently viewed, it would be preferable to challenge altogether the way male historians have structured the past, treating all unequal relationships as political, and then asking how they were established and maintained, or occasionally, opposed by women.

Is it conceivable that to incorporate women into history we must not stop at being revisionists, but must go all the way to a revolution against history itself? Perhaps a better way to put it is: Can we deconstruct history and still remain historians? To some extent we probably can, since the structures and abstract concepts of the discipline are already undergoing a continual process of challenge and change by historians. But this cannot be our complete agenda.

The sheer weight of the research and production in women's history has won it a (perhaps grudging) recognition by the historical establishment. The question is, in which direction to move? Most practitioners believe that there must be an integration of women's history with the main body of history in the long run. But how long, and by what means? Up to now women's history in the United States has operated partly as a sub-section of social history, and partly as an independent field with many sub-sections of its own. We have followed the path of trying, first, to find original sources stemming from women themselves; then, to use categories that pertain to the real lives of women; and, above all, to examine historical issues that are still relevant to women today. It should be possible to proceed from where we are now, deepening our concept of social history to include elaboration of the complex web of relationships and discourses in a society, using the 'thick description' of the anthropologists.[69] Gender history, incorporating both women's and men's history, may also help to change the paradigms of traditional history.

On the other hand, Louise Tilly has recently emphasised the necessity of analytical, problem-solving studies in women's history, which provide explanations. One advantage of such work would be that the findings could be connected to 'questions already on the historical agenda'.[70] Such a focus would certainly help to assimilate into the historical canon the tremendous base of factual material on women in the past that has been established in the last twenty years. It would also enable us, as historians, to arrive at explanations for decisions made in a particular society about such matters as access to education, equal pay, and other topics of prime interest to women. One would hope that we could keep our history connected to the mainstream of the past without perpetuating the traditional categories of historical discourse that have until recently rendered women almost invisible.

Meanwhile, we face certain immediate problems. One concern, recently discussed at a meeting of the Berkshire Conference of Women Historians,[71] has been that not only women's history, but women historians themselves may be 'ghettoised' in US colleges and universities. There are instances where woman practitioners of the field have been considered to be 'only' historians of women (!), no matter what their qualifications. In other cases it has been assumed that women's history is the chief interest of women historians, even those who are engaged in political, diplomatic, or military history. These assumptions may adversely affect hiring and tenure decisions.

This concern relates to a problem of interest to all teaching women historians, whether their research is or is not in women's history: how to integrate women's history into the other courses we are expected to teach in schools and universities. In each field, the introduction of women changes the corpus of knowledge in major ways, and requires a wholesale reordering of priorities. This may or may not be accepted by the academy. In general the approach used is taken from social history, which lends itself best to the inclusion of non-elites. But the problem has not been solved. The ideal solution awaits the full integration of women's history into the accepted canon of the discipline.

Like all intellectual developments, women's history has been subject to pressures inherent in the desire or need to publish. While some of the women's history produced outside the academy suffers from the lack of fertilisation by theory, some produced within the academy suffers from serious restraints. Not only do dissertations written for the doctorate have to satisfy advisors, often male; but the one or two articles reserved for women's history in a collection on some other topic must satisfy the editors. This often means adjusting the presentation to fit the methodology already accepted in the particular field. So the process of educating ourselves involves one of educating our male, and sometimes even our female colleagues. Not only must our historical production be acceptable to the academy; it is also dependent upon the whims of publishers, who have their own tastes in women's history.

One solution, which has proven highly successful, is for women scholars to publish their own academic journals,[72] and to obtain control of publishers' series of works on women. At the same time, networks of women historians, such as the Conference Group on Women's History, have encouraged the market for these works by publicising work in progress and publishing outlines of courses where they might be used, in newsletters produced, reproduced and mailed by volunteers at the lowest possible cost. However, there is still justified concern about the influence exercised by publishers over the history they choose to publish.

Over the years, historians in the United States have produced solid scholarship on women in every area of the world and every historical period. Perhaps the best comment on this corpus is the fact that men have been practising in the field of women's history in considerable numbers since the 1970s. Special issues of historical journals have been devoted to the field.[73] When the time comes for the full integration of women's history into the general body of historical knowledge, we are hopeful that women historians in the United States will not be alone, but will be able to draw upon considerable support from their male colleagues.

NOTES

1. This was actually the case in a Women's History seminar of the Institute for Research in History in New York, where the effort to divide it into two seminars of manageable size by splitting off the US historians from the rest always foundered, because the non-US historians enjoyed having contact with the veritable wealth of material available to the US historians, who in turn were fascinated by the theorising of the others. There is still only one seminar.

2. The actual name of the Columbia University seminar that includes women faculty of the New York area from the fields of history, literature, art history, anthropology, sociology, and law.

3. The first Berkshire Conference on the History of Women was held at Douglass College, Rutgers University, in 1973. See Mary S. Hartman and Lois W. Banner (eds.), *Clio's Consciousness Raised: New Perspectives on the History of Women* (New York: Harper & Row, 1974).

4. Natalie Zemon Davis, '"Women's History" in Transition: The European Case', *Feminist Studies*, 3, nos. 3-4 (1976), pp. 83-103.

5. Joan Kelly, 'Did Women Have a Renaissance?' in Renate Bridenthal and Claudia Koonz, *Becoming Visible: Women in European History* (Boston: Houghton-Mifflin, 1977), pp. 137-64.

6. Ann D. Gordon, Mari Jo Buhle, and Nancy Schrom Dye, 'The Problem of Women's History', in Berenice A. Carroll (ed.), *Liberating Women's History: Theoretical and Critical Essays* (Urbana: University of Illinois Press, 1976), p. 81.

7. Most useful were Michelle Zimbalist Rosaldo and Louise Lamphere (eds.), *Woman, Culture and Society* (Stanford: Stanford University Press, 1974); and Rayna R. Reiter (ed.), *Toward an Anthropology of Women* (New York: Monthly Review Press, 1976).

8. See John Demos, *A Little Commonwealth: Family Life in the Plymouth Colony* (New York: Oxford University Press, 1970); Carl N. Degler, *At Odds: Women and the Family in America from the Revolution to the Present* (New York: Oxford University Press, 1980); Tamara K. Hareven, 'The History of the Family as an Interdisciplinary Field', *Journal of Interdisciplinary History*, 2, no. 2 (1971), pp. 399-414, and 'Modernization and Family History: Perspectives on Social Change', *Signs: The Journal of Women in Culture and Society*, 2, no. 1 (1976), pp. 190-206; Mary P. Ryan, 'The Explosion of Family History', *Reviews in American History*, 10, no. 4 (1982), pp. 181-95.

9. Louise A. Tilly and Joan W. Scott, *Women, Work, and Family* (New York: Holt, Rinehart & Winston, 1978).

10. Heidi Hartmann, 'The Family as the Locus of Gender, Class and Political Struggle', *Signs*, 6, no. 3 (Spring, 1981), pp. 366-94; Louise Tilly and Miriam Cohen, 'Does the Family Have a History? A Review of Theory and Practice in Family History', *Social Science History*, 6, no. 3 (1982), pp. 131-80; Louise Tilly, 'Women's History and Family History: Fruitful Collaboration or Missed Connection?', *Journal of Family History*, 12, nos. 1-3 (1987), pp. 303-15.

11. Nancy Cott, *The Bonds of Womanhood: 'Woman's Sphere' in New England, 1780-1835* (New Haven: Yale University Press, 1977).

12. Carroll Smith-Rosenberg, 'The Female World of Love and Ritual: Relations Between Women in Nineteenth-Century America', *Signs*, 1, no. 1 (1975), pp. 1-29. This article, and 'The New Woman as Androgyne: Social Disorder and Gender Crisis, 1870-1936', may be found in her *Disorderly Conduct: Visions of Gender in Victorian America* (New York: Oxford University Press, 1986).

13. Ellen C. DuBois, Gail P. Kelly et al., *Feminist Scholarship: Kindling in the Groves of Academe* (Urbana: University of Illinois Press, 1985), pp.185-6.

14. Donna Gabaccia, 'The Transplanted: Women and Family in Immigrant Societies', *Social Science History*, 12 (1988), p. 248. For examples of work including women in immigration history see also Gabaccia's *From Sicily to Elizabeth Street: Housing and Social Change Among Italian Immigrants* (Albany: State University of New York Press, 1984); Virginia Yans-McLaughlin, *Family and Community, Italian Immigrants in Buffalo, 1880-1939* (Ithaca, NY: Cornell University Press, 1977); Judith E. Smith, *Family Connections: A History of Italian and Jewish Immigrant Lives in Providence Rhode Island, 1900-1940* (Albany: State University of New York Press, 1985); S.J.Kleinberg, *The Shadow of the Mills: Working Class Families in Pittsburgh, 1870-1907* (Pittsburgh: University of Pittsburgh Press, 1989); Sarah Deutsch, *No Separate Refuge: Culture, Class and Gender on an Anglo-Hispanic Frontier in the American Southwest, 1880-1940* (New York: Oxford University Press, 1987); and Sydney Stahl Weinberg, *The World of Our Mothers: The Lives of Jewish Immigrant Women* (Chapel Hill: University of North Carolina Press, 1988). The information on immigrant history was obtained from a talk by Sydney Weinberg at the Columbia University Seminar on Women and Society in January of 1990.

15. Paula E. Hyman, 'Immigrant Women and Consumer Protest: The New York City Kosher Meat Boycott of 1902', *American Jewish History*, 70, no. 1 (1980), pp. 91-105.

16. Gerda Lerner (ed.), *Black Women in White America: A Documentary History* (New York: Pantheon Books, 1972); Jacqueline Jones, *Labor of Love, Labor of Sorrow: Black Women, Work and the Family from Slavery to the Present* (New York: Basic Books, 1985); Deutsch, *No Separate Refuge*; and other works cited in note 12.

17. Gerda Lerner, 'New Approaches to the Study of Women in American History', in Berenice A. Carroll (ed.), *Liberating Women's History*, pp. 367-8.

18. Lerner, *New Approaches*, p. 361.

19. Hilda Smith, 'Feminism and the Methodology of Women's History', in Carroll (ed.), *Liberating Women's History*, p. 383.

20. Linda Kerber, 'Separate Spheres, Female Worlds, Woman's Place: The Rhetoric of Women's History', *Journal of American History*, 75, no. 1 (1988), pp. 9-39.

21. Sheila Ryan Johansson, '"Herstory" A History: A New Field or Another Fad?', in Carroll (ed.), *Liberating Women's History* , p. 404.

22. See Martha Vicinus, *Independent Women: Work and Community for Single Women, 1850-1920* (London: Virago Press, 1985); Martha Vicinus (ed.), *Suffer and Be Still: Women in the Victorian Age* and *A Widening Sphere: Changing Roles of Victorian Women* (Bloomington: Indiana University Press, 1972 and 1977); Ruth Rosen, *The Lost Sisterhood: Prostitution in America, 1900-1918* (Baltimore: Johns Hopkins University Press, 1982); Judith R. Walkowitz, *Prostitution and Victorian Society: Women, Class and the State* (New York: Cambridge University Press, 1980); Theresa M. McBride, *The Domestic Revolution: The Modernization of Household Service in England and France, 1820-1920* (New York: Holmes and Meier, 1976); Lillian Faderman, *Surpassing the Love of Men: Romantic Friendship between Women from the Renaissance to the Present* (New York: William Morrow, 1981); Blanche W. Cook, '"Women Alone Stir My Imagination": Lesbianism and the Cultural Tradition', *Signs*, 4, no. 4 (1979), pp. 718-39. An entire issue of *Signs*, 9, no. 4 (1984), was devoted to interdisciplinary articles about lesbianism.

23. Gerda Lerner, 'Black and White Women in Interaction and Confrontation', in *The Majority Finds Its Past: Placing Women in History* (New York: Oxford University Press, 1979), p. 94.

24. See Natalie Zemon Davis, 'Women and Religious Change' and 'Women on Top', in her *Society and Culture in Early Modern France* (Stanford: Stanford University Press, 1975).

25. Elizabeth Fox-Genovese, 'Culture and Consciousness in the Intellectual History of European Women', *Signs*, 12, no. 3 (1986), p. 531.

26. See Gerda Lerner, 'The Community Work of Black Clubwomen', in *The Majority Finds Its Past*; Paula Giddings, *When and Where I Enter: The Impact of Black Women on Race and Sex in America* (New York: William Morrow and Company, 1984); and Evelyn Brooks, *Righteous Discontent: The Women's Movement in the Black Baptist Church*, forthcoming.

27. Gerda Lerner, 'Black Women in the United States', p. 69.

28. See also Phyllis Marynick Palmer, 'White Women/Black Women: The Dualism of Female Identity and Experience in the United States', *Feminist Studies*, 9, no. 1 (1983), pp. 151-70.

29. Sharon Harley, 'Black Women in a Southern City: Washington, D.C., 1880-1920', and Dolores Janiewski, 'Sisters Under the Skin: Southern Working Women, 1880-1950', in Joanne V. Hawks and Sheila L. Skemp (eds.), *Sex, Race and the Role of Women in the South* (Jackson: University of Mississippi Press, 1983).

30. For instance, the chapters devoted to black women in Barbara Mayer Wertheimer, *We Were There: The Story of Working Women in America* (New York: Pantheon Books, 1977) and the book devoted to black working women by Jacqueline Jones, *Labor of Love, Labor of Sorrow.*

Other examples of articles on black women included in general collections are Rosalyn Terborg-Penn, 'Discontented Black Feminists: Prelude and Postscript to the Passage of the Nineteenth Amendment', in Lois Scharf and Joan M. Jensen, (eds.), *Decades of Discontent: the Women's Movement, 1920-1940* (Westport, Conn.: Greenwood Press, 1983); 'Survival Strategies among African American Women Workers: A Continuing Process', in Ruth Milkman (ed.), *Women, Work and Protest: A Century of US Women's Labor History* (New York: Routledge & Kegan Paul, 1985); Christie Farnham, 'Sapphire? The Issue of Dominance in the Slave Family, 1830-1865', and Dolores Janiewski, 'Seeking a New Day and a New Way: Black Women and Unions in the Southern Tobacco Industry', in Carol Groneman and Mary Beth Norton (eds.), *To Toil the Livelong Day: America's Women at Work, 1780-1980* (Ithaca, N.Y.: Cornell University Press, 1987).

A collection devoted to black women is Bert James Loewenberg and Ruth Bogin (eds.), *Black Women in Nineteenth Century American Life* (University Park: The Pennsylvania State University Press, 1976).

31. Elizabeth H. Pleck, 'A Mother's Wages: Income Earning Among married Italian and Black Women, 1896-1911', in Pleck and Nancy F. Cott (eds.), *A Heritage of Her Own: Toward a New Social History of American Women* (New York: Simon and Schuster, 1979), pp. 367-92.

32. Suzanne Lebsock, *The Free Women of Petersburg: Status and Culture in a Southern Town, 1784-1860* (New York: W.W. Norton & Company, 1984), particularly chapter 4.

33. Elizabeth Fox-Genovese, *Within the Plantation Household: Black and White Women of the Old South* (Chapel Hill: University of North Carolina Press, 1988).

34. Dolores Janiewski, 'Sisters Under Their Skins' and *Sisterhood Denied: Race, Gender, and Class In a New South Community.* (Philadelphia: Temple University Press, 1986).

35. Jacqueline Dowd Hall, *Revolt Against Chivalry: Jessie Daniel Ames and the Women's Campaign Against Lynching* (New York: Columbia University Press, 1979).

36. Joan Kelly, 'The Social Relations of the Sexes', *Signs*, 1, no. 4 (1976), pp. 809-23.

37. Renate Bridenthal, 'The Dialectics of Production and Reproduction', *Conceptual Frameworks for Studying Women's History* (Bronxville, NY: Sarah Lawrence College, 1975); Tilly and Scott, *Women, Work and Family.*

38. Quoted in Joan Kelly, *Women, History, and Theory* (Chicago: University of Chicago Press, 1984), p. 9.

39. These questions were raised by Jane Flax in 'Postmodernism and Gender Relations in Feminist Theory', *Signs*, 12, no. 4 (1987), pp. 621-43.

40. On 9-10 March 1990 a Conference on Men in the Middle Ages took place at Fordham University in New York. The keynote address, 'Die Herrenfrage [The Man Question]', by Joanne Macnamara of Hunter College, City University of New York, examined such topics as why male culture included a glorification of war. On the other hand, Lois Banner, in her presidential address to the Women's Breakfast at the American Studies Association meeting in New York in 1987, objected to the concept of men's studies as an attempt, by a field not analogous to women's studies, to co-opt feminist scholarship in the universities. Banner's talk is summarised in the *Study of Women and Men in Society Newsletter* (Spring 1988), University of Southern California, pp. 1-2.

41. See Joan Wallach Scott, *Gender and the Politics of History* (New York: Columbia University Press, 1988) pp. 3-6, and 'Deconstructing Equality versus Difference: or, the Uses of Poststructural Theory for Feminism', *Feminist Studies*, 14, no. 1 (1988), p. 47.

42. Bell Gale Chevigny, 'Daughters Writing: Toward a Theory of Women's Biography', *Feminist Studies*, 9, no. 1 (1983), pp. 79-102.

43. See Shari Benstock, *The Private Self: Theory and Practice of Women's Auto-biographical Writings* (Chapel Hill: University of North Carolina Press, 1988).

44. See Joan M. Jensen and Darlis A. Miller, 'The Gentle Tamers Revisited: New Approaches to the History of Women in the American West', *Pacific Historical Review*, 49, no. 2 (1980), pp. 173-213; the special issue of *Frontiers*, 7, no. 3 (1982) devoted to 'Women on the Frontier'; Susan Armitage and Elizabeth Jameson (eds.), *The Women's West* (Norman: University of Oklahoma Press, 1987); Karen J. Blair (ed.), *Pacific Northwest Women's History: An Anthology* (Seattle: University of Washington Press, 1988); Ellen Carol DuBois and Vicki L. Ruiz (eds.), *Unequal Sisters: A Multi-Cultural Reader in US Women's History* (New York: Routledge, 1990); Vicki L. Ruiz, Lillian Schlissel, and Janice Monk (eds.), *Western Women: Their Land, Their Lives* (Albuquerque: University of New Mexico Press, 1988).

45. Sharon Harley and Rosalyn Terborg-Penn (eds.), *The Afro-American Woman: Struggles and Images* (Port-Washington, NY: Kennikat Press, 1978); Gerda Lerner (ed.), *Black Women in White America*; Dorothy Sterling (ed.), *We Are Your Sisters: Black Women in the Nineteenth Century* (New York: Feminist Press, 1984); Paula Giddings, *When and Where I Enter: The Impact of Black Women on Race and Sex in America* (New York: William Morrow, 1984); Audre Lorde, *Sister Outside: Essays and Speeches* (Trumansberg, New York: Crossing Press, 1984); Jacqueline Jones, *Labor of Love*; Gloria T. Hull, Patricia Bell Scott, and Barbara Smith (eds.), *All the Women Are White, All the Blacks Are Men, but Some of Us Are Brave: Black Women's Studies* (Old Westbury, NY: Feminist Press, 1982).

46. Joan Wallach Scott, *Gender and the Politics of History*, p. 102.

47. *Ibid.*, pp. 97-103. Scott's examples are from mid-nineteenth century France.

48. Joan Scott, 'French Feminists and the Rights of Man: Olympe de Gouges' Declarations', *History Workshop*, 28 (Autumn, 1989), p. 9.

76   *Phyllis Stock-Morton*

49. Gerda Lerner, *The Creation of Patriarchy* (New York: Oxford University Press, 1986).

50. Karen Offen, 'On the French Origins of the Words Feminism and Feminist', *Feminist Issues*, 8, no. 2 (1988), pp. 45-51.

51. Karen Offen, 'Defining Feminism: a Comparative Historical Approach', *Signs*, 14, no. 1 (1988), pp. 119-57.

52. United States District Court for the Northern District of Illinois, Eastern District, Equal Employment Opportunity Commission v. Sears, Roebuck and Co. Material on the historians' role in the case, including testimony, has been deposited in the Schlesinger Library at Radcliffe College, Boston, Massachusetts. See Sandi Cooper and Jacqueline Dowd Hall, 'Women's History Goes to Trial', *Signs*, 11, no. 4 (1986), pp. 751-79; also Ruth Milkman, 'Women's History and the Sears Case', *Feminist Studies*, 12, no. 2 (1986), pp. 375-400.

53. Rosenberg is the author of *Beyond Separate Spheres: The Intellectual Roots of Modern Feminism* (New Haven: Yale University Press, 1982).

54. Kessler-Harris is the author of *Out to Work: A History of Wage-Earning Women in the United States* (New York: Oxford University Press, 1982).

55. 'Politics and Culture in Women's History: A Symposium', *Feminist Studies*, 6, no.1 (1980), pp. 26-64. See particularly the contributions of Ellen DuBois, Carroll Smith-Rosenberg, and Mari Jo Buhle. A discussion of this problem as it affects the law can be found in Eileen Boris, 'Looking at Women's Historians Looking at Difference', *Wisconsin Women's Law Journal*, 3 (1987), pp. 213-38.

56. Lebsock, *Free Women of Petersburg*, pp. xv-xvi.

57. See Linda Kerber's contribution to 'On "In a Different Voice"': An Interdisciplinary Forum', *Signs*, 11, no. 2 (1986), pp. 304-10. Nancy Hewitt's 'Yankee Evangelicals and Agrarian Quakers: Gender, Religion, and Class in the Formation of a Feminist Consciousness in Nineteenth-Century Rochester, New York', *Radical History Review*, nos. 28-30 (1984), pp. 327-42, had already indicated that family and class were as important in the formation of women activists as shared gender relations.

58. Jacqueline Jones, '"My Mother Was Much of a Woman"': Black Women, Work, and the Family Under Slavery', *Feminist Studies*, 8, no. 2 (1982), pp. 235-69.

59. Kessler-Harris, *Out to Work*, pp. 20-72.

60. Nancy F. Cott, 'Comment' on Offen, *Signs*, 15, no. 1 (1989), pp. 203-5.

61. Campaigns for women's education, property rights and suffrage would conform to this definition. See Nancy F. Cott, *The Grounding of Modern Feminism* (New Haven: Yale University Press, 1987).

62. See Karen Offen, 'Reply' to Cott, *Signs*, 15, no. 1 (1989), pp. 206-9.

63. Margot Badran, 'Dual Liberation: Feminism and Nationalism in Egypt, 1870s to 1925', *Feminist Issues*, 8, no. 1 (1988), p. 16.

64. Karen Offen, 'Ernest Legouvé and the Doctrine of "Equality in Difference" for Women: A Case Study of Male Feminism in Nineteenth-Century French Thought', *Journal of Modern History*, 58, no. 2 (1986), pp. 452-84; Sharon Sievers, 'Dialogue: Six Feminists in Search of a Historian', *Journal of Women's History*, 1, no. 2 (1989), pp. 142-3; Asuncion Lavrin, 'Comment', *ibid.*, p. 154.

65. Offen, 'Reply' to Cott (see n. 62).

66. Mary Poovey, 'Feminism and Deconstruction', *Feminist Studies*, 14, no. 1 (1988), pp. 51-65.

67. Sharon Sievers, 'Dialogue', p. 138, and Janet Afary's comment on Sievers, J. Afray, 'Some Reflections on Third World Feminist Historiography', *Journal of Women's History*, 1, no. 2 (1989), p. 150.

68. Janet Afary, 'Some Reflections on Third World Feminist Historiography', p. 151.

69. Such as Clifford Geertz.

70. Louise A. Tilly, 'Gender, Women's History and Social History', *Social Science History*, 13, no. 4 (1989), pp. 439-62.

71. May 1989, at Mohonk, New York.

72. For example, *Feminist Studies* and *Signs*, which have published many articles on women's history, and the new *Journal of Women's History*, which is totally devoted to it.

73. For example, *Third Republic/Troisième République*, nos. 3 and 4, (1977); *History of Education Quarterly* (Spring, 1984); *American Historical Review*, 89, no. 3 (1984); *French Historical Studies*, 16, no. 1 (1989); and *American Historical Review*, 95, no. 4 (October 1990).

5

Experience, Difference, Dominance and Voice in the Writing of Canadian Women's History[1]

Ruth Roach Pierson

Despite our embattled position within the profession and our struggle to assert the right of and need for women's history,[2] until recently feminist historians of women, with a few notable exceptions, have tended to undertheorise our work. Of late, however, feminist women's history seems to be enjoying a flurry of theorising as feminist historians come under the sway of French-derived deconstructivist literary theory[3] and discourse analysis.[4] Joan Wallach Scott's effort to theorise the category of 'gender' is, undoubtedly, the most acclaimed example to date.[5]

Rarely, however, are any of these theoretical systems taken up systematically. We historians continue to proceed in an eclectic way, taking from here and there what is useful to our purposes, what seems to work to open up our sources, or give us an 'angle' on a topic. Perhaps this 'eclecticism', like the non- or anti-theoretical bent of much history writing, has to do with the intrinsically empirical nature of our discipline. The chaos and complexity of human activity as embodied in concrete empirical data do not easily allow themselves to be contained by the schemata of tight systems. Some of that recalcitrant human matter inevitably seems, instead, to leak out through the cracks of any grand theory and, thus uncontained, to pose a challenge to totalising claims.

One could, of course, argue that our empiricism, our reliance on 'sources', is itself a theoretical stance. And I suppose I would have to agree. Reality is 'nothin' but a collective hunch', declares Trudy, the 'bag lady', played by Lily Tomlin in *The Search for Signs of Intelligent Life in the Universe*.[6] Historians tend to operate on two such collective hunches, one ontological, that there was a reality out there in the past, and the second epistemological, that that reality is knowable, albeit imperfectly and incompletely. In other words, while few historians in the twentieth century would claim that it is possible to know precisely '*wie es eigentlich gewesen*' (how it really was), most would maintain that we can establish *daß es gewesen ist* (that it really was).[7] Historians on the whole are still 'locked within' what Michèle Barrett would call 'a very traditional philosophical framework' that 'presupposes a somewhat optimistic confidence in empirical method and ontological reality'.[8]

Yet ours is not necessarily a naive empiricism. While it is held that the past is in some way knowable from 'sources' that have survived, it is generally recognised that these sources are almost infinite in their variety, ranging from the physical artifacts relied on by the students of material culture through the official documents of government archives to individual memories as conveyed in diaries and oral testimonies. Moreover, it is assumed that these 'sources' cannot be taken at face value, but rather require deciphering and decoding, for which critical skill and social contextual knowledge are necessary. Beyond this point, however, the floor is open to discussion, and it is precisely the profound and perpetual disagreement over questions as to how these 'texts' are to be read, as well as which ones and how many, that not only gives rise to the great diversity of fields of historical inquiry and kinds of historical writing but also designates historical discourse as a site of political struggle.

Empiricism implies, at least by one definition, a reliance on 'experience' as a source of knowledge, as opposed, say, to revelation or *a priori* deduction.[9] Women's historians of Europe and European-derived cultures, specifically feminist women's historians, have used the concept of 'women's experience' to challenge the universality of the 'grand narratives'[10] of western history, the narratives of 'the Renaissance' and 'the French Revolution'.[11] Joan Kelly exposed the partiality of the perspective of male elite experience that governed the assignment of the label 'the Renaissance' to a historical period and, given the different experience of women, including that of female members of Italy's ruling families of that time, questioned whether one could speak of women's having had a renaissance at all.[12] Kelly and others have also questioned whether the French Revolution was a progressive turning point for women in the same sense that male adherents of the republican tradition have claimed it to have been for men.[13]

What, in these and other instances, do we women's historians mean by 'experience'; how do we use the concept? If, as Joan Scott has persuasively argued, 'gender' has needed theorisation,[14] so the concept of 'experience' needs to be problematised.[15] This article represents a preliminary attempt to interrogate the concept of 'experience' as it has been used, unreflectively on the whole, by women's historians, particularly feminist women's historians, with a focus on historians of women in

Canada. As we shall see, 'experience' is inextricably entwined with other concepts, above all those of 'difference', 'dominance', and 'voice'.

At the beginning of the tremendous revival of women's history occasioned by the revival of feminism in the early 1970s, much attention was focused on women's having been 'hidden from history'.[16] Women's historical invisibility was seen to have been the work of the creators of the historical record and the designators of historical significance – an elite of almost exclusively male chroniclers, archivists, and historians. In their hands, history had become the record of men's experience.[17] The task, those interested in the history of women's past experience contended, was to recover women's 'voice'. For the women of many periods and places, however, these voices were 'muffled'[18] or, still worse, irrecoverable, lost forever. The reasons for the silence of these multitudes of women were many: they could have lived at a time and in a society that granted women no leisure in which, nor materials with which, to write; or they could have belonged to an entirely pre- or non-literate culture or class; or they could have been prevented, as members of an oppressed race, from learning to write; or, as a mark of their subordination as women despite their high, and highly literate, social status, writing was disallowed them. Rather than consign such women to a continuing oblivion, determined women's historians made do with indirect channels to women's past experience, and pieced together a picture of women's lives from the hints and traces left behind in the writings of others, usually men and sometimes men from a different culture.

An excellent example of this kind of imaginative excavation in Canadian women's history is Sylvia Van Kirk's *'Many Tender Ties': Women in Fur-Trade Society, 1670-1870.*[19] Until her work,[20] the Western Canadian fur trade was studied as a totally male endeavour, an economic system run by white male Europeans with the assistance of male Indians. The great accomplishment of Van Kirk's study is to have uncovered the indispensable contribution of women, Indian women and 'mixed-blood' women, not only to the society but also to the economy of the fur trade. In 'bona fide marital union[s]'[21] with the white European men, not merely casual liaisons, these women acted as guides, interpreters, and diplomatic intermediaries between the tribes and the trading companies. Less spectacularly but perhaps even more importantly, their labour and skills made possible the very survival of the white European male in a land of wilderness and long winters, for it was the native women who pounded and dried the buffalo meat into pemmican, ground the corn into sagamité, made snow shoes and moccasins, dressed furs, and helped fashion birch bark into canoes. With the arrival, in the course of the nineteenth century, of white European women, increasing numbers of male European missionaries, and the full blown white racism of an imperialist culture, women of Indian stock were gradually displaced, and the fur trade itself was superseded by settlement and other forms of economic development.

But what of the experience of the Indian and 'mixed-blood' women who were drawn into, or who apparently took the initiative to enter,[22] the society and economy of the fur trade? As Van Kirk was writing at a time when the language of 'sex roles' had not yet been superseded by the language of 'gender',[23] she wrote of 'reconstructing the role of women in'[24] the fur trade. Roles can be observed from outside, and if one regards experience as constituted in part by positions occupied and tasks performed, and also by the 'discourses' dominating and shaping the social/historical context, then Van Kirk's study captures important dimensions of the experience of Native women in the fur trade. But if one reserves experience for the 'interiority' of human life, that is, for the phenomena of the realms of consciousness and subjectivity, then Van Kirk would have been exceeding the bounds of her sources to claim that she had reconstructed the experience of Native women in the fur trade. In candid acknowledgement of the limitations of her sources, Van Kirk laments the fact that 'Indian women have not left a record of their views on the fur trade or their reasons for becoming traders' wives'. She then continues:

> A reconstruction of their perspective can only be derived from the writings of the fur traders who, perhaps inadvertently, provide some remarkable insights into the behaviour of the women.[25]

Van Kirk was distanced from her subjects by race. Furthermore, her sources were distanced from her subjects not only by race but also by sex/gender and, as one reviewer of her book observed, by class as well, for the literate fur traders who left accounts of their 'experiences' were 'from the upper echelons of fur trade society'.[26] Nevertheless, as 'behaviour', like role, belongs to 'exteriority', that is, can be observed from the outside,[27] Van Kirk respects the limitations of relying on male European accounts insofar as she explores Indian women's active agency in, and not just passive victimisation by, the fur-trade society and economy.

Claiming to reconstruct the 'perspective' of the Native women, however, is another matter. While Van Kirk is rightly critical of the male Europeans' widely held belief 'that the condition of women in Indian society was deplorable',[28] she is less suspicious of the fur traders' evaluations of their relations with Native women. For instance, can one read as accurate the reports from both major fur-trading companies 'that an Indian woman who had lived with and borne children to a white man could expect a ready welcome back into her tribe'?[29] Or should such reports be read more as a rationalisation for the European fur traders' practice, enforced by official regulation in the case of the Hudson's Bay Company, of leaving the 'wife' and children in North America when the man's connection with the company ended and he returned to Britain? And is not the very use of the phrase 'many tender ties' to represent the prevailing emotional tenor of most of the 'mixed' marriages of fur-trade society thrown into question by the fact that the phrase came from the pen of Chief Factor James Douglas of Fort Vancouver rather than from that of his part-Cree wife?

I would say that the uneasiness triggered by the knowledge claims implicit in the two above cases derives from a conception of experience as having a 'core' of subjectivity knowable first-hand only by those whose minds and bodies 'lived' the experience (hence the otherwise apparently redundant usage 'lived experience'). The unanswered (and unanswerable) question left nagging us in the two above examples is: what did the person immediately affected, that is, the Indian or 'mixed-blood' woman, think and feel about the situation? While we can get at some of the social meanings attached to Native women's participation in the society and economy of the fur trade, we are less able to get at what meaning that participation had for Native women.

In a hierarchy of knowledges we women's historians, particularly we feminist women's historians, have assigned a privileged place to knowledge claims based on 'lived experience'. And for good reason, we might argue, since the spark of feminism, or 'proto-feminism', has been seen, by Joan Kelly among others, to be ignited in a woman's consciousness at that moment when she senses a discrepancy between the cultural definition of 'woman' and her own experience of herself or of other 'women'. Kelly named this state of mind oppositional consciousness and traced instances of its occurrence back to Christine de Pizan (1365-1430?). According to Kelly, Christine was in the beginning 'out of touch with the ground of truth, her own and other women's experience', and was hence 'overcome by men's contempt for women'. In Kelly's reconstruction of Christine's revolutionary change in viewpoint, an examination of her own experience as a woman and of other women's experience led her to a recognition of the androcentrism and misogyny behind the assertions of women's inferiority so prevalent in the high culture of her day. 'Universal as it might seem, the disparagement of women was not validated by [Christine's] own and other women's experience', Kelly asserts, here positing experience as a wellspring of more 'authentic' or 'purer' knowledge, that is, of knowledge not fully contaminated by, and hence productive of opposition to, the dominant culture.[30]

Virginia Woolf captured the essence of such a flare up of oppositional consciousness in her account, in *A Room of One's Own*, of the anger that rose in her when, researching the subject 'women' in the British Museum, she encountered the myriad contradictory pronouncements on the nature of 'woman' written by men. The 'monumental work entitled *The Mental, Moral, and Physical Inferiority of the Female Sex*', by the hypothetical 'Professor von X.', becomes the symbolic focus of Woolf's anger. In the course of reflecting on 'the professor's statement about the mental, moral and physical inferiority of women' and of imagining the sort of man the professor might be, Woolf wrote, drawing on her sense of class superiority,

> My heart had leapt. My cheeks had burnt. I had flushed with anger. There was nothing specially remarkable, however foolish, in that. One does not like to be told that one is naturally the inferior of a little man – I looked at the student next me – who breathes hard, wears a ready-made tie, and has not shaved this fortnight. One has certain foolish vanities. It is only human nature.[31]

The non-recognition of self in definitions of 'women' underlies the contestation over the definition of 'women' that Denise Riley identifies as at the heart of feminism, the indeterminacy and ambiguity of the term providing the founding terrain of, the condition of possibility for, feminism. 'Feminism has intermittently been as vexed with the urgency of disengaging from the category "women" as it has with laying claim to it', Riley notes and then characterises feminism as 'the site of the systematic fighting out of [the] instability' of the category 'women'.[32] She herself was prompted to enter the fray by her own inability to 'recognise' herself 'in this [or that] contracting description' of 'women', be it 'the timelessly frozen properties of maternity as exemplified in the housewife-mother figure' of 1940s British social policy, or the 'hypostatisation' of 'the [female] body' in Irigarayan theory.[33]

That experience of non-recognition of self (or of other women) or, put differently, the recognition of a gulf between one's experience and the 'official' account of 'womankind' has been one of the mainsprings of feminist women's history. The early and continuing 'compensatory'[34] urge of women's history, as discussed above, to fill in the empty spaces in those representations of the past in which hardly any or no women appear stemmed and continues to stem, in part, from looking out at the figures in the landscape of one's own world and seeing that half of them are, after all, women. Or the urge is to set the record straight if, in their 'discursive' appearance, the women have been twisted beyond recognition.

Thus, Joan Sangster tells us that her writing of *Dreams of Equality: Women On The Canadian Left, 1920-1950* was in reaction both to the 'resounding silence' on the 'intersection of socialist and feminist politics' in Canada's past and to the dismissal of 'women's contribution to socialist parties as negligible' in the few historical accounts that mentioned them.[35] And clearly it was also in reaction to the treatment of socialist women's concerns as derisory in recent histories of the Canadian left. Sangster cites the case of David Lewis' *The Good Fight* (Toronto, 1981) in which a disparaging reference to the looks of one aging woman socialist and the 'chortles of laughter' which greeted another woman's report on birth control discussion groups are represented as providing comic relief for the 1936 National Convention of the Co-operative Commonwealth Federation.[36]

For ultimate 'authenticity' and 'accuracy' we feminist historians have sought (and still seek) the accounts of 'women's experience' in women's own 'voices'.[37] One of the goals of the Women in Canadian History Documentary Series, in the words of the series editor, has been 'to retrieve and make accessible. . .records of the past as the women of Canada experienced it'.[38] A kind of 'epistemic privilege'[39] has been given, in these collections of selected documents, to those in women's own words, as they were set down in letters or diaries or transcribed from tape-recorded oral interviews.[40] 'The perspective that we bring to our material', state the three editors and compilers of excerpts from diaries and letters written by Nova Scotia women over the past century and a half, 'is a feminist one, prompting us to give primary emphasis to the experience of women as they themselves describe it'.[41] The heavy valorisation of 'the category of experience' that Michèle Barrett has found 'in popular feminist discourse'[42] is perhaps never heavier than in the kind of women's history that seeks not only to recover but also to validate a separate sphere of 'women's culture'.

This valorisation of 'the category of experience' has definite repercussions in relation to men's teaching in women's studies and men's writing of women's history. Once again we find the connection between 'lived experience' and the perception of what is a rightful claim to 'voice'. One source of our unease and ambivalence when faced with a man leading a women's studies course or with male authorship of women's stories is the sense that men's capacity to understand is limited by the fact that they have not had the experience of being women. As Renate Duelli Klein has noted, that distance from women's experience has been read in the academy as providing greater 'objectivity':

> So in its apparent 'impartiality' (which I regard as a product of men's socialisation and certainly not their biology) [men] are constrained from grasping in full the complexity, nuance, and reality of female experience with the result that their work is more

likely to be praised as 'objective' and 'rigorous', to be simply, clearly and convincingly presented and even to be preferred to a woman's work, where the struggle to do justice to the intricate fabric of women's experiences encourages assessments such as 'subjective', incoherent, and even 'implausible'.[43]

From the perspective of a women's studies advocate like Duelli Klein, it is precisely the vaunted 'detachment' of the male historian (or sociologist) of women that constitutes the barrier to his 'grasping in full the complexity, nuance, and reality of female experience', to his doing 'justice to the intricate fabric of women's experiences'.

Nonetheless, there is the rare male historian who has been accepted into the canon of women's history, indeed feminist women's history. In Canadian women's history, Angus McLaren comes to mind.[44] While some of McLaren's work on the history of birth control and abortion has been co-authored with his wife, Arlene Tigar McLaren,[45] it is not through partnership and collaboration with a woman scholar that he has gained absolution. Rather, his acceptability has come through his employment of what Uma Narayan has called 'methodological caution' and 'methodological humility'.[46] His work is characterised by a focus on social and government policy, on the demographic data of infant and maternal mortality rates and the latter's relation to illegal abortion, and on political discussion of the issue of birth control, that is, on the careful reconstruction of the social, legal, medical and political context of women's experience of fertility control and childbirth. Also, insofar as women's 'lived experience' has been included, he has studiously avoided any attempt to speak for women, taking care instead to let women 'speak for themselves' in quoted passages from letters, speeches, and newspaper articles.[47] And while this care means foregoing the attempt to grasp the 'full. . .complexity, nuance, and reality of female experience', not all female women's historians have been able to attain this goal either.

In the disqualification of the male historian on the grounds of inexperience, are we not putting male scholarship into a double bind? On the one hand we have been vociferous in our castigation of male historians for failing to include women in their accounts, and on the other we are justifiably suspicious or resentful of their attempts to do so. The suspicion derives from our continuing experience of the displacement or disfigurement of the female point of view in the hands of some male writers as in the David Lewis case mentioned above.[48] The resentment relates to our own 'lived experience' of the political struggle to create a space for women's history within the curriculum of departments of history, in the pages of academic journals of history, and on the programmes of the annual meetings of historical associations. Once the space has been created, we understandably find it difficult to stand by and watch a man, who may or may not have been an ally in the struggle, take occupation.

Here, our experience of the ongoing struggle to legitimate and create a space for women's history is the lived experience of power in the sense of domination, that is, the experience of subjugation, the experience of oppression. And thus, while we have mobilised difference in experience to redefine the criteria of historical significance, we have done so in the context of power relations, for it is not simply a matter of men's different experience. What is crucial, rather, is that the most important constituent of that difference has to do with dominance. In the feminist challenge to male-dominated historical writing and teaching, it has been women's difference, particularly difference in experience, that has been to the fore. Although ideally, difference might be manifested without power inequalities, in current society, not only how difference is recognised but that difference is recognised is a social construction involving a power relationship. For white, middle-class feminists the power imbalance between the sexes has been of central concern. It has been the power exercised through the dominance of the male point of view, the universalisation of that perspective and the establishment of the male as normative and as the standard of significance that we have challenged, as elsewhere in society, in the writing of history and the staffing of history departments.

With increasing urgency over the years, however, not just gender difference but the issue of difference between and among women has been raised within feminist circles. In Canada, women of colour, aboriginal women, immigrant and working-class women, lesbians, women with disabilities and non-English speaking women have challenged the dominance and universalisation, within Canadian feminism, of a white, middle-class, heterosexual, able-bodied and Anglophone point of view. Women who have felt oppressed as 'women' are being asked to confront the fact that other women less advantaged than ourselves have experienced us as the oppressor. Particularly in the area of cultural production, including the writing and teaching of history, we women who have attained positions of privilege in academe and publishing are being told that we have been guilty of silencing other less privileged women, of treating them as 'other', and of contributing to the perpetuation of disfiguring stereotypes.

Complicating matters in Canada is the historic Anglophone-Francophone conflict that criss-crosses the other hierarchies of power and difference. While in no way perfectly resolved, there had been, until the recent constitutional crisis, a lessening of the power differential between Anglophones and Francophones and a greater acceptance of the 'French fact' in Anglophone Canada, as a result of the Quiet Revolution in

Quebec, the resurgence of Quebec nationalism, and the federal
government's commitment to bilingualism. Nonetheless, the speaking of
English has still dominated at 'national' conferences, such as the Annual
General Meeting of the Canadian Historical Association, including within
the meetings and communications of the Canadian Committee on Women's
History, although a decision was taken at the 1989 meeting to ensure that
future issues of its *Newsletter/Bulletin* will appear in French as well as in
English. Moreover, the phenomenon of the 'two solitudes'[49] has persisted
in Canadian feminism and in the writing and teaching of Canadian
women's history as elsewhere. Evidence of this is to be found in a
tendency on the part of both Anglophone and Francophone women's
historians to set linguistic cultural boundaries to the scope of their
work.[50] Nor has the commitment to bilingualism meant that every
university-educated person in Canada is fluent in both official languages;
consequently many academics are still dependent on translations, even
though, given the precariousness of Canadian publishing in general, it is
difficult to find an English-language publisher willing to finance the
translation of a Francophone work and vice versa. It took five years, for
example, for the textbook history of Quebec women by the Clio Collective
to be published in English translation.[51] Now, following the failure of the
Meech Lake Constitutional accord to be ratified[52] (and in the face of
Francophone Quebec's renewed resolve to achieve a larger measure of
self-determination independently of the other provinces), the continuation
of the Confederation of Canada unchanged seems unlikely.

While differences between English-speaking and French-speaking
Canadian women thus remain a source of tension, women who have
experienced oppression along other axes of difference have also requested
and are requesting a hearing. Attention to class difference has been present
in the writing of Canadian women's history from early on, many studies
from the beginning to the present being devoted to the work and family
experience of working-class as well as other working women.[53]
Nonetheless, Sangster was motivated to recover the history of socialist
feminism, not only because the male-authored histories of the left had
ignored the subject, but also because 'historians of Canadian women [had]
concentrated [either] on middle-class feminism[54] or on the lives of
working women',[55] thus eclipsing the history of working-class socialist
feminism.[56] Beyond the English/French difference and differences in
class, the possibilities for obscuring other 'differences' behind the face of
a dominant Anglophone or Francophone, middle-class or working-class
norm are manifold in Canada, given the enormous ethnic diversity of the
Canadian population. Not only is Canada's population overwhelmingly
immigrant in origin, there is also the vast regional diversity of the country,
extending as it does from the Atlantic to the Pacific and from the 49th

parallel to the Arctic. The difficulties of accommodating both ethnic and regional differences[57] have spawned women's histories specific to region[58] or race/ethnicity.[59] Moreover, the campaign for gay and lesbian rights has engendered histories specific to sexual orientation.[60] The connection between experience and identity politics[61] here links up with writing history to challenge the tendency towards metropolitanism[62] (the dominance of urban over rural Canada, central Canada over the periphery and southern Canada over the North)[63] and to challenge the tendency towards ethnic, racial, and sexual homogeneity in the picture of Canadian women that emerged from some of the earliest works of historical retrieval.[64] These tended to suppress the specific experiences of many women in Canada, necessitating a corrective disaggregation along lines of region, ethnicity, race, sexuality, and other differences of identity.[65] It is noteworthy that much of the ethnically- and racially-centred work in Canadian women's history has been done by members of the ethnic or racial group being studied, owing not merely to language facility and access to private sources, but also presumably to both a curiosity and a familiarity stemming from cultural identity.[66] In much of this work, a connection between identity and the experience of difference would appear to underlay and indeed forge a connection between an experienced difference in identity and the decision to write the history of the group identified as different.

The most serious challenge to Canadian feminism and Canadian feminist scholarship of late has been the charge of racism, racial difference now being understood in the sense not of the French/English divide but of the dominance of European-derived whites over the Native peoples, Chinese Canadians, Japanese Canadians, Afro-Canadians, and East and West Indian, African, and Asian immigrants.[67] Disagreements over how to implement anti-racism within the oldest feminist press in Canada, the Toronto Women's Press, reached a crisis point in 1988, sending seismic vibrations through the feminist community in Toronto. In the debate, the charge of racism was levelled at the Press' list of titles, which included a number of the major works in Canadian women's history.[68] The outcome by 1989 was a splitting into two presses, the Women's Press, under new leadership, and the Second Story Press, led by eight of the oldest members of the original Women's Press collective. Ultimately at issue was the question of whether a white middle-class woman writer of fiction has the right to create major characters whose experience is different from hers, by virtue of race or ethnicity, or to use cultural forms originating in parts of the world currently oppressed by the writer's own culture. Those who formed 'the Front of the Bus Caucus to promote an anti-racist strategy at the Press' and who eventually took over the Press have now developed

Anti-Racist Guidelines For Submissions.[69] The kinds of writing the Press
says it will henceforth avoid publishing include:

> . . .manuscripts in which the protagonist's experience in the
> world, by virtue of race or ethnicity, is substantially removed
> from that of the writer;
> . . .manuscripts in which a writer appropriates the form and
> substance of a culture which is oppressed by her own;
> . . .a manuscript whose analysis includes women of colour as a
> supplement to a text, rather than incorporating Women of Colour
> into the overall content and structure.[70]

Some members of the Writers' Union have cried censorship, arguing that
'hard and fast rules are inimical to the creative process'. Others in support
of the Press' policy, however, like dub poet and reggae artist Lillian
Allen, have pointed out that

> 'White writers have to know what they don't know. . .When
> you're in a situation of dominance, it's hard for you to know what
> you don't know. It's simple arrogance'.[71]

In the triangle of experience, difference and dominance and its relation to
voice, it is not inexperience or difference in experience alone but different
experience combined with 'power over' that disqualifies: the dominant
group's power systemically and systematically to negate or disfigure the
experience of others separates it from the oppressed group's lived
experience of that negation or disfigurement. What the Women's Press is
asking for is recognition of the 'epistemic privilege of the oppressed'.[72]
There does seem to be a compelling reason to accept as 'true' an
oppressed person's account of the lived experience of the oppression.
There seems to be an equally compelling moral argument against the right
of a member of the dominant group to appropriate the oppressed person's
story.[73]

Where does that leave the reclaiming of women's experience as the
object of the writing of women's history? Must we conclude that the only
legitimate feminist women's history is autobiography?

If contemporary feminism has contributed to the modernist and
postmodern undermining of Enlightenment certainties[74] by invoking
'women's different experience' to challenge the 'grand narratives' of
western history, feminism, as we have seen, has also 'heavily valorised'
women's own narratives, women's stories of their own experience. Indeed
this valorisation has urged women's historians in the direction of oral
history as the methodology, next to autobiography, promising to bring the

researcher closest to the 'reality' of women's lives. We have valorised oral history because it validates women's lives. As one oral historian of women on the Alberta frontier has testified:

> The women who spoke with me were eager to tell their stories, eager, I think, to participate in the creation of a world in which women have a place, a place they would make public and visible. They were seeking historical validation, a sense of continuity. . . .They wanted to leave a trace of themselves, not to disappear unnoted.[75]

The greater the past subjugation of the women, the greater the need through the gathering of oral histories to vouchsafe to them that sense of history that is perceived as so essential to one's sense of identity.[76] As Dionne Brand, the co-ordinator of an oral history project on 'The Lives of Black Working Women in Ontario' has remarked, 'If Black life in Canada as a whole has been absent or ill served by Canadian scholars, Black women's lives have been doubly hidden'.[77] Missing from or added only as an afterthought in white Canadian women's histories, Black Canadian women have also been made to disappear within the generic, apparently 'genderless', that is, male, Black protagonist of the few existing histories of Blacks in Canada. Oral history recommended itself as *the* method for rescuing the lives of Black women from this double obscurity.[78]

We should not, however, 'simply accept at face value' oral testimony any more than the written records of women's memories, for, as Joan Scott warns, 'we cannot assume that women's remembered experience lies outside officially constructed texts, as a definably separate, "purer" commentary on politics'.[79] As Natalie Zemon Davis and others have demonstrated, the stories we tell to explain ourselves to others and even to ourselves are shaped in myriad ways not only by narrative devices and conventions of storytelling but also by cultural notions of believability and hegemonic explanatory theories, of which we, as storytellers, may or may not be aware.[80] As collectors and recorders of the stories of others, therefore, we cannot accept a woman's recollection uncritically, that is, as unmediated by cultural/historical context. Instead, we need to contextualise women's narratives, for to be understood they have 'to be thoughtfully situated in time and place'.[81] For instance, if a woman remembers the Second World War as having done 'a lot to finish off the idea that a woman's place and her only place was in the home',[82] we need to examine that memory in relation to the powerful wartime discourses of gender reinforcement:[83] the temporal containment of women's increased labour force participation by the concepts of 'war emergency' and 'for the duration'; the assurances given women that enrolment in the armed forces or taking jobs in non-traditional trades would not endanger their 'femininity'; and the rhetorical 'domestication' or 'feminisation' of sectors of military and industrial employment to mask the gender disruption entailed by the entrance of women into what had been masculine preserves.[84]

Moreover, we the inscribers of the narratives of other women need to be sensitive to 'the importance of the political and institutional contexts' not only of the narrator but also of ourselves, the recorders and interpreters.[85] Indeed we listeners to the narratives of other women may have difficulty hearing the echoes of the 'discourses' reverberating through the story teller's account because of our own implication within discourses of domination. As Dionne Brand has observed:

> The historical relationship between Black peoples in Canada and the 'mainstream' society has been one of subordination which doubtlessly taints the historical record as it is often written, spoken and interpreted by those in power within the relationship.[86]

Perhaps the greater the gulf between the oppressor and the oppressed, the greater the requirement that the interviewer have shared the experience of oppression of the interviewee,[87] which, given the double oppression of Black women in Canada, would mean, for the gathering of their personal narratives, being preferably not only Black but also a woman.

In her endeavour to reclaim the past experience of women of a different race and culture, Sylvia Van Kirk was separated from her subjects, according to the criterion of the shared experience of oppression, not only by her membership in the white oppressor group but also by time. While arguably Native women of today are similarly separated by time from their fur-trading foremothers, their continued lived experience of oppression might move them closer to the perspective of the insider. In any case, statements regarding subjective experience that are made in the absence of any written record of the subject's feelings on the matter are more likely to reflect the discursive world of the speaker than that of the spoken about. Thus, Sylvia Van Kirk's claim, that a second- or third-generation 'mixed blood' wife as compared with the first generation of Indian women to 'marry' European fur traders 'did not have to struggle with a sense of divided loyalty' because 'her interests were more closely identified with that of the traders'[88] assumes an easy ascendancy, in the subjectivity of the woman of Indian descent, of a white European perspective, thereby suppressing the possible long-term survival of conflicted identity. The 'epistemic humility' being enjoined here on white Canadian women historians entails, particularly in certain political moments, a stepping back from the centre to let the marginalised narrate their own 'reality', express their 'lived experience' in their own voices. But no greater 'epistemic humility' is being insisted on than we white, middle-class feminist historians have required of men undertaking to write histories of the (formerly) undifferentiated category 'women'.

* * * * *

We have seen that we feminist historians of women used the concept of 'women's different experience' to challenge the hegemony and universality of male-centered history. In response to the invisibility and/or misrepresentation of women, it became a major goal of reclaiming women's history to enable women of the past to 'speak with their own voices'. In order to get at 'women's experience', the methodology of oral history, in the absence of women's otherwise recorded voices, was valorised as validating women's lives. The 'valorisation' of women's 'lived experience' was enhanced by the notion that it figured in the birth of feminist consciousness. In both Kelly's reconstruction of Christine de Pizan's transformation of consciousness and Woolf's account of discovering a vast repository of misogyny's accumulated wisdom in the British Museum, they seem to have posited a core of experience uncontaminated by the disfigurements of the dominant culture and, once tapped, capable of serving as a base from which to challenge that culture.

Initially, for white, heterosexual, middle-class feminists, including historians, the difference that mattered was that between men's experience and women's. Over the years women 'different' from the dominant female norm by virtue of race, class, sexuality, and/or disability, have insisted on the need to particularise the category 'women'. More importantly they have insisted on their right to be heard in their own voices, thus, like the earliest advocates of 'women's history', asserting a connection between 'lived experience' and a rightful claim to 'voice'. Women occupying these 'different' social positions have also insisted on our understanding that their 'lived experience' has been one of 'lived oppression' in which we white, able-bodied, heterosexual feminists are implicated. Dominance needs to be seen, in other words, as integral to the experience of difference and as capable of rendering the dominant insensible to the 'lived experience' of the oppressed.

The request coming from the Toronto Women's Press as well as from other quarters for the recognition of 'the epistemic privilege of the oppressed' can be read as a claim that the 'lived experience of oppression', especially in its most systemic or violent forms, can be voiced only by those who have known that experience first hand. The request can also be translated into the requirement that the women's historian recognise (and state) the position from which she herself speaks. If the women's historian is also in a relationship of dominance with respect to the subjects whose history is being recovered, she should proceed with 'methodological caution' and 'epistemic humility'. And, because the historian is always in some sense in a position of control over the past, proceeding with methodological and epistemological caution and humility is obviously as necessary for the medievalist or for the Euro-Canadian historian of ancient China as for the historian of more contemporary societies.[89]

Should Sylvia Van Kirk, then, not have undertaken to write a history of Native women in the Canadian fur trade? Here distinctions between the interiority of 'lived experience' and experience externally observed, and between narrow experience and its wider, 'discursive' context can be usefully deployed in relation to the question of dominance. It is only in the attempt to resurrect the interior experience of women whose specific experience of oppression Van Kirk does not share and for which no written records in their own voices exist that Van Kirk may have overstepped the bounds. The reconstitution of the society and economy of the fur trade and the recovery of Native women's indispensable place within it Van Kirk accomplished with both skill and respect.[90] It has, after all, never been the job of the historian only to reclaim voices. That would result in a naive empiricism. No, the task has been equally, and just as importantly, to contextualise the individual voices, to reconstitute the 'discursive' world which the 'subjects' inhabited and were shaped by.

A conception of experience lies at the intersection of theory and practice in women's history writing. The distinctions between 'discursive' reality and 'lived experience' we understand at one level to be merely analytical in view of their interaction and the impossibility of establishing any clear-cut line between the 'subject to' and the 'subject of' dimensions of experience.[91] Yet, as feminists, we also understand the importance of appealing to a core of lived experience as the unassailable source of our knowledge of subjugation. In our efforts to redefine what we know about society in the past, we must be prepared to listen with humility to the 'voices of experience' of those different from ourselves and, most especially, of those vis-à-vis whom we stand in a relationship of dominance.

NOTES

1. I would like to thank Sherene Razack, Philinda Masters, Marjorie Cohen and Dwight Boyd for helping to free me, each at different junctures, from one or more of the many cul-de-sacs in which my thinking became trapped as I was writing this article. I am also grateful to Alison Prentice and Veronica Strong-Boag for their very helpful suggestions for revision of the penultimate draft.

2. Margaret Prang, 'Personal Reflections on a Career in History', Linda Kealey, 'Women Historians in Canadian Universities: A Report on the Canadian Historical Association Survey', and Lykke de la Cour, Karen Dubinsky, Nancy Forestell, Mary-Ellen Kelm, Lynne Marks, and Cecilia Morgan, '"Here's where we separate the men from the boys": Comments on Women's Experiences as Graduate Students in History Programmes', papers presented at a Joint Session of the Canadian Historical Association and Canadian Women's Studies Association, Canadian Learned Societies Meetings, University of Victoria, Victoria, British Columbia, 27 May 1990. See also Linda Kealey, 'Highlights of the CHA Survey on the Status of Women, 1989', *Canadian Historical Association Newsletter*, 16, no. 2 (Spring 1990), pp. 1, 4-5.

3. See, for example, Mary Poovey, 'Feminism and Deconstruction', *Feminist Studies*, 14, no. 1 (Spring 1988), pp. 51-65.

4. Carroll Smith-Rosenberg, 'Writing History: Language, Class, and Gender', in Teresa de Lauretis (ed.), *Feminist Studies/Critical Studies* (Bloomington: Indiana University Press, 1986), pp. 31-54.

5. See, Joan Wallach Scott, 'Gender: A Useful Category of Historical Analysis', ch. 2 of *Gender and the Politics of History* (New York: Columbia University Press, 1988). First published in the *American Historical Review*, 91, no. 5 (December 1986), pp. 1053-75. For an example of an article in Canadian women's history influenced by the new conceptualisation of gender, see Ruth Roach Pierson, 'Gender and the Unemployment Insurance Debates in Canada, 1934-40', *Labour/Le Travail*, no. 25 (Spring 1990), pp. 77-103.

6. Jane Wagner, *The Search for Signs of Intelligent Life in the Universe* (New York: Harper & Row, 1986), p. 18.

7. For E. H. Carr's famous reference to the Leopold von Ranke aphorism, see *What is History?* (Harmondsworth: Penguin Books, 1964; first published by Macmillan, 1961), p. 8.

8. Michèle Barrett, 'The Concept of "Difference"', *Feminist Review*, no. 26 (July 1987), pp. 32-3.

9. Dagobert D. Runes (ed.), *Dictionary of Philosophy* (Paterson, NJ: Littlefield, Adams & Co., 1961), p. 89.

10. Jean-François Lyotard, *The Postmodern Condition: A Report on Knowledge*, trans. by Geoff Bennington and Brian Massumi (Minneapolis: University of Minnesota Press, 1984). Originally published as *La Condition postmoderne: rapport sur le savoir*, (Paris: Editions du Seuil, 1979).

11. Feminist historians have not been the only feminist scholars to use women's 'experience' to test hypotheses. According to Sandra Harding, 'One distinctive feature of feminist research [in general] is that it generates its problematics from the perspective of women's experiences. It also uses these experiences as a significant indicator of the "reality" against which hypotheses are tested'. S. Harding, 'Introduction: Is There a Feminist Method?', in S. Harding (ed.), *Feminism and Methodology* (Bloomington and Indianapolis: Indiana University Press, 1987), p. 7.

12. Joan Kelly, 'Did Women have a Renaissance?', ch. 2 of *Women, History, and Theory: The Essays of Joan Kelly* (Chicago and London: The University of Chicago Press, 1984), pp. 19-50. First published in Renate Bridenthal and Claudia

Koonz (eds.), *Becoming Visible: Women in European History* (New York: Houghton Mifflin Co., 1977), pp. 137-64.

13. Joan Kelly, 'The Social Relation of the Sexes: Methodological Implications of Women's History', ch. 1 of *Women, History, and Theory: The Essays of Joan Kelly*, 1st pub. in *Signs: Journal of Women in Culture and Society* 1, no. 4 (Summer 1976), pp. 809-23. According to Joan Wallach Scott, 'French Feminists and the Rights of "Man": Olympe de Gouges's Declarations', *History Workshop*, no. 28 (Autumn 1989), pp. 1-21, 'For women, the legacy of the French Revolution was contradictory: a universal, abstract, rights-bearing individual as the unit of national sovereignty, embodied, however, as a man' (p. 1). In Joan B. Landes' interpretation, the bourgeois organisation of the public sphere that emerged in the aftermath of the Revolution 'was predicated on removing women, and women's speech' (p. 204). The task bequeathed to feminists then became 'to open a discursive space for women *within* the modern public sphere' (p. 206). Landes, *Women and the Public Sphere in the Age of the French Revolution* (Ithaca and London: Cornell University Press, 1988). In Michèle Le Doeuff's interpretation, the French Revolution abolished the division of society into orders that had applied to women as well as to men and replaced it with a system that drew distinctions among men according to property and occupation while introducing the political treatment of women *en bloc*. It is in that 'historical passage from one system of discrimination (by estate) to another (by sex)' that diversity and plurality came to characterise the category 'men' while unity and homogeneity came to characterise the category 'women'. Le Doeuff, 'Pierre Roussel's Chiasmas: From Imaginary Knowledge to the Learned Imagination', *Ideology & Consciousness*, no. 9 (Winter 1981/82), pp. 52-3. See also Jane Abray, 'Feminism in the French Revolution', *American Historical Review*, 80, no. 1 (February 1975), pp. 43-62; and Cecile Dauphin et al., 'Women's Culture and Women's Power: Issues in French Women's History' in this volume.

14. For a stunning historical analysis of gender and class relations in two Canadian settings, see Joy Parr, *The Gender of Breadwinners: Women, Men, and Change in Two Industrial Towns 1880-1950* (Toronto, Buffalo and London: University of Toronto Press, 1990).

15. Teresa de Lauretis has recognised the crucial importance of the notion of experience to feminist theory for some time. T. de Lauretis, *Alice Doesn't: Feminism, Semiotics, Cinema* (Bloomington: Indiana University Press, 1984), ch. 6 'Semiotics and Experience', pp. 159-86.

16. Sheila Rowbotham, *Hidden from History: 300 Years of Women's Oppression and the Fight Against It* (London: Pluto Press, 1973).

17. Susan Mann Trofimenkoff and Alison Prentice, 'Introduction', *The Neglected Majority: Essays in Canadian Women's History*, vol. 1 (Toronto: McClelland and Stewart, 1977), p. 7; Veronica Strong-Boag and Anita Clair Fellman, 'Introduction', *Rethinking Canada: The Promise of Women's History* (Toronto: Copp Clark Pitman, 1986), p. 1.

18. Susan Mann Trofimenkoff has uncovered the 'muffled quality' of, and examined the forces 'muffling', the voices of the 102 women witnesses (out of a total of close to 1,800 people who testified) before the Royal Commission on Capital and Labour of the late 1880s. S. Trofimenkoff, 'One Hundred and Two Muffled Voices: Canada's Industrial Women in the 1880's', *Atlantis: A Women's Studies Journal*, 3, no. 1 (Fall 1977), pp. 66-82.

19. *'Many Tender Ties': Women in Fur-Trade Society in Western Canada, 1670-1870* (Winnipeg, Manitoba: Watson & Dwyer Publishing Ltd., 1980).

20. And that of the historical anthropologist Jennifer S. H. Brown, *Strangers in Blood: Fur Trade Company Families in Indian Country* (Vancouver and London: University of British Columbia Press, 1980).

21. Van Kirk, *'Many Tender Ties'*, p. 51.

22. *Ibid.*, p. 8.

23. See Natalie Zemon Davis, '"Women's History" in Transition: The European Case', *Feminist Studies*, 3, nos. 3/4 (Spring-Summer 1976), pp. 83-103.

24. Van Kirk, *'Many Tender Ties'*, p. 6.

25. *Ibid.*, p. 75.

26. Robin Fisher, Review of *'Many Tender Ties': Women in Fur-Trade Society in Western Canada, 1670-1870*, by Sylvia Van Kirk, in *The Canadian Historical Review*, 64, no. 2 (June 1983), p. 238.

27. The distinction between the 'internality' of subjective experience ('history from the inside') and the 'externality' of social structures and discourses ('history from the outside') and their intermingling in human agency are discussed by Shula Marks, 'The Context of Personal Narrative: Reflections on *"Not Either an Experimental Doll"--The Separate Worlds of Three South African Women'*, in Personal Narratives Group (ed.), *Interpreting Women's Lives: Feminist Theory and Personal Narratives* (Bloomington and Indianapolis: Indiana University Press, 1989), p. 40.

28. Van Kirk, *'Many Tender Ties'*, p. 80. See also p. 17.

29. *Ibid.*, p. 46.

30. Joan Kelly, 'Early Feminist Theory and the Querelle des Femmes, 1400-1789', ch. 4 of *Women, History, and Theory*, pp. 79-80. An earlier version of this chapter appeared in *Signs: Journal of Women in Culture and Society*, 8, no. 1 (Autumn 1982), pp. 4-28.

31. Virginia Woolf, *A Room of One's Own* (London: The Hogarth Press, 1929), p. 48.

32. Denise Riley, *'Am I That Name?': Feminism and the Category of 'Women' in History* (London: Macmillan; Minneapolis, MN: University of Minneasota Press, 1988), pp. 4-5.

33. For Riley, it is not simply 'a matter of there being different sorts of women, but of the effects of the designation, "women"'. Riley, *'Am I That name?'*, p. 111. Hence her choice of Desdemona's perplexed query in Othello 'Am I that name, Iago?' as the motto for her book. See also pp. 58, 102. As Jacqueline Rose has pointed out, Riley's 'strong argument' is 'that the apparently transparent category of "women" - the place in which the real lived experience of women as a group can be found, against the vagaries of ideological distortion and fantasy that accrue to the category of "Woman" - offers in fact no such transparency'. J. Rose, Review of *'Am I That Name?' Feminism and the Category of 'Women' in History*, by Denise Riley, *History Workshop*, no. 29 (Spring 1990), p. 159.

34. The term 'compensatory history' was used by Gerda Lerner, *The Majority Finds Its Past: Placing Women in History* (New York and Oxford: Oxford University Press, 1979), p. 145, who was borrowing it from Mari Jo Buhle, Ann G. Gordon, and Nancy Schrom, 'Women in American Society: An Historical Contribution', *Radical America*, 5, no.4 (July/August 1971), pp. 3-66.

35. *Dreams of Equality: Women on the Canadian Left, 1920-1950* (Toronto: McClelland and Stewart, 1989), p. 7.

36. *Ibid.*, pp. 110, 249n.

37. As editor Mary Crnkovich observes in her Introduction to the recently published *"Gossip": A Spoken History of Women in the North*, 'GOSSIP symbolizes and celebrates the significance of and value in women recording their own ideas in their own words. Often these experiences and viewpoints have been re-created through the interpretations of male historians and anthropologists. Within feminist writing experiential writing is recognized and valued as a significant contribution'. M. Crnkovich, 'In Our Spare Time. . .', *"Gossip"* (Ottawa: Canadian Arctic Resources Committee, 1990), p. xvi.

38. Alison Prentice, 'Introduction to the Series', in Beth Light and Alison Prentice (eds.), *Pioneer and Gentlewomen of British North America 1713-1867* (Toronto: New Hogtown Press, 1980). The other volumes in the series are: Beth Light and Joy Parr (eds.), *Canadian Women on the Move 1867-1920* (Toronto: New Hogtown Press and the Ontario Institute for Studies in Education, 1983); and Beth Light and Ruth Roach Pierson (eds.), *No Easy Road: Women in Canada 1920s-1960s* (Toronto: New Hogtown Press, 1990).

39. See the clarification of the feminist notion of the 'epistemic privilege of the oppressed' by Uma Narayan, 'Working Together Across Difference: Some Considerations on Emotions and Political Practice', *Hypatia*, 3, no. 2 (Summer 1988), pp. 31-7.

40. See, for example, Pat Staton and Beth Light, *Speak with Their Own Voices: A Documentary History of the Federation of Women Teachers' Associations of Ontario and the Women Elementary Public School Teachers of Ontario* (Toronto: Federation of Women Teachers' Associations of Ontario, 1987).

41. Margaret Conrad, Toni Laidlaw, and Donna Smyth, 'Introduction', *No Place Like Home: Diaries and Letters of Nova Scotia Women 1771-1938* (Halifax, Nova Scotia: Formac Publishing Company Ltd., 1988), p. 1.

42. Michèle Barrett, 'The Concept of "Difference"', *Feminist Review*, no. 26 (July 1987), p. 31. The consciousness raising process so popular during the early years of 'second wave' feminism was based on the recounting and sharing of personal experiences in a non-challenging group atmosphere. See, for example, 'Consciousness Raising Meetings – What Goes On', *The Northern Woman*, 2, no. 3 (Fall 1975), p. 5. This sharing of personal experiences led to the discovery of 'shared' experiences. The very 'sharedness' of the subjective experiences established their sociality and revealed the permeability of the subjective/social boundary. That revelation underwrote the fundamental proposition of 'second wave' feminism, that is, that 'the personal is political', at the same time that the 'counter discourse' of feminism made possible both individual and political contestation of the hegemonic constructions through a redefinition of these 'shared' experiences as instances of oppression.

43. Renate Duelli Klein, 'The "Men-Problem" in Women's Studies: The Expert, the Ignoramus and the Poor Dear', *Women's Studies International Forum*, 6, no. 4 (1983), p. 414.

44. Another good example is Graham S. Lowe, *Women in the Administrative Revolution: The Feminization of Clerical Work* (Toronto and Buffalo: University of Toronto Press, 1987). And for a male historian who, in incorporating

gender analysis into class analysis, genuinely seeks to give equal time to women and men and to the class-based constructions of femininity as well as to the class-based constructions of masculinity, see Mark Rosenfeld, "'It Was a Hard Life": Class and Gender in the Work and Family Rhythms of a Railway Town, 1920-1950', *Historical Papers/Communications historiques*, The Canadian Historical Association/La Société historique du Canada (1988), pp. 237-79.

45. Angus McLaren and Arlene Tigar McLaren, *The Bedroom and the State: The Changing Practices and Politics of Contraception and Abortion in Canada, 1880-1980* (Toronto: McClelland and Stewart, 1986); A. McLaren and A.T. McLaren, 'Discoveries and Dissimulations: The Impact of Abortion Deaths on Maternal Mortality in British Columbia', in Katherine Arnup, Andrée Levésque, and Ruth Roach Pierson (eds.), *Delivering Motherhood: Maternal Ideologies and Practices in the 19th and 20th Centuries* (London and New York: Routledge, 1990), pp. 126-49.

46. Narayan, 'Working Together Across Difference', p. 37.

47. See, for example, the 1930s letter from a prairie woman to Saskatchewan feminist Violet McNaughton, quoted in A. McLaren and A. T. McLaren, *The Bedroom and the State*, pp. 28- 30.

48. For another example, see W. Peter Ward, *Courtship, Love and Marriage in Nineteenth-Century English Canada* (Montreal: McGill-Queen's University Press, 1990).

49. Hugh MacLennan, *Two Solitudes* (Toronto: Collins; New York: Duell, Sloan and Pearce, 1945).

50. Examples include Carol Lee Bacchi, *Liberation Deferred? The Ideas of the English-Canadian Suffragists, 1877-1918* (Toronto: University of Toronto Press, 1983); Nadia Fahmy-Eid and Micheline Dumont (eds.), *Maîtresses de maison, maîtresses d'école: femmes, famille et éducation dans l'histoire du Québec* (Montréal: Les Éditions du Boréal Express, 1983); Micheline Dumont and Nadia Fahmy-Eid, *Les couventines: l'éducation des filles au Québec dans les congrégations religieuses enseignantes 1840-1960* (Montréal: Les Éditions du Boréal Express, 1986); Veronica Strong-Boag, *The New Day Recalled: Lives of Girls and Women in English Canada, 1919-1939* (Toronto: Copp Clark Pitman Ltd., 1988); Andrée Lévesque, *La Norme et les déviantes: Des femmes au Québec pendant l'entre deux-guerres* (Montréal: Les Éditions du remue-ménage, 1989).

51. The Clio Collective (Micheline Dumont, Michèle Jean, Marie Lavigne, Jennifer Stoddart), *Quebec Women: A History*, trans. by Roger Gannon and Rosalind Gill (Toronto: The Women's Press, 1987). Originally published as *L'Histoire des femmes au Québec depuis quatre siècles* (Montréal: Les Quinze, 1982).

52. From the time of Confederation in 1867, the Constitution of Canada resided in Britain as an act of the British Parliament called the British North America Act. One of Liberal Prime Minister Pierre-Elliot Trudeau's great political ambitions was to 'bring the constitution home'. While 'patriation' of the Canadian constitution was achieved on 17 April 1982, the then separatist-led Province of Quebec refused to sign the document. One of the political ambitions of Progressive Conservative Prime Minister Brian Mulroney was to have Quebec become a signatory to the constitution. In 1987, at the resort of Meech Lake, Mulroney and the ten provincial premiers signed an accord granting Quebec the status of a 'distinct society'. Almost immediately strong objections were voiced: by women's groups (principally in

Anglophone Canada) who feared an erosion of the sex equality guaranteed by the
federal Charter of Rights and Freedoms; by Native groups who objected to the
non-recognition of their distinct society status and to their non-inclusion in the
process of constitutional reform; and by the peoples and governments of the Yukon
and the Northwest Territories whose admission to provincial status seemed
endangered. Later, both western and eastern provinces began to insist that Senate
reform providing equal and elected provincial representation precede ratification of
the accord in order to offset the increased power of central Canada, particularly
Quebec, in Confederation. As the deadline of 23 June 1990 for ratification of the
accord by all ten provinces approached, the crisis deepened. In the end, ratification
foundered on the objections of the above-mentioned groups, particularly Native
peoples and the Liberal government of Newfoundland.

  53. See, for example, Marie Lavigne and Jennifer Stoddart, 'Les
Travailleuses montréalaises entre les deux guerres', *Labour/Le Travailleur*, no. 2
(1977), pp. 170-83; Francine Barry, *Le Travail de la femme au Québec: l'évolution
de 1940 à 1970* (Montréal: Les presses de l'Université du Québec, 1977); Veronica
Strong-Boag, 'The Girls of the New Day: Canadian Working Women in the 1920s',
Labour/Le Travailleur, no. 4 (1979), pp. 131-64; Meg Luxton, *More Than a Labour
of Love: Three Generations of Women's Work in the Home* (Toronto: The Women's
Press, 1980); Marilyn Barber, 'The Women Ontario Welcomed: Immigrant
Domestics for Ontario Homes, 1870-1930', *Ontario History*, 72, no. 3 (September
1980), pp. 148-72; Marie Lavigne and Yoland Pinard, *Travailleuses et féministes:
Les femmes dans la société québécoise* (Montréal: Les Éditions du Boréal Express,
1982); Ruth Frager, 'No Proper Deal: Women Workers and the Canadian Labour
Movement, 1870-1940', in Linda Briskin and Lynda Yanz (eds.), *Union Sisters:
Women in the Labour Market* (Toronto: The Women's Press, 1983), pp. 44-64;
Marta Danylewycz, Beth Light and Alison Prentice, 'The Evolution of the Sexual
Division of Labour in Teaching: A Nineteenth-Century Ontario and Quebec Case
Study', *Histoire sociale/Social History*, 16, no. 31 (May 1983), pp. 81-109; Bettina
Bradbury, 'Women and Wage Labour in a Period of Transition: Montreal,
1861-1881', *Histoire sociale/Social History*, 17, no. 33 (May 1984), pp. 115-31; B.
Bradbury, 'Pigs, Cows and Boarders: Non-Wage Forms of Survival Among
Montreal Families, 1861-1891', *Labour/Le Travail*, no. 14 (Fall 1984), pp. 9-46;
Judith Fingard, 'Gender and Inequality at Dalhousie: Faculty Women before 1950',
Dalhousie Review, 64, no. 4 (Winter 1984-85), pp. 687-703; Gail Cuthbert Brandt,
'"Weaving It Together": Life Cycle and the Industrial Experience of Female Cotton
Workers in Quebec, 1910-1950', in Alison Prentice and Susan Mann Trofimenkoff
(eds.), *The Neglected Majority: Essays in Canadian Women's History*, vol. 2
(Toronto: McClelland and Stewart, 1985), pp. 160-73; Joy Parr, 'Women at Work',
in W. J. C. Cherwinski and G.S. Kealey (eds.), *Lectures in Canadian Labour and
Working-Class History* (St. John's, Nfld.: Committee on Canadian Labour History,
1985), pp. 79-88; Marilyn Porter, '"She was Skipper of the Shore-Crew": Notes on
the History of the Sexual Division of Labour in Newfoundland', *Labour/Le Travail*,
no. 15 (Spring 1985), pp. 105-23; Paula Bourne (ed.), *Women's Paid and Unpaid
Work: Historical and Contemporary Perspectives* (Toronto: New Hogtown Press,
1985); G. C. Brandt, 'The Transformation of Women's Work in the Quebec Cotton
Industry, 1920-1930', in Bryan D. Palmer (ed.), *The Character of Class Struggle*
(Toronto: McClelland and Stewart, 1986), pp. 115-37; M. Danylewycz and A.

Prentice, 'Teachers's Work: Changing Patterns and Perceptions in the Emerging School Systems of Nineteenth and Early Twentieth Century Central Canada', *Labour/Le Travail*, no. 17 (Spring 1986), pp. 58-80; B. Bradbury, 'Women's History and Working-Class History', *Labour/Le Travail*, no. 19 (Spring 1987), pp. 22-43; Yolande Cohen and Michelle Dagenais, 'Le métier d'infirmière: savoirs féminins et reconnaissance professionnelle', *Revue d'histoire de l'Amérique française*, 41, no. 2 (automne 1987), pp. 155-77; Margaret Hobbs and Ruth Roach Pierson, '"A Kitchen That Wastes No Steps. . .": Gender, Class and the Home Improvement Plan, 1936-40', *Histoire sociale/Social History*, 21, no. 41 (May 1988), pp. 9-37; Michèle Dagenais, 'Itinéraires professionnels masculins et féminins en milieu bancaire: Le cas de la Banque d'Hochelaga, 1900-1929', *Labour/Le Travail*, no. 24 (Fall 1989), pp. 45-68; Nancy M. Forestell, 'Times Were Hard: The Pattern of Women's Paid Labour in St. John's Between the Two World Wars', *Labour/Le Travail*, no. 24 (Fall 1989), pp. 147-66; Margaret E. McCallum, 'Separate Spheres: the Organization of Work in a Confectionery Factory: Ganong Bros., St. Stephen, New Brunswick', *Labour/Le Travail*, no. 24 (Fall 1989), pp. 69-90; Ruth Compton Brouwer, *New Women for God: Canadian Presbyterian Women and Indian Missions, 1876-1914* (Toronto, Buffalo, London: University of Toronto Press, 1990), particularly ch. 4 'Women's Work in Central India', pp. 92-129.

    54. See, for example, Jennifer Stoddart, 'The Woman Suffrage Bill in Quebec', in Marylee Stephenson (ed.), *Women in Canada* (Toronto: New Press, 1973), pp. 90-106; Deborah Gorham, 'English Militancy and the Canadian Suffrage Movement', *Atlantis: A Women's Studies Journal*, 1, no. 1 (Fall 1975), pp. 83-112; D. Gorham, 'The Canadian Suffragists', in Gwen Matheson (ed.), *Women in the Canadian Mosaic* (Toronto: Peter Martin Associates, 1976), pp. 23-56; Veronica Strong-Boag, 'Canadian Feminism in the 1920's: The Case of Nellie L. McClung', *Journal of Canadian Studies*, 12, no. 4 (Summer 1977), pp. 58-68; Wayne Roberts, 'Six New Women: A Guide to the Mental Map of Women Reformers in Toronto', *Atlantis*, 3, no. 1 (Fall 1977), pp. 145-64; C. L. Bacchi, *Liberation Deferred? The Ideas of the English-Canadian Suffragists, 1877-1918*; Ernest Forbes, 'The Ideas of Carol Bacchi and the Suffragists of Halifax: A Review Essay on *Liberation Deferred? The Ideas of the English-Canadian Suffragists, 1877- 1918*', *Atlantis*, 10, no. 2 (Spring 1985), pp. 119-26.

    55. Sangster, *Dreams of Equality*, p. 7.

    56. At the time Sangster was researching and writing, other women's historians were also beginning to study Canadian socialist feminism. See Linda Kealey, 'Canadian Socialism and the "Woman Question", 1900-1914', *Labour/Le Travail*, no. 13 (Spring 1984), pp. 77-100; and L. Kealey, 'Women in the Canadian Socialist Movement, 1904-1914', Varpu Lindström-Best, 'Finnish Socialist Women in Canada, 1890-1930', and Janice Newton, 'From Wage Slave to White Slave: The Prostitution Controversy and the Early Canadian Left', in Linda Kealey and Joan Sangster (eds.), *Beyond the Vote: Canadian Women and Politics* (Toronto, Buffalo, and London: University of Toronto Press, 1989), pp. 171-95, 196-216, 217-36. Also recently published is a history of the contemporary women's movement in Canada written from a socialist-feminist and lesbian-sensitive perspective. Nancy Adamson, Linda Briskin, and Margaret McPhail, *Feminist Organizing for Change* (Toronto: Oxford University Press, 1988). For a race- and class-sensitive history of a contemporary middle-class feminist organisation, see Sherene Razack, *Feminism*

Applied to Law: The Women's Legal Education and Action Fund (LEAF) (Toronto: Second Story Press, 1991).

57. Given the even greater difficulties of accommodating the differences of race, class and sexuality as well, attempts at synthesised, 'total' histories will almost inevitably make themselves vulnerable to criticism. For the first courageous and impressive effort to deal with both French and English Canada in a synthesis of Canadian women's history, see the textbook by Alison Prentice, Paula Bourne, Gail Cuthbert Brandt, Beth Light, Wendy Mitchinson, and Naomi Black, *Canadian Women: A History* (Toronto: Harcourt Brace Jovanovich, 1988).

58. See, for example, Ruth Pierson, 'Women's History: The State of the Art in Atlantic Canada', *Acadiensis*, 7, no. 1 (Autumn 1977), pp. 121-31; Barbara Latham and Cathy Kess (eds.), *In Her Own Right: Selected Essays on Women's History in B.C.* (Victoria, B.C.: Camosun College, 1980); Jennifer Stoddart, 'Le paysage de l'histoire change: la production française récente en histoire des femmes', *Resources for Feminist Research/Documentation sur la recherche féministe*, 10, no. 3 (November 1981), pp. 4-11; Barbara K. Latham and Roberta J. Pazdro (eds.), *Not Just Pin Money: Selected Essays on the History of Women's Work in British Columbia* (Victoria, B.C.: Camosun College, 1984); Susan Jackel (ed.), *A Flannel Shirt & Liberty: British Emigrant Gentlewomen in the Canadian West, 1880-1914* (Vancouver: University of British Columbia Press, 1982); Mary Kinnear and Vera Fast, *Planting the Garden: An Annotated Archival Bibliography of the History of Women in Manitoba* (Winnipeg: The University of Manitoba Press, 1987); Mary Kinnear (ed.), *First Days, Fighting Days: Women in Manitoba History* (Regina: Canadian Plains Research Center, University of Regina, 1987); Georgina M. Taylor, '"Should I Drown Myself Now or Later?" The Isolation of Rural Women in Saskatchewan and their Participation in the Homemakers' Clubs, the Farm Movement and the Co-operative Commonwealth Federation, 1910-1967', in Kathleen Storrie (ed.), *Women: Isolation and Bonding – the Ecology of Gender* (Toronto: Methuen, 1987), pp. 79-100; Marilyn Porter, 'Mothers and Daughters: Linking Women's Life Histories in Grand Bank, Newfoundland, Canada', *Women's Studies International Forum*, 11, no. 6 (1988), pp. 545-58.

59. See the essays collected in Jean Burnet (ed.), *Looking into My Sister's Eyes: an Exploration in Women's History* (Toronto: The Multicultural History Society of Toronto, 1986).

60. See, for example, Becki Ross, 'The House That Jill Built: Lesbian Feminist Organizing in Toronto, 1976-1980,' *Feminist Review*, no. 35 (Summer 1990), pp. 75-91, which, in providing a history of the Lesbian Organization of Toronto, or LOOT, comments on the underrepresentation of 'working-class lesbians, lesbians of colour, young, disabled and older lesbians' among its members (p. 81).

61. See Mary Louise Adams, 'There's No Place Like Home: On the Place of Identity in Feminist Politics', *Feminist Review*, no. 31 (Spring 1989), pp. 22-33, for a critical examination of the danger in identity-based feminist organising that, by using experience of oppression as the measure of 'authentic' feminism as well as of 'authentic' identity, we fall into the competitive trap of rank ordering our oppressions.

62. Another kind of metropolitanism affecting Canadian women's history is the assimilation of the Canadian experience to the British model. For an excellent example of a work countering this tendency and arguing that the history of Canadian

women's labour cannot be assimilated to the model of what happened to women in Britain during the Industrial Revolution, see Marjorie Griffin Cohen, *Women's Work, Markets, and Economic Development in Nineteenth-Century Ontario* (Toronto: University of Toronto Press, 1988).

63. A major theme of M. Crnkovich (ed.), *"Gossip": A Spoken History of Women in the North*.

64. See, for example, Eve Zaremba (ed.), *Privilege of Sex: A Century of Canadian Women* (Toronto: Anansi, 1974); Veronica Strong-Boag, *The Parliament of Women: The National Council of Women of Canada, 1893-1929*, History Division Paper no. 18 (Ottawa: National Museums of Canada, 1976); Ramsay Cook and Wendy Mitchinson (eds.), *The Proper Sphere: Woman's Place in Canadian Society* (Toronto: Oxford University Press, 1976); Margaret A. Ormsby (ed.), *A Pioneer Gentlewoman in British Columbia: The Recollections of Susan Allison* (Vancouver: University of British Columbia Press, 1976); Wendy Mitchinson, 'Canadian Women and Church Missionary Societies in the Nineteenth Century: A Step towards Independence', *Atlantis: A Journal of Women's Studies*, 2, no. 2, part 2 (Spring 1977), pp. 57-75; Mary Vipond, 'The Image of Women in Canadian Mass Circulation Magazines in the 1920's', in Susan Mann Trofimenkoff and Alison Prentice (eds.), *The Neglected Majority: Essays in Canadian Women's History*, vol. 1 (Toronto: McClelland and Stewart, 1977), pp. 116-24; S. Jackel (ed.), *A Flannel Shirt & Liberty: British Emigrant Gentlewomen in the Canadian West, 1880-1914* (1982).

65. In her Introduction to *"Gossip": A Spoken History of Women in the North*, Mary Crnkovich observes that 'more recently, the preponderance of feminist works about the experiences of white women of Euro-Canadian descent has been recognized and is beginning to be balanced with the words of women from different cultures' (p. xvi). Her book contains transcribed oral testimony from, as well as written government and academic reports by, women from each of the four major cultural/ethnic groups living in the Northwest Territories - the Dene, Metis, Inuit, and Euro-Canadian.

66. For example, Varpu Lindström-Best, '"I Won't Be a Slave!" – Finnish Domestics in Canada, 1911-30'; Marilyn Barber, 'Sunny Ontario for British Girls, 1900-30'; Paula J. Draper and Janice B. Karlinsky, 'Abraham's Daughters: Women, Charity and Power in the Canadian Jewish Community'; Apolonja Kojder, 'Women and the Polish Alliance of Canada'; Eleoussa Polyzoi, 'Greek Immigrant Women from Asia Minor in Prewar Toronto: the Formative Years'; Lillian Petroff, 'Contributors to Ethnic Cohesion: Macedonian Women in Toronto to 1940'; Isabel Kaprielian, 'Creating and Sustaining an Ethnocultural Heritage in Ontario: the Case of Armenian Women Refugees'; Dora Nipp, '"But Women Did Come": Working Chinese Women in the Interwar Years'; and Franca Iacovetta, 'From Contadina to Worker: Southern Italian Immigrant Working Women in Toronto, 1947-62', in Burnet (ed.), *Looking into My Sister's Eyes*. See, also, Varpu Lindström-Best, *Defiant Sisters: A Social History of Finnish Immigrant Women in Canada* (Toronto: Multicultural History Society of Ontario, 1988); and Frances Swyripa, 'The Ideas of the Ukrainian Women's Organization of Canada, 1930-1945', and Ruth A. Frager, 'Politicized Housewives in the Jewish Communist Movement of Toronto, 1923-1933', in L. Kealey and J. Sangster (eds.), *Beyond the Vote: Canadian Women and Politics*, pp. 239-57, 258-75.

There are, of course, exceptions to this pattern, like the study of nuns in Québec by Marta Danylewycz, a multi-lingual Canadian citizen of Ukrainian descent whose life was tragically cut short in 1985. See Danylewycz, *Taking the Veil: An Alternative to Marriage, Motherhood, and Spinsterhood in Quebec, 1840-1920* (Toronto: McClelland and Stewart, 1987). See also the work of Gail Cuthbert Brandt cited in note 53.

67. For an account, in their own words, of the lives and struggles of working-class West Indian women employed as domestics in Canada, see Makeda Silvera, *Silenced* (Toronto: Williams-Wallace Publishers Inc., 1983). See also Tania Das Gupta, *Learning From Our History: Community Development by Immigrant Women in Ontario, 1958-1986* (Toronto: Cross Cultural Communication Centre, 1986); and for the Japanese Canadian experience, from a woman's point of view, of persecution, incarceration, expropriation, and forced labour during and after the Second World War, see Muriel Kitagawa, *This Is My Own: Letters to Wes & Other Writings on Japanese Canadians, 1941-1948*, ed. by Roy Miki (Vancouver: Talonbooks, 1985), and the acclaimed novel by Joy Kogawa, *Obasan* (Toronto: Lester and Orpen Dennys, 1981). Mounting exhibitions of photographs and other visual documentation also serves to reclaim the history of specific groups of women in Canada. For example, under the sponsorship of the Chinese Women's Photo Exhibit Planning Committee with the assistance of the Ontario Women's Directorate and the Ministry of Citizenship and Culture, and with the further sponsorship of the Mon Sheong Foundation, the Chinese Canadian National Council, the Chinese Canadian National Council Women's Issues Committee, and the Toronto Chinese Business Women's Network, '"But women did come': 150 Years – Chinese Women in North America' was exhibited at the Metropolitan Toronto Reference Library, 12 September – 12 October 1987, and expanded to include material on Chinese women in Canada. See also Peggy Bristow, 'Black Women in Nineteenth-Century Ontario', in *Survival and Resistence: Black Women in the Americas*, Proceedings of the Symposium held at the Schomburg Center for Research in Black Culture, New York, New York, 9-10 June 1989 (forthcoming).

68. Particularly Janice Acton, Penny Goldsmith, and Bonnie Shepard (eds.), *Women at Work: Ontario 1850-1930* (Toronto: The Canadian Women's Educational Press, 1974); Linda Rasmussen et al. (ed.), *A Harvest Yet to Reap* (Toronto: Women's Educational Press, 1976); and Linda Kealey (ed.), *A Not Unreasonable Claim: Women and Reform in Canada 1880s-1920s* (Toronto: The Women's Press, 1979).

69. Susan G. Cole, 'Writing out Racism', *NOW*, 23-29 March 1989, pp. 10-12, 19.

70. 'Women's Press Anti-Racist Guidelines', *Broadside*, 10, no. 3 (December 1988/January 1989), p. 4.

71. Cole, 'Writing out Racism', pp. 12, 19.

72. See Narayan, 'Working Together Across Difference: Some Considerations on Emotions and Political Practice'.

73. In '"Woman's Truth" and the Native Tradition: Anne Cameron's *Daughters of Copper Woman*', *Feminist Studies*, 15, no. 3 (Fall 1989), pp. 499-523, Christine St. Peter examines some of the 'questions about cultural imperialism' raised by white writer Anne Cameron's retelling of North Pacific Native women's 'woman-centered' tales in her widely read *Daughters of Copper Woman* (Vancouver:

Press Gang Publishers, 1981). Ameliorating Cameron's cultural imperialism, in St. Peter's view, is Cameron's accountability to her sources (she had the permission of the women whose stories she retold and they 'vetted every word she wrote') and her decision to turn over all royalties from the sale of the book to Native projects, including the preparation of an anthology of Native women's writings by the Native women's collective Ts'eku.

Another kind of cultural imperialism occurs when studies of Canada's past are appropriated as examples of American history, as has happened recently to Sylvia Van Kirk's *'Many Tender Ties'* in articles on revisionist historians of the American West (see Richard Bernstein, 'Unsettling the Old West', *New York Times Magazine*, 18 March 1990, p. 56; and Larry McMurtry, 'How the West Was Won or Lost', *The New Republic*, 22 October 1990, p. 35) and to Joy Kogawa's *Obasan* in an article on 'Japanese American Women's Life Stories' (see Shirley Geok-Lin Lim, 'Japanese American Women's Life Stories: Maternality in Monica Sone's *Nisei Daugghter* and Joy Kogawa's *Obasan*', *Feminist Studies*, 16, no. 2 (Summer 1990), pp. 289-312.

74. Jane Flax, 'Postmodernism and Gender Relations in Feminist Theory', *Signs: Journal of Women in Culture and Society*, 12, no. 4 (Summer 1987), pp. 621-43.

75. Eliane Leslau Silverman, 'Introduction', *The Last Best West: Women on the Alberta Frontier 1880-1930* (Montreal and London: Eden Press, 1984), p. viii

76. For a moving statement by an Afro-American on the importance to her self-identity of recovering her history, of 'recapturing. . .that which had escaped historical scrutiny, which had been overlooked and underseen', see Patricia J. Williams, 'On Being the Object of Property', *Signs: Journal of Women in Culture and Society*, 14, no. 1 (Autumn 1988), pp. 5-24. She writes: 'I, like so many blacks, have been trying to pin myself down in history, place myself in the stream of time as significant, evolved, present in the past, continuing into the future. To be without documentation is too unsustaining, too spontaneously ahistorical, too dangerously malleable in the hands of those who would rewrite not merely the past but my future as well. So I have been picking through the ruins for my roots' (p. 5).

77. Dionne Brand, 'Doing Oral Histories of Black Women: Some Methodological Considerations', paper submitted for an independent reading course, the Ontario Institute for Studies in Education, May, 1989, p. 6. Dionne Brand's first book of short stories, *Sans Souci and Other Stories* (Toronto: Williams-Wallace, 1988), has received rave reviews; and for her sixth book of poems, *No Language Is Neutral* (Toronto: Coash House Press, 1990), she has been short-listed for a Canadian Governor General's literary award in the poetry category.

78. Recently, Black women in Canada have made effective use of the method of oral history in the medium of film to rediscover and celebrate their past. *Black Mother, Black Daughter*, directed by Sylvia Hamilton and Claire Prieto, distributed by National Film Board of Canada (1989, colour, 16mm, 28 min.), commemorates the bonds forged between Nova Scotian Black mothers and daughters in the struggle to survive and maintain a sense of pride and identity. *Older, Stronger, Wiser*, directed by Claire Prieto and Dionne Brand (assoc. dir.), distributed by National Film Board of Canada (1989, colour, 16 mm, 28 min.), is the first of a planned three-part series entitled *Women at the Well* which seeks to recover the history of Black Ontario women through interviews with community elders.

79. Joan W. Scott, 'Rewriting History', in Margaret Randolph Higonnet, Jane Jenson, Sonya Michel, and Margaret Collins Weitz (eds.), *Behind the Lines: Gender and the Two World Wars* (New Haven and London: Yale University Press, 1987), p. 29.

80. See, in particular, Natalie Zemon Davis, *Fiction in the Archives: Pardon Tales and Their Tellers in Sixteenth-Century France* (Stanford, CA: Stanford University Press, 1987), and '"On the Lame" – AHR Forum: *The Return of Martin Guerre*', *American Historical Review*, 93 (June 1988), pp. 572-603. See also Carolyn Steedman, *Landscape for a Good Woman: A Story of Two Lives* (New Brunswick, NJ: Rutgers University Press, 1987).

81. Personal Narratives Group, 'Origins', in Personal Narratives Group (ed.), *Interpreting Women's Lives*, p. 12.

82. Barry Broadfoot, *Six War Years 1939-1945: Memories of Canadians at Home and Abroad* (Toronto: Doubleday Canada, 1974), p. 358, quoted in Prentice et al., *Canadian Women: A History*, p. 317.

83. To say nothing of the powerfully regendering discourses of the postwar anti-feminist backlash.

84. See, for example, Ruth Roach Pierson, *'They're Still Women After All': The Second World War and Canadian Womanhood* (Toronto: McClelland and Stewart, 1986), and Ruth Roach Pierson, 'Beautiful Soul or Just Warrior: Gender and War', *Gender & History*, 1, no. 1 (Spring 1989), pp. 77-86.

85. Personal Narratives Group, 'Origins', p. 12.

86. Brand, 'Doing Oral Histories of Black Women', p. 11.

87. As Dolores E. Janiewski has commented in *Sisterhood Denied: Race, Gender, and Class in a New South Community* (Philadelphia: Temple University Press, 1985), 'Even oral histories, despite earnest efforts, sometimes fail to topple the social barriers between interviewer and subject. Black people and white women demonstrated particular reticence in interviews conducted by comparative strangers, particularly if the stranger also differed in race or sex' (p. 118).

88. Van Kirk, *'Many Tender Ties'*, p. 113.

89. I am grateful to Nanna Damsholt for this insight.

90. That, until very recently, no one else undertook to build on the work of Van Kirk and Jennifer S. H. Brown attests to the difficulty of their undertaking and to the systemic exclusion from the Canadian academy of women historians of aboriginal descent. See Lorraine Littlefield, 'Women Traders in the Maritime Fur Trade', and Jo-Anne Fiske, 'Fishing is Women's Business: Changing Economic Roles of Carrier Women and Men', in Bruce Alden Cox (ed.), *Native People/Native Lands: Canadian Indians, Inuit and Metis* (Ottawa: Carleton University Press, 1988), pp. 173-85, 186-98.

91. Drawing on Michel Foucault and Teresa de Lauretis, Louis A. Montrose's formulation reads: 'my invocation of the term "Subject" is meant to suggest an equivocal process of subjectification: on the one hand, shaping individuals as loci of consciousness and initiators of action – endowing them with subjectivity and with the capacity for agency; and, on the other hand, positioning, motivating, and constraining them within – subjecting them to – social networks and cultural codes that ultimately exceed their comprehension or control'. L.A. Montrose, 'Professing the Renaissance: The Poetics and Politics of Culture', in A. Aram Veeser (ed.), *The New Historicism* (New York and London: Routledge, 1989), p. 21.

6

Women's Culture and Women's Power: Issues in French Women's History

Cécile Dauphin, Arlette Farge, Geneviève Fraise,
Christiane Klapisch-Zuber, Rose-Marie Lagrave,
Michelle Perrot, Pierrette Pézsert, Yannick Ripa,
Pauline Schmitt-Pantel, and Danièle Voldman

The trials and tribulations of women's history and its current forms clearly reveal its place within the discipline of history. These explain in part the current choice of topics studied by historians and the specific methods they use. In the past ten years important shifts in how to identify and analyse historical material have taken place. Within this large movement, so far hardly subjected to critical analysis, women's history has met with widely divergent systems of exclusion, tolerance and, today, banalisation that should be brought to light. Doing so would achieve two objectives: to remain critical towards women's history's own formulations and to raise different questions about the necessary relationship between this particular field and history as a whole. This represents an ambitious project whose difficulty we acknowledge, for it is always easier to ask questions than to answer them. But history is not just the production of new knowledge, it is also the formulation of questions. The questions it raises and that are asked of it constitute a specific site of research that urgently calls for open discussion. The choice of *Annales* as a forum is neither fortuitous nor indicative of a desire to carve out a niche in a journal which at first did not readily accept women's history, although it did not ignore it.[1] Rather, this choice offers an opportunity to openly question the methods used to analyse *rôles sexuels*,[2] methods often expounded in *Annales: E.S.C.*, and to query how a certain recent strain of historiography has managed to appropriate the field of study of female-male relationships.

What follows is a brief description of the history of women's history, whose twists and turns have not been perceived by everyone. Women's history really took off in 1970, with the realisation that it had been neglected and denied. It was helped along by the explosion of the feminist movement, the progress made by anthropology and the history of 'mentalités',[3] the new knowledge produced by social history and the new studies on popular consciousness. This was a key period when feminist activists were writing women's history before women historians themselves. After this initial impulse, French universities initiated research groups and instituted new topics and themes. This intense intellectual activity was governed by two principles: giving women a central place in a history which so far had neglected differentiation by sex, and demonstrating their exploitation and oppression under male domination. In this particular context, where ideology and identification are part and parcel of the object under examination, women's history is an addition to general history. At times, male historians have added a chapter of women's history but this was a mere token offering to a feminism that was overtaking them. Feminism but not the history of feminism: the confusion between them is cleverly maintained when a distinction should be drawn, since these are two separate entities. Is one a sub-category of a category that the discipline of history is already so reluctant to recognise? Or is their relationship not more complex insofar as feminism historically exceeds women's history by the very questions it raises? At any rate, as the facts show, women's history remains for the most part a women's task, a task either tolerated or viewed as marginal by a discipline on which it has no direct impact.

As soon as this new area of research became more organised and more important, some female historians realised the grave danger of intellectual isolation which could only lead to excessively tautological studies. Since they wanted to reach the whole discipline, they had to hone their concepts and critically evaluate their works. The time has come to assess what has been done so far, to create groups of critics[4] and, with government help, an ongoing colloquium[5] and to set up a Centre for the Study of Women and Feminism at the Centre National de la Recherche Scientifique (CNRS).[6] For some women's historians, this official recognition made the questions they had about the usage of their concepts more urgent and reawakened their fear that women's history might never become the spearhead for the discipline of history, or even a gadfly, because of its weaknesses. These include:

(1) the still noticeable preference for certain topics such as the female body, sexuality, motherhood, female physiology and occupations closely related to a feminine 'nature';

(2) the continual use of the dialectic of domination/oppression which can scarcely get beyond a tautological statement, unless it can be shown how such domination exerts its power in different periods and places;

(3) too many studies on prescriptive discourses, which hardly take into account social practices and the forms of resistance to these discourses. Such studies sometimes lead to a sort of hypnotic auto-fascination with misfortune;

(4) a poor knowledge of the history of feminism and its connections with political and social history;

(5) lack of methodological and especially theoretical reflection.

Along with these uncertainties, history itself was changing in ways that were not always obvious at the time, except for the sudden and noteworthy male contribution to research on the differentiation of *rôles sexuels* by historians and anthropologists such as Maurice Godelier and Georges Duby, whose work exemplifies a more general awareness.[7] This consciousness evolved along a direction common to historical research, which today no longer finds very fashionable the history of 'mentalités' and the unearthing of new topics such as sexuality, criminality, death, food, and deviance. These topics, so much in vogue just a little while back, do not attract much attention today, although the problems studied then are very far from being solved. New encompassing themes have emerged, such as fear, sin, and links between private and public life, which threaten to blur the analysis of social relations. At the same time, a new area of research, the history of social and cultural representations, and to a lesser degree, that of political representations, is developing. In this context the concept of 'women's culture' has emerged, through which gestures and practices are analysed as such.

There is no doubt that the success of cultural history and that of representations, plus the increasing contribution of ethnology and anthropology, have taken research on *rôles sexuels* in a new direction. This new direction needs to be examined all the more intently since it is becoming more and more important and since it is backed by a brilliant and innovative historiographical trend. In attempting to describe women's roles, a certain number of specific practices have been discerned and out of these practices, through a pattern of compensations, interferences or symbolic meanings, the traits of a women's culture have been sketched, without which the social fabric itself would disappear.[8] Similarly, the ever-changing interplay of symbolic oppositions between feminine and masculine, whose shifts in meaning vary according to given periods and themes, indicates that *rôles sexuels* are strongly constituted as a means to fight against all forms of undifferentiated roles, which are considered fatal to societies. Although we do not plan systematically to question this approach, we must nevertheless point out its limitations and its deleterious effects. We must also propose a methodological analysis capable of revealing its contributions as well as its limitations.

Having 'some' power

The cultural approach to the sexes

It is accurate to say that belonging to one or the other sex colours one's attitudes, beliefs, and codes in a given society. It is also accurate to point out that such attributions differentiate societies from one another. This parameter has opened up new areas of research that have already yielded stimulating results. Among these are the identification of objects, places and behaviours deemed specifically female, and the slightly different inflections of the concept male domination/female oppression, which used to underlie any study of *rôles sexuels*.

Naming, identifying, and measuring women's presence in places, situations, and roles which are theirs, seemed to be a necessary and long overdue step. The categories of the masculine and feminine, blurred of late by a kind of gender neutrality that only benefited men, were thus clearly established. Since modes of masculine sociability, such as *abbayes de jeunesse*,[9] military conscription, cafés, *chambrettes*[10] or hunting parties had been studied, it became legitimate to study feminine sociability, using the same criterion of separation between the sexes. This produced insightful studies on communal laundries and ovens, on the market place and the household, and certain insights about these female sites that are more or less connected with productive tasks, whereas male sites are, for the most part, related to leisure activities. Work such as Yvonne Verdier's[11] was also done on the significant events in life (birth, marriage or even death). This ethnologist showed how socially and symbolically coherent were the gestures of the laundress, the seamstress, and the cook. She also identified the strand (a sort of Ariadne's thread) that wove together in a coherent way the conversations, gestures, techniques, and roles played by women in a Burgundian village. At the very heart of women's culture lay the extraordinary power of their bodies, characterised as a series of prohibitions and of privileged relations with time.

Similarly, Agnès Fine described clearly, in her study on women's trousseaux, how the objects they contained were identified with their owners.[12] Using a slightly different approach, Jacques Gélis[13] focused on the rituals surrounding birth from the fifteenth to the nineteenth century, and thus came up with an inventory of numerous collective and individual gestures meant to encourage life and to repel death's threat. In this survey of specific female sites and behaviours, works on convent life and women's associations must also be included.[14]

On the other hand, some works suffered from a restricted and restrictive approach which focused solely on the dialectics of domination and oppression, without any attention being paid to existing systems of frequent and complex variations or to exclusively feminine forms of power. Relations between the sexes cannot be reduced to a single, unalterable and universal explanation, i.e., men's supremacy. Indeed, if women have their own view of the *sens social*, if they are allowed practices meant to help the entire community pass from birth to death, they obviously have 'some' power. And such a power should change the direction of the general debate, and open up new possibilities for interpretation. It could lead to studies free from paralysing tautology and capable of explaining a reality that is ever-changing.

Take, for example, the work of Martine Segalen,[15] which deals with nineteenth-century rural society. This author clearly shows how male authority and female powers jointly structure space, work, sexual life and the couple's relationship with the community, and are inscribed in rituals as well as in representations. In the same vein, the anthropologist Annette Weiner, re-examining an archetypical case (the Trobriand Islands),[16] freshly observed the exchange of traditional objects belonging to women (banana leaves) during mourning ceremonies. She questioned her predecessors' interpretation of how wealth circulates and discovered a new system of social explanation based on a knowledge of female roles, previously undetected. This emphasis on female powers represents a definite plus, enriching the inventory of private life as described by nineteenth-century historians and researchers through a rereading in terms of power and an analysis of the real and symbolic confrontations between public and private life.

However, this emphasis on female powers is fraught with danger – that of using it too freely or in a somewhat fallacious fashion. To realise that women possess powers within the framework of culture can lead to the espousal of an attitude of appeasement, juxtaposing the two cultures as at once diverse yet complementary, while forgetting that relations between the sexes are also fraught with violence and inequality. Only theoretical rigour can prevent the emergence of new stereotypes, hidden behind modern formulations.

Deadends

The concept of complementarity utilised in many rural studies[17] has been so successful that it has led to a definitive representation of the partition of space, time, and daily activities, and rituals between men and women, and has presented a world in equilibrium in which roles and tasks are neither antagonistic nor competitive. Social life seemed to be organised around two apparently equivalent poles: male authority on the one hand, and female powers on the other. Even though it has sometimes been demonstrated that the sexual division of tasks is not fixed, and that there are overlapping zones of intersection and exchange that disrupt the opposition between female domestic work and male production work, the notion of complementarity is quite ambiguous. For example, domestic tasks are never performed by men: dealing with water, fire and food preparation are female activities that are devalued when men perform them. Men do not try to take them over, in any case, either materially or symbolically. Conversely, it so happens that the chores usually performed by men do require women's participation for their completion. In this instance, women do not acquire any extra prestige, the necessary feminine 'touch' said to be innate in nature offsetting any value attributable to skill acquired through apprenticeship. This kind of reasoning is at the basis of all the classifications of contemporary professions and activities. In short, women are not 'disqualified', they are never 'qualified'.

Indeed, complementarity can account for real instances in which female-male association is necessary, but it also erases the fact that the distribution of tasks has, after all, a positive and a negative pole and contains implicitly a hierarchical system. The roles may be complementary, but one is subordinate to the other. The concept of complementarity should have, at the very least, taken into account the distinction between complementarity of subordination and complementarity of emulation made by Lucienne Roubin as early as 1970.[18] Consider the case of agriculture where the technical division of labour between the two sexes (men plough and sow, women weed and harvest) can be analysed in terms of complementarity, if we consider it only at the technological level. However, since peasant society encodes and values this technical complementarity differently, 'ploughing and sowing' are seen as noble tasks whereas 'weeding and harvesting' are seen as subordinate ones. Complementarity thus becomes a principle for hierarchical organisation of roles; we are clearly confronting here a complementarity of subordination or a 'complementary opposition', which leaves intact the husband's and wife's divergent or convergent interests, their inequalities before the law and their contradictory relations as a couple.[19] From now on, as these studies and others suggest, one must take into account not only the technical division of chores but also the values and symbols that go with it.

This pattern can be illustrated by further examples. The trousseau may be a long task involving mother and daughter, the cooking of pig's blood may be as essential as the stabbing of the animal, still no one can deny the existence of a hierarchical difference between activities attributed to men and to women. This difference may also entail a certain kind of violence, as exemplified by the killing of pigs. Even if the cooking of the animals' blood does represent some form of nurturing, it nevertheless can be performed only after the killing on whose accomplishment it depends.

Similarly Jacques Gélis conveys to the reader, with his thorough inventory of daily rituals and customs surrounding birth, an overall impression of great violence apparently unbeknownst to the author himself, because he does not deal with it and does not seem to realise its full extent. Yet he shows how a woman in labour is dominated by the effort she must put forth, and how she tackles the physical and the supernatural elements involved in order to give birth successfully. Burdened by precepts that constantly seek to bring about a perfect order between her and the cosmos, which will ensure her success, she ends up haunted by the fear of failure. She has to engage in ceaseless activity so that neither God nor nature will betray her. The situation of the woman in labour, incompletely described inasmuch as the author omits behaviours not in compliance with the norm, suggests a permanent state of imbalance which she must redress most often alone, in order not to appear inadequate. Obviously there is no complementarity in this instance, only violence and fear which shape female rituals and behaviours, and which are rarely mentioned in the literature.

The shadow of contestation is kept at bay by the very reassuring concept of complementarity which neutralises this threat ahead of time, in order to avoid the recognition of its modalities and its specific manifestations. Women's sweetness and peace-keeping qualities are sovereign in such a context, and the analysis of the masculine and the feminine comes to a deadend, the possibilities of tension and conflict, of rivalry or accession to power being pushed under the rug. The study of 'mentalités' as practised by some, can encourage such a view. The cultural definition of female and male worlds can lead to the statement of a real and symbolic balance between them, from that confrontations and violence are absent. Consequently, the assumed need that these two symbolic and practical positions have of each other within a system of equivalent values blurs somewhat the stakes at hand (e.g., compensation, consent, confrontation). Formulated in this way, the daily reality with its difficulties and contrasts becomes hidden, and a slippage easily occurs from the notion of gender difference (*de différence des sexes*) to the view of a binary structure of society which masks the sharpness of this difference. Although tempting, this approach is reductive.

The shift towards the recognition of a 'women's culture' took place in the wake of studies dealing with moments in history when such a culture still existed and could be recorded. In these studies, stereotypically rural society enjoys a special status and is described with few references to its historical context, or to the crucial changes that occurred in the nineteenth and the beginning of the twentieth centuries (railroads, postal services, schools, 'universal' suffrage,[20] migrations, wars, urbanisation), or to internal factors of mutation such as technical innovations and the price of land. Although the culture in question was a culture already on the wane, it was presented as a stable ahistorical society, one that leaves the reader with a strange sensation of timelessness. In these studies, the 'historical facts', purged both of events and conflicts, acquire their meaning from the repetition of gestures, rites, statements that bring to light constants, even universals, which are used to characterise the relationship between the sexes. By regarding village society as frozen, researchers chose to use only data that could be included in a mythological discourse. Works by specialists in folklore, literary or plastic representations, prescriptive discourses, even proverbs, all raise a problem of validity since they describe rural culture in a temporal vacuum and without giving voice to the peasants themselves. They mix innocence and nature, animal sexuality and human sexuality, salacious turn of mind and women's submission. The origin of these stereotypes, the way they are transmitted, their specificity to nineteenth-century rural society are hardly touched upon. Incorporating the teachings of ethnographers, this view of rural culture, and of its female-male relations prefers to focus on unchanging structures rather than on moments of evolutionary flux, of confrontation or questioning.

At best, the history of relations between the sexes can be seen as part of the 'longue durée' or long-term history,[21] but the few attempts to distinguish between 'long-term' and 'short-term' history have not been too successful. Agnès Fine, in the conclusion of her article on the trousseau, uses two such notions of history to analyse the relations between the sexes. According to her, the political, economic, and social conditions of women's place in a given society belong to a precise chronology, i.e., a short-term chronology, whereas the system of sexual symbols, the sexes' perception of their relations, belong to long-term history. The latter aspects thus fall within the domain of permanence rather than that of change. This distinction is not without its problems.

The dialectic between the short-term and the long-term, familiar to historians of the past two decades, most often deals with separate topics. But, in this particular instance, it operates within the same field, that of the relations between the sexes. How, then, can one combine a 'symbolic of the sexes', static by nature, with a practice of sexual division that is subject to change? Logically, in the logic of a theory of representations which emphasises, no matter how complex, the relations between the imagination and socio-political structures, such a combination is unthinkable. Either nothing changes – neither women's place nor the thinking about the division of the sexes – or everything changes. From a methodological point of view, such a distinction between real time dominated by history, and the time of 'mentalités' set more or less outside history, is not really satisfactory. The distinction between two temporal 'levels of analysis' remains strictly formal and the insertion of the concept of 'women's culture' into a long-term history remains the privileged approach.

Even from this perspective, however, things remain obscure. Let us examine seriously the insertion of 'women's culture' in light of Michel Vovelle's critical analysis which reveals all the risks entailed.[22] According to him, all the domains pertaining to long-term history (history of the family, the couple, child, love) are precisely those that bring the *différence des sexes* (gender difference) into play most frequently; but attention is not paid directly to this difference. In other words, if we feel reticent about this approach involving the 'longue durée', it is because none of the studies in anthropological history on themes related to the *différence des sexes* nor any of the studies that focus more specifically on women, has managed to analyse differently and historically the problem of the relations between the sexes – despite the fact that their authors have opted for a long-term approach.

Rethinking women's culture. We will now go beyond reconstructing specifically feminine discourses and knowledge and even beyond attributing to women some forgotten power. We must analyse how a women's culture evolves within a system of unequal relations, how it hides this system's flaws, how it reactivates conflicts, how it maps time and space, and finally how it views its own particularities and its relationship with society as a whole. Two works which we consider exemplary will help to do so.

In her study on bourgeois women in nineteenth-century northern France, Bonnie Smith shows how these women, excluded after 1860 from the management of businesses in which they had until then been associates, significantly changed their roles in society.[23] They had henceforth to supervise their households, composed of a large family and of servants and, thus, had to change the image of themselves, especially in fiction, which their social group came to control. They also had to invent their own values, often in opposition to the male ideology of the time. Thus, for example, they advocated faith against reason, charity against capitalism, domestic matriarchy against economic management, acute moral awareness against money.

Is women's misfortune men's happiness? This is the question asked by Marie-Elisabeth Handmann about a small Greek village in the 1960s.[24] She shows how sexual antagonism lies at the heart of both men's and women's identities; yet this antagonism does not create sex solidarity, especially among women. Isolated and confined to their homes, they have only cunning left to help them survive man's violence. In a society that is economically closed and subjected to rigid socio-cultural codes, the two-faceted instrument of human misfortune functions in a cultural manner: the denial of any liberty for women and their subjugation to permanent sexual control become sources of frustrations for men. The latter's virility cannot be experienced in a climate of mutual exchange and often is expressed violently since it must follow the principle of domination. Consequently, a woman's identity remains confined to the necessarily unhappy status of wife and mother, from which she cannot deviate, transgression being punished by exclusion or by a violence that sometimes proves fatal.

Lessons can be drawn from these two periods, two societies, two cultures, two approaches to the history of women. One must first accept the heritage of the double meaning of the word culture. In the standard usage, it encompasses intellectual faculties and the products of the mind. Conversely, the anthropological meaning refers to discourse or behaviour having the least to do with 'culture': inherited models rooted in symbols and in all the forms of expression that enable individuals to communicate, retain and develop their knowledge and attitudes about life.[25] In studies on women, the shift from a standard meaning to an anthropological one is an implicit way of getting around a problem, since the refusal to consider women within the realm of intellectual activities does away with the need to analyse the mechanisms by which they are excluded from intellectual activities, and especially to 'consider sexual differences (*les différences de sexe*) in the same abstract theoretical light as kinship, political, and economic issues'.[26]

Then – all that remains on this deserted beach are gestures, techniques, and discourses from the past.[27] Simply giving significance to daily activities cannot explain the mechanisms by which some became specific to one or the other sex nor can it explain the 'disqualification' that took place when one of these activities is reassigned to the other sex. It is more important to analyse the pattern made by the different cultural elements. Consequently, the problem of whether to call 'feminine' what is created by women or what is assigned to them becomes a pseudo-problem.

In the study of the Greek village, the relevance of M.-E. Handmann's approach is clear. She analysed the mechanisms by which categories of fundamental thought can become internalised schemes, as in the case of male domination which perpetuates itself from generation to generation thanks to women's internalisation of this domination. Among the bourgeoisie of northern France, the triumphant figures of women ruling over their households go hand in hand with a fragile system of signs that is complex, rigid, intelligible to them alone. Women's presence, strong, yet contained within the family, invades public and private imaginations. This contradictory combination can be seen in practices and norms, as well as in fiction. Thus, the following question arises: how can a mental world so dominated by the feminine element exist in a society where only men have power?

The consensus by which members of a community live and which is inherently contained in the anthropological definition of culture, establishes the existence and the vitality of that culture. In this sense, women's culture indeed concerns the whole community, but each cultural element must be analysed in terms of dependence on and relationship to the other sex, to the social group, to the political and economic context, to the overall culture. It is important to determine the positions of each sex, since sexual division is never neutral, and since a value system based on division is not automatically based on equivalence. Thus, stressing the importance of women's roles should not overshadow the crucial problem of male domination. In the contemporary Greek village as well as in the towns of nineteenth-century northern France, a relationship of inequality indeed lies at the heart of unspoken masculine forms of resistance, just as it lies at the heart of accusations and alibis by those women who found themselves torn between their aspirations and their assigned roles.

The history of women's culture cannot set aside existing conflicts and contradictions. It must, on the contrary, focus on them since, as any other culture, women's culture evolves amid tensions that produce symbolic equilibria, contracts and compromises of a more or less temporary nature. Specific practices as well as mere silence or absence organise these conflicts, which at times legitimise, reorient or control the logic of the powerful,[28] and which finally must be accounted for by historians.

Having power

'Women, how powerful!'[29] This near aphorism is not just meant to be a consolation prize for women. It also expresses a conviction felt by most people in the past as well as by most contemporary historians who believe that 'mores', i.e., private and public domains, are after all more important than political events or the state. Contemporary ideologies and events, marked by the failure of volunteerism and by the forces of inertia, view the social as more important than 'the illusion of the political'. Consequently, the movements associated with the 1968 revolt emphasised the determining role played by peripheral groups, such as dissidents, minorities and women, and the creative invention of everyday life. This type of analysis, possessing considerable heuristic value and fitting perfectly within long-term socio-cultural history, nevertheless presents the drawback of eliminating existing conflicts and tension, including class and sexual struggles. This return to a certain kind of 'political history' rather

than to a 'history of the political' (*histoire du politique*)[30] does not mean
a return to an account in which events are central, but rather a reflection
on the stakes, the agents, the forms of mobilisation, and on consent as well
as seduction and resistance. The gender dimension of such an analysis is
not, however, obvious at first glance. As a participant in a recent
colloquium strongly insisted: 'political relationships can exist only between
social groups'.[31] How, then, can we introduce this dimension and at the
same time enrich women's history with the new insights such an approach
brings to history?

The modalities of male domination. To answer the above question, we can
first remind readers that the relations between the sexes are social relations
since they are not natural but social constructions. Hence, they should be
studied like other relations, equal or unequal, between social groups. From
this perspective, male domination is just one form among others of unequal
relations. This inequality, not specific to the western world, can be found
in many societies, whatever their development may be, and to unmask it
wherever it exists does not constitute an act of exaggerated
ethnocentricism.[32] The Amazons notwithstanding, 'no irrefutable proof
of the existence of societies exempt from male domination has so far been
forthcoming'.[33] The phenomenon of male domination does not stem from
some moral judgment but from scientific observation. This is widely
known but at the same time repeatedly questioned.

We expressed our concern that the concept of male domination and
its corollary, female subordination, may constitute an impasse for women's
history, a concern not alleviated by the new notion of women's culture.
And now this concept re-emerges at the very centre of the description of
sexual relations as a form of social relationship. However, in the
perspective adopted here, male domination is not an invariable 'constant',
but the expression of an unequal social relationship whose mechanism can
be understood and whose characteristics, changing with time, can be
analysed. As such, male domination represents an indispensable tool for
understanding the overall logic of all social relations. It can even be said
that the relations of the sexes and their expression, male domination, are
closely connected to other types of inequalities, and that their
interconnectedness must be kept in mind. Since there is no need to add to
the already long list of the manifestations and modalities of male
domination in the abstract, a few examples will suffice to recall the
connections between this type of domination and other unequal forms of
social relations.

When one analyses the mechanisms, concrete or symbolic, by
which male domination is exercised, one realises that it is not
accomplished in a straightforward manner, but rather by defining or

re-defining social positions or roles related, not specifically to women, but to the reproduction system of the entire society. For example, in nineteenth-century Greece, the assignment of women to domesticity, and its periodic valorisation, are the surreptitious results of a re-definition of children's status[34] and the transformation undergone by Greek cities at the time. Male domination manifests itself in places and ways which at first glance have nothing to do with relations between the sexes. Unfortunately, there are not yet enough studies to deepen our knowledge of these mechanisms, which are less easy to detect than the violence that accompanies direct confrontation.

Both in pre-capitalist and industrialised societies, male domination cannot be dissociated from a mode of production of goods that denies women the benefit of their labour. In domestic production, women are exploited as workers and as child-bearers since the products of their labour belong to their legal guardian and procreation is under the control of the community. Thus, women become a 'consumer good', a situation not specific to archaic societies alone. This mode of domestic production continues, in other forms, in capitalist societies, as exemplified in family-based modes of production[35] in craft, commercial or agricultural enterprises. Whether in the bakery trade[36] or in agriculture, male domination can be seen in the taking over by men of the status, the techniques of a trade which they also inherit as males.[37] The history of the dowry offers another example of women's 'dispossession' that is structurally linked to the inequality between the sexes and to society's mode of production. Finally, the social division of labour among salaried workers, need we repeat, is simultaneously a sexual division of labour.[38]

If we re-position male domination within an ensemble of unequal social relations and examine its specificity and its banality (since it so often combines with class domination in order to maintain the status quo), we can study it, and thus grasp what has all too often been regarded as unavoidable and ineluctable. We now must squarely confront it in order to better understand it, but as we shall see, the confrontation of male domination has in the past already elicited many different strategies. We will now discuss some of these earlier responses.

Compensations and resistances

As a result of male domination, women are, especially as procreators (*agent de la reproduction*), subjected to government manipulation. Such manipulation is not uniform, but takes on different nuances as evidenced by varied practices and discourses which have at heart the interests of the family, society and the state. The level of constraint exercised upon women varies from one time period to another. But at the same time women derive from the system all kinds of compensations, including a certain number of powers, which may explain the degree to which they consent to a system that would not function without such consent.

For example, in contemporary industrialised societies, women's 'weakness' and 'maternal capital' have brought them a degree of protection in the form of specific labour legislation. French women stopped working underground in mines as early as 1850.[39] They were forbidden to work at night or to work long hours, but these restrictions also served to exclude them from certain factory jobs. During World War I, their entry in great numbers into armaments factories led to improved sanitation of the premises and the creation of a new supervisory position: that of female factory overseer. This ambiguous protection had perverse effects since it led to sexist discriminations and to the temporary retreat of women to what were supposedly less dangerous and more 'feminine' sectors such as sweated labour. Still, women were spared the brutality of heavy industry just as they were spared war and military service.

Women's exceptional longevity probably stems from this formal and informal protection rather than from a biological advantage which diminishes as they adopt a masculine lifestyle. The gap between men's and women's death rates in industrialised societies keeps increasing. In France, it has reached eight percentage points, among women of all classes. Could French women be 'more modern than their male counterparts? Why is it increasingly the weaker sex, especially in France, the sex that tradition keeps thinking of as the stronger one?' asks the demographer M. L. Levy.[40] As survivors and often as managers of family fortunes, women as widows remain for many years (often the years of their greatest power) the guardians of family memory, whereas other women live in increasing loneliness and poverty.[41]

Women's weakness has also justified a presumed irresponsibility which, at least in the nineteenth century, earned them the leniency of the courts. According to Michelet, 'Women are not punishable'. This, of course, does not entirely explain women's lower delinquency rate, as contemporary criminologists, such as Lombroso in his 1895 study, *Criminal Woman*, tried to do in terms of 'nature'. Their lack of mobility and the suppressed violence that characterises their forms of expression and vengeance offer equally convincing explanations. Nevertheless, the idea that women are minors who, as such, 'deserve' paternal treatment, weighs on the deliberations, even in trials for infanticide or abortion which very often ended in acquittal. The fact that their bodies were viewed as sources of fertility may have also reduced the sentences inflicted upon them since few women were condemned to hard labour and even fewer received capital punishment.[42] In 1911, a law abolished the death penalty for crimes of infanticide. A low crime rate and lenient sentences thus became the hallmarks of women's penal situation in industrialised societies, a fact which had intrigued Tocqueville in America in the 1830s. No matter how surprising it may seem, the present claim by women for the right to violence and retribution must be understood in the light of their espousal of equal responsibility for both sexes. But, for most women, to be able to escape police involvement and jail, even suspicion, represented instead a privilege which they used and were sometimes asked to use, as was the case in the resistance movements against occupying forces.

Gallantry, that bastardised form of courtship ritual, the many stratagems of seduction, the subtle games of flattery and love please not only men. Women find compensations in awaiting a love declaration, in being the one to be conquered, 'adored, spoiled, fulfilled', to use the nineteenth-century phrase of Baudelaire. And for many of them, these compensations became their main concern, their delights and dreams. These slave's pleasures were – and still are – attractive. Even social obligations, which seem so fastidious to us, offered sources of satisfaction to leisure-class women. Often being unaware of the inherent traps, women reveled in touching shimmering fabrics, selecting cashmeres for wedding presents, wearing a dress for the first time or brightening up men's somber world, as the Impressionists have so masterfully showed us. Can we plot the economy of human desire? In fact, it would be an act of courage to undertake it since the complete silence imposed upon it by feminist movements has helped no one, least of all feminism itself. So far, it has been studied only in terms of women as sex objects or as temptresses.

The history of women's and men's seduction and sexual desire, illustrated for example by the history of physical appearance,[43] make-up, clothing, cooking, housing or even advertising, should show that both men and women are caught in a complex game whose keys belong to neither sex alone. Yet, the precise code, which can be deciphered and recovered, changes quickly from age to age, revealing not only where the sexes stand in relation to each other but also how a society views sexual attraction and conquest. There is no reason not to consider them as historical materials, as has been done for taste, intimacy, or privacy.

Women's invasion of men's imagination, the celebration of 'famous women' during the Renaissance, the nineteenth-century worshipping of the Muse and the Madonna,[44] and Marianne and the Modern Style New Eve[45] represented also compensation for women's eviction, if not from public space, at least from the political arena which was more than ever dominated by the Father. Many women derived satisfaction from playing the roles of Muses or fairies – queens of the night – preferring the comfort of working in the shadows to the inevitably harsh competition with men. At the turn of the century, such preferences drove many feminists such as Madeleine Pelletier to despair.

The compensations received by women were not entirely of a passive nature. They also enjoyed some power, delegated or not, especially in the home, where their influence became so entrenched that they expressed their resentment at men's participation in cooking and cleaning. Even today, lower-class female factory workers remain unwilling to share household chores and insist on retaining the management of the budget, a privilege they acquired in the nineteenth century, probably after a fierce battle. They exercised their power first on their children, especially their daughters. Insofar as children became more important in the nineteenth century, requiring a greater investment, the mother's role was reinforced, often to the detriment of the father.[46] Maternal power became inflated as is evidenced by tyrannical mothers such as Baudelaire's, Flaubert's and Mauriac's, or literary mothers such as Madame Vingtras in Jules Vallès' *The Child* or Madame Lepic in Jules Renard's *Poil de Carotte*, both largely autobiographical novels. They constitute the constellation of mothers (the Milky Way) that made André Breton shiver. These mothers, especially those from the petty bourgeoisie, so eager for recognition and distinction, became scrupulous guardians of morality and propriety after internalising the goals of social mobility. Overwhelmed with rules, duties, feelings of shame and culpability, they turned themselves into paragons of virtue and became cogs in a power system which could only satisfy them if they submitted to it, the price for rebellion often being insanity itself.

Maternal power, perhaps at its peak at the turn of the century, served as justification for men's 'virile' rebellions against mothers and against the blandness of women. This phenomenon can be seen in men's literary magazines from which mothers are absent,[47] as well as in detective stories which represent a reaction against sentimental serialised novels.[48] It is even more blatant in militantly anti-feminist literature,[49] as well as in J. Le Rider's essay which equates the feminine principle with an absence of strength.[50] Richard Sennett, in his way, also makes this point his own.[51]

This power can also be exercised over other women – over the servants in bourgeois households[52] where female solidarity disappears, over daughters and daughters-in-law in large, extended families[53] where patriarchal authority perches on a pyramid of subsequent or adjacent powers.[54] In this instance, some kind of domestic career for women seems possible, a career capable of stifling rebellions and fulfilling aspirations, since these oppressed women will eventually reign, as mothers-in-law or widows, in their turn. This 'turn over' in power, which lends itself to manipulation, shatters women's solidarity. The status of widow deserves special attention. In *Les Gynographes* (published in 1777), Restif de la Bretonne depicted widows as the moral power within the community. But access to this recognised power requires both the death of their own sex (menopausal women supposedly are no longer in the sexual game) and the death of their husbands. What a lugubrious victory to look forward to![55]

What changed in the relationship between the private and the public in the nineteenth century was the glorification of a 'social power', at first mostly masculine[56] but progressively conceded to women who were invited to go beyond the sweet pleasures of the home and enter the outside world. Both the churches and the republican state exalted the 'social power of women',[57] regarded as essential to the development of the welfare state. In Germany, it took the form of a veritable 'social motherhood'.[58] Upper-middle-class women then assisted, educated, and controlled poor working women. Fired up by philanthropic associations, they changed from 'visitors to the poor' (Gérando's phrase) to volunteer investigators, from lady do-gooders to social assistants, the precursors of social workers. During the war (1914-1918), the female factory supervisors introduced by the socialist Minister of War, Albert Thomas, came from and would continue to come from the leisured classes.[59] Similarly, doctors used women as their allies in the fight for better hygiene, which also provided a means of moralising the misery hidden behind the filth. Many women found in this kind of work an outlet for their energies and the bad consciences they had about their idleness in a society that increasingly valued usefulness and work.

How did women take advantage of the powers given to them, of the portions accorded to them, of the missions entrusted to them? How was their potential identity crushed in the process? How did they know, at a given time, in a given circumstance, how to get around prohibitions, how to use trickery – the weapon of the weak – which they supposedly utilise so often and which has been shown by M.E. Handmann and Susan Rogers to eventually void male domination of its real content? To answer these questions, one would have to examine the subtle interplay of powers and counter-powers that constitute the secret web of the social fabric by using an approach – largely inspired by Michel Foucault – that would introduce the dimension of the relations between the sexes. Such a new but difficult approach would go beyond simplistic dichotomies and make possible a history of power – familial, social and political – viewed from the inside.

Obviously, women's response to domination lies not only in an indifferent, resigned or joyful consent, but also in a resistance whose forms have just begun to be analysed. Over the course of time, open revolts against masculine power have assuredly been rare. The battle of the sexes has little to do with confrontation between orders or classes, and, except in a few radical utopias (whose timing, even whose cycles, would be fascinating to study), the victory of one cannot be accomplished by the extermination of the other!

Women's interventions in public life have usually been extensions of their family function, as can be seen in the food riots which have been the main form of public action by women in traditional societies and in France until the mid-nineteenth century. Women acted in the name of moral economics to redress a destructive imbalance which they attributed to the greed of merchants. They valued this role, and the disappearance of such disturbances, due to a more orderly market, partly explains why women withdrew from public life during the second half of the nineteenth century. During the troubles ensuing from the high cost of living in the early twentieth century (1910-1911), the unions forced women to remain silent or to adopt more formal, and more 'virile' methods of organisation, with the consequence that this housewives' rebellion was aimed not only at the merchants but also at men's intention of taking women's place in the market riots that had, since time immemorial, been their prerogative.

Frequently, however, women acted as men's assistants in the more or less conscious hope of obtaining some recognition of their identity and rights, but such hopes were more often than not dashed during wars or struggles for national independence.[60] These disappointments have had a considerable impact on women's developing consciousness of their sex; Hirschman's theories on the role of disappointment in public/private cycles[61] could surely be applied to the feminist movements.

Even the strictly feminist interventions, the direct expressions of women's rights, are the recent products of liberal and democratic societies whose logical continuation they somehow represent (if women are individuals, then they must be born free and equal in rights) and they take place most often in the void left by the weakening of political systems, or by the flaws of revolutions or governmental crises. It is as if a latent claim seized the opportunity to make itself known.

We will return to the radical novelty of feminism and to its importance, which is more political than social. In the past, women's resistance and revolts expressed themselves in civil society. They took on private, even secret forms, or joined together in such a way as to make the checking of male domination possible. For example, the demand made by nineteenth-century housewives to manage their husbands' wages gave them the right to oversee their work. This informal 'feminism' sometimes carried enormous stakes, such as birth control. McLaren sees in the increasing number of abortions undergone by married women with several children in late nineteenth-century France the emergence of a popular 'feminism'. And if Algerians were often hostile to their wives' becoming cleaning women in the households of Europeans, it was certainly out of national pride, but it was also because they feared that their wives would learn about these 'deadly secrets', and thus about the control of procreation, which had been considered the foundation par excellence of male power.[62]

Latent conflicts and open violence permeate family intimacy and the relations between the sexes. As stakes in the system of honour, women are more often than men the victims of vengeance.[63] But at the heart of women's 'misfortune', we often find a clash of wills. In her study on so-called crimes of passion in the nineteenth century, Joëlle Guillais-Maury depicts the vitality and forcefulness of lower-class Parisian women's desires and the retribution they engendered from men who were unable to accept free and strong-willed women.[64] When the arbitration of the law replaced husbands' violence, thanks to legislation permitting separation or divorce (between 1792 and 1816, and again in 1884), observers were amazed that those who took advantage of it were in the great majority women.[65]

It is obvious from the above pages that we have ceased to view the relations between the sexes as the harmonious complementarity of nature or duty; the 'invisible hand' is no more at work here than in the social or political order.

The political stakes

In women's history, the political stakes are not obvious; where can we situate the politics and how can we describe them? In using the concept of domination and in stating its universality and its effects, that is, women's exclusion from politics, we offer an observation but certainly not an analysis. If one stops here, it may be because the emphasis on domination through oppression and rebellion prevents our understanding of it as a dialectical relationship. Most of the time, we go no further than the confrontation between dominant/dominated, which sheds little light on its mechanism and none on its causes. However, by affirming that the relations between the sexes are social relations, we are led to make a distinction between what is social and what is political, and thus to refine the concept of domination. Indeed, if what is political finds its origins in what is social, what makes the former different from the latter is its specific function, i.e., the making of common rules to govern society. But if it seems rather easy to identify political power, it proves more difficult to understand how, insofar as it structures, regulates, coordinates and controls society, the political element defines and apportions what, historically, belongs to public or private life. Is it enough to state that men have been assigned to deal with public matters and women with private ones, then to add that the private sphere is subject to political influence? In fact, it should perhaps be asked how political change has come to be seen as determining the definition and distribution of power. Thus, we would go beyond the mere opposition between social and political, which has been seen as incorporating the opposition between private and public, when in fact these two oppositions should perhaps be considered in conjunction with each other. To see this theoretical problem as particularly relevant to the history of women constitutes in itself a new methodological approach.

By reintroducing a political dimension in the study of feminine/masculine, more importance is given to what is public insofar as it implies the consideration of the social, the economic and the political, without discarding, however, the importance of private life. The opposite approach, which would infer the public from the private, proves to be nearly impossible. The feminist Jeanne Deroin told Proudhon, the famous advocate of women's 'confinement' to the home, that since men already possessed the public arena *and* the family, women also could add the public arena to the family.[66] She emphasised that women's presence in the outside world left the family intact whereas their absence from it had always been purported to offer a satisfactory representation of feminine life.

Instead of underscoring women's absence from political life or adhering to accounts which systematically minimise women's interventions, we suggest a re-evaluation, from a political perspective, of the various historical events in which women have taken part. We will re-evaluate, that is to say, we will consider as political intervention acts that are usually regarded as social, or in other words, we will perceive women in a historical framework where the uniqueness of an event is as important as the repetition of cultural facts. By using this approach, we can reformulate women's role in an eighteenth-century riot or in nineteenth-century social struggles, or in twentieth-century feminist actions. As an immediate result, women's history would no longer be thought of in terms of a more or less progressive evolution of a 'feminine condition'.

Women live with decisions they have not made, and which they cannot make. The political arena has been built around the decision to refuse making political subjects of women. Such a statement adds another dimension to any feminine intervention outside women's traditionally assigned place and to any historical event in which they take part. We are aware that it also indicates our return to a concept of power that 'crowns' the multiple powers which social scientists, since Michel Foucault and others, have sought to describe, as well as to a 'return of the event' which has been acknowledged in the last few years. This represents a necessary and salutary approach in a field of research where the ambiguous use of the various meanings of the word *power* translates all too easily into a system of compensation.

Should we associate the concept of power only with political thinking? Here again, we face a question of method: what would happen if instead of asking questions about women's power, we talked about women's freedom? We would probably be forced to change our system of representation and to give up present categories of hierarchy or compensation. As the history of feminism shows, we encounter not only the problem of women's power, but also that of their emancipation and liberation. To what re-evaluation of the public and political aspects would this lead?

Indeed, it is interesting to emphasise the similarities between Athens and nineteenth-century France at the crucial moments when both were forging autonomous political systems, and this despite major temporal and geographical differences. Both thought about public life in terms of individual citizenship and political responsibility; both represented, under the cover of a generic universality, the right of the individual to participate in the exercise of power. But in thinking universally both 'forgot' women, since such an exercise of citizenship was impossible inside the gynaeceum and since the 'universal' suffrage of 1848 concerned only men. How could there be universality in such circumstances, cut in half as it were? Besides, this political exclusion of women was not directly expressed in political terms. For example, in nineteenth-century France, it was deduced from civil rights.[67] Consequently, the concept of universality functioned as the 'unthought' of in a binary sexual partition of society. Meanwhile, the representation of the difference between the sexes continued to function at different levels of social life. This paradoxical situation in democratic societies needs to be rethought as problematic.

In addition, a contrary movement, stemming from the very status of the individual in contemporary democratic societies, allows us to speak of women's 'inclusion' in public and political life. On the one hand, we can describe how women's condition has been improved during the last few centuries and, on the other, how feminist struggles have forced democracies and industrialised societies to include women, thus putting an end to the binary division of so-called sex roles and allowing individuals to exercise their right to choose for themselves. This leads to a new problem, that is, the temptation, from now on, to neutralise the difference between the sexes. Such a prospect frightens Ivan Illich who sees unisex triumphing in the new society.[68] Objecting to women's exclusion might lead to the production of a 'neuter'; achieving equality might provoke the loss of sexual identity.

To think in such terms betrays a certain confusion, for if the neuter could be thought of as an opportunity to include women in a reinterpretation of universal categories, the difference between the sexes will still remain where it matters, namely in the relationship between one sexed person and another. It also means going in the opposite direction to that taken by history, which by creating the difference between the sexes at the social level destroyed it symbolically at the political level by excluding women. This neuter category is useful only insofar as it is temporary and operational. In any case, it has the merit of provoking a reassessment of the public and the political in such a way as to reintroduce later the real division between the public and private, but in a more original and less traditional way.

A working hypothesis

In the face of a historical cataclysm, how does the difference between the sexes function? In the case of a significant event, a juridical, technological, economic or political watershed, how does either sex represent and redefine itself and its relationship to the other? Analysing the causes and effects of some of these historical watersheds or ruptures should lead to a better understanding of how women, and the difference between the sexes, can be inscribed in historical time. Then, cross-checking masculine chronology, which has always been in existence, with the history of women's interventions would be possible and productive. Women's history would necessarily have to be rewritten in a form at once less global and less atomised. By preferring the term 'watershed' (*une rupture*) to that of 'event' we could avoid the questionable opposition between long-term and short-term history and from neglecting one for the other. Furthermore, we would be able to go beyond the study of women as agents of a given historical moment (a problem particular to the history of feminism)[69] as well as remaining mindful of their intervention, however minimal, and of their participation and reactions within the social, political and 'cultural' arena as it was redefined earlier in this article.

This working hypothesis poses several sets of questions, methodologically as well as theoretically. Based on the study of certain ruptures – transformations or upheavals – involving women directly or indirectly, we could then inquire about the subsequent evolution of the relations between the sexes, and study the eventual modification of the representational systems then in place. This should enable us to better identify all the parameters that compose these relations, and more specifically to ascertain which ones stem from a push for equality, from oppression, from women's desire for revenge or from all of these at once. Should these relations evolve, we could determine the causes, consequences and goals of the evolution in question. In the final analysis, this kind of study would stimulate a re-interpretation of history in general and of women's history in particular.

Now let us consider a few examples concerning social, political, economic and professional life, examples that will clarify this working hypothesis. Take, for instance, a new law, a judicial event bearing directly on women's lives, such as the institution of the dowry during the late Middle Ages or the right to divorce between 1792 and 1816, or an event not involving the difference between the sexes directly, such as the French Revolution which, however, can be interpreted in various ways depending on whether the point of view is Man's, men's or women's. Can we say that this social and political upheaval viewed and accepted as progress by some, was necessarily experienced and interpreted as such by nineteenth-century women? By introducing into the analysis contradictions, or at least paradoxes of this kind, we create the opportunity to place historical facts in an entirely different light. The institution of the dowry has commonly been recognised as a positive development in women's condition, but a study of its practical consequences in fact reveals that women derived only apparent economic power from it, since they could lose it through misappropriation either by management or by inheritance. We see also that by granting women a symbolic importance, subtle mechanisms of identification are established, which lead women to accept a domination whose strategies are not always easily detectable.

The erratic history of the right to divorce, once granted, then taken back and regranted in 1884, offers an opportunity to analyse in depth the acts of liberation or consent it engendered within a few decades. These juridical hesitations reveal perhaps less a fear of women's independence (which would be understandable since they filed for divorce in much greater numbers than men) than anxiety about seeing private and public spheres blend – since the act of divorce makes what is private public. Here was a burning issue if ever there was one in the nineteenth century, an issue that has relevance far beyond the writing of a chapter in women's history. Finally, let us consider the right to vote granted to French women in 1944. Once we accept the fact that it was inevitable and that France lagged behind other countries in this matter, we can reflect upon women's intervention in politics. Although the consequences of this law are still debated, the way it came about may be even more interesting. Written as it were as an addendum to a legislative bill that bore no direct relation to women's lives, it appears on the surface to have little or no connection with the feminist struggles that contributed to obtaining it.

The act of researching what preceded and succeeded an event that caused a profound change makes one far more aware of what really happened. It also challenges the idea, which is still alive in the minds of historians both male and female, that women's history has been one of steady improvement. In short, we are calling for contrasting and contradictory historical perspectives.

NOTES

From the French 'Culture et pouvoir des femmes', published in *Annales: Economies, Sociétés, Civilisations*, no. 2 (March-April 1986). The original English translation by Camille Garnier, funded by the American Association of University Women, was published in the *Journal of Women's History*, 1, no. 1 (Spring 1989) and is used here by permission. In this revised version some spellings and punctuation have been altered by the editors and a number of phrases have been retranslated. Explanatory footnotes have been embedded in the endnotes, and corrections have been made in the footnotes.

1. A systematic inventory of articles on women and the masculine/feminine in *Annales: E.S.C.* (between 1970 and 1982) was published in Arlette Farge's article, 'Pratique et effets de l'histoire des femmes', in Michelle Perrot (ed.), *Une Histoire des femmes est-elle possible?* (Marseilles: Rivages, 1984), pp. 18-35.
2. The French *rôles sexuels* has been left in the translated text, as no direct equivalent exists in English and the connotation lies somewhere between sex roles and gender roles.
3. The term 'Mentalités' designates unconscious assumptions and common ways of thinking. [Tr.]
4. In Paris, as well as outside Paris, numerous study groups were formed, both connected and unconnected with universities.
5. Colloquium *Femme, féminisme, recherche*, Toulouse, 1983.
6. Action thématique programmée: Recherches sur les femmes, recherches féministes, 1984-1988.
7. Maurice Godelier, *La Production des grands hommes* (Paris: Fayard, 1982); Georges Duby, *Le Chevalier, la femme et le prêtre* (Paris: Hachette, 1981).
8. Jacques Revel, 'Masculin/féminin: Sur l'usage historiographique des rôles sexuels', *Une Histoire des femmes est-elle possible?*, pp. 120-40.
9. 'Abbayes de jeunesse': particular forms of adolescent male gangs in early modern French villages who acted to 'police' social behaviour through charivaris, and other forms of ritual harassment. [Tr.]
10. 'Chambrettes': men's gatherings in the villages of Southern France (Lucienne Roubin has written most interestingly about these; see below, note 18). [Tr.]
11. Yvonne Verdier, *Façons de dire, façons de faire: La laveuse, la couturière, la cuisinière* (Paris: Gallimard, 1979).
12. Agnès Fine, 'A Propos du trousseau, une culture féminine?', *Une histoire des femmes est-elle possible?*, pp. 156-80.
13. Jacques Gélis, *L'Arbre et le fruit. La naissance dans l'Occident moderne, XVIe-XIXe siècles* (Paris: Fayard, 1984).
14. 'Femmes et associations', special issue of *Pénélope*, no. 11 (Autumn 1984).
15. Martine Ségalen, *Mari et femme dans la société paysanne* (Paris: Flammarion, 1980).

16. Annette Weiner, 'Plus Précieux que l'or: Relations et échanges entre hommes et femmes dans la société d'Océanie', *Annales: E.S.C.*, no. 2 (1982), pp. 222-45.

17. Ségalen, *Mari et femme.* . .; See also the bibliography in 'Femme et terre', *Pénélope*, no. 7 (Autumn 1982), pp. 136-46.

18. Lucienne Roubin, 'Espace masculin, espace féminin en communauté provencale', *Annales: E.S.C.*, no. 2 (1970); Rose-Marie Lagrave, 'Bilan critique des recherches sur les agricultrices en France', *Etudes rurales*, no. 92 (Octobre – Décembre 1983), pp. 9-40.

19. *Etudes rurales*, no. 92 (Octobre – Décembre 1983), pp. 9-40.

20. Frenchmen obtained the right to vote in 1848, women not until 1944. [Tr.]

21. The term 'longue durée' in 'histoire de longue durée' encompasses many centuries, not decades, and comes from the perceptions of Ferdinand Braudel, long-time editor of *Annales: E.S.C.* [Tr.]

22. Michel Vovelle, 'L'Histoire et la longue durée', *La Nouvelle histoire* (Paris: Encyclopédie du savoir moderne, 1978), pp. 316-43.

23. Bonnie G. Smith, *The Ladies of the Leisure Class: the Bourgeoises of Northern France in the XIXth Century* (Princeton: Princeton University Press, 1981).

24. Marie-Elisabeth Handmann, *La Violence et la ruse. Hommes et femmes dans un village grec* (Aix-en-Provence: Edisud, 1983).

25. Clifford Geertz, *The Interpretation of Culture* (New York: Basic Books Inc., 1983), p. 89.

26. Annette Weiner, *La Richesse des femmes ou comment l'esprit vient aux hommes (îles Trobriand)* (Paris: Seuil, 1983).

27. What Verdier has called 'les façons de dire et de faire'. [Tr.]

28. Michel de Certeau, *L'Invention du quotidien*, vol. 1. *Arts de faire* (Paris: 10/18, 1980), pp. 18 ff. The reference here is to a French folk saying: 'la raison du plus fort est toujours la meilleure', i.e., the arguments of the strongest are always the best. [Tr.]

29. According to Michelet's phrase.

30. See René Remond's *Pour un histoire politique* (Paris: Editions du Seuil, 1988), especially the concluding essay 'Du politique'.

31. Cited by Nicole Mathieu, 'L'Arraisonnement des femmes', *Cahiers de l'Homme*, 1985, p. 171.

32. *Ibid.*

33. Maurice Godelier, in preface to Handmann, *Violence et la ruse*, p. 7.

34. Eleni Varikas, 'La Révolte des dames: Genèse d'une conscience féministe dans la Grèce du XIXe siècle, 1833-1908', doctoral thesis, University of Paris VII, 1986.

35. Reference to the concept introduced by Christine Delphy in *Close to Home: A Materialist Analysis of Women's Oppression*, trans. and ed. by Diana Leonard (London: Unwin, 1984).

36. I. Bertaux-Wiame, 'L'Installation dans la boulangerie artisanale', *Sociologie du travail*, 34 (1982).

37. D. Barthélemy, A. Barthez, P. Labat, 'Patrimoine foncier et exploitation agricole', Paris, SCEES, Collection de statistiques agricoles, *Etude*, no.

235 (October 1984). Rose-Marie Lagrave, 'Egalité de droit, inégalité de fait entre hommes et femmes en agriculture', *Connexions*, no. 45 (1985), pp. 93-107.

38. R. Sainsaulieu, *L'Identité au travail* (Paris: Presses de la Fondation Nationale des Sciences Politiques, 1977).

39. In fact, Frenchwomen were legally barred from mine work in 1874. [Tr.]

40. M.-L. Levy, 'Modernité, mortalité', *Population et sociétés*, no. 192 (June 1985).

41. Arlette Farge, Christiane Klapisch et al., *Madame ou mademoiselle? Itinéraires de la solitude des femmes, XVIIIe-XIXe siècles* (Paris: Montalba, 1984).

42. In the US this is referred to as the chivalry factor. [Tr.]

43. Philippe Perrot, *Le Travail des apparences* (Paris: Seuil, 1984).

44. Stephane Michaud, *Muse et Madone: Visages de la femme de la Révolution française aux apparitions de Lourdes* (Paris: Seuil, 1985).

45. Maurice Agulhon, *Marianne au combat (1789-1880): L'Imagerie et la symbolique républicaine* (Paris: Flammarion, 1979); M. Quiger, *Femmes et machine de 1900: Lectures d'une obsession Modern Style* (Paris: Klincksieck, 1979).

46. As is suggested by Elisabeth Badinter's *L'Amour en plus: Histoire de l'amour maternel, XVIIIe-XIXe siècles* (Paris: Flammarion, 1980).

47. D. Bertholet, 'Conscience et inconscience bourgeoises: La mentalité des classes moyennes française, décrit à travers deux magazines illustrés de la Belle-Epoque', Ph.D. thesis, University of Geneva, 1985.

48. Anne-Marie Thiesse, *Le Roman du quotidien: Lectures populaires à la Belle-Epoque* (Paris: Le Chemin Vert, 1984).

49. Annelise Maugue, *L'Identité masculine en crise au tournant du siècle* (Marseille: Rivages, 1987).

50. Jacques Le Rider, *Le Cas Otto Weininger: Racines de l'antiféminisme et de l'antisémitisme* (Paris: Presses Universitaires de France, 1982).

51. Richard Sennett, *Les Tyrannies de l'intimité* (Paris: Seuil, 1978), and even more to the point, *La Famille contre la ville: Les classes moyennes de Chicago à l'ère industrielle* (Paris: Recherches, 1980). According to Sennett, ambitious and cantankerous women, anxious and diminished husbands are the price to pay for self-centred and 'feminised' families.

52. As is shown by Geneviève Fraisse in *Femmes toutes mains: Essai sur le service domestique* (Paris: Seuil, 1979).

53. In this regard, Lourdes Mendez Perez's thesis is quite convincing. See 'L'Evolution de la vie quotidienne des paysannes à l'intérieur de Lugo entre 1940 et 1980: L'Exemple du Municipio d'Abadin', University of Paris, 1985.

54. Elisabeth Claverie and Pierre Lamaison, 'L'Impossible mariage: Violence et parenté en Gévaudan (XVIIe, XVIIIe et XIXe siècles)* (Paris: Hachette, 1982).

55. In François Mauriac's *Le Baiser au lépreux*, young Néomie, Jean Péloueyere's widow, can only retain her right to oversee the couple's fortune if she does not remarry: 'Small, she had to be great; a slave, she had to govern. This somewhat rotund middle-class woman could not surpass herself since all avenues were closed to her except renunciation'. [Paris: Éditions Gallimard, 1, p. 499].

56. In this respect, see P. Rosanvallon's *Le Moment Guizot* (Paris: Éditions Gallimard, 1984).

57. This is the very title of a book by one of Auguste Comte's disciples, Georges Deherme, published in 1914.

58. Paper presented at Princeton (March 1985) by Christoph Sachsse, professor in Kassel (Germany).

59. Annie Fourcaut, *Femmes à l'usine* (Paris: Maspero, 1982).

60. A colloquium on the role of war in the relations between the sexes was held at Harvard (January 1984). See Margaret Randolph Higonnet, Jane Jenson, Sonya Michel, and Margaret Collins Weitz (eds.). *Behind the Lines: Gender and the Two World Wars* (New Haven, Conn.: Yale University Press, 1987), and also Françoise Thébaud, *La Femme au temps de la guerre de 14* (Paris: Stock, 1986). On wars of resistance, see Djemila Amrane, 'Le Rôle des femmes algériennes dans le guerre d'indépendance algérienne', Ph.D. thesis in history, University of Reims (France), 1988.

61. A. Hirschman, *Bonheur privé, action publique* (Paris: Fayard, 1983).

62. C. Brac de la Perrière, 'Les Employées de maison musulmanes au service des Européens pendant la guerre d'Algérie', Ph.D. thesis (third cycle), University of Paris VII, 1985.

63. Claverie and Lamaison, *Impossible marriage*; J. Gomes Fatela, 'Le Sang et la rue: l'espace du crime au Portugal (1926-1946)', Ph.D. thesis (third cycle), University of Paris VII, 1984.

64. Joëlle Guillais-Maury, 'Recherches sur le crime passionnel Paris au XIXe siècle', doctoral thesis (third cycle), University of Paris VII, 1984, to be published by Éditions O. Orban.

65. Dominique Dessertine, *Divorcer à Lyon sous la révolution et l'Empire* (Lyon: Presses universitaires de Lyon, 1981); B. Schnapper, 'La Séparation de corps de 1837 à 1914, essai de sociologie juridique', *Revue historique*, nos. 4-5 (1978).

66. In 1849, Jeanne Deroin and Proudhon carried on this controversy in the newspapers *Le Peuple* and *L'Opinion des femmes*.

67. Geneviève Fraisse, 'Droit naturel et question de l'origine dans la pensée féministe du XIXe siècle', in *Stratégies des femmes* (Paris: Tierce, 1984), pp. 375-90.

68. Ivan Illich, *Le Genre vernaculaire* (Paris: Seuil, 1983).

69. Geneviève Fraisse, 'Historiographie critique de l'histoire du féminisme en France', *Une histoire des femmes est-elle possible?*, pp. 189-204; Laurence Klejman and Florence Rochefort, 'Féminisme, histoire, mémoire', *Pénélope*, no. 12 (Spring 1985), pp. 129-138; Michèle Riot-Sarcey, 'Mémoire et oubli', *ibid.*, pp. 139-68.

7

Global Women's History: Organising Principles and Cross-Cultural Understandings

Ida Blom

A little over a century ago, Friedrich Engels formulated the theory of 'the world historical defeat of the female sex'. He insisted that the original matriarchal order had been turned into patriarchy by the emergence of the concept of private property. In order to protect inheritance rights, men had to be certain of their paternity. This made them develop a system of control over women, especially over women's sexuality, but also over their labour.[1] Although Engels' theory has been energetically discussed and even refuted, it is tempting to retain the basic notion of a common history for women world-wide. As research in women's history progresses, the need has grown to summarise historical processes over wider geographical regions, as these processes affect women and as women have affected them.[2]

An effort to address this need is being made by ten Scandinavian scholars who are currently writing a *Women's History of the World from the Earliest Times to the Present Day*.[3] As the general editor, trying to solve the many problems inherent in such an undertaking over the past five years, I have become acutely aware of questions central to women's history worldwide and to the sensitivities of historians involved in researching this history. Since women's history is in essence cross-cultural, treating as it does individuals of different classes and ethnicities even when limited to the nation state or to local histories such as the history of a town, some of the questions facing the authors of a women's world history may be of interest to all historians of women.

At the outset we faced two important problems. The first was whether it would be possible to unite all ten scholars around one unifying theoretical approach, that is, whether we could agree upon one theory of relevance to all historians of women, one that was helpful for studying women's history in a variety of periods and cultural settings? The second question was: would it be possible to overcome our inborn eurocentrism and write a women's world history in the spirit of cross-cultural understanding that a true multicultural approach required?

Our discussions of the possibility of finding a theoretical framework common to all ten researchers revolved around the concept of patriarchy.[4] Would theories of patriarchy lead us to produce a narrative focusing exclusively on women's oppression and resistance to oppression? Important as this theme is, would such a theoretical framework make it difficult to express all the richness and cultural variations in women's history? If we did not agree on a theory of patriarchy, would we run the risk that some authors might gloss over the painful problem of women's subordination, including women's acceptance of subordination throughout history as well as their long struggle against it?

We did not manage to agree on a single theory of patriarchy. Instead we solved the problem of common approach in a very simple way, perhaps the only way open to us. Each writer has been allowed ultimate freedom of interpretative choice within the parameters set by a common obligation to address the problem of women's oppression as embodied in theories of patriarchy.

Our discussions mirror a problem well-known to many historians of women's history: the problem of explaining gender differences throughout history. This problem is highlighted by writing a narrative that shows obvious similarities in women's history within different cultures.

Let us look at just one striking example of how gender difference has taken different forms but assumed similar importance within different cultures: greater restrictions on women's mobility, and on the spaces they occupy, as compared with men's. This common feature regarding mobility manifests itself variously in different cultures. Over the centuries, for example, groups of Chinese women had their feet bound at a very early age, and many Muslim women observed purdah, some living their lives in harems. In both cultures the result was physically limiting for women. In Europe and America women's mobility was also restricted, though rarely by such direct physical means. Instead ideological and psychological approaches taught women and men that respectable women must not appear unescorted except in certain well-defined areas. Failure to respect these boundaries made women more or less legitimate victims of male violence.

How do we explain these recurring inequalities between women's and men's mobility? Various explanations have been given for foot-binding, for purdah and harems, and for limiting women's mobility in Euro-American culture: one such explanation has been that these customs maintained a vital distinction between women and men, that they maintained the division of labour and of responsibility that assured the most satisfactory functioning of family and society. Another explanation has been that limiting some women's mobility served to distinguish between women of different social standing; women from the higher social ranks would in any culture have the most restricted mobility. Foot-binding has also been explained as having had a sexual function, in the belief that it resulted in, or signified, a narrower vagina. Tiny feet were also said to comply with specific ideals of feminine beauty. Control of women's sexuality also seems to be a principal factor in explanations for restricting western women's mobility. For women to avoid certain well-defined areas of a town was seen as a protection of women from male aggression, whereas other women, the prostitutes, were limited precisely to exactly the areas avoided by virtuous women so as not to expose men to unplanned temptations. In each individual culture the fact that women themselves seemed to accept these limitations to their mobility, and even to impress them on each other, has provided a strong argument for maintaining them. Feminist research has, however, pointed to the sheer exertion of male power and male preferences – the patriarchal power-relations – inherent in these traditions, and to the psychological mechanisms at work when women internalised such power-relations. But research has also stressed class and caste implications to such traditions. Seeing that limited mobility was not applied to all women in a certain culture, that some women remained unhampered by these traditions, 'free' to take up onerous work loads, class/caste has been put forward as the most relevant of analytical categories to explain the tenacity of such traditions. Finally, it should not be forgotten that in spite of limited mobility many women managed to move around and to take part in social and economic activities, even to the extent of becoming leaders.[5]

These considerations illustrate the well-known dilemma of the relative importance of class and gender as analytical categories in historical research, and the problem of how we go about combining the category of gender with other important categories. We constantly return, therefore, to the question of whether there is a single theory in relation to gender analysis that will be applicable worldwide, such as the theory of patriarchy, or whether each culture requires specific, more culturally limited, theories to make sense of its gender arrangements.

Recently Evelyn Fox Keller has discussed what she considers to be at the centre of feminist theory. Much of what she says holds true also for a feminist history of women.[6] She outlines theoretical changes that began in the 1960s with the distinction between sex and gender, between biological and social realities. Although from the outset there was a certain amount of tension between theoretical and activist interests within women's studies, Fox Keller maintains that there was agreement on the social and analytic *importance* of gender.

Subsequently a number of qualifications were made. Gender continued to be viewed as an important analytical tool, but it soon became evident that other categories were at least as important. Ethnicity and class – and I would add, for some parts of the world, caste as well – cut across gender divisions. Other more recent approaches deriving from poststructuralist theory may seem to dissolve the concept of gender by deconstructing the binary oppositions of female/male, woman/man, and thereby introducing a variety of genders and gender identities. And finally, the development of new reproductive technologies today looms as a means of eradicating the most fundamental of gender-specific characteristics – women's capacity to bear children.

However, Fox Keller posits that one vital process has until the present day compelled all societies to distinguish between individuals, and that is precisely the process of producing new life. Only one kind of individual, women, produces human offspring. The study of 'what people have made of this observation, the meaning they have given it, the social uses to which they have put it' is for Fox Keller central to feminist theory. The task of the researcher is, therefore, to expose and examine (and I would add *explain*) the enormous variability between cultures, and over time within the same culture, of what has been made of the fact that women bear children. I think in a basic sense we may safely say that this is also what much research in women's history is about.

If the contributors to our women's history – and women's historians as a group of individual researchers – choose different theoretical platforms, they will contribute in different ways to our knowledge of how different cultures at different times have translated into social institutions the biological fact that women and not men give birth to human offspring. They may also – following Gisela Bock's lead in her recent article in *Gender & History* – show that 'biology' itself cannot be understood as a given physiological phenomenon. It should be seen rather as a method of arguing that physical differences legitimise pre-existing social relations, that gender relations as well as racial relations must both be understood as power relations.[7]

Moreover, gendered power relations, as French historians have pointed out, must be considered part of a social system, embedded in a hierarchy that also includes men.[8] Consider, for example, the withdrawal of middle-class women in England at the end of the eighteenth century from gainful employment to unpaid work in the domestic sphere. This change was one important step in the formation of the English middle class – and later of the middle classes of many other nations – giving middle-class families a characteristic that separated and distinguished them distinctly from the working class.[9] Class hierarchy is therefore represented in part by the way women function within the different classes, much in the same way as 'respectable' women in some cultures can be seen as the measure of family honour.

Such power hierarchies among men as well as among women could hardly be maintained unless women to some degree accepted their assigned roles. They did that – according to the same French historians – because although they were less powerful than men in the same social group, women received significant compensations: they expected to enjoy the gallantry of men's protection; and they had less responsibility, even to the point of not being punished as severely as men for any crimes they might commit. In European and American culture women lived – and still live – longer than men, possibly in part because they were not – and still are not – exposed to as many physical dangers. These are examples of passive compensations, but women may also receive active compensations for accepting inequality, such as control over the family budget, and influence over children, sometimes even over grown-up sons. In some cultures they gain with age important influence over other women within the family, such as mothers-in-law over young wives. Finally, women's private influence over men through other channels of power than those currently used in public power relations should not be neglected.[10] However, the fact that in some cultures women are more exposed to malnutrition than men, and sometimes even forcefully killed because they are women, should remind historians that men's use of force may provide the ultimate explanation of why women internalise gender inequality. Power takes many forms and should be studied in all its varieties.

Applying gender as an analytical tool – not stopping short at analysing women's oppression but also continuing to locate their strengths and their participation in class, caste and ethnic power hierarchies – yields important knowledge as to how societies have functioned. Such analysis reveals that every area of society, be it the family, the workplace or the political arena, is gender-structured. Inheritance rules, divisions of work and of authority, beliefs as to psychological characteristics of an individual, even political power relations are structured around dichotomies of gender. Gender history may mean to analyse and explain the importance of gender in any historical context.[11]

In Scandinavia Yvonne Hirdman has pioneered the concept of the 'gender system', maintaining that relations between women and men rest on two main principles: the first is that the two genders, women and men, must be separated, allocated different fields of work, different spaces, different areas of influence. The second principle is that of male supremacy – whatever is the masculine arena will always be allocated the most authority, dignity, and worth. In an important article, 'Power and

Sex', Yvonne Hirdman questions whether this will always be so, or whether these principles will some day prove to be only of historical interest.[12]

This definition of the concept of a 'gender system' seems very close to definitions of patriarchy. It may also be important for historians to study other aspects of gender relations than 'separate spheres' and power relations. If historians of women have shown some of the consequences gender has had for women, the time has also come for historians to reveal the consequences gender has had for men, and to study how changes in the conditions of one gender affect the conditions of the other. This methodology may enable the researcher to focus not only on men's power over women, but also on men's dependence on women, and on gender relations of affection and reciprocity.[13]

All these theories have been proposed by researchers within a Euro-American historical tradition. They also come easily to mind for a European historian when writing the history of African and Asian women. But as Bolanle Awe's article in this volume reminds us, we should ask whether such theories are applicable outside the European tradition, or whether women of Asian, African and Latin American cultures require other theories to explain gender differences? Grethe Jacobsen, one of the contributors to our women's world history, has introduced the concept of 'gender parallels', that is, the existence of two different but equally important sectors, with equal power, one for women, another for men. She maintains that this was the situation in some Latin American societies before the European invasion. This concept is also used by Swedish anthropologists studying gender relations in some African cultures.[14] But if the concept of 'gender parallels' may to some extent also be applied, for instance, to gendered work divisions and economic responsibility in the agrarian societies of Europe, the fact remains that authority, the legitimate power to enact decisions, embodied in state legislation as well as in popular traditions, in the final analysis rested with men. One must be extremely cautious, then, when transferring theories from one culture to another. Whether Euro-American theories explaining gender inequalities may apply to all cultures, whether theories generated within other cultures may be applied to Euro-American history, or whether specific culturally determined theories are needed, is a fascinating problem that deserves closer scrutiny as women's history moves on to wider comparative studies.

The second problem we wanted to resolve as we began to write our women's world history was that of eurocentrism. Although we could learn a good deal from anthropologists who have dealt with this issue for some time already, we felt the need to discuss its possible consequences for our own work. Initially, we have had to admit that, to be precise, language problems, our lack of knowledge of Italian, Spanish, Portuguese, or any of the Slavic languages, for example, necessarily narrows our eurocentrism to a specific *northern European perspective*. Translations of Italian, Spanish and other southern European research in women's history are badly needed to broaden even our European outlook. So what should we say of our lack of understanding of Chinese, Japanese, Urdu or some of the many African languages?

It should be perfectly legitimate to write history from a clearly defined perspective. We are writing with a Scandinavian audience in mind, and this does to some extent make eurocentrism a natural perspective. We want our readers to feel at home in the cultures they read about, to find their own history, their own perspective, their own identity. The problem arises when it comes to making it possible for our readers to *understand* - not just to marvel at - the history of women outside our own cultures. The problem becomes even more acute when we attempt to convey a narrative of that part of women's history which would be acceptable to women from these other cultures. And this is important because even a Scandinavian audience increasingly comprises people from other cultures - Asian, African and Latin American cultures - and we do, of course, want to write for our new compatriots, too. How does one accomplish this?

* * * * *

We have decided in favour of one guiding principle: to concentrate within each volume on *important new* phenomena specific to the period in question. We have chosen as the focus for our narrative what was new and what brought change.

The decision as to what are considered important new trends in history will of course be determined by what has been *important for women*. Therefore, for instance, the 1960s are seen as an epoch-making period: the new women's movement started in North America and spread to Europe and to certain other parts of the world. In many countries women fought for and won the right to choose whether to have children, when and how many. Laws and regulations were enacted to make this possible.

Although these struggles may be seen as more applicable to European and North American women, other events of the 1960s had vital importance for women in other parts of the world: the fight for independence led in many countries to the end of colonial status, which directly affected women's lives in decisive ways. But we still have to consider the question of whether the fundamentally gendered economic, social and political conditions created during the colonial period have been changed with independence. In European and American history, by analogy, gaining national independence has been generally regarded as exemplifying an important event affecting both women and men, but to some degree affecting them in different ways.[15]

The same may also be said of European events, such as the Renaissance and the First World War. Both are of historical importance to women and men, and both affected women and men in different ways.[16] So, because of this gender difference, we will treat these events as important for other reasons than those presented in previous world histories. In contrast, the Renaissance had relatively little impact on the history of Asian and African women; therefore, choosing the Renaissance as a phenomenon worthy of discussion is a choice determined by a European perspective.

To concentrate on what are considered important innovative trends has an influence on which parts of the world will be given the most emphasis for any specific period. Thus, in volume one, Africa is featured as the birthplace of humankind, and Asia and the Middle Eastern areas are considered important as the earliest cultures organised around agrarian settlements, and therefore witnesses of significant changes in gender relations. For the period termed the 'Middle Ages' we have divided the world into four cultural areas – China/Japan, India, the Muslim world and the Christian world. For later periods the choice is more difficult, but we have found some justification in giving Europe a prominent place after 1500 in that *new* trends, such as global voyages of exploration and the instigation of new forms of aggressive contact between the continents, did eventually have decisive importance also for non-European women – and men. This eurocentrism seems even more justifiable when we come to the eighteenth and nineteenth centuries. The ideas of gender expressed during the period of Enlightenment were vital for reorganising gender relations not only during the French Revolution and for subsequent European women's history, but also because they manifested themselves during the formation of the United States of America. These ideas also assumed importance for aspects of Asian and Middle Eastern women's resistance to imperialism. The establishment of a capitalist industrial economy also affected women's lives first in Europe, later in other parts of the world, and it therefore serves as another justification for eurocentrism. So does the European – and North American – economic and military expansion during the period of imperialism from the late nineteenth century until the middle of the twentieth century.

In the fifth and final volume all these events are studied as they affect women outside Europe and the United States. We think it is important to discuss questions such as to what degree changes in women's lives in Asia, Africa and Latin America during the nineteenth and twentieth centuries, and especially during the past four or five decades, were sparked off by the influence of western ideas and imperialist expansion or by the working out of national historical traditions and developments. It is easy, for instance, to fall into the trap of seeing the growth of women's organisations in India, as well as the changes in Indian women's legal position and their growing opportunities for education during the nineteenth and early twentieth centuries, as a result of British influence, forgetting or obscuring that Indian decisions could have been motivated by distinctively Indian historical traditions. Some Indian researchers maintain that Indian women's access to higher education and to jobs in the civil administration should not be seen as a result of British colonial rule and contact with British feminism, but rather as a result of the transition from a caste system with group mobility to a class system with individual mobility. This transition marks a transformation in the ways women were used to indicate social status, from an insistence that women observe purdah to an insistence that they be educated, and in some cases even gainfully employed.[17] What should be studied in such a case is when and why the two channels of innovation – the British and the Indian – run parallel, supporting each other, and when and why they result in conflicts.

The final volume will also deal with the different impacts on women and men of the current worldwide conflicts resulting from economic and technological inequalities, and from political problems being addressed by raw military power, the problems brought about by the many waves of refugees, and finally with the problems of global pollution and the human capacity to exhaust natural resources.

We find that one way to avoid an overly eurocentric approach is to learn as much as possible from historians of women who have written about their own cultures. This helps us to situate various phenomena in the suitable cultural context. A striking example may be a discussion on *sati*, the Indian traditional practice that insists on a widow's dying on the funeral pyre of her deceased husband.[18] An outsider to this tradition may with good reason concentrate on the horror and utter disregard for female lives it embodies. But it is important to recognise that this would also be the case with most narratives written by women familiar with the cultural setting of *sati*. Nevertheless, we cannot overlook what was revealed by comments from an Indian historian, to the effect that some instances of *sati* give witness to a frame of mind that exemplifies women's strength, individuality and even revolt, which served to inspire other Indian women.

Another problematic example is how we should write of such a phenomenon as clitoridectomy and other forms of female circumcision in African and Muslim cultures, at once understanding and analysing how this rite functions in the culture in question, and yet acknowledging that we view it as a maltreatment of female bodies and consider the abolition of such rites an important amelioration of women's condition.[19]

Highlighting divisions of opinion within the cultures in question as to the legitimation of such traditions thereby becomes important, and it may be wise to remind ourselves as well as our readers that understanding why and how something happened is not the same as accepting it uncritically. Understanding does not necessarily imply agreement.

These are but two examples of practices in certain cultures that are extremely difficult to treat in a perspective of cross-cultural understanding. Such phenomena may mirror fundamentally different values from the values prevalent in the culture of the researcher.

Whereas the European-North American civilisation (since at least the seventeenth century) has increasingly viewed individuals as the basic unit of society, individual self-fulfilment and self-determination, and individual responsibility as the goal of social developments, many other cultures value group solidarity, family and kinship solidarity, collective responsibility and collective realisation of goals as fundamental. Whereas European culture has increasingly let the state take over responsibility for individual members of society who are unable to provide for or take care of themselves, other cultures still leave this responsiblity to family and kinship networks, relying on their sense of collective responsibility and group solidarity.

To a European eye, individual self-determination has been one of the important gains, enabling first men, and later women, to free themselves of dependence on the family, and eventually to attain goals such as education, economic independence and some measure of political influence. This has been possible in part because state and municipality have to some degree taken over responsibilities that used to be family responsibilities, including childcare, and care of the sick and the aged.

The historian may ask whether individual self-determination is possible by means of other roads than individualisation, whether for example it is possible within a system of collective and group solidarity. The historian may also ask whether group solidarity has to build exclusively on family and kinship. Is it not solidarity at the state level, the solidarity of economically self-sufficient groups with less privileged groups that forms the principle of the modern welfare state, and enables women to acquire and exercise more autonomy?

The problems of different culturally-determined basic values and of eurocentrism are important problems, but they reflect a more general problem that is common to all historians: the problem of understanding and analysing the lives of people very different from ourselves. Although the problem of cross-cultural understanding looms large in a world history, we know, for instance, that the same issues have been discussed within North American women's history. Outspoken criticism from Afro-American women has pointed to the fact that white historians of women have tended to ignore black women's history.[20] Similarly, western European and American researchers working with the post-war history of women from socialist countries of eastern Europe have in some instances – probably correctly – stressed the double burden of work and family responsibility for women in these countries. But they may have overlooked the importance of women's paid work for changing women's self-perception, for making them aware of their capabilities and providing them with a sense of self-reliance that has given them more autonomy and respect, in their public as in their private lives.[21] In all such cases, for the historian to transgress her own limited cultural and class background it is necessary to openly acknowledge this background, and then to make efforts to study and to try to understand different cultures and social groups.

Finally, it is important to stress that if the priority given in the choice of problems to be researched may often be biased by the cultural background of the researcher, the ensuing analysis does not necessarily suffer from the existence of a certain distance between the researcher herself and the culture studied. The advantage of 'coming from outside' may in some instances bring into clearer focus the distinctive patterns of behaviour and structures of gender interaction, a focus that may elude a person who is identifying intimately with the culture studied.[22]

Establishing a dialogue between researchers of different cultural backgrounds may in fact be the best way of reaching a cross-cultural agreement on how to analyse and explain gender inequalities in various cultures. It is at this point that contact and exchange of ideas between historians of different cultures becomes important. The International Federation for Research in Women's History may offer an important channel for facilitating better research in global women's history.

NOTES

1. Friedrich Engels, *The Origin of the Family, Private Property and the State*, 1st ed. 1884, translated by Ernest Untermann (Chicago: C.H. Kerr and Company, 1902). See Rosemary Agonito, *History of Ideas on Women: A Source Book* (New York: Paragon Books, 1977), pp. 271-88.

2. See Elise Boulding, *The Underside of History: A View of Women through Time* (Boulder: Westview Press, 1976), which although containing a broad chapter on non-European women, focuses on 'western women'; Marilyn French, *Beyond Power: On Women, Men and Morals* (London: Abacus, Sphere Books Ltd., 1985), the central question of which concerns the moral danger inherent in a patriarchal system and the need for alternative feminine values; Rosalind Miles, *The Women's History of the World* (London: Penguin Group, 1988), which despite its

title concentrates on western women; Bonnie S. Anderson and Judith P. Zinsser, *A History of Their Own: Women in Europe from Prehistory to the Present*, 2 vols. (New York: Harper & Row Publishers, 1988); Cheryl Johnson-Odim and Margaret Strobel (eds.), *Restoring Women to History: Teaching Packets for Integrating Women's History into Courses on Africa, Asia, Latin America, the Caribbean and the Middle East* (Bloomington, Indiana: Organization of American Historians, 1988); see also Cheryl Johnson-Odim and Margaret Strobel, 'Conceptualizing the History of Women in Africa, Asia, Latin America and the Caribbean, and the Middle East', and reviews by Marilyn R. Waldman, Claire Robertson, Nupur Chaudhuri, June E. Hahner, and Leila Ahmud in *Journal of Women's History*, 1, no. 1 (Spring 1989), pp. 31-62 and pp. 115-33.

   3. This five-volume history will appear in Danish, Norwegian and Swedish in 1991-1992. (Publishers: J. W. Cappelens Forlag A.s., Oslo; Politikens Forlag A.s., Copenhagen. The Swedish publisher is not yet decided.) The authors include Eva Maria Lassen and Grethe Jacobsen, Nanna Damsholt and Bente Rosenbeck, all University of Copenhagen, Sølvi Sogner and Kari Vogt, University of Oslo, Sverre Bagge, Ida Blom and Jørgen Christian Meyer, University of Bergen, and Rita Liljestrøm, University of Gothenburg.

   The present article is based on the personal thoughts and reflections of the general editor, Ida Blom.

   4. The question of the value of theories of patriarchy may be seen clearly by juxtaposing Gerda Lerner, *The Creation of Patriarchy* (New York: Oxford University Press, 1986) and Karin Hausen, 'Vom Nutzen und Nachteil eines Konzepts für Frauengeschichte und Frauenpolitik [On the Advantages and Drawbacks of a Concept Applied to Women's History and Women's Politics]', *Journal für Geschichte*, no. 5 (September/October 1986), pp. 12-21 and 58. See also Ida Blom, 'Patriarkatsteorier i kvinnehistorisk forskning [Theories of Patriarchy in Research on Women's History]', *Nytt om Kvinneforskning* 2 (1987), pp. 7-15.

   5. On footbinding, see, for instance, Florence Ayscough, *Chinese Women: Yesterday and Today* (New York: Houghton Mifflin, 1937), p. 28; Helen Snow Foster, *Women in Modern China* (The Hague: Mouton, 1967), pp. 18-19; Harald Bøckman, 'Kvinneliv i det gamle Kina [Women's Lives in Traditional China]' and Marina Thorborg, 'Kvinneliv i Kina fra 1800 til i dag [Women's Lives in China from 1800 until Today]', in Kari Vogt, Karin Gundersen, and Sissel Lie (eds.), *Orientens kvinner. Kvinnenes kulturhistorie*, 3 (Oslo: Universitetsforlaget, 1988), pp. 18-19, 41-42 and 44.

   On harem and purdah, see Elisabeth Cooper, *The Harim and the Purdah: Studies of Oriental Women* (New York: Century, 1915); Hannah Papanek, 'Purdah in Pakistan: Seclusion and Modern Occupations for Women', *Journal of Marriage and the Family*, 33 (1971), pp. 517-30. Afaf Lutfi al-Sayyid Marsot, 'The Revolutionary Gentlewomen in Egypt', in Lois Beck and Nikki Keddie (eds.), *Women in the Muslim World* (Cambridge, Mass.: Harvard University Press, 1978); Saphinaz-Amal Naguib, 'Harem', in Vogt, Gundersen, and Lie, *Orientens kvinner*, pp. 225-29.

   On western women and limited mobility, see, for instance, Karin Hausen, 'Frauenräume [Women's Spaces]', in *Journal für Geschichte*, no 2 (March-April 1985), pp. 12-15; and Karin Hausen, 'Offentlichkeit und Privatheit. Gesellschaftspolitische Konstruktionen und die Geschichte der

Geschlechterbeziehungen [The Public and the Private: Socio-political Constructions and the History of Gender Relations]', in *Journal für Geschichte*, no. 1 (February 1989), pp. 16-25. Leonore Davidoff and Catherine Hall, *Family Fortunes: Men and Women of the English Middle Class 1780-1850* (London: Hutchinson, 1987) shows very clearly the importance of religion and domesticity to middle-class identity, discussing the question of mobility and gender explicitly on pp. 403-5. For an early contribution to the discussion on the concept of 'domesticity', see Nancy F. Cott, *The Bonds of Womanhood: 'Women's Sphere' in New England, 1780-1835* (New Haven: Yale University Press, 1977).

6. Evelyn Fox Keller, 'Holding the Center of Feminist Theory', *Women's Studies International Forum*, 12, no. 3 (1989), pp. 313-18.

7. Gisela Bock, 'Women's History and Gender History: Aspects of an International Debate', *Gender & History*, 1, no. 1 (Spring 1989), pp. 7-30.

8. Cécile Dauphin, Arlette Farge, Geneviève Fraisse, Christiane Klapisch-Zuber, Rose-Marie Lagrave, Michelle Perrot, Pierrette Pezerat, Yannick Ripa, Pauline Schmitt-Pantel and Danièle Voldman, 'Culture et pouvoir des femmes: Essai d'historiographie', *Annales:e.s.c.*, 41, no. 2 (mars-avril 1986), pp. 271-93, translated into English in *Journal of Women's History*, 1, no. 1 (Spring 1989), and appearing as Chapter 6 in this collection. The comments by Karen Offen, Nell Irvin Painter, Hilda L. Smith, and Lois W. Banner (published in the same issue of *Journal of Women's History*) suggest the problems involved in transferring theories and models developed in a specific philosophical tradition and within a specific historical tradition to other and different settings. That may however, also reveal fundamental theoretical differences among historians.

9. Davidoff and Hall, *Family Fortunes*.

10. Ida Blom, 'Women's Politics and Women in Politics in Norway since the End of the Nineteenth Century', *Scandinavian Journal of History*, 12, no. 1 (1987), pp. 17-33. Reprinted in S. Jay Kleinberg (ed.), *Retrieving Women's History: Changing Perceptions of the Role of Women in Politics and Society* (Oxford: Berg/Unesco Comparative Studies, 1988), pp. 254-77.

11. Joan W. Scott, 'Gender: A Useful Category of Historical Analysis', *American Historical Review*, 91, no. 5, (December 1986); reprinted in Joan W. Scott, *Gender and the Politics of History* (New York: Columbia University Press, 1988), pp. 28 -50. For the Norwegian/Swedish debate see Ottar Dahl, '"Kvinnehistorie" – kategorihistorie eller samfunnshistorie? ["Women's History" – History of a Category or History of Society?]', (Norsk) *Historisk Tidskrift*, 64, no. 3 (1985), pp. 262-74; Ida Blom, 'Kvinnehistorie – ledd i historieforskningen og ledd i kvinneforskningen [Women's History – Part of Historical Research and Part of Feminist Research]', (Norsk) *Historisk Tidsskrift*, 64, no. 4 (1985), pp. 414-24; Eva Österberg, 'Några krummelurer till Ottar Dahls inlägg om kvinnohistoria [Some Tentative Objections to Ottar Dahl's Article on Women's History]', (Norsk) *Historisk Tidsskrift*, 64, no. 4 (1985), pp. 425-28; Ottar Dahl, 'Kvinnehistorie [Women's History]', (Norsk) *Historisk Tidskrift*, 65, no. 1 (1986); and Gro Hagemann, 'Kvinnehistorie – faglig blindspor eller fruktbar disiplin? [Women's History – an Impasse or a Fruitful Discipline?]', (Norsk) *Historisk Tidsskrift*, 65, no. 3 (1986), pp. 343-60.

12. Yvonne Hirdman, 'Makt og kön, [Power and Gender]', in Olof Petersson (ed.), *Maktbegrepet* (Stockholm: Carlsson Bokförlag, 1987), pp. 188-206.

13. Blom, 'Patriarkatsteorier....'

14. Grethe Jacobsen, unpublished manuscript for volume 3 of the Women's History from the Earliest Times to the Present Day (forthcoming); Lena Gemzöe, Tove Holmqvist, Don Kulick, Britt Marite Thurén, and Prudence Woodford-Berge, 'Sex, genus och makt i antropologiskt perspektiv [Sex, Gender and Power in an Anthropological Perspective]', *Kvinnovetenskaplig Tidskrift*, 1 (1989), pp. 44-52, in which the authors, Swedish anthropologists, build partly on Colin M. Turnbull, 'The Ritualization of Potential Conflict Between the Sexes Among the Mbuti', in Eleanor Leacock and Richard Lee (eds.), *Politics and History in Band Societies* (Cambridge: Cambridge University Press, 1982).

15. Richard J. Evans, *The Feminists: Women's Emancipation Movements in Europe, America and Australasia 1840 – 1920* (London: Croom Helm, 1977), although rightly criticised for inaccuracies, discusses the importance of nationalism to women's suffrage. See Kumari Jayawardena, *Feminism and Nationalism in the Third World* (London: Zed Books Ltd., New Delhi: Kali for Women, 1986), and Odim and Strobel (eds.), *Restoring Women to History...*, for a number of examples of how national independence affected women and men in different ways. Another example is to be found in Onu Kazuko, *Chinese Women in a Century of Revolution, 1850 – 1950* (Stanford: Stanford University Press, 1989), 2nd edition, edited by Joshua A. Fogel and Susan Mann. The 1st edition (Tokyo: Heibonsha Ltd., Publishers, 1978) was published in Japanese.

16. See, for example, Joan Kelly, 'Did Women Have a Renaissance?', in Renate Bridenthal and Claudia Koonz (eds.), *Becoming Visible: Women in European History* (Boston: Houghton Mifflin Company, 1st edition, 1977), republished in the 2nd edition, 1987. See also Diana Condell and Jean Liddiard, *Working for Victory? Images of Women in the First World War 1914-1918* (London: Routledge and Kegan Paul Ltd., 1987); Gail Braybon and Penny Summerfield, *Out of the Cage: Women's Experiences in Two World Wars* (London and New York: Pandora Press, 1987); Margaret Randolph Higonnet et al. (eds.), *Behind the Lines. Gender and the Two World Wars* (New Haven: Yale University Press, 1987); and Sandra M. Gilbert, 'Soldier's Heart: Literary Men, Literary Women and the Great War', in Marilyn J. Boxer and Jean H. Quataert (eds.), *Connecting Spheres: Women in the Western World, 1500 to the Present* (New York and Oxford: Oxford University Press, 1987), pp. 232-45.

17. Jayawardena, *Feminism and Nationalism*, pp. 73-108; Joanne Liddle and Rama Joshi, *Daughters of Independence: Gender, Caste and Class in India* (London: Zed Books Ltd., 1986).

18. Dorothy K. Stein, 'Women to Burn: Suttee as a Normative Institution', and Vina Mazumdar, 'Comment on Suttee', in *Signs*, 4, no. 2 (Winter 1978), pp. 253-73.

19. Anne Raulin, *Femme en Cause. Mutilations sexuelles des fillettes africaines en France aujourd'hui* (Paris: Collection Recherches, Centre Fédéral, 1987).

20. One of the latest expressions of this situation may be found in Evelyn Brooks Higginbotham, 'Beyond the Sound of Silence: Afro-American Women's History', *Gender & History*, 1, no. 1 (Spring 1989), pp. 60-67.

21. Maria-Barbara Watson-Franke, ' "I Am Somebody!" – Women's Changing Sense of Self in the German Democratic Republic', in Boxer and Quataert (eds.), *Connecting Spheres*, pp. 256-66.

22. For an early discussion of these problems as they were perceived by anthropologists and researchers of comparative politics, see Hanna Papanek, 'Women in South and Southeast Asia: Issues and Research', *Signs*, 1, no.1 (Autumn 1975), pp. 193-214, and Peter H. Merkl, 'The Study of Women in Comparative Politics – Reflections on a Conference', *Signs*, 1, no. 3, part 1 (Spring 1976), pp. 749-56.

PART TWO

THE STATE OF THE ART IN WOMEN'S HISTORY

8

Writing the History of Australian Women

Patricia Grimshaw

Australia is a continent with an ancient past, the history of which has been sustained through legends, traditions and more recently the craft of archaeologists and anthropologists. Its very recent history, since the occupation of Aboriginal land by Europeans commenced in 1788, has been the province of historians who shifted over years from viewing Australia as a segment of Britain's empire to interpreting its story as that of a significant, if admittedly small, independent country. Women, as has been noted elsewhere, were strangely absent from these tales of nation building. When women's history emerged in the early 1970s, it stood in an adversarial position to the accounts of mainstream historians. In the 1980s the field of women's history has become more diverse in methodological approaches and in perceptions. It remains, however, for the most part a separate development intellectually, respected yet not integrated into the central debates. The course of women's history needs to be understood in the context of the development of Australian historiography as a whole.

Women's history emerged as a forceful voice in Australia in the wake of the women's liberation movement, which first organised around the year 1969 in Sydney and Melbourne and spread rapidly through the other urban centres of the country. The anti-Vietnam war movement had been strong in Australia, and intensified when conscripts were sent into the fighting. The New Left, and campus groups such as Students for a Democratic Society, spearheaded a sharp reappraisal of western capitalist societies, and gave their support to a range of liberationist groups, including those articulating anger about racism and the oppression of Aborigines. It was in this context of challenge and dissent, and particularly in the anti-war movement, that women began questioning their own situations as Australian women in relation to Australian men. Accounts of the activities of American radical feminists reacting against sexist

151

behaviour and attitudes in left-wing groups reached Australia, and struck a ready, sympathetic chord among their Australian counterparts. 'Only the Chains Have Changed', proclaimed the leaflet distributed at an anti-war march in Sydney in December 1969, inviting women to a separate meeting to discuss oppression nearer at home than the paddy fields of Vietnam or the towers of Wall Street.

Women began meeting in women-only groups, excited and elated at the sudden insight many experienced for the first time as they read Kate Millett's *Sexual Politics* (1970), Shulamith Firestone's *The Dialectic of Sex* (1970) and Juliet Mitchell's *Woman's Estate* (1971). Most of these early participants in the women's liberation movement were young, students or ex-students, often single and childless, at a stage of life where they could most freely entertain radical critiques of the structures of their society, not just of the underpinnings of class, but of the underpinnings of the gender order. The energy, intelligence and commitment of these first revolutionary activists quickly made an impact on the media, and their assault on accepted conventions received a high, if not always sympathetic, profile. The women's liberation movement was followed in 1972 by a second, more reformist group, the Women's Electoral Lobby, which adopted methods of political agitation centred on pressuring politicians and government agencies. The WEL group shared, however, an attachment to the trenchant critique of gender emerging from the socialist liberationist women.[1]

It was the activists of the women's movement who pioneered the writing of the history of Australian women in terms recognisable by, if not acceptable to, academic historians. Women's history did not come from inside the academy. Its first practitioners were for the most part tertiary educated, part of the generation which gained increased access to universities in the affluent fifties and sixties, but without established positions in academic life; an occasional, temporary tutor constituted the exception. A few tenured female academic historians, left-wingers, eventually responded to this changing paradigm about Australian women, but their number was small: most of the few women in academe were clustered in the temporary, low-waged nether end of the academic hierarchy. The first writing of the history of women emerged in small journals and magazines established by the women's movement, *Refractory Girl*, *Hecate*, *Mejane*, *Scarlet Woman*, among others. The work was written by feminists to be read by feminists. It undertook a massive revision of Australian history in the light of feminist theory.

It was possibly only this sharp intellectual thrust from outside the university that could have made an initial impact on the smug mainstream belief that the writing of Australian history to that date had been about capturing the truly significant events and trends that led to the Australian people – presumably women included – becoming what they were in the modern age. Ann Curthoys, a founder of women's liberation in Sydney, a postgraduate student in history and a socialist, made the first attempt to prick this bubble of complacency. In an article in the left-wing journal *Arena* written in 1970, Ann Curthoys pointed out that:

> Women do not appear in most Australian histories in any important way. The nature and effect of the family in Australian society is not discussed. Sexual habits and beliefs have not been studied, nor have the rate and reasons for the entry of women into the work force.

Her challenge was followed a few years later by a similar broadside from another prominent Sydney liberationist (until recently editor of the American *Ms* magazine), Anne Summers:

> Most Australian history works are so closed, so suffocating, so self-assured in their preoccupation with the activities of men that such questions could not even occur to the reader. To read them is to be lulled into the false assumption that women did not even exist.[2]

The reasons for the invisibility of women in academic history have been well-rehearsed, and are applicable to Australian historiography. Historians never have nor could attempt to record everything that occurred in a nation's past. On the contrary, historians have been forced to select certain features of past life to describe and analyse, and those features have usually been those affairs that 'common sense' dictated as important: the major economic and political changes that appeared to shape future development, the country's dramatic events, and the figures (usually men) who were the chief actors in these dramas. The history of social life outside the public sphere – and this included most women – was deemed an inherently trivial pursuit left for amateurs. As sceptics about women's history claim, historians have looked where the power to make change resides, and it is, as one male historian (J.H. Hexter) has asserted, through no conspiracy of the historians that 'the College of Cardinals, the Consistory of Geneva, the Parliament of England, the Faculty of the Sorbonne, the Directorate of the Bank of England and the expeditions of Columbus, Vasco da Gama and Drake have been pretty much stag affairs'.[3]

Yet, on the face of it, a distant and casual observer could well have thought that the situation would work out somewhat differently in Australia. Here was a country which lacked a solid, entrenched landed aristocracy and high bourgeoisie in the pioneering days of the nineteenth century, and which celebrated the egalitarian, democratic nature of its urbanised, industrialising society in the twentieth. Women, Aboriginal and European, were a sizeable proportion of the population from the mid-nineteenth century and equalled men in numbers through the twentieth; Anglo-Australian women had the vote in two colonies, South Australia and Western Australia, since 1894 and 1899 respectively, and all women could vote in the federated Commonwealth of Australia since 1902; women's civil status in law was liberalised ahead of women in Britain and Ireland, whence most white Australian women, or their parents, had come. Aborigines, women and men, were, however, not enfranchised until 1967.

Yet neither the earlier liberal historians who portrayed Australia as an improved version of enlightened British society, nor the left-wing post World War II historians who emphasised the emergence of an egalitarian and democratic society from indigenous features of the Australian environment, found reason to perceive women as a significant category for analysis, or as agents in the creation of the Australia they presented. For behind the façade of important events that are presented as the formative issues in a country's past lies the need of a society to understand itself through a reading of its history. Just as an understanding of personal history is vital to an individual's sense of social identity, so it is to a society's establishment of a cultural tradition. While that reading will vary in detail according to the political predilections of the writer, the construction of history is rooted in the present. And when Australian historians, almost exclusively men, asked the key question, namely, what were the influential factors which turned a British imperial outpost into a separate nation, it was essentially the creation of a distinctively male sense of national identity that preoccupied them. What Australian women were like, what had produced their characteristic qualities (if such existed), and how this process related to the influences shaping the lives of Australian men, were questions that were simply not posed.[4]

It would be difficult to point to a national historical tradition which more clearly represented a celebration of white male achievement. There is astonishingly little about women in Australian historical works written before the 1970s. The earliest histories from the turn of the century presented the history of Australia as a tale of exciting progress: the taking of a continent, the establishment of an outpost of British civilisation, the federation of colonies into a promising new state. Such historians began a process of myth-making, of aligning a reading of the past with the search of men of their generation for a sense of identity as Australians, that has had a powerful influence on Australian history for much of this century. Women as a whole (unlike rabbits, sheep and horses) were not discussed, except by virtue of the social effects of their absence: the distorted sex ratio of the colonies, for example, and its effects on population increase. Only a very few remarkable women surfaced when, by chance, they fitted this narrative.

In the post-World War II period an alternative version of Australian history was posed by a group of historians (the so-called 'radical nationalist' school) in which boundary riders, shearers, convicts, labourers and unionists replaced governors, entrepreneurs and prime ministers as the central figures of the tale, but despite these historians' left-wing egalitarianism, it was the role of men that continued to be emphasised. Rather than stressing the flowering of middle-class English liberalism on Britain's antipodean frontier, the radical nationalists focused on the conjunction of the local physical environment and the needs of (white) working men. In Russel Ward's *The Australian Legend*, which appeared in 1958 and became a seminal text in Australian history, the stereotypical Australian was described as:

> a practical man [*sic*], rough and ready in his manners and quick to decry any appearance of affectation in others. He is a great improviser . . . He swears hard and consistently, gambles heavily, and often, and drinks deeply on occasion.

Not only did Ward not consider whether the stereotypical Australian might be female, but he proceeded to discuss the origin of this myth in the pressures on men to bond together, to develop 'mateship', on the womanless Australian frontier. Hence historically women were virtually obliterated from the core of the narrative. (When the New Left rebuttal of the radical nationalists was presented by Humphrey McQueen in *The New Britannia* in 1970, the effects of this paradigm were reflected in the unusual index entry: 'women, ignored, page 13'). The radical nationalist version of Australian history constituted the reading of their country's past to which most of the women who entered the women's liberation movement were previously attached: it was radical, left-wing, giving agency to the working class, and the absence of women in the texts was so ordinary as to go initially unremarked, by them as by anyone else.[5]

What was more unusual by 1970, compared with northern historiographies, was the existence of little serious social history written in Australia in academic circles. It was within studies of social history and historical demography that the lives of women were beginning to be addressed in most western countries, in the United States and Europe. It is true that in this genre women's experiences were often treated in a descriptive manner, and certainly key feminist questions about power and status were generally absent, but through such studies women were being accorded at least some recognition. The sole significant monograph of this nature was entitled (somewhat unpromisingly) *Men of Yesterday: A Social History of the Western District of Victoria, 1834-1890*, written by Margaret Kiddle, a senior tutor in the History Department at the University of Melbourne, and published in 1960, two years after her premature death. Margaret Kiddle had been a student in the History Department with a number of male students who subsequently rose to professorial level in Australian universities: her own contribution, a biography of Caroline Chisholm published in 1950, as well as this study of the squatting experience in a rich pastoral district of Victoria, rivalled anything her male contemporaries produced. The few women who had attained lecturing positions during the twentieth century had seldom shown any self-consciousness about their gender, or about gender in history. Margaret Kiddle was an exception, and although she lacked a theoretical context for discussing women's lives, she recorded the experience of squatters' wives and daughters in a style unusual in Australian historiography. Even in the 1950s Australian history (seen as new, raw and unsophisticated) was barely admitted to the curriculum in the country's tertiary institutions, which emphasised British and European traditions. It was not surprising that a serious study of social life was slow to emerge amidst such an intellectual climate.[6]

There had in fact existed a muted voice in Australian history, established outside of the academy, of women writing about and for women, that reached back to the early twentieth century. It was a tradition that resembles Natalie Zemon Davis's category of 'women worthies': that is, of largely eulogistic biographical studies of individual women (or groups of women in organisations in the Australian instance) divorced from their broader social and political context. Davis suggests that in Europe these biographies had a polemical purpose, 'to provide exemplars, to argue from what some women had done to what women could do, if given the chance and education'. One such Australian book published in 1939 was actually entitled *Certain Worthy Women*. The author, E. Marie Irvine, admitted that her central characters were not, in any sense, 'heroines', but the manner in which they overcame the trials of a new country was surely heroic. They were 'representative figures and worthy in the true sense of the word'. The anniversaries of the foundation of states and the Commonwealth of Australia, centenaries and sesquicentenaries, regularly saw the publication of such collections of biographies, put together by women who knew that the activities of men were sure to dominate the official accounts – as, indeed, occurred.[7]

These women writers essentially said that women certainly contributed to the creation of Australia, and that all Australian women should feel justly proud of pioneer women's efforts, of which later

Australian women were beneficiaries. There was modesty about their claims, however, for these women writers knew their place. As Norman MacKenzie, editor of the *New Statesman*, wrote in his 1962 study, *Women in Australia* (commissioned by the Social Science Research Council of Australia), it was scarcely surprising that we knew so little about women in Australia's early years, 'for few among this anonymous regiment reached officer rank'. One or two with unusual gifts or fortunate circumstances could break through the barriers into public life. 'The majority had to face more immediate problems in the domestic world to which both custom and necessity confined them'. Concentrating on 'women worthies' was not going to suffice to undermine a canon of historical relevance that MacKenzie's comment so graphically illustrated. In the post-war period, a few such women writers, Alexandra Hasluck, Mary Durack and Marnie Bassett in particular, wrote studies of female pioneers that began to supersede some of the limitations of the older work, but there was scant recognition of any of these publications within the academy.[8]

The feminist writers of the 1970s had none of the humility of these earlier women writers, and no such notion of relevance as evidenced by MacKenzie. With a conviction and energy born of political commitment, and a security in their skills and competency derived from educational opportunities, they proceeded to forge an interpretation of the life experiences of Australian women, past and present, that stood in stark and hostile contrast to the prevailing models. Other members of the New Left were engaged in a sharp reappraisal of Australia's past, describing the majority of nineteenth-century immigrants as petit-bourgeois, and castigating historians for the omission of racism, of a story of Australia told from an Aboriginal perspective. The radical feminists had their own new insights to explore, and it was an alternative version, a female-centred version, of the radical nationalist tradition that first appeared. This women's history was explicitly part of a current political debate in Australia as well as a debate about historical experience. The first writing appeared in advance of intensive archival research on sources generated by women themselves. The most important general histories were Anne Summers' *Damned Whores and God's Police: The Colonisation of Women in Australia*, and Miriam Dixson's *The Real Matilda: Women and Identity in Australia 1788 to 1975*, which appeared within months of each other in the mid-seventies. In some senses, they accepted the general thrust of the radical nationalist school – namely, that conditions in Australia had been conducive to improved life chances in an egalitarian context – but this, they claimed, applied only to men. The very same conditions offered a life of alienation and oppression for women. Miriam Dixson pictured male immigrants to Australia imbued with denigratory attitudes towards women

common among the Irish and English poor, reaching a country where the
sexual exploitation of female convicts and the harsh conditions for
pioneering women served only to perpetuate sexist oppression. Summers,
too, portrayed convictism as sexually exploitative, and the life of the bush
wife as isolated and demoralising, while it may indeed have promoted
bonding for the more mobile males. As settled urban life developed,
Summers saw women controlled by the manipulation of two dominant
female stereotypes, 'damned whore' and 'God's police', labelled as deviant
outcasts where they were not loyal upholders of a conventional morality
deeply restrictive of female autonomy. Women would be admitted
cautiously to participation in public life, but only if they acceded to
definitions of female behaviour that accorded with an inferior status for
their sex.[9]

This characterisation of Australian history was a far cry from that
male story of communitarian progress: a far cry too, of course, from that
cherished female myth of the pioneer woman. Summers' and Dixson's
works were widely read, sold very well and remain in print. They were
extremely influential in establishing the tone and style of women's history
in the country. American historians of women were simultaneously bent
on establishing the importance of women in all the events and social
transformations of their history: colonial times, the Revolution,
industrialisation, antebellum reform, the Civil War, the Progressive period.
Australian historians of women, by contrast, set out to demonstrate, not
women's agency in given situations, but the multifarious ways in which
they were oppressed, or granted apparent influence only in order to
oppress others. The work of the American historians could more readily
be accepted into their country's mainstream history: the new Australian
women's history stood in a hostile relation to mainstream accounts. How
could an historian stress boldly the egalitarian thrust of Australian history,
only to proceed to suggest that it did not hold up for exactly half the
population? Historical integration was clearly not feasible. What the radical
feminist model certainly did reflect was the genuine anger of women's
liberationists in the seventies at the pervasive social denigration of women,
even if it often occurred in subtle ways that others (including many
women) shrugged off as negligible, or fanciful.

Other significant studies of working women appeared alongside
those of Dixson and Summers: Beverley Kingston's *My Wife, My Daughter
and Poor Mary Ann: Women and Work in Australia*; Edna Ryan and
Anne Conlon's *Gentle Invaders: Australian Women At Work 1788-
1974*; and a collection edited by Ann Curthoys, Susan Eade (Magarey),
and Peter Spearritt, *Women At Work*, as well as the interdisciplinary
collection, *The Other Half: Women in Australian Society*, edited by Jan
Mercer, a founder of the Women's Electoral Lobby. *Women At Work* was

a compilation put together from articles already published in the journal *Labour History*, which had been swift to respond to the feminist initiative historically, as it continued to do through the eighties. (The radical feminist historians, while of the left, were challenging the left theoretically and politically; nevertheless, it was from men of the left that their main support came.) Another important initiative was afoot headed by Kay Daniels, an historian from Tasmania, whose ideas have proved highly influential for feminist scholars. With co-workers, she compiled a listing of sources of research in women's history from the holdings of the country's principal archives, published under the title *Women in Australia: An Annotated Guide to Records*. This proved the first of a series of such finding guides. A common rejoinder to feminist complaints about the invisibility of women in history had been the plea that sources to research women's lives did not exist. Kay Daniels' publication showed clearly that, while much of importance may never have been written down, and much had been destroyed, nevertheless a very considerable body of sources was freely available in accessible locations. It proved a valuable stimulus to research.[10]

Kay Daniels' introduction was also influential: the aim of women's history, she wrote, should be the integration of women into the fabric of the country's past, not a separate, unrelated thread that might be ignored by those uninterested in women's lives. A few years later, reviewing women's history of the seventies in a collection entitled *New History*, Daniels made a plea for greater attention to a new social history, to 'a reconstruction of life from below in the context of an analysis of basic social relationships'. Only this way, she believed, would the historical questions which women's historians raised be adequately answered. Dixson, Summers and Kingston, she suggested, shared problems in writing with other Australian historians: 'a narrow unimaginative methodology, a tradition of using a limited range of sources, an inadequate conceptual framework'. Daniels, trained in British history, clearly found Australian historiography thin in texture by comparison. Yet, to a certain extent, the intensive development of an indigenous Australian historiography in the fifties, sixties and seventies had been dependent on a determination to discover distinctive qualities about Australian historical transformations by looking inwards. The introversion of Australian historiography – and that included the new women's history – was an integral part of its originality and vitality.[11]

As recently as 1986 Donald Denoon, author of a comparative study of British settler societies, was still complaining that 'Australian historians usually write for a restricted, knowledgeable, Australian audience. They eschew those general terms and general themes which would make their ideas and evidence more widely accessible. Whatever its

applicability to the wider field of Australian historiography, historians of
women during the eighties were decidedly showing the impact of major
developments in the discipline, including cultural history, structuralism and
poststructuralism, particularly Michel Foucault's work. In addition, their
exploration of women's lives, while not necessarily explicitly comparative,
has reflected insights developed within other historiographical traditions.
The work of some American and British historians has been specially
important, among them Carroll Smith-Rosenberg, Nancy Cott, Mary Ryan,
Linda Gordon, Ellen DuBois, Joan Scott, Leonore Davidoff, Sally
Alexander and Barbara Taylor. While not losing the continuous thread of
radicalism derived from its origins in the early seventies, nor the stimulus
coming from outside the academy, the field of women's history has
become increasingly diverse. Daniels forecast in her *New History* essay
that the field would begin to diverge markedly into practitioners of the
political right and the left. On the contrary, the most explicit debate has
come from protagonists of socialist and radical feminisms. Ann Curthoys,
for one, expresses concern that concentrating on gender analysis has led
historians to lose sight of class issues; others have asserted the primacy of
gender. This has been essentially a debate conducted within the left. There
are historians who focus more exclusively on women's structural
disadvantages, while others by contrast attempt an analysis that gives more
credence to women in constructing their own worlds. Some emphasise
women's representation at a symbolic and ideological level, others the
material aspects of women's productive and reproductive experience. The
lines of debate, however, are not sharply drawn: the dividing line remains
in the eighties, as it was in the seventies, far more rigorously drawn
between enthusiasts for women's history, and those indifferent or hostile
to its claims.[12]

Perhaps one area of justifiable resentment in the area of women's
history, as in Australian historical debate more widely, has been the
treatment by historians of European origin of issues of race and ethnicity.
'White Australia has a black history', ran the graffiti in 1988, the
bicentennial year, the celebrations of which prompted a reappraisal of the
treatment of Aborigines both in current society and in historical texts. As
in other European and American contexts, barriers of language, culture
and historic oppression of blacks by whites have proved stumbling blocks
to a searching examination of intercultural relations in Australia, where the
numbers of Aborigines with tertiary qualifications are lamentably few, and
those few under great pressure to undertake tasks as activists in Aboriginal
policy making. Aboriginal and intercultural history are neglected areas
partly, too, because of demographic features of settlement. The majority
of the Aboriginal population, approximately 160,000 in all, live in the
northeast and west, the majority of the white population (sixteen million)

in the south-eastern cities, where white historians do not face racial issues at the immediate level of daily life. The anthropologist Diane Barwick, who contributed to the collection *Woman's Role in Aboriginal Society*, which appeared in the early days of the women's movement, produced work which embraced an historical dimension; Diane Bell, notably in *Daughters of the Dreaming*, wrote similarly. Among historians Lyndall Ryan and Ann McGrath have undertaken significant work. Aboriginal women, like women of European origin, have been more and more active in telling their own stories through autobiography and oral history, inside and outside an academic context. Further scholarly research in the area will, and must, be undertaken.[13]

The diversity of approaches to the history of women can be illustrated by a comparison of three major monographs, each of which appeared within a short space of time in the mid 1980s and dealt with white women during the first decades of the twentieth century: Jill Matthews' *Good and Mad Women: The Historical Construction of Femininity in Twentieth Century Australia*; Kerreen Reiger's *The Disenchantment of the Home: Modernising the Australian Family 1880-1940*; and Janet McCalman's *Struggletown: Public and Private Life in Richmond 1900-1965*. Each book was well reviewed and sold well. Each was different in methodological and theoretical approaches, yet they did not so much contradict each others' findings as stand separately, one appealing more than another to different readers and scholars of Australian history.

Jill Matthews in *Good and Mad Women* used a series of casenotes on women admitted to a psychiatric hospital to explore the normative standards of behaviour by which these women, designated deviant, were judged. Matthews built up a powerful case to display the rigidity of cultural constructs of femininity that sharply limited the autonomy of women, supposedly free and equal in terms of civil rights and meritocratic upward mobility. This was a study owing much to contemporary theorists such as Foucault, yet firmly anchored in the stream of radical feminism stretching back to Summers' other dichotomy, that of 'damned whores' and 'God's police'. Matthews, like Summers, had been part of the early women's liberation movement.[14]

Kerreen Reiger's *Disenchantment of the Home* also drew on the work of social theorists, such as Jacques Donzelot, along with socialist feminist theory, to explore women's lives historically, and she, too, displayed forcibly the outward pressures to which women, adult married women in particular, were subjected. Yet her study was focused differently, on the role of the state and the emerging ranks of professionals in restructuring Australian family lives on 'scientific' and 'efficient' lines. Reiger looked more closely than Matthews at the extent to which housewives, including working-class wives, received the messages from the professionals and made them part of their own world view, or not. She attempted to examine from a feminist perspective the construction of both outward social forces and inward cultural values to explain the character and pace of the highly important reorientation of ordinary women's lives in this century.[15]

Janet McCalman's work, *Struggletown*, stands more obviously in the tradition of social history as she explored intensively the women, along with the men, of an inner-urban, working-class industrial suburb of Melbourne. In terms of feminist theory the study is reticent: there is implicitly a strong advocacy for these working-class women, which is manifested through the selection of the questions explored and the findings displayed, although the work reflects a feminist basis in that the women's lives are generously and sympathetically explored, in marked contrast to so many local history studies in Australia. The difficult obstacles in the path of those working-class girls' and women's pursuit of health, education, jobs, resources and satisfactory human relationships, and their strategies for survival, are movingly portrayed. McCalman, who undertook extensive interviewing, gives due weight to the ways in which the women constructed their worlds and made sense of them – all this by contrast to the men's experiences, which she similarly presents. All three studies constitute constructive and illuminating work, an indication that in the decade since Summers and Dixson wrote, the field of women's history continued to pick up a strength and an intellectual force of no mean order.[16]

Because of its current diversity, it is difficult to categorise women's history neatly. Women's history has a debate, established by its first historians, to which to respond, modify or challenge. It faces the need to establish the contours of women's lives at the level of detailed research. It has to explore, continually, the task of placing issues relating to women in a position of importance in the country's historiography, while at the same time demonstrating that giving attention to women's concerns may indeed turn around the focus of mainstream debates. The following description provides at least some indication of preoccupations over the past decade in Australia.

A cluster of important books and articles attempt to throw fresh light on the lives of middle-class women in the nineteenth and early twentieth centuries, providing a women-centred analysis to set beside earlier models of social control exercised by affluent women over the working class. Susan Magarey has written an important full-length biography of the South Australian reformer Catherine Spence, entitled *Unbridling the Tongues of Women*, and there are now a number of interesting shorter studies of first-wave feminists, like those in Marilyn

Lake and Farley Kelly's collection *Double Time: Women in Victoria – 150 Years*. While there remains as yet no definitive study of nineteenth-century feminism, these short biographical studies take reformers' and feminists' activities in a direction more constructive that the seventies offered. Particularly, they trace the ways in which such women manipulated ideologies of femininity to find a legitimate place in public life, or to gain legal and civil emancipation for their sex. Marian Simms is one among several historians who have continued this story to look at women, mostly middle-class, in politics, inside and outside political parties, in the twentieth century. Educational historians have contributed generously to this area of understanding, not only in their studies of the education of girls, but in the history of women teachers, part of a renewed interest in women's professional work generally. Women writers, and women artists, have been the subjects of shorter or full-length studies, Drusilla Modjeska's and Janine Burke's perhaps the most interesting.[17]

Marilyn Lake has picked up on this revisionist portrayal of late nineteenth-century feminist and temperance reform to engage in the debate on the emergence of a distinctive national identity, proposing that the feminists, understandably, promoted a rival version of the acceptable Australian male to oppose the frontier version of freewheeling, free-drinking, anti-woman manhood. She continued this question with her investigation of the ideas of male supremacy sustained by such apparent unionist egalitarians as the socialist William Lane; to provide for, and simultaneously to dominate, a wife lay at the heart of notions of masculinity. Her two articles immediately attracted the attention of mainstream historians, since they addressed the issue at the core of Australian historiography. Another historian, Portia Robinson, has also entered into this discussion, in her case with a treatment of the experiences of convict women distinctly at odds with the earliest radical feminist version. In *The Brood and Hatch of Time* she depicts the early New South Wales penal colony as a relatively positive environment for transported women, given their distinctly gloomy prospects had they stayed in London or Dublin. Her work, and that of other scholars associated with her, is subject to some debate, but the enormously detailed level of her research is undeniable. Marian Aveling's interpretation of convict women, as confronted with hard choices but nevertheless making those choices, perhaps remains the most illuminating interpretation. A third area which challenges the male hegemony of the national identity debate is a burgeoning interest in women and war, covered previously as quintessentially a male experience leading to the enhancement of male nationalism.[18]

Women's waged and unwaged labour continues to attract historical attention. Interesting work on women's wages, on the gendered structuring of the labour force, and on work processes has emerged, much of which should appear in due course in full-length monographs: studies by Raelene Francis, Jenny Lee, Gail Reekie and Desley Deacon are to the fore in shaping understanding of the conditions of women's paid public work. Some studies of women's unpaid labour, the structuring of the family, sexuality, marriage and childbearing, have focused on the law and its role in defining expected behaviour. Judith Allen's work on domestic violence, infanticide and abortion has been of critical importance here, along with Hilary Golder's on divorce, and Kay Daniels' on prostitution. Australia did not keep manuscript schedules of censuses, a loss which has hampered the work of those who have investigated the circumstances of women's domestic-related labour. Nevertheless historians interested in family structures have produced such studies, using birth, death and marriage certificates held by government statisticians. Unlike demographers, these social historians have linked demography with the detailed concerns of everyday life within households and communities: Margaret Anderson's work has been notable. Three such studies which I have undertaken with colleagues have combined an examination of the structuring of families in early colonial settlements with a study of domestic labour and resource generation in a mining town, an agricultural town and a working-class industrial suburb of Melbourne. We have emphasised the continuing importance of women's informal economic contribution to the family economy and the colonial economy in the nineteenth century, as well as in the peopling of Australia.[19]

It is difficult to assess the impact of women's history in Australia. That there is lively interest in the area on the part of many Australian women, including undergraduates, postgraduate students and faculty members (no longer temporary and junior) is undeniable, and for a country with a fairly small population, the volume of research and published work must count as impressive. Under Susan Magarey's editorship *Australian Feminist Studies*, founded in 1984, flourishes, and has contained important articles ·in women's history; a collective of postgraduate students in Melbourne produces a women's history journal, *Lilith*; *Hecate* and *Refractory Girl* remain valued forums for discussion and *Australian Historical Studies* (formerly *Historical Studies*) now matches *Labour History* in its inclusion of content on women, and by women. Several collections in women's studies have given generous space to historians, and if the number of substantial monographs is still at present not large, work in progress promises several important studies within the foreseeable future. Courses in women's history are taught on most tertiary campuses, and historians are notable for their participation in teaching women's studies, including master of arts degrees based on course-work. An historian, Susan Magarey, heads the Centre of Research on Women at

Adelaide University, Jill Matthews convenes women's studies at the Australian National University, Lyndall Ryan at Flinders University, Marilyn Lake at La Trobe University, and Judith Allen at Griffith University. Conferences are frequent and well-attended, seminars and, recently, summer schools abound. Despite the cut-back in academic appointments, women with an interest in women's history continue to enter the profession at the lectureship level. They receive male support, particularly from left-wing men, to win at least a share of the positions in a tight job market, aided by the fact that women's history courses usually attract high student numbers.

Yet one would not have to be an utter pessimist to suggest that, in some curious way, this lively initiative in the subject area has dented the consciousness of the majority of academic researchers and teachers only to a superficial degree: enough to create some unease, some embarrassment, perhaps, but insufficiently to inspire a resolution to follow through the implications of women's history for traditional modes of thinking. If one adopted as a test case the prestigious ten-volume history of Australia published in the bicentennial year, one would be far from satisfied with the conclusion. A feminist historian, Marian Aveling, co-edited one volume which shows a marked and mostly successful effort to integrate women, and women's issues, firmly into the narrative, and Ann Curthoys co-edited another. By and large, however, critics have objected that women's lives were dealt with partially, or in separate sections, in an enterprise still dominated numerically by men. The situation was, of course, very different from that of the sesquicentenary year fifty years earlier. Women's past experiences then were relegated to a separate volume written and edited by dedicated female volunteers from outside the academy. (It was entitled, interestingly enough, in a year of increasing militarism, *The Peaceful Army*.) One might ask, however, why the bicentennial volumes did not represent a more marked orientation away from the traditional style in relation to women's history, since the writers did diverge from the usual positivist narrative of Australia's past.[20]

From the mid 1970s onwards feminist scholars have asserted that to incorporate women's past experiences into a nation's historiography demanded far more than filling in gaps. On the contrary, it constituted a challenge to the central canons of relevance widely accepted and taken for granted. Scholars imbued with the values of an empiricist training that has prioritised the experiences of men, have found objectionable what appears as a threat from a political and polemical source to the fabric of their craft. In reply feminists have undertaken important theoretical studies into epistemology and hermeneutics, pointing to the inevitable value system that underlies the construction of all knowledge. In the intellectual context of poststructuralism, their case should be more readily heard. Yet the

particular character of Australian historiography, the central paradigms
which remain widely accepted, combined with the resistance of historians
generally to theory, make the acknowledgment of the validity of gender
issues, as formulated by feminist historians, particularly difficult. It will
be some years before the realisation of the feminist hope that their
endeavour will result in not only a new history of Australian women, but
the effective writing of a new history of Australia.[21]

NOTES

1. See Patricia Grimshaw, 'Only the Chains Have Changed', in Verity
Burgmann and Jenny Lee (eds.), *Staining the Wattle: A People's History of Australia*
(Melbourne: McPhee-Gribble\Penguin 1988), pp. 66-86; Marian Simms, 'The
Australian Feminist Experience', in Patricia Grimshaw and Norma Grieve (eds.),
Australia Women: Feminist Perspectives (Melbourne: Oxford University Press 1982),
pp. 227-39; Susan Magarey, 'Jane and the Feminist History Group', *Australian
Feminist Studies*, nos. 7/8 (Summer 1988), pp. 115-53.

2. Ann Curthoys, 'Historiography and Women's Liberation', *Arena*, 22
(1970), p. 37; Anne Summers, 'An Object Lesson in Women's History', in Jan
Mercer (ed.), *The Other Half: Women in Australian Society* (Melbourne: Penguin
1975), p. 51.

3. Quoted in Berenice A. Carroll, 'Mary Beard's *Woman as Force in
History*: A Critique', in Berenice A. Carroll (ed.), *Liberating Women's History:
Theoretical and Critical Essays* (Urbana: University of Illinois Press, 1976), p. 34.

4. For a fuller discussion of the issue of women in the history of
Australian historiography, see Patricia Grimshaw, 'Women in History:
Reconstructing the Past', in Jacqueline Goodnow and Carole Pateman (eds.), *Women,
Social Science and Public Policy* (Sydney: George Allen and Unwin, 1985), pp. 32-
55. See also Michael Roe, 'Challenges to Australian Identity', *Quadrant*, (April
1978), pp. 34-40.

5. Russel Ward, *The Australian Legend* (Melbourne: Oxford University
Press, 1974 [1958]), pp. 1-2; Humphrey McQueen, *A New Britannia* (Melbourne:
Penguin, 1975 [1970]), p. 261.

6. Margaret Kiddle, *Men of Yesterday: A Social History of the Western
District of Victoria, 1834-1890* (Melbourne: Melbourne University Press, 1960); and
Caroline Chisholm (Melbourne: Melbourne University Press, 1950).

7. Natalie Zemon Davis, '"Women's History" in Transition: The European
Case', *Feminist Studies*, 3, no. 3/4, (Spring-Summer 1976), pp. 83-102; E. Marie
Irvine, *Certain Worthy Women* (Sydney: New Century Press, 1939), p. 12. Examples
of anniversary collections include: Flora Eldershaw (ed.), *The Peaceful Army: A
Memorial to the Pioneer Women of Australia, 1788-1938* (Sydney: Sesquicentennial
Committee, 1938); Louise Brown et al. (eds.), *A Book of South Australia: Women
in the First Hundred Years* (Adelaide: Rigby, 1934).

8. Mary Durack, *Kings in Grass Castles* (Sydney: Corgi, 1959); Marnie Bassett, *The Hentys: An Australian Colonial Tapestry* (Melbourne: Melbourne University Press, 1954); Norman MacKenzie, *Women in Australia* (Melbourne: Angus and Robertson, 1962), p. 10; Alexandra Hasluck, *Portrait with Background: A Life of Georgiana Molloy* (Melbourne: Oxford University Press, 1955).

9. Anne Summers, *Damned Whores and God's Police: The Colonisation of Women in Australia* (Melbourne: Penguin, 1975); Miriam Dixson *The Real Matilda: Women and Identity in Australia 1788 to 1975* (Melbourne: Penguin, 1976).

10. Beverley Kingston, *My Wife, My Daughter and Poor Mary Ann: Women and Work in Australia* (Melbourne: Nelson, 1975); Edna Ryan and Anne Conlon *Gentle Invaders: Australian Women at Work 1788-1974* (Don Mills: Thomas Nelson and Sons, 1975); Ann Curthoys, Susan Eade, and Peter Spearritt (eds.), *Women At Work* (Canberra: Australian Society of Labour History, 1975); Mercer (ed.), *The Other Half;* Kay Daniels, Mary Murnane and Anne Picot (eds.), *Women in Australia: An Annotated Guide to Records*, 2 vols. (Canberra: Australian Government Printing Office, 1977). Kay Daniels and Mary Murnane also compiled a book of documents for women's history, one of four published at this time: *Uphill All the Way: A Documentary History of Women in Australia* (Brisbane: University of Queensland Press 1980), as did Beverley Kingston, *The World Moves Slowly: A Documentary History of Australian Women* (Sydney: Cassell, 1977). Anne Summers with Anne Bettison compiled a bibliography: *Her Story: Australian Women in Print 1788-1975* (Sydney: Hale and Iremonger, 1980). Other bibliographies and finding guides to archives appeared in this period.

11. Kay Daniels, 'Women's History', in Graeme Osborne and William Mandle (eds.), *New History: Studying Australia Today* (Sydney: George Allen and Unwin, 1982), p. 36. In the same chapter Daniels described two of my earlier papers as indications of a divergence from a radical feminist basis towards a more conservative orientation: 'Women and the Family in Australian History: A Reply to *The Real Matilda*', *Historical Studies*, 18, no. 72 (April 1979), reprinted in Elizabeth Windschuttle (ed.), *Women, Class and History: Feminist Perspectives on Australia 1788-1978* (Sydney: Fontana, 1980); and (with Graham Willett) 'Family Structure in Colonial Australia: An Exploration of Family History', *Australia 1888*, Bulletin 4 (May 1980), reprinted in: Grimshaw and Grieve (eds.), *Australian Women: Feminist Perspectives*. See my reworking of the argument in '"Man's Own Country": Women in Colonial Australian History', in Norma Grieve and Ailsa Burns (eds.), *Australian Women: New Feminist Perspectives* (Melbourne: Oxford University Press, 1986).

12. Donald Denoon, 'The Isolation of Australian History', *Historical Studies*, 22, no. 87 (October 1986), p. 254; Ann Curthoys, *For and Against Feminism: A Personal Journey into Feminist Theory and History* (Sydney: Allen and Unwin, 1988). See also the discussion in *Australian Feminist Studies*, nos. 7/8 (Summer 1988), pp. 171-92.

13. Diane Barwick, 'And the Lubras Are Ladies Now', in Fay Gale (ed.), *Woman's Role in Aboriginal Society* (Canberra: Australian Institute of Aboriginal Studies 1970); also '"This Most Resolute Lady": A Biographical Puzzle', in Diane Barwick, Jeremy Beckett, and Marie Reay (eds.), *Metaphors of Interpretation: Essays in Honour of W.E.H. Stanner* (Sydney: ANU Press, 1985); and Isobel White, Diane Barwick, and B. Meehan (eds.), *Fighters and Singers: The Lives of Some*

Australian Aboriginal Women (Sydney: ANU Press, 1985); Diane Bell, *Daughters of the Dreaming* (Sydney: George Allen and Unwin, 1983); Lyndall Ryan, *The Aboriginal Australians* (Brisbane: University of Queensland Press, 1981); Ann McGrath, *'Born in the Cattle': Aborigines in Cattle Country* (Sydney: George Allen and Unwin, 1987).

14. Jill Julius Matthews, *Good and Mad Women: The Historical Construction of Femininity in Twentieth Century Australia* (Sydney: George Allen and Unwin, 1984).

15. Kerreen Reiger, *The Disenchantment of the Home: Modernizing the Australian Family 1880-1940* (Melbourne: Oxford University Press, 1985).

16. Janet McCalman, *Struggletown: Public and Private Life in Richmond 1900-1965* (Melbourne: Oxford University Press, 1984).

17. Susan Magarey, *Unbridling the Tongues of Women: A Biography of Catherine Helen Spence* (Sydney: Hale and Iremonger, 1985); Marilyn Lake and Farley Kelly (eds.), *Double Time: Women in Victoria – 150 Years* (Melbourne: Penguin, 1985); Judith Allen, '"Our Deeply Degraded Sex" and "The Animal in Man": Rose Scott, Feminism and Sexuality 1890-1925', *Australian Feminist Studies*, nos. 7/ 8 (Summer 1988), pp. 65-94 (see also the work by Susan Sheridan and Jenni Mulraney in the same issue); Marian Simms (ed.), *Australian Women and the Political System* (Melbourne: Longman Cheshire, 1984); Marian Sawyer and Marian Simms, *A Woman's Place* (Sydney: George Allen and Unwin); Alison Mackinnon, *The New Women: Adelaide's Early Women Graduates* (Adelaide: Wakefield Press, 1986); Patricia Grimshaw and Lynne Strahan (eds.), *The Half-open Door: Sixteen Australian Women Look At Professional Life and Achievement* (Sydney: Hale and Iremonger, 1982); Drusilla Modjeska, *Exiles At Home: Australian Women Writers 1925-1945* (Sydney: Angus and Robertson, 1981); Janine Burke, *Australian Women Artists, 1840-1940* (Melbourne: Greenhouse Publications, 1980). Recent studies of girls' education include: Helen Jones, *Nothing Seemed Impossible: Women's Education and Social Change in South Australia 1875-1915* (St. Lucia, Queensland: University of Queensland Press, 1985); Noeline Kyle, *Her Natural Destiny: The Education of Women in New South Wales* (Sydney: New South Wales University Press, 1986); Ailsa Zainu'ddin, *They Dreamt of A School: A Centenary History of Methodist Ladies' College, Kew 1882-1982* (Melbourne: Hyland House, 1982).

18. Marilyn Lake, 'The Politics of Respectability: Identifying the Masculinist Context', *Historical Studies*, 22 (April 1986), pp. 116-131, also 'Socialism and Manhood: The Case of William Lane', *Labour History*, 50 (May 1986), pp. 54-62; Portia Robinson, *The Hatch and Brood of Time: A Study of the First Generation of Native-born White Australians 1788-1828*, 1 (Melbourne: Oxford University Press, 1985); Marian Aveling, 'She Only Married to Be Free: Or Cleopatra Vindicated', in Grieve and Grimshaw (eds.), *Australian Women: Feminist Perspectives*; see also another monograph on the period, Katrina Alford, *Production or Reproduction? An Economic History of Women in Australia 1788-1850* (Melbourne: Oxford University Press, 1984); Gail Reekie, 'Industrial Action by Women Workers in Western Australia During World War II', *Labour History*, 49 (November 1985), pp. 75-82; Judith Smart, 'Feminists, Food and the Fair Price: The Cost of Living Demonstrations in Melbourne, August-September, 1917', *Labour History*, 50 (May 1986), pp. 113-31. For a more popular history, see Patsy Adam-Smith, *Women At War* (Melbourne: Nelson, 1984).

19. Raelene Francis, '"No More Amazons": Gender and Work Process in the Victorian Clothing Trades, 1890-1939', *Labour History*, 50 (May 1986), pp. 95-112; Jenny Lee, 'A Redivision of Labour: Victoria's Wages Boards in Action 1896-1903', *Historical Studies*, 22, no. 88 (April 1987), pp. 352-72; Gail Reekie, '"Humanising Industry": Paternalism, Welfarism and Labour Control in Sydney's Big Stores, 1890-1930', *Labour History*, 53 (November 1987), pp. 1-19; Desley Deacon, *Managing Gender: The State, The Middle Class and Women Workers 1830-1930* (Melbourne: Oxford University Press, 1989); see also Edna Ryan, *Two-thirds of a Man: Women and Arbitration in New South Wales 1902-08* (Sydney: Hale and Iremonger, 1984), and Penelope Johnson, 'Gender, Class and Work: The Council of Action for Equal Pay and the Equal Pay Campaign in Australia During World War II', *Labour History*, 50 (May 1986), pp. 132-46; Judith Allen, *Sex and Secrets: Crimes Involving Australian Women Since 1880*, (Melbourne: Oxford Unversity Press, 1990); also 'Abortion, (Hetero) Sexuality and Women's Bodies', *Australian Feminist Studies*, no. 5 (Summer 1987), pp. 85-94; also 'The Invention of the Pathological Family: A Historical Study of Family Violence in New South Wales', in Carol O'Donnell and Jan Craney (eds.), *Family Violence in Australia* (Melbourne: Longman Cheshire, 1981); also 'Octovius Beale Reconsidered: Infanticide, Baby Farming and Abortion in New South Wales, 1880-1939', in Sydney Labour Group, *What Rough Beast? The State and Social Order in Australian History* (Sydney: Allen and Unwin, 1984); Margaret Anderson, 'The Family', in C.T. Stannage (ed.), *A New History of Western Australia* (Perth: University of Western Australia Press, 1981); also '"Helpmeet for Man": Women in Mid-Nineteenth Century Western Australia', in Patricia Crawford (ed.), *Exploring Women's Past: Essays in Social History* (Melbourne: Sisters Press, 1983); Patricia Grimshaw and Charles Fahey, 'Family Structure and Community in Nineteenth Century Castlemaine', and Patricia Grimshaw et al., 'Families and the Land in Colonial Horsham', in Patricia Grimshaw, Chris McConville, and Ellen McEwen (eds.), *Families in Colonial Australia* (Sydney: George Allen and Unwin, 1985); Jane Beer, Charles Fahey, Patricia Grimshaw, and Melanie Raymond, *Colonial Frontiers and Family Fortunes: Two Studies of Rural and Urban Victoria* (Melbourne: Melbourne University History Monographs, 1987); Marilyn Lake, *The Limits of Hope: Soldier Settlement in Victoria 1915-1938* (Melbourne: Oxford University Press, 1987).

20. Marian Aveling and Alan Atkinson, *Australians in 1838* (Sydney: Fairfax, Weldon and Syme, 1987), in the series *Australians: An Historical Library*; Flora Eldershaw (ed.), *The Peaceful Army: A Memorial to the Pioneer Women of Australia 1788-1938* (Sydney: Centennial Committee, 1938); Jill Matthews, 'A Female of All Things: Women and the Bicentenary', and Kay Daniels, 'Slicing the Past', *Australian Historical Studies* 23, no. 91 (October, 1988), pp. 130-40; Heather Goodall et al., review of *Australians: A Historical Library*, in *Labour History*, 54 (May, 1988), pp. 114-19.

21. See Carole Pateman and Elizabeth Grosz (eds.), *Feminist Challenges: Social and Political Theory* (Sydney: Allen and Unwin, 1986); Barbara Caine, Elizabeth Grosz, and Marie de Lepervanche (eds.), *Crossing Boundaries: Feminisms and the Critique of Knowledges* (Sydney: Allen and Unwin, 1987).

9

The Development of Women's History in Japan

Noriyo Hayakawa

Research on women's history really began in Japan during the period 1945 through the early 1960s, although a few eminent researchers such as Takamure Itsue were at work prior to that time. The main achievements of this period were two general histories of women. Inoue Kiyoshi, a historian of modern Japan, published his book on women's history in Japan in 1948; in it he described the history of women since ancient times from a perspective of women's liberation based on class struggle.[1] In the preface he pointed to the absence of women from almost all the published accounts of Japanese history and remarked that the few existing books on women's history had been written from a male perspective that took women's subordination for granted. His own declared purpose in writing women's history was to show how women were to be liberated from their subjection to men, which had been structured by the emperor system. This book greatly influenced a large number of women who had had experience with ideas of democratic reform, such as the demand for women's suffrage, and who longed for their own emancipation.

Takamure Itsue published her three-volume general history of women between 1954 and 1958.[2] She had already completed 'Research on the Matrilineal System'[3] as well as 'Research on Matrilocal Marriage'.[4] She insisted in these works that there had not been a patriarchal family in the ancient society of Japan and that after the fourteenth century the marriage system in Japan completely changed from matrilocal marriage to patrilocal marriage, which caused a deterioration of women's social status in matters such as the loss of inheritance rights. However, Takamure Itsue's work was ignored by almost all other scholars. She repeated this argument in her general history of women, where she described the commercialisation of sexuality and of labour as central to women's history. Her book was not as popular amongst women as Inoue's, because the

171

women's liberation movement at that time had a strongly marxist perspective. A ten-volume collection of her essays, which included her poems and diary, was published in 1966.[5]

In 1959 Murata Shizuko wrote about the modern period in her biography of Fukuda Hideko, an activist in the Freedom and Popular Rights Movement during the Meiji era.[6] Tatewaki Sadayo, who was herself a liberal in the pre-war period, published her book on women in Japan in 1957.[7] A few women historians including Mitsui Reiko, Nagahara Kazuko, and Murata Skizuko had already set up the research group for women's study in 1946 as a section of the Japanese Researchers' Congress. In 1963 they published a chronological table of women's movements.[8]

From the late 1960s through the early 1970s research on women's history began to be taken up by ordinary people as well as by academically-trained women historians. The reasons for this can be summarised as follows: the popular movement of the 1960s powerfully influenced Japanese researchers, and women, whether academic researchers or merely ordinary women, experienced an increasing desire to analyse the roots of sexual discrimination. Women's history began to blossom in the wake of these experiences.

This new research on women's history had three main characteristics. First of all, the lives of women who were considered to have undergone the harshest experiences were brought to light. For example, Yamamoto Shigemi described the working life of young women in the silk factories of Nagano prefecture around 1900-30 in his book *Nomugi Toge*, published in 1968.[9] Yamazaki Tomoko completed her research on women who went to Southeast Asia in the 1900-1945 period to work as prostitutes. Her book, *Sandakan Hachiban Shokan*, appeared in 1972.[10] Both these historians based their research on copious interviews, and both emphasised the fact that their subjects had not only been neglected but had also been discriminated against, even though their labour had contributed greatly to the development of the Japanese empire. These books remain very popular among women even now. Another important publication was the autobiography of Kobayashi Hatsue, a Buraku woman (a woman of the outcast class, which was officially abolished in 1871 and whose descendants still experience social discrimination).[11] This woman described the harsh experiences of her grandmother and mother as well as her own.

Additionally, such new research stimulated the publication of new general histories of women. The most important of these was the four-volume 'Women's History of the Meiji Era' by Murakami Nobuhiko.[12] He tried to describe every aspect of the daily lives of women including their consciousness. He wrote about the daughters and wives of the declining samurai class, ambitious girls who went up to Tokyo to study, working women, peasants' wives, and so on. He also published other related books such as the history of dress. Based on all these works, he insisted that the description of the women's movement alone did not convey a true picture of most ordinary women, but only dwelt on the famous ones.[13]

Finally, controversy arose between Murakami and other historians of women who had published works on the history of women in modern Japan and who had emphasised the women's movement. Of these historians, Yoneta Sayoko deserves particular mention; according to her view, the history of the women's movement is necessarily based on the daily lives of women. Were it not, she argued, one could not understand why women took part in the movement. She also insists that it is most important to articulate the process by which women participated in political movements.[14] Yoneta and Mizuta Tamae mainly discussed topics such as the concept of family in a capitalist society.[15] These debates led women historians to pay more attention to the daily lives of women than to the movements.

Indeed, since the late 1970s women's history has made remarkable progress. An increasing number of women have been engaged in research of this nature, and in Japan in particular these researchers are not exclusively academics but also include ordinary housewives. There are now two main women's history societies,[16] and over seventy local history societies in Japan.[17] About twenty of these local societies publish their own bulletins, and since 1977 four have sponsored nationwide conferences.[18] Roughly 150 people attended the first conference, whilst there were 500 in attendance at the fourth in 1986. These conferences have been staged with the collaboration of both professional and non-professional researchers. A conference report was edited for each one. The *Rekishi Hyoron* (a monthly review of history) has encouraged these researchers by editing a special issue on women's history every March since 1974.

Another feature of recent work is the stream of publications including republication of older documents and periodicals. Of particular value is the ten-volume *Nippon Fujin Mondai Shiryo Shusei* [A Series of Archives on Women in Modern Japan], which won the publication prize of the Mainichi Newspaper Company.[19] A second important collection is the thirty-two volume *Kindai Fujin Mondai Meicho Senshu* [Selected Collection of Essays on Women's Studies in Modern Japan], which includes articles by feminists such as Oko Mumeo and Yamada Waka, and also social surveys undertaken by local governments.[20]

In 1982 there appeared a five-volume collection of essays on women's history in Japan, which covers the period from primitive times to the present.[21] In the preface to this work, the editorial collective describes the purpose of this publication in these words: 'we intend to portray an authentic and total image of women by analysing what role the social structure has played in forming a sexual division of roles as well as female consciousness, and we hope that we can create a new feminist history that will replace both the history of marriage and the history of women's liberation movements'. These important essays have stimulated considerable further research, particularly on the pre-modern periods. Two complementary volumes, bibliographies of research in women's histories, published in 1983 and 1988, list much of this research, as well as earlier work.[22] The first volume covers research done between the 1880s and 1981, and the second includes research completed between 1982 and 1987. Both the five-volume collection on women's history in Japan and the two bibliographies were edited by the Kyoto Women's History Society (Joseishi Sogo Kenkyukai), with a grant from the Japanese Ministry of Education. Another important publication, which received the Research Prize of the Asahi Newspaper Company, is the two-volume *Bosei wo Tou* [Historical Essays on Motherhood], which treats changing aspects of motherhood from primitive times to the present.[23] A new series on the history of Japanese women's lives by the Kyoto Women's History Society is scheduled for publication by the end of 1990. Finally, several collections of essays by feminists such as Hiratsuka Raicho and Yamakawa Kikue have been reprinted.[24]

The scope of the new research in Japanese women's history is broad indeed. Research in the fields of ancient history as well as in the medieval periods has progressed greatly. Moreover, a focus on women's history has appeared in the discipline of archaeology.[25] Research on both ancient and medieval periods began as a critical response to the thesis put forward by Takamure in the 1970s. Based on her research into the structure of marriage among aristocrats, she had argued that the family in the ancient period had been organised according to matrilineal descent, which guaranteed women's ownership of property. Some historians, including Sekigucti Hiroko and Yoshie Akiko, point out that the family in the ancient period was neither a patriarchal family nor a matrilineal system.[26] They insist that descent was either bilineal or bilateral. Their theories have had a significant influence on traditional academics who argued that a despotic society in the ancient period was based on the patriarchal extended family. As a result of these findings, not a few researchers have had to change their opinions and to confront women's history in order to deepen their own research. Women historians now suggest that the periodisation for the establishment of a patriarchal family type must be located in the eleventh century. This research has also stimulated a lively discussion about family and kinship in the medieval period.

Researchers in women's history have since extended our knowledge in several areas, including the relationship between ownership of property and the form of marriage, the formation of political clans, and changes in women's right of inheritance and the decline of their political status.[27] Current investigations of this period also cover subjects such as the household as an economic unit, women's role in domestic labour as well as in business, ideas of motherhood, women's participation in community meetings, female politicians, changes in girls' names, and female entertainers including prostitutes.[28] The Society of Buddhism and Women has held an annual seminar every year from 1984 to 1988; in 1989 members of the society published a four-volume collection on women and Buddhism in Japan.[29] Almost all the articles treat topics in the ancient and medieval periods.

Full-scale academic research on the early modern period of Japanese history from a perspective of feminist history has just begun, although many researchers and literary figures have already published on women of this period. Both Inoue Kiyoshi and Takamure Itsue had assumed that in this time women were completely oppressed. In 1986 and again in 1990 a society for research on women's history published collections of essays on this period.[30] Current research addresses the following subjects: the establishment of the *bakuhan* system (the system of government during the Edo era, from the seventeenth to the nineteenth century which is often described as centralised feudalism) and the legal status of women, including women's right of inheritance, their economic activities in urban areas, and their agricultural labour; women's lifecycle; the education of girls and adult females; the thought of religions headed by married women such as Tenri-kyo; women's travel diaries; prostitution, divorce, and so forth.[31] These inquiries indicate that the real status of women in the household as well as society was actually higher than their legal status, and that women had more freedom than previous research had suggested. For example, women were not excluded from inheritance, divorce and remarriage were far from rare, and to live as a single woman was possible.[32]

Topics in modern Japanese women's history include the *ie* system (the family system in place from 1898 to 1947, which provided no rights to women), education for girls, women's work in silk and the textile industry, women's movements including those of women workers and suffragists, ideas of women's liberation, and so on. In addition to these topics, new areas of study have recently developed. First, numerous local women's histories have been published. Some of these have been issued by local history groups,[33] while others have been edited by local authorities. Professional researchers from other countries have also published important contributions to localised Japanese women's history, as for example, Gregory M. Pflugfelder's *Seiji to Daidokoro* [Politics and Kitchen-History of the Suffragist Movement in Akita Prefecture].[34] Many of these works are based on extensive use of oral history.

Additionally, studies on the wartime period (1931-1945) have also appeared. These deal with women workers, women's agricultural labour, women's organisations, women's health, the politics of motherhood, and the activities of famous women leaders, among other topics. Some of these works point out that ordinary women as well as women leaders positively supported war, although ordinary women have more frequently been considered to be only victims of war. Implicit in this new work is the notion that all women have to reconsider their responsibilities so that they are not mobilised into the war system.[35]

Lastly, scholars have begun to examine new topics such as the history of nursing, the co-operative association movements, the birth control movement, and the history of childrearing.[36] A final significant feature of this new work on the modern period is the large number of biographical and autobiographical publications. It must also be mentioned that research on peoples who have been discriminated against, such as the *Burakumin*, *Ainu* and *Koreans*, has just begun.[37] Two new general histories of women have also appeared.[38] One of these, the new *Nippon Joseishi* [Women's History in Japan] (1987) was the work of twenty-five women researchers.

As an indicator of the progress made in developing research in women's history, it is noteworthy that in the 1980s two prizes were created, one in memory of Yamakawa Kikue (the feminist mentioned above), and a second in honour of the distinguished historian Aoyama Nao. These prizes are awarded annually for outstanding works on women's history.

It should be apparent from this brief survey that research on women's history in Japan has made great advances in recent years. It seems worth mentioning, however, that the outburst of interest in women's history has not been associated with academic women's studies, as is the case in the United States and some other countries. What is more, there are few researchers who have analysed other historical topics from the standpoint of gender. The gender perspective as a tool of analysis for history has not been introduced among Japanese women historians. But we have been forced to re-examine social and private structures such as the family from a feminist historical perspective, because traditional research has dealt with the family as one of the most important social forms. Already in 1976, Kano Masanao[39] pointed to the necessity of rethinking periodisation from the standpoint of women's history. Thus, it might be said that Japanese historians have actually been researching women's history from a gendered perspective without being conscious of the concept of gender.

NOTES

1. Inoue Kiyoshi, *Nippon no Joseishi* [Women's History in Japan] (Tokyo: Sanichi-Shobo, 1948).

2. Takamure Itsue, *Josei no Rekishi* [Women's History in Japan], 3 vols. (Tokyo: Kodansha, 1954-58).

3. Takamure Itsue, *Bokeisei no Kenkyu* [Research on the Matrilineal System] (Tokyo: Kosei-kaku, 1938).

4. Takamure Itsue, *Shoseikon no Kensku* [Research on Matrilocal Marriage] (Tokyo: Dainipponyubenkaikodansha, 1953).

5. *Takamure Itsue Zenshu*, 10 vols. (Tokyo: Riron-Sha, 1966-67).

6. Murata Shizuko, *Fukuda Hideko* (Tokyo: Iwanami-Shoten, 1959).

7. Tatewaki Sadayo, *Nippon no Fujin* [Women in Japan – The Development of the Women's Movement] (Tokyo: Iwanami-Shoten, 1957).

8. Mitsui Reiko (ed.), *Gendai Fujinundoshi Nenpyo* [The Chronological Table of Women's Movements] (Tokyo: Sanichi-Shobo, 1963).

9. Yamamoto Shigemi, *Nomugi Toge* [Unmarried Women Workers in the Silk Factories of Nagano Prefecture] (Tokyo: Asahi Shinbun-Sha, 1968).

10. Yamazaki Tomoko, *Sandakan Hachiban Shokan* [Japanese Women as Prostitutes in Southeast Asia] (Tokyo: Chikuma-Shobo, 1972).

11. Kobayashi Hatsue, *Onna Sandai-Kanto no Hisabetsuburaku no Kurashi kara* [Three Generations of Women – The Lives of the Discriminated Buraku People in East Japan] (Tokyo: Asahi Shinbun-Sha, 1974).

12. Murakami Nobuhiko, *Meiji Joseishi* [Women's History of the Meiji Era], 4 vols. (Tokyo: Riron-Sha, 1969-72).

13. Murakami Nobuhiko, 'Joseishi Kensky no Kadai to Tenbo [Theoretical Problems in Research on Women's History]', *Shiso*, no. 549 (1970), pp. 93-5.

14. Yoneta Sayoko, 'Gendai no Fujinundo to Joseishi no Kadai [Contemporary Women's Movements and Research on Women's History]', *Keizai*, no. 83 (1971), p. 88.

15. *Shiryo-Joseishi Ronso* [Documents – The Debates on Women's History] (Tokyo: Domes-Shuppan, 1987), includes important articles referring to these debates.

16. Joseishi Sogo Kenkyukai in Kyoto and Sogo Joseishi Kenkyukai in Tokyo.

17. These include Hokkaido Joseishi Kenkyukai in Asahikawa, Niigata Joseishi Kenkyukai in Niigata, Hiroshima Joseishi Kenkyukai in Hiroshima, Kazokushi Kenkyukai in Kumamoto, and Okinawa Joseishi Kenkyukai in Naha.

18. The first conference was called by Aichi Joseishi Kenkyukai in Nagoya, 27-28 August 1977. The second was held by Hokkaido Joseishi Kenkyukai in Asahikawa, 7-8 August 1981. The third took place in Yokohama, 9-10 August

178   *Noriyo Hayakawa*

1983, sponsored by Kanagawa Fujinundoshi Kenkyukai. The forth, in Matsuyama, was held by Ehime Joseishi Kenkyukai, 9-10 August 1986.

19. Maruoka Hideko, Ichikawa Fusae, Akamatsu Yoshiko et al. (eds.), *Nippon Fujin Mondai Shiryo Shusei* [A Series of Archives on Women in Modern Japan], 10 vols. (Tokyo: Domesu-Shuppan, 1976-80).

20. Nakajima Kuni and Gomi Yuriko (eds.), *Kindai Fujin Mondai Meicho Senshu* [Selected Collection of Essays on Women's Studies in Modern Japan], 32 vols. (Tokyo: Nippon Tosho Centre, 1982-85).

21. Joseishi Sogo Kenkyukai (president, Wakita Haruko) (ed.), *Koza, Nippon Joseishi* [Essay Collection on Women's History in Japan], 5 vols. (Tokyo: Tokyo University Press, 1982).

22. Joseishi Sogo Kenkyukai (ed.), *Nippon Joseishi Kenkyu Bunken Mokuroku* [Bibliography of Research on Women's History], 2 vols. (Tokyo: Tokyo University Press, 1982-89). Vol. 1 (1880s-1981) is 343 pages, containing about 5000 references. Vol. 2 (1982-87), at 300 pages, provides some 3000 additional references.

23. Wakita Haruko (ed.), *Bosei wo Tou* [Historical Essays on Motherhood in Japan], 2 vols. (Kyoto: Jinbun Shoin, 1985).

24. See, for example, *Yamakawa Kikue Shu* [Yamakawa Kikue Essay Collection], 10 vols. [Iwanami-Shoten, 1981-82); *Hiratsuka Raicho Chosaku Shu* [Hiratsuka Raicho Essay Collection], 7 vols. (Tokyo: Otsuki-Shoten, 1983-84).

25. Tsuro Hideo, 'Genshidoki to Josei [Primitive Earthenware and Women]', in *Koza Nippon Joseishi*, vol. 1; Kagiya Akiko, 'Bosei no Tayosei [Motherhood and Its Variety]', in *Bosei wo Tou*, vol. 1.

26. See Sekigucho Hiroko, 'Kodai Kazoku to Koninkeitai [The Family and Marriage in the Ancient Period]', in *Koza Japanese History*, vol. 2 (Tokyo: Tokyo University Press, 1985], and Yoshie Akiko, *Nippon Kodai no Ugi no Kozo* [Clan Structure in Ancient Japan] (Tokyo: Yoshikawa Kobunkan, 1986).

27. See, for example, Fukuto Sanae, 'Heian Jidai no Sozoku ni tsuite [Inheritance in Heian Japan]', in *Kazokushi Kenkyu*, vol. 2 (Otsuki Shoten, 1980); Tabata Yoshiko, *Nippon Chusei no Josei* [Women in Medieval Japan] (Tokyo: Yoshikawa Kobunkan, 1987); Zenkindai Joseishi Kenkyukai (ed.), *Kazoku to Josei no Rekishi-Kodai, Chusei* [Family and Women in Ancient and Medieval Japan] (Tokyo: Yoshikawa Kobunkan, 1989).

28. See, for example, Iinuma Kenji, 'Joseimei karamita Josei no Shakaitekichi [Women's Social Status in Medieval Japan from the Perspective of Female Naming]', *Rekishi Hyoron*, no. 443 (1987). See also the essays in *Koza Nippon Joseishi*, vols. 1 and 2.

29. Nishiguchi Junko and Osumi Kazuo (eds.), *Series Josei to Bukkyo* [Series - Woman and Buddhism] (Tokyo: Heibonsha, 1989).

30. Kinsei Joseishi Kenkyukai (ed.), *Kinsei Joseishi* [Essay Collection - Women's History in Early Modern Japan] (Tokyo: Yoshikawa Kobunkan, 1986); *Edojidai no Joseitachi* [Essay Collection - Women in the Edo Era] (Tokyo: Yoshikawa Kobunkan, 1990).

31. See the collections *Kinsei Joseishi*, *Edojidai no Joseitachi*, *Koza Nippon joseishi*, vol. 3; *Bosei wo Tou*, vol. 2.

32. See, for example, Katakura Hisako, 'Edo Machikata ni okeru Sozoku [Inheritance in a Merchant Household in Edo]', in *Kinsei Joseishi*; Oguchi Yujiro, 'Kinseikoki ni okeru Nosonkazoku no Keitai [Heiresses in a Nineteenth-Century Farmer's Family]', in *Koza Nippon Joseishi*, vol. 3. See also Shiba Keiko, 'Tabinikki kara mita Kinseijosei no Ichikosatsu [Women's Travel Diaries in Early Modern Japan]', in *Edojidai no Joseitachi*, and Takagi Tadashi, *Mikudarihan* [Divorce and Women in the Edo Era] (Tokyo: Heibonsha, 1987).

33. Sappolo Joseishi Kenkyukai (ed.), *Kita no Joseishi* [Women's History in Hokkaido] (Sappolo: Hokkaido Shinbun sha, 1986); Okayama Joseishi Kenkyukai (ed.), *Kindai Okayama no Onnatach* [Women in Okayama Prefecture] (Tokyo: Sanseido, 1987); Kazokushi Kenkyukai (ed.), *Kindai Kumamoto no Onnatachi* [Women in Kumamoto] (Kumamoto: Kumamoto Nichinichi Shinbun sha, 1976).

34. Gregory M. Pflugfelder, *Seiji to Daidokoro* [Politics and Kitchen-History of the Suffragist Movement in Akita Prefecture] (Tokyo: Domes-shuppan, 1986).

35. Kano Mikiyo, *Onnatachi no Jugo* [Women and the Homefront] (Tokyo: Chikuma-Shobo, 1987); Suzuki Yuko, *Feminism to Senso* [Feminism and War] (Tokyo: Marujusha, 1986); Hayakawa Noriyo, 'Joseishi Kenkyu to Rekishitekisekinin [Theoretical Problems in Research on War]', in *Rekishi wo Manabu Hitobito no tameni* (Tokyo: Sanseido, 1988).

36. Kameyama Michiko, *Kindai Nippon Kangoshi* [History of Nursing in Modern Japan], 4 vols. (Tokyo: Domesu Shuppan, 1983-85). See also *Koza Nippon Joseishi*, vols. 3 and 4; *Bosei wo Tou*, vol. 2, etc.

37. Suzuki Yuko, *Suiheisen wo Mezasu Onnatachi* [Women's Movements of Burakumin] (Tokyo: Domesu Shuppan, 1987); Takahashi Mieko, *Hoddaido no Onnatachi-Utari* [Ainu Women in Hoddaido] (Tokyo: Domesu Shuppan, 1976); Kojima Kyoko, 'Dentoteki Ainushakai ni okeru Josei no Yakuwari [Women's Role in Ainu Society]' (see note 27 above), in *Kazoku to Josei no Rekishi-Kodai*.

38. Kano Masanao and Horiba Kiyoko, *Sobo, Haha, Musume no Jidai* [Women's History in Modern Japan] (Tokyo: Iwanami Shoten, 1985); Wakita Haruko, Hayaski Reiko, and Nagahara Kazuko (eds.), *Nippon Joseishi* [Women's History in Japan] (Tokyo: Yoshikawa Kobunkan, 1987).

39. Kano Masanao, 'Aru Kanso [Some Comments on Research on Women's History]', *Rekishi Hyoron*, no. 311 (1976), p. 21.

10

Women's History in India:
An Historiographical Survey

Aparna Basu

It is well known by now that women receive little or no attention in traditional historical writing. One reason for this is that traditional history has tended to focus on areas of human activity in which men were dominant – politics, wars, diplomacy – areas in which women had little or no role. As I begin to reflect on women's history in India, my mind goes back to my school textbooks. Etched in my memory are the beautiful Mumtaz Mahal who moved Shah Jehan to build the Taj Mahal for her, Noor Jehan who was much abler than her husband, Jehangir, and was the real power behind the throne, or the brave Rani Laxmibai of Jhansi who fought to retain her husband's kingdom. The only women who found a place in traditional history text books were either women who successfully performed male roles or whom great men loved.

Women's history in India began as an act of reclamation. It has developed in the direction charted by the titles of leading works in the English-language in the 1970s. Since women had been 'hidden from history', the aim was to have 'Clio's consciousness raised' by 'liberating women's history' from ignorance and neglect, and, in the resulting work, women in history were 'becoming visible'.[1] Our view of the past has dramatically widened in scope in the last few years. History is no longer just a chronicle of kings and statesmen, of people who wielded power but of ordinary women and men engaged in manifold tasks. Women's history is an assertion that women have a history, although that history has been distorted, even erased by the biases that pervade our culture and scholarship. We have to see women as a force in politics, as reformers, revolutionaries, searching for an identity in their nation, their class, themselves. Women as producers, peasants, workers, artisans, domestic servants, in their roles in the family, as wives, daughters and mothers have

181

to become visible. The totality of women's lives is the concern of women historians. Women's history is developing into a new area of research at a particularly exciting time. It has been stimulated by two related but essentially independent developments, the maturation of social history and the growth of an active women's movement. In India, a significant landmark in the field of women's studies was the publication in 1974 of *Towards Equality*, the Report of the Committee on the Status of Women in India, which concluded on the basis of a countrywide investigation that the *de jure* equality guaranteed by the Indian Constitution had not been translated into reality and that large masses of women had remained unaffected by the rights guaranteed to them. It drew the attention of scholars to the neglect in the social sciences of women's role and inputs. Indian scholars were also influenced by the growth of the feminist movement in the west.

In spite of the high visibility of women's subordination in Indian society, historical work on the origin and development of the patriarchal system does not yet exist. It is also being recognised that women's history cannot be studied in isolation from what we may call 'mainstream' history. Given the regional, class and caste variations of patriarchal practices and their diverse histories in Indian society, it is obviously necessary to have specific studies before we can construct any useful theory. In 1989, Sangari and Vaid have made an excellent attempt in this direction.[2] Maria Mies has also written on Indian women and patriarchy.[3] In this article I have undertaken a broad historiographical survey of work done in the field of women's history in India by both foreign and Indian scholars. The paper is divided into three main sections, ancient, medieval and modern. While there is considerable work on women in ancient and modern India, the medieval period has so far been neglected. There was a sharp increase in research publications on women after 1921 and this can be traced to the impact of the participation of women in the freedom movement. A decline in the number of publications on women is evident between 1947 and the 1970s, as in the years immediately after independence it was felt that since women had been granted equal rights in the Constitution, their disadvantages would soon disappear. The themes on which most work has been done are women's position in society, and women's education and their role in the freedom struggle. On the other hand, there is a paucity of research on women's role in the economy, in art and in culture. In the last few years there has been a shift in the methodology of research from broad historical analysis to a more intensive and specialised examination of current problems. So far there has been little theoretical work but such questions are now being raised and debated.

Ancient Indian history

Women in ancient India have been the focus of scholarly attention since the nineteenth century. Both Indian and British scholars undertook to study the position of women in early India, although from different perspectives. Indologists and Sanskritists unearthed useful information about women in early India from archaeological excavations, religious and literary texts, inscriptions, and so forth. As British missionaries, administrators and scholars criticised Hindu society, particularly the degraded position of women, Indian historians bent over backwards to prove that women occupied a very exalted position in ancient India which had gradually declined over a period of time. Some nineteenth-century western scholars such as Clarisse Bader also had a tendency to romanticise and idealise the early Indian situation, possibly explicable in terms of their disillusionment with a western civilisation in the throes of industrialisation.[4]

A. S. Altekar's *The Position of Women in Hindu Civilization: From Pre-history to the Present Day* has been the most influential and widely used text in colleges and universities where courses or topics on women's history have been offered.[5] The treatment of the subject is both chronological and thematic and provides a detailed picture of the social, cultural and economic status of women at different times. Moreover, this work presents several hypotheses, which have subsequently been widely accepted, regarding the decline in the position of women. The exposition is based on meticulous research and a deep knowledge of Sanskrit texts and of cultural histories. It includes a comparative study of the status of women in various civilisations of the world at a particular point of time. The scope of the book is, however, limited, as the analysis is restricted to elite women within the Vedic Aryan tradition. The author relies exclusively on Brahmanical sources and is mainly concerned with women in upper caste families. He makes no attempt to examine regional or caste/class differences.

Altekar's work has in the last few years been criticised by a number of feminist scholars. In 1981, Suvira Jayaswal contended that society in the Rig-Vedic period was still predominantly pastoral and nomadic and did not produce enough surplus to allow any sector of society to be completely withdrawn from the process of production.[6] This, according to her, explains the better position of women in the Vedic period in terms of access to education, religious rights, freedom of movement, and other such issues. Though the historical data is insufficient for a full understanding of the links, she posits a connection between the rise of the caste system and the decline in the position of women from 500 B.C. to 1800 A.D.

Uma Chakravarti points out how Altekar and other historians were influenced by nationalist ideas and the need to instil national pride at a time when Indians needed to build up their cultural self-confidence in face of attacks by western scholars.[7] These historians, therefore, created a picture of a golden age in the ancient past when women held a very high position in society. A portrait of Hindu women based on mythology, literature and history was proposed by these nationalist historians. This idealised version of Hindu women's lives provided an answer to the critics of Hindu society about its treatment of women. Chakravarti accuses Altekar of sexist and racist biases.

The influence of nationalist historians manifests itself in the works of several post-independence historians also. The notion that the Vedic age was a golden age is reiterated time and time again and is rarely challenged. An example is Indra's *Status of Women in Ancient India* published in 1955.[8] R. M. Das in *Women in Manu and the Seven Commentators* virtually justifies the text and all early Indian practices and precepts.[9] Similarly, Talim argues that the Buddha was justified in his reluctance to confer the right of renunciation on women as 'perhaps he also knew that *sanyas dharma* would never be in harmony with womanhood'.[10] The tendency to confine women's history to family relations and to marginalise the role of women in production is still evident in works such as S. Gulati's *Women and Society in the 11th and 12th Centuries in North India* (1985).[11] One of the few studies of a category of women outside the socio-legal framework is Motichandra's *World of Courtesans* (1973), which, however, merely lists references to courtesans or prostitutes culled from different texts and organised in terms of sources.[12]

The pioneering works of Dharmanand D. Kosambi, Romila Thapar and Ram Saran Sharma in the late 1970s and early 1980s made an important contribution to our understanding of early Indian social and economic history, but they do not incorporate an analysis of gender.[13] Sharma does, however, put forward the traditional marxist view that women's inferior status is rooted in private property and a class-divided society. His discussion on the equation of women with property and with *sudras* (the lowest caste in the hierarchy of Aryan society, who were servants of the three higher castes) focuses attention on certain significant connections.

Despite certain limitations, post-independence scholars show some awareness of the need to view the women's question within a wider perspective. P. Thomas brings in non-Aryan women and collates useful information on types of marriage and variations in kinship patterns in different parts of the country.[14] This is a change from the earlier tendency to concentrate only on Aryan women. Scholars such as Suvira

Jayal, writing in 1966, recognise the need to interpret data in terms of a sociological or anthropological approach.[15] Prabhati Mukherjee and Saroj Gulati (1985) also recognise the need to study women within a given socio-economic context.[16] Uma Chakravartri's papers on 'The Rise of Buddhism as Experienced by Women' and 'The Sita Myth',[17] and Sukumari Bhattacharya's 'Women in Mahabharata'[18] have made a beginning in reconstructing ancient Indian history from a women's perspective and reinterpreting the lives of traditional women like Sita, Savitri, Draupadi, and Kunti (who have been role models for generations of Indian women) and showing how they symbolised strength.

Medieval India

Little work has been done on women in medieval India, which as far as women are concerned is regarded as the 'dark' period of Indian history. Some references are found to women who wielded power as queens, such as Sultan Razia in the thirteenth century, who is one of the extremely rare examples of a woman who succeeded to the throne legitimately, or Chand Bibi in the sixteenth century, or Noor Jehan who is usually portrayed as a power-hungry woman. There are books and theses on women in Mughal courts or in the harems. Ila Mukherji's book, *Social Status of North Indian Women* (1972),[19] studies the status of women during the period of the Mughals in India. Scholars generally agree that women enjoyed a high status during the Vedic period but that during the subsequent periods there was a steady decline. This decline is generally held to have reached a *nadir* during Muslim rule. Mukherji provides a graphic picture of the position of women during the two hundred years of Mughal rule and of the condition of women in all phases of their lives as well as an idea of the social laws, customs and traditions which governed their lives. The study is based on the written texts of contemporary vernacular literature, mainly Hindi, Bengali, and Oriya, and accounts of foreign travellers. The detailed account of women's contribution in various fields of art and literature during this period and of their dress and jewellery makes interesting reading but the book is not useful in understanding women's subordination. Rekha Misra has depicted the position of women, chiefly of the aristocratic class, during the Mughal period.[20] Currently some work is being done on women and land rights by scholars at Aligarh Muslim University, including Pushpa Prasad on 'Women and Land Rights in Early Medieval India', B. L. Bhandari on 'Women's Land Rights in 17th century Rajasthan', and Rafat Bilgrami on 'Muslim Women and Land Grants'.

Modern India

The Women's Movement

The Indian women's movement can be broadly divided into three phases. The first began around the 1880s and grew out of the socio-religious reform movements initiated by male intellectuals to eliminate obscurantist customs, practices and beliefs. Charles Heimsath and S. Natarajan both provide a comprehensive account of these movements.[21] The first man to speak out publicly against the injustices perpetrated on women in the name of tradition and religion was Raja Ram Mohan Roy who in an 1818 tract condemned *sati* (the burning of a woman on her husband's funeral pyre). He also attacked *kulin* (high caste Hindu Brahmins) polygamy and spoke in favour of women's property rights. Roy vividly described the degraded state of Indian society and held the condition of women as one of the causes responsible for this. Following his example, improving the condition of women became the first tenet of the Indian social reform movement. Their generally inferior status, their enforced seclusion, their early marriage, and lack of education were facts documented by reformers throughout the country. Roy's mobilisation of Hindu reformist opinion against *sati* created a climate which made it possible for Lord William Bentinck to pass a law banning *sati* in 1829. Ram Mohan Roy's role in the modernisation of India was reassessed in the bicentenary of his birth, 1975.[22] One hundred and fifty-eight years after the banning of *sati*, Rupmati, an 18-year-old girl, burnt herself on the funeral pyre of her husband in Deorala, a village in Rajasthan. This incident aroused a great deal of scholarly and public interest in the whole practice. Mention may be made of V. N. Datta's *Sati* (1988), of Kumkum Sangari's article on '*Sati* in Modern India', and that by Lata Mani entitled 'Contentious Traditions: the Debate on *Sati* in Colonial India', in which she analyses the connections between public concern with women, the discursive reconstruction of Hindu tradition and strategies for colonial legitimacy.[23] Her concern with the debate on *sati* is not so much with who was for or against the practice, but rather with how these ideological positions were argued by the British officials, the social reformers and the orthodox Hindus.

Ishwar Chandra Vidysagar (1820-1891) championed the cause of Hindu widows which, unlike the *sati* agitation which had been confined to Bengal, became a cause that attracted English-educated men across the sub-continent and led to the passing of the Hindu Widows Remarriage Act of 1856. The customary and statutory aspects of the Act have been examined by Lucy Carroll.[24] Autobiographies of Hindu widows in the second half of the nineteenth and early twentieth centuries have been found in recent years and based on this, work is being done on widowhood. Rosalind O'Hanlon, in her paper on 'Issues of Widowhood, Gender, Discourse and Resistance in Colonial Western India', argues that in the whole debate on *sati* and other issues of social reform:

> woman stands as signifier and Hindu tradition as signified, whose associative total in Roland Barthes' term, constitutes Hindu womanhood as sign. At this level what matters is not so much whether good or bad figurings of the feminine and tradition were employed, than that Hindu womanhood became instituted as a sign or mode of communication between male subjects, both colonizers and colonized.[25]

The issue of child marriage was taken up by social reformers like Keshub Chandra Sen (1838-1884), Vidyasagar and Gopal Hari Deshmukh. Unlike *sati*, polygamy and widow remarriage, which affected mainly the upper castes, child marriage was widespread among the lower castes also. Behramji Malabari (1853-1912) launched an all-India campaign for the passing of a Bill to raise the age of consent of marriage of Hindu girls, which led to a bitter controversy between the orthodox and the reformers. This controversy has been dealt with by historians such as Stanley Wolpert and others as part of the debate between those who were defending and those who were attacking tradition.[26] Despite a storm of protest from the orthodox, an Act raising the age of marriage was passed by a legislature which was predominantly British. Dagmar Engels has argued that British officials were not really concerned with the plight of Hindu women but in employing what they took to be their acute deprivation as evidence for the moral unfitness of Hindu society itself.[27] Joanna Liddle and Rama Joshi have argued that the British used gender divisions in India as a vehicle for proving their liberality, as a demonstration of their superiority and as a legitimisation of their rule.[28] Mrinalini Sinha presented a paper at the Women's Studies Conference held at Chandigarh in 1986 on 'Colonial Politics and the Ideal of Masculinity: The Example of the Age of Consent Act of 1891 in Bengal' in which she attempts to draw a connection between imperialism and the ideal of manliness and to show how colonial politics was mediated through a set of gender relations, and argues that gender identities and gender relations were vital features in the ideological defence of the Raj.[29]

One of the first to make a connection between caste oppression and women's oppression was Jotiba Phule, a Maharashtrian of low caste who led the anti-Brahmin struggle in Maharashtra, also opposing child marriage, polygamy and advocating women's education and widow remarriage. Phule, ignored by earlier historians, is now receiving scholarly attention.[30]

All the nineteenth-century social reformers were concerned with some issue or other relating to women and the reasons for this have been explored, among others, by Charles Heimsath and Veena Mazumdar.[31] A re-examination of the ideology of reformers regarding women and a reassessment of their role in liberating women are also being undertaken. One such attempt is Madhu Kishwar's work on Dayanand Saraswati and the powerful social reform movement he founded in 1875, the Arya Samaj.[32] Kishwar argues that while the Arya Samaj worked for women's education and widow remarriage and against child marriage, it did not advocate women's equality. According to her and a number of other feminist historians, this is true not only of the Arya Samaj but of all the social reformers and their organisations. Kishwar focuses on the hegemony the urban educated elite acquired in defining the women's question in North India. She attempts to answer questions such as why the women's issue became one of the central issues for reformers and why women's education came to occupy such an important place in the social reform movement. Women's response to the process of social change, she argues, was not just one of being passive recipients of welfare. Their participation gave rise to self-generated activity by individual pioneers and women's organisations. Reformers like Dayanand Saraswati were not concerned with women as individuals but recognised women only in their familial roles as wives and mothers. According to her, the Arya Samaj wanted to reform women rather than the social conditions which oppressed them. The women's question was a central issue in the debate over social reform in the early- and mid-nineteenth century. What has perplexed historians is the rather sudden disappearance of such issues from the agenda of public debate towards the end of the century. Sumit Sarkar and Partha Chatterjee have both recently given different answers to this question.[33]

Few studies exist of Muslim women in India. Patricia Jeffrey has looked at a small group of Muslim women in an area of Delhi.[34] Gail Minault has examined Muslim women's lives and men's view thereof in her paper 'Purdah and Boundaries: Images of Women and the Emergence of Indo-Muslim Identity'.[35] For the emerging Muslim middle class, as for their Hindu counterparts, women were symbolic of all that was wrong with their cultural and religious life but also of all that was worth preserving. She holds that the movement for women's education and social reform among Muslims was a part of an overall process of Islamisation taking place in India in the late nineteenth century. This was not a movement for women's liberation but rather for reform of a patriarchal sort. The movement for women's education was an integral part of the process of Muslim identity formation but it did not envisage the removal of *Purdah*.

By the end of the nineteenth century, women emerged from within the reform movement who formed their own organisations and the emergence of a rudimentary women's movement in India can be traced from this time. Swarnakumari Devi, sister of the poet Rabindranath Tagore, started a Ladies' Society in 1882. She discarded *purdah* and together with her husband, edited a Bengali journal, *Bharati*, having thus earned the distinction of being the first Indian woman editor. Significant changes were taking place in the lives of upper caste/class Bengali women in the second half of the nineteenth century and a number of books and articles have dealt with this in the last ten years, including those by Meredith Borthwick, Ghulam Murshid, Srabashi Ghosh and Malavika Karlekar.[36] Bengal has been most extensively studied because of the availability of material in the vernacular language in the form of women's autobiographies, journals, newspapers, novels, and so on. But a new awakening also took place among women in Western India, references to which can be found in Neera Desai's *Women in Modern India* (1977), which studies the changing position of women in India in various historical epochs and explores some of the fundamental factors which affect the status of women in modern India, as well as in her *Social History of Gujarat*, published in 1978.[37] In the same year that Swarnakumari Devi founded *Sakhi Samiti*, Pandita Ramabai Saraswati formed the Arya Mahila Samaj and went on to start a series of women's associations in various towns of Bombay Presidency. Pandita Ramabai was a remarkable woman who first lost her parents in the most tragic circumstances and then her husband. A young Hindu widow, with an infant daughter, she faced enormous odds in waging a life-long battle for the rights of women. Numerous biographies have been written about her, including that by Padmini Sengupta. In the 1980s, both Meera Kosambi and I have written of her life and work.[38]

The early women's associations had been confined to a locality or city. The first all-India organisation was the Women's Indian Association established in 1917 by Dorothy Jinarajadas, together with Annie Besant and Margaret Cousins. Barbara Ramusack has studied the work of these foreign women and their contribution to the Indian women's movement.[39] Conscious of their political rights and influenced by democratic values, these elite women worked actively to generate political consciousness among women. They took up the issue of votes for women when the Secretary of State for India, Lord Edwin Montagu, came to India to discuss the demands for political reform. The Southborough Franchise Committee was initially reluctant to give women the right to vote but because of the sustained campaign launched by the women's organisations and the support given to them by the Indian National Congress and other political parties, it was finally left to the provincial legislatures to decide the matter. Geraldine Forbes has considered the whole issue of votes for women (1979).[40] Madras was the first province to grant votes to women in 1920, followed by Bombay in 1921. The franchise was, of course, extremely restricted and when the first provincial elections were held in which women could vote, less than one per cent of the female population could exercise the right. Kamaladevi Chattopadhyaya contested the election as an independent candidate but was defeated by a narrow margin of fifty votes. Kamaladevi has discussed her views on the women's movement, and has well described this election in her article on the 'Women's Movement Then and Now' and in *Indian Women's Battle for Freedom* (1983).[41]

It was assumed by the men that women in legislatures would confine themselves to debates on social issues affecting women and children, and the women leaders themselves gave assurances that despite the vote, they would continue to be good wives and mothers. Gail Pearson shows how middle-class women wanted women to be pre-eminent in the household, to be respected and to have the right to education but that they did not challenge the patriarchal social order.[42] Neither Sarojini Naidu nor Begum Shah Nawaz Khan who led the women's deputation asking for votes for women, were feminists. They argued that women should be given the vote because of their role in the household. Votes for them were necesary, said Sarojini Naidu, so that they could imbue their children with ideas of nationalism. Pearson feels that there was little difference in the views of women of different political wings on the women's movement or on the role that women should play at home and outside.

In 1927, the All India Women's Conference (AIWC) was founded in Poona by Margaret Cousins and a group of Indian women with the modest objective of promoting women's education. But they soon found that this was not possible without looking at other issues such as *purdah*, child marriage, and so forth. The AIWC was the most representative women's organisation in the pre-independence period and had branches all over the country. Jane Everett and I have both examined the foundation and history of the AIWC.[43] Bharati Ray and I are both at present engaged in the project 'From Silence to Activism: A History of the AIWC'. Everett's study compares the historical development of the Indian women's movement in the late nineteenth and early twentieth centuries with that of the feminist movement of the west. The author has sought answers to the question: to what extent can the origin, ideology, success and failure of the Indian women's movement be explained by the same factors that explain the course of the movement in the west and to what extent by factors specific to the Indian experience. She also examines why the campaign for political representation for women in India did not provoke the type of hostility experienced in Britain and the USA and brings out the weaknesses of the women's movement in India and the west and their inability to affect mass mobilisation. Kalpana Shah attempts to understand the working of the AIWC or Akhil Hind Mahila Parishad in its historical and all-India perspective.[44] She holds the view that welfare programmes undertaken by a middle-class women's movement unintentionally strengthened the traditional image of women and, therefore, performed a restricted and, perhaps, a regressive role. Pratima Asthana has also dealt with the women's movement in India, while Vijaya Agnew's work, *Elite Women in Indian Politics* (1979), traces the historical background to the women's movement in her first chapter.[45] In 1980 Renu Chakravarti published a study of *Communists in the Indian Women's Movement.*[46]

  While on the one hand women were fighting for their rights and trying to improve their status through education and legal reforms, the women's movement entered a new phase with the arrival of Mahatma Gandhi on the Indian political scene. From the very inception of the Indian National Congress in 1885, its membership was open to women and ten women attended the fourth session at Bombay in 1889. In 1917, Annie Besant became the first woman President of the Indian National Congress. As studied by Bharati Ray, women had taken part in the *swadeshi* ('of one's own country') movement during the anti-partition agitation in Bengal from 1905 to 1911.[47] But as I wrote in 1976, women were hardly visible on the Indian political scene until the coming of Gandhi.[48] It was he who gave them a new direction and actively involved them in the freedom struggle. Women's role in the freedom movement is one area in which considerable work has been done in the last few years. Manmohan Kaur gives a descriptive account of women's participation in various phases of the freedom struggle since 1857.[49] Kumari Jayawardena highlights women's participation in revolutionary and democratic movements in India and other countries of the third world and also deals with the early movement for women's emancipation.[50] In *Indian Women's Battle for Freedom* (1983), Kamaladevi Chattopadhyaya tells the story of women's battle for freedom from the late nineteenth century to the present.[51] This book highlights the role played by pioneering women and the odds faced by them. Gail Minault's *Extended Family: Women and Political Participation in India and Pakistan* (1981) is an important contribution to the study of the Indian women's movement. The collection of articles here examine the participation of women in political movements in a historical perspective, starting from the reform movements of the nineteenth century, through the freedom movement to the contemporary period. Minault's contention is that women's participation in the Gandhian movement was in a sense an extension of their role within the family. Women were traditionally supposed to sacrifice themselves and participation in politics was internalised as a special form of sacrifice in an essentially religious process. The language, imagery, and idiom of nationalist protest remained steeped in tradition and religion as self-conscious alternatives to alien Western norms. It is held by many scholars that while such strong traditional moorings permitted the political involvement of thousands of women, at the same time it inhibited the extension of radicalisation to other spheres.

There is a growing recognition among scholars that women should not be treated as an undifferentiated, homogenised category but that an attempt must be made to seek the connection between the nature of a particular political movement and the social composition of the women participants. The need to explore the wider effect of politicisation and its impact on the domestic milieu and ethos and whether it led to radicalisation in other aspects of women's lives and status is also recognised.[52] A number of M.Phil. and Ph.D. theses and articles are being written on women's role in the freedom struggle in different regions of India and even at the district level. Mention may be made of Usha Bhatt's thesis on Ahmedabad, of the work of Chitra Ghosh, and Mita Mukherji on Bengal, of my work on Gujarat, and that of Uma Rao on U.P.[53] Work has also been done on Karnataka, Andhra, Assam, Bihar and Orissa. Some of these papers were presented at the third women's studies conference held at Chandigarh in 1986 and have not been individually cited here. Work has also been done on women in the armed revolutionary movement in Bengal. Many of these studies are based not only on archival and written records but also on oral interviews.

A number of articles have appeared in the last two or three years critically assessing Gandhi's role in the movement for women's emancipation. While the earlier view, to which most Indians still subscribe, was that Gandhi played a crucial role in bringing women out of their homes by having immense faith in their inner strength and their moral appeal, a number of feminists have questioned how far he really liberated women insofar as he viewed the woman's role primarily as that of a mother and wife. Among the interesting articles on this subject mention may be made of those by Madhu Kishwar, Sujata Patel, and Karuna Chanana Ahmed.[54] Shashi Joshi has written on 'Feminism, Mass Movement and Gandhian Ideology'[55] and examined the uniqueness of the Gandhi-led mass movement in the history of revolutions and national liberation struggles of the twentieth century.

Although the pre-independence women's movement was successful in achieving many of its goals, it never mobilised the mass of women in the fight against female subordination in the same way that Gandhi mobilised them for civil disobedience. In this they missed the opportunity to broaden support for their causes. The women's organisations which were led by middle-class urban women failed to form any links with rural struggles in which women played an important role. Recently Peter

Custers has shown how rural poor women in Bengal defended their villages and homes from police raids and set up their own *nari bahini* during the *Tebhaga* movement in 1944-46.[56] Similarly, Indra Saldanha Munshi describes the heroic role of tribal women in the Warli revolt in Maharashtra in 1946, and Vasantha Kannabiran and K. Lalitha have written about women in the Telangana People's Struggle.[57] By and large, historians of the peasant movement have so far ignored questions regarding gender and only now is this being remedied and research carried out on women's participation in various peasant and tribal struggles. Deepti Mehrotra and Kapil Kumar have both written on women's activism in Avadh.[58] The emphasis which had so far been on urban elite women is now shifting to the lesser known, poorer women in the cities and villages. Scholars are interested not only in what women did but in the impact political participation may have had on women's lives and self-perceptions, as Bharati Ray has done in a well-researched paper.[59]

Women's education

The history of women's education in the modern period is an area on which a number of monographs have been published since the mid-1960s, such as those by L. Misra and Y. B. Mathur, the latter of which concentrating on educational policy and is based on educational records, quinquennial reports, and so forth.[60] J. C. Bagal's *Women's Education in Eastern India, the First Phase* is a detailed study based on contemporary records, tracing the beginnings of female education and the role played by missionaries, Europeans and Indians.[61] Unfortunately very few studies exist on women's education in ancient and medieval India. Christian missionaries played a pioneering role in bringing modern education to women in India. A. Jeyasekharan has written on the 'Church of Scotland's Early Educational Endeavours for Girls in Madras, 1841-1861'.[62] Vidyut Khandwala prepared a useful bibliography on 'Education of Women in India, 1850-1967', but unfortunately twenty years have elapsed and it is now out of date.[63] While the studies in the pre-independence period and in the 1950s and 60s dealt with the growth of women's education and the role of missionaries, government and Indian social reformers, a number of recent works have tried to examine issues such as what changes education actually brought about in women's lives, the debates over the kind of education women ought to receive, the curriculum in girls' schools, and so forth, using sources such as women's autobiographies, contemporary journals, and the magazines and writings of reformers. G. Murshid and Meredith Borthwick offer excellent accounts of the lives of Bengali women and their exposure to education through schools as well as the *zenana* system, which was a system of privately educating women at home (where they lived in secluded quarters, the *zenana*) by employing women teachers, usually Christian missionary ladies.[64]

Scholars have been working extensively on the growth of education in various states in India. The motivations and desires of those who wanted to introduce education for women as well as the agents themselves have been identified. What is highlighted is that while the direction of social change helped women, there was the overriding consideration that masculine and feminine roles should not be blurred through education for women. In other words, the socialisation process at home was not to be counterbalanced by the processes going on in schools; in fact the latter was supposed to reinforce the former. These points are made in a volume of essays, *Women, Education, and Socialisation*, edited by Karuna Chanana (1988).[65] In this volume, I have written of the life histories, biographies and autobiographies of seven women who were among the first few to receive modern education in western India. All of them were Brahmin by caste and belonged to middle-class families. From these accounts, one gets an idea of the orthodox reaction to the 'new woman', who was seen as a threat to the family. The fear was that exposure to English education would result in disrespect for the traditional norms and values. I argue that education does affect women in ways that push them towards modernisation and social change and helps them to widen their horizons by making them step out of the boundaries of their homes. Chanana's paper, 'Social Change or Social Reform: The Education of Women in Pre-Independence India', argues that the growth and expansion of women's education in colonial India have to be seen and understood within the social context that determines the educational campaign's goals and functions. She looks at women's education from 1921 to 1947, a period of intense political awakening and social reform in India. She demonstrates the linkages between the debates on curriculum changes for girls, and enrolment of girls in co-educational schools to the notion of the role of a girl as a daughter, housewife and a mother. Again the differential response to education by different religious groups and different regions is viewed in relation to socio-economic and cultural practices such as *purdah* and the segregation of sexes in certain areas and by some groups. Karlekar's paper in the same volume argues that the participation of women in education and employment in non-traditional areas has brought about a substantial change in the notions of femininity. She traces the genesis of women's education in nineteenth-century Bengal and links it to the differential perceptions of its functions for boys and girls. She looks at existing reality to see the continuity of traditional role models and observes that asymmetrical relations between the sexes have influenced and shaped the system of education during the colonial period and after.[66]

Research is being done on women's education in the different Indian states and among different communities and groups such as Muslims, tribals, and scheduled castes.[67] Since most of the work on education has focused on middle-class urban women, the Women's Studies Conference in 1986 had a special sub-theme on women's struggles for education with reference to the weaker sections and the minorities. The inequalities in women's education between various states, communities, castes and between urban and rural areas are being explored. While there is a history of Bethune College in Calcutta, the oldest women's college in India (established in 1849), published in its centenary year, there is still really no good scholarly study of any women's school or college or even of the first women's university, Seth Nathibai Damodar Thackersey University (known as SNDT), founded in 1916.

Women and the economy

Women's role in social production has been the subject matter of intensive research in the recent period. The alarming decline in women's participation in economic production highlighted in the report of the Committee on the Status of Women (1974) focused attention on female employment.

The relationship of women to the economy is a special problem in the area of Indian women's studies. Data for the ancient period is not easy to find and one has to rely on inscriptions and literary texts. Vijaya Ramaswamy has recently written a paper on women and work in South India, based on *Sangam* literature which essentially consists of two major collection of songs composed between the first century BC and sixth to seventh centuries AD.[68] She examines the various occupations in which women played a role, including agriculture, dairy farming, handloom industry, and so forth. She finds that rural rather than urban women were co-sharers with men in economic activities.

Gregory Kozlowski describes some aspects of the processes by which Muslim women in North India succeeded or failed to obtain material goods and the influence they wielded during the era of Mughal ascendancy which lasted from the early sixteenth century to mid-eighteenth century.[69] The British had different definitions of wealth and different administrative establishments which brought about fundamental changes in Muslim women's control over property.

Mention has already been made of research being done on women and land rights in medieval India. While the role of unequal land rights in determining the status of different caste and class groups in India has been the subject of much debate, their impact on women's status has generally escaped attention. In fact the patriarchal bias of the social and legal system gives rise to the assumption that once the men of the family have land, women's needs are automatically taken care of. The impact of land rights on women is seldom fully comprehended. Land inherited by sons only, deprives daughters of land and leads to dowry. The position of tribal women is different and some attention is now being focused on them.

The reconstruction of women's economic history often has to rely on informed guesses since reference to women's economic activities is extremely infrequent in Indian history. Our first records come from travellers' accounts, administrative reports, official documents and the Census. In the Census reports we get rough quantitative estimates that tell us something of the range and degree of the economic involvement of women. The records of the colonial period are subject to many biases and inaccuracies and like all historical records have to be used with great caution. They are nevertheless extremely useful as source material. Beginning in the late eighteenth century, the British introduced new systems of land tenure in India. A 1983 study on Kerala traces the impact on women due to historical changes in land rights in the colonial period and land reform legislation after independence.[70] Kerala had a matrilineal system where women long enjoyed rights of ownership.

Despite the overwhelming importance of the agricultural sector for female employment, research on women in agriculture is a relatively new area of concern. Women's role in agricultural production is now being examined. Women's work and survival strategies among tribal groups in Bihar has been studied and it has been found that women had rights of ownership, control over earning and also a role in decision making in the pre-colonial system of agricultural production. Women's access to land and productive resources in Awadh in the period 1856-1947 have been investigated by Smita Tewari Jessal, who finds that women of different castes and communities had enjoyed a wide variety of rights in land which they gradually lost.[71] The question of course is how they lost these rights. Customary laws often gave women more rights than did the codified Hindu or Muslim laws. Development of the legal system clearly affected the pattern of landholding and the new concepts and definitions of property raised innumerable problems for women. Minoti Kaul has since written on women's access to land in Punjab, for the same period, 1849-1947.[72]

The pattern and trends in women's occupations excited the attention of scholars like D. R. Gadgil, whose book *The Industrial Evolution of India in Recent Times* appeared in 1954.[73] Throughout the last hundred years, two features stand out with regard to women's economic activities: (1) continuous and impressive decline in the number of women reported in the work force; and (2) major shifts in their occupational distribution. We need to study the forces that determine the degree of involvement women have had in different economic activities and under what conditions they have been altered.

Scholars have recently been doing work on women's role in specific occupations. Atchy Reddy has given a vivid description of the large number of free female farm servants in the Nellore district and how these women were more numerous than males right up to 1951.[74] He also discusses the special system of female agricultural supervisors or *maletas* as well as the presence of some high caste women as agricultural labourers and their high status a century ago. A sad story of the decline in women's livelihood is traced by Mukul Mukherji who records the devastation brought by the introduction of power-driven rice processing mills on women who had rice dehusking as their major source of livelihood.[75] Nirmala Banerji's 1980 study of Bengal traces the disappearance of the spinning industry and the stagnancy of silk manufacturing as a result of the import of British yarn from the 1820s onwards.[76] Thousands of workers were thrown out of work, half of them being women.

In the mid-nineteenth century the first factories were set up in India. Cotton textile mills came to Bombay and jute mills to Bengal. Only recently has research begun on women in the trade unions and the professions. Though women were initially employed as factory labour, there was sharp decline after 1901. In the 1970s J. N. Sinha and J. Ambannavar have tried to map the changes in different sectors of female employment.[77] Ambannavar disaggregates each sector and compares the new industries with the old. Scholars have attempted to identify the factors responsible for the decline in female labour participation. The biggest decline occurred in those sectors which had traditionally relied on the *jajmani* system of reciprocal exchange. The system covered not only the needs of the cultivators, such as agricultural implements but also other goods such as footwear, clothes, pottery, utensils, and so forth. This method guaranteed a secure source of livelihood to women and its disappearance caused great hardship to those who could not readily move out of their villages or find alternative employment. The effect of this on women's health has not yet been fully investigated. Famines, epidemics and disease all took a heavy toll of women throughout the eighteenth, nineteenth, and twentieth centuries. Bidyut Mohanti has worked on 'Famines and Sex Ratio in Orissa Division between 1881 and 1921'.[78]

Women constituted a high proportion of the work force in the cotton textile industry in Bombay between 1919-1936, their numbers rising to 22.95 per cent of the whole in 1926. By 1939, however, the proportion was only 14.9 per cent. Radha Kumar hypothesises that underlying this decline were attempts to reform the working-class family.[79] At the centre of all these activities stood the concept of woman as mother. Wage work for women was considered secondary and not regarded as essential for their survival. The attitude of the state, the capitalists and the reformers towards working-class families, all tended to reinforce the notion that women's wage labour was supplemementary to the family income, which was earned by the male worker.

The family

Sociological literature is flooded with family studies which describe roles without examining the inequalities within the family. Family history has become a new area of study among European and American scholars. By and large, it is as yet, an unexplored area among Indian historians. Nevertheless, Iravati Karve provided in 1968 a descriptive analysis of Indian family and kinship systems, which enables us to understand the similarities and differences between the different regions of India.[80] A study of the family and the relation between its size and nuclearity or jointness is provided with the help of an analysis of Gujrati families by A. M. Shah.[81] Kapadia's work on marriage and family in India (1980, 3rd ed.) is recognised as a standard textbook on the subject.[82] Alice Clark has examined the effect of long term demographic behaviour on *Leva Kanbi Patidar* women in central Gujarat in the nineteenth century.[83] The two major themes she discusses are female infanticide and the entrenchment of the marriage system which entailed increased levels of female subordination and mortality. She looks at female infanticide from a structural viewpoint, in the context of the wider ecological, economic and political constraints among which it emerged. Among the *kanbi patidars*, hypergamy and dowry are practised. Her data from central Gujarat also shows that male domination within families varied according to the family's social status. As family status rose, there was greater emphasis on family purity and on controlling the lives of women. An inter-generational study of four generation of women in urban upper-caste families, exploring the changes and continuities in the lives and perceptions of women, was completed in 1988.[84]

Law

A neglected area of research is women's situation in the law. In India, scholars have not made significant use of legal records or criminal proceedings to study the position of women. Some work has been done on the acts passed in the pre-Independence period, such as on the Hindu Widows' Remarriage Act, the Age of Consent Act or the Child Marriage Restraint Act (all mentioned above), but much more could be done. Lotika Sarkar holds the colonial policy of divide and rule, whereby separate personal laws were instituted, responsible for the difficulty in bringing about changes through social legislation.[85] She discusses the various laws pertaining to marriage, divorce, guardianship, and inheritance and examines their effect on the status of women. In her 1985 study Indira Jaisingh evaluates the changes in the law relating to women passed during the decade 1975-1984.[86] At the second Women's Studies Conference held at Trivandrum in 1984, there was a special section on law where papers on women and family law, Muslim family law, dowry, and land legislation and women were presented.

Women and religion

In recent years, a few studies of women in religious movements have also been undertaken. Ursula King has looked at the effect of social change on religious self-understanding by examining the lives of some women ascetics in modern India. She has also studied the status and images of women in the major religious traditions of contemporary India.[87] Some work has been done on women poets and saints of medieval India, both Hindu and Muslim. Neera Desai has written on 'Women in the Bhakti Movement' and so has Madhu Kishwar.[88] Sarojini Shintri has worked on 'Women in the Virasaiva Movement', while Gautam Neogi has studied the Brahmo Samaj and women in Bengal.[89] In 1989 Julie Leslie described the Perfect Wife, the orthodox Hindu woman according to one Sanskrit text.[90] Vanaja Dhruvarajan has studied the way in which religion, ideology, and social structure have converged to subjugate women.[91]

Women in literature

The images and perceptions of women in the literature of different Indian languages is another area of interest. Scholars are working on individual women authors, such as Premchand, an eminent Hindi novelist who wrote in the 1930s and 1940s and Bankim Chandra Chaterjee, one of the most important authors of nineteenth-century Bengal, or on the literature of a region such as C. S. Lakshmi's work on Tamil Nadu (the former Madras Presidency), or Tanika Sarkar's study on Bengal.[92] Gail Minault has examined Urdu women's magazines in their historical context and describes them as brave pioneers, expanding the frontier of women's roles and consciousness at a time when these frontiers were severely limited.[93]

Women and medicine

The British introduced Western medicine as a means of showing the beneficial nature of their rule. Both childbirth practices and the role of midwives have been studied by Patricia Jeffery and Geraldine Forbes, respectively.[94] Forbes holds that in a colonial setting, the attitude of the ruling class towards the role of scientific medicine, indigenous gender roles, male-female relationships, and their own civilising mission all contributed to the rhetoric of the 'dangerous dai' as the symbol of all that was unhealthy in the customs and conditions of birthing in India. Barbara Ramusack has written on the debate over birth control in India, 1920-1940.[95]

Medicine was one of the first professions that Indian women entered but not much work has yet been done on their participation in the medical profession, on missionaries and women's medical education or on the history of women's medical colleges.

Post-independence women's political activism

In the 1960s, women were mobilised in large numbers and took part in various peasant, tribal, and industrial working-class struggles. A major source of radicalisation was the Naxalite movement which affected parts of West Bengal, Andhra Pradesh, Kerala, and Bihar. Not enough work has been done on the role of women and women's consciousness in this movement, but there is evidence that women showed remarkable courage in the face of police repression. Women like Suniti Biswakarmarkar, a tribal, or Dhaneswari Singh, an agricultural labourer, or Nayaneswari Mallik, a sharecropper, joined the movement (often with their entire families) and became local leaders. They attended meetings armed with bows and arrows, choppers and spears and many died in encounters with the police as recounted by Sunil Sen and Saswati Ghosh.[96] Women's role in the Telangana movement has also been studied. In 1972, a unique movement developed in Shahada in Dhulia district in Maharashtra among the *adivasis*, mostly Bhils, the majority of whom are landless labourers. The movement and women's role in it has been the subject of several articles including one by Maria Mies.[97] In the rural areas of Maharashtra, according to Gail Omvedt, male organisers of peasant struggles testified that 'women were the most militant; they were the first to break through police lines and fight, the most tenacious in negotiations, the inventors of new forms of struggles such as blocking of traffic on roads'.[98] During the drought in Maharashtra in 1972-73, the United Women's Anti-Price Rise Committee was formed bringing together slum dwellers, middle-class housewives and women workers. Thousands of women marched through the streets of Bombay city, singing songs and chanting slogans against rising prices. This movement has also been the subject of recent research by Gail Omvedt and Nandita Gandhi.[99]

Women in India have also played a crucial role in the movement against deforestation. They evolved a new mode of protest that has now become well-known over the world as the Chipko movement. When forest officials, contractors and others came to cut down trees, women embraced the trees to prevent their being cut down. As Kumud Sharma and S. Jain have shown, it was only because of women's militancy, initiative and active participation that the movement could be so effective.[100]

A particular feature of the post-1975 women's movement is the rise and proliferation of a number of autonomous women's groups. Their autonomy is to be understood in terms of their independence from all political parties. The distinguishing characteristics of these organisations are that they are led by women, that the fight against oppression, exploitation, injustice and discrimination against women is their first priority and that they are not subordinate to the decisions of any other party. Though the leadership of these groups is in the hands of middle-class educated urban women and they are city-based, they have formed linkages with rural groups and have taken up issues concerning agricultural labourers, marginal farmers or tribals. The social base of these autonomous women's groups, their methods of mobilisation, and the issues with which they are concerned, have been discussed by Vibhuti Patel.[101] The whole scenario of the women's movement in India in the decade for women had been very ably and comprehensively discussed by Neera Desai and Vibhuti Patel.[102]

As a result of the sustained activities in various fields by Indian women's groups, there is now a much greater social awareness about women's problems. After 1975, the government set up machinery to develop policies and programmes for women, consisting of a national committee with the Prime Minister as Chairman, a steering committee of the national committee, an inter-departmental co-ordination committee, and a women's welfare and development bureau. In 1984, a special department of women and child development was formed as part of the Ministry of Human Resource Development. The Planning Commission has also been giving greater attention to women's development. The National Council of Educational Research and Training (NCERT) and some state governments have appointed committees of women scholars and activists to remove sexism from school textbooks. Growing academic interest in women's issues is one of the noteworthy features of the women's decade. The University Grants Commission has selected a number of universities where women's studies are to be developed. Research on women with a new perspective and documentation on women's issues have been gaining prominence. The University Grants Commission, the Indian Council of Social Science Research (ICSSR), the Indian Council of Historical Research (ICHR), and many other national and international agencies are supporting research on women. The Research Unit on Women's Studies at the SNDT University in Bombay is a pioneer organisation focusing on research on women's issues. Apart from SNDT, there are two other women's universities, the Mother Teresa University in Kodaikanal and the Women's University at Tirupati. The Indian Association of Women's Studies established in 1981 is a leading institution of academicians and activists involved in research and teaching. Every alternate year it sponsors an all-India conference which encourages young scholars to write and present papers relating to different areas of women's studies. All this has encouraged scholars to produce material on women. In the last few years a number of publications devoted entirely to women's issues, in the form of books, magazines, such as *Manushi* and *Samya Shakti*, newsletters and pamphlets have appeared. Efforts are being made to prepare reading and teaching material with a feminist perspective. The *Economic and Political Weekly* brings out a special supplement on women's studies twice a year, and journals such as the *Indian Economic and Social History Review*, *Social Scientist*, *Mainstream*, *Social Change*, and *Social Action* contain scholarly and research-based articles on women, but there is no journal devoted exclusively to women's history. Many more students are today engaged in doing research on different aspects of women's history in Indian universities than a decade ago, though there are still large unexplored areas. India is a vast country and there are wide variations in the cultural, economic and social patterns across the nation; while the mainstream experiences have received more attention, this plurality has to be recognised if we are not to make quick and facile generalisations. Scholars are paying increased attention to scheduled caste, tribal,[103] and other marginalised women. Despite numerous drawbacks and limitations, historians in India have initiated processes for bringing about a greater awareness and interest in women's history.

NOTES

1. Sheila Rowbotham, *Hidden from History: 300 Years of Women's Oppression and the Fight Against It* (New York: Pantheon Press, 1975); Mary S. Hartman and Lois Banner (eds.), *Clio's Consciousness Raised: New Perspectives on the History of Women* (New York: Octagon Press, 1976); Berenice A. Carroll (ed.), *Liberating Women's History: Theoretical and Critical Essays* (Urbana: University of Illinois Press, 1975); Renate Bridenthal and Claudia Koonz (eds.), *Becoming Visible: Women in European History* (Boston: Houghton-Mifflin, 1977).

2. Kumkum Sangari and Sudesh Vaid (eds.), *Recasting Women: Essays in Colonial History* (New Delhi: Kali for Women, 1989).

3. Maria Mies, *Indian Women and Patriarchy* (New Delhi: Concept Publishing House, 1980).

4. Clarisse Bader, *La Femme dans l'Inde antique* (Paris, 1867); in English as *Women in Ancient India*, tr. by Mary E. R. Martin. (Reprint. New Delhi: Anmol Publications, 1987).

5. A. S. Altekar, *The Position of Women in Hindu Civilization* (New Delhi: Motilal Banarasidas, 1962).

6. Suvira Jayaswal, 'Position of Women in Early India', paper presented at the First National Conference on Women's Studies, Bombay, 1981.

7. Uma Chakravarti, 'In Search of Our Past', *Economic and Political Weekly* [hereafter *EPW*], 23, no. 18 (April 30, 1988). See also Uma Chakravarti and Kum Kum Roy, 'Breaking Out of Invisibility: Rewriting the History of Women in Ancient India', in S. J. Kleinberg (ed.), *Retrieving Women's History* (Oxford: Berg, UNESCO, 1988).

8. Indra, *Status of Women in Ancient India* (Banaras: Motilal Banarasidas, 1955).

9. R. M. Das, *Women in Manu and his Seven Commentators* (Varanasi: Kanchana Publications, 1962).

10. M. Talim, *Women in Early Buddhism* (Bombay: University of Bombay Press, 1972).

11. Saroj Gulati, *Women and Society in the 11th and 12th Centuries in North India* (Delhi: Chanakya Publications, 1985).

12. Motichandra, *The World of Courtesans* (New Delhi: Vikas, 1973).

13. Dharmanand D. Kosambi, *The Culture and Civilization of Ancient India in Historical Outline* (New Delhi: Vikas, 1975); Romila Thapar, *Ancient Indian Social History* (Delhi: Orient Longman's, 1978); Ram Saran Sharma, *Perspectives on the Economic and Social History of Early India* (New Delhi: Munshiram Manoharlal, 1983).

14. P. Thomas, *Indian Womanhood Through The Ages* (Bombay: Asia, 1964).

15. Suvira Jayal, *The Status of Women in the Epics* (Delhi: Motilal Banarasidas, 1966).

16. Prabhati Mukherjee, *Hindu Women: Normative Models* (New Delhi: Orient Longman's, 1978); Gulati, *Women and Society*.

17. Uma Chakravarti, 'The Rise of Buddhism as Experienced by Women', paper presented in the seminar on Women's Life Cycle and Identity, Badkal, 1981; Chakravarti, 'The Sita Myth', *Samya Shakti*, 1, no. 1 (1983).

18. Sukumari Bhattacharya, 'Women in Mahabharata', paper presented at a seminar at Indraprastha College, Delhi University, 1981.

19. Ila Mukherji, *Social Status of North Indian Women* (Agra: Shivlal Agarwal & Company, 1972).

20. Rekha Misra, *Women in Mughal India* (New Delhi: Munshiram Manohardal, 1967).

21. Charles Heimsath, *Indian Nationalism and Social Reform* (Princeton: Princeton University Press, 1964); S. Natarajan, *A Century of Social Reform* (Bombay: Asia Publishing House, 1959).

22. Vijay C. Joshi (ed.), *Rammohun Roy and the Process of Modernisation in India* (New Delhi: Vikas Publishing House, 1975).

23. V. N. Datta, *Sati* (New Delhi: Manohar Publishers, 1988); Anand Yang, 'Whose *Sati*? Widow Burning in Early 19th Century India', *Journal of Women's History*, 1, no. 2 (Fall 1989); Kumkum Sangari, '*Sati* in Modern India', *EPW*, 16, no. 31 (August 1, 1981); and Lata Mani, 'Contentious Traditions: the Debate on *Sati* in Colonial India', in Sangari and Vaid (eds.), *Recasting Women*. See also Lata Mani, 'The Production of an Official Discourse on *Sati* in Early Nineteenth-Century Bengal', *EPW*, 21, no. 17 (April 26, 1986), which documents the legislative history of *Sati*. For a suggestive discussion that early nineteenth-century *Sati* was related to socio-economic changes brought about by colonial rule, see Ashish Nandy, '*Sati*: A Nineteenth-Century Tale of Women, Violence and Protest', in Joshi (ed.), *Rammohun Roy*.

24. Lucy Carroll, 'Law, Custom and Statutory Reform, the Hindu Widows' Re- Marriage Act of 1856', *Indian Economic and Social History Review* (hereafter *IESHR*), 20, no. 4 (October-December, 1983).

25. Rosalind O'Hanlon, 'Issues of Widowhood', paper for discussion at Institute of Commonwealth Studies, London, 1988.

26. Stanley Wolpert, *Tilak and Gokhale* (Berkeley: University of California Press, 1962).

27. Dagmar Engels, 'The Age of Consent Act of 1891: Colonial Ideology in Bengal', *South Asia Research*, 3, no. 2 (1983).

28. Joanna Liddle and Rama Joshi, 'Gender and Imperialism in British India', *EPW*, 20, no. 43 (October 26, 1985).

29. Mrinalini Sinha, 'Colonial Politics and the Ideal of Masculinity: The Example of the Age of Consent Act of 1891 in Bengal', paper presented at the Third National Conference on Women's Studies, Chandigarh, October 1986.

30. Dhananjay Keer, *Mahatma Jotirava Phule* (Bombay: Popular Prakashan, 1968); Rosalind O'Hanlon, *Caste, Conflict and Ideology* (Cambridge: Cambridge University Press, 1985).

31. Heimsath, *Indian Nationalism*; Vina Mazumdar, 'The Social Reform Movement: From Ranade to Nehru', in B. R. Nanda (ed.), *Indian Women From Purdah to Modernity* (New Delhi: Vikas, 1976).

32. Madhu Kishwar, 'The Daughters of Aryavata', *IESHR*, 23, no. 2 (1986).

33. Patricia Jeffery, *Frogs in a Well: Indian Women in Purdah* (New Delhi: Vikas, 1979).

34. Sumit Sarkar, 'The Women's Question in Nineteenth-Century Bengal', in Kumkum Sangari and Sudesh Vaid (eds.), *Women and Culture* (Bombay: SNDT University Press, 1985); Partha Chatterjee, 'The Nationalist Resolution of the Women's Question', in Sangari and Vaid (eds.), *Recasting Women*.

35. Gail Minault, paper presented at the Tenth European Conference on South Asian Studies, 1988.

36. Meredith Borthwick, *Changing Role of Women in Bengal, 1849-1905* (Princeton: Princeton University Press, 1984); Ghulam Murshid, *Reluctant Debutant: Response of Bengali Women to Modernisation 1849-1905* (Rajshahi: Rajshahi University Press, 1983); Shrabashi Ghosh, 'Birds in a Cage', *EPW*, 21, no. 43 (October 25, 1986); Malavika Karlekar, 'Kadambini and the Bhadralok, Early Debates over Women's Education in Bengal', *EPW*, 21, no. 17 (April 26, 1986).

37. Neera Desai, *Women in Modern India* (Bombay: Vora & Co., 1977); and Desai, *Social Change in Gujarat* (Bombay: Vora & Co., 1978).

38. Padmini Sengupta, *Pandita Ramabai Saraswati, Her Life and Work* (Bombay: Asia Publishing House, 1970); Meera Kosambi, 'Women, Emancipation and Equality: Pandita Ramabai's Contribution to Women's Cause', *EPW*, 23, no. 44 (October 29, 1988); Aparna Basu, 'A Century's Journey: Women's Education in Western India, 1820-1920', in Karuna Chanana (ed.), *Socialisation, Education and Women: Explorations in Gender Identity* (New Delhi: Orient Longman's, 1988).

39. Barbara Ramusack, 'Catalysts or Helpers? British Feminists, Indian Women's Rights and Indian Independence', in Gail Minault (ed.), *The Extended Family: Women & Political Participation in India and Pakistan* (Bombay: South Asia Books, 1981).

40. Geraldine Forbes, 'Votes for Women', in Vina Mazumdar (ed.), *Symbols of Power* (Bombay: Allied Publishers, 1979).

41. Kamaladevi Chattopadhyaya, 'The Women's Movement Then and Now', in Devaki Jain (ed.), *Indian Women* (New Delhi: Publications Division, Government of India, 1976); and Chattopadhyaya, *Indian Women's Battle for Freedom* (New Delhi: Abhinav Publishers, 1983).

42. Gail Pearson, 'Women and the Vote in Bombay', *IESHR*, 20, no. 1 (1983).

43. Jane Everett, *Women and Social Change in India* (New Delhi: Heritage Publications, 1979); Aparna Basu, 'Sixty Years of AIWC', *Roshni* (New Delhi: AIWC, 1987, Diamond Jubilee issue).

44. Kalpana Shah, *Women's Liberation and Voluntary Action* (New Delhi: Ajanta Press, 1984).

45. Pratima Asthana, *Women's Movement in India* (New Delhi: Vikas Publishing House, 1974); Vijaya Agnew, *Elite Women in Indian Politics* (New Delhi: Vikas Publishing House, 1979).

46. Renu Chakravarti, *Communists in Indian Women's Movement* (New Delhi: People's Publishing House, 1980); Bhattacharya Malini, 'Communist Party and Indian Women's Movement', *EPW*, 17, nos. 1 and 2 (January 2 and 9, 1982).

47. Bharati Ray, 'Swadeshi Movement and Women's Awakening in Bengal, 1903- 1910', *The Calcutta Historical Journal*, 9, no. 2 (1985).

48. Aparna Basu, 'Role of Women in the Indian Freedom Movement', in B. R. Nanda (ed.), *Indian Women From Purdah to Modernity* (New Delhi: Vikas Publishing House, 1976).

49. Manmohan Kaur, *Women in India's Freedom Struggle* (Delhi: Sterling Publishers, 1968).

50. Kumari Jayawardena, *Feminism and Nationalism in the Third World* (The Hague, Netherlands: Institute of Social Studies; see also the edition published in London by Zed Books, 1986).

51. Chattopadhyaya, *Indian Women's Battle*.

52. See Tanika Sarkar, 'Politics and Women in Bengal – The Conditions and Meaning of Participation', *IESHR*, 21, no. 1 (1984).

53. Usha Bhatt, 'Women in the Freedom Movement in Ahmedabad', Ph.D. thesis, Gujarat University, 1973; Chitra Ghosh, 'Women in the Freedom Movement in Bengal', paper presented at the Third National Conference on Women's Studies, Chandigarh, 1986; Mita Mukherji, 'Women in the Civil Disobedience Movement in

Bengal', M.Phil. thesis, Delhi University, 1988; Aparna Basu, 'Gujrati women's response to Gandhi', *Samya Shakti*, 1, no. 2 (1984); Uma Rao, 'Women in the Freedom Struggle in U.P.', *Samya Shakti*, 1, no. 2 (1984).

54. Madhu Kishwar, 'Gandhi on Women', *EPW*, 20, nos. 4 and 5 (October 1985); Sujata Patel, 'Construction and Reconstruction of Women in Gandhi', *EPW*, 23, no. 8 (February 20, 1988); Karuna Ahmed, 'Gandhi, Women's Role and the Freedom Movement', occasional paper, Nehru Memorial Museum and Library, New Delhi, 1984.

55. Shashi Joshi, 'Feminism, Mass Movement and Gandhian Ideology', paper presented at the Third National Conference on Women's Studies, Chandigarh, 1986.

56. Peter Custers, *Women in the Tebhaga Uprising* (Calcutta: Naya Prakash, 1987).

57. Indra Munshi Saldanha, 'Tribal Women in the Warli Revolt, 1945-47: Class and Gender in the Left Perspective', *EPW*, 21, no. 17 (April 26, 1986); Vasantha Kannabiran and K. Lalitha, 'That Magic Time: Women in the Telangana People's Struggle', in Sangari and Vaid (eds.), *Recasting Women*.

58. Deepti Mehrotra, 'Women's Activism in Rural Avadh, 1917-1947', paper presented at the Third National Conference on Women's Studies, Chandigarh, 1986; Kapil Kumar, 'Rural Women in Oudh 1917-47: Baba Ramchandra and the Women's Question', in Sangari and Vaid (eds.), *Recasting Women*.

59. Bharati Ray, 'Freedom Movement and Women's Awakening in Bengal, 1911-1929', *Indian Historical Review*, 12 (1983-4).

60. Lakshmi Misra, *Education of Women in India, 1921-1966* (Bombay: Macmillan, 1966); Y. B. Mathur, *Women's Education in India, 1813-1966* (Bombay: Asia Publishing House, 1973).

61. Jogesh Chandra Bagal, *Women's Education in Eastern India, the First Phase* (Calcutta: The World Press Private Ltd., 1956).

62. Ambpose Jeyasekharan, 'Church of Scotland's Early Educational Endeavours for Girls in Madras, 1841-1861', paper presented at the Tenth European Conference on South Asian Studies, 1988.

63. Vidyut Khandwala, *Education of Women in India, 1850-1967: A Bibliography* (Bombay: SNDT Women's University Press, 1968).

64. Murshid, *Reluctant Debutant*; Borthwick, *Changing Role* (both cited above).

65. Karuna Chanana, ed., *Socialisation, Education and Women* (New Delhi: Orient Longman's, 1988), which includes essays by Aparna Basu, 'A Century's Journey: Women's Education in Western India, 1820-1920'; K. Chanana, 'Social Change or Social Reform: The Education of Women in Pre-Independence India', and Malavika Karlekar, 'Women's Nature and Access to Education'.

66. In a paper entitled 'Bengali Women and the Politics of Joint Family', presented at the International Interdisciplinary Congress on Women (Dublin, 1987), Bharati Ray has analysed the impact of women's education on the joint family in the context of Bengal.

67. See Farah Nizami, 'Arguments for and against Muslim Female Education in North India', paper presented at the Eighth European Association of South Asian Studies Conference, 1986; Sakina Hasan, 'Culture, Consciousness and Social Liberation', paper presented at the Third National Conference on Women's

Studies, Chandigarh, 1986; and Gail Minault, 'Purdah's Progress: The Beginnings of School Education for Indian Muslim Women', in J. P. Sharma (ed.), *Individuals and Ideas in Modern India* (Calcutta: M. L. Mukhopadhayay, 1982).

68. Vijaya Ramaswamy, 'Aspects of Women and Work in Early South India', *IESHR*, 26, no. 1 (1989).

69. Gregory C. Kozlowski, 'Muslim Women and the Control of Property in North India', *IESHR*, 24, no. 2 (1987).

70. K. Sardamoni, 'Changing Land Relations and Women: A Case Study of Palghat District in Kerala', in Vina Mazumdar (ed.), *Women and Rural Transformation* (New Delhi: Concept, 1983).

71. S. Jessal, 'Women and Access to Land and Productive Resources: Case of Awadh, 1856-1947' (Delhi: Center for Women's Development Studies, undated).

72. Minoti Kaul, 'Women's Access to Land in Punjab, 1849-1947', paper presented at the Fourth National Conference on Women's Studies, Waltair University, Vishakapatnam (1988).

73. Dhananjay R. Gadgil, *The Industrial Evolution of India in Recent Times* (Bombay: Oxford University Press, 1954).

74. Atchy Reddy, 'Female Agricultural Labourers of Nellore, 1881-1981', *IESHR*, 20, no. 1 (1983).

75. Mukul Mukherji, 'Impact of Modernisation on Women's Occupations – A Case Study of the Rice Husking Industry of Bengal', *IESHR*, 20, no. 1 (1983).

76. Nirmala Banerji, 'The Bengal Experience', seminar paper, Indian Social Studies Trust, New Delhi.

77. J. N. Sinha, 'The Indian Working Force: Its Growth, Change and Composition', *Census of India 1961*, 1 (1972); J. Ambannavar, 'Changes in Economic Activity of Male and Females in India', *Demography India*, no. 42 (1975).

78. Radha Kumar, 'Family and Factory: Women Workers in the Bombay Cotton Textile Industry, 1919-1939', *IESHR*, 20, no. 1 (1983).

79. Bidyut Mohanti, 'Famines and Sex Ratio in Orissa Division between 1881 and 1921', paper presented at the Fourth National Conference on Women's Studies at Waltair University, Vishakapatnam, 1988.

80. Iravati Karve, *Kinship Organisation in India* (Bombay: Asia, 1968).

81. Arvind M. Shah, *The Household Dimension of the Family in India* (New Delhi: Orient Longman's, 1973).

82. K. M. Kapadia, *Marriage and Family in India* (Delhi: Oxford University Press, 1980).

83. Alice Clark, 'Limitations of Female Life Chances in Rural Gujarat', *IESHR*, 20, no. 4 (1983).

84. Aparna Basu, 'Widening Horizons: an Inter-Generational Study of Social Change among Four Generations of Women', unpublished monograph, 1988.

85. Lotika Sarkar, 'Law and the Status of Women in India', in Columbia Human Rights Law Review, USA (ed.), *Law and the Status of Women: An International Symposium, Centre for Social Development and Humanitarian Affairs, United Nations* (New York, 1977).

86. Indira Jaisingh, 'Evaluation of Changes in the Law Relating to Women during the Decade 1975-1984', paper presented at seminar at SNDT University, Bombay, 1985.

87. Ursula King, 'Women and Religion: The Status and Image of Women in Major Religious Traditions', in Alfred de Souza (ed.), *Women in Contemporary India* (New Delhi: Manohar, 1980).

88. Neera Desai, 'Women in the Bhakti Movement', paper presented at the Third National Conference on Women's Studies, Chandigarh, 1986. See also Madhu Kishwar, *Women Bhakti Poets*, Tenth Anniversary Issue of *Manushi* (New Delhi 1990).

89. Sarojini Shintri, 'Women in the Virasaiva Movement', paper presented at the Third National Conference on Women's Studies, Chandigarh, 1986; Gautam Neogi, 'Religious Institution as a Dynamic of Women's Activism: A Case Study of Brahmo Samaj Movement in Bengal', paper presented at the Third National Conference on Women's Studies, Chandigarh, 1986.

90. Julia Leslie, *The Perfect Wife: The Orthodox Hindu Woman according to the Stridharmapaddhati of Tryambakayajvan* (Delhi: Oxford University Press, 1989).

91. Vanaja Dhruvarajan, *Hindu Women and the Power of Ideology* (Westport, Conn.: Bergin and Garvey Publishers, 1989).

92. See Jagdish Lal Dawar, 'Feminism and Femininity: Women in Premchand's Fiction', *Studies in History*, 3, no. 1 (1987); Geetanjali Pandey, 'Women in Premchand's Writings', *EPW*, 21, no. 50 (December 13, 1986); Jasodhara Bagchi, 'Positivism and Nationalism: Womanhood and Crisis in Nationalist Fiction: Bankim Chandra's *Anandmath*', *EPW*, 20, no. 43 (October 26, 1985). See also C. S. Lakshmi, *The Face Behind the Mask: Women in Tamil Literature* (New Delhi: Vikas, 1984), and Tanika Sarkar, 'Nationalist Iconography: Image of Women in Nineteenth Century Bengali Literature', *EPW*, 22, no. 4 (November 21, 1987).

93. Gail Minault, 'Urdu Women's Magazines in the Early 20th Century', *Manushi*, no. 48 (1988).

94. See Patricia Jeffery, 'Contaminating States and Women's Status: Midwifery, Childbearing and the State in Rural North India' (New Delhi: Indian Social Institute, 1985). See also Geraldine Forbes, 'Managing Midwifery in India', paper presented at the German Historical Institute Conference, Berlin, 1989.

95. Barbara N. Ramusack, 'Embattled Advocates: The Debate over Birth Control in India, 1920-1940', *Journal of Women's History*, 1, no. 2 (Fall 1989).

96. Sunil Sen, *The Working Women and Popular Movements in Bengal* (Calcutta: K. P. Bagchi & Co., 1985); Saswati Ghosh, 'Women in the Naxalbari Movement', paper presented at the Third National Conference on Women's Studies, Chandigarh, 1986.

97. Maria Mies, 'The Shahada Movement: Peasant Movement in Maharashtra (India)', *Journal of Peasant Studies*, 3, no. 4 (July 1976).

98. Gail Omvedt, 'Women and Rural Revolt in India', *Journal of Peasant Studies*, 5, no. 3 (April 1978).

99. Gail Omvedt, *We Will Smash This Prison* (Bombay: Orient Longman's, 1979); Nandita Gandhi, '"When the Rolling Pin Hit the Streets", the Anti-Price Rise Movement in Bombay', paper presented at the Third National Conference on Women's Studies, Chandigarh, 1986.

100. Kumud Sharma, 'Women in Struggle: A Case Study of Chipko Movement', *Samya Shakti*, 1, no. 2 (1984); S. Jain, 'Women and People's Ecological Movement', *EPW*, 19, no. 41 (1984).

101. Vibhuti Patel, 'Emergence and Proliferation of Autonomous Women's Groups in India, 1974-84', mimeographed paper, 1985.

102. Neera Desai and Vibhuti Patel, *Indian Women, Change and Challenge in the International Decade, 1975-1985* (Bombay: Popular Prakashan, 1985).

103. On the tribal women, see Manjushri Chaki Sircar, *Feminism in a Traditional Society* (Gaziabad: Shakti Books, Vikas, 1984).

11

Writing Women into History:
The Nigerian Experience

Bolanle Awe

The writing of women into the history of Nigeria, indeed into African history, has hardly begun. Compared with the history of many other parts of the world, the writing of the history of Africa itself is a fairly recent development. Efforts in this direction have had to contend with two difficult problems which are bound up with Africa's historical experience. First, African historians have the uphill task of eradicating the prejudices and misconceptions about the African past which have been perpetuated by many western writers, such as G. W. H. Hegel, Reginald Coupland, C. G. Seligman, Hugh Trevor Roper, and others who have claimed that Africa and Africans had no past to speak of, and that the only viable African history is the history of the invaders of Africa, notably, the Europeans. Secondly, while destroying this myth of the African past, African historians have also the responsibility of undertaking the scientific investigation of human development in Africa; the reconstruction of the African past with the attendant problems of writing the history of non-literate peoples posed for them a particular challenge. For this purpose, many African states, on becoming independent, established Institutes and Centres of African Studies which adopted a multidisciplinary approach to the study of African history and culture.

However, in the writing of that history, the factor of gender has been significant. While building up their own picture of African society, as distinct from western notions of that society, African historians seemed to have inherited a certain degree of Western bias, in that they have perpetuated in their writings the masculine-centred view of history; in explaining human experience in Africa, they have accepted the male experience as the norm while African women in consequence became anomalies. Thus the eight-volume *General History of Africa* published by

211

UNESCO in 1981, which summarises current significant knowledge in African history, says nothing about female contributions to that history.[1] Nearer home, the *Groundwork of Nigerian History*, the standard text on the history of this country, which was authored by many distinguished Nigerian historians, made no particular mention of the role of Nigerian women in the development of their different societies.[2] Such historians have tended to focus attention on the public domain where men held sway. Only a few scholars have pioneered the writing of history from a female perspective, largely through biographies, studies of female institutions, particularly within the political process, and their actions of protest and resistance during the colonial period. However, the output so far is fragmentary and unco-ordinated; a great deal of the material is unpublished and remains in the form of seminar papers and dissertations, with only a few articles in journals. Apart from Nina Mba's work, *Nigerian Women Mobilised*, there is no full-length synthesis in book form of women's role in Nigerian history; however, the number of monographs delineating specific subjects in narrowly defined areas is increasing, and now includes Kristin Mann's *Marrying Well* and Barbara Callaway's *Muslim Hausa Women in Nigeria: Traditions and Change*.[3]

It is quite clear therefore that these contributions are merely scratching the surface, and the work of writing women into history has therefore to begin in earnest. When in 1986, at the Nigerian Historical Society Congress, Nina Mba presented a paper on 'The Introduction of Courses on African Women's History into History Departments of Nigerian Universities: A Proposal', she was not only making a case for teaching women's history but also for studying it. Indeed, the interdependence of teaching and research in a field which has only begun to develop could not be more real; for teachers in a new field like this have to depend on the research and interpretation of scholars for what they teach. Two years after Nina Mba's paper, in 1988, that same congress agreed to the setting up of a panel on women's history and went on further to elect a woman to its executive body. That congress also saw the effective beginning of a network among historians working in the field of women's history.[4]

It is, however, important to point out that the task of writing women into history in the Nigerian context cannot be viewed in isolation from recent developments in women's studies in this country. The field of women's studies is itself a new one; writing on women began during the colonial period, 1914-1960, when missionaries, district officers and anthropologists wrote on women. The works of the Nigerian academics came to the fore during the nationalist period (1960-1976), and during the present period (1976-1988) attention has been focused on rural women. The struggle for the recognition of women's studies as an academic discipline is, however, a recent one. Writing women into history is part of this new impetus to look at the role of women in human development in a scholarly fashion.[5] The emphasis is to make women's studies an acceptable academic discipline. Scholars veering into this field have shown an acute awareness of the fact that the power of the ideas generated and the excellence of the scholarship are the most significant factors in achieving success in this endeavour.[6]

Scholarly writings in this field have been criticised for inadequacy or absence of theory. The crux of the matter lies in the development of a meaningful theoretical framework as well as the evolution of an effective methodological approach. Hitherto, the conventional approach to the study of history and human development has resulted in the invisibility of women as actors in that history; it is therefore imperative to consider new methodological and theoretical approaches to make them visible.

The Wellesley Conference of 1976 provided one of the earliest forums for expressing the need for a new methodological and theoretical approach for the study of African women, whose historical and cultural experiences showed some marked dissimilarities from those of Western women.[7] That search led to the formation of AAWORD (Association of African Women for Research and Development) and the seminar 'African Women: The Type of Methodology'. This same awareness led in 1987 to the seminar in the Institute of African Studies at the University of Ibadan on 'Women's Studies in Nigeria: The State of the Art Now'. A communiqué from that seminar recommended the incorporation of the discipline into the curriculum of higher institutions of learning, and stressed the need for a theoretical base and a sound methodology for the successful development of women's studies in Nigeria.[8] Later in January 1988 a workshop, sponsored jointly by two universities in Nigeria – Obafemi Awolowo University and the University of Ibadan – and two Canadian universities – Dalhousie University and the University of Mount St. Vincent, had as its theme 'Theoretical and Methodological Issues in the Study of Women' and examined this topic comparatively. That workshop pointed out the fact that existing theories and methodologies which emanate from western experiences are extremely limited in accounting for the historical and cultural peculiarities of Nigerian societies, and again emphasised the need for developing a sound theoretical and methodological base for that discipline in Nigeria.[9]

Availability of data is one of the most crucial determinants of the degree of progress which can be made in formulating new conceptual frameworks. For African history, and for the study of women in particular, sources have been crucial. History can only be written if the sources are available; but locating sources in African history has necessitated new methodological approaches. Sources for writing women into history cannot easily be found in the regular archives and card catalogues of public libraries. Yet there *is* a record of the contributions of these women in African societies, which are acutely aware of their past. The historian must therefore devise methodologies to unearth this past. This is a task that involves the discovery of new records and the development of an aptitude for asking the right questions even of the conventional records. Apart from the conventional sources, there are other sources which have been untapped and overlooked. For non-literate societies of Africa, the oral traditions of the people have been shown to be a repository of their history and culture. These traditions throw light on the role of each segment of their society; the women therefore are not left out. Such traditions are expressed in many forms; they are to be found in mythologies, folktales, proverbs, praise poems, oral and written literature, and so on. They are the traditions of the people which have been handed down by word of mouth from generation to generation and they encapsulate the history, norms and values of the particular society that produced them.[10]

Some information could also be gleaned from missionary and explorer accounts, private papers, archaeological excavations, language, the traditional legal code, genealogies, and land tenure arrangements. Oral histories dealing with the lives of women who, though illiterate, were eyewitnesses of momentous events in their community or whose lives symbolised the achievements of women also offer good sources. The tools borrowed from social science disciplines such as anthropology and sociology can also help to redefine the framework of women's history. It will mean weaving together a host of technical approaches to data collection including participatory strategies, focused group discussions and other methods. It will be necessary to understand the society and focus attention on those areas where women predominate; they might not be prominent in political history, which highlights male experience, but an examination of the changes which have taken place, for instance in women's work and the organisation of the household, might yield much information about their contributions.

But what are the issues around which this data gathering, teaching and networking among Nigerian scholars should revolve? What is the research agenda, what are the priorities? All scholars in the field of women's studies do recognise the importance of the historical perspective in studying Nigerian women. They are the product of a chain of historical experiences which have conditioned their attitudes and made them what they are now. With slight modification, Lawrence A. Scaff's four categories of feminist research form a useful guide for writing Nigerian women into history:

(1) the deconstructive work of revealing androcentric and misogynistic tendencies;

(2) women-centred research without much or any analysis of traditional historical thought;

(3) a dialogue with the traditions of and appropriations of concepts and theories from traditional research, and integration of these with feminist insights;

(4) establishing new feminist theories, interweaving existing helpful models of scholarship with new models.[11]

It will then be possible to focus on certain phases of and themes in women's history.

Women in the pre-colonial society. Their position within that society is as yet not fully understood; but it is important to identify salient features of their lives before the society was subjected to external pressures so as to understand the enormity of that impact on women.

The Trans-Atlantic Slave Trade. The slave trade was one of the most traumatic events for the African continent; the figures on those taken into slavery are not definite, but Paul Lovejoy calculates that 11,698,000 men and women were exported to the Americas.[12] Within the last decade attention has been paid to the age and sex composition of those slaves.

Many significant questions still remain unanswered: how many female slaves were exported and why? The sex and age composition, according to David Geggus,[13] could be significant in shaping black society in Africa and the Americas. To what extent did women participate as dealers in the trade? In Dahomey, the organisation and supply of slaves helped to create a capitalist class; what, then, was the situation among the Yoruba of Nigeria whose women owned slaves?

The Colonial Experience. There are differing views about the impact of colonialism on women. WORDOC's recent conference, 'The Impact of Colonialism on Nigerian Women', has shed much new light on many areas of women's experience under European rule.[14] The impact of colonialism differed from locality to locality, from region to region. It was not a uniform experience for all women. Furthermore colonial rule had positive consequences for women, especially in the areas of law and education, as well as negative consequences. Though women were often victims of colonial policies, they also took the initiative in resisting policies they considered harmful and in using existing situations to their advantage. Studies of the impact of colonialism would also benefit by going beyond the examination of political and social policies engendered by colonialism and looking at changing relationships of production; colonial policies had economic, social and cultural consequences for women. Further, what was the particular effect of colonialism on European women who came to Africa either as wives or as employees of the colonial service?[15]

Impact of the Foreign Religions. Christianity and Islam are two religions with definite views on women's role in society. It will be necessary to examine the constraints of Islam and Arabic culture on women and how Islam and its associated ideology operated on pre-Islamic societies where women had participated more fully in activities outside their homes.[16] Christianity's influence could be treated as an aspect of colonial experience.

Women and Nation Building. What role did women play in the nationalist struggle for independence and the development of the state during the post-independence era? Nina Mba has analysed women's role in nationalist politics in southern Nigeria, but more case studies and biographies are needed for a full understanding of the dynamics of women's contribution and leadership in urban centres and rural areas. In addition, a study similar to Mba's is needed for northern Nigeria.

This is a tall order, and it is still possible to think of more pressing issues which need to be investigated. There are, however, developments of a practical nature that are needed to encourage research and scholarship not only in history but in the field of women's studies generally.

It has, in fact, become urgent to have some type of data bank of published and unpublished materials where information on African women can be easily accessible. Most of the scholars in this field have been working in isolated pockets and the results of their findings are often scattered in learned journals, theses, students' project essays, unpublished compilations in various government ministries and research institutes. The assemblage of such data in one place will enable scholars to be conversant with new developments in the field and will also prevent the duplication of efforts.

While emphasis in the building up of a data bank should be on raw data, primary sources and original contributions, the collection of secondary material is equally important. With a new and growing discipline, there is the need to have a good library of basic texts dealing with feminist theory and the development of the many phases of women's studies as background material.

The Institute of African Studies of the University of Ibadan has recently set up a Women's Research and Documentation Centre (WORDOC) for this purpose. The objectives of the Centre include the following:

(1) to provide a focus for women's studies in Nigeria through the co-ordination of research projects on women's issues in Nigeria and the promotion of new methodologies in the study of Nigerian women;

(2) to set up a women's network and promote a more accurate understanding of the various roles and concerns of women in Nigeria and West Africa, through projects, publications, regular seminars and other activities, with a view to providing a basis for policy formulation on issues affecting women;

(3) to establish a documentation centre for use of scholars, researchers, and other interested persons;

(4) to seek sources for funding research on women and to facilitate its implementation;

(5) to provide a link with other women's research centres and international agencies in Africa, the West Indies, North America, Latin America, Europe and Asia;

(6) to develop a network among scholars working in the field.

This network will be developed at two levels. First, there must be the encouragement of a network within Nigeria for scholars working in this field to ensure effective co-ordination of research efforts. Second, there is a need to develop an international network with scholars in other countries. A network with scholars from other third world countries that have been subjected to similar historical experiences will be advantageous; so will the link with the more developed countries. Both types of international networking will provide useful comparisons for the study of women and will enrich our understanding of the subject. It will give Nigerian scholars the opportunity to learn about the experiences of women in other comparable situations and to study their responses to similar problems. It will also ensure that they remain in the mainstream of feminist studies.

The development of a network raises the question of the need to provide the means for disseminating the information contained in research findings. Workshops and seminars provide a useful forum for this purpose. Publications also provide another effective way of disseminating information. Although the idea of a Journal of Women's Studies in Nigeria has been mooted, the *Journal of the Historical Society of Nigeria* and *Tarikh* will certainly carry publications that meet their scholarly standard. A special issue of *Tarikh* devoted to 'Women in History' is in preparation. Moreover, the main problem in journal publications right now in Nigeria is to maintain regularity of appearance. Occasional publications around themes in women's history as well as a newsletter for disseminating information on a regular basis should not be ruled out of order. Teaching also provides a useful outlet for the product of research. The case for the introduction of courses on African women's history has been made by Nina Mba (see above). Their acceptability will depend on how successful scholars in this field have been in establishing the study of women in history as an academic discipline.

The major problem which a programme of research and teaching in women's history is likely to encounter is that of funding. At present, Nigerian universities are finding it difficult to give out research grants to scholars even for established programmes, and the current financial crisis is having an adverse effect on the development of education generally. Although a great deal of emphasis is being placed on women's education, it is not certain that some of the monies earmarked for these projects will also include funding for scholarly research.

Writing women into the history of Nigeria is not an easy task; however LaRay Denzer's recent overview of the state of study concerning women during colonial rule has been well-launched.[17] A similar assessment of women in pre-colonial history would probably show that more work has been done than we think. Several departments of history, particularly those in the University of Ibadan, the University of Lagos and Ogun State University, have teachers who have encouraged research on women's subjects at the undergraduate and, more recently, the postgraduate level. Even more significantly, female lecturers in those departments have reported that their male colleagues are increasingly receptive to the need to study women as well as men in their own research and some have begun to conduct research in this area.

NOTES

1. J. Ki-Zerbo (ed.), *UNESCO General History of Africa*, vol. 1 (Berkeley: University of California Press, 1981).

2. Obaro Kime (ed.), *Groundwork of Nigerian History* (Ibadan: Heineman, 1980).

3. Nina E. Mba, *Nigerian Women Mobilized: Women's Political Activity in South Nigeria, 1900-1965* (Berkeley: University of California Institute for International Studies, 1982). See also, Kristin Mann, *Marrying Well: Marriage, Status and Social Change among the Educated Elite in Colonial Lagos* (Cambridge: Cambridge University Press, 1985); and Barbara Callaway, *Muslim Hausa Women in Nigeria: Traditions and Change* (Syracuse, NY: Syracuse University Press, 1987).

4. Panel on 'Women and History' at the 33rd Annual Congress of the Historical Society of Nigeria, Nayero University, Kano, March 28-31, 1988. Papers presented:
(1) Bolanle Awe, 'Theory and Methodology of Women's History';
(2) Nina Mba, 'Imperialism, Gender and Literature: Case Study of *Major Dane's Garden* by Margery Perham';
(3) LaRay Denzer, 'Female Employment in Government Service in Nigeria from 1869 to 1945';
(4) Judith Byfield, 'Women Entrepreneurs in Abeokuta in the Early 20th Century: A Case Study of the Adire Tirade';

(5) Adesola Afolabi, 'Women in the Agricultural Economy of South Western Nigeria: A Case Study of the Ijebu Remo Kolanut Industry';

(6) G. Thomas Emeagwali, 'Women in the Pre-Colonial Nigerian Economy'.

5. Karen Offen, 'Definining Feminism: A Comparative Historical Approach', *Signs: Journal of Women in Culture and Society*, 14, no. 1 (Autumn 1988), pp. 119-57.

6. See Filomina C. Steady, 'Research Methodology and Investigative Framework for Social Change: The Case for Nigerian Women', in the Seminar, *Research on African Women: What Type of Methodology?*, Dakar, AAWARD (December 1983). See also Winnie Tomm, 'Standards of Research in Women's Studies', paper presented to the Canadian Women's Studies Association, Learned Societies Meetings, Laval University, Quebec City, 31 May 1989.

7. See Bolanle Awe, 'Reflections on the Conference on Women and Development', in The Wellesley Editorial Committee (ed.), *Women and National Development: The Complexities of Change* (Chicago: University of Chicago Press, 1977); also in *Signs: Journal of Women in Culture and Society*, 3, no. 1 (Autumn 1977), pp. 314-17.

8. See the papers presented at the 'Seminar on Women's Studies in Nigeria: The State of the Art Now', at the Institute of African Studies, University of Ibadan, Nigeria, 4-6 November 1987, particularly: Olufemi Taiwo and Olabisi Adeleye, 'Theory and Future of Women's Studies in Nigeria'; Renee Pittin, 'Women's Studies in Nigeria: Towards Greater Interdisciplinary'; Nina Mba, 'Recent Trends in Women's Studies in Nigeria: Problems and Prospects'.

9. *Proceedings of the Seminar on Women's Studies in Nigeria and Canada: A Comparative Appoach* (Canada: Mount Saint Vincent University, 1988), and specifically G. Thomas Emeagwali, 'Women's Studies and Methodologies', pp. 43-52; Simi Afonja, 'Critical Issues in Women's Studies in Nigeria: A Sociological Perspective', pp. 55-64.

10. On oral history as a source, see E. J. Alagoa, 'Oral Tradition Among the Ijo of the Niger Delta', *Journal of African History*, 7, no. 3 (1966), pp. 405-19; Ruth Finnegan, *Oral Literature in Africa* (London: Oxford University Press, 1976); Jan Vansina, *Oral Tradition as History* (London: James Currey, 1985).

11. Lawrence A. Scaff, 'From Silence to Voice: Reflections on Feminism in Political Theory', in Susan Hardy Aiken et al. (eds.), *Changing Our Minds* (Albany: State University of New York Press, 1988).

12. Paul Lovejoy, *Transformations in Slavery: A History of Slavery in Africa* (Cambridge: Cambridge University Press, 1983), p. 19. See also Claire C. Robertson and Martin A. Klein, (eds.), *Women and Slavery in Africa* (Madison: University of Wisconsin Press, 1970).

13. David Geggus, 'Sex Ratio, Age and Ethnicity in the Atlantic Slave Trade: Data from French Shipping and Plantation Records', *Journal of African History*, 30 (1989), pp. 23-44.

14. Conference on 'The Impact of Colonialism on Nigerian Women', Women's Research and Documentation Centre, Institute of African Studies, University of Ibadan (Nigeria), 16-19 October 1989. Forty-six papers were presented in the areas of history, law, education, marriage, science and technology, culture and health.

15. Mona Etienne and Eleanor Leacock (eds.), *Women and Colonisation: Anthropological Perspectives* (New York: Praeger, 1980). See also Simi Afonja, 'Changing Modes of Production and the Sexual Division of Labour among the Yoruba', *Signs: Journal of Women in Culture and Society*, 7, no. 2 (Winter 1981), pp. 299-313.

16. See, for example, Catherine Ver Eecke, 'From Pasture to Purdah: The Transformation of Women's Role and Identity among the Adamawa Fulbe', *Ethnology: An International Journal of Cultural and Social Anthropology*, 28, no. 1 (January 1989), pp. 53-73.

17. LaRay Denzer, 'Women in Colonial Nigerian History: An Appraisal', paper delivered at the WORDOC conference, 'The Impact of Colonialism on Nigerian Women', University of Ibadan, 16-19 October 1989.

12

Women's History in Norway:
A Short Survey

Ingeborg Fløystad

In this introduction to the development and practice of women's history in Norway, I aim simply to describe some of its main characteristics. As in other western countries women's history has emerged as a new academic discipline in Norway primarily over the last twenty years.

The early years

Before 1970 there was very little literature based on research into the history of Norwegian women. There were two major contributions, one published in 1937 on the women's movement in Norway from the nineteenth century up to the 1930s,[1] and another in 1941 on the changes in women's work with the coming of industrialisation in the nineteenth century.[2] Few writers, and very few academic historians among them, had been interested in studying the history of Norwegian women.

In 1970 a male professor of social history, Edvard Bull, predicted in a speech commemorating the centenary of the Norwegian Historical Association that groups then considered outside history, such as women and children, would soon enter it. By this he meant that the recent youth movement would lead to an interest in the history of different generations and in the institution of the family, and consequently to a study of women.[3] He obviously had not noticed the new women's liberation movement which had started in the US and had already spread to Sweden and Denmark. In the autumn of 1970 the first feminist groups were organised in Norway and other groups followed. This provoked an unprecedented interest in Norwegian women's position in society and in their history, and created a demand for more knowledge of women's past lives.

221

When considering the development of women's history in Norway, it is important to remember that Norway is a country of about four million people. In 1970 the historical profession was small. But the 1970s saw a considerable increase in higher institutions teaching history and in the number of students and scholars of history. And more students than ever before were women. From the 1970s history was taught at four universities (Oslo, Bergen, Trondheim, and finally Tromsø, from 1972) and at some regional colleges established during the same period. As in other western countries, the Norwegian universities were soon confronted with the new interest in women's history. The demand came especially from below, from young women studying history, who were also active in the new feminist movement. The students wanted courses to be taught on the history of women, and some of them wanted to write theses on women's history for their final university degree in history. A few university teachers offered courses focusing on women, usually in combination with social history or demography or family history. But with one exception, Ida Blom at Bergen, the professional historians – who then included only two or three women employed at the university level -did not initiate research into women's history at the beginning of the 1970s. Generally speaking, however, they became conscious of a questioning of how historical events and structures of the past had affected women's lives. This new way of looking at history was first encountered by those professors supervising students' theses.

Research on women's history since 1970

The focus on women's history during the last fifteen to twenty years has undoubtedly had an impact on the overall teaching and research of history in Norway. We now know, of course, much more about Norwegian women in the past than we did two decades ago. This is due first of all to new scholarly analyses, and, secondly, a close second, to student dissertations on subjects in women's history. Many dissertations were presented in the second half of the 1970s and the first half of the 1980s. The majority of them remain unpublished, and are accessible only through university and college libraries. But in many cases the principal findings have been published as articles in anthologies and journals. Many of these theses have made valuable contributions to the growing body of material about women in the past. Most of these 'student historians' have been women. But after graduation it has proved very difficult for them to obtain financial support – let alone positions at university level – to continue research in women's history, and only a few have done so.

Most of the scholars who have published monographs and articles in women's history, have also been, and continue to be women. There are, however, only a few women historians permanently employed at the universities and regional colleges in Norway – only nine in all in 1989. And not all of them have a substantial part of their research production within women's history or within research of special relevance to women. For scholars who wish to work within women's history and who do not have a permanent job at the universities or at the regional colleges, it has been hard to obtain financial support to continue research. But some historians – all women – have received short-term grants from the state-financed Norwegian Research Council for Science and the Humanities to carry out research in women's history or on historical issues of special relevance to women. None of this money has yet gone to medieval historians.

The Norwegian Research Council has promoted research in women's studies in the humanities and social sciences in various ways from the 1970s onwards. The Council has arranged several conferences on women's studies, and the first interdisciplinary one was in 1975, the UN International Women's Year. Within the Council a Secretariat for Research about Women and for Women Researchers has also been functioning for some years.

The Council has offered scholarships to researchers and to students writing dissertations, supported sabbatical leaves for university faculty and given financial support for publication in women's history. It has also supported Scandinavian conferences on women's history, financed research stays abroad and participation in international congresses. From 1980 to 1984 the Research Council for the Humanities financed a special research project 'Women's Work in Family and Society in Norway 1870 -1940', a project that was also part of a Scandinavian project about women's work in the same period. Three historians, all women, were each financed for three years as senior researchers. This project was initiated and led by Professor Ida Blom at the University of Bergen, assisted by three other professors: Anne-Lise Seip and Sølvi Sogner of Oslo University and Ståle Dyrvik of Bergen University.

Ida Blom has had a great personal impact on the development of women's history in Norway from the beginning. She is the only full professor of women's history in this country. Her chair at the University of Bergen may be seen as a recognition by the university authorities and by the historical profession of the importance of women's history.

There has been, however, some discussion within the historical profession about the existence of women's history as a distinct field of academic research. Some have questioned whether it should be seen as a discipline in its own right or as part of family history. Objections to the autonomy of women's history came most explicitly from a male professor, Ottar Dahl, who began the debate in an article published in the Norwegian

Historisk Tidsskrift [Historical Journal] in 1985.[4] Women's historians replied that the focus of women's history is on women and the social construction of gender, and that such topics had not been in any way covered within the history of the family.[5] Generally speaking, however, one may say that the historical profession in Norway – and in the other Nordic countries (including Sweden, Denmark, Finland, and Iceland) – has accepted the argument that research in the history of women is important.

This first became evident at the 17th Congress of Nordic Historians held in Norway in 1977, which was followed up by the 18th Congress of Nordic Historians in 1981 in Finland. At both these conferences women's history was one of the designated themes. In 1977 it was incorporated into the main theme of the congress, the process of urbanisation in the Nordic region. This participation in Nordic congresses indicates that Norwegian women's historians are not isolated. They have frequently met with colleagues from neighbouring countries since the second half of the 1970s. Broader international contact has also been fostered through conferences, and through visits to our universities by scholars of women's history from outside Scandinavia, mainly British and American. Finally, historians of women's history have collaborated with other Norwegian scholars of women's studies in the humanities and social sciences. In the last few years interdisciplinary centres of women's studies have been established at the universities.

Traditionally historical research in Norway has focused primarily on Norwegian history, although in the last fifteen to twenty years the history of other cultures and countries has been increasingly pursued by Norwegian scholars. The historians of women's history in this country have continued on this path, in the main having studied Norwegian women's history, for reasons that are easily understood. Students researching theses have found the Norwegian sources more accessible than others. Not surprisingly, the lack of basic research into Norwegian women's history, coupled with our deep desire to know more about our own foremothers, has strongly motivated many of us to investigate the past of women in our own country.

A bibliography of the literature produced in Norwegian women's history shows that some periods and themes have been more fully investigated than others.[6] No monograph on women in Norway in the middle ages or even in early modern history has been published, though there are some unpublished theses on these periods.[7] The years after 1850, and especially the period 1870-1940, have been the most thoroughly studied. This was a time of modernisation, and of industrialisation and urbanisation in Norway as elsewhere, and a time of significant change for women in many ways. The lives of women in Norway after the Second World War, however, and especially their situation during the last twenty to thirty years, have mainly been studied by sociologists and other social scientists, less by historians as yet.

Looking at the subjects of investigation, it is evident that several topics pertaining to social and economic history have dominated research: women's organisations and their struggle for equal rights, reproduction and the family, and women's paid and unpaid work and professions. Other areas are less systematically studied.

All monographs and theses in women's history presented by historians are empirical studies. By and large, historical training in Norway has never included much study of theory, and this orientation also characterises the practice of women's history. Feminist and marxist influences are in evidence, of course, and the British and American literature on theory and methodology are well known. But in view of the literature produced, the visible results of the historian's craft, Norwegian women's history cannot be characterised as 'revolutionary' in its approach. Consequently the literature produced has not been very controversial, which has undoubtedly contributed to the general acceptance of women's history in Norway. In addition, the broad definition of women's history that Ida Blom presented at a conference in 1975[8] established the guidelines for research in women's history in this country, guidelines which have hardly been challenged until recently.[9]

Sources for research in women's history include written source material and oral history, both of which have broadened and enriched studies of women from 1900 onwards. Sources such as diaries and memoirs have not yet been systematically used by historians. Such sources were produced mostly by upper-class women, at least in the nineteenth century, and research up till now has mainly been concerned with the majority, with women from the working class, middle class and peasantry. Upper-class women have not yet been studied as a group, though some have been partially studied, usually in connection with their participation in women's organisations.

As already mentioned, research in women's history has been particularly concerned with the question of modernisation. Underlying much of it has been this basic question: how have changes in all areas of society after 1850 affected women's lives? Much of the research has been carried out as local studies, and there is little work covering the whole country. This may seem surprising since Norway has long been a country with a small and homogeneous population, except for the Lapps (and Lapp women have not yet been studied by historians). But different ways of living in towns as contrasted with in the countryside, different class identities, a scattered population and the varied geography of the country – all important factors – have tended to shape women's lives in different ways. Generalisation at the national level is still not easy.

In the 1970s much of the published research literature focused on women in the capital, Oslo (formerly Kristiania), and in other towns. Urban women led the struggle for women's rights and founded women's organisations, starting in the capital. Urban women were also studied for their work, in household service, in industry, and in prostitution, and for the extent to which they practised birth control. But the experience of women in the capital and other towns did not necessarily represent that of the majority of women, who still lived in the countryside. And the 1980s have seen more studies that have broadened our knowledge of women living in the country. Studies of rural women and particularly regional studies of peasant women may be mentioned here.[10] Norway was to a large extent an agrarian society in the first half of this century. The economic role of women on the farms was very important, not only because they were responsible for the animals and for milking and dairying. They often shouldered much of the responsibility for running the farm when the men took employment away from home in many regions, particularly in fishing and forestry. The mechanisation and capitalisation of the farms after the Second World War have, however, changed women's role in agriculture very much, and many women are now often partially employed outside the farm.

New work opportunities for women after 1870 have been well documented, and monographs for this period, 1870-1940, have been or are about to be published, on the nursing and teaching professions, and on women employed as telegraph and telephone operators and as seamstresses.[11] Women's productive and reproductive roles in the family have long been of interest to women's historians. Women's role in family planning in connection with the demographic transition, and changing conditions at childbirth, from home to hospital, have been studied in three monographs.[12] Studies of women's housework in different kinds of households, and how this has changed, can be found in several local studies of women's varied work in towns and in the countryside.[13] Women's historians have aimed to make women's work in production and reproduction visible, and to show its importance to society. They have therefore felt the need to redefine the word 'work' so that it covers much more than just paid work.

The ideal of domesticity for women began to spread, beginning in the early nineteenth century. Although Norway had no nobility after 1814, a very small economic and cultural elite of state officials and higher bourgeoisie defined the norms of behaviour for women in society. Research to date suggests that these prescriptions were not followed in practice by the majority of women until well into the twentieth century. As a result, the period during which the majority of Norwegian women were full-time housewives was in fact very short. Today's trends began to be apparent about 1970: that is, the tendency for most women to have paid work, though many work part-time, and for all young women to be offered educational opportunities.

Women's history today

Women's history today may be said to be 'institutionalised' at all levels of education in Norway. The history of women is incorporated into all history textbooks, as a condition of their use in the schools. It is part of the curriculum at college and university level, although it comprises only a very small part of the curriculum. There is now no lack of literature. There is, however, a need for a textbook that surveys the history of Norwegian women.

In the universities, however, it seems that women's history is no longer expanding. In recent years few history students have produced theses on this subject for their final degrees. Since women's history has had its fair share of the money coming from the Norwegian Research Council, women's history may not expect to get much in the near future. However, the Council now plans to support theoretical studies in women's history and women's studies. There is an increasing interest in theory, something that has been reflected recently in articles and discussions by women's historians.[14] Though it has been the aim of women's historians to integrate a gender perspective, as a natural and obvious part of all historical research, such integration remains a difficult task. Such a perspective is, for instance, missing in certain recent publications that are otherwise of high quality.[15]

Norwegian historians have a long tradition of presenting history in a form accessible to non-academic readers. This tradition is reflected in the Scandinavian project for a global women's history, due to be published in 1990-91 (and discussed elsewhere in this volume by Ida Blom). This project will result in a popular work for the Scandinavian market. The interdisciplinary *Kvinnenes Kulturhistorie* [The Cultural History of Women] provides another good example of women's historians presenting their findings to a broader range of readers,[16] as does also a recent study of changes in women's household work since 1850.[17]

As yet little has been published in English on Norwegian women's history.[18] A future task may be to place Norwegian women's experience within an international western pattern. Such a study, published in English, would certainly help to differentiate the study of European women's historical experience, which should not be represented solely by the examples of British, French and German women. This also represents a challenge to researchers in Norwegian women's history, who should be

228 *Ingeborg Fløystad*

more concerned in the future with developing an international and comparative perspective.

NOTES

1. Anna Caspari Agerholdt, *Den norske kvinnebevegelses historie* [The History of the Norwegian Women's Movement] (Oslo: Gyldendal Norsk Forlag, 1937, new editions 1973 and 1980).

2. Mimi Sverdrup Lunden, *De frigjorte hender. Et bidrag til forståelse av kvinners arbeid i Norge etter 1814* [The Released Hands. A Contribution to the Understanding of Women's Work in Norway after 1814] (Oslo: Tanums forlag, 1941, new edition 1978).

3. Edvard Bull, 'Historisk vitenskap foran 1970-årene [The Science of History Before the 1970s]', *Historisk Tidsskrift*, 3 (1970), p. 253.

4. Ottar Dahl, '"Kvinnehistorie". Kategorihistorie eller samfunnshistorie. Noen synspunkter [Women's History: History of a Category or of a Society. Some Viewpoints]', *Historisk Tidsskrift*, 3 (1986), pp. 262-74.

5. Ida Blom, 'Kvinnehistorie – ledd i historieforskningen og ledd i kvinneforskningen [Women's History – A Component in Historical Research and a Component in Women's Research]', *Historisk Tidsskrift*, 4 (1985), pp. 415-24; Gro Hagemann, 'Kvinnehistorie – faglig blindspor eller fruktbar disiplin? [Women's History – Professional Deadend or a Fruitful Discipline?]', *Historisk Tidsskrift*, 3 (1986), pp. 343-60.

6. Ingeborg Fløystad, *Kvinnehistorie i Norge, en Bibliografi/Women's History in Norway, a Bibliography* (Bergen, 1989).

7. A few articles have been published by historians on Norwegian women in the Middle Ages: see, for example, Anna Elisa Tryti, 'Kvinnenes stilling i klostervesenet [Women's Position in the Religious Orders]', *Årbok for Foreningen til norske fortidsminnesmerkers bevaring* (1987), pp. 187-208. On early modern history, two collections of articles have been published: Jørgen Eliassen and Sølvi Sogner (eds.), *Bot eller bryllup. Ugifte mødre og gravide bruder i det gamle samfunnet* [A Penance or a Wedding? Unmarried Mothers and Pregnant Brides in Traditional Society] (Oslo: Universitetsforlaget, 1981); Anna Tranberg and Harald Winge (eds.), *Kvinnekår i det gamle samfunn c. 1500-1850* [Women's Living Conditions in Traditional Society c. 1500-1850] (Oslo, 1985). (*Skrifter fra Norsk Lokalhistorisk Institutt* [Papers from the Norwegian Institute of Local History], 16.)

See also Sølvi Sogner and Hilde Sandvik, 'Ulik i lov og lære, lik i virke og verd? Kvinner i norsk Økonomi i by og på land 1500-1800 [Unequal in Law and Doctrine, but Equal in Work and Worth: Women in the Norwegian Economy in Town and Countryside 1500-1800], *Historisk Tidsskrift*, 4 (1989), pp. 434-62.

8. Ida Blom's definition was: 'Women's history is a collective term for all research on women's activities in the past and on problems particularly relevant to women in earlier times'. See Ida Blom, 'Women's History – No Longer a Neglected Field of Study'? *Research in Norway* (Norwegian Research Council, 1976), p. 6.

9. For instance, Gro Hagemann, 'Om å gjøre det enkle komplisert og det usynlige synlig. Noen dilemmaer i kvinnehistorien [On Making the Simple Complicated and the Invisible Visible: Some Dilemmas in Women's History]'. This paper was presented at the third meeting of Nordic women's historians in Stockholm, in April 1989, and will be published in *Studier i historisk metode*, 21 (1990).

10. Anna Jorunn Avdem, '... gjort ka gjerast skulle'. *Om arbeid og levekår for kvinner på Lesja ca. 1910-1930* ['... done what should be done'. Work and Living Conditions for Women at Lesja c. 1910-1930] (Oslo: Universitetsforlaget, 1984); Ingeborg Fløystad, *Kvinnekår i endring. Kvinnene sitt arbeid i Arna, Hordaland, 1870-1930* [Changing Living Conditions for Women. Women's Work in Arna, Hordaland, 1870-1930] (Oslo: Universitetsforlaget, 1986). The women in this rural community outside Bergen worked mostly on farms and in the textile industry.

11. Kari Martinsen has published *Freidige og uforsagte diakonisser. Et omsorgsyrke vokser fram 1860-1905* [Self-confident Deaconesses. The Growth of a Caring Profession 1860-1905] (Oslo, 1984). Monographs are forthcoming from Gro Hagemann on women in telecommunication and in the clothing industries, and from Kari Melby on nurses and teachers and their unions, and also on the housewives' union.

12. Sølvi Sogner, Hege Brit Randsborg and Eli Fure, *Fra stua full til tobarnskull: Om fruktbarhetsnedgangen i Norge ca. 1890-1930* [From a Full Cottage to the Two Child Family. The Decline in Fertility in Norway c.1890-1930] (Oslo: Universitetsforlaget, 1984); Ida Blom, *Barnebegrensning – synd eller sunn fornuft?* [Family Planning – Sin or Common Sense?] (Oslo: Universitetsforlaget, 1980), and *'Den haarde dyst'. Fødsler og fødselshjelp gjennom 150 år*. ['The Hard Struggle': Childbirth and Obstetrics over 150 Years] (Oslo: Cappelens Forlag, 1988).

13. See the works by Avdem and Fløystad in note 10 above.

14. See, for example, Gro Hagemann's article mentioned in note 5.

15. Gro Hagemann has criticised the three volumes published (of the five planned) of *Arbeiderbevegelsens historie i Norge* [The History of the Workers Movement in Norway] (Oslo: Tiden Norsk Forlag, 1985 and 1987) from this perspective. The authors are male historians. Gro Hagemann, 'Historien om den mannlige arbeiderklassen [The History of the Male Working Class]', *Arbeiderhistorie*, Årbok for arbeiderbevegelsens historie, 2 (1988), pp. 124-51.

16. Kari Vogt, Sissel Lie, Karin Gundersen, Jorunn Bjørgum (eds.), - *Kvinnenes Kulturhistorie* [A Cultural History of Women] 1, *Fra antikken til år 1800* [From Antiquity to 1800], 2, *Fra år 1800 til vår tid* [From 1800 to Our Time] (Universitetsforlaget, 1985); Kari Vogt, Karin Gundersen, Sissel Lie (eds.), *Kvinnenes Kulturhistorie. Orientens kvinner* [The Cultural History of Women: Women of the Orient] (Oslo: Universitetsforlaget, 1988).

17. Anna Jorunn Avdem and Kari Melby, *'Oppe først og sist i seng'. Husarbeid i Norge fra 1850 til i dag* ['Up First and the Last to Bed': Housework in Norway from 1850 till Today] (Oslo: Universitetsforlaget, 1985).

18. The following articles have all been published in the *Scandinavian Journal of History*: Sølvi Sogner, '"... a Prudent Wife is from the Lord". The Married Peasant Woman of the Eighteenth Century in a Demographic Perspective', 9, no. 2 (1984), pp. 113-33; Ida Blom, 'The Struggle for Women's Suffrage in Norway 1885-1913', 5, no. 1 (1980), pp. 3-22, and 'Women's Politics and Women

in Politics in Norway since the End of the 19th Century', 12, no. 1 (1987), pp. 17-33; Gro Hagemann, 'Feminism and the Sexual Division of Labour: Female Labour in the Norwegian Telegraph Service Around the Turn of the Century', 10, no. 2 (1985), pp. 143-54; Ole Jørgen Benedictow, 'The Milky Way in History: Breast Feeding, Antagonism between the Sexes and Infant Mortality', 10, no. 1 (1985), pp. 19-53; Kari Melby, 'The Housewife Ideology in Norway between the Two World Wars', 14, no. 2 (1989), pp. 181-93. See also Ida Blom, 'A Centenary of Organized Feminism in Norway', *Women's Studies International Forum*, 5, no. 6 (1982), pp. 569-74. Ida Blom has also published articles in English in various anthologies. For other publications in English, see the bibliography in Norwegian women's history.

13

The State of Women's History in Denmark

Nanna Damsholt

It is a characteristic feature of Danish research in women's history – just as it is a characteristic feature of all Danish research in the humanities – that it does not take place in ivory towers but, for better or for worse, grows and flourishes in the open. It is influenced not only by what happens in research at universities, but also by what happens in society at a global as well as at a national level. In Denmark, university-based women's history is primarily attached to the humanities, that is, to Faculties of Arts, and this is, for the time being, not an advantageous position. Because of the current economic situation in Denmark, there is a general cutback in state funding. This general retrenchment particularly affects that part of the state budget allocated to research in the humanities, because this kind of research is not expected to benefit business or promote exports. As a consequence, scholars in the humanities, and among them women historians, have to spend quite a lot of time and energy on legitimising their work and making themselves visible in order to survive professionally. We feel we are required to prove that history is useful and are encouraged to write in an immediately comprehensible way to reach as wide an audience as possible. Our research is expected to be of current interest and exciting to read, not dry as dust. This challenge is, at one and the same time, both paralysing and stimulating, and the demands that are being made are legitimate as well as illegitimate. On principle I dissociate myself from the idea that the humanities need to prove themselves useful. To know one's history is part of human life and need not be judged on its utility. It is a human right more than an asset.

During the last years some important changes have taken place in our country's educational system. For the first time the university has opened its gates to people who have not qualified in traditional ways and one of the consequences is that mature students, including women, make up an increasing proportion of those enrolled. The fact that an increasing number of mature women are visible in the university classroom is due to this open-door policy. That an increasing proportion of students in women's history courses are mature women is also due to the fact that the interest in women's history among younger students is declining. This decline reflects the situation in the women's movement, which is still alive and thriving, but has come of age, matured and is not primarily led by the young generation. Of course, we mature feminists discuss this situation intensively, and we have noticed, with some optimism, that a number of young women are forming a new political party, a women's party, and that is something new in Danish politics.[1]

Among researchers in women's history are a growing number of mature women like myself. What can we do to rally the young women to an interest in women's history? An important step in the right direction has been taken with a reform of the teaching of history in upper-secondary schools. Beginning in 1989 it has become a compulsory part of the curriculum to learn about the different conditions of men and women in both the present and the past. This is actually a very advanced educational policy statement, and we who were members of the working group appointed by the Secretary of State for Education to advise on the national curriculum for history and who contributed to the formulation of this policy are justifiably proud of it. We hope that this change in the history curriculum will mean that women's history will become an integral part of the teaching of Danish history. In this connection it is worth mentioning that history as a school subject in primary and lower-secondary schools has recently been strengthened.

Themes in current historiography

What are Danish feminist historians currently writing about? In general one could say that research on the themes from the first period of feminist history continues but in greater depth and breadth. The most popular period is still the last century, from about 1850 till today, and it is still groups of women, women's organisations and women from a particular social class, that are studied. An important publication is *Kvindefællesskaber* [institutions where women get together to work, to help each other, or to celebrate something], an anthology of articles on women's history in the nineteenth and twentieth centuries, focusing on the tension between autonomy and isolation, power and powerlessness.[2] There is a lively interest in female school teachers, their professional and private lives.[3] A great deal has also been written about female philanthropists, that is, about bourgeois ladies who took care of poor children, the sick and the outcast.[4] Research into the history of the YWCA (Young Women's Christian Association) resulted in the article 'Ungpigekultur i provinsen [Teenage culture in a provincial town]'.[5] A monograph on farmers' wives is forthcoming.[6] It will show how living conditions for these women were altered with the structural changes in Danish agriculture from the 1880s onwards.[7]

Another popular framework for studies in women's history focuses on decades, that is, women in the 1930s, in the 1970s, in the 1980s. A very popular book is *Tidens Kvinder* [Modern Women],[8] a fine collection of articles on women in the 1930s. These studies contribute to the important task of proving how the conditions for women have changed and of proving the historicity of femininity. The theme of the historicity and the social construction of femininity is, I believe, one of the most interesting aspects of Danish feminist historiography. In the book *Kvindekøn* [Womankind], published in 1987,[9] Bente Rosenbeck has shown, firstly, how this notion was constructed in Denmark in the period 1860-1960 and, secondly, how it was shaped – torn, as it were – by the tension between two tendencies, the tendency towards equality and the tendency towards sexual polarisation. Rosenbeck argues convincingly that the scientific biologisation of femininity has been an important factor in the attempt to keep women in an unequal position in spite of the introduction of a degree of formal equality.

In the last few years there has been a greatly increasing interest in the history of the body and of sexuality. This is due not only to the growing understanding of psychosomatic disease, but also to the sexual preferences of individual female historians and to the growing feminist insistence on attending to the connections between body and soul. In *Hvad hjertet begærer* [What the heart desires], Karin Lützen, a highly qualified ethnologist, has treated the subject of women's sexuality and of love between women in the last century with great charm and a sense of humour.[10]

So far I have only mentioned works in women's history from the fairly recent past. They tend to steal the show. But with respect to research on women in the middle ages, we Danish feminist historians are actually in a fairly strong position. We started early with an international symposium in 1976, the proceedings of which were published in 1978 under the title *Aspects of Female Existence*,[11] and the edited papers from the second symposium in 1987 have appeared under the title *Female Power In The Middle Ages*.[12] In the interim we have held several Nordic symposia on, *inter alia*, women's work in the middle ages and medieval women's economic conditions. Recently *Kvinders Rosengård* [Women's Rose Garden] has appeared, a report from a symposium on medieval women's health and sexuality.[13] All these reports have summaries in English.

Among historians working on medieval history Grethe Jacobsen is doing research on women in Danish urban society, revealing how women's lifecycle, determined by their gender, in turn determines their activities in reality but is ignored in the town laws.[14] I myself have written a book on the image of women in medieval Denmark as it appears in hagiography and historiography written in Latin by the clergy of that time.[15] I found that the literary image is not one definite image but several. I demonstrate that the genre of a text has determined the image of women but I also show that certain traits cut across genres: the more localised, private and concerned with concrete events, the more varied and lively the depiction of women. Conversely, the more universal, official and abstract a work, the more schematic and lifeless is its image of women.

A very recent trend in Danish women's historical writing involves students exploring religious and ethical questions. A new generation of students is ready to accept that religious faith, or belief in God, has historical agency. Such students are interested in holy women, their religious experiences and expressions.[16] This new interest is probably a reaction to the predominance of materialism in the 1970s and also, I suspect, a consequence of the fact that the global problems, the increasing disparity between the have and have-not nations and the resulting disease, poverty, militarism and threat to the environment, are getting more and more urgent for us to tackle. Addressing these global problems calls for an understanding of other cultures which will be deficient without attention to the religious dimension.

Choice of communicative form

Among the historical best sellers of the 1988-89 season have been two biographies of women, written by women: *Christine* by Helle Stangerup and *Skriverjomfruen* [The female writer], by Mette Winge.[17] Both are fictional biographies but based on a thorough study of the lives of the protagonists. *Christine* retrieves the life of a Renaissance princess; *Skriverjomfruen* reclaims the life of a learned author, translator, and playwright from the eighteenth century. These successes have presumably furthered a trend, already in existence, for feminist historians of women to cast the results of their research in the form of a biography. This trend is related, I believe, to a general trend in Western Europe towards focusing on the individual and the revival of the narrative form.

The seventeenth and eighteenth centuries have so far been rather neglected, except for the ongoing work of Marianne Alenius, a classical philologist, who writes about the fairly large group of learned ladies from these centuries.[18] Between 1500 and 1800 the names of 160 learned women from the Nordic countries have been preserved, among them about 120 Danish women. That Danish women were so highly represented is probably due to the predilection for record keeping of Danish male scholars in that period. As mentioned above, the interest in female school teachers is great and a biography on a pioneering educator from the nineteenth century is forthcoming.[19]

Female historians share with other writers the desire to make our articles and books good and exciting reading. And I think we can be seen to have been fairly successful on that score insofar as our books are bought in large numbers and widely read. The first modern history of Danish women from 1600 to the present, *Kvindfolk* [Womenfolk], appeared in 1984[20] and was published in a paperback edition a few years later. This pioneering work can easily be criticised and will no doubt one day be replaced by a new history based on more up-to-date research findings. Nevertheless, *Kvindfolk* must be credited with having played an important part in the revival of interest in women's history in Denmark.

Methods and theories

Research based on the theory of femininity as a social construction has already been mentioned. In addition, some of our theoretical discussions turn on the question of whether women's history should be cultivated as a special discipline, in isolation from general history, or whether it should be studied within the framework of gender history. Some colleagues, including myself, believe that the problem may be tackled by using a theory of patriarchy, because the concept of patriarchy automatically entails attention to the relations between the sexes, above all the power relations between men and women. To analyse and describe society as a patriarchy, and to place within this framework the lives and conditions of women, seems to me, as a medievalist, a natural thing to do, because patriarchy was the legitimate, normal state of affairs in the middle ages. It would be useful if a number of books on patriarchy in various parts of the world at various times were to appear. This would enable us to do a better job of describing, understanding and fighting the changeable, slippery and tough institution called patriarchy.

An important element in current feminist theoretical debates concerns the relation of feminism to postmodernism. At our Centre for Feminist Studies in Copenhagen, which is an interdisciplinary institution, this debate is first and foremost raised by the literary historians, and so far, I believe, the most important outcome has been the realisation that postmodernists and feminists have something in common: namely the wish to deconstruct – for our part androcentrism in the sciences and in the dominant world view.

This essential debate bears on the two most urgent problems we women face in our attempt to write our own history. The first is how we can write our own history into the general history, and this is difficult in itself. The second and no less intricate problem is how we can make the academy integrate what we have already achieved into the academic mainstream. In Denmark our male colleagues continue to ignore or minimise what has already been written by feminists in general, including feminist historians. For instance, the first volumes of a projected ten-volume history of Denmark are beginning to appear but the prospect of finding much women's history in this series seems unlikely.[21]

Organisation

Only a few of the Danish women historians have succeeded in securing permanent academic positions that make it possible to concentrate on research work. Therefore, private initiatives have meant a lot to the development of studies in women's history and these initiatives have quite often been supported by authorities empowered to make grants. As mentioned above, since 1983 Nordic conferences on women's history have been held with themes such as women's work, sexuality and fertility, women's organisations and socialisation. These conferences have been well-attended and have resulted in the editing and publication of proceedings and reports.[22] The most recent initiative is the setting up of a women's network, Klio, with the purpose of helping women historians to keep in contact.

* * * * *

Even if the problems confronting us as historians of women in Denmark are manifold, we have not lost either our courage or our strength. A great number of unemployed women or temporarily employed women work very energetically and ambitiously on the researching and writing of Danish women's history. I trust that the reform of the history curriculum for the upper-secondary schools will bring a change in the status of women's history, in schools and at university level, with the result that we gain a more secure foothold in the academy. We women must be optimistic just as we must use our strength wherever we are active as scholars, teachers, and mothers.

NOTES

1. This initiative does not appear to have got off the ground.

2. Anna-Birte Ravn and Marianne Rostgård (eds.), *Kvindefællesskaber* (Aalborg: Aalborg Universitetscenter, 1985).

3. Hanne Rimmen, Birgitte Possing, and Adda Hilden are working on this subject.

4. See, for example, Tinne Vammen, *Rent og urent* [Pure and impure] (København: Gyldendal, 1986).

5. Hilda Rømer Christensen, 'Ungpigekultur i provinsen [Teenage culture in a provincial town]', in Hilda Rømer Christensen and Hanne Rimmen Nielsen (eds.), *Tidens Kvinder* [Modern Women] (Aarhus: Håndbibliotekets Veninder, 1985), pp. 104-23.

6. The author is Bodil K. Hansen, 'Rural Women in Late Nineteenth-Century Denmark', *Journal of Peasant Studies*, 9, no. 2 (January 1982), pp. 225-40.

7. Anna-Birte Ravn has written about smallholders. Anna-Birte Ravn, 'Patriarchy in smallholding families in Denmark after 1945', in Anna-Birte Ravn, Bente Rosenbeck and Birte Siim (eds.), *Capitalism and Patriarchy* (Aalborg: Aalborg University Press, 1983), pp. 79-86.

8. Hilda Rømer Christensen and Hanne Rimmen Nielsen (eds.), *Tidens kvinder* [Modern Women] (Aarhus: Håndbibliotekets Veninder, 1985).

9. Bente Rosenbeck, *Kvindekøn* [Womankind] (København: Gyldendal, 1987).

10. Karin Lützen, *Hvad hjertet begærer* [What The Heart Desires] (København: Gyldendal, 1986).

11. B. Carlé, N. Damsholt, K. Glente and E. Trein Nielsen (eds.), *Aspects of Female Existence* (København: Gyldendal, 1978).

12. Karen Glente & Lise Winther-Jensen (eds.), *Female Power In The Middle Ages: Proceedings from the 2nd St. Gertrud Symposium, Copenhagen, August 1986* (København: C.A.Reitzel, 1989).

13. H. Gunneng, B. Losman, B. Møller Knudsen, and H. Reinholdt (eds.), *Kvinders Rosengård* [Women's Rose Garden] (Stockholm: Skriftserie från Centrum för kvinnoforskning vid Stockholms Universitet, no. 1, 1989).

14. Grethe Jacobsen, 'Women's Work and Women's Role: Ideology and Reality in Danish Urban Society, 1300-1550', *Scandinavian Economic History Review*, 31, no. 1 (1983), pp. 3-20.

15. Nanna Damsholt, *Kvindebilledet i dansk højmiddelalder* [The Image of Women In Medieval Denmark] (København: Borgen, 1985). Summary in English.

16. Several historians are doing research in this field: Hilda Rømer Christensen, Tinne Vammen, Hanne Rimmen Nielsen, Karin Lützen, Birgitte Possing, Adda Hilden and Sidsel Eriksen all study female teachers and female leaders in religious organizations and the religious aspects of life in schools and in charity work.

17. Helle Stangerup, *Christine* (København: Gyldendal, 1988); Mette Winge, *Skriverjomfruen* [The Female Writer] (København: Samleren, 1988).

18. Marianne Alenius' works include her edition of the autobiography of Charlotte Dorothea Biehl as well as a monograph about her: *Charlotta Dorothea Biehl: Mit ubetydelige Levnets Løb* [Charlotta Dorothea Biehl: My Insignificant Life]

(København: Museum Tusculanum, 1986); *Brev til eftertiden* [A Letter for Posterity] (København: Museum Tusculanum, 1987).

19. Birgitte Possing is writing a biography of Nathalie Zahle.

20. Anne Margrete Berg, Lis Frost and Anne Olsen (eds.), *Kvindfolk* [Womenfolk] (København: Gyldendal, 1984).

21. Olaf Olsen (ed.), *Gyldendal og Politikens Danmarks Historie* [A History of Denmark] (København: Gyldendal og Politiken, 1988).

22. Gro Hagemann (ed.), *Nordisk Kvinnehistoriemøte Oslo, 20.-23. februar 1983. Konferanserapport, Arbeidsnotat 1/84* (Oslo, 1984); Inge Frederiksen and Hilda Rømer (eds.), *Kvinder, Mentalitet, Arbejde* [Women, Mentality and Work] (Aarhus: Aarhus Universitetsforlag, 1986).

14

The State of Women's History in Sweden:
An Overview

Yvonne Hirdman[1]

Academic history and women historians

The first woman in Sweden, and for that matter in the Nordic countries, to defend a doctoral thesis in history was Ellen Fries. The year was 1883, the place Uppsala University and the subject was the history of the diplomatic relationship between Sweden and the Netherlands in the seventeenth century. This event was seen by some radical professors as a sign of a better and more equal world to come, but by others (the majority) as the opposite: as a sign of the decline of scholarship. They hoped that she, as well as being the first, would also be the last as, in fact, she was for a long time.[2] The first woman ever to become a professor in history in Sweden was Ingrid Hammarström (Stockholm University), who, in the late 1950s, wrote a very good dissertation on Swedish trade in the sixteenth century. The second female professor was Birgitta Odén (Lund University), also a brilliant historian, who later developed a keen interest in 'the theoretical aspects of' history and, in the 60s, engaged in the debate between 'the new' history and the old empirically-oriented history. Outside university circles, Ellen Fries, who had connections with the women's movement, published biographical essays about famous women in Swedish history. The interests of the two later female professors, however, lay strictly within mainstream historiography.[3]

When I was a young historian choosing a theme for my dissertation in the red years of the 60s, the idea of 'women's history' was still very distant. The topic suggested to me by my professor – the impact of the Second World War on family life in Sweden – sounded to me rather insulting. In the spirit of the time I chose instead to write about the Swedish Communist Party.

Yet I had read by then Gunnar Qvist's dissertation, 'The Woman Question in Sweden 1809-1840', which appeared in 1960.[4] It dealt with legal prohibitions against women, mainly within the fields of commerce and craft during the first half of the nineteenth century, and with the political efforts to abolish these restrictions. His main thesis was rooted in a materialistic interpretation of history: it was the need of capitalism for free labour that brought an end to the old restrictions. These reforms were not initiated for the sake of the emancipation of women, but rather for the benefit of capital. Qvist continued to write about women and the labour market in the second half of the nineteenth century and into the twentieth. He worked at the University of Gothenburg, and in the early 1970s he created an interdisciplinary seminar around 'his' topic – thus creating the first women's history group, which profited by the fact that since 1958 an archive of women's history had been established at the Gothenburg University Library.[5]

The new feminists and the development of women's history

It could perhaps be said that women's history in Sweden had two immediate sources: one academic, linked to the Gothenburg seminar, and one feminist, linked to the new women's movement outside the universities. From this 'second wave' of feminism in the 1970s, ideas about women's studies emerged and took shape in small feminist groups at various universities. Among the first generation of those women scholars who built up new institutions to support women's studies, women historians interested in women's history turned out to be in the majority. At every university a 'Forum for Women's Research and Female Researchers' was being constructed, partly from below – that is by women students, teachers and researchers at the universities – and partly from above, as the universities obtained some money from the government in order to increase the quota of women at the research level in all disciplines.

As feminists and historians, the main issues for us at that time were problems concerning positions (at the university, in the labour market), raising money for new projects, and dealing with the humiliating treatment we received from our male colleagues (who did not listen to us at seminars, and when they did listen, belittled our contributions, or so we had good reason to think). We concerned ourselves far less at that time with the question of what women's history might be. The questions we raised were the questions of the women's movement, translated to the realm of academic life and culture. We were not then concerned with more specifically epistemological problems, such as whether there exists a special kind of female knowledge? What does women's studies mean? And, more recently, what is women's history?

As to the work done in history or the work that we intended to do, once we found money to do it (and now I speak from my own perspective in the second half of the 1970s), our focus was mainly on women and work, and/or women and the labour movement. The connection with the rising interest in labour history was self-evident, as the spirit of the time was indeed radical. Perhaps this emphasis was stressed even more in Sweden than elsewhere, due to the great success of the Swedish labour movement, with the strongest trade union in the world and with a political party, the Social Democratic Party, which has held power in Sweden almost without interruption since the early 1930s.

Theoretical discussions

This interest in women and work and women and the labour movement raised some fundamental theoretical issues, though issues very much of their time, for Swedish historians of women. Of course, Heidi Hartmann's argument about the dual system (capitalism and patriarchy) reached us quite early and played an important role in our developing understanding of women, capitalism and socialism.[6]

But the work by the German sociologist Ulrike Prokop also played a very important role, and her book about the unlimited desires and utopian strategies of women was widely read and commented upon.[7] Prokop's use of the concept 'female productive forces' was seen as a means of getting away from one of the problems of 'contribution history', how to explain the non-participation, or weak participation, of women in the great struggle between labour and capital. Put another way, this was the question of Professor Higgins: Why can't a woman be more like a man? Where the Hartmann explanation placed the oppression of women by women in the centre of our understanding, the Prokop argument insisted more on the complex nature of female wishes and dreams.

Theoretical perspectives were indeed needed. Very early a debate emerged in Scandinavia among feminist scholars, concerning the interpretations of the results that were bound to appear when one looked at women in history (or society) from a male perspective (that is, the perspective of a radical male of the leftist 1960s). The results were (inevitably) misery and/or deviation, where women were indeed the victims of history (and men) rather than participants and actors. Here the Hartmann dual system analysis could be used, but it did not alter the overall view of women as outsiders. In opposition to this 'Research of Misery', as the Norwegian women scholars called it, 'Research of Dignity' developed, where the Prokop approach could be used. This was a branch

very much like, and not surprisingly inspired by, the women's culture
trend within the historiography of women's history in the United States.

This shift away from a politically oriented view of women's
history towards a more descriptive, apolitical, nostalgic interpretation,
found its main spokeswomen within other disciplines, particularly
sociology.[8] Contrary to other countries, in Sweden there never was a 'herstory' or 'women's culture' trend within women's history.[9] One reason
why it did not spread to history was probably that quite early the issue was
transformed from being an ideological dilemma for feminists into a subject
of historical research.[10] For four days in June 1982 a so-called 'Women's
University' was held at Umeå University. It was an interdisciplinary
symposium, with hundreds of participants from all over Sweden,
discussing women's studies, new methods, new theories and new
problems. One of these problems concerned the feminist predicament of
the opposing ideologies of 'equality' (in the sense of 'sameness') and
'difference' (the old debate over whether men and women are essentially
the same kind of human being or whether they are of two fundamentally
different kinds, almost as if they belonged to separate species, like cats and
dogs). As an historian, I had seen this dilemma causing much confusion
and bitterness within the earlier women's movement of the late nineteenth
and early twentieth centuries. At the Women's University I tried to share
this experience, telling the story of the previous conflict, beginning with
Ellen Key, a 'difference feminist', versus the women within the suffrage
movement, (*kvinnosakskvinnorna*) who were 'sameness' or equality
oriented.[11] This famous conflict had begun in 1896 when Ellen Key
published a little booklet entitled *Missbrauchte Frauenkraft* [Misused
Women-power], in which she accused the 'feminists' of provoking a world
war because of their unfair, false and unnatural demands for equality.[12]

Indeed, the extent to which these different positions were rooted
in their own time was startling, and made it easier to contemplate this
dilemma as a scholar. The case for 'difference' seemed to occur at times
when the future seemed dark and expectations had shrunk. The case for
'equality', on the other hand, seemed to come alive in brighter and more
optimistic times. Hence, the different answers to the issue of the 'nature'
of woman seemed to be a question of the 'Zeitgeist' (spirit of the times),
a structural question to be explained in connection with other social and
economic structures. Another striking observation was that these shifts
occurred both within the socialist and in the bourgeois women's
movements. In other words, the answer to the question 'what is a woman?'
was not part of an explicit ideology, although it did shape feminist
strategies for social and political change.[13]

One way of resolving the theoretical dilemma that women
obviously acted differently from men in history, without accepting the old

misogynist (or the new feminist-fundamentalist) arguments of 'natural' causes for this different behaviour by women, was the idea of a female 'perspective'. This perspective was to be held by the woman researcher - who was trying to define women in history as both victims of oppressive structures and as actors, conscious of both the possibilities and restrictions. Yet it could also easily become a rather idealistic, heroine-centred perspective which did not actually resolve the problem.

With the subsequent advancement of theories of gender and gender system, it seemed that we might overcome the unfruitful dichotomy between 'equality' and 'difference' (created by 'modernity'). In the light of a new understanding of the historically constructed nature of gender, the dichotomy debate became an important historical issue. Of course, there is still a lively debate in Sweden as elsewhere, concerning the concept of gender, in Swedish *genus*, which continues to have a purely grammatical meaning. Those who argue against the *genus* concept claim that such a concept already exists, that of 'socially constructed sex' (*socialt kön*), and that *genus* might diminish the central role of women within women's studies. Those in favour of the new concept, however, claim that there is a qualitative difference - that *genus* should be seen as a category in which 'culture' and 'nature' are interwoven. They also find the concept useful just because of its neutrality and 'emptiness' and, thus, its unseen possibilities. They further emphasise its strategic value in infiltrating other theoretical systems.[14] However, whether one uses the concept of 'socially constructed sex' or 'genus', the main understanding of the complex and changing nature of the construction of human beings is shared - as well as a more complex understanding of women's history.

Research: the present and the future

Given that Sweden is a small country, with only a handful of universities (the oldest and most important being those of Lund and Uppsala) and history departments, and that each year only about ten to twenty dissertations in history (including economic history) are completed, the results of research within the field of women's history in Sweden are necessarily quite modest. Yet they are fertile in new interpretations.

As the interest in women's history in the beginning was part of the new interest in the lives of ordinary people, their work and their political struggles, some scholars began to investigate the role of women in the processes of industrialisation and democratisation by focusing on the Social Democratic Labour Movement. Two important scholars in this area are Christina Carlsson and Anita Göransson, both of whom started their research in the early days of women's history, and only recently finished their theses. The many difficulties they met – the 'sexless' source material, the lack of interest in their institutions, the dearth of models of interpretation – of course prolonged their work. But precisely these difficulties make the work of these two historians good illustrations of the ways in which models and explanatory theories have been developed within women's history itself.

Women and work

The work by Anita Göransson, *Från family; till fabrik* [From Family to Factory] is a study of the changes in the class and gender systems that the new production and the new labour system created between 1830 and 1877.[15] Her main theses are that the division of labour that existed in the home was taken over and 'translated' at the factory level. She argues that the rise of a labour aristocracy and the gender division of labour are but two sides of the same coin. Her empirical material is mostly taken from the textile industry, but also from the early tobacco industry in the city of Norrköping, the former centre of the textile industry in Sweden. To emphasise her points, she also examined the household position of workers and their responsibility for children, the age of marriage, and so on.

In her work on the history and development of women's work in the pottery factory of Gustavsberg, Ulla Wikander also addresses the development of a gender division of labour. But her perspective is directly opposed to that of Göransson. She tries to isolate the processes of gender segregation and hierarchy in the relations of production inside a factory, without introducing the concept of 'the private' into her explanatory model. Her findings are rather disappointing: from 1880 to 1980, despite dramatic technological innovations and new forms of work organisation, a constant imbalance remained between men and women in the workplace. The position of women was subordinate, they were given the most monotonous and least well-paid jobs, and was constantly recreated, even during periods that strongly favoured the integration of men's and women's work.[16] Together with Lynn Karlsson, Ulla Wikander has also published a short overview of women's work and the gender division of labour in Swedish industry, 1870-1950.[17]

Work in progress in the history of women and work includes women and bookbinding, women and the tobacco industry,[18] women typographers,[19] women in a candle factory,[20] and women as dairy maids.[21] Some studies also deal with more 'typical' women's occupations, such as midwifery and nursing.[22] Other studies under way of a broader and more complex kind include: an examination of the mobility of the female labour force 1880-1930;[23] and examination of women as part of the working force in Gothenburg;[24] and a comparative study of the different paths to employment for women in Sweden, the United States,

Great Britain and Finland from 1939 to the present.[25] For the post-war period, another important study is that by Gunhild Kyle (the first professor of women's history at Gothenburg and my immediate predecessor) *Gästarbeterska i manssamhället* [Guestworkers in Male Society] (1979), a study of the condition of women factory workers in Sweden.[26]

Women historians have also dealt explicitly with the difficulties and obstacles confronting women in paid work – as, for instance, does Gunhild Kyle, in an article about the conflict between production and reproduction.[27] Ulla-Britt Lithell deals in her recently published study with the dual burden of women's work and childcare in the northern part of Finland during the eighteenth and nineteenth centuries.[28] Other more direct obstacles to female employment in Sweden are being studied, especially the legislation passed at the beginning of the twentieth century against women's night work.[29] There is also a study under way at the University of Gothenburg on the efforts made in the inter-war period – to a great extent spearheaded by the trade unions – to prohibit married women from working.[30]

Since women's work also includes unpaid work, some historical studies have been done on different aspects of that topic. Outside the academic institutions, Brita Åkerman set up an impressive team project with many contributors, both researchers and historical actors such as Brita Åckerman herself, on women and the vast area of 'reproduction'. I, as historian on this project, wrote the article 'The Socialist Housewife: The Social Democratic Women's League and the Issue of Housework, 1900–1940', which focused on the ideological conflict of how to adapt marxist and socialist ideology to fit the lives of women in the working class. The conclusion pointed to the inability of marxist ideology to explain and interpret the experiences of women's lives, thus opening the way for alternative theoretical approaches.[31]

Given the emphasis on studies of women and work in a broad sense, it is interesting that the study of women and trade unions has not yet begun, except for an overview based on statistical material, written by Gunnar Qvist in the late 70s. Qvist had collected material for a larger study but it remained uncompleted when he died in 1980.[32]

This neglected area is an important one, as Swedish women formed their own trade union at the beginning of the century, but were forced back into the male trade unions as a result of the so-called Big Strike in 1909. The inter-war period is also almost blank as far as historical research on women is concerned. This may seem very surprising insofar as it was precisely then that the famous 'Swedish Model' was constructed; yet, surprisingly the part of women within it has never been problematised. The post-war period is also terrain sadly neglected by historians, though certainly it is one of the most dramatic periods as far as can be judged from the statistics. At this time large numbers of women entered the labour market, or 'stepped outside' or were 'drawn out' of the home.[33]

Women and politics

Christina Carlsson's study, mentioned above, deals with the rise and early development of the socialist labour movement in Sweden. In her search for the attitudes, policies and actions, relevant to women's issues within the movement, Carlsson has thoroughly investigated all the official source materials at various levels of the party from its beginnings in the 1880s to 1910. The result shows very plainly the movement's complete lack of interest in the entire matter, in spite of its vague theoretical commitments. Actually, women's issues were put aside and belittled and never inspired political actions. The richness of the book lies in its double approach, since it addresses both attitudes towards women and the actions of women themselves within the labour movement.[34] In my study of the socialist housewife, I dealt with the Social Democratic Women's League during its first forty years, but in a more general way. In a related study, I wrote of 'the Female Idol' of the Social Democratic women, the conscious and unconscious image of what a true woman should be like, as portrayed in their magazine, *Morgonbris*.[35]

There is as yet, however, no general history of the Social Democratic Women's League and its impact upon the history and shaping of the Swedish welfare state, although some areas of its history have been intensively studied. As early as 1974 Ann Katrin Hatje wrote her dissertation on the debate on the population issue in the 1930s and 40s.[36] A few years later the Uppsala historian Ann-Sofie Ohlander dealt with this topic in her book (published in English) *More Children of Better Quality?*[37] In an edited collection of articles about the Social Democratic Party in Sweden, Ann-Sofie Ohlander has also published an overview of the impact of the Women's League on welfare politics.[38] This is part of her continuing research project on 'Women, Motherhood and Social Policy in Sweden 1900-1945'.[39]

In my own work *Att lägga livet tillrätta* [The Making of Everyday Life] (1990), in which the population issue is also prominently featured, I deal with the reform of everyday life. In this book, the making of the welfare state is discussed from the perspective of gender, indicating the implicit but urgent need to resolve the conflict between women and society that underlay the reforms.[40] The reason for the interest in this particular issue lies in its important role in shaping modern Swedish society, where women in many respects were both the means and the goal of social policies. Interest in the Social Democratic women and their very special status in the successful welfare state of Sweden is shared by another scholar, Gunnel Karlsson, who is about to finish her dissertation at the University of Gothenburg. She is writing about the Social Democratic women in the post-war period, and deals especially with the relationship between the Party and the Women's League.[41]

The focus of these twentieth-century studies has to date combined work on the politics of the government concerning women, the so-called social policy or family policy, with work on the actions and reforms suggested by women politicians themselves. Anna-Greta Nilsson Hoadley, an historian from Stockholm, takes a different approach in her forthcoming dissertation about the women in the Social Democratic Women's League and their struggle against Swedish atomic weapons in the 1950s and 60s.[42]

The hegemonic status of the Social Democrats in the historiography of Swedish women is sharply underlined when one compares its large output with the much more limited quantity of ongoing research on other political parties and their women's organisations. For instance, there are only two studies under way that investigate the history of the Association of Conservative Women.[43] More astonishing is the fact, that the history of the women's suffrage movement in Sweden is not yet written[44] except for a few articles, including one by Gunhild Kyle, '"Why Must Women Wait?": Gender Arguments in Connection with Women's Suffrage'.[45] There is, however, one study in progress of the first feminist association in Sweden, the Fredrika Bremer Förbundet, and its perceptions of 'Woman'.[46] There is also a study on the leftish-liberal so-called Fogelstad group of the inter-war period.[47]

Otherwise, it seems to be the recent women's movement, both here and in the United States, that has attracted most interest.[48] This could also be explained by the rather hegemonic status not only of the Social Democrats in Sweden but also of socialist-feminist ideology. Writing about 'bourgeois' women has obviously not had the same priority as writing about socialist women. This is, however, changing.[49] Another way to study the emancipation of women in the nineteenth century is to examine more subversive strategies, for instance, that of philanthropy. Could philanthropy be a possible route towards, a school of learning for, political participation for women, or was it merely a socially approved way of transferring the exploitation of unmarried women's labour without any kind of economic or social reward?[50]

Family and sexuality

Very few studies have been done on women and sexuality in Swedish history. Two studies are under way on the regulation of prostitutes in the two major Swedish cities.[51] Nonetheless the distinctive history of sexual ethics in Sweden is still mainly untold. One aspect of its history has, however, been studied by Beata Losman in her book on the thoughts and lives of young female students at the beginning of the twentieth century, and their struggle to solve the impossible demands of being both 'manly' intellectuals and 'feminine' women, and both mothers and lovers in accordance with Ellen Key's high ethical standards for maternal caring and free love.[52] If we give the category of heterosexuality a wider meaning, however, and include within it the offspring of procreative sexual intercourse, namely children, other studies can be cited. In Swedish women's historiography, one finds a special interest in the situation of the unmarried mother and her child, as well as in orphans, in the past.[53]

And if we include marriage, family and divorce in this category the range of studies is broader still. The Stockholm historian Margareta Matovic has investigated family formation and choice of partners in Stockholm from 1850 to 1890 in the so-called 'Stockholm Marriage'.[54] Her main argument is that the women in her study were rational and calculating, preferring not to marry, but to live together with the men of their choice (also bearing them many children) in such a 'Stockholm marriage', in order not to lose control of the possibilities of their own earning power.[55] The story, or rather stories, of how to obtain a divorce during the nineteenth century in the northern parts of Sweden, has been told by the Umeå historian Marja Taussi Sjöberg.[56] Based on vast demographic evidence from the county of Värmland in the nineteenth century, Beata Losman (Gothenburg) has written about family structures (500 families) and the life-cycles of men and women (1,000 altogether). The most remarkable finding was that men moved around in order to survive, whereas women remained in the same place.[57]

Women's education

Women's education is a field that is attracting more and more attention. In the 1970s Gunhild Kyle wrote on nineteenth-century girls' schools in Sweden from an historian's perspective.[58] More recently Marie Nordström has published her investigation of the development of co-education in Sweden form 1866 to 1962.[59] In Umeå, the historian Christina Florin has been working with a combined theory of professionalisation and gender, in order to describe and understand the development and fascinating history of elementary school teachers from 1860 to 1906.[60]

The middle ages

As can easily be seen from the examples above, the domination of modern history (since 1800) is overwhelming. Women's history in Sweden is heavily concentrated on the last two hundred years, with the emphasis on the last century. This also mirrors the situation in history departments more generally. There are only a handful of scholars working within the field of women's history in the middle ages. But in spite of the small number of scholars, the results of their work are significant. This is due in no small part to inspiring collaboration by historians from the Nordic countries of Sweden, Norway, Denmark, Finland and Iceland. This collaboration, based on their common history, has resulted in five anthologies.[61] Work in progress includes the research project of Hedda Gunneng (Stockholm) and Birgit Sawyer (Gothenburg) on the inheritance laws of the middle ages.

Early modern history

Even less research has been done on early modern history in Sweden. At the University of Umeå, however, Inger Knobblock is writing her thesis on sexuality in seventeenth and eighteenth century Sweden. And in 1988 Ulla-Britt Lithell (Uppsala) published a book about women's work and childcare in eighteenth- and nineteenth-century Österbotten.[62]

The future of women's history in Sweden

The crucial question is 'How many historians are there?' One has to count historians, since the number is relevant not only to today's situation but also to that of the future. The total number of postgraduate students writing their dissertations in the field of women's history (including economic history and history of ideas) is only about forty-five. Moreover, there is a tendency towards a 'middleageisation' of those female historians dealing with women's history. This tendency may change, but at the moment most students doing their dissertations are over thirty. The younger women who no longer have, as we had, a strong women's movement to back them, hesitate to enter this field of study, perhaps simply because of the aura of 'old fashionedness' that lingers with us today as 'survivors' from the 70s. With a more 'realistic' approach to the world than we had, women students wanting to make a proper academic career, hesitate before entering the field of women's history, since it is still seen as a separate branch of history, which does not give them the same 'unassailable' qualifications as other fields of study, qualifications that are essential in applying for jobs in history departments.

And these 'jobs' are few. The situation in the humanities in Sweden is fairly desperate, compared to the situation in the natural or social sciences where there is an alternative labour market. Hence the furious battles over the few chairs available. Only five per cent of *all* professors are women. At the level just below, the so-called *docents* (senior lecturers, assistant professors) only about fifteen per cent are women. In history, the total number of chairs in the entire country is fourteen. One of them, a chair in Women's History at the University of Gothenburg, was only established in 1982. The first holder of the chair was Gunhild Kyle. When she retired in 1987, a very bitter but interesting conflict erupted over her successor, a conflict worth relating although one in which I was personally involved.

In the final round, there were two candidates for the chair, Yvonne Hirdman and Christer Winberg. The latter had no published work in women's history, and his main claim to consideration lay in the fields of social history and demography. He was, however, initially chosen by the department of history at Gothenburg, and then confirmed by the University of Gothenburg, on these grounds: his research, although not in the field, would make a splendid contribution to women's history. What he lacked in this field he could easily pick up. My work, on the other hand, much of which was within women's history, was said to be too theoretical and too frivolous (and partisan) so that, although it clearly met the requirements, it was not judged to be of sufficient quality according to mainstream historical criteria. Women's history was thus defined by these mainstream historians as simply a focus on the history of women, with no need for any special theoretical or methodological tools. I appealed this decision to the Education Ministry and the issue also aroused various women's organisations throughout Sweden. In April 1988 the government decided against the University of Gothenburg and I was appointed to the chair.

Contrary to most gender conflicts in Sweden (which are usually solved, or diminished, or taken off the agenda, by the achievement of a bland consensus) this case aroused very sharp and antagonistic feelings which were, for once, publicly expressed. As a result there is now considerable evidence on, first, the different definitions of women's history, and second, the relationship between men and women in the Swedish academic world of the late 1980s.[63]

The question of integration

In every department of history in Sweden, not only in Gothenburg's, a small women's history seminar group exists. The group at Uppsala, headed by Ann-Sofie Ohlander, is one of the largest. In the Department of

Economic History at Uppsala University a strong group of female scholars also exists, gathered around Ulla Wikander, who holds one of five research positions (and the only one in history) created by the government in order to encourage women's studies. The 1988 battle over the Gothenburg chair underscored the existence of this new academic field of women's history, and the interest of some male mainstream historians has now been aroused.

There is, for instance, an increasing demand for women historians as commentators on mainstream papers at conferences and seminars. This could be one path to integration. But it could just as well illustrate a new kind of segregation, where women are given their space, or their parallel area of study, so that everybody and everything can go back to normal. The logic of gender seems to make this trend irrevocable; thus we have also been given space in *Historisk Tidskrift* (the main Swedish historical journal) with two special numbers devoted to women's history',[64] just as we have been given space to teach our own courses (which are, of course, not compulsory).[65]

The question of integration is a difficult one, and is much discussed in Sweden of late. There is a striking change of emphasis since the early days, when we asked ourselves whether we wanted to participate or not, whether we should infiltrate and change the male bastions from within or not, or rather build our own universities or institutions, to today's question focusing on the possibilities of integration.

Integration of course does mean adding: you add women to a male-dominated institution. But adding women has never been enough, and the real claim from our side is to alter the general view of history by taking into account theoretical and empirical constructions, the fact that humankind is doubly gendered and that this fact plays an intriguing (and critical) part in shaping human societies. This question of integration was formally debated in 1988 when a conference was held on the initiative of the Arbetarrörelsens Arkiv [Archive for Labour Movement Research]. The theme for discussion was how the 'female perspective' could be applied to the history of the Swedish labour movement. A great deal of confusion was exhibited both by mainstream (male) historians and also by women historians. In fact, the two groups seemed to be talking about different subjects. One mainstream labour historian defended furiously what one might call the 'despotism of events', in which women were simply not involved at all or only to a very small degree. What could one do to alter history? The women historians tried to argue for another kind of history, that of other 'non-evident' events, as well as for another (gendered) interpretation of the mainstream 'events'. In spite of the lack of a definitive outcome, this discussion does indicate the existence of a rising interest in women's history among some of our male colleagues, and suggests that such a dialogue among ourselves can also be very fruitful. But we must not forget that in Sweden interest in women's history is not restricted to university circles. More pronounced is the interest from ordinary people, from women outside the university, from the media, from publishers and politicians. This public interest may therefore compensate for some of the other, gloomier trends discussed above.

NOTES

1. This is, of course, an overview from my particular perspective, based on my knowledge, formed by my bias. I thank Ulla Wikander and Beata Losman for helping me to avoid some fundamental mistakes. I am also in debt to Lynn Karlsson for her biographical help. I have tried to be consistent in the system of references, giving the Swedish title only for *published* articles, dissertations and books. As for Ph.D. theses in progress, I give the title only in English.

2. From an article by Ann-Sofie Ohlander, 'Kvinnliga forskarpionjärer i Norden [Female Research Pioneers in Scandinavia and Finland]', *Historisk Tidskrift*, no. 1 (1987).

3. The lack of interest in 'the woman question' has been commented upon by Birgitta Odén herself, in an interesting article on women students at the university during the twentieth cenu'ry, 'Kvinnostrategier i studentmiljö [Female Strategies at the Universities],' in *Scandia*, 54, no. 1 (1988).

4. Gunnar Qvist, *Kvinnofrågan i Sverige 1809-1846. Studier rörande kvinnans näringsfrihet inom de borgerliga yrkena* [The Woman Question in Sweden 1809-1846] (Götenborg: Gumpert, 1960).

5. One of the founders of this library was Asta Ekenvall, who wrote her dissertation (History of Ideas, Gothenburg University, 1966) on ideas about male and female qualities from Aristotle onwards.

6. Heidi Hartmann, 'The Unhappy Marriage of Marxism and Feminism: Towards a More Progressive Union', in Lydia Sargent (ed.), *Women and Revolution: A Discussion of the Unhappy Marriage of Marxism and Feminism* (Boston: South East End Press, 1981), pp. 1-41.

7. Ulrike Prokop, *Kvinnors Livssammanhang. Begränsade Strategier och Omättliga Önskningar* [Women's Life Conditions: Limited Strategies and Unlimited Desires] (Stockholm: Rabén & Sjögren, 1981).

8. One important scholar was Rita Liljeström, who wrote with Edmund Dahlstrom about women in trade unions, *Arbetarkvinnor i hemarbete och samhällsliv* [Working Women in Home, Work and Society] (Stockholm: Tiden, 1981).

9. This is a view shared by Rolf Danilelson in an evaluation of Swedish historiography, *Historia i beslysning: Sex perspektiv på svensk historisk forskning* [History in the Spotlight: Six Perspectives on Swedish Historiography] (Stockholm: HSFR, 1988), p. 93.

10. This does not mean that the dilemma does not exist among feminists – it certainly does. But it did not divide women historians.

11. The distinction was never such a simple one, but in her charge against the women's movement Ellen Key herself made this one over-simplification. At the University of Stockholm, in the Department of the History of Ideas, Ulla Manns is writing a dissertation on the self-image of women within the women's movement. The same issue, of different female-ideologies, is also the topic of a study by Margareta Lindholm at the Department of Sociology at the University of Gothenburg, where she examines and relates the thoughts of Elin Wägner (a 'difference' feminist) to those of Alva Myrdal, who was an outspoken 'equality' or 'sameness' feminist. See also Yvonne Hirdman, 'Alva Myrdal – en studie i feminism [Alva Myrdal – a Study in Feminism]', *Kvinnovetenskaplig Tidskrift*, no. 4 (1988).

12. Ellen Key, *Missbrauchte Frauenkraft* (Paris: Albert Langen, 1898).

13. See Yvonne Hirdman, 'Mellan likhet och särart – kvinnorörelesens historia i ett annat perspektiv [Between Sameness/or Equality/and Difference – the History of Women's Movement in Another Perspective]', in the collection *Rapport fran Kvinnovniversitet: Vetenskap, patriarkat och makt* [Knowledge, Patriarchy and Power] (Stockholm: Akademilitteratur, 1983), and Yvonne Hirdman, 'Särart och likhet: Kvinnorörelsens Scylla och Karybdis? [Difference and Equality – the Scylla and Charybdis of the Women's Movement]', in the edited anthology, *Kvinder, Mentalitet, Arbejde* (Aarhus, 1986).

14. The debate has taken place within *Kvinnovetenskaplig Tidskrift*, no. 4 (1987), Maud Landby Eduards and Ulla Manns, 'Om genus och genussystem [About Gender and the Gender System]'; no. 3 (1988), Yvonne Hirdman, 'Genussystemet – reflextioner kring kvinnors sociala underordning [The Gender System – Thoughts about the Social Subordination of Women]'; and no. 1 (1989), Lena Gemzöe et al., 'Sex, genus och makt antropologiskt perspektiv [Sex, Gender and Power in Anthropological Perspective]'.

15. Anita Göransson, *Från familj till fabrik. Teknik, arbetsdelning och skiktning i svenska fabriker 1830-1877* [From Family to Factory: Technology, Division of Labour, and Stratification in Swedish Factories, 1830-1877]' (Lund: Arkiv, 1988). History as a subject at Swedish universities is divided into three institutions or departments: 'History' – which originally meant political history, but which today also includes social history, family history, demography, and so on, under which women's history is placed; 'Economic History', with its own departments; and the 'History of Ideas', also with its own departments.

16. Ulla Wikander, *Kvinnors och mäns arbeten. Gustavsberg 1880-1980* [Women's Work – Men's Work: Gustavsberg 1880-1980] (Lund, 1988).

17. Lynn Karlsson and Ulla Wikander, 'Kvinnoarbete och könssegregering i svensk industri 1870-1950: tre uppsatser [Women's Work and Sex Segregation in Swedish Industry 1870-1950: three papers, with a summary in English]', *Uppsala Papers in Economic History*, Research Report no. 9, 1985.

18. See also the project at the Department of History at the University of Stockholm: Els-Magret Moberg Carlsson, 'Women Workers in the Bookbinding Industry in Stockholm 1870-1920', Ph.D. thesis in progress; and Kristina Rossland, 'From Male Handicraft to Women's Factory Work: Women in Stockholm's Tobacco Industry 1870-1930', Ph.D. thesis, in progress.

19. Inger Humlesjö, 'Women Typographers: The Position of Women on the Labour Market in Industrial Work and in Union Activities 1910-1939', Ph.D. thesis in progress, Economic History, Stockholm.

20. Kerstin Norlander, 'Women's and Men's work at Liljeholmens Candle Factory 1839-1939', Ph.D. thesis in progress, Economic History, Umeå University.

21. Lena Sommerstad, 'From Dairymaid to Dairyman: How Men Appropriated a Female Sphere of Competence', Ph.D. thesis in progress, Economic History, University of Uppsala.

22. Midwives: Margareta Wallman, 'The Association of Swedish Midwives 1886-1986', research project, College of Health Care (Vårdhögskolan) Uppsala; Ulla Wikander, Christina Romlid, and Lisa Öberg, 'Midwives in the 19th century' research project, Economic History, University of Uppsala; Lisa Öberg, 'Midwives in Stockholm 1850-1920', Ph.D. thesis in progress, History, University of Stockholm. Nurses: Arneta Emanuelsson, 'Professionalisation among Swedish Medical Workers during the 20th century: With special focus on the differences between Nurses, Assistant Nurses and Nurses' Assistants', Ph.D. thesis in progress, History, University of Uppsala; Anita Göransson, 'Women in the Swedish Service Sector 1970-1988' (part of a larger research project dealing with technological change and human resources development in the service sector), Economic History, University of Umeå. Childcare: Ann-Katrin Hatje, 'Society and Childcare in a Women's History Perspective Between 1900-1960', research project, History, University of Stockholm.

23. Jarl Torbacke, 'The Mobility of the Female Labour Force in Sweden 1880-1930', research project, History, University of Stockholm.

24. Christina Sundberg, 'Women's Employment in Gothenburg, 1920-1970', Ph.D. thesis in progress, Economic History, University of Gothenburg.

25. Håkon Leifsrud, 'Different Paths to Women's Employment – A Comparative Study of the U.S., Great Britain, Finland and Sweden 1939-1985', research project, Sociology, University of Uppsala.

26. Gunhild Kyle, *Gästarbeterska i manssamhället. Studier om industriarbetande kvinnors villkor i Sverige* [Guestworkers in a Male Society: Studies on the Conditions of Women Factory Workers in Sweden] (Stockholm: Liberforlag, 1979).

27. Gunhild Kyle, 'Kvinnan unter 1900 – talat – Konflikten mellan produktion och reproduction [Twentieth Century Women – The Conflict Between Production and Reproduction] *Historisk Tidskrift*, 3 (1980).

28. Ulla-Britt Lithell, *Kvinnoarbete och barntillsyn i 1700- och 1800-talets Österbotten* [Women's Work and Childcare in 18th and 19th-Century Österbotten] (Stockholm: Alonqvist and Wiksell, 1988; Uppsala: Academicus Ubsallensis, 1988).

29. Lynn Karlsson, 'Protection or Discrimination: The Regulation of Women's Night Work in Sweden 1911-1962', Ph.D. thesis in progress, Economic History, University of Uppsala; Ulla Wikander, 'The Prohibition Against Women's Night Work in an International Perspective 1890-1919' (part of an international project: the Sexual Division of Labour and Protective Labour Legislation), research project, Economic History, University of Uppsala.

30. René Frangeur, 'Male Power and Women's Responses: Attempts to Prohibit the Employment of Married Women During the 1920s and 1930s. The Actions of Employers, Unions and the Women's Movement', Ph.D. thesis in progress, History, University of Gothenburg.

31. See Brita Åkerman, editor of three anthologies: *Den okända vardagen - om arbetet i hemmen* [The Unknown Everyday Life about Home Work] (Stockholm: Akademilitteratur, 1983); *Vi kan, vi behövs! Kvinnorna går samman i egna föreningar* [We are Able, We are Needed! Women Form their Own Organisations] (Stockholm: Akademilitteratur, 1983); and *Kunskap för vår vardag. Utbildning och forskning för hemmen* [Knowledge for Our Every-Day Life: Education and Research for the Homes] (Stockholm: Akademilitteratur, 1984). See also, Yvonne Hirdman, 'The Socialist Housewife: The Social Democratic Women's League and the Issue of Housework 1900-1940', in Åckerman (ed.), *Vi kan, vi behövs!*; and Jan-Erik Hagberg, *Tekniken i kvinnornas händer, Hushållsarbete och hushållsteknik under 20-och 30-talen* [Housework and Technology during the 1920s and 1930s] diss. (Linkoping: Universitetet i Linkoping distrib. by Malmo: Liber, 1986).

32. Gunnar Qvist, *Statistik och politik. Landsorganisationen och kvinnorna på arbetsmarkanden* [Statistics and Politics: The Swedish Confederation of Trade Unions and Women on the Labour Market] (Stockholm: Prisma, 1974).

33. There is going to be a massive project on the subject, 'LO (The Swedish Confederation of Trade Unions) and the Women', under the supervision of Yvonne Hirdman, which will start within the next two years and be completed in 1998, when LO will celebrate its 100th anniversary.

34. Christina Carlsson, *Kvinnosyn och kvinnopolitik. En studie i svensk socialdemokrati 1880-1919* [Perceptions of Women and Women's Politics: A Study of Swedish Social-Democracy 1880-1910] diss. (Lund, 1986).

35. Yvonne Hirdman, '*Morgonbris* and the Female "Idols" 1900-1940', to be published in *Studies in Women's History* (forthcoming, spring 1991).

36. Ann-Katrin Hatje, *Befolkningsfrågan och välfärden. Debatten om familjepolitik och nativitesökning under 1930-och 1940-talen* [The Population Issue and the Welfare Policy: The Debate in the 1930s and 1940s] diss. (Stockholm: Allmanna Forlag, 1974).

37. Ann-Sofie Kälvemark, *More Children of Better Quality? Aspects of Swedish Population Policy in the 1930s* Studia historica Upsaliensia, vol. 115 (Uppsala, 1980).

38. Ann-Sofie Ohlander, 'The Invisible Child - the History of the Social Democratic Family Policy', in the collection *Socialdemokratins samhälle. SAP och Sverige under 100 år*, ed. Klaus Misgeld, Kare Molin, Klas Åmark (Stockholm: Tiden, 1989).

39. See also, at the Department of History, Uppsala University, Elisabeth Elgan, 'Women, Motherhood and Social Policy 1900-1945: A Comparative Study of Social Policy with Respect to Women as Mothers in Sweden and France', Ph.D. thesis in progress; and also in Uppsala, Jan Gröndahl, 'The Growth of the Welfare State in a Women's Perspective - Social Policy in Gävle Towards Single Women with Small Children', Ph.D. thesis in progress. The development and history of the Swedish Social Security System between 1913-1980 from a female perspective has been studied by Kerstin Abukanfusa, *Piskan och moroten. Om könens tilldelning av skyldigheter och rättigheter i det svenska socialförsäkringssystemet 1913-1980* (Stockholm, 1987).

40. Yvonne Hirdman, *Att lägga livet tillrätta. Studier i svensk folkhemspolitik* [The Making of Everyday Life: Studies in Swedish Reform Policy 1930-1950] (Stockholm: Carlssons, 1990).

41. Gunnel Karlsson, 'Social-Democratic Women During the Post-War Period', Ph.D. thesis in progress, History, University of Gothenburg.

42. Anna-Greta Nilsson-Hoadley, *Atomvapnet som partiproblem. Sveriges socialdemokratiska kvinnoförbund och frågan om svenskt atomvapen 1955-1960* (The Swedish Social-Democratic Women's Association and the Question of Swedish Atomic Weapons 1955-1965) diss. (Edsbruk, 1989).

43. Stina Nicklasson, 'The Association of Conservative Women and their Activities in Connection with Schools Reform 1940-1965', Ph.D. thesis in progress, History, University of Uppsala. See also, Inger Ström-Billing, 'Conservative Women's Associations in Swedish Politics 1912-1972', research project, History, University of Stockholm. For the Farmers' Party see Anita Dahlgren, Ole Elgström, and Hans Albin Larsson, 'Kvinnor påverkar . . . Centerns kvinnoförbund ur tre vetenskapliga perspektiv' (Women contribute . . . The Women's league of the Centre Party in three scientific perspectives) (Stockholm, 1985); for the Liberal party see Louise Drangel, 'The Liberal party and Equality-Status Policy' in the collection *Liberal ideologi och politik, 1934-1984* (Stockholm: Folk and Samhalle, 1984).

44. Except for a dissertation in the History of Literature Department; see Bertil Björkenlid, *Kvinnokrav i manssamhälle. Rösträttskvinnorna och deras metoder som opinionsbildare och påtryckargrupp i Sverige 1902-1921* [Female Demands in Male Society: The Suffragettes and their Methods as Opinion-moulders and Lobbyists in Sweden 1902-1921] (Uppsala: Avdenlningen f_ or litteratursociologi, 1982).

45. In *Kvinnovetenskaplig Tidskrift*, 2 (1983).

46. Ulla Manns, 'The Fredrika Bremer Association's Perceptions of Women 1884-1921', Ph.D. thesis in progress, History of Ideas, University of Stockholm.

47. Lena Eskilsson, 'The Women's School for Citizenship at Fogelstad – Ideas on the Content and Meaning of Women's Citizenship,' Ph.D. thesis in progress, History of Ideas, University of Umeå.

48. Ann-Marie Berggren, *Likhet eller särart – harmoni eller Conflikt? En analys av kvinnorörelsens idéer med utgångspunkt i utvecklingen i USA under 1960- och 70-talen* [Equality or Difference – Harmony or Conflict? An Analysis of the Ideas of the Women's Movement based on the Developments in the United States during the 1960s and 1970s]. diss., History, University of Gothenburg (Göteborg, 1987), and Ann-Sofie Juhlén, 'The Vitalisation of the Women's Movement in Sweden during the 1960s and 1970s', Ph.D. thesis in progress, History, University of Stockholm.

49. See, for example, Anita Göransson, 'Kinship as Power: The Rise of the Swedish Bourgeoisie 1780-1880', research project, Economic History, University of Umeå. See also Angela Rundquist, *Blått blod och liljevita händer. En etnologisk studie av aristokratiska kvinnor 1850-1900* [Blue Blood and Lily-White Hands: An Ethnology, University of Stockholm. Ethnological Study of Aristocratic Women 1850-1900], diss. (Malmö, 1989). Also: Gunhild Kyle, 'The Baker's Wife and the Worker's Wife', in the collection, *Den dolda historien, 24 uppsatser om vårt okända förflutna* (Stockholm: Forfatlarforlaget, 1984), and Gunhild Kyle, 'Genrepictures of

Women: A Study in the Bourgeois Family Hierarchy at the Turn of the Century', *Historisk Tidskrift*, 1 (1987).

50. Birgitta Jordansson, 'Poverty, Philanthropy and Women's Charity Work – One Route Towards Women's Emancipation, 1850-1916', Ph.D. thesis in progress, History, University of Gothenburg; see also, Ingrid Åberg, 'Women in the Association and Mass Organisations of the 19th Century: Religious Revival, Philanthropy and Emancipation', research project, History, University of Uppsala.

51. Gunilla Johansson, 'Women Prostitutes in Stockholm 1850-1918', Ph.D. thesis in progress, History, University of Stockholm; Gunnel Karlsson, 'Regulated Slavery: Prostitutes in Gothenburg 1865-1918', research project, History, University of Gothenburg. See also Tommie Lundqvist, 'Den diciplinerade dubbelmoralen. Studier i den reglementerade prostitutionens historia i Sverige 1859-1918 [Studies in the Regulation of Prostitution in Sweden 1859-1918]', diss., University of Gothenburg, 1983.

52. Beata Losman, *Kamp för nytt kvinnoliv. Ellen Keys idéer och deras betydelse för sekelskiftets unga kvinnor* [Striving for a New Existence: Ellen Key's Ideas and their Influence on Young Women at the Turn of the Century] (Stockholm: Liberforlag, 1980). See also the discussion on the creation of a state ethics of sexuality in the 30s in Yvonne Hirdman's 'The Making of Everyday Life' (see above, note 39).

53. Sigrid Håkansson, 'Illegitimate Children and their Mothers – A Regional Comparison', Ph.D. thesis in progress, History, University of Stockholm; Birgit Persson, 'A Study of Foster Children Boarded Out From Stockholm's General Orphanage during the 1830s', Ph.D. thesis in progress, History, University of Stockholm; Louise Lönnroth, 'Providing for Poor Children in Gothenburg 1800-1950', Ph.D. thesis in progress, History, University of Gothenburg.

54. Margareta Matovic, 'The Stockholm Marriage' (Stockholm, 1984).

55. See her forthcoming research project 'The Formation of Families and Household Structure in Stockholm 1820-1850', History, University of Stockholm. See also Monika Edgren, 'The Working Class Family in Norrköping 1820-1900', Ph.D. thesis in progress, History, University of Lund.

56. Marja Taussi Sjöberg, 'Skiljas. Trolovning, äktenskap och skilsmässa i Norrland på 1800-talet [Getting Divorced: Engagement, Marriage and Divorce in Norrland During the 19th Century]', diss., History, University of Umeå (Stockholm, 1988). Sjöberg has also published a book on female prisoners, *Duvans fångar: Brottet, straffet och människan i 1800-talets Sverige* [Prisoners of the Dove: Crime, Punishment and the Individual in Nineteenth-Century Sweden] (Stockholm, 1986).

57. Beata Losman, *Kvinnor, män och barn på 1800-talets svenska landsbygd: livsöden för människor födda i Väse församlilng, Värmland, 1800-1840* [Women, Men and Children in a Swedish Parish in Nineteenth-Century Värmland, (Goteborg: Acta Universätatis Gothoburgensis, 1986). See also, Bengt Anklarloo, 'Wives in Karlshman: A Collective Biography of the Lives of 181 Women in a Marriage Cohort 1848-1853', research project, History, University of Lund; see also, Eva Durhán, 'Strategies Among Different Generations in Agrarian Society in Norrland 1750-1900', Ph.D. thesis in progress, History, University of Umeå; Ulla Britt Lithell, 'Breast-Feeding and Reproduction: Studies in Marital Fertility and Infant Mortality in 19th-Century Finland and Sweden', diss., History, University of Uppsala, 1981.

58. Gunhild Kyle, 'Svensk flickskola under 1800-talet [Swedish Girl-Schools during the 19th Century]', diss. (Göteborg, 1972).

59. Lund, 1987.

60. Kristina Florin, 'Who Should Sit in the Teacher's Chair: Feminisation and Professionalisation Among Swedish Elementary School Teachers 1860-1909' (Umeå: Universitatet i Umea, 1987). In a forthcoming project she is going to study 'The Secondary School as a Social and Cultural System, 1850-1914'.

61. 1) As a result of the symposium at Kungälv in 1979: Hedda Gunneng and Birgit Strand, eds., *Kvinnans ekonomiska ställning under Nordisk medeltid* [The Economic Position of Women during the Nordic Middle Ages] (Sweden: Kompendiet, Lindome, 1981); 2) From a symposium in Iceland in 1981: Silja Adalsteinsdottrir and Helgi Thorlakson (eds.), *Förändringar i kvinnots villkor under medeltiden* [Changes in Women's Conditions during the Middle Ages] (Rejkavik: Sagnfra Distofnun haskola Islands, 1983); 3) From a symposium at Gotland: Hedda Gunneng, Beata Losman, Bodel Moller Knudsen, and Helle Reinholdt (eds.), *Kvinnors Rosengård. Medeltidskvinnors liv och hälsa, lust och barnafödande* [The Women's Rose Garden: The Life and Health, Lust and Childbearing of Women of the Middle Ages] (Visby, 1987). See also, Birgit Sawyer, 'Kvinnor och män i Gesta Danorum [Women and Men in Gesta Danorum]', diss., History, University of Gothenburg, 1980, and by the same historian, 'Inheritance and Property Relationships in Medieval Scandinavia ca 1000-1350', research project; Ruth Rajamaa, 'Education and Training in the Convent at Vadstena 1384-1524', Ph.D. thesis in progress, Pedagogy, University of Stockholm. See also, *Kvinnovetenskaplig Tidskrift*, 2 (1986), special issue on 'Perceptions of Women in the Middle Ages'. Although not in this category, I still want to mention the dissertation (Department of Theology, Uppsala University) by Lilian Portefaix, *Sisters Rejoice: Pauls Letter to the Phillipians and Luke: Acts as Received by First-Century Phillipian Women* (written and published in English) (Stockholm, 1988).

62. See also the articles by Kekke Stadin, 'The Forgotten Labour Force: Townswomen in Production During the Seventeenth and Eighteenth Centuries', in *Historisk Tidskrift*, 3 (1980); 'Women's Taxes', in *Manliga strukturer och kvinnliga strategier. En bok till Gunhild Kyle* (Goteborg: Historiska Institutionen, 1987).

63. One paper has already been written on this subject, in the Department of the History of Ideas, University of Gothenburg.

64. *Historisk Tidskrift*, 3 (1980) and 1 (1987).

65. There does exist some kind of 'automatic' integration and that is the policy of research projects in Sweden, for instance those on the rise of the industrial working classes (Stockholm), on social movements (Uppsala), and on old age (Lund) to which topics concerning 'women' are often added.

15

Women's History Behind the Dykes: Reflections on the Situation in the Netherlands

Francisca de Haan

Dutch women's history: the 'infrastructure'

In the Netherlands questions about the history of women and about the male-dominated traditional version of history were first raised by students around 1974. In the fifteen years since then, women's history has developed a strong 'infrastructure'. This infrastructure and its history are described in the first part of the article. Debates and developments in Dutch women's history in the 1980s will be described in the second part.

Between 1974 and 1976 women's history groups were organised by students at the Universities of Amsterdam, Groningen, Nijmegen and Utrecht. The group at the University of Amsterdam took the initiative for a national meeting, to co-ordinate existing groups and to start new ones. At this national meeting, on 13 March 1976, the *LOV* (Landelijk Overleg Vrouwengeschiedenis), a national association of feminist historians, was born. Its membership then consisted entirely of students. Every three months one of the associated women's history groups organised a national meeting, where both the results of research and organisational questions were discussed. In this form the *LOV* functioned until 1988. By then it had become impossible for the associated groups to organise these meetings. The *LOV* was changed into a regular association with individual members and an active 'board'.[1]

From the very beginning local groups and the national organisation, *LOV*, struggled to get teachers and researchers in women's history appointed at the universities. Since 1979 women's historians have been appointed at all universities except Maastricht. However, most of these women work part time and in temporary assignments. There are still no chairs in women's history, which means that we lack the kind of

259

institutional base from which women's history could be further developed and consolidated. Though there sometimes seems to be an increased awareness of the meaning and importance of women's history on the part of traditional historians, the limits placed on women's history and women's historians at the universities outweigh 'recognition' in the form of lipservice.

An important date in the history of the *LOV* is 6 May 1978 when a very successful 'Women's History Day' was held in Utrecht. This was organised to give more publicity to women's history, and make connections with the women's movement outside the universities.[2] As a result of this day a collection of articles was published, aimed at non-academic readers and called: *Een Tipje van de Sluier* [Lifting the Veil]. It sold out immediately and was reprinted twice.[3] Trying to make the results of women's history accessible to a wider audience has been an important aspect of the work of Dutch women's historians ever since. The book *Een Tipje van de Sluier* was turned into a series.[4] And a number of exhibitions on women's history were organised, like 'Alsof je een emmer leeg gooit' [on the daily life of women in the Netherlands in the twentieth-century], 'Kaatje, ben je boven?' [on the life and work of domestic servants], 'Van onze oud-tantes. . .' [on the life and work of five Dutch female novelists and historians], 'Een half miljoen boerinnen in de klas. Landbouwhuishoudonderwijs vanaf 1909' [about women in the countryside and education for girls as future farmers' wives] and 'Zij telt voor twee' [or: 'She counts for two', about various kinds of women's work in the province of Brabant]. Those exhibitions were visited by thousands of people. More than other branches of the historical discipline in the Netherlands, women's history has succeeded in crossing the boundaries of the universities and reaching a wider audience.[5]

Besides the *LOV-Vrouwengeschiedeniskrant* [*LOV*-Women's History Paper] for communication within the organisation and the series *Een Tipje van de Sluier* for a wider audience, there was a need for a more academic periodical. This was realized in the form of the *Jaarboek voor Vrouwengeschiedenis* [Women's History Yearbook], which appeared for the first time in 1980.[6] It was and still is the only periodical in the Netherlands entirely devoted to women's history[7] and as such the ten years of its existence have been very significant. In November 1989 the tenth *Jaarboek voor Vrouwengeschiedenis* appeared: since 1980 more than 80 articles have been published in the journal. Six issues of the *Jaarboek* were devoted each to a special theme: 'Women in the History of Christianity' (1983), 'The First Feminist Wave' (1985), 'Women in the Dutch Colonies' (1986), 'Women's Lives 1500-1850' (1987),[8] 'Learned Women' (1988) and 'The Mystery of Women's History' (1989). If I were to try to characterise the *Jaarboek voor Vrouwengeschiedenis*, I would say that it has always aimed at being an 'academic' and 'professional' journal.[9] It is often called 'solid', and does not offer too many surprises, attempts at theory or 'avant-garde' articles, though there are exceptions to this rule.[10] Through translation and publication in the *Jaarboek*, a number of path-breaking articles on women's history, which originally appeared in American or English women's studies journals, have been made accessible to Dutch students and other practitioners of women's history.[11]

In 1980 the organisational structure of Dutch women's history was strengthened by the establishment of the Kontaktadres *LOV* or *KLOV* [the contact address for women's history]: it was in fact a little office, where someone was available once a week to answer questions about women's history. Beginning in 1983 the Dutch government subsidised the *KLOV* by paying a woman to do this work, but, unfortunately, government funding ended in January 1989. This is particularly sad since women's history will be a compulsory subject in the final examinations in history at all Dutch high schools in 1990 and 1991 – an extremely important result of the work that has been done in the field of women's history. Students will be examined on the history of women in the Netherlands and the United States in the period between first and second wave feminism, 1929-1969.[12]

This short survey of the infrastructure of Dutch women's history would not be complete without mentioning some of the libraries and archives. The first and oldest is the Internationaal Informatiecentrum en Archief voor de Vrouwenbeweging [International Information Centre and Archives for the Women's Movement], *IIAV*, originally founded in 1935 as *IAV*, Intenationaal Archief voor de Vrouwenbeweging [International Archives for the Women's Movement].[13] The initiative for the *IAV* was taken in the 1930s by three well-known feminists, Johanna Naber,[14] Rosa Manus and Willemijn Posthumus-van der Goot. The purpose of the *IAV* was to collect and save all material relating to the women's movement, in the broadest sense of the word. This material was to provide the foundation for historical studies on women and the women's movement. In 1985 the *IIAV* celebrated its 50th anniversary with a programme that commemorated these original intentions.[15] The collection of archives at the *IIAV* is rapidly expanding. In 1989 there were some 200 metres (600 feet) of archives.

In 1982 Maaike Meijer published an article in the journal *Lover*, about the Lesbian Herstory Archives in New York.[16] Very soon the idea of starting a lesbian archives in the Netherlands as well was picked up. A group of women who called themselves *LOLA* [Landelijk Overleg Lesbische Archieven] carried out this plan and decided for several reasons to establish more than one lesbian archive. In 1989 there were lesbian archives in Amsterdam, Nijmegen and Leeuwarden.[17]

Flamboyant is a centre for black/immigrant women (in Dutch: zwarte/migranten vrouwen) in Amsterdam. It began in 1985 and its goal is to support the emancipation of black/immigrant women in the Netherlands. One of its activities is the building up of a library to provide documentation about black women. In the last two years three bibliographies about black women have been published, which contain a wealth of information. So far little historical material has been gathered, mainly due to lack of time and money.[18] In view of all these activities in the field of women's history, it could certainly be argued that women's history in the Netherlands has a relatively strong foundation or what I have called 'infrastructure'.[19] Maria Grever reaches the same conclusion in her historiographical essay on Dutch women's history.[20] However, it should not be forgotten that this strength is a result mainly of the – largely unpaid – efforts of many devoted women. 'Official' recognition in the form, for instance, of academic appointments and funding is scarce. Women's history, though on the one hand a prospering field, on the other hand still has a marginal position within the Dutch academic world and its policies.[21]

Debates and developments in Dutch women's history

In 1985 Ine Megens published *Zicht op een vrouwelijk verleden* [View on a Female Past], the first of several historiographical essays on Dutch women's history in the seventies and eighties.[22] Megens described, in chronological order, the most important approaches, themes and subjects, and I will very briefly summarise them here. In the seventies, marxism, social history and socialist-feminism were the most important influences on women's history. Women's paid and unpaid work, industrialisation, the development of the nuclear family, the marxist-feminist debate on reproduction and the history of socialist or socialist-feminist women were the topics that dominated this period. Gradually, marxist analysis proved to be inadequate and new questions arose. How could forms of repression other than the economic be explained and what could be known about other forms of women's resistance, besides the organised and public? The influence of radical feminism grew, as seen for instance in the attention by Dutch scholars to Adrienne Rich's essay on 'Compulsory hetero-sexuality'.[23] Ideology, motherhood, prostitution, different approaches to sexuality, religion and constructions of femininity came to the centre of attention. In these years a debate began that was inspired by questions about 'a female world' and women-identified concepts. Ine Megens summarised the different positions in this debate as 'Herstory' or 'the rewriting of history'.[24]

I shall continue the story where she left it in March 1985 and rename the discussion 'integration or autonomy'. Secondly, I would like to describe the debate about 'differences', which can be seen as a key word in describing recent developments in Dutch women's history. The analysis of these discussions, and the underlying differences of opinion about feminism, history, politics and feminist history, is of great importance to the development of women's history.[25]

Integration or autonomy

The debate about 'integration or autonomy' in women's history began in 1980 when the first *Jaarboek voor Vrouwengeschiedenis* [Women's History Yearbook] was published. From the start the *Jaarboek* was not just the main women's history publication in the Netherlands, but also the most academic. If traditional historians were interested in women's history at all, it was likely that they would turn to the *Jaarboek*. What was said about women's history by the editors? In the introduction to the first number they wrote:

> We doubt whether women's history should be seen as a separate new specialism; we tend to see it as only a form of criticism of the existing historical science or a manoeuvre to catch up. From this point of view we are in favour of integrating women's history into the academy and remain on our guard against being ghettoized.[26]

Though at first sight this seemed to be a clear definition of women's history and the way it should develop, there were some ambiguities as well. The editors did not explain how they envisioned this integration, whether it was primarily conceptual, institutional or both.[27] They added that differences of opinion existed within their group as well. The *Jaarboek voor Vrouwengeschiedenis* itself was (and is) an autonomous women's history publication and as such it embodied a contradiction in the integrationist point of view.

In the next three *Jaarboeken* (1981-1983) there was room for more than one vision of women's history. An example of this is the publication in the second volume (1981) of translations of both Natalie Zemon Davis' article on women's history in Europe, in which she advocated the use of 'sex' as a historical category and the study of both men and women, *and* of Carroll Smith-Rosenberg's article about 'the female world of love and ritual', devoted to a nineteenth-century women's world and the meaning of women's relationships.[28]

In 1982-3 *Lover* published a series of articles about the writing of lesbian history, raising such questions as: is it possible and desirable to develop this sort of history? What concepts should be used and what source-material is available? In this series the historian Mineke Bosch published a mainly historiographical article, which was an inspired attempt to build a bridge between women's and lesbian history by proposing an alternative way of looking at women, their relationships, the meaning of 'lesbian', and at resistance and the women's movement.[29] Bosch recorded the discussions in American women's history on the reinterpretation of Mary Beard's ideas, and especially of Beard's idea that women should not be seen just as passive victims, but as active historical agents as well, who had in many different ways reacted to their oppression. She pointed to the resemblances or the parallels between this way of looking at women and the concepts of 'the outsiders' (Virginia Woolf), a 'lesbian continuum' (Adrienne Rich) and that of 'women's culture' as it had been developed in the work of women like Carroll Smith-Rosenberg, Gerda Lerner, Nancy Cott, Mary Ryan and Estelle Freedman, and discussed in the debate published by *Feminist Studies* in 1980.[30] Furthermore, Bosch wrote that it is no longer a question of whether certain relationships between women *were* lesbian, but that we could call them that, or not. We could choose to do so, or not, as part of our attempt to build a new symbolic universe. The choice of concepts was thus, in her words, 'a political act'.[31] To understand her ideas, it is important to see that Bosch argued from a non-essentialist epistemological point of view, seeing the historian as actively making sense of an otherwise chaotic past.[32]

Both on the side of 'lesbian history' and of women's history this particular article provoked an enormous response, probably because Bosch's nominalism was either rejected or not understood. As Ine Megens pointed out, within 'lesbian history' a debate developed between a 'romantic' and a 'sexual' school,[33] while in women's history a fierce reaction came from the side of the editors of the *Jaarboek voor Vrouwengeschiedenis*.[34]

In *Jaarboek* 5 (1984) the editors repeated and reinforced their adherence to the integrationist point of view and added that the 'rewriting of history' was their goal, and not the development of a new specialism. The phrase the 'rewriting of history' was of course borrowed from Joan Wallach Scott, whose article in *Past and Present* (1983) was translated and published in this same issue.[35] Joan Wallach Scott was very welcome as one who argued the case against 'herstory' and for integration, and who furthermore elaborated theoretically how 'integration' was supposed to happen, by introducing 'gender' as the concept or the tool that would make the 'rewriting of history' possible. The editors proclaimed themselves in favour of her 'programme' and even argued that this was what the

Jaarboek had always aimed at.[36] There were other ways in which they showed their enthusiasm. The original English title of Joan Scott's article: 'Women in History. II. The Modern Period', was changed in the Dutch translation, without any explanation, into: 'Women's History: the Rewriting of History. The "Debate" of the Last Ten Years'. In other words: women's history was equated here with 'the rewriting of history'. This was not what Joan Wallach Scott meant: she was *not* including all sorts of women's history in the 'rewriting of history' concept or project. The term 'rewriting of history' had a very specific meaning in her text, which she did not elaborate on, but presented as self-evident.[37] Scott distinguished three sorts of women's history, called 'herstory', women's history as social history and gender history. This allowed her to introduce a hierarchy within women's history, a hierarchy which placed 'gender' history at the top and women's history that was 'only' about women, at the bottom. Although Scott *introduced* the various kinds of women's history as being equally included in the 'rewriting of history' project, in her final argument this was no longer the case: only gender history turned out to be a real contribution to the 'rewriting of history', and other kinds of women's history were perceived as of a lower order.[38]

What did all of this mean to the debate on 'integration or autonomy' in women's history?[39] By publishing Scott's article, by changing its title, and by doing this without any critical note, the editors of the *Jaarboek* took over her hierarchy and introduced it into Dutch women's history.[40] Besides, they used Scott's denunciation of 'herstory' in the next *Jaarboek voor Vrouwengeschiedenis* 6 (1985), which was a special issue about the so-called *First Feminist Wave*. The hostility here was partly concealed. In a historiographical article by two of the editors, Ulla Jansz and Tineke van Loosbroek, such words as 'demagoguery', 'circular reasoning' and 'reactionary' were used to describe the arguments of Gerda Lerner and Carroll Smith-Rosenberg in their contribution to the debate on 'Politics and Culture' in *Feminist Studies*.[41] The Dutch historian Mineke Bosch was accused among other things of 'moralism', without her name being mentioned and without any discussion of the ideas that she proposed in the *Lover* article, even though these were of direct relevance to the topic in question: the history of the women's movement. Her name and article only appeared in a footnote.[42]

In a number of book reviews the *Jaarboek* was severely criticised.[43] Both Mineke Bosch and Maria Grever reacted to the articles by Scott in *Jaarboek* 5 and by Jansz and van Loosbroek in *Jaarboek* 6. In her contribution to the International Conference on Women's History (ICWH) in 1986, Mineke Bosch formulated her objections to the Jansz and van Loosbroek article and the *Jaarboek*'s embrace of Joan Scott.[44] In 1987 she published a fine article, called 'Women's Culture in Women's

266 Francisca de Haan

History: Historical Notion or Feminist Vision?'. As the title indicated,
Bosch made a distinction between women's culture as a perspective for
looking at history, as a feminist vision, and women's culture as a specific
historical concept. In the debate in *Feminist Studies* that distinction had
been blurred. The meaning of the concept had been restricted to a 'specific
phenomenon in 19th-century America' and associated with women's
friendships, women's networks, women's sphere and with women as
'better', higher moral human beings. In this one-dimensional
interpretation, according to Bosch, the concept of 'women's culture'
'greatly lost in expressiveness compared to the visionary quality it had in
the thought of Mary Beard'.[45] Meanwhile Maria Grever published a
historiographical article on women's history in the Dutch *Tijdschrift voor
Sociale Geschiedenis* [Journal of Social History] in which she criticised
Scott's thesis that 'herstory' was not a form of the 'rewriting of history'
and pleaded for an appreciation of different kinds of women's history, to
be given equal merit instead of being ranked in hierarchical order.
According to her it was necessary for women's history to remain institutionalised as a separate specialism. Women's history should only strive
for integration from a strong position. She also pleaded for an ongoing
reflection on and debate about underlying ideas, questions and methods in
women's history, all of which I heartily agree with.[46]

I have elaborated upon this discussion for two reasons. First, I
think that it shows how, partly without acknowledging it (and perhaps
without intending it), one kind of women's history was legitimised in the
Jaarboek voor Vrouwengeschiedenis and another kind was denounced and
excluded. The women's history that was favoured argued for 'integration'.
The women's history that was denounced did not take traditional history
as its norm and tried to create an 'autonomous' feminist tradition.

Secondly, the debate has a follow-up in and is the background to
what is happening at the moment: every self-respecting academic women's
historian has to employ the concept of gender and to refer to the work of
Joan Wallach Scott.[47]

Differences

In 1979 the women's history group at the University of Amsterdam
published a brochure simply called *Vrouwengeschiedenis* [Women's
History]. In this brochure it was argued that:

> Women should not be considered as a homogeneous
> group, since class differences, and differences in social
> roles, should be taken into account. It is also important to

note that the class position of women is not derived from
their own status, but from that of their husbands.[48]

When read in 1989/90, this statement clearly sounds like a pronouncement
from the seventies. As a consequence of the socialist-feminist background
of many women's historians at that time, class differences between women
were seen as *the* issue. Only the women with the most difficult lives
seemed to deserve attention, and studies about women in the middle and
higher classes were 'not done'.[49]

Ten years later we are more accustomed to read and write about
differences between women, not only in respect to class (as in the above
quotation), but also in respect to ethnicity, colour, sexual preference,
marital status, age and religion. In other words, differences between
women have become a major issue. It is no longer self-evident to whom
we are referring in the terms 'women' or 'women's history'. What
happened in the Netherlands in this respect?

In the 1980s three incentives seem to have led to this growing
recognition of differences between women. First, the norm of heterosexuality was revealed and discussed, both at women's studies conferences
and in articles.

Secondly, the fact that it is of crucial importance for feminism and
for feminist history to recognize differences between women, has been put
forward very strongly by black women. At the International Conference
on Women's History in March 1986 in Amsterdam, black and white
women protested strongly against the white and ethnocentric character of
this gathering. The criticism was not just aimed at the programme of the
conference, but at the way in which women's history was practised, the
conference being a reflection of this.[50] While in other parts of Dutch
women's studies attention had been paid to 'the colour of women's studies'
– even though this had an incidental character – this had not happened in
women's history. To give one example: Philomena Essed, a Dutch
anthropologist, had in 1982 published an article called 'Racism and
Feminism' in a well-known feminist series, the *Socialisties-Feministiese
Teksten* [Socialist-Feminist Texts]. In this illuminating article she describes
racism and ethnocentrism, in both everyday life and the women's
movement, and she illustrates these with a number of examples that one
can recognise from one's own experience. She also describes how the
women's movement in the United States, in both the nineteenth and the
twentieth centuries, had roots in the movement for racial equality, a
historical background that has seldom been recognised by white Dutch
women's historians, as Essed points out. The dominant image of the
women's movement is one of a movement carried by white women (with
pioneers like Betty Friedan).[51]

At the conference in 1986 the debate about the colour of women's history was a passionate one, raising fundamental issues. In order to follow this up, a number of women organised a *LOV* day about 'Racism and Women's History' in November 1987. In an introduction to the collection of papers the organisers wrote:

> Suffragettes, women workers, housewives, mothers, witches, prostitutes, teachers, lesbian women, farming women, female historians: they have all been put in the centre of attention by historians. However, they often turn out to be all white and the questions asked come from a white perspective.[52]

As the organisers remarked, in view of the work of Gerda Lerner, well-known in Dutch women's history circles, and that of Philomena Essed, which had been available for years, it was all the more remarkable that this white bias had never been noticed.[53]

The programme of the day on Racism & Women's History consisted among other things of a number of workshops. One of these workshops was on 'The seventh *Jaarboek voor Vrouwengeschiedenis* (1986) "Women in the Dutch Colonies" and anti-racist women's history'. Very regrettably, the issue of racism was not addressed in that *Jaarboek*. The fact that it was largely conceptualized and written before the outburst over racism at the International Conference on Women's History cannot be an excuse – the work of Lerner and Essed (and many others, of course) had offered possible starting-points. Though the discussion in the workshop about the *Jaarboek* and anti-racist women's history could only be seen as a first attempt, in my view it was useful because it demonstrated a willingness at least to address the issue.

Unfortunately, one does not always see the impact of these developments in women's history publications. As I mentioned before, in 1989 two new issues have appeared in the series *Een Tipje van de Sluier*, a series that is published under the flag and responsibility of the *LOV*.[54] In both these last two *Tipjes* the women are white and heterosexual – without any discussion of this – as if no critique had ever arisen. Nevertheless, by 1990 it is no longer 'acceptable' to point only to class as a social category and to neglect other forms or elements of inequality and difference between women.

Other recent publications in the field of women's history show signs of yet another theoretical development: the debate on poststructuralism. While in the debates described so far differences between women (black and white women, heterosexual and lesbian women) were the issue, leaving 'women' as a category unchallenged, here the concept of 'women' itself is being questioned. What sort of unity is suggested or organised by means of this concept, that is to say, by means of language? If 'woman' and 'women' are historical constructs,[55] what does this mean for feminist theory and history? How does the concept of 'women' relate to 'real' historical women? And, what is the meaning of poststructuralism for the debate on the concept of gender?

As in the earlier debate on gender, the work of Joan Scott is again very influential.[56] The questions raised by poststructuralism do not only concern 'women', but are directed as well to history as a discipline. What is the meaning of narrativism – poststructuralist par excellence – for women's history? Is history a social science or a literary genre? Should we try to explain or to interpret? What is the meaning of style? How do different sorts of texts and of source-material relate to each other? Questions like these are being asked, for instance, in the tenth *Jaarboek voor Vrouwengeschiedenis* (1989) and in *Naar het leven. Feminisme & biografisch onderzoek*,[57] a collection of essays in which the authors have combined the results of their biographical research (and fascination with the subject) with questions on biography as a genre in feminist studies or history. In some cases the questions remain implicit, in other cases they are at the centre of attention, as in the article by Geertje Mak about the meaning of poststructuralist theory for 'women's' and 'lesbian' history.[58] One should not conclude from this survey that all Dutch historians of women are equally interested in theoretical matters. Some do not see the relevance of feminist theory for women's history, others wonder, for instance, whether poststructuralism is not deconstructing the women's history 'building', which we have only just begun to create. However, a growing interest in questions concerning feminist theory and the nature of history is visible, and forms part of the prospering field of Dutch women's history.

NOTES

For their critical remarks and support I would like to thank: Mirjam de Baar, Mineke Bosch, Maria Grever, Jacqueline de Haan, Ulla Jansz, Annette Mevis, Marjan Schwegman, Barbara Smeets, Dineke Stam and Jane Rendall.

1. These university-based women's history groups still exist. Some of them are more autonomous than in the past, and they are still very active. For instance, in the last couple of years, courses of lectures on women's history have been organised in Amsterdam, Nijmegen, Utrecht and Rotterdam. In 1978 the first *LOV-Vrouwengeschiedeniskrant* [Women's History Paper] appeared. It was meant primarily for communication between members of the *LOV*, and has been

supplemented, since 1988, by a newsletter. At a meeting in March 1990 it was decided to change the name of the organisation to Vereniging voor Vrouwengeschiedenis [Women's History Association].

2. Wietske van Agtmaal et al. (eds.), *Een Tipje van de Sluier. Vrouwengeschiedenis in Nederland* [Lifting the Veil: Women's History in the Netherlands] (Amsterdam: *LOV*, 1978), p. 7.

3. These are sold out as well, so that 5000 copies in all have been sold, proportionately an enormous figure.

4. Numbers 5 and 6 in the series have just appeared: Carla Wijers et al. (eds.), *Tussen aanpassing en verzet. Vrouwen voor het voetlicht 1929-1969* [Between Adjustment and Resistance: Women in the Footlights 1929-1969] (Culemborg: Lemma, 1989); Fransje Backerra et al. (eds.), *Vrouwen van het land. Anderhalve eeuw plattelandsvrouwen in Nederland* [A History of Rural Women since 1830] (Zutphen: De Walburg Pers, 1989).

5. Since 1978 women's history days have been organized by the *LOV* about witches, sexuality, women's history and racism, and girls' education. Two recent books on women's history that were aimed at a wider reading public and sold very well are: Maria Grever and Annemiek van der Veen (eds.), *Bij ons moeder en ons Jet. Brabantse vrouwen in de 19de en 20ste eeuw* [At Home with Our Mother and Our Jet: Women in the Province of Brabant in the 19th and 20th Centuries] (Zutphen/s'Hertogenbosch: St.Brabantse Regionale Geschiedbeoefening/De Walburg Pers, 1989); Marieke Hilhorst, *Bij de zusters op kostschool. Geschiedenis van het dagelijks leven van meisjes op Rooms-Katholieke pensionaten in Nederland en Vlaanderen* [At School with the Nuns: A History of the Daily Life of Girls at Roman-Catholic Convent Schools in the Netherlands and Flanders] (Utrecht: Bruna, 1989).

Yet another way in which women's history was made visible and accessible has been the composition and publication of women's history walks, for instance, Leontine Bijleveld and Dineke Stam, *Sporen van vrouwen. Zes historische wandelingen door Amsterdam* [Traces of Women: Six Historical Walks through Amsterdam] ('s-Gravenhage: Bzztoh, 1987).

6. For a critical discussion of both the series *Een Tipje van de Sluier* and the *Jaarboek voor Vrouwengeschiedenis* until 1985, see Leontine Bijleveld, 'Het Groot Boek der Geschiedenis. Het Tipje van de Sluier en het Jaarboek voor Vrouwengeschiedenis' [The Encyclopedia of History: The series Lifting the Veil and the Women's History Yearbook], *Lover*, 12, no. 3 (1985), pp. 211-17.

7. Dutch journals like the *Tijdschrift voor Vrouwenstudies* [Journal of Women's Studies], *Lover* [the name Lover is an abbreviation of Literatuuroverzicht voor de Vrouwenbeweging or: Survey of Literature for the Women's Movement] and *Lust & Gratie* [a lesbian cultural journal] publish articles on women's history as well – and very exciting ones too – but it is not their main subject.

8. It is important to note that there are Dutch women's historians working in the field of ancient, medieval and early modern history. In 1988 a Studiegroep Vrouwengeschiedenis van de Vroegmoderne Tijd [a study group on early modern women's history] was established by Els Kloek and Mirjam de Baar. See also note 22.

9. Josine Blok et al. (eds.), *Jaarboek voor Vrouwengeschiedenis* 1 (Nijmegen: SUN, 1980), editorial introduction; Selma Leydesdorff, 'Wij en de geschiedenis' [We and History], *Te Elfder Ure 39. Dilemma's van het Feminisme*, 29, no. 1 (1986), pp. 135-49, especially pp. 135-7.

10. The articles by Aerts and Schwegman in the second *Jaarboek voor Vrouwengeschiedenis* are certainly among these exceptions. Both questioned accepted views and introduced new concepts, namely 'constructions of femininity' and 'layers of reality' ('constructies van vrouwelijkheid' and 'lagen der werkelijkheid'). Mieke Aerts, not a historian herself, was a pioneer in Dutch women's history with respect to the rejection of 'historical realism' and the introduction of 'constructions of femininity'. Mieke Aerts, 'Op zoek naar konstrukties van vrouwelijkheid. Naar aanleiding van drie katholieke vrouwenorganisaties in het interbellum' [Looking for Constructions of Femininity: Research into Three Roman Catholic Women's Organisations in the Interwar Years], in Josine Blok et al. (eds.), *Jaarboek voor Vrouwengeschiedenis* 2 (Nijmegen: SUN, 1981), pp. 132-45; Marjan Schwegman, 'Lagen der werkelijkheid. Italiaanse en Nederlandse vrouwen tijdens het interbellum' [Layers of Reality: Italian and Dutch Women in the Interwar Years], in *ibid.*, pp. 110-31.

11. Els Kloek, 'Vrouwengeschiedenis en het vaktijdschrift: een inventarisatie. Bijlage: Overzicht 10 Jaarboeken voor Vrouwengeschiedenis [Women's History and the Historical Journal: An Overview. Appendix: Table of Contents of 10 Women's History Yearbooks]', in Francisca de Haan et al. (eds.), *Het raadsel vrouwengeschiedenis. Tiende Jaarboek voor Vrouwengeschiedenis* (Nijmegen: SUN, 1989). On the occasion of the tenth anniversary of the *Jaarboek voor Vrouwengeschiedenis*, a symposium was held on 17 March 1990 called 'The Future of Women's History'. At this symposium Natalie Zemon Davis and Gisela Bock spoke on women's history and gender history, with Mineke Bosch and Marjan Schwegman acting as commentators. The papers from this meeting will be published in the Fall 1990 issue of *Jaarboek voor Vrouwengeschiedenis*. As well, the 'Johanna W. A. Naber' prize was installed (see note 14).

12. The examinations are based on a book published by the VGN, the Association of History Teachers: Maria Grever and Carla Wijers (eds.), *Vrouwen in de twintigste eeuw. De positie van de vrouw in Nederland en de Verenigde Staten van Amerika 1929-1969* [Women in the 20th Century. The Position of Women in the Netherlands and the United States 1929-1969] (IJsselstein: VGN, 1988). 22 May 1990 was the historic day when the exams took place for the first time. A great deal of public interest and publicity surrounded this event. Several newspapers wrote about it in advance and mostly favourably, as for example, *NRC-Handelsblad*, 21 November 1989; *De Volkskrant*, 18 April 1990; and *Trouw*, 9 May 1990. Jan Bank, professor of Dutch history at the University of Leiden, commented afterwards in the *NRC-Handelsblad* on the questions which had been posed in the exam. Last but not least, Joan Scott's response to the questions was published in *De Volkskrant* of 23 May.

13. For a description of the IIAV, see: Ineke Jungschleger, *De vergeelde blauwkous. Vijftig jaar Internationaal Archief voor de Vrouwenbeweging* (Amsterdam: IAV, 1985). Also published as: *Bluestockings in Mothballs: 50 Years International Archives for the Women's Movement* (Amsterdam: IAV, 1987). In 1987 the IAV, *Lover* and the IDC became one organization, the IIAV: *International*

Information Centre and Archives for the Women's Movement. This means that the IIAV consists of a library and an archives sector, a sector for information and documentation and the journal *Lover*. The address is: Keizersgracht 10, 1015 CN Amsterdam.

14. Johanna W. A. Naber was the most important historian of the Dutch women's movement at the end of the nineteenth and the beginning of the twentieth century. On the occasion of its tenth anniversary in 1989, the *Jaarboek voor Vrouwengeschiedenis* instituted a biennial 'Johanna W. A. Naber' prize (or award) for the best thesis in women's history, thus making a connection between the historical work of women in several periods. The first 'Johanna W.A. Naber award' was won by Monique Stavenuiter and Jeanette Dorsman, who together wrote a thesis on single women in Amsterdam in the second half of the nineteenth century.

15. At the celebration of the 50th anniversary of the IAV, two books appeared based on the archival collections. Annette Mevis (ed.), *In verloren minuten. Dagboeken en herinneringen van vrouwen 1896-1979* (Weesp: Fibula-van Dishoeck, 1985) is a selection from the 'ego-documents' or personal documents of women that had been actively collected at the IIAV since 1983. The same collection of 'ego-documents' has recently been used by a theatre-group, Lopend Vuur, as the basis of a performance called 'Strikt persoonlijk' or: 'Strictly personal'. See also Mineke Bosch, 'A Woman's Life in a Soap-Box: The Collection of Personal Documents of Women in the Internationaal Archief voor de Vrouwenbeweging in Amsterdam', *History Workshop Journal*, 24 (1987), pp. 167-70. The second publication, Mineke Bosch and Annemarie Kloosterman, *Lieve Dr. Jacobs. Brieven uit de Wereldbond voor Vrouwenkiesrecht 1902-1942* (Amsterdam: Sara, 1985), is forthcoming as Mineke Bosch, with Annemarie Kloosterman (eds.), *Politics and Friendship: Letters from the International Woman Suffrage Alliance, 1902-1942* (Columbus: Ohio State University Press, 1990).

16. Maaike Meijer, 'De roddel van de een is de geschiedenis van de ander [What's Gossip to One is History to Another]: The Lesbian Herstory Archives in New York', *Lover*, 8, no. 4 (1982), pp. 172-6.

17. There was a lesbian archive in Utrecht as well, but it has been closed down. The Lesbian Archives in Leeuwarden started on 17 April 1982. The archivists there are very active, not just in collecting material but also in initiating research.

18. *Flamboyant Newsletter*, undated, p. 17. In June 1989 the Netwerk-ZMV or 'Zwarte/Migranten Vrouwen met hogere opleiding [Network of Black/Immigrant Women with a higher education]' was officially established. The goals of this network are to influence government's decisions on black/immigrant women, to stimulate academic research for, by and with black/immigrant women and to have contacts with similar organisations in other countries.

19. One could point to the women's bookstores as part of this infrastructure too: Xantippe and Lorelei (antiquarian) in Amsterdam, De Feeks in Nijmegen, Savannah Bay in Utrecht, Trix in Den Haag, Dikke Trui in Groningen, Boeken Nel in Eindhoven, Helleveeg in Arnhem and Shikasta in Wageningen. Some of these have a very good collection of women's history books.

20. Maria Grever, 'Het verborgen continent. Een historiografische verkenning van vrouwengeschiedenis in Nederland [The Hidden Continent: A Historiographical Search into Dutch Women's History]', *Tijdschrift voor Sociale Geschiedenis*, 12, no. 3 (1986), pp. 221-68, especially p. 227.

21. Very cautiously, one might say that in the first half of 1990 there seems to have been a growing recognition of the sophisticated importance of women's history and of the stage of development of the field. This change (if one may call it that) has been brought about by the publicity about the March 1990 symposium, 'The Future of Women's History', and especially by the publicity about the final examinations in women's history in May 1990 (see note 12). The fact that a number of Ph.D. theses have recently been completed may have played a part as well. In Fall 1991 papers on women's history will be given at the yearly meeting of the Dutch Historical Association [Nederlands Historisch Genootschap].

22. Ine Megens, 'Zicht op een vrouwelijk verleden. Ontwikkelingen binnen vrouwengeschiedenis in Nederland [View on a Female Past. Developments within Women's History in the Netherlands]', in Ine Megens et al. (eds.), *Met andere ogen. Vrouwengeschiedenis in Nederland 1975-1985* [From another Point of View. Women's History in the Netherlands 1975-1985] (Groningen: Werkgroep Universitaire Publicaties, 1985). The others were: Maria Grever, 'Het verborgen continent [The Hidden Continent]', see note 20. In revised form it appeared as: 'Het vrouwelijk oculair. Een historische beschouwing van vrouwengeschiedenis in de VS en West-Europa vanaf circa 1970 [The Female Point of View: A Historical Reflection on Women's History in the United States and Western Europe since 1970]', in *DIGO*, Didactiek in het geschiedenisonderwijs, 10, no. 4 (1987) and, updated again, in the book which Maria Grever edited with Carla Wijers, *Vrouwen in de twintigste eeuw* [Women in the 20th-Century], see note 12.

Margo Brouns, 'Geschiedwetenschappen [The historical sciences]', in *Veertien jaar vrouwenstudies in Nederland: een overzicht* [Fourteen Years of Women's Studies in the Netherlands: An Overview] ('s-Gravenhage: Ministerie van Onderwijs en Wetenschappen, 1988), pp. 98-113. Brouns intends to give a complete overview, but she hardly pays attention to research on women in antiquity, for instance, the work by Josine Blok and Emilie Hemelrijk, or on women in the early modern period.

23. Adrienne Rich, 'Compulsory heterosexuality and lesbian existence', *Signs: Journal of Women in Culture and Society*, 5, no. 4 (1980), pp. 631-60, translated into Dutch as 'Gedwongen heteroseksualiteit en lesbisch bestaan', in Selma Sevenhuijsen et al. (eds.), *Feministies-Socialistiese Teksten* [Socialist-Feminist Texts] 6, (Amsterdam: Sara, 1981), pp. 44-80. Also published as a brochure by the Stichting Lust & Gratie (Nijmegen, 1981).

24. Ine Megens, 'Zicht op een vrouwelijk verleden [View on a Female Past]', pp. 28-30.

25. I think I should add here that I have been co-editor of the *Jaarboek voor Vrouwengeschiedenis* from 1986 to 1989. The *Jaarboek* plays a dominant role in my story.

26. *Jaarboek voor Vrouwengeschiedenis*, 1 (1980), p. 8.

27. Leontine Bijleveld pointed to a number of contradictions and underlying notions about history in the editorial introductions to the *Jaarboeken*: for instance, the idea of history as a science which has the writing of the one and only Encyclopedia of History (in her words: 'het Groot Boek der Geschiedenis') as its task. Leontine Bijleveld, 'Het Groot Boek der Geschiedenis', *Lover*, 12, no. 3 (1985), pp. 211-17.

28. Natalie Zemon Davis, '"Women's History" in Transition: the European Case', *Feminist Studies*, 3, no. 3/4, (1976), pp. 83-103, translated as 'Vrouwengeschiedenis in verandering. Het Europese voorbeeld'; Carroll Smith-Rosenberg, 'The Female World of Love and Ritual: Relations between Women in Nineteenth-Century America', *Signs: Journal of Women in Culture and Society*, 1, no. 1 (1975), pp. 1-29, translated as 'De vrouwenwereld van liefde en rituelen. Relaties tussen vrouwen in Amerika in de negentiende eeuw'. By mentioning these articles as two examples of different approaches, I do not mean to say that 'gender' and 'women's culture' are mutually exclusive, nor to suggest that 'women's culture' in Smith-Rosenberg's work tends to an essentialist meaning.

29. Mineke Bosch, 'De geschiedenis van een en ander. Naar een discussie tussen lesbische en vrouwengeschiedenis [The History of One and Another: Towards a Debate between Lesbian and Women's History]', in *Lover*, 10, no. 3 (1983), pp. 115-25. Bosch's title refers to the earlier articles in *Lover* by Maaike Meijer, Mieke Aerts and Saskia Grotenhuis on lesbian history.

30. Virginia Woolf, *Three Guineas* (London: Hogarth Press, 1938, and Harmondsworth: Penguin, 1977); Rich, 'Compulsory Heterosexuality and Lesbian Existence'; and 'Politics and Culture in Women's History: A Symposium', *Feminist Studies*, 6, no. 1 (1980), pp. 26-64.

31. Mineke Bosch, 'De geschiedenis van een en ander [The History of One and Another]', *Lover*, 10, no. 3 (1983), pp. 115-25, especially pp. 121 and 124. And, one might add, just as labelling women as 'lesbian' on the basis of any other definition – be it sexological, psychiatric, sexual or whatever – is a political act.

32. See also Mineke Bosch, 'Women's Culture in Women's History: Historical Notion or Feminist Vision?', in Maaike Meijer and Jette Schaap (eds.), *Historiography of Women's Cultural Traditions* (Dordrecht-Holland/ Providence-USA: Foris Publications, 1987), pp. 36-52.

33. On this debate see Myriam Everard, 'Verandering en verschil: Lesbische geschiedenis in Nederland [Change and Difference: Lesbian History in The Netherlands]', *Lover*, 10, no. 4 (1983), pp. 198-201 and 253-4; Paula Koelemij, 'Pendelen van sexus naar socia. Lesbiese geschiedenis of vrouwengeschiedenis? [Commuting between 'Sexus' and 'Socia': Lesbian or Women's History?]', *Tijdschrift voor Vrouwenstudies*, 19, 5, no. 3 (1984), pp. 290-307.

34. Ine Megens, 'Zicht op een vrouwelijk verleden [View on a Female Past]', pp. 27, 28-39.

35. Joan Scott in her turn borrowed 'to rewrite history' from Virginia Woolf, who originally used these words in *A Room of One's Own* (1929), but not in the Scottian sense. Woolf's picture was on the cover of *Jaarboek voor Vrouwengeschiedenis*, 5 (1984). Thus, Virginia Woolf, of 'the outsiders', was in a way appropriated by Joan Scott and the *Jaarboek* editors, champions of integration, for an altogether different women's history project. Joan Wallach Scott, 'Women in History. II. The Modern Period', *Past and Present*, 101 (1983), pp. 141-57, translated as 'Vrouwengeschiedenis: de geschiedenis herschrijven. De 'diskussie' van de afgelopen tien jaar' in Jeske Reys, et al. (eds.), *Jaarboek voor Vrouwengeschiedenis*, 5 (Nijmegen: SUN, 1984), pp. 131-52.

36. *Jaarboek voor Vrouwengeschiedenis*, 5 (1984) Editorial introduction, p. 8. They 'proved' this by mentioning some earlier published (translated) articles

which took this view of the 'rewriting of history', while leaving out others, such as Carroll Smith-Rosenberg's.

37. Maria Grever pointed to Scott's very specific interpretation of the term 'rewriting of history' in her article 'Het verborgen continent [The Hidden Continent]', *Tijdschrift voor Sociale Geschiedenis*, 12, no. 3 (1986), pp. 221-68.

38. Two quotations from Scott's article can make this clear: 'There are several positions in the debate, which is less a debate than *a different set of approaches to the "rewriting of history"*. Most scholars working in women's history assume that their work will transform history as it has been written and understood; they differ on the questions of how that will be accomplished....'

Later in the article she writes: 'In a sense, if "her-story" tends to too separatist a position, much of the social history of women has been too integrationist, subsuming women within received categories of analysis. Both approaches offer supplements to history, but they have not found a way to convince or demonstrate to other historians that it is essential to take their findings into account. *They have not, in other words, "rewritten history". That rewriting is the project of the third position in the "debate" I have constructed*, and it builds on, indeed is made possible by, the work of both "her-story" and the social history of women'. Joan Wallach Scott, 'Women in History. II. The Modern Period', *Past and Present*, 101 (1983), pp. 145 and 152.

39. Scott and others speak of 'separatism' (a recent example is Theresa McBride, 'Integration or Separation? Constructing the History of European Women', *Gender & History*, 1, no. 2 (1989), pp. 213-18). I would prefer to speak of 'autonomy'. Separatism seems to imply a 'reacting against', which is not what I wish to emphasize. Autonomy stresses the development of an independent feminist tradition.

40. In a series about history, the 4 July 1985 issue of *NRC-Handelsblad*, a highly respectable, liberal-academic Dutch newspaper, published an article on women's history, based on an interview by Tom van der Meer and Hubert Smeets with Els Kloek, co-founder and editor of the *Jaarboek voor Vrouwengeschiedenis*, and Fia Dieteren. The headline of the article was: 'Women's History is an outdated term [Vrouwengeschiedenis is een achterhaalde term]'. Women's history was thus publicly declared old-fashioned, not really necessary any more. A critical reaction to this interview by Helene Vossen and Carolien Salomon appeared in the *LOV-Vrouwengeschiedeniskrant*, 9, no. 1, z.j. (1986).

41. Ulla Jansz and Tineke van Loosbroek, 'Nieuwe literatuur over de eerste feministische golf: "herschrijven van de geschiedenis" [New Literature on the First Feminist Wave: "The Rewriting of History"]', in Jeske Reys et al. (eds.), *De Eerste Feministische Golf [The First Feminist Wave]. Jaarboek voor Vrouwenges-chiedenis* 6 (Nijmegen: SUN, 1985), pp. 10-29, especially pp. 20 and 27. In the 'Politics and Culture' debate, Lerner and Smith-Rosenberg argued with Mari Jo Buhle for the women's culture approach, while Ellen DuBois was on the 'politics' side.

42. Jansz and Van Loosbroek spoke in their article of 'a number of recent Dutch publications' (p. 28). In a note they referred to Mineke Bosch and to Ine Megens (who had 'done' nothing but describe and thus interpret the positions in the debate until March 1985, as I mentioned earlier).

276 *Francisca de Haan*

43. In a review of this *Jaarboek voor Vrouwengeschiedenis*, 6 (1985), Marjan Schwegman criticised Jansz and Van Loosbroek among other things for a limited choice of literature and a lack of arguments for their rejection of the women's culture approach 'per se' and concluded that their article was more irritating than stimulating. She also remarked that, fortunately, history will never be definitively 'rewritten'. This review appeared in *Tijdschrift voor Vrouwenstudies*, 26, no. 7 (1986), no. 2, pp. 236-9.

Two years later, in a review of *Jaarboek voor Vrouwengeschiedenis* 8 (1987), Jannie Poelstra came back to this matter. She criticised Joan Scott for her rejection of 'herstory' and of women's-history-as-social-history and Jansz and van Loosbroek for the way in which they formulated their critique of 'herstory' and women's culture. She also remarked that, fortunately, the editors had let go of their earlier tight embrace of Joan Scott's 'programme'. This review appeared in *Tijdschrift voor Vrouwenstudies*, 34, no. 9 (1988), no. 2, pp. 213-16.

44. This conference was organised by women from the *LOV* and took place in Amsterdam in March 1986. Recently a selection of papers from this conference was published: Arina Angerman et al. (eds.), *Current Issues in Women's History* (London and New York: Routledge, 1989). For Bosch's reaction see: Mineke Bosch, 'On the Meaning of Gossip in a Women's History of Women's Suffrage', in Lilian de Bruijn and Annemarie de Wildt (eds.), *International Conference on Women's History. Programme and outlines of papers*, pp. 135-8.

45. Mineke Bosch, 'Women's Culture in Women's History: Historical Notion or Feminist Vision?', in Maaike Meijer and Jette Schaap (eds.), *Historiography of Women's Cultural Traditions* (Dordrecht-Holland/Providence-USA: Foris Publications, 1987), p. 49.

46. Maria Grever, 'Het verborgen continent [The Hidden Continent]', *Tijdschrift voor Sociale Geschiedenis*, 12, no. 3 (1986), pp. 261-2. See also her article, 'Het vrouwelijk oculair [The Female Point of View]', *DIGO*, Didactiek in het geschiedenisonderwijs, 10, no. 4 (1987).

47. Especially since Joan Scott's article, 'Gender: A Useful Category of Historical Analysis', *American Historical Review*, 91 (1986), pp. 1053-75. Scott's work has become so dominant that other interpretations of 'gender', for instance Gisela Bock's, are hardly discussed. See Gisela Bock, 'Women's History and Gender History: Aspects of An International Debate', *Gender & History*, 1, no. 1 (1989), pp. 7-30.

48. Suzanne van Norden et al., 'Het feminisme en vrouwengeschiedenis', in *Vrouwengeschiedenis*, brochure published by the Women's History Group, University of Amsterdam (1979), p. 10.

49. Ine Megens, 'Zicht op een vrouwelijk verleden [View on a Female Past]', pp. 14-15; Maria Grever, 'Het verborgen continent [The Hidden Continent]', *Tijdschrift voor Sociale Geschiedenis*, 12, no. 3 (1986), pp. 240, 244.

50. *Racisme & Vrouwengeschiedenis* [Racism and Women's History], a collection of articles that appeared on the occasion of the *LOV* day about this topic (*LOV*, 1987), p. 9.

51. Philomena Essed, 'Racisme en feminisme', Selma Sevenhuijsen et al. (eds.), *Socialisties-Feministiese Teksten* 7 (Amsterdam: Sara, 1982), pp. 9-41, especially pp. 30-40. In January 1990 Philomena Essed received her Ph.D. at the

University of Amsterdam with 'Understanding Everyday Racism: An Interdiscipli-nary Theory and Analysis of the Experiences of Black Women'.

52. *Racisme & Vrouwengeschiedenis* (*LOV*, 1987), p. 11.

53. Gerda Lerner, 'Black Women in the United States: A Problem in Historiography and Interpretation', in *The Majority Finds its Past: Placing Women in History* (New York, Oxford: Oxford University Press, 1979), pp. 63-82; *Racisme & Vrouwengeschiedenis* (*LOV*, 1987), p. 11. The remark itself reveals a white and academic perspective. Someone who experiences the consequences of racism everyday does not need a text to make her realize this.

54. See note 4.

55. Denise Riley, 'Am I That Name?' Feminism and the Category of 'Women' in *History* (Basingstoke: Macmillan Press, 1988), pp. 1-2.

56. Joan Wallach Scott, 'Deconstructing Equality-Versus-Difference: Or, the Uses of Poststructuralist Theory for Feminism', *Feminist Studies*, 14, no. 1 (1988), pp. 33-50, translated as 'Deconstructie van gelijkheid-versus-verschil. De bruikbaarheid van de post-structuralistische theorie voor het feminisme', in *Het raadsel vrouwengeschiedenis. Tiende Jaarboek voor Vrouwengeschiedenis* [The Mystery of Women's History. Women's History Yearbook 10] (Nijmegen: SUN, 1989); and *Gender and the Politics of History* (New York: Columbia University Press, 1988).

57. Mieke Aerts et al. (eds.), *Naar het leven. Feminisme & biografisch onderzoek* (Amsterdam: SUA, 1988).

58. Geertje Mak, 'De verklede werkelijkheid? Analyse van aan vrouwen toegekende "mannelijkheid", 1625-1920 [Dressed Reality? An Analysis of "Masculinity" Attributed to Women]', *Jaarboek voor Vrouwengeschiedenis* [Women's History Yearbook 10], pp. 113-15. In this article, Mak, among other things, criticises the unproblematic way in which Rudolf Dekker and Lotte van de Pol use concepts such as homosexuality and hermaphroditism in their pioneering study of Dutch passing women, *Daar was laatst een meisje loos. Nederlandse vrouwen als matrozen en soldaten* (Baarn: Amboboeken, 1981). In 1989 this book was substantially rewritten and published in Dutch as *Vrouwen in mannenkleren. De geschiedenis van een tegendraadse traditie. Europa 1500-1800* (Amsterdam: Wereld bibliotheek, 1989), and in English as *The Tradition of Female Tranvestism in Early Modern Europe: Women Living as Men in the Dutch Republic* (Basingstoke: Macmillan, 1989).

16

The State of Women's History in Austria

Brigitte Mazohl-Wallnig

Women's studies in the narrow sense, that is, as an academic programme of study which leads to a degree (undergraduate or post-graduate), does not exist in Austria. Women's studies in a broader sense, meaning teaching and research activities focusing on women, have developed only in the past decade. Only very recently, in October 1988, was Claudia von Werlhof appointed to the first university chair in Austria to include women's studies, the chair in 'Political science with particular reference to women's studies' at the University of Innsbruck. Compared to other western industrialised countries, even the introduction of women's studies in Austria has proceeded slowly. This is due, among other reasons, to the fact that the expansion of higher education in general has taken place slowly in Austria.

Thus, a precondition for the further development of women's studies at universities is that women attain an adequate share of university teaching and research positions. For this to happen a corresponding number of university-educated women are needed as teachers so that more women may complete the higher school grades necessary for university studies. In Austria, the general expansion of education (which, as in other countries, entailed a substantial increase in female students and academics) began later than in other European countries. Consequently, an increase in the proportion of girls in *Gymnasien* and higher school grades (and therefore in those entering university) was also later in coming.

Only the last twenty years have brought decisive quantitative changes in this situation, wherein a close correlation exists between the growth in the proportion of girls in high schools offering a general education and the increase in female university students. The following statistical data may illustrate this point: the expansion of secondary schools, and consequent higher secondary-school enrolment, in the sixties led to higher numbers of students qualified for university entrance in the seventies: between 1970 and 1980 their number increased by 82 per cent. The proportion of girls graduating from secondary schools ('Matura') amounted to 35 per cent in the sixties; in 1986 it exceeded 50 per cent. The number of women who went on to university after secondary school also increased. In 1970, 41 per cent of women who qualified for university entrance went on to university; in the eighties the pertinent percentage is 52 per cent.

As a result of these changes, the proportion of women in first-year university enrolment rose from 29 per cent in the academic year 1970/71 to 50 per cent in the academic year 1985/86. The proportion of female students rose from 25 per cent (1970/71) to 44 per cent (1985/86). In the same period the number of female students quintupled: at present 64,000 female students are enrolled at Austrian universities and colleges of art and music. In technical disciplines the proportion of women rose from 6 per cent (1970) to 17 per cent (1986), although in engineering (mechanical, electrical, civil engineering) their share is still only 5 per cent.

Although by now first-year university enrolments have achieved a numerical balance between the sexes, graduations show a completely different picture. In the academic year 1984/85 about 39 per cent of the graduates were women. The percentage of female postgraduates is still lower (29 per cent). The census of 1981 shows that there are 34,000 female graduates in employment which means that 26 per cent of the academic labour force are women. In September 1986, 54 per cent of graduates out of work were women. Thus unemployment has hit female graduates harder than male graduates.

Along with the increase in the number of female graduates, women's share of teaching and research staff positions at the universities rose - although less and in a hierarchically staggered manner. In 1986, some 18 per cent of university assistants were women, ranging from about 30 per cent in the humanities to 5 per cent in technical disciplines. Since 1980, 1,130 men, but only 88 women qualified as university readers (*Habilitation*) which means an average of 8 per cent per year. Nevertheless, the percentage of women who have qualified as university readers has risen since the seventies when it was only about 3 per cent. In the academic year 1985/86, 142 out of the 2,295 readers (*Dozenten*) at Austrian universities were women (6 per cent). For professors, the percentage of women is still lower: 2 per cent of the full professors (19 out of 1,100), and 5 per cent of the associate professors (25 out of 516) are women. At colleges of art and music, the proportion of women teachers is higher: at the level of professors it amounts to 15 per cent (55 out of 367).

With regard to the election of their academic administrators, universities remain inflexible. There is no woman to be found among the rectors of the twelve Austrian universities, and only one female dean (out of 38). In 1978, Prof. Brigitte Scheer-Schäzler (professor of American literature) was elected dean at the University of Innsbruck. There is only one female university director (head of the administration at a university). One of the six colleges of art and music has a female rector.

This statistical overview suggests that women's studies activities at universities must rely heavily on individual commitment and external support.[1]

Official concern for the role of women in Austrian society was manifested in 1981 with the appointment of an Undersecretary for Women's Affairs (*Staatssekretariat für Frauenfragen*) and consequently with the introduction of a Programme for the Advancement of Women in Public Service (*Förderungsprogramm für Frauen im Bundesdienst*). Much of the official activity in the realm of research and teaching has been carried out in connection with this committee, although it has to be stressed that the actual activities were always initiated by independent individuals and groups at the various universities. Co-ordination and communication between and among these individuals and groups are, however, regardless of the smallness of the country, rather poor. Various privately initiated conferences have increased contacts, but every newcomer has to find her own way.

Women's studies activities so far have ranged from individual courses (mainly in history, literature and the humanities in general) to interdisciplinary lecture series (*Ringvorlesungen*) at all universities, the possibility of electing women's studies as a minor (University of Vienna), the organisation of conferences of women in history and in art history, conferences on specific topics, the installation of women's committees at the universities and so on. Of general interest is the Centre for Documentation for Research By, About and for Women (*Dokumentationsstelle für Frauenforschung*) at the Institute for Science and Art (*Institut für Wissenschaft und Kunst*) in Vienna, which collects bibliographical information on women's studies, including M.A. and Ph.D. theses from Austrian universities.[2] A subject index on computer now makes this material available to researchers.

Given these circumstances, it is important to differentiate between three levels of status within the field of historical women's studies. The first level is occupied by university courses of various kinds. The Universities of Vienna and Graz offer university credits for those courses organised by each institution's standing committee on historical women's studies (*Arbeitsgruppen für historische Frauenforschung*). The Federal Ministry of Science and Research also funds special courses within an extracurricular national programme, that is, a set number of 'paid lectures at university level' (*Lehraufträge*) devoted to women's studies outside the regular number of hours allotted to the universities. These special lectures are important in two ways: they help to initiate women's studies courses in university towns where there is departmental opposition to them and they provide financial support for the large number of women scholars who work outside official institutions (a two-hour teaching appointment at a university carries with it the full range of social security benefits). The main drawback of this programme is the fact that the courses that are funded remain, in most cases, a fringe phenomenon, and the lecturers are dependent on the good will of their students. Finally, individual feminist-minded professors do offer courses on women's topics within the 'normal' realm of required classes. This, however, is left to the initiative of the individual professors.[3]

A second and much more important level consists of supra-university research funding - financed either via the Ministries of Science or Social Affairs, or directly through the Federal Scientific Research Fund. Once authorised, such projects usually run for two years and include a renewal option. This stratum is closely connected to research done at the university level. In many cases feminist-oriented members of the academic staff apply for funding, which they then pass on to graduate students and postgraduate colleagues, so that the research project and university levels mix. Typical of this 'research mix' are the non-university research institutes, such as the Ludwig Boltzmann Institute for Labour History in Linz and Salzburg (named after the renowned scientist, who incidentally, is notorious for his sexist attitudes towards female colleagues), the Salzburg Institute for the Study of Everyday Culture (*Institut für Alltagskultur*), and the Viennese Institute for Science and Art.

The third level is occupied by a very active student community. Feminist students now organise annual networking meetings, circulate a newsletter put out successively by local groups in the university towns of Vienna, Salzburg, Graz, Klagenfurt, and Innsbruck, and have initiated, to date, four women's summer schools (*Frauen-Sommer-Universität*), the results of which have been partially published.[4] An 'activist-mix' exists especially between these student groups and the previously-mentioned research project level, as well as with the university standing committees on historical women's studies. This intermingling of the three levels has admittedly led to conflicts and disagreements concerning a definition of such terms as the 'best form of feminism'.

I will now elaborate on a few of the most important research results and current initiatives in our field in Austria. Starting in 1986, various lecture series (*Ringvorlesungen*) have been held in Salzburg, Graz, and Vienna, enabling the few female researchers interested in feminism to interact in an interdisciplinary setting. The titles of these lecture series are very general, signalling intent rather than content. The results of the first Salzburg as well as the first Graz *Ringvorlesungen* entitled 'Women's Images/Women's Roles/Women's Studies' and 'Women's Life/Man's World and Science' respectively, have now been published, containing reports from the fields of history, literature, sociology, and philosophy.[5] In the past year the lecture series in the cities of Vienna and Salzburg, entitled 'Gender in Bourgeois Society' and 'Feminist Science - Outlook and Methodology' respectively, exchanged speakers, an example of inter-urban co-operation. The published results of both interdisciplinary lecture series are now in preparation.[6]

A scientific 'coming-out' has also taken place. Last year's series saw a lively discussion of the feasibility of a feminist 'long march through the institutions'. Students also played an important role in preparing the lecture series which included 'non-establishment' speakers active outside the realm of direct university research.

With respect to the federally funded university-level courses on women's topics, which currently total 200 credit hours annually, it is now possible to look at the spread of topics as recorded in official government sources. Theoretical/methodological reflections are of great importance, emphasising the assumption that women's studies does not merely constitute a new field of research, but rather a completely new scientific approach. Secondly, there is increasing interest in oral sources, especially in relation to the study of the female victim/culprit paradigm during the Nazi period, as well as of the position of political emigrants and Jews. Finally, the field of education – and the variety of influences women's role models play in this area – are attracting attention.[7]

The research project level is, however, of even greater importance than university teaching per se, when considering the direction women's studies is now taking. The breadth of such projects, all of which will be or have been in part published, is documented in the following summary. One can clearly discern from this overview the focus that has to date characterised historical research on women in Austria. Up to now interest has been focused primarily on the twentieth century (and within it above all on the problematic of National Socialism and the Resistance), and secondarily on the problem of the women's movement and the position of women at the turn of the century. One can equally well discern a specific interest in the question of women in relation to the historiography of the working class. Only most recently has attention also been devoted to the nineteenth century and the world of bourgeois life. The following list will provide some idea of current projects:
- 'Unemployment in Austria from the First World War until the 1950s'. The original title was changed during the preliminary research phase,

dropping the term 'without work' (*arbeitslos*) in favour of the term 'without employment' (*erwerbslos*) in order not to negate housework. The initial results of this project are already available in published form.[8]

- 'Female Homosexuality' is a project in which the historical forms of love, friendship and sexuality between women are investigated. Here also reference can now be made to a publication.[9]

- 'Autobiographies and Gender-specific Identity'. This is a methodologically very demanding project that inquires into the influences of gender identity not only on the individual life itself but also on the modes and means of its autobiographical linguistic articulation. Research has just begun on this project by Christa Hämmerle and Edith Saurer.

- 'The Bourgeois Women's Movement in Vienna at the Turn of the Century'. This is an extremely important research project since, in contrast to the already well-developed historiography of the German women's movement, no comprehensive account yet exists of the history of the no less significant Austrian women's movement. The principal investigators are Ingrid Cella and Harriet Jane Anderson, editor of the Rosa Mayreder diaries.[10]

- 'The Female Students of the University of Vienna'. This volume, to be published in 1990, will present a sociological historical analysis by Waltraud Heindl, Marina Tichy and Jutta Avrat, of all women who studied at the university since the admission of women. This study will not only provide a statistical analysis of 12,000 female students at the University of Vienna since 1897 with reference to their social origin (place of birth, parental home, father's occupation), their nationality and educational level, it will also investigate the socio-political function of the university within the system of the state and its politics vis-à-vis women.

- 'Feminist Film Theory' is a project, undertaken by Gabriele Jutz, Claudia Preschl and Gloria Withalm, which analyses American and European films from the 1930s to the present from the perspective of female representational forms, that is, with regard to the transmission of clichés about women.

- A proposal for a project on 'Bourgeois Female Culture in nineteenth Century Austria' has been submitted by Sigrid Schmid (German literature), Ulrike Jenny and Gabriele Hammer-Tugendhat (art history), and Brigitte Mazohl-Wallnig. With this project an attempt will be made to carry out, for the first time, interdisciplinary research in this field. The scholars in German literature hope to unearth forgotten female authors, and the art historians will analyse the visual arts along the lines of the ideology of femininity. The historians will study the role bourgeois women played in public life (and not only in the familiar 'private' sphere). The Vienna World's Fair of 1873 will be the point of departure. Special emphasis will be placed on a display of women's labour in the women's pavilion at the fair. This research project will be organised on a comparative basis providing insights by references to visual arts, public display and journalistic and literary reports. The researchers on the project are Gunda Barth, Margret Friedrich (history), Christa Gürtler, Theresia Klugsberger (German literature), and Marie Luise Angerer, Irene Nierhaus, and Judith Schöber (art history).

Other significant projects currently in progress include:
- 'Courtesans in Rome in the Sixteenth Century' is an investigation by Monika Kurzel-Runtscheiner of prostitution in Renaissance Italy which will be based especially on legal and judicial documentary sources (such as wills and decrees) from the Vatican Archives.
- 'Women's Experiences in the Nazi Period' is an oral history project by Ingrid Bauer and Helga Embacher.[11] A very wide range of source material has been collected for this investigation. It will cover not only resistance fighters in opposition to the Nazi regime but also active and convinced National Socialist women as well as 'unpolitical' women whose personal lives were influenced only indirectly and subliminally by the women's politics of National Socialism.
- 'Women in the Viennese Labour Movement' is being co-ordinated by Edith Prost at the Institute for Science and Art (*Institut für Wissenschaft und Kunst [IWK]*) in Vienna. The history of the Austrian labour movement was very thoroughly explored in the 1970s at the time of the socialist government. A few of these studies also devoted some attention along the way to women-specific points of view within the history of the labour movement.[12]
- 'Women in Post-War Vienna', an investigation by Irene Bandhauer-Schöffmann, Michaela Hornung, and Erika Weinzierl,[13] is dedicated to recovering the large yet until now hardly noticed role of women in the work of reconstruction after World War II. Since many men had died in battle or found themselves in prisoner-of-war camps, it fell above all to women to secure day-to-day survival and to carry out the crucial work of rebuilding. Oral sources will provide an important basis for this project also.
- 'The Resistance of Austrian Women in Concentration Camps during the Nazi Period (1938-1945)' is a project designed by Karin Berger, Elisabeth Holzinger, and Ida Podgornik. In historical research in Austrian contemporary history generally, more space is being given to the collecting and editing of the writings and other legacies of former concentration camp inmates. It is crucial in this context also not to overlook the women among them. Some results of this project are already available in published form.[14]
- 'Women and Everyday Life in Vienna during the Nazi Period 1938-1945'. This project by Brigitte Lichtenberger-Fenz parallels that by Ingrid

Bauer and Helga Embacher. The latter concentrates on the provincial city
of Salzburg while Lichtenberger-Fenz pursues the same set of questions for
the metropolis and capital city of Vienna.
- 'Biographical Dictionary of Important Austrian Women since 1918', by
Ruth Aspöck and Erika Weinzierl, is a kind of counter dictionary to the
Austrian Biographical Dictionary, which – like most similar national
biographical dictionaries – is distinguished by its treating almost
exclusively of male subjects.

    All of these projects share the weakness that they are generally
carried out either by non-university institutes or by university faculty with
outside funding. This exacerbates the already existing lack of co-
ordination. And most importantly, only those projects in already-developed
thematic areas find very slow admittance into the university, that is, into
the everyday practice of teaching and research. At universities traditional
male-dominated course content remains unaltered, and university structures
remain almost totally unaffected by research undertaken outside the
academy itself. Many applications for funding are now coming from
individuals without direct institutional ties, a sign of the times not only in
Austria. Here as in most European countries research activities have
moved to institutions outside the universities. But in this way the important
positions within universities still remain firmly in male hands, a situation
that naturally has decisive consequences for research and teaching, above
all for perpetuating the lack of interest in research on women.

    Student initiatives now focus on establishing an intra-Austrian
network in order to improve their strategies for dealing with the general
public and the government. The Austrian Society for Historical Women's
Studies was recently established in Salzburg as a *Verein* or officially
recognised association.[15] This legal status facilitates government subsidy
applications and the hiring of employees. The most recent intra-Austrian
women's co-ordinating meeting was held in Innsbruck from 23 to 25 June
1989. Its principal objective was to gain an overview of the different
initiatives in research on women in Austria and to develop some common
strategies for better establishing and co-ordinating research on women and
women's studies within Austrian universities.[16]

    Above and beyond these mainly organisational activities, the
women's studies student groups have initiated many highly visible projects,
such as the commemorative exhibit in Salzburg in 1988 – 'Forward to
Victory on the Battle Field and in the Nursery' (*Sieg der Waffen – Sieg der
Wiegen*), demonstrating the effect the Anschluß of 1938 had on the lives
of Austrian women.[17] The Viennese exhibit '70 Years of Political
Franchise', marking the introduction of voting rights for women in 1918,
is now touring the country. The recent introduction of town tours and
walks, a novelty in Austria, enables visitors and residents alike to become

acquainted with streets and squares named after prominent women and with landmarks that played an important role in women's history. Such tours now exist in Vienna and in Graz.[18]

Finally, one major point of conflict now divides Austrian women's research as does no other, and I assume that this difference of opinion plays an important role in many other countries as well, namely, the tensions and controversies between the activist, political 'movement' and the theoretically and scientifically active 'research community'. The former consider the latter to have sold out to the establishment, to support the status quo, and to be lacking in political enthusiasm. The second group claims that for women it is impossible to be active in scholarship and politics at the same time, since such a double engagement results in a loss of quality in both fields.

The dividing line between the two camps is, however, not clearly defined, and many students are active in both, serving to connect them. This is especially true in the fields of political science and sociology. On the one hand research on such topics as the homeless, unemployment, and cleaning women unite both groups.[19] On the other, it is in these particular disciplines that the conflict has reached a new high. The recently appointed professor for women's studies in Innsbruck, Claudia von Werlhof, fundamentally rejects current forms of academic feminism as merely attempts by women to find a place in a male-dominated world without changing the conditions necessary for the recognition of women's rights.[20]

Nevertheless a group has recently constituted itself among Austrian women's historians that has set itself the goal of publishing a feminist historical journal. The editorial committee of this journal is composed of the same scholars who belong to the Austrian National Committee of the International Federation for Research in Women's History. The first issue of this journal, which will be entitled *L'Homme: Journal for Feminist Historical Science*, will appear in fall 1990. At present, no journal of this type exists in the German-speaking world. Through this journal Austrian female historians hope to realise their plans to develop their understanding of feminist historiography as an entirely new perspective and not merely an expanded field of research. The main intention of this journal will be to produce historical scholarship that highlights the role of gender as a social category in history and from this perspective really to rewrite history.

As has always been the case in our history, Austria has again fallen behind, perhaps by several generations. However, this makes catching up all the more invigorating. At the moment the feminist discourse is not only relevant within institutionalised and informal women's circles, it has also begun to shake the foundations of academic institutions.

NOTES

*Text translated in part by Ruth Roach Pierson.

1. Elsa Hackl, *Women's Studies at Universities* (Vienna: Ministry of Science and Research, Statistical Data, 1986).
2. The documentary centre will soon start compiling a 'Bibliography of Women's Studies Research', including abstracts mainly of those works published after 1968. A 'List of Research Gaps' is also planned. The address of the documentary centre is: Institut für Wissenschaft und Kunst, Berggasse 19, 1090 Vienna, Austria.
3. See, for example, the conference which took place at the University of Salzburg, 24-26 October 1984: 'Women and Historiography in Austria'. One of the results of this conference was the article by Fritz Fellner, 'Frauen in der österreichischen Geschichtswissenschaft [Women and Historiography in Austria]', *Jahrbuch der Universität Salzburg* (1981-1983), pp. 107-23.
4. Anni Bell, Eva Fleischer et al. (eds.), *Furien in Uni-Form? Dritte österreichische Frauensommeruniversität Innsbruck 1986* [Furies in Uni-form: Third Austrian Summer University for Women in Innsbruck 1986] (Innsbruck: Vor-Ort, 1987).
5. Christa Gürtler, Brigitte Mazohl-Wallnig et al. (eds.), *Frauenbilder – Frauenrollen – Frauenforschung* [Women's Images – Women's Roles – Women's Studies] (Vienna and Salzburg: Geyer, 1987); Beate Frakele, Elisabeth List, and Gertrude Pauritsch (eds.), *Über Frauenleben, Männerwelt und Wissenschaft* [Women's Life, Man's World and Science] (Vienna: Verlag für Gesellschaftskritik, 1987). See also the publication of the 5th conference of female historians in Vienna in 1984: Wiener Historikerinnen, *Die ungeschriebene Geschichte* [The Unwritten History] (Vienna: Wiener Frauenverlag, 1984). Another collection of articles written by Viennese female historians was published in 1981: Autorinnengruppe Uni Wien, *Das ewige Klischee* [The Eternal Cliché] (Vienna and Graz: Böhlau, 1981).
6. Including historical articles, for example: Brigitte Mazohl-Wallnig, 'Männergeschichte – Frauengeschichte/n. Historische Frauenforschung als wissenschaftliche Alternative [Men's History, Women's (His)-Stories. Feminist History as an Alternative Science]'; Edith Saurer, 'Sind Frauen schuldig geboren? Theologische Diskussionen zum Thema Sünde und Frau [Are Women Born Guilty? Theological Discussions about Women and Sin]'; Ingrid Bauer and Helga Embacher, '"Um Politik hab' ich mich damals nicht viel gekümmert": Frauenerfahrung und Nationalsozialismus. Ergebnisse mündlicher Geschichte ["I didn't care about politics at the time": Women's Experiences and National Socialism – Results of Oral History]'. In the meantime (after having finished this article) the Viennese Ring – lecture has been published, see: Heide Dienst and Edith Saurer (eds.), *'Das Weib existiert nicht für sich'. Geschlechterbeziehungen in der bürgerlichen Gesellschaft*

[Women Do Not Exist Separately or Only for Themselves: Gender Relations in Bourgeois Society] (Vienna: Verlag für Gesellschaftskritik, 1990).

7. Bundesministerium für Wissenschaft und Forschung, *Überblick über frauenspezifische Lehraufträge 1988* [Summary of Women-specific Lectures in 1988] (Vienna: Bundesministerium für Wissenschaft und Forschung, 1989).

8. See, for example, Erna Appelt, Andrea Lösch, and Edith Prost (eds.), *Stille Reserve? Erwerbslose Frauen in Österreich* [Secret Reserves: Unemployed Women in Austria] (Vienna: Verlag für Gesellschaftskritik, 1987), and Erna Appelt, *Von Ladenmädchen, Schreibfräulein und Gouverneranten. Die weiblichen Angestellten Wiens zwischedn 1900 und 1934* [Shop-assistants, Secretaries and Governesses: Female Employees in Vienna between 1900 and 1934] (Vienna: Verlag für Gesellschaftskritik, 1985).

9. Hanna Hacker, *Frauen und Freundinnen. Studien zu weiblichen 'Homosexualität' am Biespiel österreich* [Women and Friendship: Studies of Female 'Homosexuality': The Austrian Example 1870-1938] (Weinheim and Basel: Beltz, 1987).

10. Harriet Anderson (ed.), *Rosa Mayreder, Tagebücher 1873-1937* [Rosa Mayreder, Diaries 1873-1937] (Frankfurt/Main: Insel, 1988). Also on Rosa Mayreder, one of the best known Austrian representatives of the early women's movement, see 'Rosa Mayreder, 1858-1938', *Mitteilungen des Instituts für Wissenschaft und Kunst (Vienna)*, 44, no. 1 (1989). See also the exhibition catalogue: *Aufbruch in das Jahrhundert der Frau? Rosa Mayreder und der Feminismus in Wien um 1900* [Dawn of the Century of the Woman? Rosa Mayreder and Feminism in Vienna 1900] (Vienna: Museen der Stadt Wien, 1990).

11. Other projects at the Boltzmann-Institutes of Salzburg and Linz: Ingrid Bauer, *Frauenleben vom Ersten Weltkrieg bis zum Beginn der Neuen Frauenbewegung* [Women's Lives from the First World War to the Beginning of the New Women's Movement]; Helga Embacher, *Emigrantinnen. Zum Problem jüdischer Identität nach 1945* [Female Emigrants: The Problem of Jewish Identity after 1945]; Erika Thurner, 'Österreicherinnen im antifaschistischen Widerstand [Austrian Women in the Resistance during the Nazi Period]'.

12. The following publications have resulted from this project: Edith Prost (ed.), *'Die Partei hat mich nie enttäuscht. . . .' Österreichische Sozialdemokratinnen* ['The Party never disappointed me . . .' Austrian Female Social Democrats] (Vienna: Verlag für Gesellschaftskritik, 1989); Wolfgang Maderthaner (ed.), *Sozialdemokratie und Habsburgerstaat 1867-1918* [The Social Democratic Party and Habsburg Monarchy 1987-1918] (Vienna: Löcker, 1988), which also includes articles on female Social Democrats.

13. See a first report on this topic: Brigitte Mandl, 'Frauen im Wien der Nachkriegszeit [Women in Post-War Vienna]', *Österreichische Hochschulzeitung* (Vienna), 7/8 (1989).

14. Publications on this topic: Karin Berger et al. (eds.), *Der Himmel ist blau. Kann sein. Frauen im Widerstand. Österreich 1938-1945* [The Sky is Blue. Maybe. Women in the Resistance. Austria 1938-1945] (Vienna: Promedia, 1985); Karen Berger et al. (eds.), *Ich geb Dir einen Mantel, daß Du ihn noch in Freiheit tragen kannst. Widerstehen im KZ. Österreichische Frauen erzählen* [I give you a coat so that you can still wear it when you are free. Resistance in Concentration Camps – Austrian Women Remember] (Vienna: Promedia, 1987).

15. The address of this Association is: Gesellschaft für Historische Frauenforschung, Haydngasse 6, 5020 Salzburg, Austria.

16. At the Institute of Political Sciences, University of Innsbruck.

17. This exhibit took place 4-28 October, 1988 at the Mozarteum in Salzburg.

18. Arbeitsgruppe Frauengeschichte – Gesellschaft für Feministische Forschung, *Konzept einer Frauenrundfahrt* [Programme of a Feminist City-Tour] (Graz: Arbeitsgruppe Frauengeschichte, 1989).

19. See the projects at the Institute for Everyday Culture in Salzburg: *Frauenarbeitslosigkeit und Öffentlichkeit* [Female Unemployment and the Public] including the Exhibit: *Frau und Arbeit* [Women and Work] at the same Institute; *Weibliche Arbeitskräfte in Reinigungsberufen* [Female Workers in Cleaning Jobs]; *Obdachlose Frauen* [Homeless Women].

20. Claudia von Werlhof, 'Männliche Natur und künstliches Geschlecht [Male Nature and Artificial Gender]'. Lecture presented at the University of Salzburg, 17th of June 1989 (to be published).

17

Historical Research on Women in the Federal Republic of Germany

Ute Frevert
Heide Wunder
Christina Vanja

PART ONE

Women's history: between a social movement and an academic discipline

Academic work on women's history has been underway in West Germany for more than fifteen years.[1] In the meantime, just as in the USA and Great Britain, although with a decided chronological delay, women's history has become an established field of research. It has generated its own publication series, conferences, university chairs and, accompanied by a comparatively lively public and media response, it has created a new and independent 'product market'.[2]

In this country, too, interest in the history of women arose in the context of the new, autonomous women's movement, which came into existence in West Germany at the beginning of the 1970s. It not only exposed the need for political action and change, but beyond that, it also sought a historical foundation that could allow current desires and goals to be situated within a broad and chronologically widespread context. It received little support or help with information from the professional discipline of history. Even as the traditional, politically-oriented history had nothing to report about women, since statesmanship, diplomacy and war had always been reserved as manly activities, so social history, which had been expanding since the late 1960s, also remained silent about the new women's issues. Even though social history dealt with the history of social structures and processes, the development of classes and social strata, families and socialisation, demography and reproductive behaviour, organisations, mentalities and social protest, its published results then

291

contained but little information about the life conditions, actions, and experiences of women.

Hardly any social-historical work considered the fact that the processes and structures being researched did not, as a rule, take place in a gender-neutral way, and that a look at gender-differentiated forms of work, behaviour and thought patterns would perhaps reveal a very different historical reality: a different classification, explanation, and evaluation of such developments. Indeed, the very system of categories with which social history worked did not allow for gender-specific differentiation, but demanded general validity. However, social history implicitly remained 'male-focused', in that it focused on those topics in which male behaviour and experience were portrayed. Even when social historians became more interested in the motives and subjective actions of people, and related the development of collective movements to the history of individual experiences and expectations, the word people [*menschen*] almost exclusively meant 'men'.

Female students and doctoral candidates who inquired about 'female people' received little attention from professors or thesis supervisors. If not rejected outright, research on women's issues was under no circumstance encouraged or promoted. This attitude in turn made clear to the female historians and history students connected with the women's movement that women's history was not a 'normal' research field but a kind of special area of inquiry, pushed forward by women for women, and belonging outside the established research institutions. The disadvantages of such an approach are obvious: exclusion from the research undertaken at the universities meant in particular exclusion from financial and material resources. But the advantages should not be underestimated: the consequent freedom allowed 'free' thought, the possibility of crossing disciplinary boundaries, of operating on the other side of established patterns of argumentation and outside of the powerful pressures for methodological conformity.

The half-forced, half-chosen isolation in a woman-focused subculture did not last long, however. As women's issues gained greater public attention and became politically more important, systematic research on such questions achieved a solid position in the book trade and a base in a number of research institutes. Even so, one still searches for discussions of such issues in the journals and on the bookshelves of established history publishers almost in vain. In contrast, for example, with sociology (and also in contrast with developments in the USA and Great Britain), the historical brotherhood of West Germany persistently resists (with only a few exceptions) women's history and up to now has hardly deigned to notice the results. The fact that there are now three chairs for women's history research at West German universities (Bonn,

Bielefeld, and Berlin) has not changed the situation much. More the product of political and administrative pressures than the deliberately-planned children of history faculties, they seem like alien elements in the more generally-oriented range of subjects in German universities. Only the future will tell whether they will succeed in staving off the ghettoisation of women's history and in promoting its general acceptance.

The slow erosion of the collegial front, due both to indifference and to defensiveness, can be seen at the bi-annual conferences of German historians. Not until 1984 were women's history issues included in the official program. Four years later, in 1988, there were two organised sections out of thirty-three. These developments, however, did generate some publicity for women's history research and thereby successfully circumvented the male strategy of suppression and devaluation.

The conditions for such a 'coming-out' have clearly improved during the last twenty years. Although the 'change of perspective' promulgated by female historians at the beginning of the 1980s relied mainly on US works or as yet unpublished research projects, there have since been a considerable number of publications on women's history in West Germany. These will be introduced in the following short survey.

Ruptures and continuities: research on the Weimar Republic and National Socialism

At first glance, West German women's history seems to offer a colourful diversity of themes, interpretations and theoretical approaches that make it advisable to avoid rash classifications and arbitrary systematisation. Such diversity, which is more welcome than not, can be explained not least by the fact that there are hardly any centres and institutions where 'schools' specialising in women's issues could develop, to propose, steer, and co-ordinate research work. Since 1977, in fact, women historians have been able to put forward their theses and research results for discussion at almost yearly conferences on women's history.[3] Such a selective market of opportunities is, however, incapable of providing a continuing and concentrated exchange and dialogue. Thematic and conceptual diversity is thus offset by contingency and isolation from discussion, and by the lack of a broader, overarching level of theoretical debate that could formulate questions, describe central problems, and design work strategies.

Despite the anarchy prevailing in the research process, there is a certain chronological and topical clustering in published work in women's history in West Germany. Initially, the interest of female historians was directed toward the twentieth century, and more precisely to the period of the Weimar Republic and the 'Third Reich'.[4]

The preoccupation with the recent past in this case had the immediate function of establishing identity: we sought the history of mothers and grandmothers and the traces that this history had left behind in the consciousness of the daughters and granddaughters. The question of how National Socialism marked earlier generations of women, why it had so many followers among women, as well as men, and so few opponents, what changes it caused in female life and what continuities it advanced were all the object of intense debates. Heated controversy arose about both the quality and quantity of female resistance.[5]

Although initially what we might call a 'victim perspective' dominated, gradually a more differentiated picture of National Socialist women's politics developed, one that revealed the contradictory nature of intentions as well as the diversity of effects and reactions. According to age, religion, ethnic background and social class, women experienced National Socialism very differently.[6] Differences between women could be as great as life and death, as in the case of the difference between Jewish and non-Jewish women.[7] This variety makes it very difficult to arrive at a general assessment and interpretation of National Socialist women's politics that can encompass these differences. One cannot insist, as Sebastian Haffner did, that women's emancipation made 'great strides' between 1933 and 1945, nor can one describe the 'Third Reich' as a time of complete humiliation for women, as a 'relapse into a degraded existence deprived of rights'.[8] There were winners and losers among women, just as there were among men. Under no circumstances can women be seen only as sacrificial victims of a male-organised, omnipotent and completely repressive power system.

It is perhaps no coincidence, though, that the studies in women's history that concentrate exclusively on the period of National Socialism veer more often than not towards a perspective that stresses loss of status and deprivation of rights, thereby, however, contributing to an exaggeration of the successes of women's emancipation, or more precisely of the degree of equal rights achieved, during the 1920s. Because of this, however, women historians who have studied the Weimar Republic have successfully and repeatedly shown how limited and contradictory post-war modernisation was for women, and how deep the gap between constitutional equality and existing conditions in the economy, society and politics.[9] Even though the signs of radical cultural change in relations between the sexes cannot be overlooked, and many young women profited from this liberation, the collapse of the empire in 1918 did not ring in an 'era of the liberated woman'. Neither the feminisation of the expanding white-collar labour force, nor the sex reform movement offset the inequality of male and female life styles.[10] With new freedoms came new dependencies, constraints, and duties.

Although the positive aspects of Weimar 'modernisation', including the fact that young women did have a wider field of job opportunities, cannot be ignored, nevertheless historians of German women are inclined to emphasise the elements of continuity with the Third Reich, rather than perceiving 1933 as sharp break, an end (as it were) to experiments in emancipation. Women's history cannot be written strictly according to a political chronology; other possible periodisations must also be considered. There is much to be said for the notion of connecting the Weimar and NS-periods, although there may be a danger of stretching the continuity argument too far and underrating the new quality of National Socialist rule and politics, which did have its own severity and coerciveness. Among other things, the frequent use of 'oral history' may have contributed to this tendency. Many (surviving) women experienced the NS seizure of power to be less of a break in their life-histories than the outbreak of World War II. Due to the fact that the immediate victims of this 'seizure of power' cannot, as a rule, give interviews, a certain - although unwanted - 'bias' cannot always be avoided.

That the period of the 'Third Reich' was obviously favoured as a subject of women's historical research was not due solely to the fact that, transmitted through 'oral history' or family historical connections, it triggers or presupposes a particular personal concern. National Socialism also commends itself as a women's history research area because it politicised - and made suitable for politics - the relation of the sexes and especially, in a hitherto unsurpassed way, the particular situation of women.[11] Whether it concerned women's housework, which was budgeted and taxed as an economic resource,[12] women's paid labour in serving the war economy,[13] or their ability to bear children and raise them, every element of female work capacity was used and exploited in the interest of the new political system. Unfortunately, to date there are only a few studies that have thoroughly researched and analysed the internal connections between the National Socialist system and women's politics. Despite continual references to the effect and omnipresence of fascist women's ideology, there is still no broad survey that embeds this ideology in the overall plan of NS power structures and imagination.[14]

In contrast, Gisela Bock's extensive study on forced sterilisation[15] offers a convincing attempt to relate the history of National Socialism to women's history. By means of a very complex and nuanced argument, she characterises the supposedly gender-neutral sterilisation policies of the 1930s and 1940s as an element of women's politics, designed to be - contrary to previously prevailing opinions - anti-procreative, rather than the other way around. By showing how politics around women interlocked with racial, social, and population politics, she succeeds in presenting a new picture of National Socialist politics towards women as well as in explaining and clarifying the status of such policies within the power structure of the 'Third Reich'.

Women's labour in historical perspective

Gisela Bock's work also marks the return to a political social history, which had been lost for some time among women historians, even though they had focused initially on political and institutional themes - female behaviour at the polls,[16] party and labour union politics,[17] and the women's movement.[18] By the end of the 1970s the focus of women's history research had shifted and narrowed down more and more to social historical questions and approaches. As social history broke away from the concentration on organisations and associations, steering increasingly towards more complex social constellations and realities of life, so women's history also turned to examine structures and long-term processes, processes that can be designated by the key-words: industrialisation, modernisation and rationalisation.

In the centre of these developments - and here too women's historians followed a general trend - stood the development of women's paid labour. Large-scale quantitative surveys based on mass statistical data[19] outlined the increasing integration of women in work processes outside the house that were mediated by the job market. At the same time, however, these surveys drew attention to the fact that men and women were affected differently by the structural economic changes set in motion by the industrial revolution. This inequality was not reduced, but rather increased, as industrialisation continued. Even in the so-called modern professions, gender-specific segregation patterns and hierarchies were immediately established.

Although a series of historical studies of women's workers – nurses,[20] homeworkers,[21] domestic servants,[22] factory workers,[23] office workers,[24] teachers[25] - are now available, not enough is yet known about the motives and conditions that are responsible for this form of social differentiation. How did it come about that male and female work in factories or offices was so clearly segregated? How was the process of gender-specific division of labour made empirically concrete? What were the driving forces and what forms did resistance take? What is the basis for the very visible connection between the feminisation of a profession and its social degradation? Complex questions of this kind are still not taken up often enough,[26] and all too many works confine themselves to isolated accounts and demonstrations that come dangerously close to a mindless historical chronicling.[27]

Despite this failing, however, almost all the new studies of women's gainful employment stand apart from the older surveys,[28] insofar as they relate the occupations of women outside the house to the work done in the household and family. Rosmarie Beier's study of female workers in the clothing industry, Elisabeth Plössl's examination of Bavarian female factory workers and Josef Ehmer's dissertation on 'family structure and the organisation of work in early industrial Vienna' all show how this integrative starting point can be used. They provide informative results about the reciprocal constraints between family situation and female labour force participation during the process of industrialisation.[29] Ute Daniel expands the study of this intersection, pursuing the connections, at the time of the First World War, between and among women's paid labour, family labour and state politics. In doing so, she not only acquires new insight into the dynamics of female paid labour, seeing continuity instead of a break, but also provides a modified perspective on the relations between the state and society in wartime. As in Gisela Bock's book, the new aspect lies in the political dimension, in a systematic reconstruction of the alternating and multiple relations between the rulers and the ruled.[30]

The fact that in this way a new light is cast on the former as well as the latter means that we have obtained a two-fold increase in our knowledge. Firstly, women's history profits, because the economic and social situation of working-class women between 1914-1918, their dependency on political factors and their influence on political decisions are all analysed at the source. Secondly, from this follows a completion and simultaneously a revision of 'general' research results bearing on the political and social history of the First World War. In the future, overall analyses of wartime society will hardly be able to overlook that in reality, and in the eyes of its administration, society consisted mainly of women whose work and behaviour were crucial to the achievements and shortcomings of the 'home front'. Thus have studies in women's history filled important gaps in research and collected new, hitherto unknown information about un(der)exposed issues and groups of people. Such studies also challenge the traditional view of history, question current interpretations and shift the weight of single topics and formulations of questions on the general scale of importance.

Of course, it would be unrealistic to expect revolutionary results and fundamental re-evaluations with each new publication on women's history. Even though most women historians are aware of the demand to rewrite history from the perspective of women, this goal often has to be postponed in view of what are still serious gaps in information and an abundance of topics needing to be researched. Before the history of education can be rewritten, for example, more has to be learned about the development of higher girls' schools, about the forms and intentions of co-education in elementary schools, about the typical content of female education and curricula, and about modalities of women's education since the early twentieth century.[31] A similar situation characterises the history of the academic vocations and their professionalisation, for which so far only a few pieces of the mosaic have been gathered as regards women.[32]

Class and gender: women in bourgeois society

Even when dealing with topics in social history in a narrow sense, with the development of classes or social strata, their movements and conflicts, the formulation of women- or gender-specific questions has just begun. We are relatively well-informed about the conditions of the lower classes in German cities, thanks to extensive research on working-class families and female paid labour. However, far less is known about the relations between the sexes among the peasants, the bourgeoisie or the aristocracy.

Only recently has a tendency appeared in women's history to inquire about women from the bourgeoisie and upper classes, with an emphasis on their life styles, thought patterns and forms of culture. The politically and morally motivated concentration in research on the lower classes is giving way to a noticeable interest in the obviously diversified and changeable structures of female bourgeoise life patterns and 'discourses'. The recent turn to topics and questions on the history of ideas and culture seems to reinforce this tendency.

At the end of the eighteenth century and the beginning of the nineteenth century, moreover, the enthronement of modern gender relations took place within the bourgeoisie. These relations were quickly generalised and continue to have an effect even today. This class encompassed the most radical supporters of these relations as well as the sharpest critics. In addition, the bourgeoisie spawned those social movements and trends that consistently centred on the inherent (and potentially destructive) contradictions of bourgeois gender models (the women's movement, the youth movement, psychoanalysis, and so on). All these reasons justify our looking beyond current fashions and political 'changes' and occupying ourselves with the history of women (and men).[33] In so doing, the bourgeoisie should also be viewed as a social class and be investigated using gender-historical formulations of questions. Until now this has been done mainly with a focus on the educated, responsible academic portion of that class. The various and all-absorbing functions of educated bourgeois women as thinking members of society, careful mothers and good homemakers have been clearly worked out.[34] On the other hand, we still know relatively little about how women's roles were defined in the bourgeois economic milieu. The observable changes in bourgeois gender relations in Germany during the nineteenth century have received only slight attention.

At least as important as the social historical dimensions of these relations are the institutional manifestations in the areas of law, politics, economy, and religion. Only a few studies have examined the ways in which nineteenth-century bourgeois law regulated and controlled the relations between German women and men. This is a central question, equally important for understanding the self-image of bourgeois societies and the scope of allowable action for women.[35] Also the political theory and praxis of gender relations have hardly been researched. Although there are some women's history studies of the philosophical discourse of the late eighteenth century,[36] there are for instance no analyses of the debates on the right to vote in the bourgeois period. An intensification of research interest can be observed only in research on protest and revolution.[37]

There is a notable lack of research on religious history. In what is available, the subject 'women and the church' has been examined mainly from social and organisational perspectives, rather than from perspectives of ideology and norms.[38] The same can be said about the emergence of academic disciplines. If anything, only the exclusion of women from German universities has been researched; the definition of women by the various disciplines, which is at least as 'exclusive' and significant, has not yet been examined. Here education, philosophy, medicine, and history played an especially active role.

Cultural anthropological interests

Taken altogether, the range of subjects in women's history research in West Germany clearly reflects that the whole of history has been addressed. This corresponds to the institutional setting of such research. In contrast to the USA, West German women's historians now work, as a rule, within 'regular' university faculties, and therefore in relatively close relationship to the research foci and approaches in these faculties. In consequence, the topics they treat - women's paid labour, political actions, social movements - find their place in a more or less traditionally conceived catalogue of social history and are merely given a gender-specific twist.

Some studies, however, have clearly taken a minority or outsider's position. These concentrate on the uniqueness of female forms of existence in history, that is to say, they do not rely on examples obtained from men and standards that apply to male or 'general human' experience. Besides the development of modern housework as a historically new 'natural resource'[39] ascribed to all women *qua* gender, these unique forms include such topics as prostitution,[40] and sexuality and corporeality (the latter terms encompassing pregnancy, birth, and motherhood).[41] In France, body-themes have for years provided a strong link between anthropology and historical science, but in West Germany historians of women have only approached such topics very cautiously. This situation reflects, above all else, our general underexposure to entry points and approaches derived from cultural anthropology. Whether this will change in the next few years, through the energetic co-operation of women historians, remains to be seen.[42]

PART TWO

Early modern period

As is the case for the middle ages and modern periods, German historical research on women in the early modern period has only begun.[43] There has been no institutional base in the universities, publication series are lacking, and there has been little financial sponsorship for conferences on these research activities. At the 1983 conference on 'Women in the Germany Economy' in Essen, the early modern period was scarcely represented.[44] In contrast, three interdisciplinary conferences on the theme of 'Women's Images and Women's Roles in the Late Middle Ages and Early Modern Times' (sponsored by the Werner Reimers Foundation in Bad Homburg in 1987-88) devoted themselves overwhelmingly to the early modern period.[45] The particularly neglected theme of women in the countryside was the topic of an exploratory working conference at the University of Kassel in 1989.[46] There the common work of the various scholarly disciplines, historians from various specialties, Germanists (language and literature), art historians, representatives of the disciplines of folklore, theology and sociology, proved to be very successful in expanding knowledge and in framing new questions. At the same time research gaps became apparent, especially in the areas of work,[47] law, religion and church.

Furthermore, this gathering revealed that whole areas of knowledge on the history of women which were well-known up to the eighteenth century have to be made accessible again, in order for us to understand the contemporary positions on the 'woman question' of those times and also to work on the continuum of the 'woman question' in an appropriate way. The publication of the woman theologian Elisabeth Gössmann, 'Archive for Philosophical and Theological Women's History Research',[48] is dedicated to this task.

Interdisciplinarity has already become common for conferences and exhibits organised by women Germanists and art historians. This development is exemplified, for example, in the interdisciplinary symposium 'Marriage, Love and Sexuality in the Sixteenth Century: Discourses and Historical Change' (Berlin, 1989), two conferences on the French Revolution, held in Marburg and Osnabrück (1989), as well as the recent Frankfurt exhibition, 'Slave or Citizeness? The French Revolution and the New Womanliness, 1760-1830'.[49]

Significantly, research on women's history in the early modern period started with a series of studies by American scholars, who succeeded in introducing the impulse of the new women's movement into their research faster than was the case in West Germany. Thematically, they refer to women's work, the position of women during the Reformation and the Reformation's effect on the position of urban women (Merry Wiesner, Susan Karant-Nunn, Miriam Christman). Programmatic and conceptually interdisciplinary proposals for women's history in the early modern period came also from the United States, with the work of Natalie Zemon Davis, referring, in this instance, to French history. Not so in Germany, where for the longest time, approaches to women's history coming from the women's movement clashed with academic disciplines, largely because both 'parties', relying on research results from the 1920s rather than doing new research, insisted on maintaining their respective 'prejudices'.

This situation becomes more comprehensible when one considers that in those years social history made its breakthrough as an historical social science, under the mantle of which women could also be 'taken care of'. As a matter of fact the new 'Expanded Social History' and the new historical subdisciplines (historical demography,[50] family history research,[51] and research on proto-industrialisation[52]) provided valuable databases for research in women's history, but they concentrated mainly on formulating their own questions – in which women were not presented as historical 'subjects' but were incorporated into groups and social strata. However, the research on proto-industrialisation, beginning with the pathbreaking work of Rudolf Braun on the Zurich highlands (1960), demonstrated that the change in gender relations under the influence of industrialisation was a central aspect of societal change, an aspect which was further illuminated and historicised in the wake of the reception of anthropological and ethnological research findings.[53] Thanks to the 'Expanded Social History', which turned its attention to marginal groups and social problems like age, sickness, and poverty, we no longer have to search for the women since in these groups they are in fact over-represented.[54]

This German situation in historical research explains why theoretical discussions over the acceptance of the category 'gender' (*Geschlecht*) for the analysis of historical processes have only recently begun. Definite progress can also be seen in research on women's history:

the original goal of a 'women's history', which corresponded to the phase of looking for women and making them visible, is now being further developed into a gendered history of men and women, or as the case may be, into a history of gender relations in all areas of society, without being restricted to the family and private life.[55]

The initial preoccupation in research on early modern German women's history revolved around the phenomenon of 'witch persecution as the persecution of women', a theme which leading historians of early modern times considered until the end of the 1970s only as a part of cultural history, not of 'real' history. To the local- and regionally-specific studies were soon added an overarching interest in finding out why the highest incidence of witch persecutions took place precisely within the domain of the Holy Roman Empire. This general rather than 'particular' interest contributed to research on witch trials becoming viewed as a legitimate concern for the historical sciences. In the meantime research on this topic has become mainly a 'men's subject', as it deals with territory, collectivities, the creation of modern states and the consolidation of legal and juridical authority, and the development of theological and learned discourses.[56] The original question of why it was women who were accused of using magic has retreated into the background. Only Eva Labouvie has persisted in asking about the gender-specific relations that make women into witches and men into sorcerers.[57]

The second important emphasis in research has been on the Reformation and its aftermath, whereas there are only a few existing studies on Catholic renewal, which examine, for example, the new women's orders and the renewal of monastic life.[58] For a long time the major topic of discussion has been 'the common man' in the Peasant Wars and Reformation Era, but now we are questioning the role of women in the religious reform movement[59] and in the Peasant Wars.[60] Recent studies focus on the role of women as understood by the Reformers, particularly their marriage doctrines, and their own practice of marital life, as well as the establishment of the pastor and his wife as *the* exemplary married couple.[61]

In this case also, co-operation with cognate disciplines has proven to be helpful: the controversy over the marriage of priests,[62] as well as the propaganda on Reform conceptions of marriage in prescriptive literature on married life,[63] as demonstrated in literary histories, show that marriage was not the private concern of a few individuals, but an important new element contributing significantly to the Christian society of the Reformation Era.

Closely connected with this research are studies on marriage, family, home emotions, and sexuality, which are carried out partly by historians in the fields of family research, the history of everyday life, and the history of culture,[64] and partly by researchers in women's history. Even though the questions they formulate are closely related, an important difference remains in the perspective taken, that is, whether one simply describes the development of the specific context, or whether one directly interrogates it with respect to the quality of relations between men and women. The literary historian Ursula Hess has given a new 'reading' to the discourse of the humanists, by holding up to scrutiny the humanist marriage as exemplified by the married couple Conrad Peutinger and Margarete Welser.[65] Similarly the folklorist Silke Göttsch has examined the marriage initiation rite characteristic of villages, the *'Fenstern'* [the practice whereby a young man or suitor sneaks through the window into the bedchamber of an unmarried girl at night: Eds.]. But she looks at this practice from the perspective of the women, not as usual from that of the young men, and has discovered the great extent to which these young women were exposed to male violence.[66]

A third focal point of research is on the education of girls, 'learned women', poetesses and other women writers, women artists and their specialties, which are, of course, presented by women Germanists and women art historians, but also by women educational scholars and women sociologists. This aspect of research has, in general, progressed further than the narrower, old fashioned history, which has either remained anecdotal in the older style of culture history or has retained its preference for biography. As an exception, one should mention Rolf Engelsing, who treats the history of readers as social history, and gives consideration therein to women as readers.[67] In addition there is the general overview by Barbara Becker-Cantarino[68] and the 'German Women's Literature' series edited by Gisela Brinker-Gabler,[69] as well as the encyclopedia of famous women in the arts and sciences.[70] 'Historical' studies still remain very necessary if one does not wish to minimise the historical context, as is the case, for example, with Becker-Cantarino. In contrast, Anne Conrad succeeds in showing, through the example of the Catholic reform of girls' education by the reformed orders of the *Englischen Fräulein* [a Catholic Reform women's religious order: Eds.] and the Ursulines, that our views on the origin of girls' education are prejudiced. It is true that the Protestant Reformers demanded an elementary school education for girls as well as boys, and to a limited extent they were able to push it through. But whereas women remained excluded from universities in German-speaking areas, the tradition of 'higher education' for women continued in the Catholic cloister schools, and in the Reformed orders with an instructional programme modeled on the schools of the Jesuits.[71] Similar to the research on 'Women in the Reformation', major contributions have come from America, particularly

Cornelia Niekus-Moore's work of literature for girls.[72] Niekus-Moore's study has not yet found followers in Germany.

This research situation, briefly described here (for the great number of individual studies I refer readers to the following paragraphs), is determined, last but not least, by the fact that the early modern period is not yet so well established as a field of research as is the middle ages or the modern period. On the one hand, many studies of the middle ages continue into the sixteenth century, and on the other hand, studies of the 'modern' history of women go back into the eighteenth century. I believe, however, that for women's history research, as has become the case for economic and social history research, the fifteenth century should be included in 'the early modern period' and that the era should extend to the 1750s. These three centuries are marked by very pronounced and dynamic social processes. Research in women's history in the early modern period should therefore be oriented toward re-examining the complex and already much-researched process of transformation with women in view and from women's perspective, and toward reconstructing our understanding of that process by considering the changing gender relations.

Work

The history of women's work in early modern times is not treated as an independent subject within historical research in the German-speaking part of the world. In comprehensive social and economic history studies, women's work is generally only mentioned in connection with putting-out systems and work houses, even though examining women's work on the mass scale on which it occurred during the seventeenth and eighteenth centuries is indispensible to an understanding of proto-industrialisation and industrialisation.

As early as 1981, in her sketch 'On the Position of Women in Working Life (15th-18th Centuries)', Heide Wunder made clear the connection between the development of women's work and the overall structural change of society. The extension of grain cultivation (*Vergetreidung*) of the high middle ages, the increase of women's work in agriculture, the formation of 'professions' and the 'masculinisation' of fields of activity or the social rise of certain groups within the population and the emancipation of women from manual work thus appeared to be closely connected and could be analysed - in contrast to isolated studies of the history of women's work that referred exclusively to the 'patriarchy'.[73]

During the last few years the main subject of discussion has been the question of changes within the area of women's work since the late middle ages. As separate studies have appeared, various works have challenged the thesis of the 'displacement' of women's work in the early modern period, while showing changes in the character and meaning of women's activities.[74] Thus Merry Wiesner has demonstrated that in the towns of southern Germany during the sixteenth and early seventeenth centuries an increase in official regulations made the formally 'unqualified' women's work increasingly impossible. At the same time, however, a multitude of female jobs were left unaffected.[75] Similarly, Lyndal Roper has pointed to fundamental changes in the field of prostitution that lost more and more of its public character without, however, disappearing.[76] In spite of all the restrictions imposed on urban crafts, women of the eighteenth century were still able to work, as is shown by, among others, Petra Eggers' study on women bookbinders in Hamburg.[77]

Dorothee Rippmann and Christina Vanja have examined women's work in rural areas. They explain that women were integrated into the expanding cash and market economy in a variety of ways. Even women in villages possessed financial resources, acquired through sales business and wage labour, which contributed significantly to the support of their households. Furthermore, Rippmann has shown for the Basel area that the shift from payment through goods to payment by cash could bring a worsening situation for women.[78]

The subject of industrial mining in the early modern period, hitherto considered as a male domain, is treated as an area of significance for women's work in the comprehensive study done by Christina Vanja and also in a single study on the Erz Mountains by Susan Karant-Nunn. These studies clearly reveal not only that women performed a multitude of tasks in mining itself, but also that women's supportive and supplementary labour as part of the division of labour between men and women was what made the mining business possible. At the same time mining illustrates in an exemplary way the significance of professionalisation for the division of labour between men and women in the early modern period.[79]

Similarly, for the longest time, women in public service remained invisible in the history of administration. Recently, however, different individual studies have demonstrated that the expanding administration of the early modern period depended to a large extent on (married) women's work. It was very common, for example, for women to administer hospitals, refuges for the poor and the sick, the insane, and orphans.[80] At the same time, midwives played an important role, throughout the entire early modern period, although their work became increasingly restricted through midwives' decrees and intensified control by physicians.[81]

In the areas of distribution and manufacturing systems, women's work has often been mentioned but rarely treated systematically. An exception is the dissertation of Rita Bake, which uncovers the miserable living conditions of women workers in Hamburg's manufacturies during the eighteenth century.[82]

Other areas of women's work in the early modern period should be referred to briefly. The social scientist Johanna-Luise Brochmann has specifically studied the role of the wet-nurse, highlighting the wet nurse's ambivalent role as a desired yet feared helper (because a 'believer in superstitions').[83] The sociologist Irine Hardach-Pinke is currently preparing a study on governesses as important representatives of intellectual women in the eighteenth century.[84]

A special category is formed by studies on the life and works of artistic and literary women, studies which were mainly written by representatives of the corresponding disciplines. Some years ago Gisela Brinker-Gabler published an anthology on poetesses from the sixteenth century to the present.[85] Other anthologies on the history of women's literature followed, which filled a gap in our knowledge, rediscovering numerous women writers and allowing us to perceive literary production from a new perspective.[86] Correspondingly Eva Walter made the work situation of women writers around 1800 the subject of a monograph.[87]

The memoirs of an eighteenth-century actress, Karoline Schulze-Kummerfeld, have been published by Inge Buck. They enable us to gain deep insight into the harsh everyday working life, and the aspirations of members of this newly-established profession for women.[88]

The position of women composers has scarcely been explored. An initial overview of 'five hundred years of women composers' was put together by the music journalist Eval Weisweiler.[89] A more negative approach to this subject was taken in some individual studies that revealed the exclusion of women from the production of music, exemplified through Bach and Mozart.[90] Still unsolved is the reason for the discrimination against women in the field of art.

Far better was the situation for women in the discipline of painting, especially in the seventeenth and eighteenth centuries, when many women were employed in handicraft workshops and also in officially-recognized artistic production for the court. Various exhibiton catalogues deal with individual biographies and the working conditions of women painters. A more general treatment emphasising sociohistorical questions will soon be published by the art historian Berthold Hinz.[91]

The first general overview of the situation of women's work in the eighteenth century will soon be published by Christina Vanja. She points to the divergent developments in women's work, caught between expansion and marginalisation, corporate control and freedom from restriction, as the necessary prelude to the general disqualification of women's work in bourgeois industrial society.[92]

Poverty, age, disease, medicine

Even though women were particularly subject to poverty, as unmarried women, widows, and as usually low-paid wage workers, for example servants, the subject of women's poverty in the early modern period has rarely been treated explicitly. Poor women are mentioned in the context of the representation of beggars and brigands, as well as in studies on hospitals, prisons, work houses, and welfare for the sick and old, but the history of their lives is never comprehensively examined from the perspective of what was specific to women.

The historian Rita Bake deals with poor urban women in wage-dependent positions in a case study based on the city of Hamburg. While orienting itself insufficiently within the societal context of the early modern period, this study nevertheless shows clearly that women in the new pre-industrial or early industrial areas of work and life either became the victims of employment in sectors of labour that were unqualified, badly paid, and marginalised, or also the victims of the new urban living conditions that were cut off from agricultural resources.[93]

Helfried Valentinisch has studied the similarly miserable fate of poor women in the countryside of Styria (southern Austria), who were leading a vagrant life of intermittent wage labour, beggary, and prostitution. Among other things, he has traced the life of a 'loose' woman in the eighteenth century. This woman, who came from a small village, was not able to settle down in her native village nor in a town and thus fell more and more into the clutches of the authorities, who often imprisoned her.[94]

As for institutions specially created for poor women, there are studies of the urban maternity hospitals of the eighteenth century. Typical of these institutions was their double character as institutions of welfare and social discipline for single mothers.[95]

Specific studies of the situation of old women in the early modern period would be valuable. So far this has only been dealt with in the more general context of inheritance laws and the position of widows.[96]

A pioneering study entitled 'Disease: Woman' by Esther Fischer-Homberger has become one of the standard works, without, however, exhausting the subject entirely, particularly in regard to the early modern period.[97] 'History under the Skin' is the title of Barbara Duden's study of an Eisenach doctor and his women patients around 1730. She demonstrates in a striking way the changing attitude towards the female body and corporeality during the eighteenth century by applying, in content and method, the techniques of historical anthropology.[98] Edith Stolzenberg has investigated 'Female Weakness - Male Strength' as

'Cultural Images of Women in Medical and Anatomical Dissertations at the Turn of the Eighteenth Century'.[99]

City and Country

Following the broad trends in historical research, women's history research has also focused on the 'big cities'. Altogether, however, the number of publications has been restricted to a few subjects. Special attention has been paid to 'employed' women, particularly craftswomen and tradeswomen, whose positions are evaluated with respect to changes since the middle ages. Despite various restrictions, authors find a general deterioration, particularly in regard to the possibilities of independent business initiatives for women.[100]

Closely connected to the question of women's economic situation are the investigations of the urban household. Margarethe Freudenthal's classic sociological study of bourgeois and proletarian households in the eighteenth and nineteenth century (published in 1934) contains preliminary analyses and interesting references to documents. Freudenthal clearly shows the extensive scope of housewives' duties, but also demonstrates the liberation from manual labour in eighteenth-century bourgeois circles.[101]

A unique source of information on the life course of an urban bourgeois clergyman's wife in the eighteenth century, the memoirs of Margarete Milow of Hamburg, have recently been republished by Rita Bake and Birgit Kiupel. These memoirs belong to a genre of family-history works written by women, which are not yet sufficiently well-known (or made known).[102]

A research project, financed through the *Deutsche Forschungsgemeinschaft* [German Research Council] and supervised by Heide Wunder, analyses the situation of women of the new academic bourgeoisie, especially in the city of Leipzig. This is accomplished through the examination of funeral sermons to trace and analyse life courses (see the paragraph on 'marriage' in this essay).

On the situation of female urban domestic servants, see above all the numerous studies written by Rudolph Engelsing. Maids and other female domestic servants lived and worked in large numbers in capital cities, where they outnumbered their male co-workers without being able to attain a comparable social position.[103] Scarcely examined is the situation of women in small towns, which probably varies in a number of aspects from that in large towns, such as Nuremburg, Augsburg, Frankfurt or Cologne. One must also consider the importance of agricultural work done by women. Collections of material in this area have mainly been done in folklore, particularly the works of Karl-Sigismund Kramer, and, among historians, Gerd Wunder.[104]

Comparing women in the countryside to urban women, Edith Ennen assesses the situation of the former more negatively because the latter had no rights and were subject to the authority of the husband as master.[105] In contrast, Christina Vanja points out the active role women played in village society, influencing events in the village, for example, through 'women's courts'.[106] Heide Wunder demonstrates, through the example of the rural society of Prussian Lithuania in the sixteenth and seventeenth centuries, that investigations of the position and role of women must take into account the complexity of the entire society. Her evidence suggests that widespread notions, which hold that women were, in general, oppressed and exploited beings, cannot be sustained any longer.[107] Michael Mitterauer, Reinder Beck, and the folklorist Silke Göttsch deal with questions of marriage proposals, sexuality, and illegitimacy. Göttsch singles out in particular the violent assaults on farmhand women by farm labourers and stable boys.[108]

In December, 1989, a conference held by the interdisciplinary study group 'Women's Research' at the comprehensive high school and University of Kassel, under the direction Heide Wunder and Christina Vanja, focused attention for the first time in a thorough-going way on 'Women in Rural Societies during the Early Modern Period' (see above in this essay). Under the major themes of 'work, public office, profession' and 'order, chaos, change', not only peasant women in villages were the subject of discussion but also women in public office (*Amtsfrauen*), governesses, women in pietism, and vagrant beggars living in the countryside. It became apparent that the countryside was not merely a place of life and work for peasant women. Moreover, rural women played a part in societal change.

Women's images and women's education: the Enlightenment and the French Revolution

The decisive impulse for the break with a tradition dominant for a long time of denouncing the negative images of women in the works of medieval and early modern philosophers and theologians came from the ground-breaking work of Elisabeth Gössmann. Since 1984 Gössmann has published the 'Archive for Women's History Research in Philosophical and Theological History' with pamphlets on the *querelle des femmes*. The rediscovery of texts written by men and women who presented themselves as 'friends of women' and 'enemies of women' reflect the controversies – lasting well into the eighteenth century – over the equal standing, the complementarity, the inequality, and the hierarchy of the sexes. Women intervened in these, arguing eloquently for their 'humanity'.[109]

Especially the atmosphere of the Enlightenment, with its pedagogical impetus, permitted 'womanly learnedness' towards the end of the early modern period. Learned women in the eighteenth century, who owed their education primarily to the teaching they received in the bourgeois academic households of their fathers and husbands, formed a unique 'cultural type', which was soon offset, however, by the new type created by the 'Sensibility' movement.[110] Recent new work on a series of outstanding women of both types have revealed the very often difficult, even tragic, situation of their lives, as existing living conditions did not provide the opportunities for such women to develop according to their ideals. Women were not able to make a profession out of their education.[111]

On the occasion of the 1989 Bicentennial of the French Revolution, questions were also posed regarding the situation of women in the German-speaking part of the world at that time. To what extent did they notice the events in France, criticise their own 'ancien regime', or become politically active? How did their life and work situation present itself? Did social change from a women's perspective mean 'emancipation' for them, too?

'The French Revolution and the New Womanliness, 1760-1830' was the theme of a comprehensive exhibition in the Historical Museum of Frankfurt that, under the direction of Viktoria Schmidt-Linsenhoff, combined a rich collection of documents and ideas.[112] At the same time an interdisciplinary conference on 'Freedom – Equality – Sisterhood', held at the University of Marburg, focused predominantly on German situations and circumstances during the era of the French Revolution.[113] Both these events approached this many-sided subject from a critical angle. Whether women became 'Slaves or Citizenessess' in consequence of the revolutionary events, must certainly be discussed further in the years to come.

NOTES

Ute Frevert is responsible for Part One of this essay, and Heide Wunder and Christina Vanja for Part Two. The text has been translated from the German by Ria Bleumer and Christine Muelsch, with Ruth Roach Pierson and Karen Offen. Endnotes and references translated and edited by Christine Muelsch, with Karen Offen and Ruth Roach Pierson. Some publishing information has been added by the editors. The German term *'Geschlecht'*, which carries the double meaning of 'sex' and 'gender', has here been translated as 'gender'.

1. This overview deals exclusively with developments in West Germany, or as the case may be, with works written on the history of German women. The fact that so many of the early works were written by women historians in Great Britain and North America indicates - yet again - the leading position of Anglo-American women's history and its significant influence on West German research.

2. Since 1979 the Schwann publishing house has issued a series 'Frauen in der Geschichte [Women in History]', edited by the Bonn historian Annette Kuhn. As of 1987 this series included eight volumes and half a dozen thematically-oriented publications. In 1988 this series continued as a publication of Centarus, 'Frauen in der Geschichte und Gesellschaft [Women in History and Society]', under the editorship of Annette Kuhn and Valentine Roth. Within two years Centarus has issued more than twelve volumes in this series.

Interest in regional or local women's history has increased significantly during the last few years, as is evidenced by the following monographs and anthologies: Christiane Eifert and Susanne Rouette (eds.), *Unter allen Umständen. Frauengeschichte(n) in Berlin* [Under all Circumstances: Women's History(ies) in Berlin] (Berlin: Rotation, 1986); Ilse Brehmer and Juliane Jacobi-Dittrich (eds.), *Frauenalltag in Bielefeld* [Women's Everyday Life in Bielefeld] (Bielefeld, 1986); Birgit Panke-Kochinke, *"Dienen lerne beizeiten das Weib..." Frauengeschichten aus Osnabrück* ['Learn How to Serve Betimes, O Woman...': Womanstories from Osnabrück] (Pfaffenweiler: Centarus, 1990); Karen Hagemann and Jan Kolossa, *"Gleiche Rechte - Gleiche Pflichten?" Frauenkampf für die "staatsbürgerliche" Gleichstellung. Ein Bilder-Lese-Buch zu Frauenalltag und Frauenbewegung in Hamburg* [Equal Rights - Equal Duties: Women Campaign for Equal Citizenship. A Picture-Reading Book On Women's Everyday Life and the Women's Movement in Hamburg] (Hamburg: Verlag für das Studium der Arbeiterbewegung, 1990).

The following collections provide more general information: Karin Hausen (ed.), *Frauen suchen ihre Geschichte. Historische Studien zum 19. und 20. Jahrhundert* [Women Seek Their History: Historical Studies on the 19th and 20th Centuries] (Munich: Beck, 1983); John C. Fout (ed.), *German Women in the Nineteenth Century: A Social History* (New York: Holmes & Meier, 1983); Ruth-Ellen B. Joeres and Mary Jo Maynes (eds.), *German Women in the Eighteenth and Nineteenth Centuries: A Social and Literary History* (Bloomington: Indiana University Press, 1986). A social history-oriented overview of German women's history in the nineteenth and twentieth centuries is Ute Frevert, *Frauen-Geschichte. Zwischen Bürgerlicher Verbesserung und Neuer Weiblichkeit* (Frankfurt/Main: Suhrkamp, 1986; in English translation as *Women in German History: From Bourgeois Emancipation to Sexual Liberation* (Oxford: Berg, 1989).

3. To date the following meetings of women historians have taken place (with a trend toward increasing numbers): 1977 in Gaiganz (see Ute Frevert, 'German Women Historians' Meeting, 26-27 March 1977', *History Workshop*, 4 (1977), pp. 235-6); and 1978 in Berlin on the theme 'Women in the Weimar Republic and under National Socialism'; a Women's Studies Workshop, 18-20 January 1980 in Bremen on the theme 'Muttersein und Mutterideologie in der bürgerlichen Gesellschaft [Motherhood and Motherhood Ideology in Bourgeois Society]' (mimeographed proceedings); 1981 in Bielefeld (*Frauengeschichte. Dokumentation* [Women's History: Proceedings], Munich, 1981); 1983 in Berlin (*Dokumentation 4. Historikerinnentreffen*, Berlin, 1983); 1984 in Vienna (*Die*

ungeschriebene Geschichte [The Unwritten History]. Dokumentation, Vienna, nd.); 1985 in Bonn (Jutta Dalhoff et al. [eds.], *Frauenmacht in der Geschichte. Beiträge des Historikerinnentreffens 1985 zur Frauengeschichtsforschung* [Women's Power in History: Contributions of the Meeting of Women Historians in 1985 to Women's History Research], Düsseldorf, 1986); 1986 in Amsterdam.

4. It was not until recently that the early history of the Federal Republic was treated from a women's history perspective: See the work of Sibylle Meyer and Eva Schulze, *Wie wir das alles geschafft haben. Alleinstehende Frauen berichten über ihr Leben nach 1945* [How We Managed: Single Women Report on their Lives After 1945] (Munich: Beck, 1984); Meyer and Schulze, *Von Liebe sprach damals keiner. Familienalltag in der Nachkriegszeit* [No One Spoke of Love Then: Everyday Family Life in the Post War Era] (Munich: Beck, 1985); the documentary edition by Doris Schubert, *Frauen in der deutschen Nachkriegszeit* [Women in Post-War Germany], vol. 1 - *Frauenarbeit 1945-1949. Quellen und Materialien* [Women's Work 1945-49: Sources and Documentation] (Düsseldorf: Schwann, 1984); Klaus-Jörg Ruhl (ed.), *Unsere verlorenen Jahre. Frauenalltag in Kriegs- und Nachkriegszeit 1939-1949* [Our Lost Years: Women's Everyday Life in the War and Post-War Eras] (Darmstadt: Luchterhand, 1985); Ruhl (ed.), *Frauen in der Nachkriegszeit 1945-1963* [Women in the Post-War Period 1945-1963] (Munich: Deutscher Taschenbuch Verlag, 1988); Annette Kuhn (ed.), *Frauen in der deutschen Nachkriegszeit, vol. 2 - Frauenpolitik 1945-1949. Quellen und Materialen* (Düsseldorf: Schwann, 1986), as well as the anthology by Anna E. Freier and Annette Kuhn (ed.), *Frauen in der Geschichte V.: 'Das Schicksal Deutschlands liegt in der Hand seiner Frauen'. Frauen in der deutschen Nachkriegsgeschichte* ['Germany's Destiny Lies in the Hands of its Women': Women in the History of Post-War Germany] (Düsseldorf: Schwann, 1984). See also Renate Wiggershaus, *Geschichte der Frauen und der Frauenbewegung in der Bundesrepublik Deutschland und in der Deutschen Demokratischen Republik nach 1945* [History of Women and the Women's Movement in the Federal Republic of Germany and the German Democratic Republic After 1945] (Wuppertal: Hammer, 1979); Nori Möding, 'Die Stunde der Frauen? Frauen und Frauenorganisationen des bürgerlichen Lagers [A Historic Moment for Women? Women and Women's Organisations of the Bourgeois Camp]', in Martin Broszat et al. (eds.), *Von Stalingrad zur Währungsreform. Zur Sozialgeschichte des Umbruchs in Deutschland* [From Stalingrad to Currency Reform: On the Social History of the Radical Change in Germany] (Munich: Oldenbourg, 1988, pp. 619-47.

5. A systematic study of women's resistance during National Socialism is still needed. So far existing publications deal predominantly with the subject from a biographical perspective: Gerda Szepansky, *Frauen leisten Widerstand: 1933- 1945* [Women Resist, 1933-1945] (Frankfurt/Main: Fischer, 1983); Hanna Elling, *Frauen im deutschen Widerstand 1933-45* [Women in the German Resistance] (Frankfurt/Main: Roderberg, 2nd ed., 1981); Sigrid Jacobeit and Liselotte Thoms-Heinrich, *Kreuzweg Ravensbrück. Lebensbilder antifaschistischer Widerstandskämpferinnen* [Martyrdom Ravensbruck: Portraits of Antifascist Women Resisters] (Leipzig: Verlag für die Frau, 1987); Ingrid Strobl, *'Sag nie, du gehst den letzten Weg'. Frauen im bewaffneten Widerstand gegen Faschismus und deutsche Besetzung* [Never Say You Take the Final Step: Women in the Armed Resistance against Fascism and German Occupation] (Frankfurt/Main: Fischer, 1989). Various

areas of female resistance are documented in the informative source collection of Annette Kuhn and Valentine Rothe (eds.), *Frauen im deutschen Faschismus* [Women under German Fascism], 2 vols. (Düsseldorf: Schwann, 1982).

6. See also the two following collections: Frauengruppe Faschismusforschung, *Mutterkreuz und Arbeitsbuch. Zur Geschichte der Frauen in der Weimarer Republik und im Nationalsozialismus* [Mothers' Crosses and Workers' Passbooks: Contributions to the History of Women in the Weimar Republic and under National Socialism] (Frankfurt/Main: Fischer, 1981), and Renate Bridenthal et al. (eds.), *When Biology Became Destiny: Women in Weimar and Nazi Germany* (New York: Monthly Review, 1984). Biographical examples of this diversity can be found in Irmgard Weyrather (ed.), *'Ich bin noch aus dem vorigen Jahrhundert'. Frauenleben zwischen Kaiserreich u. Wirtschaftswunder* ['I'm Still From the Last Century': Women's Lives between the Wilhelminian Empire and the German Economic Miracle] (Frankfurt: Fischer, 1985); Charles Schüddekopf (ed.), *Der alltägliche Faschismus. Frauen im Dritten Reich* ['Ordinary' Fascism: Women in the Third Reich] (Berlin: Dietz, 1982), as well as Angelika Ebbinghaus, *Opfer und Täterinnen. Frauenbiographien des Nationalsozialismus* [Victims and Victimisers: Women's Biographies under National Socialism] (Nördlingen: Delphi Politik, 1987).

7. Very little monographic work has yet been done by German historians of women on the experience of German Jewish women under the nationalist socialist regime. Some material can be found in Gudrun Schwarz, *Nationalsozialistische Lager* (Frankfurt am Main: Campus Verlag, 1990); in the special issue of *Dachauer Hefte*, no. 3 (1987) on 'Frauen: Verfolgung und Widerstand'; and in the chapter entitled 'Geburtenkrieg im Weltkrieg [A Birth War during the World War]' in Gisela Bock, *Zwangssterilisation im Nationalsozialismus. Studien zur Rassenpolitik und Frauenpolitik* [Compulsory Sterilisation under National Socialism: Studies in Racism and Sexism] (Opladen: Westdeutscher Verlag, 1986). See also Vera Laska (ed.), *Women in the Resistance and in the Holocaust: The Voices of Eyewitnesses*, Contributions in Women's Studies, no. 37 (Westport, Connecticut/London, England: Greenwood Press, 1983).

8. Sebastian Haffner, *Anmerkungen zu Hitler* [Notes on Hitler] (Munich: Kindler, 1978), p. 48. Examples of a 'humiliation' perspective include: Rita Thalmann, *Frausein im Dritten Reich* [Being a Woman in the Third Reich] (Frankfurt/Main: Ullstein, 1984; Renate Wiggershaus, *Frauen unterm Nationalsozialismus* [Women Under National Socialism] (Wuppertal: Hammer, 1984); Margret Lück, *Die Frau im Männerstaat* [Women in a Male State] (Frankfurt/Main: Lang, 1979); more nuanced interpretations can be found in Dorothee Klinksiek, *Die Frau im NS-Staat* (Stuttgart: Deutsche Verlags Anhalt, 1982). This author does not successfully demonstrate the influence of NS women's politics, but limits herself to describing the outward expressions of these policies. See also the very broadly conceptualised new study by Claudia Koonz, *Mothers in the Fatherland: Women, the Family, and Nazi Politics* (New York: St. Martin's, 1987), as well as Gisela Bock's critique, 'Die Frauen und der Nationalsozialismus. Bemerkungen zu einem Buch von Claudia Koonz [Women and National Socialism: Reflections on a Book by Claudia Koonz]', *Geschichte und Gesellschaft*, 15 (1989), pp. 563-79.

314   *Ute Frevert, Heide Wunder and Christina Vanja*

9. See the groundbreaking essay by Renate Bridenthal and Claudia Koonz, 'Beyond Kinder, Küche, Kirche: Weimar Women in Politics and Work', in Bridenthal et al. (eds.), *Biology*, pp. 33-65. See also the detailed work by Karen Hagemann, *Frauenalltag und Männerpolitik. Alltagsleben und gesellschaftliches Handeln von Arbeiterfrauen in der Weimarer Republik. Untersucht am Beispiel des sozialdemokratischen Milieus in Hamburg* [Women's Daily Life and Men's Politics: The Everyday Life and Social Action of Working-Class Women in the Weimer Republic, based on the Example of the Social Democratic Milieu in Hamburg] (Bonn: Dietz, 1990), as well as Karin Hausen, 'Unemployment also Strikes Women: The New and the Old Woman on the Dark Side of the Golden Twenties in Germany', in Peter Stachura (ed.), *Unemployment and the Great Depression in Weimar Germany* (Basingstoke: Macmillan, 1986), pp. 78-120; and Susanne Rouette, 'Die Erwerbslosenfürsorge für Frauen in Berlin nach 1918 [Unemployment Benefits for Women in Berlin after 1918]', *Internationale Wissenschaftliche Korrespondenz*, 21 (1985), pp. 295-307.

10. On the sex reform movement, see Atina Grossmann, '"Satisfaction is Domestic Happiness": Mass Working-Class Sex Reform Organizations in the Weimar Republic', in M. N. Dobkowski and I. Wallimann (eds.), *Towards the Holocaust* (Westport, Conn.: Greenwood, 1983), pp. 265-93; and Grossmann, 'The New Woman and the Rationalization of Sexuality in Weimar Republic', in Ann Snitow et al. (eds.), *Powers of Desire: The Politics of Sexuality* (New York: Monthly Review, 1983), pp. 153-71. See also Kristine von Soden, *Die Sexualberatungsstellen der Weimarer Republik, 1919-1933* [The Sex Information Centres in the Weimar Republic] (Berlin: Hentrich, 1988). On the feminisation of white collar professions, see Ute Frevert, 'Vom Klavier zur Schreibmaschine. Weiblicher Arbeitsmarkt und Rollenzuweisungen am Beispiel der weiblichen Angestellten in der Weimarer Republik [From the Piano to the Typewriter: Female Job Market and Role Assignments: A Study based on Salaried Women Employees in the Weimar Republic]', in Annette Kuhn and Gerhard Schneider (eds.), *Frauen in der Geschichte I* (Düsseldorf: Schwann, 1979), pp. 83-112; and Frevert, 'Traditionale Weiblichkeit und moderne Interessenorganisation: Frauen im Angestelltenberuf 1918-1933 [Traditional Womanhood and Modern Interest Groups; Women in Salaried Occupations], *Geschichte und Gesellschaft*, 7 (1981), pp. 507-33.

11. This politicisation is reflected last but not least on the organisational level; see Jill Stephenson, *The Nazi Organisation of Women* (London: Croom Helm, 1981); see Dagmar Reese's case study of the mobilisation of girls supported by local historical data, Dagmar Reese, *Straff, aber nicht stramm - herb, aber nicht derb. Zur Vergesellschaftung von Mädchen durch den Bund Deutscher Mädel im sozialkulturellen Vergleich zweier Milieus* ['Firm but not Sturdy; Severe but not Rough': The Nationalisation of Young Women in the German Girls' League] (Weinheim: Beltz, 1989); also Nori Möring, '"Ich muss irgendwo engagiert sein, fragen Sie mich bloss nicht, warum". Uberlegungen zu Sozialisationserfahrungen von Frauen in NS-Organisationen ["I Have to be Involved Someplace; Don't Ask Me Why"? Reflections on the Socialisation Experiences of Women in Nazi Organisations]', in Lutz Niethammer et al. (eds.), *'Wir kriegen jetzt andere Zeiten'. Auf der Suche nach der Erfahrung des Volkes in nachfaschistischen Ländern* (Berlin: Dietz, 1985), pp. 256-304.

12. On this subject see Georg Tidl, *Die Frau im Nationalsozialismus* [Women in National Socialism] (Vienna: Europaverlag, 1984), pp. 115ff. This study is fairly unsystematic and restrained in its selection of materials; it is helpful though as an introduction to the activities of the *Deutsche Frauenwerk*. See also Jill Stephenson, 'Propaganda, Autarky and the German Housewife', in David Welch (ed.), *Nazi Propaganda: The Power and the Limitation* (London: Croom Helm, 1983), pp. 117-42. For an out-of-the-house dimension of 'housework', see Carola Sachse, 'Hausarbeit im Betrieb. Betriebliche Sozialarbeit unter dem Nationalsozialismus [Housework in Companies: Organisational Social Work under National Socialism]', in Carola Sachse et al. (eds.), *Angst, Belohnung, Zucht und Ordnung. Herrschaftsmechanismen im Nationalsozialismus* (Opladen: Westdeutscher Verlag, 1982), pp. 209-74. Also see Sachse, *Siemens, der Nationalsozialismus und die moderne Familie. Eine Untersuchung zur sozialen Rationalisierung in Deutschland im 20. Jahrhundert* [Siemens, National Socialism and the Modern Family: An Examination of Social Rationalisation in Germany in the 20th Century] (Hamburg: forthcoming, 1990).

13. See Dörte Winkler, *Frauenarbeit im 'Dritten Reich'* [Women's Work in the 'Third Reich'] (Hamburg: Hoffmann u. Campe, 1977), a useful book in spite of its misleading title and some misplaced formulations which suggest that 'women's work' was only performed in areas of employment. This critique also applies to Stephan Bajohr, *Die Hälfte der Fabrik, Geschichte der Frauenarbeit in Deutschland 1914 bis 1945* [Half of the Factory: A History of Women's Work in Germany 1914 to 1945] (Marburg: Verlag Arbeiterbewegung, 1979; 2nd ed., 1984).

14. Descriptive sketches like those of Christina Burghardt, *Die deutsche Frau. Küchenmagd - Zuchtsau - Leibeigene im III. Reich* [The German Woman: Kitchenmaid, Breeding Sow, Bondwoman in the Third Reich] (Münster: Verlag Frauenpolitik, 1978) do not provide an approach for this. I prefer the comprehensive study of Christine Wittrock, *Weiblichkeitsmythen. Das Frauenbild im Faschismus und seine Vorläufer in der Frauenbewegung der 20er Jahre* [Myths of Femininity: Images of Women under Fascism and their Predecessors in the Women's Movement of the Twenties] (Frankfurt/Main: Sendler, 1983; 2nd ed., 1985), which is, because of its philological character, limited to an analysis of programmatic texts.

15. Bock, *Zwangssterilisation im Nationalsozialismus* [Compulsory Sterilisation under National Socialism]; also Gisela Bock, 'Racism and Sexism in Nazi Germany: Motherhood, Compulsory Sterilization and the State', *Signs: Journal of Women in Culture and Society*, 8 (1983), pp. 400-21.

16. Annemarie Tröger, 'Die Dolchstosslegende der Linken: "Frauen haben Hitler an die Macht gebracht" [The Left's "Stab-in-the-Back" Legend: "Women Brought Hitler to Power"]', in Gruppe Berliner Dozentinnen (eds.), *Frauen und Wissenschaft: Beiträge zur Berliner Sommeruniversität für Frauen, Berlin 1976* (Berlin: Courage-Verlag, 1977), pp. 324-55; Helen L. Boak, 'Women in Weimar Germany: the "Frauenfrage" and the Female Vote', in Richard Bessel and E. J. Feuchwanger (eds.), *Social Change and Political Development in Weimar Germany* (London: Croom-Helm, 1981), pp. 155-73.

17. Mary Nolan, 'Proletarischer Anti-Feminismus. Dargestellt am Beispiel der SPD-Ortsgruppe Düsseldorf, 1890-1914 [Proletarian Anti-Feminism: The Case of the Düsseldorf SPD Local', in *Frauen und Wissenschaft*, pp. 356-77; Silvia Kontos, *Die Partei kämpft wie ein Mann. Frauenpolitik der KPD in der Weimarer*

Republik [The Party Fights Like a Man: Women's Politics in the German Communist Party during the Weimar Republic] (Basel: Stroemfeld, 1979); Werner Thönnessen, *Frauenemanzipation. Politik und Literatur der deutschen Sozialdemokratie zur Frauenbewegung 1863-1933* [The Emancipation of Women: The Rise and Decline of the Women's Movement in German Social Democracy 1863-1933] (Frankfurt/Main: Europaische Verlagsanstalt, 1969; 2nd ed., 1976); Richard J. Evans, *Sozialdemokratie und Frauenemanzipation im deutschen Kaiserreich* [Social Democracy and Women's Emancipation under the German Empire] (Berlin: Dietz, 1979); Gisela Losseff-Tillmanns, *Frauenemanzipation und Gewerkschaften* [Women's Emancipation and Unions] (Wuppertal: Hammer, 1978). On earlier socialist emancipationist theories, see Elke Kleinau, *Die freie Frau. Sozial Utopien des frühen 19. Jh.* [The Free Woman: Social Utopias of the Early 19th Century] (Düsseldorf: Schwann, 1987).

18. Margrit Twellmann, *Die deutsche Frauenbewegung. Ihre Anfänge u. erste Entwicklung 1843-1889* [The German Women's Movement: Its Beginnings and Early Development] (Meisenheim: A. Hain, 1972); Julia Meissner, *'Mehr Stolz, Ihr Frauen!' Hedwig Dohm - Eine Biographie* [More Pride, You Women!: A Biography of Hedwig Dohm] (Düsseldorf: Patmos, 1987); Richard J. Evans, *The Feminist Movement in Germany 1893-1933* (London: Sage, 1976); Barbara Greven-Aschoff, *Die bürgerliche Frauenbewegung in Deutschland 1894-1933* [The Bourgeois Women's Movement in Germany] (Göttingen: Vandenhoeck & Ruprecht, 1981); Heinz Niggemann, *Emanzipation zwischen Sozialismus und Feminismus. Die sozialdemokratische Frauenbewegung im Kaiserreich* [Emancipation between Socialism and Feminism: The Social Democratic Women's Movement under the German Empire] (Wuppertal: Hammer, 1981); Sabine Richebächer, *Uns fehlt nur eine Kleinigkeit. Deutsche proletarische Frauenbewegung 1890-1914* [We Want for Little: The German Proletarian Women's Movement 1890-1914] (Frankfurt/Main: Fischer, 1982); Florence Hervé (ed.), *Geschichte der deutschen Frauenbewegung* [A History of the German Women's Movement] (Cologne: Pahl-Rugenstein, 1983); Jean Quataert, *Reluctant Feminists in German Social Democracy, 1885-1917* (Princeton: Princeton University Press, 1979); Renate Pore, *A Conflict of Interest: Women in German Social Democracy, 1919-1933* (Westport, Conn.: Greenwood, 1981); Christl Wickert, *Unsere Erwählten. Sozialdemokratische Frauen im Deutschen Reichstag und im Preussischen Landtag 1919 bis 1933* [Our Chosen Ones: Social Democratic Women in the German Reichstag and the Prussian Landtag], 2 vols. (Göttingen: Sovec, 1986). For a successful interlinking of sociohistorical and organisational dimensions, see Herrad U. Bussemer, *Frauenemanzipation und Bildungsbürgertum. Sozialgeschichte der Frauenbewegung in der Reichsgründungszeit* [Women's Emancipation and Educated Bourgeoisie: A Social History of the Women's Movement during the Era of the Founding of the Empire] (Weinheim: Beltz, 1985).

In recent years there have been an increasing number of studies, mainly by women sociologists and political scientists, which deal with politically strategic debates within the women's movement and with their efforts to professionalise women's working skills. See Bärbel Clemens, *'Menschenrechte haben kein Geschlecht!' Zum Politikverständnis der bürgerlichen Frauenbewegung* ['Human Rights Have No Sex': Toward a Political Understanding of the Bourgeois Women's Movement] (Pfaffenweiler: Centarus, 1988); Theresa Wobbe, *Gleichheit und Differenz. Politische Strategien von Frauenrechtlerinnen um die Jahrhundertwende* [Equality and Difference: Political Strategies of Equal Rights Advocates at the Turn of the Century] (Frankfurt/Main: Campus Verlag, 1989); Hiltraud Schmidt-Waldherr, *Emanzipation durch Professionalisierung? Politische Strategien und Konflikte innerhalb der bürgerlichen Frauenbewegung während der Weimarer Republik und die Reaktion des bürgerlichen Antifeminismus und des Nationalsozialismus* [Emancipation Through Professionalisation?: Political Strategies and Conflicts within the Bourgeois Women's Movement during the Weimer Republic and the Reaction of Bourgeois Antifeminism and National Socialism] (Frankfurt/Main: Materialus, 1987); Elisabeth Meyer-Renschhausen, *Weibliche Kultur und soziale Arbeit. Die Geschichte der Frauenbewegung am Beispiel Bremens 1810-1927* [Women's Culture and Social Work: The History of the Women's Movement through the Example of Bremen] (Cologne: Bohlau, 1989); Dietlinde Peters, *Mütterlichkeit im Kaiserreich. Die bürgerliche Frauenbewegung und der soziale Beruf der Frau* [Motherliness under the Empire: The Bourgeois Women's Movement and Women's Social Professions] (Bielefeld: Kleine Verlag, 1984).

19. Angelika Willms, *Die Entwicklung der Frauenwerbstätigkeit im Deutschen Reich. Eine historischsoziologische Studie* [The Development of Gainful Employment for Women: A Historical-sociological Study] (Nürnberg: Institut für Arbeitsmarkt- und Berufsforschung, 1980); also Willms, 'Modernisierung durch Frauenarbeit? Zum Zusammenhang von wirtschaftlichem Strukturwandel und weiblicher Arbeitsmarktlage in Deutschland, 1882-1939 [Modernisation through Women's Employment?: On the Connection between Structural Economic Change and Women's Position in the Labour Market in Germany]', in Toni Pierenkemper and Richard Tilly (eds.), *Historische Arbeitsmarktforschung* (Göttingen: Vandenhoeck & Ruprecht, 1982), pp. 37-71; Walter Müller et al., *Strukturwandel der Frauenarbeit 1880-1980* [Structural Changes in Women's Work] (Frankfurt: Campus, 1983); Reinhard Stockmann, 'Gewerbliche Frauenarbeit in Deutschland 1875-1980. Zur Entwicklung der Beschäftigtenstruktur [Commercial Women's Work in Germany: The Development of the Employment Structure]', *Geschichte und Gesellschaft*, 11 (1985), pp. 447-75.

20. Claudia Bischoff, *Frauen in der Krankenpflege. Zur Entwicklung von Frauenrolle u. Frauenberufstätigkeit im 19. u. 20. Jh.* [Women in Nursing: On the Development of Women's Role and Women's Professional Activity in the 19th and 20th Centuries] (Frankfurt/Main: Campus, 1984).

21. Rosmarie Beier, *Frauenarbeit und Frauenalltag im Deutschen Kaiserreich. Heimarbeiterinnen in der Berliner Bekleidungsindustrie 1880-1914* [Women's Work and Everyday Life in the German Empire: Home Work in the Berlin Garment Industry] (Frankfurt/Main: Campus, 1983); Barbara Franzoi, *At the Very Least She Pays the Rent: Women and German Industrialization, 1871- 1914* (Westport, Conn.: Greenwood, 1985); Irmtraud Gensewich, *Die Tabakarbeiterinnen in Baden 1870-1914* [Women Tobacco Workers in Baden] (Mannheim: Universität Mannheim, 1986).

22. Uta Ottmüller. *Die Dienstbotenfrage. Zur Sozialgeschichte der doppelten Ausnutzung von Dienstmädchen in Deutschen Kaiserreich* [The Domestic Servant Question: The Social History of the Double Exploitation of Maid-Servants in the German Empire] (Münster: Verlag Frauenpolitik, 1978); Dorothee Wierling, *Mädchen für alles. Arbeitsalltag und Lebensgeschichte städtischer Dienstboten. Eine Untersuchung über Dienstboten und ihre Herrschaften* [Maid-of-all-Work: Daily

Work Routines and Biographies of Domestic Servants and their Masters] (Berlin: Dietz, 1987); Regina Schulte, 'Bauernmägde in Bayern am Ende des 19.Jh. [Maids on Bavarian Farms at the End of the 19th Century]', in Hausen, *Frauen*, pp. 110-27; Karin Walser, *Dienstmädchen. Frauenarbeit und Weiblichkeitsbilder um 1900* [Domestic Servants: Women's Work and Images of Femininity around 1900] (Frankfurt: Extrabuch, 1985).

    23. Marlene Ellerkamp and Brigitte Jungmann, 'Unendliche Arbeit. Frauen in der "Jutespinnerei u. weberei Bremen" 1888-1914 [Work Without End: Women in the "Jute-Spinning Mill and Weavery of Bremen"]', in Hausen, *Frauen*, pp. 128-43; Gajohr, *Hälfte*; Gabriele Wellner, 'Industriearbeiterinnen in der Weimarer Republik [Women Industrial Workers in the Weimar Republic]', *Geschichte und Gesellschaft*, 7 (1981), pp. 534-54.

    24. Ursula Nienhaus, *Berufsstand weiblich. Die ersten weiblichen Angestellten* [Professional Category - Female: The First Salaried Women Employees] (Berlin: Transit Buchverlag, 1982); Nienhaus, 'Von Töchtern und Schwestern. Zur vergessenen Geschichte der weiblichen Angestellten im deutschen Kaiserreich [Of Daughters and Sisters: The Forgotten History of Women Employees under the German Empire]', in Jürgen Kocka (ed.), *Angestellte im europäischen Vergleich* (Göttingen: Vandenhoeck & Ruprecht, 1981), pp. 309-30; Ellen Lorentz, *Aufbruch oder Rückschritt? Arbeit, Alltag und Organisation weiblicher Angestellter in der Kaiserzeit und Weimarer Republik* [On the Move or One Step Back? Work, Everyday Life and Organisations of Salaried Women's Employees during the German Empire and the Weimer Republic] (Bielefeld: Kleine Verlag, 1988).

    25. Helmut Beilner, *Die Emanzipation der bayerischen Lehrerin - aufgezeigt an der Arbeit des bayerischen Lehrerinnenvereins (1898-1933)* [The Emancipation of Bavarian Women Teachers: The Work of the Bavarian Teachers' Association] (Munich: Stadtarchiv, 1971); Ilse Brehmer (ed.), *Lehrerinnen. Zur Geschichte eines Frauenberufs* [Teachers: The History of a Women's Profession] (Munich: Urban & Schwarzenberg, 1980); Marion Klewitz et al. (eds.), *Frauenberufe - hausarbeitsnah? Zur Erziehungs-, Bildungs- und Versorgungsarbeit von Frauen* [Women's Professions – Extensions of Housework?: The Teaching, Educational and Public Service Work of Women] (Pfaffenweiler: Centarus, 1989).

    26. For an exception, with more programmatic intentions, see Barbara Duden and Karin Hausen, 'Gesellschaftliche Arbeit - geschlechtsspezifische Arbeitsteilung [Societal Work - Gender-Specific Division of Labour]', in Kuhn and Schneider (eds)., *Frauen I*, pp. 11-33. A fine case study of the ensemble of technical and economic development and women's employment is Karin Hausen, 'Technischer Fortschritt u. Frauenarbeit im 19. Jh. Zur Sozialgeschichte der Nähmaschine', *Geschichte und Gesellschaft*, 4 (1978), pp. 148-61; in English as 'Technical Progress and Women's Labour in the Nineteenth Century: The Social History of the Sewing Machine', in George Iggers (ed.), *The Social History of Politics: Critical Perspectives in West German Historical Writing since 1945* (Leamington Spa: Berg, 1985), pp. 259-81.

    27. As an example of such lack of direction, with consequently tedious results, see the slender volume of Anke Probst, *Helene Amalie Krupp. Eine Essener Unternehmerin um 1800* [A Woman Entrepreneur in Essen Around 1800] (Stuttgart: Steiner, 1985), and many essays in Hans Pohl (ed.), *Die Frau in der deutschen Wirtschaft* [Women in the German Economy] (Wiesbaden: Steiner, 1985).

28. Mainly Jürgen Kuczynski, *Studien zur Geschichte der Lage der Arbeiterinnen in Deutschland von 1700 bis zur Gegenwart* [Studies on the Situation of Working Women in Germany from 1700 to the Present] (Berlin: Akademie Verlag, 1963).

29. Beier, *Frauenarbeit*; Elisabeth Plössl, *Weibliche Arbeit in Familie und Betrieb. Bayerische Arbeiterfrauen 1870-1914* [Bavarian Women's Work in the Family and the Factory: Bavarian Working-Class Women 1870-1914] (Munich: UNI Druck, 1983); Josef Ehmer, *Familienstruktur u. Arbeitsorganisation im frühindustriellen Wien* [Family Structures and the Organisation of Work in Early Industrial Vienna] (Munich: Oldenbourg, 1980). Further examples of such integration include Ulla Knapp, *Frauenarbeit in Deutschland* [Women's Work in Germany], 2 vols. (Munich: Minerva, 1984), and Wellner, 'Industriearbeiterinnen'.

30. Ute Daniel, *Arbeiterfrauen in der Kriegsgesellschaft. Beruf, Familie und Politik im Ersten Weltkrieg* [Working-Class Women in Wartime Society: Jobs, Family, and Politics in the First World War] (Göttingen: Vandenhoeck & Ruprecht, 1989). See also Christiane Eifert, 'Frauenarbeit im Krieg. Die Berliner "Heimatfront", 1914-1918 [Women's Work during War: The Berlin "Homefront", 1914-1918]', *Internationale Wissenschaftliche Korrespondenz*, 21 (1985), pp. 281-95. Older works, weaker in explanatory power, include Ursula Gersdorff, *Frauen im Kriegsdienst 1914-1945* [Women in War Service 1914-1945] (Stuttgart: Deutsche Verlags Anstalt, 1969); and Anneliese Seidel, *Frauenarbeit im Ersten Weltkrieg als Problem der staatlichen Sozialpolitik. Dargestellt am Beispiel Bayerns* [Women's Work in the First World War: A Problem of State Social Politics, Based on the Bavarian Example] (Frankfurt/Main: Fischer, 1979).

31. Hitherto, only a few studies on the history of women's education have been published. The early work of Jürgen Zinnecker, *Sozialgeschichte der Mädchenbildung* [Social History of Girls' Education] (Weinheim: Beltz, 1973), offered the first overview, but as concerns detail and conception it could now stand revision. The same can be said of Elisabeth Blochmann, *Das 'Frauenzimmer' u. die 'Gelehrsamkeit'. Eine Studie über die Anfänge des Mädchenschulwesens in Deutschland* [Women and Learning: A Study of the Beginnings of Girls' Education in Germany] (Heidelberg: Quelle & Meyer, 1966). A collection recounting women's personal and school experiences is Sylvia Conradt and Kirsten Heckmann-Janz, '. . . du heiratest ja doch!' 80 Jahre Schulgeschichte von Frauen* ['You'll Get Married Anyway!': Eighty Years of Women's School History] (Frankfurt/Main: Fischer, 1985), which is supplemented by the historical excursion into twentieth-century girls' education in Monika Simmel, *Erziehung zum Weibe* [Educated to be a Woman], which promises in its subtitle to provide information on girls' education in the nineteenth century, but actually proves to be a mere history of educational prescriptions from Fénelon to Helene Lange.

In his comprehensive work, *Die Frauenzimmer-Bibliothek des Hamburger 'Patrioten' von 1724. Zur weiblichen Bildung in der Frühaufklärung* [The Women's Library of the Hamburg 'Patriots' of 1724: Female Education in the Early Enlightenment], 2 vols. (Stuttgart: Heinz, 1976), the Germanist Peter Nasse discusses the contents and dimensions of girls' education in Hamburg during the early eighteenth century. Nasse reconstructs the supply and standard of female education by means of reading recommendations made at the time, without sufficiently considering the situation of the market. A similar approach is Dagmar

Grenz, *Mädchenliteratur. Von den moralisch-belehrenden Schriften im 18. Jahrhundert bis zur Herausbildung der Backfischliteratur im 19. Jh.* [Girls' Literature: From the Moral Educational Writings of the Eighteenth Century to the Development of Teen-Age Girls' Literature in the Nineteenth Century] (Stuttgart: Metzlersche, 1981). Her study of educational literature, novels, and short stories especially written for girls deals primarily with the structure of the educational message. She therefore operates mainly on the level of educational norms and behavioural orientations. A good continuation of Grenz's study is the collection of source materials compiled by the Germanist Gunter Häntzschel (ed.), *Bildung u. Kultur bürgerlicher Frauen 1850-1918* [The Education and Culture of Bourgeois Women] (Tübingen: Niemeyer, 1986). These collected texts, selected from etiquette books, advice books, and manuals published mostly during the later nineteenth century, offer a good overview of the expectations with which young bourgeois women were approached in their private and public lives. See also the new work by Ingrid Otto, *Bürgerliche Töchtererziehung im Spiegel illustrierter Zeitschriften von 1865-1915* [The Education of Bourgeois Daughters as Reflected in Illustrated Magazines] (Hildesheim: Lax, 1989).

Dagmar Ladj-Teichmann, *Erziehung zur Weiblichkeit durch Textilarbeiten. Ein Beitrag zur Sozialgeschichte der Frauenarbeit im 19 Jh.* [Education in Femininity through Work with Textiles: A Contribution to the Social History of Women's Work in the 19th Century] (Weinheim: Beltz, 1983), examines a special aspect of female education, the training for needlework and the garment industry. The author explores the contrast between the needlework of bourgeois daughters and the sewing for pay of working-class women. On the different educational concepts for bourgeois and proletarian women, see Gerda Tornieporth, *Studien zur Frauenbildung* [Studies on Women's Education] (Weinheim: Beltz, 1977). Also see Ilse Brehmer et al. (eds.), *Frauen in der Geschichte IV. 'Wissen heisst leben . . .' Beiträge zur Bildungsgeschichte von Frauen im 18. und 19 Jh.* ['Knowledge Means Living. . .': Essays on Women's Education in the 18th and 19th Centuries] (Düsseldorf: Schwann, 1983), a collection that covers aspects of normative prescriptions and actual behaviour. Unfortunately, the authors focus on ideologies and neglect to explore institutional developments.

32. James Albisetti, 'Frauen und die akademischen Berufe im Kaiserlichen Deutschland [Women and the Academic Professions in Imperial Germany]', in Ruth-Ellen B. Joeres and Annette Kuhn (eds.), *Frauen in der Geschichte VI. Frauenbilder und Frauenwirklichkeiten* (Düsseldorf: Schwann, 1985), pp. 286- 303; also Albisetti, 'The Fight for Female Physicians in Imperial Germany', *Central European History*, 15 (1982), pp. 99-123; Claudia Huerkamp, 'Frauen, Universitäten und Bildungsbürgertum. Zur Lage studierender Frauen 1900-1930 [Women, Universities and the Educated Bourgeoisie: The Situation of Women Students]', in Siegrist Hannes (ed.), *Bürgerliche Berufe* (Göttingen: Vandenhoeck & Ruprecht, 1988), pp. 200-22; Jack R. Pauwels, *Women, Nazis and Universities: Female University Students in the Third Reich, 1933-1945* (Westport, Conn.: Greenwood, 1984).

33. A beginning is Ute Frevert (ed.), *Bürgerinnen und Bürger. Geschlechterverhältnisse im 19. Jahrhundert* [Citizenesses and Citizens: Gender Relations in the 19th Century] (Göttingen: Vandenhoeck & Ruprecht, 1988).

34. Pia Schmid, *Zeit des Lesens - Zeit des Fühlens. Anfänge des deutschen Bildungsbürgertums* [Time for Reading - Time for Emotions: The Beginning of the Educated German Bourgeoisie (Berlin: Quadriga, 1985); Eva Walter, *Schrieb oft, von Mägde Arbeit müde: Lebenszusammenhänge deutscher Schriftstellerinnen um 1800* [Wrote Often, Tired from 'Maiden's Work': Life Contexts of German Women Writers Around 1800] (Düsseldorf: Schwann, 1985); Karin Hausen, '"eine Ulme für das schwanke Efeu". Ehepaare im deutschen Bildungsbürgertum. Ideale und Wirklichkeiten im späten 18. und 19. Jahrhundert ["An Elm for the Clinging Vine": Married Couples of the Educated German Bourgeoisie - Ideals and Realities in the late 18th and 19th Centuries]', in Frevert (ed.), *Bürgerinnen*, pp. 85-117; Sibylle Meyer, *Das Theater mit der Hausarbeit. Bürgerliche Repräsentation in der Familie der vilhelminischen Zeit* [The Housework Drama: Bourgeois Representation in Families of the Wilhelminian Era] (Frankfurt: Campus, 1982). On bourgeois Jewish women, see the impressive work of Marion Kaplan, *The Jewish Feminist Movement in Germany: The Campaigns of the Jüdischer Frauenbund, 1904-1938* (Westport, Conn.: Greenwood Press, 1979; in German, Hamburg, 1981); 'Tradition and Transition: The Acculturation, Assimilation and Integration of Jews in Imperial Germany: A Gender Analysis', *Leo Baeck Institute Yearbook*, 27 (1982), pp. 3-35; 'For Love or Money: The Marriage Strategies of Jews in Imperial Germany', *Leo Baeck Institute Yearbook*, 28 (1983), pp. 263-300; 'Freizeit-Arbeit. Geschlechterräume im deutsch-jüdischen Bürgertum 1870-1914 [Leisure-Time Work: Gendered Spheres in the German-Jewish Bourgeoisie]', in Frevert (ed.), *Bürgerinnen*, pp. 157-74.

35. Ute Gerhard, *Verhältnisse und Verhinderungen. Frauenarbeit, Familie und Rechte der Frauen im 19. Jahrhundert* [Circumstances and Obstacles: Women's Work, the Family, and Women's Rights in the Nineteenth Century] (Frankfurt: Suhrkamp, 1978); Gerhard, 'Die Rechtsstellung der Frau in der bürgerlichen Gesellschaft des 19. Jahrhunderts. Frankreich und Deutschland im Vergleich [The Legal Situation of Women of the 19th Century: A Comparison of France and Germany]', in Jürgen Kocka (ed.), *Bürgertum im 19. Jahrhundert*, vol. 1 (Munich: Deutschen Taschenbuch Verlag, 1988), pp. 439-68; Ursula Vogel, 'Patriarchale Herrschaft, bürgerliches Recht, bürgerliche Utopie. Eigentumsrechte der Frauen im Deutschland und England [Patriarchal Rule, Bourgeois Law, Bourgeois Utopias: Women's Property Rights in Germany and England]', in Kocka (ed.), *Bürgertum*, pp. 406-38; Dirk Blasius, *Ehescheidung in Deutschland 1794-1945* [Divorce in Germany] (Göttingen: Vandenhoeck & Ruprecht, 1987; Blasius, 'Bürgerliche Rechtsgleichheit und die Ungleichheit der Geschlechter. Das Scheidungsrecht im historischen Vergleich [Bourgeois Legal Equality and the Inequality of the Sexes: Divorce Law in Historical Comparison]', in Frevert (ed.), *Bürgerinnen*, pp. 67-84.

36. Karin Hausen, 'Die Polarisierung der "Geschlechtscharaktere" - Eine Spiegelung der Dissoziation von Erwerbs- und Familienleben', in Werner Conze (ed.), *Sozialgeschichte der Familie in der Neuzeit Europas* (Stuttgart: Klett-Cotta, 1976), pp. 363-93; in English as 'Family and Role-Division: The Polarisation of Sexual Stereotypes in the Nineteenth Century - An Aspect of the Dissociation of Work and Family Life', in Richard J. Evans and W. R. Lee (eds.), *The German Family* (London: Croom Helm, 1981), pp. 51-83. Barbara Duden, 'Das schöne Eigentum. Zur Herausbildung des bürgerlichen Frauenbildes an der Wende vom 18. zum 19. Jahrhundert [Beautiful Property: On the Shaping of the Bourgeois Women's

Image at the Beginning of the Nineteenth Century]', *Kursbuch*, 48 (1977), pp. 125-40; Ute Frevert, 'Bürgerliche Meisterdenker und das Geschlechterverhältnis [Bourgeois Master Thinkers and Gender Relations]', in Frevert (ed.), *Bürgerinnen*, pp. 17-48.

    37. Helga Grubitzsch et al. (eds.), *Grenzgängerinnen. Revolutionäre Frauen im 18. u. 19. Jh. Weibliche Wirklichkeit u. männliche Phantasien* [Transgressing Boundaries: Revolutionary Women in the Eighteenth and Nineteenth Centuries: Female Realities and Male Fantasies] (Düsseldorf: Schwann, 1985); Carola Lipp (ed.), *Schimpfende Weiber und patriotische Jungfrauen. Frauen im Vormärz u. in der Revolution 1848-49* [Bitching Women and Patriotic Virgins: Women Before and During the Revolution of 1848-49] (Bühl-Moos: Elster, 1986). See also the collection of sources by Gerlinde Hummel-Haasis (ed.), *Schwestern zerreist eure Ketten. Zeugnisse zur Geschichte der Frauen in der Revolution von 1848/49* [Sisters, Throw Off Your Chains: Documents on the History of Women in the Revolution of 1848/49] (Münich: DTV, 1982), as well as the exhibit catalog edited by Viktoria Schmidt-Linsenhoff, *Sklavin oder Bürgerin? Französische Revolution und Neue Weiblichkeit 1760-1830* [Slave or Citizeness? The French Revolution and the New Womanliness, 1760-1830] (Marburg: Jonas, 1989).

    38. Doris Kaufmann, *Katholisches Milieu in Münster 1928-1933. Politische Aktionsformen u. geschlechtsspezifische Verhaltensräume* [The Catholic Milieu in Munster, 1928-33: Political Forms of Action and Gender-Specific Behaviour] (Düsseldorf: Schwann, 1984); also Kaufmann, *Frauen zwischen Aufbruch und Reaktion. Protestantische Frauenbewegung in der ersten Hälfte des 20. Jahrhunderts* [Women Between Uprising and Reaction: The Protestant Women's Movement in the First Half of the Twentieth Century] (Munich: Piper, 1988); Jochen-Christoph Kaiser, *Frauen in der Kirche. Evangelische Frauenverbände im Spannungsfeld von Kirche und Gesellschaft 1890-1945* [Women in the Church: Protestant Women's Organisations in Tension between Church and Society] (Düsseldorf: Schwann, 1985); A. Kall, *Katholische Frauenbewegung in Deutschland. Eine Untersuchung zur Gründung katolischer Frauenvereine im 19. Jh.* [The Catholic Women's Movement in Germany: A Study of the Founding of Catholic Women's Groups in the Nineteenth Century] (Paderborn: Schoningh, 1983); Sylvia Paletschek, 'Religiöse Emanzipation und Frauenemanzipation [Religious Emancipation and Women's Emancipation]', *SOWI*, 18 (1989), pp. 228-36; Paletschek, *Frauen und Dissens. Frauen im Deutschkatholizismus und in den Freien Gemeinden 1841-1852* [Women and Dissent: Women in German Catholicism and in the Free Parishes] (Göttingen, 1990).

    39. This complex, central for the construction of feminist theory, has not received appropriate scholarly treatment. Besides a programmatic essay by Gisela Bock and Barbara Duden, 'Arbeit aus Liebe - Liebe als Arbeit. Zur Entstehung der Hausarbeit im Kapitalismus [Working Because You Love - Love as Work: On the Development of Housework under Capitalism]', in *Frauen und Wissenschaft*, pp. 118-99, and a sociological overview by Gertrude Kittler, *Hausarbeit. Zur Geschichte einer 'Natur-Ressource'* [Housework: On the History of a 'Natural Resource'] (Munich: Frauen Offensiv, 1980), there are only sketches such as those by Meyer, *Theater*, or Karin Hausen, 'Große Wäsche. Technischer Fortschritt und sozialer Wandel in Deutschland vom 18. bis ins 20 Jh. [Washday: Technical Progress and Social Change in Germany from the Eighteenth to the Twentieth Century]',

Geschichte und Gesellschaft, 13, (1987), pp. 273-303. The household as a workplace for all women is still less well known than, for example, the various forms of women's paid employment. Also the matter of the technologising of the household, its causes and its consequences, has not been studied at all.

40. In addition to the work of Regine Schulte, *Sperrbezirke. Tugendhaftigkeit und Prostitution in der bürgerlichen Welt* [Red Light Districts: Virtue and Prostitution in the Bourgeois World] (Frankfurt/Main: Athenaeum, 1979], one can also consult the local study by Anita Ulrich, *Bordelle, Straßendirnen und bürgerliche Sittlichkeit in der Belle Epoque. Eine sozialgeschichtliche Studie der Prostitution am Beispiel der Stadt Zürich* [Brothels, Streetwalkers, and Bourgeois Morality in the Belle Epoque: A Social Historical Study of Prostitution in Zurich] (Zurich: Rohr, 1985], as well as Sybille Leitner, 'Großstadtlust. Prostitution und Münchener Sittenpolizei um 1900 [Lust in the Big City: Prostitution and Vice Squads in Munich around 1900]', in Wolfgang Hartwig and Klaus Tenfelde (eds.) *Soziale Räume in der Urbanisierung* (Munich: Oldenbourg, 1990), pp. 261-75.

41. See also the medical historical work of Esther Fischer-Homberger, *Krankheit Frau. Zur Geschichte der Einbildungen* [Disease: Woman – On the History of the Imagination] (Darmstadt: Neuwied, 1984); Fischer-Homberger, 'Krankheit Frau', in Arthur E. Imhof (ed.), *Leib und Leben in der Geschichte der Neuzeit* (Berlin: Duncker & Humblot, 1983), pp. 215-29; Claudia Honegger, 'Überlegungen zur Medikalisierung des weiblichen Körpers [Reflections on the Medicalisation of Women's Bodies]', in Imhof, *Leib und Leben*, pp. 203-13; Ute Frevert, 'Frauen und Ärzte im späten 18. u. frühen 19. Jh. [Women and Doctors in the late Eighteenth and Early Nineteenth Century]', in Annette Kuhn and Jörn Rüsen (eds.), *Frauenkörper, Medizin, Sexualität* (Düsseldorf: Patmos, 1986); and Barbara Duden, *Geschichte unter der Haut. Ein Eisenacher Arzt und seine Patientinnen um 1730* [History under the Skin: An Eisenach Doctor and his Women Patients around 1730] (Stuttgart: Klett-Cotta, 1987).

42. See among other works Regine Schulte, *Das Dorf im Verhör. Brandstifter, Kindsmörderinnen und Wilderer vor den Schranken des bürgerlichen Gerichts. Oberbayern 1848-1910* [The Village on Trial: Arsonists, Child Murdering Women, and Outlaws at the Bar of Bourgeois Justice: Upper Bavaria, 1848-1910] (Reinbek: Rowholt, 1989), especially Part II; also Schulte, 'Kindsmörderinnen auf dem Lande [Child Murdering Women in the Countryside], in Hans Medick and David Sabean (eds.) *Emotionen und materielle Interessen* (Göttingen: Vandenhoeck & Ruprecht, 1984), pp. 113-42; and Karin Hausen, 'Mütter, Söhne und der Markt der Symbole und Waren. Der "Deutsche Muttertag" 1923-1933 [Mothers, Sons and the Market for Symbols and Commodities: Mother's Day in Germany, 1923-1933]', in Medick and Sabean (eds.), *Emotionen*, pp. 473-523.

43. A brief overview is provided in Heide Wunder, 'Frauen in der Gesellschaft Mitteleuropas im späten Mittelalter und in der Frühen Neuzeit (15. bis 18. Jahrhundert) [Women in Central European Society from the Late Middle Ages to Early Modern Times (15th to 18th Centuries)', in Helfried Valentinitsch (ed.), *Hexen und Zauberer. Die grosse Verfolgung - ein europäisches Phänomen in der Steiermark* [Witches and Magicians: The Great Persecutions – A European Phenomenon in Styria] (Graz-Vienna: Leykam, 1987), pp. 123-54. This essay does not treat the legal historical aspect, which, however, is examined by Gernot Kocher in the same volume.

324   *Ute Frevert, Heide Wunder and Christina Vanja*

44. Pohl (ed.), *Die Frau in der deutschen Wirtschaft* (note 26, above).

45. Part l: 'Wandel und Stabilisierung der Geschlechterbeziehungenim 15. und 16. Jahrhundert [Change and Stability in the Relations of the Sexes in the 15th and 16th Centuries]', (September 1987); Part 2: 'Theologische Frauenbilder - Frauen in der Kirche - Frauenfrömmigkeit [Theological Images of Women - Women in the Church - Women's Piety]', (September 1988); Part 3, 'Ideale und reale Präsenz von Frauen in der Gesellschaft der Frühen Neuzeit [Ideal and Actual Presence of Women in Early Modern Society]' (November 1988). A first volume will appear in 1990/91.

46. A publication based on this contribution is being prepared.

47. See below the section on 'Work'.

48. Four volumes have appeared so far in the series 'Archiv für philosophie- und theologiegeschichtliche Frauenforschung' (Munich: Iudicium, 1984-1988).

49. Viktoria Schmidt-Linsenhoff (ed.), *Sklavin oder Bürgerin? Französische Revolution und Neue Weiblichkeit 1760-1830* [Slave or Citizeness: The French Revolution and the New Womanliness, 1760-1830] (Historisches Museum Frankfurt; Marburg: Jonas, 1989).

50. Arthur E. Imhof, 'Historische Demographie [Historical Demography]', in Wolfgang Schieder and Volker Sellin (eds.), *Sozialgeschichte in Deutschland*, vol. 2 (Göttingen: Vandenhoeck & Ruprecht, 1986), pp. 32-63; other important studies include Thomas Kohl, *Familie und soziale Schichtung. Zur historischen Demographie Triers 1730-1860* [Family and Social Strata: On the Demographic History of Trier 1730-1860] (Stuttgart: Klett-Cotta, 1985), and Peter Zschunke, *Konfession und Alltag in Oppenheim. Beiträge zur Geschichte von Bevölkerung und Gesellschaft einer gemischtkonfessionellen Kleinstadt in der Frühen Neuzeit* [Confession and Everyday Life in Oppenheim: Contributions to the History of the Population and Society of a Denominationally Mixed Small Town in the Early Modern Period] (Wiesbaden: Steiner, 1984).

51. Karin Hausen, 'Familie und Familiengeschichte [Family and Family History]', in Schieder and Sellin (eds.), *Sozialgeschichte*, 2, pp. 64-89; Michael Mitterauer and Reinhard Sieder (eds.), *Historische Familienforschung* [Historical Family Research] (Frankfurt: Suhrkamp, 1982); Conze (ed.), *Sozialgeschichte der Familie in der Neuzeit Europas* (note 35 above).

52. Peter Kriedte, Hans Medick, and Jürgen Schlumbohm, *Industrialisierung vor der Industrialisierung. Gewerbliche Warenproduktion auf dem Land in der Formationsperiode des Kapitalismus* [Industrialisation before Industrialisation: Commodity Production in the Countryside During the Formative Period of Capitalism] (Göttingen: Vandenhoeck & Ruprecht, 1977).

53. Hans Medick and David Sabean (eds.), *Emotionen und materielle Interessen. Sozialanthropologische und historische Beiträge zur Familienforschung* [Emotions and Material Interests: Social Anthropology and Historical Contributions to Family Research] (Göttingen: Vandenhoeck & Ruprecht, 1984).

54. Peter Borscheid, *Geschichte des Alters. 16. - 18. Jahrhundert* [History of Old Age from the 16th to the 18th Century] (Münster: Coppenrath, 1987); Robert Jütte, *Obrigkeitliche Armenfürsorge in deutschen Reichsstädten der frühen Neuzeit: Städtisches Armenwesen in Frankfurt am Main und Köln* [Governmental Assistance of the Poor in German Free Imperial Towns in Early Modern Times: Urban Welfare in Frankfurt/Main and Cologne] (Cologne: Böhlau, 1984); Ernst Schubert, *Arme*

Leute, Bettler und Gauner im Franken des 18. Jahrhunderts [Poor People, Beggars, and Crooks in Eighteenth Century Franconia] (Neustadt a.d. Aisch: Degener & Co., 1983).

55. Gisela Bock, 'Geschichte, Frauengeschichte, Geschlectergeschichte [History, Women's History, Gender History], *Geschichte und Gesellschaft*, 4 (1988), pp. 364-91.

56. Gerhard Schormann, *Hexenprozesse in Deutschland* [Witchcraft Trials in Germany] (Göttingen: Vandenhoeck & Ruprecht, 1981). Exemplary local studies include Wolfgang Behringer, *Hexenverfolgung in Bayern. Volksmagie, Glaubenseifer und Staatsräson in der Frühen Neuzeit* [Persecution of Witches in Bavaria: Folk Magic, Religious Zealotry, and Reason of State in Early Modern Times] (Munich: Oldenbourg, 1987), and Christian Degn, Hartmut Lehmann, and Dagmar Unverhau (eds.), *Hexenprozesse. Deutsche und skandinavische Beiträge* [Witch Trials: German and Scandinavian Contributions] (Neumünster: Wachholtz, 1983].

57. Eva Labouvie, 'Männer in Hexenprozessen. Zur Sozialanthropologie eines "männlichen" Verständnisses von Magie und Hexerei [Men in Witchcraft Trials: On the Social Anthropology of a "Manly" Understanding of Magic and Witchcraft]', *Geschichte und Gesellschaft*, 16 (1990), pp. 56-78; Ingrid Ahrendt-Schulte, 'Schadenzauber und Konflikte. Sozialgeschichte von Frauen im Spiegel der Hexenprozesse des 16. Jahrhunderts in der Grafschaft Lippe [Black Magic and Conflict: The Social History of Women as Mirrored in the Sixteenth-Century Witchcraft Trials in the County of Lippe]', in Heide Wunder and Christina Vanja (eds.), *Wandel der Geschlechterbeziehungen am Beginn der Neuzeit* [Changes in Gender Relations at the Beginning of the Early Modern Period] (forthcoming).

58. Anne Conrad, 'Ordensfrauen ohne Klausur? Die katholische Frauenbewegung an der Wende zum 17. Jahrhundert [Uncloistered Women's Orders? The Catholic Women's Movement at the Turn of the Seventeenth Century]', *Feministische Studien*, 5 (1986), pp. 31-45.

59. Lyndal Roper, '"The Common Man", "The Common Good", "Common Women": Gender and Meaning in the German Reformation Commune', *Social History*, 12 (1987), pp. 1-21; and Roper, *The Holy Household: Women and Morals in Reformation Augsburg* (Oxford: Clarendon Press, 1989).

60. Marion Kobelt-Groch, 'Von "armen frowen" und "bösen wibern" - Frauen im Bauernkrieg zwischen Anpassung und Auflehnung ["Poor Women" and "Evil Women": Women in the Peasant Wars Between Adjustment and Rebellion]', *Archiv für Reformationsgeschichte*, 79 (1988), pp. 103-137.

61. Gerta Scharffennorth, 'Martin Luther zur Rolle von Mann und Frau [Martin Luther on the Roles of Men and Women]', in Hans Süssmuth (ed.), *Das Luther-Erbe in Deutschland* (Düsseldorf: Droste, 1985), pp. 111-29; Alice Zimmerli-Witschi, *Frauen in der Reformationszeit* [Women in the Reformation Era], Ph.D. dissertation, Zurich, 1981; Luise Schorn-Schütte, '"Gefärtin" und "Mitregentin". Zur Sozialgeschichte der evangelischen Pfarrfrau in der Frühen Neuzeit ["Companion" and "Co-ruler": On the Social History of Protestant Minister's Wives in the Early Modern Period]', in Wunder and Vanja (eds.), *Wandel der Geschlechterbeziehungen*; Angelika Nowicki Pastuschka, *Frauen in der Reformation. Untersuchungen zum Verhalten von Frauen in den Reichsstädten Augsburg und Nürnberg zur reformatorischen Bewegung 1517 und 1537* [Women in

the Reformation: Studies of Women's Conduct in the Free Imperial Cities of Augsburg and Nuremberg during the Reform Movements of 1517 and 1537] (Pfaffenweiler: Centarus, 1989); Gotthardt Frühsorge, 'Die Einheit aller Geschäfte. Tradition und Veränderung des "Hausmutter"-Bildes in der deutschen Ökonomieliteratur des 18. Jahrhunderts [The Unity of Business: Tradition and Change in the Image of the "House-mother" in Eighteenth-Century German Economic Literature]', *Wolfenbütteler Studien zur Aufklärung*, 3 (1976), pp. 137-57.

62. Bernd Moeller, 'Die Brautwerbung Martin Bucers für Wolfgang Capito. Zur Sozialgeschichte des evangelischen Pfarrerstandes [Martin Bucer's Matchmaking for Wolfgang Capito: A Social History of the Status of the Protestant Minister]', in Ludger Grenzmann, Hubert Herkommer, and Dieter Wuttke (eds.), *Philogie als Kulturwissenschaft. Studien zur Literatur und Geschichte des Mittelalters. Festschrift für Karl Stackmann zum 65. Geburtstag* (Göttingen: Vandenhoeck & Ruprecht, 1987), pp. 306-25.

63. Maria E. Müller, 'Schneckengeist im Venusleib. Zur Zoologie des Ehelebens bei Johann Fischart [A Snail's Spirit in a Venus Body: The Zoology of Married Life According to Johann Fischart]', in Maria E. Müller (ed.), *Eheglück und Liebesjoch. Bilder von Liebe, Ehe und Familie in der Literatur des 15. und 16. Jahrhunderts* (Weinheim and Basel: Beltz, 1988), pp. 155-205.

64. Peter Borscheid and Hans J. Teuteberg (eds.), *Ehe, Liebe, Tod. Zum Wandel der Geschlechts- und Generationsbeziehungen in der Neuzeit* [Marriage, Love, and Death: On Changes in Sexual and Generational Relationships in Modern Times] (Münster: Coppenrath, 1983); Richard von Dülmen (ed.), *Die Kultur der einfachen Leute. Bayerisches Volksleben vom 16. bis zum 19. Jahrhundert* [The Culture of Simple People: The Common People's Lives in Bavaria from the Sixteenth to the Nineteenth Century] (Munich: Beck, 1983); Richard van Dülmen, *Kultur und Alltag in der Frühen Neuzeit* [Culture and Everyday Life in Early Modern Times], vol. 1: *Das Haus und seine Menschen. 16. - 18. Jahrhundert* [The Household and its Inhabitants, 16th-18th Centuries] (Munich: Beck, 1990).

65. Ursula Hess, 'Lateinischer Dialog und gelehrte Partnerschaft. Frauen als humanistische Leitbilder in Deutschland (1500-1550) [Latin Dialogues and Learned Partnerships: Women as Humanistic Models in Germany, 1500-1550]', in Gisela Brinker-Gabler (ed.), *Deutsche Literatur von Frauen*, vol. 1: *Vom Mittelalter bis zum Ende des 18. Jahrhunderts* (Munich: Beck, 1988), pp. 113-48.

66. Silke Göttsch, 'Weibliche Erfahrungen um Körperlichkeit und Sexualität nach archivalischen Quellen aus Schleswig-Holstein 1700-1850 [Women's Experiences of Corporality and Sexuality, from Archival Sources in Schleswig-Holstein 1700- 1850], *Kieler Blätter zur Volkskunde*, 18 (1986), pp. 29-59.

67. Rolf Engelsing, *Zur Sozialgeschichte deutscher Mittel- und Unterschichten* [On the Social History of the German Middle and Lower Classes] (Göttingen: Vandenhoeck & Ruprecht, 2nd ed., 1978); Engelsing, *Der Bürgerer als Leser* [The Citizen as Reader] (Stuttgart: Metzler, 1974).

68. Barbara Becker-Cantarino, *Der lange Weg zur Mündigkeit. Frauen und Literatur (1500-1800)* [The Long Road to Emancipation: Women and Literature] (Tübingen: Metzler, 1987).

69. Brinker-Gabler, *Deutsche Literatur*, 1.

70. Jean M. Woods and Maria Fürstenwald, *Schriftstellerinnen, Künsterinnen und gelehrte Frauen des deutschen Barock. Ein Lexikon* [Women Writers, Artists and Intellectuals of the German Baroque: A Lexicon] (Stuttgart: Metzler, 1984); for work on art history see Cordula Bischoff et al. (eds.), *FrauenKunstGeschichte. Zur Korrektur des herrschenden Blicks* [Women's Art History: Correcting Prevailing Perceptions] (Giessen: Anabas, 1984), and Ilsebill Bara et al. (eds.), *Frauen, Bilder, Männer, Mythen. Kunsthistorische Beiträge* [Women, Pictures, Men, Myths: Papers on Art History] (Berlin: Reimer, 1987). For an art-historical approach to the witchcraft issue, see especially Sigrid Schade, *Schadenzauber und die Magie des Körpers* [Black Magic and the Sorcery of the Body] (Worms: Werner'sche Verlagsgesellschaft, 1983).

71. Anne Conrad, '"Katechismusjungfrauen" und "Scholastikerinnen" - Katholische Mädchenbildung in der Frühen Neuzeit' ["Catechism Girls" and "Female Scholastics" - Catholic Girls' Education in the Early Modern Period]', in Wunder and Vanja (eds.), *Wandel der Geschlechterbeziehungen*.

72. Cornelia Niekus Moore, *The Maiden's Mirror: Reading Material for German Girls in the Sixteenth and Seventeenth Centuries* (Wiesbaden: Harrassowitz, 1987).

73. Heide Wunder, 'Zur Stellung der Frau im Arbeitsleben und in der Gesellschaft des 15. bis 18. Jahrhunderts [On the Position of Women in Working Life and Society from the Fifteenth to the Eighteenth Century]', *Geschichtsdidaktik*, 6 (1981), pp. 239-51.

74. Anke Wolf-Graaf, *Frauenarbeit im Abseits. Frauenbewegung und weibliches Arbeitsvermögen* [Women's Work on the Sidelines: The Women's Movement and Women's Work Skills] (Munich: Frauenoffensiv, 1981).

75. Merry Wiesner, *Working Women in Renaissance Germany* (New Brunswick, N. J.: Rutgers University Press, 1986); Wiesner, 'Women's Work in the Changing City Economy, 1500-1650', in Marilyn J. Boxer and Jean H. Quataert (eds.), *Connecting Spheres: Women in the Western World, 1500 to the Present* (New York: Oxford University Press, 1987), pp. 64-74.

76. Lyndal Roper, 'Mothers of Debauchery: Procuresses in Reformation Augsburg', *German History*, 6, no. 1 (1988), pp. 1-19; Roper, 'Discipline and Respectability: Prostitution and the Reformation in Augsburg', *History Workshop*, 19 (1985), pp. 3-28.

77. Petra Egger, 'Lebens- und Arbeitswelt der Hamburger Handwerksfrauen im 18. Jahrhundert. Einige methodische Probleme in der Frauengeschichtsschreibung [Life and Work for Hamburg Craftswomen in the Eighteenth Century: Some Methodological Problems in Writing Women's History]', in *Frauenalltag. Frauenforschung. Beiträge zur 2. Tagung der Kommision Frauenforschung in der Deutschen Gesellschaft für Volkskunde* (Frankfurt/Main, Berne, New York, Paris: P. Lang, 1988), pp. 274-84.

78. Dorothee Rippmann, 'Frauenarbeit im Wandel. Untersuchungen zur Arbeitsstellung, Arbeitsorganisation und Entlöhnung in der Landwirtschaft am Oberrhein (15./16. Jahrhundert) [Changes in Women's Work: Investigations of Women's Work Situation, Organisation and Remuneration in the Upper Rhine]', in Heide Wunder and Christina Vanja (eds.), *Frauen in der ländlichen Gesellschaft* (in preparation); Christina Vanja, 'Frauenarbeit in der vorindustriellen Gesellschaft. Fragestellungen - Quellen - Forschungsmöglichkeiten [Women's Work in

Preindustrial Society: Questions, Sources, Research Possibilities]', *Frauenalltag. Frauenforschung*, pp. 261-73.

79. Christina Vanja, 'Bergarbeiterinnen. Zur Geschichte der Frauenarbeit im Bergbau, Hütten- und Salinenwesen seit dem späten Mittelalter. Teil 1: Spätes Mittelalter und frühe Neuzeit [Mining Women: On the History of Women's Work in Mining, Smelting, and Saltworks in the Late Middle Ages. Part 1: Late Middle Ages and Early Modern Times]', *Der Anschnitt*, 39, no. 1 (1987), pp. 2-15; Vanja, 'Frauenarbeit im Bergbau - ein Überblick [An Overview of Women's Work in Mining]', *Frauen und Bergbau. Zeugnisse aus fünf Jahrhunderten* (Bochum: Deutsches Bergbaumuseum, 1989), pp. 11-29; Susan Karant-Nunn, 'The Women of the Saxon Silver Mines', in Sherrin Marshall (ed.), *Women in Reformation and Counter-Reformation Europe* (Bloomington, Ind.: Indiana University Press, 1989), pp. 29-46.

80. Wiesner, *Working Women*, pp. 37-74; Christina Vanja, 'Auf Geheiß der Vögtin. Amtsfrauen in hessischen Hospitälern der Frühen Neuzeit [By Command of the Overseer: Women Supervisors in Hessian Hospitals in the Early Modern Period]', forthcoming in Wunder and Vanja (eds.), *Frauen in ländlichen Gesellschaft*.

81. Ute Frevert, 'Frauen und Ärzte in späten 18. und frühen 19. Jahrhundert - zur Sozialgeschichte eines Gewaltverhältnisses [Women and Doctors in the late Eighteenth and Early Nineteenth Centuries - The Social History of a Power Relation]', in Annette Kuhn and Jörn Rüsen (eds.), *Frauen in der Geschichte II* (Düsseldorf: Schwann, 1982), pp. 177-210; Marianne Degginger, *Zur Geschichte der Hebammen im alten St. Gallen* [On the History of Midwives in Old St. Gallen] (1988); Merry Wiesner, 'Early Modern Midwifery: A Case Study', in Barbara A. Hanawalt (ed.), *Women and Work in Preindustrial Europe* (Bloomington: Indiana University Press, 1986), pp. 94-114.

82. Rita Bake, *Vorindustrielle Frauenerwerbsarbeit. Arbeits- und Lebensweisen von Manufakturarbeiterinnen im Deutschland des 18. Jahrhunderts unter besonderer Berücksichtigung Hamburgs* [Preindustrial Women's Employment: Work and Life Styles of Women Factory Workers in Germany in the 18th Century with Special Reference to Hamburg] (Cologne: Pahl-Rugenstein, 1984).

83. Johanna-Luise Brockmann, 'Die ambivalente Rolle der Amme - ein Beitrag zur Sozialgeschichte der Familie in Deutschland [The Ambivalent Role of the Wetnurse - A Contribution to the Social History of the Family in Germany]', in Jost von Maydell (ed.), *Bildungsforschung und Gesellschaftspolitik* (Oldenburg: Holzberg, 1982), pp. 63-88.

84. Irene Hardach-Pinke, 'Weibliche Intelligenz auf dem Lande: Gouvernanten im 18. Jahrhundert [Woman Intellectuals in the Countryside: Governesses in the Eighteenth Century]', forthcoming in Wunder and Vanja (eds.), *Frauen in der ländlichen Gesellschaft*.

85. Gisela Brinker-Gabler, *Deutsche Dichterinnen vom 16. Jahrhundert bis zur Gegenwart. Gedichte und Lebensläufe* [German Poetesses from the Sixteenth Century to the Present: Poems and Life Courses] (Frankfurt/Main: Fischer, 1978).

86. Hiltrud Gnüg and Renate Möhrmann (eds.), *Frauen. Literatur. Geschichte. Schreibende Frauen vom Mittelalter bis zur Gegenwart* [Women, Literature, History: Women Writers from the Middle Ages to the Present] (Stuttgart: Metzler, 1985); Gisela Brinkler-Gabler (ed.), *Deutsche Literatur von Frauen*, vol.

1: *Vom Mittelalter bis zum Ende des 18. Jahrhunderts* [German Literature by Women, vol. 1: From the Middle Ages to the End of the 18th Century] (Munich, 1988).

87. Walter, *Schrieb oft, von Mägde Arbeit müde* (note 34 above).

88. Inge Buck (ed.), *Einfahrendes Frauenzimmer. Die Lebenserinnerungen der Kömödiantin Karoline Schulze-Kummerfeld 1745-1815* [A Traveling Woman: Memoirs of the Actress Karoline Schulze-Kummerfeld] (Berlin: Orlanda Frauenverlag, 1988).

89. Eva Weissweiler, *Komponistinnen aus 500 Jahren* [500 Years of Women Composers] (Frankfurt/Main: Fischer, 1981).

90. See Luise F. Pusch (ed.), *Schwestern berühmter Männer* [Sisters of Famous Men] (Frankfurt/Main: Insel, 1985), pp. 123-54; Swantje Koch-Kanz and Luise F. Pusch, 'Die Töchter von Johann Sebastian Bach [The Daughters of Johann Sebastian Bach]', in Luise F. Pusch (ed.), *Töchter berühmter Männer* [Daughters of Famous Men] (Frankfurt/Main: Insel, 1988), pp. 117-54.

91. Neue Gesellschaft für Bildende Kunst e.V., Berlin (ed.), *Das Verborgene Museum I: Dokumentation der Kunst von Frauen in Berliner öffentlichen Sammlungen* [The Hidden Museum, vol. 1: Documentation on Women's Art in Berlin Public Collections] (Berlin: Hentrich, 1987).

92. Christina Vanja, 'Zwischen Expansion und Verdrängung, Kontrolle und Befreiung. Vortrag auf der Tagung *Frauenrollen - Frauenbilder in Spätmittelalter und Früher Neuzeit* [Between Expansion and Repression, Control, and Liberation: Lecture for the Conference on Women's Roles and Images in the Late Middle Ages and Early Modern Times], bei der Werner-Reimers-Stiftung, Bad Homburg, 1988' (forthcoming).

93. Rita Bake, 'Trotz Fleiss kein Preis. Frauenarbeit und Frauenarmut im 18. Jahrhundert [Despite Diligence, No Profit: Women's Work and Women's Poverty in the Eighteenth Century]', in Schmidt-Linsenhoff (ed.), *Sklavin oder Bürgerin?*, pp. 260-74.

94. Helfried Valentinitsch, 'Aus dem Leben eines "liederlichen Weibsbildes". Zur rechtlichen und sozialen Stellung von Randschichten der steierischen Bevölkerung im 18. Jahrhundert [From the Life of a 'Loose Woman': On the Legal and Social Position of Marginal Groups in the Population of Styria during the 18th Century]', in Kurt Ebert (ed.) *Festschrift Nikolaus Grass* (Innsbruck: Universitätsverlag Wagner, 1986).

95. Jürgen Schlumbohm, 'Ledige Mütter als "lebendige Phantome", oder: Wie aus einer Weibersache eine Wissenschaft wurde. Die ehemalige Entbindungsanstalt der Universität Göttingen am Geismar Tor [Single Mothers as "Living Phantoms", or How the Women's Cause became a Science: The Former Maternity Hospital of the University of Göttingen at Geismar Gate]', in Kornelia Duwe, Carola Gottschalk, and Marianne Koerner (eds.), *Göttingen ohne Gänseliesel* (Göttingen: Wartberg, 1988), pp. 150-63; Mary Lindemann, 'Fürsorge für arme Wöchnerinnen in Hamburg um 1800: Die Beschreibung eines "Entbindungs-Winkels" [Welfare for Newly Delivered Poor Mothers in Hamburg around 1800: The Description of a "Delivery Corner"]', *Gesnerus*, 32 (1982), pp. 395-403.

96. Peter Borscheid, *Geschichte des Alters 1600-1800* [History of Old Age, 1600- 1800] (Münster: Coppenrath, 2nd ed., 1987); Josef Ehmer, *Sozialgeschichte des Alters* [Social History of Old Age] (Frankfurt/Main: Suhrkamp, 1989).

97. Fischer-Homberger, *Krankheit Frau* (note 41 above).

98. Duden, *Geschichte unter der Haut* (note 41 above).

99. In Jochen Martin and Renate Zoepffel (eds.), *Aufgaben, Rollen und Träume von Mann und Frau* [Duties, Roles, and Dreams of Man and Woman] (Freiburg and Munich: Verlag Karl Alber, 1989), pp. 751-818.

100. Margret Wensky, 'Die Frau im Handel und Gewerbe vom Mittelalter bis zur frühen Neuzeit [Women in Trade and Business from the Middle Ages to Early Modern Times]', in Pohl (ed.), *Die Frau in der deutschen Wirtschaft* (note 26 above), pp. 30-44; Wensky, 'Die Stellung der Frau in Familie, Haushalt und Wirtschaftsbetrieb im spätmittelalterlich - früneuzeitlichen Köln [The Position of Women in the Family, Household, and Economic Management in Late Medieval and Early Modern Cologne]', in Alfred Haverkamp (ed.), *Haus- und Familie in der spätmittelalterlichen Stadt* (Cologne: Böhlau, 1984), pp. 289-330; Wensky, *Die Stellung der Frau in der stadtkölnischen Wirtschaft im Spätmittelalter* [Women's Position in the City Economy of Cologne in the Late Middle Ages] (Cologne: Bohlau, 1980); Klaus-Joachim Lorenzen-Schmidt, 'Zur Stellung der Frauen in der frühneuzeitlichen Städtegesellschaft Schleswigs und Holsteins [On the Situation of Women in Early Modern Urban Society in Schleswig and Holstein]', *Archiv für Kulturgeschichte*, 61 (1979), pp. 317-29; Peter-Per Krebs, 'Die Stellung der Handwerkerwitwe in der Zunft vom Spätmittelalter bis zum 18. Jahrhundert [The Situation of Craftsmen's Widows in the Guilds from the Late Middle Ages to the 18th Century]', Ph.D. dissertation, Regensburg, 1974; Petra Renschler, 'Lohnarbeit und Familienökonomie. Zur Frauenarbeit im Zeitalter der Französischen Revolution [Waged Work and Family Economy: On Women's Work in the Time of the French Revolution]', in Schmidt-Linsenhoff (ed.), *Sklavin oder Bürgerin?*, pp. 223-46.

101. Margarete Freudenthal, *Gestaltwandel der städtischen, bürgerlichen und proletarischen Hauswirtschaft zwischen 1760 und 1910* [Structural Changes in the Urban, Bourgeois, and Proletarian Household Economy between 1760 and 1910] (Frankfurt/Main and Berlin: Ullstein, 1986).

102. Rita Bake and Birgit Kiupel (eds.), *Margarethe E. Milow. Ich will aber nicht murren. Mein Leben* [But I Don't Want to Complain: My Life], vol. 2 (Hamburg: Dölling und Galitz, 1987).

103. Rudolf Engelsing, 'Der Arbeitsmarkt der Dienstboten im 17., 18. und 19. Jahrhundert [The Job Market for Domestic Servants in the 17th, 18th, and 19th Centuries]', in H. Kellenbenz (ed.), *Wirtschaftspolitik und Arbeitsmarkt* (Munich, 1981), pp. 159-237.

104. Karl-Sigismund Kramer, *Fränkisches Alltagsleben um 1500. Eid, Markt und Zoll im Vollkacher Salbuch* [Franconian Daily Life around 1500: Oath, Market, and Customs Duties in the Customs Book of Vollkach] (Würzburg: Echter, 1985); Gerd Wunder, *Die Bürger von Hall. Sozialgeschichte einer Reichsstadt 1216-1802* [The Citizens of Hall: Social History of a Free Imperial City] (Sigmaringen: Jan Thorbecke Verlag, 1982).

105. Edith Ennen, 'Die Frau in der Landwirtschaft vom Mittelalter bis zur frühen Neuzeit [Women in Agriculture from the Middle Ages to Early Modern Times]', in Pohl (ed.), *Frau in der deutschen Wirtschaft*, pp. 18-29.

106. Christina Vanja, 'Verkehrte Welt - Das Weibergericht in einem hessischen Dorf des 17. Jahrhunderts [A Topsy-Turvy World - The Women's Court in a Seventeenth- Century Hessian Village]', *Journal für Geschichte*, 5 (1986), pp.

22-29; see also Vanja, 'Frauen im Dorf. Ihre Stellung unter besonderer Berücksichtigung landgräflich-hessischer Quellen des späten Mittelalters [Village Women: Their Position with Special Reference to the Late Medieval Sources of the Landgrave of Hesse]', *Zeitschrift für Agrargeschichte und Agrarsoziologie*, 34, no. 2 (1986), pp. 147-59.

107. Heide Wunder, 'Zur Stellung der Frauen in Preussisch-Litauen (16./17. Jahrhundert). Ein Versuch [Women's Position in Prussian Lithuania in the 16th and 17th Centuries: A Preliminary Study]', *Preussenland, 22, no. 3 (1984), pp. 33-40.*

108. Michael Mitterauer, *Ledige Mütter. Zur Geschichte unehelicher Geburten in Europa* [Single Mothers: On the History of Out-of-Wedlock Births in Europe] (Munich: Beck, 1983); Rainer Beck, 'Illegitimität und voreheliche Sexualität auf dem Land. Unterfinning 1671-1770 [Rural Illegitimacy and Premarital Sexuality]', in Van Dülmen (ed.), *Kultur der einfachen Leute*, pp. 112-50; Göttsch, 'Weibliche Erfahrungen', (noted above).

109. See Elisabeth Gössmann (ed.), *Das wohlgelahrte Frauenzimmer* [The Well-Learned Woman] (Munich: Iudicium, 1984; Archiv für philosophie- und theologiegeschichtliche Frauenforschung, vol. 1), and subsequent volumes in this series (note 48 above).

110. Silvia Bovenschen, *Die imaginierte Weiblichkeit. Exemplarische Untersuchungen zu kulturgeschichtlichen und literarischen Präsentationsformen des Weiblichen* [Imagined Femininity: Attempts to Examine the Cultural Historical and Literary Forms of Representation of the Feminine] (Frankfurt/Main: Suhrkamp, 1979).

111. See Ursula Becher, 'Weibliches Selbstverständnis in Selbstzeugnissen des 18. Jahrhundert [Womanly Self-Understanding as Seen in Autobiographical Accounts From the Eighteenth Century], in Ursula Becher and Jörn Rüsen (eds.), *Weiblichkeit in geschichtlicher Perspektive* (Frankfurt/Main: Suhrkamp, 1988), pp. 217-33; Bärbel Kern and Horst Kern, *Madame Doctorin Schlözer. Ein Frauenleben in den Widersprüchen der Aufklärung* [Madame Doctor Schlözer: A Woman Caught in the Contradictions of the Enlightenment] (Munich: Beck, 1988); Ulrike Prokop, 'Cornelia Goethe (1750-1777). Die Melancholie der Cornelia Goethe [The Melancholia of Cornelia Goethe]', in Pusch (ed.), *Schwester berühmter Männer*, pp. 49-122.

112. Schmidt-Linsenhoff, *Sklavin oder Bürgerin?*

113. Hessische Landeszentrale für politische Bildung (ed.), *Freiheit - Gleichheit - Schwesterlichkeit. Männer und Frauen zur Zeit der Französischen Revolution* [Freedom - Equality - Sisterhood: Men and Women in the Age of the French Revolution] (Niedernhausen, 1989).

18

Historical Research on Women in the German Democratic Republic

Petra Rantzsch
Erika Uitz

By way of introduction, we should like to make two statements regarding the scope of our report on historical research on women in the German Democratic Republic (GDR). First, this report essentially covers the state of research during the last ten years. Assessments of earlier work merely serve to clarify the background of current historical research on women in the GDR. Second, the bibliographical references given in our footnotes are selective. More detailed information concerning scholarly production during the indicated period can be found in the reports on literature in the *Zeitschrift für Geschichtswissenschaft* [Journal of the Science of History].[1]

Research in women's history in the GDR has been ongoing for decades. It first developed in connection with the formation of an independent science of history in the GDR in the years following the end of the Second World War. After the elimination of fascism the principal task of the science of history in the GDR was to critically analyse reactionary interpretations of history and to rework and reassess the historical legacy. More specifically, the task was to uncover revolutionary, progressive, democratic and anti-fascist lines of development from the past and to carry them forward. With the founding in 1949 of the GDR, a working-class state linked to broad democratic social forces, historians were called upon to research the role of the people in history with particular attention to the proletarian movement since the nineteenth century. In this connection, historical research on women received some early attention, albeit not enough from our contemporary perspective.

In 1966 various research initiatives resulted in the foundation of a research group called 'The History of the Struggle of the Working Class for Women's Liberation' at the College of Education in Leipzig. In acknowledgement of its pioneering role with respect to research in women's history in the GDR, the name of 'Clara Zetkin' was bestowed on the college. Taking into account current democratising developments in the GDR from 1989, and the pressing need, clearly indicated for some time, for the expansion of research on women, this research group is now in the process of establishing a 'Women in History' research centre, and is thus overcoming previous politically-motivated restrictions on research topics. The decision to create such a centre was made in December 1989.

In 1964, following a decision reached by the Council of Ministers of the GDR, a scientific advisory committee called 'Women in Socialist Society' was established. It was the responsibility of this committee to manage, plan, co-ordinate, and initiate research projects designed to further the consolidation of women's position in all aspects of society. In accordance with the complexity of its assigned task, the advisory committee promoted interdisciplinary co-operation between sociologists, historians, philosophers, legal scholars, educators, economists, scientists specialising in the study of young people, vocational teachers, psychologists, and medical scientists.

During the sixties, investigations into the role of women in medieval social-religious movements were undertaken under the aegis of the medieval studies research group of the Institute for General History at the Karl Marx University in Leipzig. In addition, the Department of History at the 'Erich Weinert' College of Education in Magdeburg took up and thematically extended research work on the role of women in medieval feudal society.

Research in women's history is currently being carried out at the following institutions:
- The Institute for the History of the Workers' Movement, formerly the Institute for Marxism-Leninism, Berlin. Here, as a component of the history of the workers' movement, research is undertaken to help clarify the role of outstanding women, such as Rosa Luxemburg, Clara Zetkin and others, belonging to the German and international working class. Other subjects under investigation include research on the life of anti-fascist female resistance fighters; research on early theoretical-methodological achievements, in particular those of August Bebel and Clara Zetkin, contributing to the marxist approach to the women's question in history, as well as to the role of women in socialist society.
- The Central Institute for History at the Academy of Sciences of the GDR. Research on the history of women is conducted at this Institute in connection with research on the medieval bourgeoisie, and also within the framework of reworking the heritage of historical personalities. Research in women's history is also undertaken in connection with social historical investigations, mainly in the field of regional history and folklore, but also with respect to the revolution of 1848 in Germany.

- The Central Institute for Ancient History and Archaeology at the Academy of Sciences of the GDR. Historical research on women takes place here in connection with research on the development of marriage and the family in pre-capitalist social formations, and also in connection with investigations of the theoretical-methodological significance of Friedrich Engel's *The Origin of the Family, Private Property and the State*. Studies are also undertaken of the role of women in antiquity.
- The Humboldt University, Berlin. Here research in connection with the medieval studies of the early middle ages includes research on women of the period. Women are also included as subjects of some of the investigations shedding light on the role and legacy of historical personalities. Studies in the field of cultural history also encompass some research in women's history.
- The Friedrich Schiller University, Jena. Studies here in the history of modern times and cultural history include historical research on women.
- Karl Marx University, Leipzig. Research has been carried out here on outstanding female figures of the Middle Ages, such as Jeanne d'Arc, Heloise and Christine von Pizan.

Women's history research in the GDR is, to a large extent, still committed to a marxist understanding of society that sees society as a totality, of which, of course, the relation between the sexes is an integral part. In particular, August Bebel and Clara Zetkin devoted considerable attention to the historical aspect of the women's question in their writings. Unearthing the widest possible range of new sources and utilising international research results are characteristic of the founders of the marxist science of history, as well as of women's history research in the GDR.

A basic premise of marxist women's history research is the view that women's issues, as social issues, must be seen as closely bound up with the entire social process, such as the development of the economic structure of society and its accompanying conflicts. Thus, the development of relations between the sexes cannot be seen as a consequence primarily of biologically determined differences, or of a natural conflict of interests. Instead, the relations between the sexes have to be seen as a result of particular social-economic conditions. Without a doubt this basic relationship is influenced by legal, religious and cultural factors as well as historical traditions and mentalities. Even in today's GDR the continuation of inequalities between the sexes apart from the economic and legal context is obvious. In the language of the radical social changes currently taking place in the GDR, these unequal relations between the sexes can be effectively, if not with scientific exactitude, labeled as patriarchal structures. Thus, further theoretical working out of the women's question as set forth here is of the utmost importance.

Women's history research in the GDR was given a theoretical-methodological starting point for further development by Karl Marx's articulation of the view that paid labour for women is a crucial condition for women's emancipation. This he worked out in *Das Kapital*. Clara Zetkin gave further emphasis to this theoretical conception in her ground-breaking speech at the founding congress of the Second International in 1889. These theoretical-methodological views influenced the work of further conceptualisation and established a focal point for further research.

Efforts towards further theoretical disclosure resulted from the following:
- research on the proletarian women's movement since its beginning;
- research on women's roles in the building of a socialist society in the GDR;
- research on the progressive traditions within the bourgeois women's movement of Germany;
- research on the development of the social position of women in various regions and periods.

Useful theoretical-methodological research was carried out in connection with studies on the relationship of marriage, family and social structure in pre-capitalist epochs, and in particular on the role and social position of women in feudalism.[2] Other theoretical-methodological research focused on the ideologies of women's emancipation in Germany and France from 1789 to 1871, as well as on basic issues in the proletarian women's movement.[3]

Historiographical contributions to the marxist theory of women's liberation ensued. In particular, research on the position of the labour parties with respect to August Bebel's major work *Die Frau und der Sozialismus* [Women and Socialism] should be mentioned. The results of this research were presented at an international conference in 1979 celebrating the one-hundredth anniversary of the publication of *Die Frau*.[4] Furthermore, the publication of primary source materials[5] and new editions of basic works on women's emancipation[6] were begun.

Progress was made in researching the history of the German proletarian women's movement since the 1860s. These research results confirmed the basic realisation that the proletarian women's movement developed as part of the workers' movement, owing above all to its revolutionary, marxist forces. This development received particularly clear expression in the successful initiative of Clara Zetkin in 1910 to have an International Women's Day declared at the Second Socialist Women's Conference in Copenhagen. This day has since become an internationally observed tradition of the women's movement, thus developing far beyond the scope of the workers' movement.

Among other things, these historical studies document the historical attempts of the revolutionary workers' movement to win over women for the peace movement as well as the contribution of the proletarian women's movement to the struggle for peace.[7] Within the framework of a more comprehensive study, the proletarian women's movement of a large city – Leipzig – has also been studied for the first time.[8] Other studies have dealt specifically with the women's movement within the trade union movement before 1914.[9] Very comprehensive studies are now available concerning the November Revolution of 1918 in Germany, in which proletarian and other working women actively participated and women's issues gained specific recognition.[10] These findings also shed light upon the connection between the beginning of the communist women's movement and the foundation of the German Communist Party. Specific studies have been completed on the essential aspects of women's policy within the German Communist Party, especially with regard to theoretical, programmatic and socio-political issues.[11]

Studies of the German and international social democratic women's policies have also been produced. Focal points for these studies included the November Revolution, the years 1919 to 1929, and the Socialist Workers' International. These studies clarify the historical achievements of the Social Democratic Party of Germany (SPD), as well as its limitations.[12] Generally, the findings establish that the German Communist Party (KPD), in contrast to other political parties of the Weimar Republic, developed extensive ideas with respect to women's emancipation. Research has also been done on the women's policy of the German Communist Party during the period of fascism and on the role of women in the anti-fascist resistance. The comprehensive primary source materials that have been assembled substantiate the mobilizing role of the KPD in the development of various activities for women and girls in the resistance.[13] Moreover, these materials reveal the character of fascism as being absolutely hostile towards the interests of women and mothers. Specific studies of the policies towards women of the German fascist imperialism of 1933-1945 are available. These policies prove to have been demagogically manipulative and hostile to women's emancipation.[14]

Studies of the international women's movement prior to 1945 were also undertaken in order to secure a clearer perspective on, and thus a more refined appreciation of, the role of women in German history within the international context. Issues studied in particular have included: the policies towards women of the Communist International, the formation and effectiveness of the international anti-fascist women's movement, and the histories of the International Women's League for Peace and Freedom and of the International Democratic Women's Federation.[15]

To provide impetus and theoretical entry points for the practical realisation of equal rights for women in the GDR, historical research on women (and the research on women by other sociological disciplines within the GDR) turned early on to the study of women's roles in the social development of GDR as well as to the study of how the women's policies of the socialist state might be realised in the field of women's paid employment.[16] Specific studies have been devoted to the history of Women's Day.[17] Other studies have been made of social and demographic processes and family policy, all of which influenced the realisation of equal rights for women.[18]

One should not overlook the fact that many of the publications dealing with women's roles in the GDR and with the policies towards women of its ruling powers have tended to be apologetic. The authors saw themselves as more or less obliged to adhere to a stalinist conception of socialism, and thus to its corresponding view of contemporary history. These works nevertheless contain important facts and draw attention to problems of development in such countries as Bulgaria, Poland, Czechoslovakia, the USSR, and Hungary. Moreover, at their core were problems arising specifically from the incompatibility of paid employment and motherhood during the formative years of socialism. Generally speaking, it seems clear that the topics selected were not yet integrated into historical research in these countries. On the one hand, research documented the steps taken, mainly by the ruling communist parties since 1944/45, towards realising equal rights for women. On the other hand, the research revealed the manifold problems of development, particularly in this area of social policy.[19]

During the eighties, influenced by the rapprochement between the two Germanys, the science of history in the GDR took increasing account of the various trends of the bourgeois women's movement. This development corresponds with the increasing reappraisal of the entire historical heritage and the gradual overcoming of the restrictive search for the progressive traditions in Germany history only. It became valid to study the beginnings of the bourgeois women's movement, the development of the Federation of German Women's Organizations from 1894 to 1914, and the left wing of the bourgeois women's movement, as well as the effects of the Socialist October Revolution of 1917 in Russia and the November Revolution of 1918 in Germany on the bourgeois women's movement and the ensuing policies towards women of the bourgeois parties.[20] Further research has dealt with the overall process of women's emancipation during the Weimar Republic,[21] with the bourgeois women's organisations, and in particular with the lower-middle-class democratic forces of the non-marxist women's movement. Moreover, original research results have been obtained concerning the activities of the

International Women's Federation and the International Association for Maternal Protection and Sexual Reform founded in 1910.[22] Analyses concerning various groups within the non-marxist women's movement made clear that lower-middle-class democratic forces increased during the period of the Weimar Republic. These groups were fighting for peace, democracy and social progress, together with all democratic-minded people, including representatives of the workers' movement.

The growing tendency of the science of history in the GDR to analyse the entire heritage of German history was also important for women's research, insofar as it promoted biographical studies. Biographical sketches of the wives of leading politicians and theorists of the workers' movement have been produced.[23] Numerous biographical studies have been devoted to outstanding women of the social democratic and communist movements, as well as of the women's trade union movement. The life and writings of Rosa Luxemburg are available in the form of a biography, collected essays and volumes of letters. Further studies were done on the life and work of Clara Zetkin, whose selected works were published years ago.[24]

During the past few years, biographical studies have been extended to cover outstanding bourgeois women in German and general history. The biographies of two famous representatives of the lower-middle-class democratic wing of the bourgeois women's movement should be singled out for mention, namely those of Minna Cauer and Helene Stöcker.[25] Such studies are available on women of earlier times as well. For example, a biographical sketch of Maria Theresa was included in the volume *Herrscherpersönlichkeiten der Neuzeit* [Ruling Personalities of the Modern Age].[26] Another volume in this series covers the middle ages from the tenth to the thirteenth century and includes biographical sketches of nine female rulers and nuns, with the latest research results on the Empress Adelheid, Eleonore of Aquitaine, and Hrotsvit [Hrosvitha] of Gandersheim. This biographical work will be continued for the late middle ages. The series' contribution to knowledge derives from its concentration on relational structures: changes in the social balance of power, variation in the political power structures and in the role of women rulers. The series also advances our knowledge through its uncovering of the moral values and rules for living held by women in the middle ages.[27]

In accordance with our tradition of the marxist science of history and in conjunction with current modern international trends in historical research, there has been an accelerated development during the past few years of research foci that are relevant to women's history studies. We think, for example, of social-historically oriented research on family history and research projects on folklore or on the history of culture. These research trends contribute in a vital manner to the illumination of new dimensions of women's history. They also provide specific information about the situation of women in marriage and the family, and about women's ordinary lives, while taking into account family status, age and motherhood. They also reveal important information about the impact a woman's paid job has on her social position under various social conditions and in various time periods.

Studies of this kind have been produced on the social history of Saxony, Berlin and Gotha during the transitional period from feudalism to capitalism.[28] Similarly, studies of the living conditions of female servants as well as of working women and girls in big cities have investigated the way of life and everyday life of female workers at the end of the nineteenth century and the beginning of the twentieth.[29] The everyday life of female workers during the post-war period (1945-1949) has been the subject of additional investigations, as have the lives of female workers in industry in the GDR during the 1950s, including their daily struggle for equal rights in employment.[30] Another study concerned with women in the country has focused on family structure in the villages in the Magdeburger Börde during the period 1900-1960. It also draws on female self-portraits.[31]

Researchers with a focus on the role and social position of women have also turned their attention toward developments in other European and non-European countries. For instance, on the basis of travel stories and cultural traditions, the respected social position and role of women in pre-colonial Africa have been demonstrated and described convincingly.[32] Moreover, studies on the female city dweller in the Middle Ages have revealed the meaning that those social-cultural changes in feudal society, which culminated in the strengthening of medieval towns, had for the development of occupations for women living in urban centres and for the improvement of their legal position.[33]

*   *   *   *   *

If in conclusion one attempts to summarise the most important research results of the last ten years, including present trends, as well as the problems that transcend specific historical periods, it will become obvious that for the period from the end of the nineteenth century onward a very extensive body of work has been accomplished in the area of the role of women. This is particularly true with respect to the German proletarian women's movement, the women's movement of the revolutionary party of the working class in Germany prior to 1945, and in the GDR.

Some important preliminary work that lays a foundation for future research deserves special mention. Immediate access to research results is ensured by the publication of an Information Bulletin by the research centre 'Women in History' at the 'Clara Zetkin' College of Education in Leipzig. Formerly the association 'History of the Struggle of the Working Class for Women's Liberation' provided this service. One should also consult the newsletter *Die Frau in der Sozialistischen Gesellschaft* [The Woman in Socialist Society], edited by the Academy of Sciences of the GDR and published by its Scientific Advisory Council, as well as the bibliographical reference work on the history of the German working class struggle for women's liberation and on women's role in the German workers' movement.[34] Also useful is the two-volume chronological survey *Zur Rolle der Frau in der Geschichte des deutschen Volkes nach 1830* [Women's Role in the History of the German People since 1830].[35]

In numerous areas of the history of women in modern and contemporary society, however, considerable gaps remain. These will have to be researched step by step in the 1990s. The same can be more or less said for the transition period from feudalism to capitalism. For the more recent period, work remains to be done on the influence of German trade unions on working women, particularly after 1914. But work also needs to be done for the period after the founding of the Free German Trade Union, the trades' organisation of the GDR, as well as on the women's politics of the SED. The objective of this work must be the critical analysis of the degree of equality achieved by women in the GDR. To this end, the women's policies of the SED and the GDR government must be researched. The question is: To what extent did they either change or support the still remaining patriarchal structures. In the area of the history of the international women's movement, it will be important to further investigate further the activities of the International Democratic Women's Federation, the influence of international non-marxist women's organisations, the political work of women of the Socialist International of 1923-1939 and, more particularly, of the Socialist Workers' International since 1951. In addition, the policies towards women of the German bourgeoisie, its state and parties (especially after 1917) will have to be researched. A field that remains open for further research is the history of women's paid work and women's place in the development of individual classes and strata of capitalist society in Germany prior to 1945. Here too it will be possible also to connect up with international women's history research.

One of the basic problems is the very slow integration of the results of historical research on women into the more general historical overviews which essentially determine the lay person's overall picture of history. Nor are teaching curricula and lesson plans as yet satisfactory. On the other hand, increasing numbers of publications bring the results of historical research on women to a wide readership, thus introducing many more people to issues in the history of women.[36]

Great efforts will continue to be required to elucidate the role of women throughout history, and to document the concrete changes in their social position dependent on social-economical, legal and ideological conditions, in particular their efforts to improve their social and legal situation. Such work cannot be accomplished by women's history research alone. This is especially true of small countries with a relatively small number of historians. For this reason, increased interdisciplinary collaboration and, above all, the integration of women's history into general historical research are essential. By this we mean the inclusion of gender-specific questions in current historical, ethnographic and historical-cultural research as well as in other historically relevant social scientific research.[37]

Developments during the past few years indicate that this process is under way. Besides the above mentioned ethnographic and social-historical studies in the field of regional history, this trend holds true for academic history as well,[38] for research on the bourgeois revolution of 1848 and on the early history of the German feudal state, for example. Integration of gender-specific questions into the current research of various historical disciplines has the advantage of lessening the risk of isolation that women's history research on its own runs. Integration can contribute to a faster flow of information from research in women's history into general historical research as has been shown in the past by the research community of the 'Clara Zetkin' College of Education.

It is obvious that integrative women's research is dependent on rapid access to the results of international research. Therefore, bibliographical information from the International Federation for Research in Women's History is of great value and highly appreciated.

NOTES

Abbreviations:
Thesis A – [Thesis for a Doctorate in a Branch of Science]
Thesis B – [Thesis for a Doctor of Science]

The text has been translated by Ria Bleumer with the assistance of Ruth Roach Pierson, the notes by Pierson.

1. Hans-Jürgen Arendt and Fritz Staude, 'Forschungen zur Geschichte der Frauenbewegung [Studies on the History of the Women's Movement]', in 'Historische Forschungen in der DDR 1970-1980. Analysen und Berichte zum XV.

Internationalen Historikerkongreß in Bukarest 1980 [Historical Research in the GDR 1970-1980: Analyses and Reports for the 15th International Congress of the Historical Sciences in Bucharest 1980]', *Zeitschrift für Geschichtswissenschaft* (ZfG), Special Issue (1980), pp. 707-19; Hans-Jürgen Arendt , Fritz Staude, and Petra Rantzsch, 'Forschungen zur Geschichte der Frauen und der Frauenbewegung [Studies of the History of Women and of the Women's Movement]', in 'Historische Forschungen in der DDR 1980-1990. Analysen und Berichte zum XVII. Internationalen Historikerkongreß in Madrid 1990', *ZfG*, Special Issue (1990, forthcoming); see also *The Changing Role of Women in Society: A Documentation of Current Research 1984-1987*, ed. by Werner Richter, Liisa Husu, and Arnaud Marks for the European Co-operation in Social Science Information and Documentation (ECSSID) Programme, co-ordinated by the European Co-ordination Centre for Research and Documentation in the Social Sciences (Berlin: Akademie-Verlag, 1989).

    2. Joachim Herrmann and Jens Köhn, *Familie, Staat und Gesellschaftsformation. Grundprobleme vorkapitalistischer Epochen einhundert Jahre nach Friedrich Engels' Werk 'Der Ursprung der Familie, des Privateigentums und des Staats'* [Family, State and the Formation of Society: Basic Problems of Pre-Capitalist Epochs a Hundred Years after Friedrich Engels' Work *The Origin of the Family, Private Property and the State*] (Berlin: Akademie-Verlag, 1988); Erika Uitz, 'Frau und gesellschaftlicher Fortschritt in der mittelalterlichen Stadt [Woman and Social Progress in the Town of the Middle Ages]', in *ZfG*, 12 (1984), pp. 20-42; Erika Uitz, 'Zur gesellschaftlichen Stellung der Frau in der mittelalterlichen Stadt (Die Situation im Erzbistum Magdeburg) [Concerning the Social Position of Women in Towns of the Middle Ages (The Situation in the Archbishopric of Magdeburg)]', in *Magdeburger Beiträge zur Stadtgeschichte*, 1 (1977), pp. 20-42.

    3. Hans-Jürgen Arendt, 'Einige Bemerkungen zur Darstellung der kommunistischen Frauenbewegung in Arbeiten zur regionalen Parteigeschichte [Some Remarks Concerning the Representation of the Communist Women's Movement in Works on the Regional History of the Party]', in *Parteigeschichte im regionalen Vergleich. 2. Leipziger Tagung zur Geschichte der Arbeiterbewegung, 26.-27. März 1987 (Referate und Diskussionsbeiträge)* (Leipzig: Eigenverlag der Karl-Marx-Universität, 1987), pp. 70-6; Fritz Staude, 'Zu Problemen der Erforschung und Darstellung der proletarischen Frauenbewegung [Concerning the Problems of Researching and Representing the Proletarian Women's Movement]', in *Protokollband der Konferenz 'Zur Geschichte der proletarischen Organisationen'* (Potsdam: Eigenverlag der Pädagogischen Hochschule 'Karl Liebknecht', 1984), pp. 86-92; Ingrid Strehler, *den Männern gleich an Rechten. Auffassungen zur Emanzipation der Frau in Frankreich und Deutschland 1789-1871* [Equal to Men in Rights: Opinions on the Emancipation of Women in France and Germany 1789-1871] (Leipzig: Verlag für die Frau, 1989).

    4. Fritz Staude, '100 Jahre Bebels Hauptwerk *Die Frau und der Sozialismus* [100 Years of Bebel's Major Work *Women and Socialism*]', in *Mitteilungsblatt der Forschungsgemeinschaft 'Geschichte des Kampfes der Arbeiterklasse für die Befreiung der Frau* [Bulletin of the Research Team 'History of the Working Class Struggle for Women's Liberation', Department of History, 'Clara Zetkin' College of Education, Leipzig], no. 1 (1979), pp. 5-20; Ursula Herrmann, 'Die Verarbeitung von Ideen aus Friedrich Engels Schrift *Der Ursprung*

der Familie, des Privateigentums und des Staates durch August Bebel in seinem Buch *Die Frau und der Sozialismus* [The Development of Ideas from Friedrich Engels' Book *The Origin of the Family, Private Property, and the State* by August Bebel in his Book *Women and Socialism*]', in *Informationen des Wissenschaftlichen Rates 'Die Frau in der Sozialistischen Gesellschaft' bei der Akademie der Wissenschaften der DDR*, no. 6 (1985), pp. 42-58; Gerhard Becker, 'Frauen über August Bebel 1910. Artikel über den Verfasser von "Die Frau und der Sozialismus" zu dessen 70. Geburtstag [Women on August Bebel in 1910: Articles about the Author of *Women and Socialism* on His 70th Birthday]', *ZfG*, no. 1 (1990), pp. 32-57; Proceedings of the International Conference of the Central Committee of the SED, on the Occasion of the 100th Anniversary of the Publication of August Bebel's Book *Women and Socialism*, 23-25 February 1979, parts 1 and 2 (Berlin, 1979). See also the jubilee edition, edited for this occasion, of August Bebel, *Die Frau und der Sozialismus* (Berlin: Dietz Verlag, 1979).

5. For example, Eberhard Recklies, '"Die werktätige Frau und Hitlers Raubkrieg": Eine Agitations- und Propagendaschrift der KPD aus den Jahren 1944 ["Working Women and Hitler's War of Plunder": A Study of Agitation and Propaganda by the KPD from the Year 1944]', *Informationen des Wissenschaftlichen Rates 'Die Frau in der Sozialistischen Gesellschaft'*, 1 (1986), pp. 22-42.

6. For example, Eleanor Marx-Aveling and Eduard Aveling, *Die Frauenfrage* [The Woman Question], ed. by Joachim Müller and Edith Schotte (Leipzig: Verlag für die Frau, 1986).

7. Fritz Staude, 'Clara Zetkins Kampf für den Frieden – gegen Militarismus und Krieg (1889-1914) [Clara Zetkin's Fight for Peace – Against Militarism and War (1889-1914)]', *Informationen des Wissenschaftlichen Rates*, no. 3 (1986), pp. 46-54; Ursula Herrmann, 'Sozialdemokratische Frauen in Deutschland im Kampf um den Frieden vor und während des ersten Weltkrieges [Social-Democratic Women in Germany in the Fight for Peace, Before and During World War I]', *ZfG*, no. 3 (1985), pp. 213-30; Elke Böttger and Regine Danneberg, 'Chronik des Kampfes der werktätigen deutschen Frauen und Mädchen gegen imperialistischen Krieg in der Zeit vom 1. August 1914 bis zum Ausbruch der Novemberrevolution 1918 [Chronicle of the Fight of German Working Women and Girls Against Imperialistic War from 1 August 1914 to the Beginning of the November Revolution of 1918]', *Informationen des Wissenschaftlichen Rates*, no. 3 (1979), pp. 25-67.

8. Rainer Schilling, 'Die proletarische Frauenbewegung in Leipzig von 1890 bis 1908 [The Proletarian Women's Movement in Leipzig from 1890 to 1908]', Thesis A, 'Clara Zetkin' College of Education, Leipzig, 1987.

9. Dieter Peuser, 'Die gewerkschaftliche Arbeiterinnenbewegung in Deutschland (1885-1896) [The Unionized Working Women's Movement in Germany (1885-1896)]', Thesis A, 'Clara Zetkin' College of Education, Leipzig, 1979; Birgit Klaubert, 'Das Ringen der freien Gewerkschaften Deutschlands um die Organisierung der Arbeiterinnen von 1896 bis zum Ausbruch des ersten Weltkrieges [The Struggle of the Free Trade Unions of Germany to Organise Working Women from 1896 to the Outbreak of the First World War]', Thesis A, 'Clara Zetkin' College of Education, Leipzig, 1986.

10. Peter Kuhlbrodt, 'Die proletarische Frauenbewegung in Deutschland am Vorabend und während der Novemberrevolution (Herbst 1917 bis Anfang Mai 1919) [The Proletarian Women's Movement in Germany on the Eve of and During the November Revolution (Autumn 1917 to the Beginning of May 1919)]', Thesis A, 'Clara Zetkin' College of Education, Leipzig, 1981; *Die Novemberrevolution 1918/19 in Deutschland und die Frauen. Kolloquim der Forschungsgemeinschaft 'Geschichte des Kampfes der Arbeiterklasse für die Befreiung der Frau' am 27. September 1988, Referate und Diskussionsbeiträge)* [The November Revolution 1918/19 in Germany and Women: Colloquium of the Research Team 'History of the Struggle of the Working Class for Women's Liberation' on 27 September 1988, Papers and Discussions] (Leipzig: Eigenverlag der Pädagogische Hochschule 'Clara Zetkin', 1989); Hans-Jürgen Arendt and Peter Kuhlbrodt, 'Die proletarische Frauenbewegung in der Novemberrevolution 1918/19 [The Proletarian Women's Movement during the November Revolution 1918/19]', *Beiträge zur Geschichte der Arbeiterbewegung*, no. 6 (1988), pp. 761-73.

11. Hans-Jürgen Arendt, 'Die Frauenpolitik der KPD 1918-1945 [The Women's Politics of the KPD, 1918-1945]', *Konsequent, Beiträge zur marxistischen Theorie und Praxis*, hrsg. vom Parteivorstand der Sozialistischen Einheitspartei Westberlin, no. 1 (1988), pp. 97-103; Hans-Jürgen Arendt, 'Zur Frauenpolitik der KPD und zur Rolle der Frauen in der kommunistischen Bewegung Deutschlands [Concerning the Policy Towards Women of the KPD and the Role of Women in the Communist Movement of Germany]', in Ernest Bornemann (ed.), *Arbeiterbewegung und Feminismus, Berichte aus vierzehn Ländern* (Frankfurt a.M./West Berlin/Vienna: Ullstein Verlag, 1982), pp. 45-54; H.-J. Arendt, 'Zum Kamppf der Reichstagsfraktion der KPD für den Schutz von Mutter und Kind [On the Fight of the KPD Reichstag Fraction for the Protection of Mother and Child]', *Mitteilungsblatt*, no. 2 (1985), pp. 46-51; H.-J. Arendt, 'Die KPD und die werktätige Bäuerin [The German Communist Party and the Working Farm Woman]', *Wissenschaftliche Mitteilungen der Historiker-Gesellschaft der DDR*, no. 2 (1982), pp. 46-57.

12. Holger Hantzsch, 'Zur Frauenpolitik der rechten SPD-Führer und zur Sozialdemokratischen Frauenbewegung in der Zeit der Weimarer Republik (untersucht am Beispiel der Jahre 1919-1929) [Concerning the Women's Policy of the Right-wing SPD Leaders and the Social-democratic Women's Movement during the Weimar Republic (examined on the basis of the example provided by the years 1919-1929)]', Thesis A, 'Clara Zetkin' College of Education, Leipzig, 1985.

13. Eberhard Recklies, 'Zur Frauenpolitik der KPD und zur Rolle werktätiger deutscher Frauen im antifaschistischen Widerstandskampf während des zweiten Weltrieges (1939 bis 1945) [Concerning the Women's Policy of the KPD and the Role of Working Women in the Anti-fascist Resistance Fight during the Second World War (1939-1945)]', Thesis A, Educational Institute 'Clara Zetkin', Leipzig, 1985; E. Recklies, 'Zur Frauenpolitik der KPD im antifaschistischen Widerstandskampf 1933 bis 1945 [Concerning the Women's Policy of the KPD in the Anti-fascist Resistance Fight 1933 to 1945]', in *Kolloquium der Forschungsgemeinschaft 'Geschichte des Kampfes der Arbeiterklasse um die Befreiung der Frau', Leipzig, den 24. Januar 1983, Referate und Diskussionsbeiträge* (Leipzig: Eigenverlag der Pädagogischen Hochschule 'Clara Zetkin', 1983), pp. 73-83; Christian Friedrich, *Sie wollten uns brechen und brechen uns nicht . . . Zur Lage*

und zum antifaschistischen Widerstandskampf weiblicher Häftlinge im Frauenzuchthaus Cottbus 1938 bis 1945 [They Wanted to Break Us, but They Didn't Break Us . . . Concerning the Conditions and the Anti-fascist Resistance Fight of Female Prisoners in the Women's Prison of Cottbus, 1938-1945] (Cottbus: Verlag des Kreiskomitees Cottbus-Stadt der Antifaschistischen Widerstandskämpfer der DDR, 1986); Christian Klinger, 'Zum Anteil deutscher Frauen am antifaschistischen Widerstandskampf unter Führung der KPD (1933-1939) [Concerning the Participation by German Women in the Anti-fascist Resistance Fight Led by the KPD (1933-1945)]', Thesis A, 'Clara Zetkin' College of Education, Leipzig, 1975.

14. *Kolloquium der Forschungsgemeinschaft 'Geschichte des Kampfes der Arbeiterklasse um die Befreiung der Frau', Zur Frauenpolitik des faschistischen deutschen Imperialismus (1933-1945), am 27 Mai 1982, Referate und Diskussionsbeiträge* [Colloquium of the Research Team 'History of the Struggle of the Working Class for Women's Liberation', Concerning the Policies Towards Women of the Fascist German Imperialism (1933-1945), Papers and Discussions from 27 May 1982] (Leipzig: Eigenverlag der Pädagogischen Hochschule 'Clara Zetkin', 1982); see also, Hans-Jürgen Arendt, 'Mädchenerziehung im faschistischen Deutschland unter besonderer Berücksichtigung des BDM [The Education of Girls in Fascist Germany with Special Attention to the League of German Girls]', *Jahrbuch für Erziehungs- und Schulgeschichte*, 23 (1983), pp. 107-27; H.-J. Arendt, 'Grundzüge der Frauenpolitik des faschistischen deutschen Imperialismus 1933 bis 1939 [The Basic Features of the Policies Toward Women of the Fascist German Imperialism 1933 to 1939]', *Jahrbuch für Geschichte*, 24 (1981), pp. 313-49; H.-J. Arendt, 'Zur Frauenpolitik des faschistischen deutschen Imperialismus im zweiten Weltkrieg [Concerning the Policies Towards Women of the Fascist German Imperialism during the Second World War]', *Jahrbuch für Geschichte*, 26 (1982), pp. 299-333; Sigrid Jacobeit, 'Die Stellung der werktätigen Bäuerin in der faschistischen Ideologie 1933-1939. Realität und Manipulation [The Position of the Working Farm Woman in Fascist Ideology 1933-1939: Reality and Manipulation]', *Jahrbuch für Geschichte*, 27 (1983), pp. 171-99.

15. Siegfried Scholze, 'Zur Entwicklung der Frauenpolitik der Kommunistischen Internationale unter dem Einfluß Georgi Dimitroffs in den Jahren 1935-1937 [Concerning the Development of the Women's Policy of the Communist International under the Influence of Georgi Dimitroff during the Period 1935-1937]', in *Geschichte des Marxismus-Leninismus und der marxistisch-leninistischen Geschichtswissenschaft 1917-1945, Wege zu ihrer Erforschung und Darstellung* (Leipzig: Wissenschaftliche Beiträge der Karl-Marx Universität, 1985), pp. 141-7; Gisela Rannefeld, 'Der Platz des Weltkomitees der Frauen gegen Krieg und Faschismus im Kampf um die Erhaltung des Friedens in den 30er Jahren (1932-1939) [The Place of the World Committee of Women against War and Fascism in the Fight for Maintaining Peace in the Thirties (1932-1939)]', Thesis A, Educational Institute 'Clara Zetkin' College of Education, Leipzig, 1986; *40 Jahre IDFF – Zu ihrer Entstehungsgeschichte und ihrem Wirken. Kolloquium der Forschungsgruppe 'Geschichte des Kampfes der Arbeiterklasse um die Befreiung der Frau', Referate und Diskussionsbeiträge* [40 Years IDFF – Concerning the History of Its Genesis and Activities: Colloquium of the Research Group 'History of the Struggle of the Working Class for Women's Liberation', Papers and Discussions] (Leipzig: Eigenverlag Pädagogische Hochschule 'Clara Zetkin', 1986); Barbara Mücklich,

'Zum Kampf der demokratischen Frauenbewegung in den kapitalistischen Ländern Europas für Frieden und Abrüstung vom Ende der sechziger Jahre bis Anfang der achtziger Jahre [Concerning the Fight of the Domocratic Women's Movement in the Capitalist Countries of Europe for Peace and Disarmament from the End of the Sixties until the Beginning of the Eighties]', Thesis A, 'Clara Zetkin' College of Education, Leipzig, 1986; Siegfried Scholze, 'Zur Rolle des Neofeminismus [On the Role of Neofeminism]', *Chingin to Sahakaihosho* (Tokyo), no. 786 (1980), pp. 64-71; Christine Eifler, 'Zum Gesellschaftsverständnis radikaler Feministinnen [On the View of Society of Radical Feminists]', Thesis B, Zentralinstitut für Hochschulbildung, Berlin, 1989; Christine Seidel, 'Zur Rolle der Internationalen Frauenliga für Frieden und Freiheit in den Jahren 1945 bis 1975 [Concerning the Role of the Women's International League for Peace and Freedom in the Period 1945 to 1975]', Thesis A, 'Clara Zetkin' College of Education, Leipzig, 1981.

16. Hans-Jürgen Arendt, 'Zu den Etappen sozialistischer Frauenpolitik in der Geschichte der DDR [Concerning the Stages of Socialist Women's Policy in the History of the GDR]', *Informationen des Wissenschaftlichen Rates*, no. 5 (1982), pp. 40-6; Gudrun Partisch, 'Die Verwirklichung des Vermächtnisses von Karl Marx und Friedrich Engels bei der Lösung der Frauenfrage in der DDR [The Realisation of the Legacy of Karl Marx and Friedrich Engels concerning the Solution of the Women's Question in the GDR]', *Mitteilungsblatt*, no. 2 (1983), pp. 15-22; G. Partisch, 'Zu den Grundzügen sozialistischer Frauenpolitik bei Gründung der DDR [On the Essential Features of Socialist Women's Policy at the Founding of the GDR]', *Wissenschaftliche Zeitschrift der Pädagogischen Hochschule 'Clara Zetkin', Leipzig*, no. 2 (1989), pp. 8-11. In this connection, see also the documentation of law prepared by Ursula Adomeit, *Förderung der Frauen in der Deutschen Demokratischen Republik* [The Advancement of Women in the German Democratic Republic] (Berlin: Staatsverlag der DDR, 1987).

17. Marianne Ehlenbeck et al. (eds.), *Geschichte des Demokratischen Frauenbundes Deutschlands* [The History of the Democratic Women's Association of Germany] (Leipzig: Verlag für die Frau, 1989); Wilfriede Otto and Siegfried Scholze, 'The Contribution of Women in the German Democratic Republic to the Struggle for Peace, Past and Present', *Atlantis: A Women's Studies Journal*, 12, no. 1 (Fall 1986), pp. 111-21; Cornelia Klose, 'Zur Geschichte des Internationalen Frauentages in der Deutschen Demokratischen Republik von 1962 bis 1980 [Concerning the History of International Women's Day in the GDR from 1962 to 1980]', Thesis A, 'Clara Zetkin' College of Education, Leipzig, 1988; Gudrun Partisch, 'Internationaler Frauentag in der DDR in den achtziger Jahren – Kampftag für den Frieden [International Women's day in the GDR during the Eighties – Day of Struggle for Peace]', *Mitteilungsblatt*, no. 3 (1987), pp. 34-41; Jürgen Kirchner (ed.), *70 Jahre Internationaler Frauentag* [70 Years of International Women's Day] (Leipzig: Verlag für die Frau, 1980); see also, 'Studien zur Rolle der Frau im Arbeitsprozeß im Sozialismus [Studies of the Role of Women in the Work Process under Socialism]', in Rector of the Berg Academy, Freiberg (ed.), *Beiträge zur Geschichte der Produktivkräfte*, Vol. 14 (Leipzig: VEB Deutscher Verlag für Grundstoffindustrie, 1979); Gudrun Partisch, 'Zur Rolle der Frauenausschüsse in der sozialistischen Industrie und Landwirtschaft der DDR in den Jahren 1952 bis 1964/65 [On the Role of the Women's Committee in Socialist Industry and Agriculture of the GDR in the Period 1952 to 1964/65]', Thesis B, 'Clara Zetkin' College of

Education, Leipzig, 1986; Kathrin Menzel, 'Zur Geschichte des Hausarbeitstages und seiner Stellung im System der Frauenförderung [On the History of the Day of Housework and Its Position in the System of the Advancement of Women]', Thesis A, Humboldt-Universität zu Berlin, 1987; Rosemarie Eichfeld, 'Probleme der Entwicklung der Frau als Produktionsarbeiterin in den Jahren 1945 bis 1980 – dargestellt an Beispielen aus 5 Betrieben des Kreises Freiberg [Problems in the Development of the Woman as a Productive Worker in the Period 1945 to 1980 – Represented by Examples taken from 5 Factories of the District Freiberg]', Thesis B, Bergakademie Freiberg, 1988.

18. Jürgen Dorbritz, 'Familienstandsprozesse in der DDR im Zeitraum 1975 bis 1983 [Marital Status Trials in the GDR from 1975 to 1983]', *Informationen des Wissenschaftlichen Rates*, no. 6 (1985), pp. 24-41. See also, Council of Ministers of the GDR (ed.), *Frauen in der DDR. Bericht der Regierung der Deutschen Demokratischen Republik. Bilanz der Erfüllung des Weltaktionsplanes für die Dekade der Frau 1976-1985 'Gleichberechtigung, Entwicklung, Frieden'* [Women in the GDR: Report of the Government of the GDR on the Balance of the World Action Plan--Decade for Women 1976-1985: 'Equality, Development, Peace'] (Dresden: Verlag Zeit im Bild, 1985). The latter has also been published in Arabic, English, French, Russian and Spanish.

19. Astrid Spitzner, 'Zur geschichtlichen Entwicklung der Vereinbarkeit von Berufstätigkeit und Mutterschaft in der UdSSR zwischen dem XXIV. und XXVII. Parteitag der KPdSU [Concerning the Historical Development of the Co-ordination of Paid Work and Motherhood in the Soviet Union between the 24th and the 27th Party Congress of the KPdSU]', Thesis A, 'Clara Zetkin' College of Education, Leipzig, 1987; Franceska Schwabe, 'Zur historischen Entwicklung der Vereinbarkeit von Berufstätigkeit und Mutterschaft in der Volksrepublik Polen in den Jahren 1971 bis 1986 [On the Historical Development of the Co-ordination of Paid Work and Motherhood in the People's Republic of Poland, in the Period 1971 to 1986]', Thesis A, 'Clara Zetkin' College of Education, Leipzig, 1988.

20. Else Sauer, 'Die Entwicklung der bürgerlichen Frauenbewegung von der Gründung des Bundes Deutscher Frauenvereine 1894 bis zum ersten Weltkrieg [The Development of the Bourgeois Women's Movement from the Founding of the Federation of German Women's Associations in 1894 to the First World War]', Thesis A, 'Clara Zetkin' College of Education, Leipzig, 1969; Petra Rantzsch, 'Die Große Sozialistische Oktoberrevolution und die sowjetische Politik im Spiegel bürgerlichen deutscher Frauenzeitschriften (1917 bis 1927) [The Great Socialist October Revolution and Soviet Politics Reflected in Bourgeois German Women's Magazines (1917 to 1927)]', *Wissenschaftliche Zeitschrift der Pädagogischen Hochschule, Leipzig*, no. 2 (1988), pp. 62-5; E. Sauer, 'Linke Kräfte der bürgerlichen Frauenbewegung [Left Forces in the Bourgeois Women's Movement]', *'Die Revolution von 1918/19 in Deutschland und die Frauen' Kolloquium der Forschungsgemeinschaft 'Geschichte des Kampfes der Arbeiterklasse für die Befreiung der Frau', Referate und Diskussionsbeiträge* (Leipzig: Eigenverlag der Pädagogischen Hochshcule 'Clara Zetkin', 1988); E. Sauer, 'Bürgerliche Frauenbewegung und politische Parteien für und wider das Frauenstimmrecht (Zum 70. Jahrestag der Gewährung des Frauenstimmrechts in Deutschland) [The Bourgeois Women's Movement and Political Parties For and Against Women's Suffrage (To Celebrate the 70th Anniversary of the Gaining of Women's Suffrage in Germany)]', *Mitteilungsblatt*, no. 3 (1989), pp. 5-15; Klaus Hönig, 'Die Weimarer

Nationalversammlung und die Rechte der Frau [The Weimar National Assembly and the Rights of Women]', *Wissenschaftliche Zeitschrift der Pädagogischen Hochschule, Leipzig*, no. 2 (1989), pp. 60-3; 'Arbeitstagung der Forschungsgemeinschaft "Geschichte des Kampfes der Arbeiterklasse um die Befreiung der Frau" 1989: "Bertha von Suttner und ihr Friedensvermächtnis", Referat und Diskussionsbeiträge [Conference of Research Group "History of the Struggle of the Working Class for the Liberation of Women" 1989: "Bertha von Suttner and Her Peace Legacy", Papers and Discussion]', *Mitteilungsblatt*, no. 1 (1990).

21. Hans-Jürgen Arendt, 'Die bürgerlichen Frauenorganisationen in der Weimarer Republik. Ein Überblick [The Bourgeois Women's Organisations in the Weimar Republic: An Overview]', *Jahrbuch für Geschichte*, 38 (1989), pp. 167-200; H.-J. Arendt, 'Fortschritte und Rückschläge im Prozeß der Frauenemanzipation in Deutschland 1918 bis 1933 [Progress and Setbacks in the Process of Women's Emancipation in Germany, 1918 to 1933]', *Wissenschaftliche Zeitschrift der Pädagogischen Hochschule Leipzig*, no. 2 (1989), pp. 56-60.

22. Petra Rantzsch, 'Zur Bündnisfähigkeit kleinbürgerlich-demokratischer Kräfte in der Weimarer Republik im Kampf gegen Imperialismus, Faschismus und Krieg [On the Capacity of the Lower-Middle-Class Democratic Forces of the Weimar Republic for Forming Coalitions Against Imperialism, Fascism and War]', *Wissenschaftliche Zeitschrift der Pädagogischen Zeitschrift Leipzig*, no. 2 (1985), pp. 37-40; P. Rantzsch, 'Zum Imperialismusbild kleinbürgerlich-demokratischer Kräfte in der Weimarer Republik (Dargestellt am Beispiel des deutschen Zweiges der Ifff und des Bundes für Mutterschutz) [Concerning the Image of Imperialism of Petty Bourgeois-democratic Forces in the Weimar Republic (Represented by the Example of the German Branch of Ifff and of the Federation for the Protection of Mothers]', *Imperialismustheorie und -analyse der KPD im Kampf gegen Imperialismus, Faschismus und Krieg* (Leipzig: Eigenverlag der Karl-Marx-Universität, 1985), pp. 61-7; Heiner Thurm, '100 Jahre International Council of Women – Anmerkungen zu: Geschichte einer internationalen bürgerlichen Frauenorganisation [100 Years of the International Council of Women – Remarks on the History of an International Bourgeois Women's Organisation]', *Mitteilungsblatt*, no. 2 (1988), pp. 5-16; Petra Rantzsch und Gabriele Kreißler, 'Für die Rechte der Frau und den Schutz der Mütter. Zum 70. Gründungstag der Internationalen Vereinigung für Mutterschutz und Sexualreform [For the Rights of Women and the Protection of Mothers: On the Occasion of the 70th Anniversary of the Founding of the International Association for the Protection of Mothers and Sex Reform]', *Mitteilungsblatt*, no. 3 (1981), pp. 23-32.

23. Ruth Kirsch, *Käte Duneker. Aus ihrem Leben* [Käte Duneker: From Her Life] (Berlin: Dietz Verlag, 1982); Roswitha Freude, 'Ottilie Baader. Ein biographischer Beitrag zur Geschichte der deutschen proletarischen Frauenbewegung [Ottilie Baader: A Biographical Contribution to the History of the German Proletarian Women's Movement]', Thesis A, 'Clara Zetkin' College of Education, Leipzig, 1984; Wolfgang Schröder, *Ernestine. Vom ungewöhnlichen Leben der ersten Frau Wilhelm Liebknechts* [Ernestine: About the Unusual Life of the First Wife of Wilhelm Liebknecht] (Leipzig: Verlag für die Frau, 1987); W. Schröder, '"Sie können sich denken wie mir oft zu Mute war", Jenny Marx ["You Can Imagine How I Felt", Jenny Marx]', in *Briefe an eine vertraute Freundin* [Letters to a Trusted Friend] (Leipzig: Verlag für die Frau, 1989).

350   *Petra Rantzsch and Erika Uitz*

24. Anneliese Laschitza and Günter Radezun, *Rosa Luxemburg. Ihr Wirken in der deutschen Arbeiterbewegung* [Rosa Luxemburg: Her Activities in the German Workers' Movement], 12th ed. (Berlin: Dietz Verlag, 1980); *Rosa Luxemburg, Gesammelte Werke* [Collected Works], 5 vols. (Berlin: Dietz Verlag, 1970-1975); Institut für Marxismus-Leninismus beim ZK der SED (ed.), *Rosa Luxemburg, Gesammelte Briefe* [Collected Letters], 5 vols. (Berlin: Dietz Verlag, 1982-1984); Anneliese Laschitza and Georg Adler (eds.), *Rosa Luxemburg, Herzlichst Ihre Rosa* [Cordial Greetings, Your Rosa] (Berlin: Dietz Verlag, 1989); Anneliese Laschitza, 'Rosa Luxemburg – Edition und Forschung. Bilanz und Ausblick [Rosa Luxemburg – Edition and Research: Balance and Outlook]', in *Beiträge zur Geschichte der Arbeiterbewegung*, no. 4 (1986), pp. 470-91; Luise Dornemann, *Clara Zetkin, Leben und Wirken* [Clara Zetkin: Life and Activities], 6th ed. (Berlin: Dietz Verlag, 1974); Dorothea Reetz, *Clara Zetkin als sozialistische Rednerin* [Clara Zetkin as Socialist Speaker], 2nd ed. (Leipzig: Verlag für die Frau, 1986); Sonja Buchmann, 'Clara Zetkins Wirken in der internationalen proletarischen Solidaritätsbewegung von 1921 bis 1933 [Clara Zetkin's Activities in the International Proletarian Solidarity Movement from 1921 to 1933]', Thesis A, 'Clara Zetkin' College of Education, Leipzig, 1987; Katrin Wahlbuhl, 'Zum Beitrag Clara Zetkins zur Entwicklung der Theorie der politischen Organisation des Sozialismus (untersucht in den Jahren von 1919-1925) [On the Contribution of Clara Zetkin to the Development of the Theory of the Political Organisation of Socialism (studied in the years 1919 to 1925)]', Thesis A, 'Clara Zetkin' College of Education, Leipzig, 1986.

25. Ruth Götze, 'Louise Ottos Beziehungen zum Proletariat im Vormärz und in der Revolution von 1948/49 [Louise Otto's Relations with the Proletariat in *Vormärz* and During the Revolution of 1848/49]', *Wissenschaftliche Zeitschrift der Pädagogischen Hochschule Leipzig*, no. 2 (1980), pp. 85-8; R. Götze, 'Zur "Frauenzeitung" Louise Ottos [Concerning the "Women's Newspaper" of Louise Otto]', *Wissenschaftliche Zeitschrift der Pädagogischen Hochschule Leipzig*, no. 3 (1983), pp. 56-60; Manfred Gebhardt, *Mathilde Franziska Anneke, Madame, Soldat und Suffragette. Biographie* [Mathilde Franziska Anneke – Madame, Soldier and Suffragette: A Biography] (Berlin: Verlag Neues Leben, 1988); Nadja Stultz-Herrnstadt, 'Fanny Lewald. Bürgerliche Umgestaltung und Frauenemanzipation [Fanny Lewald: Bourgeois Reorganisation and Women's Emancipation]', Gustav Seeber (ed.), *Gestalten der Bismarckzeit*, vol. 2 (Berlin: Akademie Verlag, 1986), pp. 118-42; Gerlinde Naumann, *Minna Cauer – eine Kämpferin für Frieden, Demokratie und Emanzipation der Frau (1842-1922)* [Minna Cauer – A Fighter for Peace, Democracy and the Emancipation of Women (1842-1922)] (Berlin: Verlag 'Der Morgen', 1989); G. Naumann, 'Vor 100 Jahren – Gründung des Vereins "Frauenwohl" [100 Years Ago – The Founding of the Association "Women's Welfare"]', *Mitteilungsblatt*, no. 2 (1988), pp. 33-43; Petra Rantzsch, *Helene Stöcker (1869-1943). Zwischen Pazifismus und Revolution* [Helene Stöcker (1869-1943): Between Pacifism and Revolution] (Berlin: Verlag 'Der Morgen', 1984; Wolfgang Genschorek, *Florence Nightingale, Triumph des Humanismus* [Florence Nightingale: The Triumph of Humanism], 2nd ed. (Leipzig: Verlag Hirzel, 1987); Norbert Molkenbur and Klaus Hörhold, *Oda Schottmüller, Tänzerin, Bildhauerin, Antifaschistin. Eine Dokumentation* [Oda Schottmüller – Dancer, Sculptress, Antifascist: A Documentation] (Berlin: Henschelverlag, 1983); Karl-Heinz Günther (ed.), *Marie Torhorst, Pfarrerstochter, Pädagogin, Kommunistin: Aus dem Leben der*

Schwestern Adelheid und Marie Torhorst [Marie Torhorst – Pastor's Daughter, Teacher, Communist: From the Life of the Sisters Adelheid and Marie Torhorst] (Berlin: Dietz Verlag, 1986); Gertrud Bobeck, *Dr. Margarete Blank: Ein Lebensbild* [Dr. Margarete Blank: A Life Sketch] (Leipzig: Verlag des Kreiskomitees der Antifaschistischen Widerstandskämpfer, 1985); Gisela Rannefeld, 'Gabrielle Duchène. Biographische Skizze zum Wirken einer linken Pazifistin [Gabrielle Duchène: A Biographical Sketch of the Activities of a Left Pacifist]', *Mitteilungsblatt*, no. 1 (1986), pp. 43-56.

26. Rolf Straubel and Ulman Weiß (eds.), *Herrscherpersönlichkeiten der Neuzeit* [Ruling Personalities of the Modern Age] (Leipzig/Weimar/Berlin: Urania-Verlag, forthcoming).

27. Erika Uitz, Barbara Pätzold, and Gerald Beyreuther (eds.), *Herrscherinnen und Nonnen. Frauengestalten von der Ottonenzeit bis zu den Staufern* [Female Rulers and Nuns: Female Figures from the Ottonian Period until the Hohenstaufen Period] (Berlin: Verlag der Wissenschaften, forthcoming).

28. Helga Schultz, *Berlin 1650-1800, Sozialgeschichte einer Residenz* [Berlin 1650-1800: Social History of a Residence] (Berlin: Akademie Verlag, 1987); Michèle Schubert, 'Lage und Bewegung der Leipziger Dienstmädchen zur Zeit der industriellen Revolution [The Situation and Movement of Maids in Leipzig at the Time of the Industrial Revolution]', *Jahrbuch für Regionalgeschichte*, 16, no. 2 (1989), forthcoming.

29. Anneliese Neef, *Mühsal ein Leben lang. Zur Situation der Arbeiterfrauen um 1900* [Lifelong Tribulation: Concerning the Situation of Female Workers ca. 1900] (Berlin: Dietz Verlag, 1988); Petra Dunskus, 'Zur Entwicklung der Lohnarbeit von Frauen in Berlin – in den Jahren 1871 bis 1933 [The Development of Women's Paid Labour in Berlin from 1971 to 1933]', *Informationen des Wissenschaftlichen Rates*, no. 5 (1987), pp. 28-55; Leonore Ansorg, 'Erwerbsarbeit von Arbeiterfrauen im 19. Jahrhundert. Ein Beitrag zur Theorie der Frauenlohnarbeit [Work for Pay of Women Workers in the 19th Century: A Contribution to the Theory of Women's Paid Work]', *Informationen des Wissenschaftlichen Rates*, no. 6 (1989), pp. 34-43.

30. Petra Clemens, 'Frauen helfen sich selbst. Die Betriebsfrauenausschüsse der 50er Jahre in kulturhistorischer Sicht [Women Help Themselves: The Factories' Women's Committees of the 1950s in their Cultural Historical Dimension]', *Jahrbuch für Volkskunde*, 30 (new series 15) (1987), pp. 107-42.

31. Gisela Griepentrog, 'Zur Struktur und Funktion der Familie im Leben der werktätigen Dorfbevölkerung zwischen 1900 und 1960 [On the Structure and Function of the Family in the Life of the Working Population of Villages Between 1900 and 1960]', in Hans-Jürgen Rach, Bernhard Weissel and Heiner Paul (eds.), *Das Leben der Werktätigen in der Magdeburger Börde. Studien zum dörflichen Alltag vom Beginn des 20. Jahrhunderts bis Anfang der 60er Jahre* (Berlin: Akademie-Verlag, 1987), pp. 9-106.

32. Heinrich Loth, *Die Frau im alten Afrika* [Women in Ancient Africa] (Leipzig: Verlag Edition, 1986); for another work concerned with conditions for women outside Europe, see Wiebke Walther, *Die Frau im Islam* [Women in Islam] (Leipzig: Verlag Edition, 1980).

33. Erika Uitz, *Die Frau in der mittelalterlichen Stadt* [Women in the Medieval City] (Leipzig: Verlag Edition, 1988; Stuttgart: Dr. Bernhard Abend Verlag, 1988; English edition – New York: Moyer Bell/ London: Barrie & Jenkins, 1990; Japanese edition – Tokyo: Kokusai Bunka Shuppansha, 1991); E. Uitz, 'Zeitlicher Frieden im Denken von Frauen des Spätmittelalters [Timely Peace in the Thinking of Women of the Late Middle Ages]', in Ingrid Matschinegg, Brigitte Rath, and Barbara Schuh (eds.), *Von Menschen und ihren Zeichen. Sozialhistorische Beiträge zum Spätmittelalter und zur Neuzeit* (Bielefeld: Verlag für Regionalgeschichte, 1989), pp. 61-76; E. Uitz, 'Zur wirtschaftlichen und gesellschaftlichen Situation von Frauen in ausgewählten spätmittelalterlichen Hansestädten [On the Economic and Social Position of Women in Selected Hanse Towns of the Late Middle Ages]', in Barbara Vogel and Ulrike Weckel (eds.), *Frauen in der Ständegesellschaft. Leben und Arbeiten in der Stadt vom späten Mittelalter bis zur Neuzeit*, Beiträge zur deutschen und europäischen Geschichte, vol. 2 (Hamburg: [publisher] forthcoming); E. Uitz, 'Die Frau im Berufsleben der spätmittelalterlichen Stadt [Women in the Work Life of the Late Medieval City]', in *Frau und spätmittelalterlicher Alltag; Sitzungsberichte der Oesterreichischen Akademie der Wissenschaften, Philosophisch-Historische Klasse*, vol. 473 (Vienna: Verlag der Oesterreichischen Akademie der Wissenschaften, 1986), pp. 439-73.

34. Ingrid and Hans-Jürgen Arendt (eds.), *Bibliographie zur Geschichte des Kampfes der deutschen Arbeiterklasse für die Befreiung der Frau und zur Rolle der Frau in der deutschen Arbeiterbewegung von den Anfängen bis 1970* [Bibliography of the History of the Struggle of the German Working Class for the Liberation of Women and of the Role of Women in the German Workers' Movement from its Beginnings to 1970] (Leipzig: Eigenverlag der Pädagogischen Hochschule 'Clara Zetkin', 1974).

35. Hans-Jürgen Arendt and Siegfried Scholze (eds.), *Zur Rolle der Frau in der Geschichte des deutschen Volkes (1830 bis 1945). Eine Chronik* [On the Role of Women in the History of the German People (1830 to 1945): A Chronology] (Leipzig: Verlag für die Frau; Frankfurt am Main: Verlag Marxistische Blätter, 1984); Siegfried Scholze and Hans-Jürgen Arendt (eds.), *Zur Rolle der Frau in der Geschichte der DDR. Vom antifaschistisch-demokratischen Neuaufbau bis zur Gestaltung der entwickelten sozialistischen Gesellschaft (1945 bis 1981). Eine Chronik* [On the Role of Women in the History of the GDR – From the Anti-fascist New Reconstruction to the Formation of the Developed Socialist Society (1945 to 1981): A Chronology] (Leipzig: Verlag für die Frau, 1987); see also Joachim Müller et al. (eds.), *Dokumente der revolutionären deutschen Arbeiterbewegung zur Frauenfrage 1848-1974* [Documents of the Revolutionary German Workers' Movement Concerning the Women's Question 1848-1974] (Leipzig: Verlag für die Frau, 1975).

36. Friedrich Schlette, *Von Lucy bis Kleopatra* [From Lucy to Cleopatra] (Berlin: Verlag Neues Leben, 1988); Eiko Saito, *Das Bild der Frau im alten Japan* [The Image of Women in Ancient Japan] (Leipzig: Verlag Edition, 1990); Bernd Schöne, 'Posamentierer, Strumpfwirker, Spitzenklöpplerinnen [Gold Lace Makers, Hosiery Knitters, and Lace Makers]', in Rudolf Weinhold (ed.), *Volksleben zwischen Zunft und Fabrik* (Berlin: Akademie-Verlag, 1982), pp. 107-64; Luise Dornemann, *Alle Tage ihres Lebens, Frauengestalten aus zwei Jahrhunderten* [All the Days of Their Lives: Female Figures from Two Centuries] (Berlin: Dietz Verlag, 1981).

37. See, for example, Angela Schnabl, 'Vom feudalen zum bürgerlichen Eherecht. Grundlinien der deutschen Eherechtsentwicklung von 1789 bis 1870/71 [From the Feudal to the Civil Marriage Law: Baselines of the Development of the German Marriage Law from 1789 to 1870/71]', Thesis B, Karl-Marx-Universität, Leipzig, 1988; Volkmar Schöneburg, 'Sexualstrafrecht und menschliche Emanzipation in der Weimarer Republik. Zum Kampf der KPD um die Reform des Sexualstrafrechts [Criminal Law with Respect to Sexuality and Human Emancipation in the Weimar Republic: On the Fight of the Communist Party of Germany for the Reform of the Criminal Law with Respect to Sexuality]', *Informationen des Wissenschaftlichen Rates*, no. 5 (1988), pp. 33-46; Astrid Kleffe, 'Die Entwicklung des höheren Mädchenschulwesens in Berlin von 1871-1914 [The Development of Girls' Higher Education in Berlin from 1971-1914]', Thesis A, Humboldt-Universität zu Berlin, 1988; Gerlinde Naumann, 'Auffassungen Salzmans zur Mädchenbildung [Salzman's Views on Girls' Education]', *Wissenschaftliche Zeitschrift der Pädagogischen Hochschule 'Clara Zetkin', Leipzig*, no. 2 (1989), pp. 52-6.

38. Liane Zeil, 'Frauen in der Berliner Akademie der Wissenschaften (1700-1945) [Women in the Academy of Sciences in Berlin (1700-1945)]', *Informationen des Wissenschaftlichen Rates*, no. 6 (1989), pp. 57-70.

19

Women's History in Switzerland

Regina Wecker

Women's History and the Structure of Swiss Universities

The first two seminars on the history of women held at Swiss universities, in 1978 and 1979, carried English titles and German subtitles: '"To Suffer and Be Still": Die Frau im 19. Jahrhundert [Women in the Nineteenth Century]'[1] and '"Her Story": Die Frau in der amerikanischen Geschichtsforschung [Women in American Historiography]'[2] and were thus articulating the importance of American and English historiography. The bibliographies handed out to students listed mainly English and American publications, including only two books on Germany and France and one on Swiss women's history: Susanna Woodtli's study of the Swiss women's suffrage movement.[3]

This situation was typical of women's history in Switzerland, where university historians became interested in the history of women at a rather late stage. The first seminars aimed primarily at providing a survey of a new field of research in other countries – especially in the USA and England – and secondly at opening up new approaches for Swiss historians. The seminar at Zürich University produced a series of essays on the situation of women in nineteenth-century Switzerland which – although never published – served to inspire future research.

There were then very few women teaching history at Swiss universities, and hardly any doing research in women's history. Susanna Woodtli – an historian who was also an active member of the Swiss women's suffrage movement[4] – wrote her book while outside the mainstream of academic research. Those first seminars were directed by male professors but the majority of the students attending the seminars were women who were engaged in the feminist movement or who were at least familiar with discussions about women and their role in society. To

355

them this was not just a new field of research. It was through their commitment to feminism that the call for women's history at the universities became louder. It had also become obvious that it was not sufficient merely to include women in history (or in a lecture programme), but that the new approach to history would have implications for our overall understanding of history (and for the whole of the university lecture programme). Women's history became the particular concern of women.

Much research in women's history has been undertaken in Switzerland since then. But the impact of the circumstances surrounding its origins can still be felt. First of all it had a late start, unfortunately at a time when raising money for new fields of teaching and research in universities, especially in the humanities, had become more difficult. Women's history is therefore still barely institutionalised: there is no chair of women's history, as can be found in other countries, and no specific and continuous university programmes in women's history. To compensate, women at most universities try to bring the subject in, either by inviting women historians for one or two terms as guest lecturers or by occasionally making it the subject of their own lecture and seminar programme. The Swiss argument against a chair in women's history is that the structure of Swiss universities does not allow for such a specific subject matter and that it would be better to make women's history part of some already existing 'venia legendi' (the formal entitlement to teach one's subject at a university): though this possibility, in fact, has not been realised either.[5]

Since research programmes are closely attached to or linked with universities, we are faced with a similar situation in research. One finds a few women in influential university positions, where they might be able to promote research in women's history. Few such projects are financed by the Swiss National Science Foundation (the government foundation for research). Opportunities to do paid research into women's history are therefore scarce, and networking and co-operation in projects depend very greatly on individual initiative.

Besides the late start and the unwillingness of the academic establishment to reform its understanding of history, university structures and the limited size of the overall Swiss research capacity in history contribute to the comparatively weak position of women's history. There are about 2,500 university students studying history, less than a thousand of whom are women.[6] The higher one climbs in the university hierarchy, the smaller the percentage of women. About 20-25 per cent of assistants and about 10 per cent of university lecturers are women. At the very top of our profession there are about 45 history chairs held by so called 'ordinarii', or full professors. Only two of them are women (4.4 per cent).

The small number of women at the top of the hierarchy is not distinctively Swiss, but it is nevertheless obvious that the situation in Switzerland is worse than in Germany, England or the United States because the overall number of historians is so low. The hierarchical structure of our universities and the comparatively difficult situation for those in the middle of the hierarchy constitutes another factor influencing the situation of women's history.[7] A formal 'habilitation', or post-doctoral research project,[8] has become a prerequisite for a permanent university career, at least in the German-speaking universities. But there are few ways for women to raise funds for the additional research work necessary for this most important academic hurdle.[9]

On the other hand, Switzerland is a rich country with a low unemployment rate.[10] This opens up opportunities even to women. They very often finance research by taking on other employment or by finding niches where a combination of paid labour and unpaid research is possible. These circumstances seem to make the struggle for funds or positions within institutions less severe. The fact that women's history is hardly institutionalised has - notwithstanding all the disadvantages - some clear advantages, including the fact that the impulse towards utilisation or instrumentalisation of women's history for career purposes is weaker. The other advantage is - so far - that male historians do not interfere.

Topics, Methods and Approaches

A survey of recently published books on women's history still reveals the dominance of nineteenth- and twentieth-century topics. This dominance can be seen in the unique anthology of Swiss source materials,[11] as well as in various monographs. The feminist movement continues to be a very popular topic. Having obtained the right for women to vote on federal matters in Switzerland as late as 1971, the traditional women's suffrage movement had hardly achieved success, when the new feminist movement began to proclaim that suffrage was only one - and perhaps not even the most important - of women's aims. The phase of celebration by those who had actively and persistently fought for women's suffrage, and the critical analysis of their struggle by the new feminist movement and by academic historians, virtually coincided. Thus the personalised approach of pioneers like Susanna Woodtli and Lotti Ruckstuhl[12] was closely followed or, one might even say, anticipated by very critical essays about the theory and practice of the feminist movement in the nineteenth century by Brigitte Schnegg and Annamarie Stalder,[13] or detailed monographs such as Anne-Marie Käppeli's[14] on Protestant feminism. Beatrix Mesmer's work on women and women's organisation in nineteenth-century Switzerland is the most comprehensive study of this period. It analyses the process of state formation and the way women were 'excluded' [ausgeklammert] from it, but 'included' [eingeklammert] in the process of healing the wounds of an industrialising society. This book can be considered a synthesis of women's history, the women's movement, social history and the history of the political system of Switzerland.[15]

The private 'Gosteli Archiv', an archive for the history of the Swiss women's movement, offers a very useful collection of documents and sources and is a great asset to those working on the feminist movement of the last hundred years.[16] In addition, and closely connected to research on the women's movement, many publications have appeared on women in political organisations, for instance the trade unions and the socialist movement.[17]

Within nineteenth-century women's history women's work is a favoured topic. This was a traditional field for early Swiss women economists, and is also, of course, a topic dealt with frequently and from a variety of angles by researchers in women's history in other countries. Nevertheless we still lack a broad survey of the subject. Despite the work of early economists and foreign examples, the analysis of Swiss female labour remains a difficult task. Historians of women differ from economists in their approach - mainly by dealing with the mutual dependence of paid and unpaid labour. The patterns of Swiss economic and political development differ from those of other countries in important ways: the early but decentralised industrialisation, the high participation rate of women in industry in the nineteenth century, and the continuous decrease in the percentage of female wage-earners up to the middle of the twentieth century, plus the fact that Switzerland did not participate in the two world wars. Publications on domestic labour and the private sphere,[18] and on paid labour,[19] show that Swiss development followed a distinctive pattern, one that may even offer the possibility of challenging prevailing theories (by comparative study) about the impact of the wars on female labour.

Although in nineteenth- and twentieth-century historiography, a majority of publications concentrate on the feminist movement or female labour, these are by no means the only topics that have attracted scholars. Some of the biographical studies and projects, for instance those on Rosa Grimm,[20] a member of the Swiss Communist Party, and on the Women's Secretary of the Trade Union, Margarethe Faas-Hardegger,[21] deserve to be mentioned. Two researchers are editing the letters of the eighteenth-century literary figure Julie Bondeli, while another group of scholars is working on Swiss women in literature.[22] Both these scholarly teams are interdisciplinary.

The work of Esther Fischer-Homberger pioneered Swiss research into the history of women and medicine.[23] More recent publications on this topic deal with pregnancy and child birth[24] and the changing role of women in the medical professions.[25]

A very interesting research project – one of the rare examples financed by the Swiss National Science Foundation – deals with family structure in Zürich from 1820 to 1940. It concentrates on women's role within the family and on analysing development in terms of the homogenisation of family structures.[26]

Work has been published on images of women as well as on education and female roles,[27] on prostitution[28] and on women in the time of the Second World War.[29] Very often research is inspired by current political questions or issues. Three examples may suffice: the political discussion about a new law on abortion stimulated historical research on this subject;[30] the political initiative for the abolition of the Swiss army led to discussion of women's role in the Second World War;[31] and the international debate on the abolition of ILO Convention 89, which forbids women to work in factories at night, brought research on the Swiss role in international organisations and on the very interesting development of protective labour legislation in Switzerland.[32]

The dominance of nineteenth- and twentieth-century historiography does not imply that other periods are not being investigated. Recently more interest has developed in the medieval and early modern periods.[33] The eighteenth century, however, seems to be 'terra incognita'. Very little research has been done on this period apart from Brigitte Schnegg's current dissertation on women's social role during the Enlightenment.[34]

This variety of topics, and the fact that there is no centre of women's history or major project around which research could rally, contributed to a sense of isolation among researchers. In order to improve the situation, in 1983 we initiated annual meetings of women historians. Except for the very first meeting, these have always been organised by a group of students and *Assistenten* [instructors]. The five meetings to date have been held at one or another of the three German-speaking universities of Berne, Basel or Zürich. The next meeting will be held in Zürich in the autumn of 1990.[35]

Between one and three hundred women, and a few men,[36] have participated in these meetings, which aimed at providing insight into the current state of women's history, both to researchers and to an interested public. Most of those giving papers were university students or *Assistenten*, though some university lecturers and freelance historians also participated. Every woman who wanted to present a paper could do so. Accordingly, the depth and quality of the research presented varied greatly: undergraduate students presented papers written for university courses, a summary of about two or three months' work, while graduate students presented parts of their MA or Ph.D. theses, the result of four or five years' research.

This form of organisation stems from the situation in women's history but it obviously does not provide a suitable climate for a professional discussion of research results. This was of considerable concern to some advanced researchers who lacked a suitable forum for their discussions.[37] But this form of meeting can - in spite of all its problems - undoubtedly provide opportunities, if envisioned as part of the process of emancipation. Those organising the meetings are students who are doing this kind of job for the first time. The organising committee contacts more advanced researchers, raises funds, contacts newspapers and organises public relations ventures. Its members learn about a variety of aspects of women's history and, last but not least, they - very often for the first time - have the responsibility of editing a publication. These meetings and publications offer a vital framework for providing contacts for those doing women's history, even for arousing interest in it, and for informing a wider public about the state of women's history in Switzerland.[38] Even in the international context of women's history, it seems noteworthy that the first publication from our meetings was published as a special issue of the *main* historical journal of Switzerland, *Schweizerische Zeitschrift für Geschichte*.[39]

Recent Developments: Debates and Trends

Although the international debate on 'women's history versus gender history' might be called 'academic' for Switzerland, insofar as neither one nor the other is part of a curriculum or a 'venia', this debate raises important problems in at least two contradictory respects.[40] The first problem concerns our demand that women's history (or gender history?) should be continuously taught at all university levels. Here the change of paradigm involved in gender history seems to weaken our initial position, especially in addressing those who have only recently begun to understand what women's history is about. Furthermore women's history in Switzerland is – despite its origins – the domain of women historians, who currently determine the shape of the debates. Gender history makes it easier to argue for the participation of men, but this might lead to its becoming yet another field where men dominate debates and determine the issues. I think it rather suspicious that the call for gender history has been found so agreeable to those who have to date objected to the 'narrowness' of concepts of women's history along with the fact that these concepts 'only' deal with women's experience. Apart from these tactical considerations, however, the discussion among Swiss scholars about the significance of the change of paradigm and about the chances of undermining the traditional dichotomies has been very stimulating, even though it has only just begun.

Until now few projects or publications have explicitly used gender as a category of analysis. One of the exceptions is Susanna Burghartz' Ph.D. thesis on delinquency in the later Middle Ages, which will soon be published.[41] To explain the functioning of the Town Court of Zürich, Burghartz uses gender as a primary category to reveal that the court is not only an instrument for the punishment of offenders, but also the instrument and location for the regulation of typical male conflicts, conflicts that determine male status. Women are less frequently judged and punished because they have fewer such conflicts, and so appear far less often in court. Thus they lack a public place to determine their status. Another illustration of the way in which gender is beginning to be used as a research concept is provided by the annual meeting of the 'Schweizerische Gesellschaft für Wirtschafts- und Sozialgeschichte [Swiss Society for Economic and Social History]', which was organized around the theme of poverty in Switzerland, with one section devoted to 'Gender and Poverty'.[42]

A regional research project, still in progress, includes two sub-projects of which gender and gender relations are an integral part, among them a study that explicitly considers issues of masculinity.[43] This comparatively large project signals a new trend in Swiss research. It seems to be more complicated to raise money for research projects dealing with women's history, than to establish gender as one of the central categories in other research projects. For example, a very well-organised women's history project was rejected by the Swiss National Science Foundation, but regional studies establishing gender as one of the central categories are being organised. As funding has not yet been granted, it is perhaps too early to call this a new trend in Swiss academic policy. But it certainly throws new light on the 'women's history versus gender history' debate.

One other trend can clearly be recognised, and that is the determination of researchers to make their results known to a wider public. This has been accomplished by a couple of remarkable exhibitions dealing, in one case, with events and developments in women's history exclusively,[44] and in another, with women's history as part of a larger setting.[45] The plans for 'city walks' to places of interest having a special meaning for women in different Swiss cities may also be understood in this context.[46] Another interesting example is a novel written for young people by two historians, based on sources they researched for their MA thesis. This book has enjoyed a great success and has been awarded several prizes.[47]

Given the small number of women doing research, the delayed start, and the absence of extensive official support, the results so far may be considered encouraging. To improve the situation of women's history we are exploring various possibilities. One is connected with a more general attempt to raise the quota of female university lecturers. At several universities, commissions have been set up to work out plans to increase the number of women faculty and to help women with a university career. The second is – as already mentioned – that we are trying to make women's history a part of the history curriculum in such a way that it can be continuously taught and can even become part – or even the core – of some lecturers' or professors' 'venia legendi'.

What we still lack – despite the encouraging beginnings – is an ongoing forum for discussion, internationally, comparatively and nationally, to complement our annual meetings. We need more exchange of methods and results, more conferences on special subjects and networking. What we lack most is the chance to discuss our research projects with others who are also interested and working on similar topics.

International exchange, to date, has been a one-way communication. We read and discuss concepts and research results from other countries, but our own research is hardly known outside Switzerland. One reason for this stems from the situation already mentioned in this essay – the time-lag, or in other words, the fact that our research is often behind that of other countries, the small number of researchers, the limited research capacity and the missing institutional base. Beyond this, the fact that Switzerland seems to be a special case may contribute further to this impression of one-way traffic. Our country was once in a leading position – in the progress of industrialisation or in giving women access to universities, for instance – but it has seemed backward with respect to certain later developments, such as the granting of women's suffrage. As concerns the analysis of crucial European events – for instance World Wars I and II – Switzerland is simply outside the mainstream of European history. The potential of this uneven development for comparative studies in women's history has not yet been explored.

NOTES

1. Held at the University of Zürich in 1978 by Prof. Rudolf Braun and his assistant Albert Tanner.

2. Held at the University of Basel in 1979 by Prof. Hans Rudolf Guggisberg and his assistant Regina Wecker.

3. Susanna Woodtli, *Gleichberechtigung. Der Kampf um die politischen Rechte der Frau in der Schweiz* [Equal Rights: Women's Struggle for Political Rights in Switzerland] (Frauenfeld: Huber, 1975, 1983), also published as *Du Féminisme à l'égalite politique* (Lausanne: Payot, 1977). Esther Fischer Homberger's research

on the history of medicine (see below, note 24) was obviously at that time not well known to historians.

4. Swiss women were enfranchised at the federal level only in 1971.

5. The 'venia legendi' entitles a person to lecture at a university and specifies his or her field of teaching, such as 'The History of the Middle Ages', or 'The History of Eastern Europe'. The incorporation of women's history as such a 'venia' is one of the aims of the 'Leitbild für die Geschichtswissenschaft an der Universität Basel [Guidelines for the Organisation of the History Department of the University of Basel]', 1988.

6. *Statistisches Jahrbuch 1987/88* [Yearbook of Statistics 1987/88] (Basel: Birkhauser Verlag, 1989), p. 447, for the years 1986/87.

7. *Assistenten* hold their posts only for a limited period, and few positions last more than three years.

8. A 'habilitation' consists of a research project after the Ph.D. and a formal presentation of its results to the faculty.

9. This is a problem for male historians as well, but it is especially galling for women, because the unpaid family work usually rests on their shoulders. Because of the absence of childcare facilities, women must make private arrangements or rely on their partners' agreement to do part-time work, if they want to combine a family and a university career. Thus their research must be paid work. It seems to be a vicious circle: without the research necessary for a 'habilitation' there are no paid university positions, and women cannot afford to do the necessary research, precisely because it is unpaid.

10. The rate was about 0.5 per cent in 1989.

11. The only anthology of general source materials is Elisabeth Joris and Heidi Witzig (eds.), *Frauengeschichte(n), Dokumente aus zwei Jahrhunderten zur Situation der Frauen in der Schweiz* [Women's Stories: Documents of Two Centuries on the Situation of Women in Switzerland] (Zürich: Limmat Verlag, 1986).

12. Woodtli, *Gleichberechtigung*; Lotti Ruckstuhl, *Frauen sprengen Fesseln, Hindernislauf zum Frauenstimmrecht in der Schweiz* [Women Throw off Their Yoke: The Hard Road Towards Women's Suffrage] (Bonstetten: Interfeminas Verlag, 1986).

13. Brigitte Schnegg and Anne-Marie Stalder, 'Ueberlegungen zu Theorie und Praxis der schweiz. Frauenbewegung um die Jahrhundertwende [Reflections on Theory and Practice in the Swiss Women's Movement at the Turn of the Century]', in Wiener Historikerinnen (ed.), *Die ungeschriebene Geschichte* (Wien: Wiener Frauenverlag, 1984), pp. 37-46.

14. Anne-Marie Käppeli, 'Le Féminisme protestant de Suisse romande à la fin du XIXe et au début du XXe siècles', Ph.D. thesis, Université de Paris VII, 1987.

15. Beatrix Mesmer, *Ausgeklammert – Eingeklammert. Frauen und Frauenorganisation in der Schweiz des 19. Jahrhunderts* [Excluded – Included: Women and Women's Organisations in 19th-Century Switzerland] (Basel: Helbing und Lichtenhahn, 1988).

16. Gosteli Archiv. Archiv zur Geschichte der schweizerischen Frauenbewegung [Archive for Research into the Swiss Women's Movement], Altikofenstrasse 186, CH 3048 Worblaufen/Switzerland.

17. Annette Frei, *Rote Patriarchen, Arbeiterbewegung und Frauenemanzipation in der Schweiz um 1900* [Red Patriarchs: The Working-Class Movement and Women's Emancipation in Switzerland ca. 1900] (Zürich: Chronos Verlag, 1987); Yvonne Pesenti, *Beruf: Arbeiterin: soziale Lage und gewerkschaftliche Organisation der erwerbstätigen Frauen aus der Unterschicht in der Schweiz, 1890-1914* [Profession: Worker. The Social Situation and Trade Union Organisation of Women Working for Pay in Switzerland, 1880-1914] (Zürich: Chronos Verlag 1987); Brigitte Studer, '"...da doch die verheiratete Frau vor allem ins Haus gehört". Die Stellung der Frau im SGB und die gewerkschaftliche Frauenpolitk unter dem Aspekt des Rechts auf Arbeit, 1880-1945 ["...a Woman's Proper Place is in Her Home". The Role Of Women in the Swiss Trade Union and The Right to Work, 1880-1945]' in Bernard Degen et al. (eds.), *Arbeitsfrieden-Realität eines Mythos* (Zürich: Widerspruch-Sonderband, 1987).

18. Geneviève Heller, *'Propre en ordre', Habitation et vie domestique 1850-1930: l'exemple vaudois* ['Nice and Orderly', Housing Conditions and Private Life 1850-1930: the Canton Vaud] (Lausanne: Edition d'en bas, 1979); Beatrix Mesmer, 'Reinheit und Reinlichkeit [Cleanliness and Neatness]', in Nicolai Bernard and Quirinus Reichen (eds.), *Gesellschaft und Gesellschaften, Festschrift für Ulrich Imhof* (Bern: Wyss Verlag, 1982).

19. Yvonne Pesenti, *Beruf: Arbeiterin*; Regula Bochsler and Sabine Gisiger, *Dienen in der Fremde, Dienstmädchen und ihre Herrschaften in der Schweiz des 20. Jahrhunderts* [Female Servants and Their Masters in Switzerland in the 20th Century] (Zürich: Chronos Verlag, 1989); Liliane Mottu-Weber, 'Les Femmes dans la vie économique de Genève, XVI-XVIIIe siècle [Women in Economic Life in Geneva from the 16th to the 18th Century]', *Bulletin de la Société d'Histoire et d'Archeologie de Genève*, 16 (1979), pp. 381-401; Madelaine Denisart and Jaqueline Surchat, *Le Cigar et le fourmis. Aperçu sur l'histoire des ouvrières vaudoises* [The Cigar and the Ant: On the History of Working Women in the Canton Vaud] (Lausanne: Editions d'en bas, 1988).

A new attempt at a survey has been made in a series of essays in Marie-Louise Barben and Elisabeth Ryter (eds.), *Verflixt und zugenäht! Frauenberufsbildung - Frauenerwerbsarbeit 1888-1988* [Women's Occupational Training – Women's Work 1888-1988] (Zürich: Chronos Verlag, 1988).

In progress: Regina Wecker, 'Zwischen Ideologie und Ökonomie. Leben und Arbeit erwerbstätiger Frauen in Basel 1870-1910 [Between Ideology and Economy. The Life and Work of Women in Basel 1870-1910]', and Beatrice Ziegler Witschi's research on Swiss women in war and crisis between 1919 and 1945.

20. Brigitte Studer, 'Rosa Grimm (1875-1955): Als Frau in der Politik und Arbeiterbewegung – Die Grenzen des weiblichen Geschlechts [Rosa Grimm (1875-1955): A Woman in Politics and the Working Women's Movement]', in Arbeitsgruppe Frauengeschichte (eds.), *Auf den Spuren weiblicher Vergangenheit* (Zürich: Chronos, 1988).

21. Monica Studer, 'L'Organisation syndicale Suisse et les femmes: L'Action de Margarethe Faas-Hardegger [Swiss Unions and Women: Margarethe Faas-Hardegger]', MA thesis, University of Geneva, 1975.

22. Brigitte Schnegg and Angelica Baum will edit the letters of Julie Bondeli. Sabine Kubli and Doris Stump are working on Swiss women's literature in a research project funded by the Swiss National Science Foundation.

23. Esther Fischer-Homberger, *Krankheit Frau und andere Arbeiten zur Medizingeschichte der Frau* [An Illness Called Woman and Other Publications on the History of Medicine] (Berne, Stuttgart, Wien: Verlag Hans Huber, 1979).

24. Maya Borkowsky, *Krankheit Schwangerschaft? Schwangerschaft, Geburt und Wochenbett aus ärztlicher Sicht seit 1800* [Pregnancy as Illness? Pregnancy, Birth and Confinement since 1800] (Zürich: Chronos Verlag, 1988).

25. Josiane Ferrari-Clement, *Marguerite, sage-femme vaudoise ou la naissance autrefois* [Marguerite, Wise Woman from the Canton Vaud, or Childbirth in Former Times] (Lausanne: Edition de l'Aire, 1987).

26. Heidi Witzig and Elisabeth Joris, 'Der Abbau regionaler und schichtspezifischer Verhaltensmuster und die Homogenisierung der Familienstrukturen [The Deconstruction of Different Regional Patterns of Behaviour and the Homogenisation of Family Structures]'.

27. Monique Pavillon, *La Femme illustrée des années 20, Essai sur l'interprétation de l'image des femmes dans la presse illustrée 1920-1930* [Illustrations of Women from the Twenties. Essay on the Interpretation of Women's Pictures in Journals] *Histoire et Société contemporaines*, 4 (Lausanne, 1986); Ursi Blosser and Franziska Gerster, *Töchter der guten Gesellschaft, Frauenrolle und Mädchenerziehung im schweizerischen Grossbürgertum um 1900* [Daughters in the Best Circles: Women's Role and Education in the Upper Classes in Switzerland around 1900] (Zürich: Chronos Verlag, 1985).

28. Danielle Javet, *La Prostitution à Lausanne au XIXe siècle* [Prostitution in Lausanne in the 19th Century] *Histoire et Société Contemporaines* 2 (Lausanne, 1984); Anita Ulrich, *Bordelle, Strassendirnen und bürgerliche Sittlichkeit in der Belle Epoque* [Brothels, Prostitutes and Middle-Class Morality in the Belle Epoque] (Zürich: Druckerei Schulthess, 1985); Alberto Cairoli, Giovanni Chiaberto and Sabina Engel, *Le Déclin des Maisons Closes – la Prostitution à Genève à la fin du XIX siècle* [The Decline of Brothels – Prostitution in Geneva at the End of the 19th Century] (Genève: Edition Zoe, 1987).

29. Monique Pavillon, *Les Immobiliseés. Les femmes suisses en 39-45* [The Unmobilised: Swiss Women 1939-1945] (Lausanne: Edition d'en bas, 1989).

30. Annamarie Ryter, 'Abtreibung in der Unterschicht zu Beginn des Jahrhunderts. Eine empirische Untersuchung [Abortion in the Working Class at the Beginnings of this Century]', MA thesis, University of Basel, 1983; Ursula Gaillard and Annik Mahaim, *Retards des règles. Attitudes devant le contrôle des naissances et l'avortement en Suisse du début du siècle aux années vingt* [Overdue Periods: Attitudes toward Birth Control and Abortion in the Twenties] (Lausanne: Edition d'en bas, 1983).

31. Irene Vonarb, Catherine Sokoloff, 'Wie d'Fraue dr Schwyzer Huushalt verteidigt han [How Women Defended the Swiss Household]', in Nadia Guth and Bettina Hunger (eds.), *Reduit Basel 39/45* (Basel: Friedrich Reinhardt, 1989).

32. Regina Wecker, 'Protective Labour Legislation and Women's Waged Work: The Swiss Case', paper presented at the Bellagio Conference on Women's Waged Work and Labour Legislation in Europe and the USA, August 1989.

33. The last meeting in Berne in 1988 was intended to survey research into this period. The main contributions on the early modern period were given by Heide Wunder, Katharina Simon-Muscheid and Dorothea Rippmann. Unfortunately the papers have not yet been published. An earlier study of the Reformation was Alice

Zimmerli-Witschi's 'Frauen in der Reformationszeit [Women at the Time of the Reformation]', Ph.D. thesis, University of Zürich, 1981. Another area of research in early modern history is the history of witches and witch-hunting. See, for example, Susanna Burghartz, 'The Equation of Women and Witches: A Case Study of Witchcraft trials in Lucerne and Lausanne in the Fifteenth and Sixteenth Centuries', in Richard Evans (ed.), *The German Underworld: Deviants and Outcasts in German History* (London and New York: Routledge, 1988).

34. Brigitte Schnegg, 'Öffentliche Stellung – Gesellschaftliche Rolle der Frau in der Schweiz der Aufklärung [Women's Social Role in Switzerland during the Enlightenment]', University of Berne, Ph.D. thesis in progress.

35. The main theme of this meeting will be 'Women in the Public Sphere'.

36. Men were admitted to the meetings but did not present papers.

37. It was because of this lack of a forum that the group, now forming in part the membership of the Swiss IFRWH committee, was constituted.

38. There have been four publications from the annual meetings on women's history: Regina Wecker and Brigitte Schnegg (eds.), 'Frauen. Zur Geschichte weiblicher Arbeits- und Lebensbedingungen in der Schweiz [Women: On the History of the Conditions of Life and Work in Switzerland]', *Schweizerische Zeitschrift für Geschichte*, 34, no. 3 (1984), pp. 326-493; Annamarie Ryter, Regina Wecker and Susanna Burghartz (eds.), *Auf den Spuren weiblicher Vergangenheit. Berichte des 2. Schweizerischen Historikerinnentreffens in Basel, Oktober 1984* [Tracing Women in History: Essays from the Second Meeting of Women Historians in Basel, October 1984] (Basel: Itinera 2/3 1985); Lisa Berrisch et al. (eds.), *3. Schweizerische Historikerinnentagung, Zürich 1985: Beiträge* [The Third Meeting of Women Historians, Zürich 1985: Contributions] (Zürich: Chronos Verlag, 1986); Arbeitsgruppe Frauengeschichte Basel (eds.), *Auf den Spuren weiblicher Vergangenheit (2) Beiträge der 4. Schweizerischen Historikerinnentagung in Basel* [Tracing Women in History (2), Contributions to the Fourth Meeting of Women Historians] (Zürich: Chronos Verlag, 1988).

39. Gisela Bock mentions this in 'Women's History and Gender History: Aspects of an International Debate', *Gender & History*, 1 (1989) p. 7. She stresses in 'Geschichte, Frauengeschichte, Geschlechtergeschichte', *Geschichte und Gesellschaft*, 14 (1988), p. 367, that apart from the *American Historical Review* only a few non-feminist and non 'women-oriented' historical journals have published issues on women's history written exclusively by women.

40. In her report for the 'Schweizer Wissenschaftsrat [Swiss Council of Science]' Brigitte Studer outlined some of the implications of Swiss research policy. See Brigitte Studer, *Frauen-/Geschlechtergeschichte (Historische Frauenforschung)* [Women's History/Gender History (Research on Women)] (Berne: Schweizer Wissenschaftsrat, 1987).

41. Susanna Burghartz, 'Das Zürcher Ratsgericht als Sanktionierungs- und Konfliktregelungsinstanz. Untersuchungen zur Kriminalitäts – und Mentalitätsgeschichte einer städtischen Gesellschaft Ende des 14. Jahrhunderts [The Zürich Town Court as Instrument for Sanctioning and Regulating Conflicts: On the History of the Criminology and Mentality of an Urban Society Towards the End of the 14th Century]', Ph.D. thesis, University of Basel, 1987.

42. Anne-Lise Head and Brigitte Schnegg (eds.), *Armut in der Schweiz (17.-20.Jh.)* [Poverty in Switzerland (17th-20th Century)], Schweizerische Gesellschaft für Wirtschafts- und Sozialgeschichte 7 (Zürich: Chronos Verlag, 1989).

43. Kuno Trüeb, 'Männerrollen im Wandel. 20. Jahrhundert [The Changing Role and Image of Men in the 20th Century]', in progress.

44. The catalogues give a very good overview of the research done for these exhibitions: Marie-Louise Barben and Elisabeth Ryter (eds.), *Verflixt und zugenäht!, Frauenberufsbildung – Frauenerwerbsarbeit 1888-1988* [Tied in Knots: Women's Vocational Training and Women's Paid Work 1888-1988]; Verein feministische Wissenschaft (ed.), *Ebenso neu als kühn. 120 Jahre Frauenstudium an der Universität Zürich* [New and Daring: The 120th Anniversary of Women Students at the University of Zürich] (Zürich: efef-Verlag 1988).

45. For instance, the exhibition in Luzern in 1986, for the 700th anniversary of the Canton: Fridolin Kurmann, Martin Leuenberger and Regina Wecker (eds.), *Lasst hören aus neuer Zeit. Gesellschaft, Wirtschaft und Politik im Kanton Luzern seit dem ersten Weltkrieg* [Society, Economy and Politics in Canton Luzern since World War I] (Luzern: Luzerner Lehrmittel Verlag, 1986), and the 1989 exhibition on conditions in Basel during World War II: Nadia Guth and Bettina Hunger (eds.), *Reduit Basel 39/45* (Basel: Friedrich Reinhardt 1989).

46. This idea has been successfully realised in some German towns, for instance in Hamburg and Köln [Cologne].

47. Karin Grütter and Annamarie Ryter, *Stärker als ihr denkt* [More Powerful than You Think] (Solothurn: Aare Verlag, 1988).

20

Women's History in Brazil:
Production and Perspectives

Maria Beatriz Nizza da Silva

Brazilian universities and women's studies

As an interdisciplinary field and, most of all, as a fluid area of knowledge, women's studies has had some difficulties in finding a place at Brazilian universities. The existing academic structure is too conservative to abandon certain old courses and replace them by new ones. Only very recently the University of São Paulo has accepted the idea of a Women's Studies Centre, but this is simply an auxiliary centre that tries to bring together scholars who share this common interest. The initiative was taken by female sociologists and very little has as yet been done at this Centre by historians. We have reason to complain about sociological imperialism. Let me give an example. This last June a conference on 'Society, Politics, and Social Relations of Gender' took place and no historian was invited to speak – only sociologists, political scientists, one anthropologist and one psychologist. Even the journal published this year with a first issue on 'Social Relations of Gender and Relations of Sex' gave little space to historians; it contained just one article on a women's periodical in Greece in the late nineteenth century.[1]

In my opinion historians have to fight their own war at the universities and try to bring women's history into departments of history. At my own university it is now possible to lecture on women's history as an option for undergraduate students and to insert it in the larger field of social history for graduate students. But it will be very hard to achieve the same status for women's history as for other traditional courses on ancient or modern history. For the next decade women's history will continue to be viewed either as a feminist problem or as a simple curiosity not worth much attention. This situation may be a consequence of the theoretical and

369

methodological issues raised by the emergence of an autonomous field called women's history. Even so we can find some support at the universities in the growth of historical demography, family history, and the history of everyday life.

The Carlos Chagas Foundation and Research on Women

Since the late 1970s the role that could have been played by Brazilian universities (with their very recent centres for women's studies) has been assumed by the Carlos Chagas Foundation in São Paulo.

The researchers who work at this Foundation began to collect material for a bibliography on Brazilian women's studies publications since 1976. The book appeared (with the financial aid of the Ford Foundation) in 1979, following the institution's call in 1978 for projects on women.[2] This bibliography was a very useful instrument of research and covered not only the social sciences but also historical studies. In it we can count 177 historical articles and books, but most of them belong to what we may perhaps call 'heroic women's history'. The only exceptions to this tendency were the works by American historians such as Ann Pescatello, Susan Soeiro and June Hahner (see below). Some Brazilian research also pointed in new directions, including the study of such subjects as foundlings in the nineteenth century, dependent women who lived in someone else's household, manumission of female slaves, female criminality in nineteenth-century Bahia, dowries, illegitimate children, and divorce. My first article on 'The System of Marriage in Colonial Brazil', published in 1976, was included in this bibliography.[3]

In 1980 the Carlos Chagas Foundation published the results of the First Project on Women (1978) with the title *Vivencia (History, Sexuality, and Feminine Images)*. Four historical studies appeared in this book: Ilana Novinsky's 'Heresy, Women and Sexuality (Some Notes on the Brazilian Northeast in the Sixteenth and Seventeenth Centuries)'; Miriam Moreira Leite's 'The Double Documentation on Women in Travel Literature (1800-1850)'; Pedro Maia Soares' 'Feminism in Rio Grande do Sul: First Notes (1835-1945)'; and my own 'Divorce in São Paulo Captaincy', now also translated in English by Asunción Lavrin for the forthcoming collection, *Sexuality and Marriage in Latin America*.[4]

The Second Project on Women, again with a grant from the Ford Foundation, took place in 1980 and the results were published in a volume entitled *Woman, Women* in 1983. Three articles by historians were included: one on the slave wetnurses, based on advertisements in the daily press of Rio de Janeiro between 1850 and 1880; the second on female workers during the first Republic; and the third on a woman belonging to the anarchist milieu in the beginning of the twentieth century.[5]

The historical production resulting from the Third Project on Women in 1982 was less abundant: just one article was published in the Carlos Chagas Foundation's journal [*Cadernos de Pesquisa*], a piece on black women, both freedwomen and slaves, in the Captaincy of Minas Gerais (the mining district) in the eighteenth century.[6]

The researches presented to the Fourth Project on Women in 1986 have just been published in a book entitled *Rebellion and Submission: Studies on the Feminine Situation*. My own contribution to this volume deals with 'The Image of the Concubine in Colonial Brazil'.[7]

As should be clear, the role played by the Carlos Chagas Foundation in the development of women's studies is a very important one, even though the presence of social scientists remains stronger than that of historians. Every project has been followed by a book or a collection of articles. Here as elsewhere the historians are mostly women. Men are not especially interested in this field at the present time.

The new historical production in Brazil

A genuine documentary revolution was necessary before women's history became possible. And this revolution first erupted in the related fields of historical demography, social history, and family history. These specialists looked for their sources in ecclesiastical archives rather than in public ones. When bishops finally opened the gates of these well-organised archives to researchers, a wealth of documentation concerning everyday life was found: baptism, marriage and death registers; marriage permissions for those who wanted to marry kin; divorce suits; investigations of those who lived in concubinage; admonitions to priests who did not observe religious celibacy and had illegitimate children, and so on.

The use of this new documentation brought with it a transition from a macrosocial to a microsocial level of analysis and a new kind of attention to both female and male populations. Very different from political sources, these new sources had the advantage of throwing a new light on women and men simultaneously.

After this experience with ecclesiastical archives (especially in Catholic countries), historians went back to national and state archives with a new perspective on documentation and began to search for other kinds of sources such as lists of inhabitants, inventories and wills, judicial and notarial sources, and petitions.

In Brazil the question of defining a new field named women's history depends less on the discovery of adequate sources than on the establishment of a distinct boundary separating it from other fields in which the same documentation is employed. This current lack of definition has another consequence: historians of women tend to work in the same time period as historians of the family or of demography – that is, roughly 1750 to 1850.

The more recent period from the mid-nineteenth century to the second decade of the twentieth century (when the historians began to examine the feminist movement) is covered only by a few studies on the history of female education and on female work, including prostitution.[8]

The American contribution

As women's history underwent a rapid growth in the United States in the 1970s, several American historians began to research and write about Brazilian women's history. In 1972 Ann Pescatello published in the *Hispanic American Historical Review* 'Dona e prostituta: Growing Up Female in Brazil', which anticipated her 1976 book *Power and Pawn: The Female in Iberian Families, Societies, and Cultures*.[9] With her article, 'The Social and Economic Role of the Convent: Women and Nuns in Colonial Bahia, 1677-1800', in the same journal, Susan Soeiro signaled the completion of her Ph.D. thesis, 'A Baroque Nunnery: The Economic and Social Role of a Colonial Convent, Santa Clara do Desterro, Salvador, Bahia, 1677-1800'.[10] Unfortunately, this important study has not yet been translated into Portuguese and only a few Brazilian specialists have access to the University Microfilms International version. No Brazilian historian has yet followed the path carved out by Soeiro when she wrote: 'Since few women have had the opportunity to record their own history, the archives of the female orders are doubly valuable both for their disclosure of the operations of the Church and for their revelations concerning the women who wrote them'. Susan Soeiro is better known to Spanish readers, due to the republication of her article (in translation) in the Spanish language edition of the book (originally edited in English in 1978 by Asunción Lavrin): *Las Mujeres Latino-americanas: Perspectivas historicas*.[11]

June E. Hahner is well known to Brazilian researchers because in 1981 a longer version of her study, 'The Nineteenth Century Feminist Press and Women's Rights in Brazil', was published in Portuguese.[12] Her article on this subject has also been translated into Spanish for the Lavrin volume.[13] Before undertaking that research, Hahner had also published 'Women and Work in Brazil, 1850-1920: A Preliminary Investigation', in *Essays Concerning the Socioeconomic History of Brazil and Portuguese India*.[14]

As a complementary research for her book *Household Economy and Urban Development: São Paulo, 1765 to 1836*, Elizabeth Anne Kuznesof has published a very stimulating article, 'The Role of the Female-Headed Household in Brazilian Modernization: S. Paulo 1765 to

1836'.[15] I myself am following this line of research for my study on women's work in colonial São Paulo, not in the town of São Paulo as Kuznesof has done but in the townships of the Captaincy.

More recently Muriel Nazzari has submitted her Ph.D. thesis on 'Women, the Family and Property: The Decline of Dowry in São Paulo, Brazil (1600-1870)'.[16] As the author writes in her abstract: 'This study traces changes in the practice of dowry, seeking to explain its decline and ultimate disappearance. In the seventeenth century most São Paulo property owners gave their daughters dowries, contributing much of the land, cattle, agricultural tools, and Indian slaves necessary for the support of the newly married couple. By the nineteenth century few families gave dowries, and those that did gave smaller ones with a different content, so that they no longer contributed much to the support of the newly weds'.

In 1988 a very interesting book by Sandra Lauderdale Graham appeared, entitled *House and Street: The Domestic World of Servants and Masters in Nineteenth Century Rio de Janeiro*.[17] As the author says in the Introduction, 'to take servants as an occupational group dispels the stereotype that only slaves were servants or that domestic work was exclusively slaves' work'. Attempting to discover the range of possible experiences that could characterise servant women's lives, Graham accepted the challenge 'to trace both the cultural patterns that made dominance possible and pervasive and the ways by which servant women achieved some independence'.

Amid this cluster of female historians I can at last mention one male: A. J. R. Russell-Wood. For the book organized in 1978 by Asunción Lavrin, he wrote a very interesting survey article, 'Woman and Family in the Economy and Society of Colonial Brazil'.[18] This essay has a twofold purpose: first, to argue that women played a significantly more important role in the ideological, economic, and social development of colonial Brazil than has been acknowledged; and, second, to focus attention on potential sources for the history of women in colonial Brazil that had not been adequately used or had been ignored by earlier scholars.

History of the Brazilian feminist movement

If it is somewhat difficult for historians who come to women's history from historical demography, family history and social history to separate off from those fields, for others guided by a feminist perspective this problem is less difficult. They do not hesitate: they choose to analyse women's publications and the development of female education in order to ascertain the origins of the feminist movement at the turn of the century.

As early as 1974, Rachel Soihet submitted a master's thesis on one of the leaders of the Brazilian feminist movement, 'Berta Lutz and the

Social Ascension of Women, 1919-1932'; in 1986 another master's thesis by Sonia Machado Lino studied 'Feminist Ideas in Brazil (1918-1932)'. [19] In such studies, one invariably attempts to compare the Brazilian feminist movement with the American and European ones; some underscore the elitist and bourgeois character of the struggle for the right to vote. An outstanding expression of feminist militancy was the master's thesis presented in 1977 at Rio de Janeiro by a sociologist, Branca Moreira Alves, 'Looking For Our History; The Movement for the Feminine Vote in Brazil, 1919-1932'. [20] But in the 1980s feminist militancy and scholarly research stand quite separately, at least in history, if not in sociology.

Characteristics of women's history in Brazil

One of the main characteristics of women's history in Brazil is the close fit between the questions asked by historians and the documentation at their disposal. This does not indicate intellectual poverty on the part of the questioner but rather a certain dose of realism about sources. Thus, for instance, it is easier to find adequate, though fragmentary, answers to our questions about women's work in colonial Brazil than about their sexuality. Nevertheless, for the sixteenth and seventeenth centuries the investigations directed by the Inquisition permit us to know something about sexual practices extant in colonial society but condemned by the Church. For another period, a younger generation of historians has attempted to extend their knowledge about female sexuality through medical theses submitted to the Faculties of Medicine during the nineteenth century, and through medical reports by sanitary authorities dealing especially with prostitution. [21] In a study practically unknown to Brazilian scholars because it was presented in London at the Institute of Latin American Studies, Luis Carlos Soares has analysed 'Prostitution in Nineteenth-Century Rio de Janeiro'. He examined the reports written by police chiefs on brothels and the sanitary [hygienic] measures adopted by the government. [22]

In contrast, our questions about contraceptive practices and abortion, especially in the colonial period, will receive only vague and unsatisfactory answers, even though there is abundant documentation on abandoned children since the second half of the eighteenth century. With the exception of medical treatises, colonial documents keep silent also about childbirth and its rituals and mother/child relationships. Moralists hold forth on mothers' duties but we know very little about women's actual behaviour. Children are the great absentees in colonial documentation, unless we take a purely demographic point of view. With regard to women's education, the only aspects that can be spoken of in this period are the rules and the fees of the first schools for girls during the early nineteenth century.

Due to a high degree of illiteracy, we cannot directly recover women's thoughts and sensibilities during three and a half centuries of Brazilian history. Female desires, decisions and complaints can only be guessed at through the bureaucratic language of petitions written by men. In Brazil we have to date found practically no women's diaries, no letters, no novels.

We have to wait until the middle of the nineteenth century to read an anonymous *Humanitarian Pamphlet* (1853) written and published in Rio de Janeiro by a woman, whose literary name would later be Nisia Floresta. In 1832 she made a free translation of Mary Wollstonecraft's *A Vindication of the Rights of Woman* under the title *Direitos das mulheres e injustiças dos homens* [Women's Rights and Men's Injustices]; and from 1837 she directed a school for girls.[23] But this exception only confirms the rule: women in Brazil spoke only through men's writings until the second half of the nineteenth century. So there are a certain number of questions we could hardly expect to answer with the available documentation and this limitation is strongly felt by Brazilian historians who certainly envy the written women's sources available to their English, American, and French colleagues.

Another important characteristic seems to be the neat distinction established between the study of norms concerning female behaviour established by the State, the Church, and medical authorities, and the study of female behaviour itself. Brazilian historians are fully conscious that these rules could have been accepted, forgotten, and denied. So they concentrate their attention on evaluating the gap between prescription and practice.

For instance, Catholic norms prohibited cohabitation and sexual intercourse outside marriage, but these norms found little acceptance in colonial Brazil, as seen in an examination of the investigations ordered by the bishop of the mining region in 1737. Research by Luna and Costa has found that of 350 crimes against the faith, 306 were concubinages and amongst these 76.8 per cent were committed by single men and women - that is to say, by couples who could have married if they had wanted to.[24]

A third characteristic should also be emphasised: women's history in Brazil is not for the most part concerned with theories, either theories imported from other social sciences or theories formulated by historians themselves. The desire to listen to a majority that has remained silent for a long period and the curiosity about the new documentation seem, for the time being, more urgent than the need for theoretical explanations.

Nevertheless, we can discern a certain amount of conceptual sophistication, especially when historical studies keep in touch with the social sciences. In a very recent master's thesis directed by an anthropologist, we find a chapter entitled 'Some theoretical issues', where the concept of culture is thoroughly analysed.[25] In general, marriage and family, and the rules presiding over these institutions provide the required conceptual framework even when sexual intercourse and procreation take place outside them. Concepts of work and economic survival also play a central role in historical studies on women, not perhaps with the primary purpose of denouncing the exploitation of female labour but with a strong curiosity about the strategies developed by women in their everyday life. We also find a clear preference for the analysis and evaluation of the spheres of decision that belonged to women in past societies, over the study of rebellion and nonconformity.

By the end of the 1980s, we stand at a considerable distance from the heroic women's history of more traditional historians. Now our aim is to write of women from all social groups and in all stages of life in their daily activities, though some historians still find it easier to focus on elite women.

Perspectives

In Brazilian historiography the main trend seems to be the inclusion of women's history in broader fields such as family history, through the emphasis on the assymetry in female and male roles, and in historical demography, a field where the variable of sex has always had the same relevance as age or race. The links with social history will certainly become more frequent, because women's history is not the history of an abstract entity but of women belonging to different social groups and (most important in Brazil) to different ethnic groups. We must not forget that Brazilian women are variously white, indian, black, 'mulattas' and other sorts of *mestizas*; furthermore there were for almost four centuries free-born, slave and freed women. Until the 1980s, the history of slavery itself was written without taking into consideration the differences between slave men and slave women, not only in their market prices but also in their abilities as workers. Today historians tend to recognize the specificity of the way of life of slave women.

The history of immigration continues to suffer from gender insensitivity, but the same development as in the history of slavery is to be expected: a new focus on the experiences of immigrant women. In the nineteenth century and even in the twentieth century, immigration was largely a male phenomenon, but this does not mean that a small contingent of single women and widows were not courageous enough to leave their countries to try another way of life in Brazil.

When immigration was no longer an individual affair and became a family project, the role of those wives and daughters who simply followed their husbands and parents to the new country should not be underestimated. They contributed to maintaining their original country's values and traditions – language and religion, as well as technological, cooking and family traditions. And their role in Brazilian society was quite different from that of Brazilian-born women. Much work must be done to analyse the sexual division of labour in immigrant families (from Italian, German, Spanish, Japanese, and Arab backgrounds), along with the activities of women who immigrated alone during the nineteenth century, becoming teachers, dressmakers, servants, and even working in urban brothels.

The most striking omission in Brazilian women's history to date is a concern with age. The concept of the lifecycle is little employed except by those who came to women's history from historical demography. Historians are now beginning to do some research on children, but not specifically on young girls. Though fecundity is an important phenomenon in historical demography, most studies on women's history speak of women as ageless, with just a bare reference to their civil status (single, married and widows). Old age seems to have been completely forgotten, yet we may hope for some development in this topic given the recent sociological interest in older people.

To conclude, let me underscore once again the dominant trend of Brazilian historiography on women: an emphasis on the variety and complexity of roles and functions, rather than any exclusive interest in the political advancement of women.[26]

NOTES

1. *Relações Sociais de Gênero x Relações de Sexo*, Universidade de São Paulo, Departamento de Sociologica, Área de Pós-Graduação, Núcleo de Estudos da Mulher e Relações Sociais de Gênero, 1989; the historical article is Eleni Varikas, 'Jornal das Damas, Feminismo no séc. XIX na Grécia', pp. 46-60.

2. *Mulher Brasileira. Bibliografia anotada* [Brazilian Women: A Critical Bibliography] (São Paulo: Brasiliense e Fundação Carlos Chagas, 1979), vol. 1.

3. *Ciência e Cultura* (São Paulo), 28, no. 11 (1976), pp. 1250-63.

4. M. Cristina Brischini and Fúlvia Rosemberg (eds.), *Vivência (História, Sexualidade e Imagens Femininas)* (São Paulo: Brasiliense e Fundação Carlos Chagas, 1980). See Ilana W. Novinski, 'Heresia, mulher e sexualidade (algumas notas sobre o Nordeste brasileiro nos séculos XVI e XVII)', pp. 227-56; Miriam M.

Leite, 'A dupla documentação sobre mulheres nos livros de viagens (1800-1850)',
pp. 195-226; Pedro M. Soares, 'Feminismo no Rio Grande do Sul: primeiros
apontamentos (1835-1945)', pp. 121-50; and Maria Beatriz Nizza da Silva, 'O
divórcio na Capitania de S. Paulo', pp. 151-94.

5.   Carmen Barroso and Albertina O. Costa (eds.), *Mulher, Mulheres*
[Woman, Women] (São Paulo: Cortez Editora e Fundação Carlos Chagas, 1983). See
Elizabeth Magalhães and Sonia Giacomini, 'A escrava ama-de-leite: anjo ou
demônio? [The Slave Wetnurse: Angel or Devil?]', pp. 73-88; M. Valéria J. Pena
and Elca M. Lima, 'Lutas ilusórias: a mulher na política operária da Primeira
República [Deceptive Fights: Women in Workers' Policy During the First
Republic]', pp. 17-33; and Miriam M. Leite, 'Maria Lacerda de Moura. Imagem e
reflexo [Maria Lacerda de Moura: Image and Reflection]', pp. 35-53.

6.   Luciano Figueiredo and Ana M. Magaldi, 'Quitandas e quitutes: um
estudo sobre rebeldia e transgressão feminina numa sociedade colonial [Pedlars and
Delicatessen: A Study of Female Rebellion and Transgression in Colonial Society]',
Cadernos de Pesquisa (São Paulo: Fundação Carlos Chagas), no. 54 (August 1985),
pp. 50-61.

7.   Albertina O. Costa and M. Cristina Brischini (eds.), *Rebeldia e
submissão. Estudos sobre a condição feminina* (São Paulo: Vértice e Fundação
Carlos Chagas, 1989), including Maria Beatriz Nizza da Silva, 'A imagem da
concubina no Brasil colonial: ilegitimidade e heranca [Images of the Concubine in
Colonial Brazil: Illegitimacy and Inheritance]', pp. 17-59.

8.   See Zuleika M. F. Alvin, 'A participação política da mulher no início
da industrializacão em São Paulo [Women's Political Participation during the
Beginning of Industrialisation in São Paulo]', *Revista de Historia* (São Paulo), 114
(1983), pp. 61-84; Magali G. Engel, 'O médico, a prostituta e os significados do
corpo doente [Doctors, Prostitutes, and the Meaning of Sick Bodies]', in Ronaldo
Vainfas (ed.), *História e sexualidade no Brasil* [History and Sexuality in Brazil] (Rio
de Janeiro: Graal, 1986), pp. 169-90; Esmeralda Moura, *Mulheres e menores no
trabalho industrial* [Women and Minors in Industrial Work] (Petrópolis: Vozes,
1982); Esmeralda Moura, 'Trabalho feminino e condição social do menor em São
Paulo (1890-1920) [Female Labour and the Social Situation of Minors in São Paulo
(1890-1920)]', *Estudos Cedhal* (São Paulo), 3 (1988), pp. 4-38; Marinete dos Santos
Silva, 'Escravidão e prostituição - das várias utilidades de uma escrava negra [Slavery
and Prostitution - The Several Uses of a Slave Woman]', *Anais da VII Reunião* (São
Paulo: Sociedade Brasileira de Pesquisa Histórica, 1988), pp. 119-22; Marinete dos
Santos Silva, 'Die Prostitution in Rio de Janeiro im 19. Jahrhundert', in Ursula A.
J. Becher and Jörn Rüsen (eds.), *Weiblichkeit in geschichtlicher Perspektive,
Fallstudien und Reflexionen zu Grundproblemen der historischen Frauenforschung*
(Frankfurt am Main: Suhrkamp, 1988), pp. 292-305; and Luiz Carlos Soares, 'Da
necessidade do bordel higienizado. Tentativas de controle da prostituição carioca no
século XIX [The Need for Hygienic Brothels: Attempts at Controlling Prostitution
in Nineteenth Century Rio de Janeiro]', in Ronaldo Vainfas (ed.), *História e
sexualidade no Brasil* (Rio de Janeiro: Graal, 1986), pp. 143-68.

9.   (Westport, Conn.: Greenwood Press, 1976).

10.   Susan A. Soeiro, 'The Social and Economic Role of the Convent:
Women and Nuns in Colonial Bahia, 1677-1800', *Hispanic American Historical
Review*, 54, no. 2 (1974), pp. 209-32; see also, Susan A. Soeiro, *A Baroque*

Nunnery: The Economic and Social Role of a Colonial Convent, Santa Clara do Desterro, Salvador, Bahia, 1677-1800, Ph.D. thesis, New York University (Ann Arbor, Michigan: University Microfilms International, 1974).

11. Asunción Lavrin (ed.), *Latin American Women: A Historical Perspective* (Westport, Conn.: Greenwood Press, 1978); in Spanish as Asunción Lavrin (ed.), *Las mujeres latino-americanas: Perspectivas historicas* (Mexico City: Fondo de Cultura Economica, 1985).

12. June E. Hahner, *A mulher brasileira e suas lutas sociais e políticas, 1850-1937* [Brazilian Women and their Social and Political Struggles, 1850-1937] (São Paulo: Brasiliense, 1981). See also her earlier collection, *A mulher no Brasil* [Women in Brazil] (Rio de Janeiro: Civilização Brasileira, 1978).

13. June E. Hahner, 'La prensa feminista de siglo XIX y los derechos de las mujeres en el Brasil', in Lavrin (ed.), *Mujeres latino-americanas*, pp. 293-328. See also Hahner's historiographical article, 'Recent Research on Women in Brazil', *Latin American Research Review*, 20, no. 3 (1985), pp. 163-179.

14. Dauril Alden and Warren Dean (eds.), *Essays Concerning the Socioeconomic History of Brazil and Portuguese India* (Gainesville: University Presses of Florida, 1977).

15. Elizabeth Anne Kuznesof, *Household Economy and Urban Development: São Paulo, 1765 to 1836* (Boulder, Colo: Westview, 1986); 'The Role of the Female-Headed Household in Brazilian Modernization: São Paulo 1765 to 1836', *Journal of Social History*, 13, no. 4 (1980), pp. 589-613.

16. Ph.D. thesis, Yale University, 1986; available through University Microfilms International (Ann Arbor, Michigan), 1988.

17. Sandra L. Graham, *House and Street. The Domestic World of Servants and Masters in Nineteenth-Century Rio de Janeiro* (Cambridge: Cambridge University Press, 1988).

18. A. J. A. Russell-Wood, 'La mujer y la familia en la economia y en la sociedad del Brasil durante la epoca colonial [Woman and the Family in Brazilian Economy and Society during the Colonial Period]', in Lavrin (ed.), *Mujeres latino-americanas. Perspectivas historicas*, pp. 74-120.

19. Rachel Soihet, 'Berta Lutz e a ascensão social da Mulher, 1919-1937', M.A. thesis, Universidade Federal Fluminense, 1974; Sonia Machado Lino, 'As ideias feministas no Brasil (1918-1932)', M.A. thesis, Universidade Federal do Parana, 1986.

20. *Em busca de nossa história: o movimento pelo voto feminino no Brasil, 1919-1932: factos e ideologia*, Universidade de Rio de Janeiro, 1977. Published as Branca Moreira Alves, *Ideologia e feminismo. A luta da mulher pelo voto no Brasil* [Ideology and Feminism: Women's Fight for the Vote in Brazil] (Petrópolis: Vozes, 1980).

21. See especially Magali G. Engel, *Meretrizes e doutores. Saber médico e prostituição no Rio de Janeiro (1840-1890)* [Whores and Doctors: Medical Knowledge and Prostitution in Rio de Janeiro (1840-1890)] (São Paulo: Brasiliense, 1989).

22. See the article by Luis Carlos Soares, 'Da necessidade do bordel higienizado' (note 8).

23. This free translation was made from a French version. See the Introduction written by Peggy Sharpe-Valadares for a new edition of the *Opúsculo Humanitário* [Humanitarian Pamphlet] (São Paulo: Cortez e INEP, 1989), p. xvii.

24. Francisco Vidal Luna and Iraci del Nero da Costa, 'Devassa nas Minas Gerais: observações sobre casos de concubinato', *Anais do Museu Paulista* (São Paulo) 31 (1982), pp. 221-34.

25. Maria Fernanda Baptista Bicalho, *O BELLO SEXO—Imprensa e identidade feminina no Rio de Janeiro em fins do século XIX e início do século XX* [The Beautiful Sex, the Press, and Female Identity in Rio de Janeiro in the late 19th and early 20th centuries], Federal University of Rio de Janeiro, 1988. See the published summary in Maria Fernanda Bicalho, 'O Bello Sexo: Imprensa e identidade feminina no Rio de Janeiro em fins do século XIX e início do século XX [The Beautiful Sex: The Press and Feminine Identity in Rio de Janeiro during the Late Nineteenth- and Early Twentieth Century]', in Costa and Bruschini (eds.) *Rebeldia e submissão*, pp. 79-99.

26. Some of these observations (with additional bibliography) were previously published as 'A História da Mulher no Brasil: Balanço da Produção e Perspectivas', *Ler História* (Lisbon), 12 (1988), pp. 95-110, and in *Revista do Instituto de Estudos Brasileiros* (University of São Paulo), 27 (1987), pp. 75-91, under the title 'A Historia da Mulher no Brasil: tendências e perspectivas'.

21

Two Decades of Women's History in Spain: A Reappraisal

Mary Nash

Women's history has been undoubtedly the area of greatest development in Spanish scholarship in women's studies over the past fifteen years.[1] It is still, however, to a large extent seeking legitimisation and normalisation in Spanish academic circles. In general, we can say women have become somewhat more visible in historical studies and other disciplines over the past two decades. The major currents of women's history in Spain today may be situated mainly within the parameters of 'contributive history'. Over the past decade women's history in Spain has developed into a complex discipline which cannot, of course, be reduced to a single methodological or theoretical framework.[2] This survey indicates the major trends within this field but does not claim to offer an exhaustive overview. Rather it proposes only to identify the most significant topics and patterns of research and to point out the most important interpretative schemes in Spanish women's history over the past fifteen years.

Patterns of development in women's history

Among women in Spanish academe today the drive is to develop women's studies within mainstream curricula. In the past women considered education as a crucial tool to achieve women's rights and improvements in their status; today the thrust to develop women's studies can be described as the key to changing women's worldview and perspectives. As the intellectual tool of feminism, women's studies is now pioneering, from a plurality of methodological stances and theoretical frameworks, the construction of new terms of reference for the understanding of how women shaped their lives, and how gender interrelates with societal change. Women's studies is slowly formulating the means to female advancement, empowerment and self-identity, although the path is still extremely arduous and fraught with obstacles.

In Spain, women's history has been the pioneering field within women's studies. It has achieved a significant degree of development in the academic world. Nonetheless, it, too, is far from receiving widespread recognition, research facilities and acceptance in the academy. Furthermore the development of the historiography on women over the past two decades has in practice undoubtedly been constrained by the restrictions of the state university system, the current state of the discipline of history in Spanish academic life and the overall growth of feminist theory and its integration into historical studies on women.[3]

Two main stages can be discerned in the development of women's history in Spain since the early seventies. The first stage ran from 1974 to 1981. This was the time of the first methodological formulations, and of the presentation of the first results in scholarship, and especially, it was the time when a very small number of female scholars chose to focus on women's issues in their research. Of course, women's history developed in Spain at a later date than in other European countries or the US. The fact that the first masters dissertations in women's history were not presented until 1974[4] must be understood not only in the context of the incipient women's movement of the time but also in the context of the socio-political development of Spain in the final years of the Franco regime.[5] The upsurge of the women's movement can be identified not so much with the generation of 1968 but rather with the anti-Franco movement. The overall collective historical amnesia which had characterised the post-war period in Spain, together with the distortion and marginalisation of historical social movements and political processes by Francoist historiography, had led to a blurring or misrepresentation of Spanish social reality prior to the conclusion of the Spanish Civil War in 1939. Spanish historiography thus set about to redress this imbalance in contemporary history and so insisted on the development of a more politicised and political history of the pre-war period.[6] Not surprisingly, historical amnesia on women was even more acute; there was a general lack of awareness and knowledge on what women's collective historical experience had been in Spain. And so, the first studies in women's history focused on political issues in contemporary history, such as female suffrage and the working-class movement.

Women's history developed initially from the idea of the negation and neglect of women in historical studies; one of the first stages in its growth was precisely the elementary observation of the silences in historical discourse.[7] Just as in other countries, pioneer works in Spain focused on the recovery of historical memory and on including women as active collective agents in the dynamics of historical change. However, in contrast to the development of women's history in other European countries such as Italy or France,[8] where a significant body of anthropologically-based scholarship had examined the private sphere and a socio-cultural approach to everyday life, the body, reproduction or motherhood, in Spain most pioneering studies focused on the public arena of politics, suffrage and the labour movement. In reflecting what was happening in mainstream Spanish historiography, women historians also investigated more political issues while the late development of the social history of the period since 1800 generated methodological problems in dealing with women in the private sphere and with socio-cultural aspects of women's collective historical experience.

During the seventies women's history constituted one of the fields in the *avant-garde* of scholarship, research and teaching in women's studies. It was through women's history that women's studies first gained some degree of recognition in the academy with the introduction in 1974 of the first course on the Social History of Women in mainstream curricula at the Department of Contemporary History at the University of Barcelona, the first such course within the Spanish university system. Shortly afterwards the Centre d'Estudis Històrics Internacionals organised the first forum for academic debate on women in a series of seminars which ran in the spring of 1975, at a time when the women's movement was holding mass conferences in Madrid and Barcelona.[9] Thus, the development of women's history in the seventies is closely associated with the development of the women's movement and the growing sensitivity of women scholars to feminist and women's issues. However, women's history was still exceptional and precarious, facing undoubted hostility in many academic circles. In this first phase, the practice of women's history was limited to individual scholars, with extremely inadequate academic support and little scholarly visibility in the academy. In these initial years of the development of women's history, the contributions of Hispanists represented an important stimulus to the development of historiography on women. Studies by journalists and writers, together with the memoirs and autobiographical writings of women activists (particularly from the Civil War and the movement of resistance to Franco), all made important contributions to our knowledge of the historical experience of women in Spain.[10]

The second phase in women's history extends from the early eighties to the present. During this period scholarship itself underwent important changes and achieved a greater degree of legitimisation. The increasing consolidation of the women's movement, and the overall development of feminist consciousness, together with the increase in the number of female academics with tenure, have all helped the development of women's history and of women's studies in Spanish universities over the past few years. Furthermore, the political transformation and the consolidation of democracy in Spain led to the creation in 1984 of the first official state bureau designed to protect women's interests, which in turn led to the creation of other regional official bodies. These changes also stimulated interest in research on women's issues, although only more recently in the field of history. Since 1986 Spain's integration into the European Community has compelled the implementation of European policies on equality and this development has also generated a greater degree of sensitivity to and acceptability of women's studies.

Although nothing in Spain compares to the degree of institutionalisation which has occurred in some European countries and in the US, since the early eighties there has nevertheless been a remarkable degree of activity. In this second stage women's history has been characterised by rapid expansion, greater consolidation, an increase in research projects, a diversification of the topics studied and an opening up of fields and disciplines, including the history of art and literature. The past six years in particular have been a time of greater visibility for women's issues in academe as a greater number of female scholars (and some males) now dedicate themselves to the study of women as their primary area of research. This period is also one of greater institutionalisation in the academic world and one of growing recognition of the legitimacy of such studies in academic research and teaching. Even so we are still very far from obtaining widespread recognition of the scientific rigour and value of such studies or their integration into mainstream university curricula.

The efforts undertaken to develop women's studies have differed somewhat in their strategy and objectives. The majority of endeavours to develop research on women has been centred within the universities. There are, however, several notable exceptions, such as the Feminist Centre for Studies and Documentation in Madrid which held an important exhibition on Women's Work in History in 1985, the feminist press La Sal, located in Barcelona, which has reprinted an important collection of literature by women, and the courses held by the Instituto de Promoción de Estudios Sociales in the Basque Country. Although some grass roots interest exists in women's history, academic women's history has been the main forum for its development and diffusion.

In the early eighties two patterns emerged in the development of forums for women's studies. One strategy developed was that of the Centre d'Investigació Històrica de la Dona (CIHD) [Centre for Research on Women's History, University of Barcelona] which was founded in 1982 as an autonomous section of an already existing University Institute.[11] It is unique in the sense that it acquired a legal status and formal administrative base within the university. It also differs from other seminars on women because of its official status and also because it focused on women's history, though with an interdisciplinary approach. The legal status of the CIHD has allowed it since 1987 to introduce pioneer post-graduate and master's courses on women's history and in women's studies and to create an infrastructure of bibliographical resources and research on women's history.

The more general pattern was that of loosely structured interdisciplinary seminars on women such as the Seminario de Estudios de la Mujer [Women's Studies] at the Autonomous University of Madrid and more recently at the Complutense University of Madrid and at the universities of the Basque Country, Valencia, Malaga and Granada. These seminars have channeled their main activities into organising conferences and seminars on women's issues; many of their members carry out some individual research on women. Until very recently they have tended not to maintain a permanent relationship with their constituency of university students and female university faculty. The Seminar on Women at the Autonomous University of Madrid, in collaboration with the Complutense University, Madrid, has organised more than half a dozen conferences since its creation in 1981. These conferences have centred on history (ancient, medieval, modern, contemporary), art, sociology, literature and economics. The published proceedings from some of these conferences have made a decisive contribution to the development of research in women's studies. More recently seminars have been established in two university institutes, the Fundación Ortega y Gasset (Madrid) and the Instituto Universitario de Estudis e Desenvolvemento de Galicia (Santiago de Compostela). Another formula has been used in the Basque Country where the Seminar on Women at the Basque University has been developed with funding provided by the local government.

In the past two years there has been a decided change in strategies in the field of women's studies towards seeking to increase the institutionalisation of the seminars on women as formally structured centres and university institutes. The issue of women's studies versus feminist studies is being debated[12] and for the moment the dominant tendency is quite clearly to create interdisciplinary women's studies university centres. Within these centres historians have played a major role and women's history continues to be the predominant field.

There is in Spanish universities no tradition of incorporating specific subjects dedicated to women into mainstream curricula. This can be ascribed to a complex situation which encompasses both ideological and structural difficulties, linked to the contemporary situation of the state university system. Obstacles to the consolidation of women's studies include the overt hostility of male academics, and structural problems within the highly inflexible and centralised Spanish university systems.

The area which appears most receptive to the introduction of women's studies at present is the newly created post-graduate Third Cycle programmes. A small number of courses on women's history are being introduced in these programmes, which offer greater flexibility of curricula and a larger degree of specialisation. Another formula for introducing studies on women has been through short university lecture series and seminars.

In this second period, Spanish historians of women have shown increased interest in the range of topics developed in French and Italian women's history, (in, for instance, the history of everyday life, of reproduction, of private sphere, and of domestic work). Until recently more conventional 'contributive history,' focusing on the description of the activities of women, their status and oppression in a social context defined by men within a patriarchal society, has been the core of women's history in Spain. There is considerable agreement among Spanish historians of women on the need to develop our methodological and theoretical framework. Despite the attention drawn at recent conferences to the need[13] for such a framework, gender theory, feminist theory and theories on women's history have as yet to be fully integrated into historical studies on women. Nevertheless, some advances have been made in this direction.[14] Spanish women's history has been variously influenced by Anglo-American and Italian and French historiography, although as yet it has not reached an overall level of sophisticated gender and/or feminist analysis. The increasing interest on and writing of women's history, and the awareness of the need to encourage further theoretical and methodological reflection, offer positive signs of the growing development of this discipline in Spain.

Historiographical patterns

Bibliographical, documentary and archival resources

Much attention has been given to the task of identifying documentation for the history of women in Spain. Most of the bibliographical guides include publications documenting the nineteenth and twentieth centuries. The available published catalogues tend to present a general overview with particular attention to the material available in Madrid archives,[15] although there are some articles with a thematic focus.[16] In 1988 the CIHD at the University of Barcelona completed an exhaustive compilation of historical bibliography on women – *An Historical Bibliography on Women in Catalonia, 1800-1939* – located in more than twenty archives and libraries in Barcelona. Currently it is developing a computerised database of the 3000 abstracts compiled. A thesaurus of non-sexist language for women's history has also been drawn up from this historical material.[17] Few historical bibliographies are as yet available on Spanish women in the medieval and early modern periods.[18] In 1988 the CIHD initiated a project which aims to compile a guide to documentary sources for the history of women in Catalonia in the medieval and early modern periods. Considerable attention has been given to the indexing of periodicals published by or directed towards women in the late nineteenth and early twentieth centuries, although there is as yet no complete guide available for all of Spain.[19] So far research resources in Spain have allowed little development of scholarship by Spanish historians on women outside the Spanish context; a number of review articles with an international perspective on women's history have been published,[20] together with some anthologies and articles on international women's history.[21]

Another aspect of the task of developing an infrastructure aimed at creating the foundations for the study and diffusion of women's history has been the publication of anthologies of historical texts, such as those published in the collection of Catalonian Classics by the feminist publisher La Sal. Of particular interest for the medieval period are Isabel de Villena, *Protagonistes femenines a la 'Vita Christi'*,[22] and the ninth-century work by Duoda, *De mare a fill*.[23] In contemporary history the pioneering work of Amalia Martín Gamero, *Antologia del feminismo* (1978), a selection of feminist texts by Spanish and international authors from the sixteenth to the twentieth centuries has provided a very useful general overview. A selection of key articles by two prominent nineteenth-century Spanish women – the lawyer and prison reformer Concepción Arenal and by the writer Emilia Pardo Bazán[24] – and the twentieth-century suffragist Clara Campoamor,[25] together with an anthology of historical texts on topics such as family, work, prostitution, and the image of women[26] allow us to trace the growth of Spanish feminist thought and to survey the social condition of women in late-nineteenth and early-twentieth-century Spain. An anthology of historical documents on the anarchist women's organisation 'Mujeres Libres' [Free Women] throws light on the development of feminist theory and practice from the perspective of a working-class women's alternative feminist proposal for revolutionary change during the Civil War of 1936-1939.[27] In view of the usefulness of such anthologies, particularly for teaching purposes, this genre of scholarly production in women's history needs to be further encouraged.

Medieval history from the fourth to the fifteenth century

Although the number and scope of works on the history of women in the Iberian Peninsula in the middle ages[28] is still quite small, there has been a decisive growth in such studies over the past few years. Prior to the early seventies historiography on women was characterised by the absence of interest in defining the object under study (women are assumed to be notable figures, or functional goods for exchange between families, or courtesans in the Muslim capitals). Literary and judicial sources predominate in studies written mainly by male historians and characterised by a neo-positivist methodology. These characteristics are perceptible in important studies on women in Al-Andalus and in the Christian kingdoms.[29] This kind of history of women continues to be written,[30] but it is now flanked by a parallel historiography that reveals new attitudes, new theoretical frameworks and a broadening of topics characteristic of studies published during the last decade.

In the late seventies a growing nucleus of women historians began to write and reflect on women in medieval Spanish history although their explicit conceptual preoccupation with women's history and feminist theory was not yet manifest in their published works. Most of these women historians only began to write the history of women at a later stage in their careers. Although their works reveal an increasingly ideological commitment to a feminist conceptual framework for women's history, most of these studies still reflect the approach of 'contribution history' in their research. Currently there is a growing desire to develop theoretical approaches to medieval women's history and some published studies have begun to introduce general feminist theory to studies on the middle ages. The topic for the next conference on medieval women (to be held at the Complutense University, Madrid, in 1991) will be the theoretical bases and primary sources for the history of women. A series of thematic conferences on women in the medieval history has been held during the past five years.[31] Major topics of discussion have included the legal aspects of women's social condition,[32] women in Muslim Spain,[33] aspects of female religiosity,[34] everyday life, the body and reproduction,[35] work, family and the economic role of women,[36] medieval thinkers on women,[37] and women in the medieval Europe.[38] This significant increase in studies on women in medieval period, should make it increasingly difficult for established academic historians in Spain to persist in ignoring such studies as minor themes in mainstream medieval historiography.

Women in early modern history from the sixteenth to the eighteenth century

For the early modern period the new history on women has developed alongside the introduction of new historiographical trends in Spanish historiography. Of particular significance are the works of E.P. Thompson on social history, Michel Vovelle on the history of mentalities, and Michel Foucault on the study of new institutions, the prison and the asylum. More recently women's history in this period has been greatly influenced by the publications of Natalie Zemon Davis. In contrast to historical writings on more recent periods, studies of early modern history in Spain have taken a less political and more socio-cultural approach to women's history.

One of the first themes within the early modern period to be examined more systematically has been the social condition of women in relation to the judicial norms of the *Antiguo Regimen*.[39] Attention has been paid to the significant restrictions on women as increasingly repressive legislation discriminated on the basis of social status. Another line of research has been the study of discourses on the role and image of women, particularly from religious and medical sources.[40] The role of religious and scientific discourse in the cultural construction of gender is gradually being documented as are also changes in male and female roles in the context of societal changes in the eighteenth century.[41]

Considerable attention is also being paid to education[42] and accordingly to the relationship between knowledge and power and its gender connotations.[43] The role of religion, religiosity and convent life and their significance for the cultural, personal and economic status of women is another topic being studied,[44] while the lives of saints, such as Teresa of Avila, and heterodox religious women[45] are being re-examined in the light of the development of female potential in religious and cultural arenas.[46] Attitudes towards women are being culled not only from a greater knowledge of women's role in religion but also through other areas of research such as the history of the family.[47] Studies of noble women have underscored the increasing restrictions placed on their socio-political role and their continued subordination within the closely entwined family and social order of the Spanish *Antiguo Regimen*, although some instances of female resistance to normative behaviour have also been documented. Family structures and matrimonial strategies represent another area of research although to date such studies often take a more conventional approach to women. A gender perspective on inheritance systems and male/female roles in the family has also been developed recently and new studies point out that the legal regulation of matrimony in the *Antiguo Regimen* strengthened the subordination of married women from the late sixteenth century on.[48]

The area of women's work in the early modern period is another which has grown over the past few years. Studies of different economic sectors have examined women's labour in domestic service, medicine and nursing, religious work, and in developing industries (tobacco and textile sectors). Advances have been made in studying women in the guilds despite difficulties in documenting their specific role.[49] Most studies deal with women's paid work within the labour market, although most urban women in this period were housewives dedicated to household production and the running of their homes.[50] However, this is an area of research that requires further expansion both for early modern and for the contemporary history of women in Spain. Another area of research has been on the work of nuns.[51] A recent study on the important treatise on women by Fray Luis de León, *La Perfecta Casada* [The Perfect Married Lady] (1583), suggestively reinterprets a work previously known only as a treatise on morals and proper dress. By introducing a new conceptual framework based on feminist economic theory, M. Angeles Duran treats the work as a treatise on domestic work considered as a complex economic activity distinct from the regular labour market.[52] Major emphasis must be given in the future to the development of a theoretical framework which places Spain and Spanish women in the overall context of pre-industrial Europe, while considerably more attention must be dedicated to investigating the role of women in rural Spain.

Another topic of research in early modern women's history concerns female delinquency and prostitution[53] and the role of social institutions in dealing with these issues.[54] Inquisition sources are as yet little exploited but preliminary studies indicate their extraordinary possibilities for examining the social history of women and exploring the history of *mentalités*.[55] Few studies as yet address the issue of women and power but these are being developed from the perspective of both formal and informal power structures.[56] Another major area of research addresses the power the Catholic Church held over women through confessional and spiritual direction, given that Church belligerency during the Counter Reformation era particularly emphasised religious control over women. Other early modern studies have focused on the study of private life, the relationship between sexuality and honour, both formal and informal codes concerning personal relationships and the instrumentalisation of the institution of marriage as a means of assuring the social integration of women. The variety of family models (Muslim, *moriscas*, *conversas*, Christian), points to very different family structures and arrangements of public and private spaces in Spain prior to 1800.[57] Another topic of research has been picaresque women (characterised by their unorthodox and roguish behaviour) in the seventeenth century and the effect of the economic crisis of that period on the development of misogynistic attitudes towards women.[58]

Modern history, from 1808 to the present

The disintegration of the *Antiguo Regimen* and the consolidation of a new constitutional political system in the 1830s gave rise to new parameters for the social condition of women. The frailty of the liberal state and the deep conservatism of the Spanish ruling class throughout the nineteenth century underlined the traditional nature of existing social structures, and where women were concerned, reinforced existing religious and cultural mores and values. In a scenario where politics was the privilege of a minority elite, it is not surprising to find women absent from the political domain with the exception of the female representatives of the throne, the regent, Maria Cristina and the queen, Isabel II. The intensity of the struggle for power between conservative and progressive liberals throughout the nineteenth century left no room for considering the need to redress the political inequality of women. The new values of citizenship and national sovereignty had a specific gender dimension; they did not apply to women. There are as yet few studies which examine the relationship of women to politics in the nineteenth century; however, those that exist point to a degree of female activism in socio-political events despite the limits on their intervention in the public sphere and their lack of political rights.[59]

The complex political system established at the restoration of the Bourbon Monarchy (1875), based on the fraudulent malfunctioning of the parliamentary system, operated to guarantee the existing social structures and political hegemony of the dynastic conservative parties, but also restricted progress in the field of women's rights. The fragility and the misuse of the liberal representative system in the last quarter of the nineteenth century was very unfavourable toward the development of liberal political feminism such as had arisen in Great Britain and the United States. Among Spanish liberals and democrats, the core of the political struggle was to gain power and consolidate an effective modern liberal or democratic state. They were not interested in voicing a claim for citizenship for women and even in the late nineteenth century there are very few voices who broach the question of women's rights. At the same time the acute polarisation of social tensions led the more radical parties and labour movements to focus on strategies that were, on the whole, indifferent to the legal, economic, political and educational injustices perpetrated on women.

Initially many of the early studies on women in modern Spanish history drew on the interpretative scheme of the victimisation and oppression of women. Preferential attention has thus been given to political feminism, to the redressing of political grievances and to the attainment of political rights. Studies of the women's press, literature and prescriptive literature have defined the archetypal woman for the nineteenth and early twentieth centuries in terms of the 'Perfecta Casada' (the perfect married lady),[60] although it is also quite clear that women themselves were often far from identifying with this prescribed model.

The development of Spanish feminism has represented one of the core fields in women's history over the past two decades. Preliminary studies on women in the Spanish socialist-utopian movement point to a significant degree of socio-political consciousness by a small elite of women whose feminist consciousness led them to articulate certain strategies for attaining the emancipation of women.[61] Our knowledge of the characteristics and development of first wave feminism is still quite fragmentary and we cannot yet establish a definitive typology of feminist groups. However, it appears that in both the nineteenth century and in the early decades of the twentieth century Spanish feminism can be characterised more by its social than its political aspirations[62] and, on the whole, the Spanish women's movement then was not singularly suffragist. Despite the significant identification with the feminist cause by some exceptional late nineteenth-century women, such as Concepción Arenal and Emilia Pardo Bazán, organisation among women was still quite weak and there was no concerted drive to develop a strong feminist movement until the early twentieth century. Even then the women's movement was not always openly suffragist but had, rather, a socio-cultural character.

One of the difficulties that arises in the study of historical feminism is the lack of definition and theoretical reflection on the use of the concept of feminism in historical analysis.[63] Indeed a topic that deserves further analysis is the appropriation and readaptation of the concept 'feminism' by women activists in the early twentieth century.[64] Many of the women's movements in early twentieth-century Spain were actively involved in the Catholic social reform movement and thus redefined a version of feminism more in consonance with their ideological convictions. Women's organisations were not always overtly feminist and the move for women's emancipation tended not so much to be associated with a conception of feminism based on equal rights and political equity but rather (more in line with the situation in France and Italy), with a feminism based on maternal and family rights.[65]

Recent scholarship has also shown the existence in twentieth-century Spain of a minority of more explicitly feminist women activists (Suceso Luengo, Belén Sárraga, Clara Campoamor, Carmen de Burgos, or Maria Martinez Sierra)[66] and groups (Asociación Nacional de Mujeres Españolas, Unión de Mujeres de España, Mujeres Libres) who openly advocated women's rights in the political and social arenas. The development of feminist thought in Spain has still, however, to be fully studied. We have few biographical studies of women suffragists and know little about the interconnection between the organised feminist movements, the process of achieving a feminist consciousness or the meaning of their identification with feminism for women activists.[67] It is nevertheless clear that within the autonomous women's groups in the early twentieth century there were many ways of understanding feminism and many strategies for the emancipation of women.

The regional diversity of the historical process in Spain is another factor that must be considered. It is quite significant that the mechanisms of organisation among women in Catalonia and in the Basque Country were articulated primarily through women's adherence to the nationalist cause.[68] The symbolic discourse on the female figure, the mobilisation of women within the canons of conservative, nationalist discourse, and the socio-political intervention of women activists, all constitute issues that have provided considerable insights into the actual development of Catalan and Basque nationalism in the early twentieth century. Indeed the trajectory of the women's movement in Spain challenges the classical interpretation of the development of first wave feminism in areas of greater economic and industrial growth and of a wider middle class. This approach is not necessarily valid in Spain where precisely in the two main areas of industrial growth the movement to promote women was less suffragist, more traditional and carried strong conservative, nationalist and Catholic reformist impulses. Furthermore, in Catalonia, the development of the women's movement was also linked with the struggle for the modernisation of the state and socio-economic structures. This led, in turn, to a growing interest in the creation of a national Catalan version of the 'new modern woman' consonant with the parameters of modernity but also as the guardian of conservative Catalan cultural values. The development of sport, cultural activities, professional training and the politics of motherhood were all shaped by this overall traditional ideology.[69] Some studies have also been developed on international feminism, where a comparative approach has underscored the significance of religious plurality and Protestant culture in the formation of the first wave of Anglo-American feminism compared to the Roman Catholic tradition in Spain.[70] A complementary area of international research on historical feminism by Spanish historians has focused on the Arab-Islamic world.[71]

The political debate on women's suffrage in Spain is now better understood but we must still investigate the particular importance of the acquisition of political and civil equality for women as a social collectivity and also undertake a more detailed study of their political and electoral behaviour. Studies have now underscored the inadequacy of interpretative schemes based on the supposedly unconditional commitment of women to right-wing conservative political options. But in the 1930s, even with the consolidation of a democratic representative system under the Second Republic, legal equality did not give rise to immediate gender equality and we need to explore the nature of such processes.[72]

Another area of major research in nineteenth- and twentieth-century Spain has been on women and social change. Historians have investigated the dynamics of social transformation by analysing female activism in the working-class movement, social conflicts, and revolutionary processes. Studies on women in the labour movement have only begun to rehabilitate female activists and challenge prior historiography on the absence of women from social conflict in Spain.[73] Despite the subordinate role played by women in the different tendencies of the organised labour movement (anarchist and socialist), women's extensive social mobilisation is well documented.[74] Studies being developed from a gender perspective show that female mobilisation seems to have responded to motives and patterns different from those of male workers. The very high level of women's participation in strikes has been documented somewhat more clearly for the early twentieth century. Despite the impressionistic information available, this participation seems to follow motives common to union struggles in general (wage increases, improvement in working conditions). However, women workers also appear to respond in more specifically gendered circumstances such as sexual harassment.

Work on female collective action shows that the active presence of women in these conflicts is related to a defence of their living conditions.[75] The interpretative model which relates involvement in conflicts to their acceptance of the sexual division of labour and to their consequent defence of their social function as providers for the family, is very useful to the understanding of female involvement in social conflicts that develop outside the organised working-class movement. Further research must attempt to trace the link between female consciousness, collective action and actual feminist awareness.

Spanish women have also developed resistance strategies within working-class associations since the creation of the labour movement,[76] although women workers have kept a low profile until the early twentieth century. By the late nineteenth century we find the first isolated formulation of the connection between social struggle and the emancipation of women, particularly by anarchist women such as Teresa Claramunt, and also the first attempts to set up autonomous working-women's associations.[77] This development within the anarchist movement led to the first experience of the collective strategy of dual struggle – socialist and feminist – proposed by the anarchist women's organisation Mujeres Libres [Free Women] in 1936.[78] Regional studies are underway to trace the development of feminism within the socialist and anarchist movements.[79] Working women had a very low profile in the development of cultural activities and popular associations[80] and also in the development of popular sex reform movements.[81] Gender cultural norms and value codes which impeded the presence of women in the public sphere appear to have been decisive in restricting women's activism in these spheres; working women's organisations and cultural activities flourished only under the specific initiative of women as the male-dominated working-class movement ignored women's issues in practice.

The relationship between the process of social transformation and the modifications of patriarchal structures has been studied in some detail for the period of the Civil War.[82] Recent studies seem to suggest that this process of social transformation did not per se signify a substantial modification in the social condition of women or in mental attitudes towards women's social role. It appears rather to point out that changes occurred particularly to the extent that they were fomented by the initiative of women themselves and also to the degree of sensitivity towards the 'woman question'. Such studies raise questions about the association between the models of new 'revolutionary' women developed at the time and women's emancipation. On the contrary they underscore the continuing restrictions on women's socio-political horizons.[83] The gender asymmetry in the breakdown between socio-political structures and changes in mentality is indeed quite noticeable. On another level, the development of women's activity in voluntary work and production, points to the need to reconsider the war economy from a gender perspective.[84]

Further research has been done recently on women under the Franco regime. Studies on the *Sección Femenina*, the fascist women's organisation, point to its significant role not only in the political indoctrination of women but also on a socio-ideological level.[85] They also analyse the basis for the social construction of gender models and the mechanisms of transmission of female stereotypes during the Franco regime.[86] The role of religion in the development of Francoist discourse on women has shown how the regime relied heavily on traditional religious canons for the construction of its ideological discourse on women.[87] Studies on gender models of sainthood and, on another level, research on the discourse on motherhood and family point to the need to explore the links between conservative canons in pre-Franco Spain and Francoist thought on women. The close link between state policies, political processes and women has been clearly shown in research on pronatalist and family policies in the construction of the early Franco regime.[88] On another level, through personal memoirs, studies on women's role in the political opposition to Franco and on women's dismissal of population policies, women's resistance to the Franco regime is being documented.[89] Again, a gender-aware perspective points to the need to establish a gendered history of women's different modes of resistance and reaction to Franco.

Women and work has been another area of research in women's history; however, it is still quite an underdeveloped field. The state of historiography in this area is still very limited. We still know very little, for instance, about the role and significance of women in the first stages of industrial development in Spain. For the twentieth century we have established the characteristics of the female work force, the evolution of the active female population and the regulation of women's paid unemployment.[90] Despite the difficulties involved in documenting women's work we can nevertheless trace its development in the twentieth century.[91] As in other European countries, wage discrimination, gender segregation and the subdivision and segmentation of the labour process characterise women's paid work in this period. Many studies point to the consequences of traditional hostility towards women's paid employment[92] and to the relationship between wage labour and the reproduction of the sexual division of labour through which women's oppression is articulated.[93] Some studies are being developed from the perspective of the relationship between wage labour, domestic labour, female consciousness and family strategies.[94] Although there are still few studies of the irregular labour market, a connection has been established between homework, the gender division of labour, and strategies for survival within the family economy of the working class.[95] Demographic factors have also been analysed in relation to women and the labour market.[96] Recent studies of different occupational sectors offer insights into the development of wage labour, the changing patterns of professional occupations and women's social condition. The areas most studied so far are commerce, office work, administration,[97] the garment trade, the tobacco industry,[98] homework and religious work.[99] Women's paid employment in the course of industrialisation is now being explored region by region, which will undoubtedly allow us to develop a more exact overview of its significance in the varied patterns of economic development in Spain.

More recently women's voluntary unpaid work is being studied and points to the extraordinary importance of such work in the service sector, not only at exceptional moments such as the Civil War[100] but also in the development of educational, charitable and social assistance services.[101] Little research has so far been done in the field of domestic work and female labour within the home,[102] while we also know all too little about peasant women and their role in rural economies.[103]

Spanish historiography on women has devoted close attention to issues in education. The development of the official school system and the institutionalisation of education for girls and women have been traced most thoroughly for the early twentieth century.[104] The deficiencies of the official school system, and the predominance of church-controlled schools, together with the obstacles to the introduction of innovative pedagogies in female education, all determined the frankly unfavourable educational picture for Spanish women of whom over 71% were still illiterate in 1900. A subordinate gender model of education for girls led to educational discrimination against women even in the more innovative and progressive attempts at female schooling. The *Krausista* educational reform in the late nineteenth century, which proposed a rationalist, secular and innovative perspective on female education, never presented an overall critique of women's situation in Spanish society. Official education for girls at the time was primarily devoted to needle work, piety, deportment and proper social behaviour. Despite their development of a more rational and broader education for women, the *Krausistas* viewed it as a means by which women might achieve a better performance in their traditionally assigned roles as wives and mothers.[105] Further educational reforms were introduced in the twentieth century on both an unofficial and official level, such as the experiment in coeducation during the Second Republic in the 1930s. Nevertheless, educational values were still oriented towards the construction of schematic gender roles, and aimed at educating and socialising women in their traditional roles as mothers, daughters and wives. Such was also the case during the Franco regime.[106] Little is yet known about more informal channels of female education such as innovative reform proposals, working-class schools or the circulation of cost free educational text books.[107] Recent studies also show the slow development of higher education for women, which was not officially allowed until 1910; despite this impediment women with university careers have been documented since the late nineteenth century.[108] Furthermore the significant role of women in the medical profession has been studied both for the nineteenth and early twentieth centuries.[109]

Spanish work on the history of the private sphere, including that on the history of the family, reproduction, everyday life, and interpersonal relations, has flourished in the past few years. Although most demographic studies and family history have not yet introduced a gender perspective, they are still very useful for women's history. The relationship between demographic patterns, family structure and the social condition of women are now becoming somewhat clearer particularly for the early twentieth century.[110] The overt legal discrimination against women in Spanish family law is an important explanatory factor in the subordination of married women prior to the legal reforms introduced under the democratic regime in the 1930s, but even then, despite changes in marriage laws, a genuine egalitarian status was far from being achieved.[111] Differential gender patterns are evident in divorce trends in the thirties[112] while marriage appears even then to be the only culturally accepted outlet for women.

The politics of reproduction in early twentieth-century Spain is now being researched from the viewpoint of both the discourse on and the practice of birth control and abortion.[113] In the case of both birth control and abortion attention has been drawn to the existence of two levels of gender reality – public male discourse and legal or medical regulation and the private female clandestine reality of its practice.[114] Linking with demographic trends, the incidence of birth control and abortion, and the mechanisms leading to the breakdown in traditional cultural values in a predominantly Roman Catholic country, are being traced from both a gender and a class perspective. The adoption of family planning and the control of reproduction is being axamined for its specific significance for women. Despite the difficulties the sources present, for instance, we can now trace the path of the anarchist birth control movement and the reformist professional eugenics movement in Spain, and the development and diffusion of popular and medical knowledge on birth control. The politics of motherhood are being traced through eugenic, demographic, medical, religious and popular discourses together with official regulation of birth control and motherhood.[115] The gender connotations of sex reform are also being studied in the framework of a highly conservative society whose cultural parameters were shaped by Roman Catholic doctrine on this issue; here as in other areas, research points to a decided degree of discrepancy between prescription and practice.

Abortion is another practice on which considerable research has been done from a legal, medical and gender perspective.[116] Despite the strong conservative and Roman Catholic cultural canons, studies have now shown the ambivalent treatment in legal regulation of therapeutic abortion since 1848 – a treatment which implicitly admits its practice.[117] The failure of the progressive 'Eugenics Reform of Abortion' in 1936, which legalised voluntary abortion, has been interpreted not only from the perspective of the actual difficulties involved in its application in the circumstances of the Civil War, but also from the perspective of the male medical profession and the unchanging attitudes of women towards voluntary abortion. There are still few studies so far on the history of sexuality and its relation to women.[118] Existing studies on prostitution give insight on the existing double sexual code of conduct. The regulation of prostitution was seen essentially as a sanitary health problem[119] until the new initiative for the creation of prostitution *Liberatorios* (centres for the liberation and rehabilitation of prostitutes) during the Civil War.[120] Everyday life and rituals of personal relations linked with life cycles are now being more fully documented for the early twentieth century, although our knowledge is still very fragmentary in this field.[121]

In the field of women and literature research is less developed when compared to women's history. The study of women through literature as a historical source represents an analytical approach that is still little known in the academic world in Spain and of itself presents important methodological problems. Current research in this field has focused primarily on the image and figure of women. Topics have focused on women in general literature (studies of women as literary characters;

as a literary theme or as authors);[122] women as a symbol in hegemonic discourse (women in Catalan and Basque nationalist discourse; women in the mentality of a historical period or as its projection in a class society and women as the transmitters of family or cultural values); women and education (the study of sexist content in text books, the female role in literary discourse, female archetypes and models of women, and women and Catholic morals); women and everyday life in literature, (the wife, the bourgeois lady, prostitution, and marginal and domestic work).

Studies on women in literature have dealt mainly with the following areas of research. In the medieval period studies have centred on courtly love while in the early modern period recent research has dealt with picaresque women and also uncovered the works of enlightened women.[123] There are many studies on women in nineteenth- and twentieth-century literature; on romanticism, realism and nationalisms in the late nineteenth century,[124] and on novelists of the Franco period such as Carmen Laforet, Ana Matute, Carmen Martín Gaite, Mercé Rodoreda, Montserrat Roig and Carme Riera.[125] Another major area of research has been on international literature, particularly Anglo-American[126] while popular literature and the construction of gender has also been studied recently.[127] A recent recommendation for future research in literature on women by women historians has proposed the development of this field of inquiry through theoretical studies on western thought which allow us to establish a methodology compatible with intellectual history and feminist literary criticism. It also recommends the use of literary discourse, together with other sources, to reconstruct gender systems and the role of women in society.[128]

NOTES

1. I should like to thank the representatives of the Spanish National Commission of the International Federation for Research on Women's History for their bibliographical contributions and comments on this survey: Cristina Dupláa and Milagros Rivera (Centre d'Investigació Històrica de la Dona, University of Barcelona); Rosa Maria Capel (Instituto Ortega y Gasset, Madrid); Candida Martinez (Seminario de Estudios de la Mujer, University of Granada); Reyna Pastor (Provisional Seminario Libre de Historia de la Mujer, Centro de Estudios Históricos, C.S.I.C. Madrid); Maria Xosé Rodriguez (Instituto Universitario de Estudios e Desenvolvemento de Galicia, University of Santiago de Compostela); Dolores Ramos (Seminario de Estudios Interdisciplinarios de la Mujer, University of Malaga); Gloria Nielfa (Instituto de Investigaciones Feministas, Complutense University, Madrid); Merché Ugalde (Emakumeari Buruzko Ikerketarako Mintegia, University of the Basque Country); Ana Aguado (Seminario Permanente de Historia de la Mujer,

University of Valencia); Margarita Ortega and Teresa Gonzalez (Seminario Interdisciplinar sobre la Mujer, Autonomous University Madrid).

2. Due to considerations of space only published works and papers presented at Conferences are included. However a considerable number of Ph.D. and M.A. dissertations have been presented on women's history over the past few years. For additional bibliography, see Montserrat Carbonell, Mary Nash, and Milagros Rivera, 'La storia delle donne in Spagna [The History of Women in Spain]', *Quaderni Storici*, 63 (December 1986), pp. 995-1008; Mary Nash, 'Nuevas dimensiones en la historia de la mujer [New Dimensions in Women's History]', in *Presencia y protagonismo: aspectos de la historia de la mujer* [Presence and Protagonism: Aspects of Women's History] (Barcelona: Serbal, 1984); Mary Nash, 'Modelli di sviluppo della storia delle donne in Spagna [Models of development of Women's History in Spain]', in Ginevra Conti Odorisio (ed.), *Gli studi sulle donne nelle Università: Ricerca e trasformazione del sapere* [Women's Studies in the University: Research and Transformation of Knowledge] (Rome: Edizioni Scientifiche Italiane, 1988).

3. See Pilar Domínguez, Concha Fagoaga, Mari Carmen García Nieto et al., 'Interacción de pensamiento feminista e historiografía en España (1970-1986) [Interaction between Feminist Thought and Historiography in Spain (1970-1986)]', in *Mujeres y hombres en la formación del pensamiento occidental* [Women and Men in the Formation of Western Thought] (Madrid: U.A.M. 1989).

4. Rosa Maria Capel, *El sufragio femenino en la Segunda República* [Female Suffrage during the Second Republic] (Granada: Universidad de Granada, 1975); Mary Nash, *Mujeres Libres. España 1936-1939* [Free Women: Spain 1936-1939] (Barcelona: Tusquets, 1975); Teresa Vinyoles, *Les barcelonines a les darreries de l'Edat Mitjana, 1370-1410* [Barcelona Women in the Late Middle Ages, 1370-1410] (Barcelona: Fundació Vives Casajoana, 1976).

5. See, for an overview, Pilar Díaz Sánchez and Pilar Domínguez Prats, 'Las mujeres en la historia de España. Siglos XVII-XX [Women in the History of Spain: Seventeenth to Twentieth Centuries]', in *Bibliografía comentada* [Annotated Bibliography] (Madrid: Instituto de la Mujer, 1988); Montserrat Carbonell, Mary Nash, and Milagros Rivera, 'La storia delle donne'; Mary Nash, 'Nuevas dimensiones'.

6. José Alvarez Junco and Manuel Pérez Ledesma, 'Historia del movimiento obrero. ¿Una segunda ruptura? [A History of the Working-Class: A Second Rupture?]', *Revista de Occidente*, 12 (March-April 1982), pp. 19-41; José Maria Jover Zamora, 'Corrientes historiográficas en la España Contemporánea [Historiographical Trends in Contemporary Spain]', in Juan José Carreras Ares (ed.), *Once ensayos sobre la historia* [Eleven Essays on History] (Madrid: Fundación Juan March, 1976).

7. Mary Nash, 'Nuevas dimensiones', p. 11.

8. Cécile Dauphin, Arlette Farge, Geneviève Fraisse et al., 'Culture et pouvoir des femmes: essai d'historiographie', *Annales: Economies, Sociétes, Civilisations*, 2 (March-April 1986), pp. 271-93 (see English translation in this volume); Michelle Perrot and Alain Paire (eds.), *Une histoire des femmes est-elle possible?* [Is a Women's History Possible?] (Marseille: Édition Rivage, 1984); Mary Nash, 'Michelle Perrot: La vida privada i la dona [Michelle Perrot: Private Life and

Women]', *L'Avenç*, 108 (October, 1987), pp. 34-9. See also *Memoria, Penelope, Donna Women Femme*.

9. See Amparo Moreno, *Mujeres en lucha. El movimiento feminista en España* [Women in struggle: The Feminist Movement in Spain] (Barcelona: Anagrama, 1977).

10. Carmen Alcalde, *La mujer en la guerra civil española* [Women in the Spanish Civil War] (Madrid: Cambio 16, 1976); Condesa de Campo Alange, *La mujer en España. Cien años de su historia* [Women in Spain: A Hundred Years of their History] (Madrid: Aguilar, 1964); M.A. Capmany, *El feminisme a Catalunya* [Feminism in Catalonia] (Barcelona: Nova Terra, 1973); Teresa Pàmies, *Quan érem capitans. (Memòries d'aquella guerra)* [When We were Captains. (Memoirs of that War)] (Barcelona: Dopesa, 1974); Ramona Via, *Nit de reis. Diari d'una imfermera de 14 anys* [The Night of the (three) Kings: Diary of a fourteen-year-old nurse] (Barcelona: Club Editor, 1966).

11. See *Memòria del Centre D'Investigació Històrica de la Dona* [Report of the Centre for Research on Women's History], 1983-1986 and 1987-1989.

12. 'Estudis sobre la dona [Women's Studies]', *Papers, Revista de Sociologia*, 30 (1988), pp. 13-32.

13. 'Mujer, ciencia y práctica política [Women, Science and Political Practice]', Seminario de la Mujer, Universidad Complutense, 1985; 'Desde la casa a la fábrica, la mujer como elemento de transformación social [From Home to Factory: Women as a Factor of Social Change]', Centre d'Investigació de la Dona, Universidad de Barcelona, 1986; 'Mujeres y hombres en la formación del pensamiento occidental [Women and Men in the Formation of Western Thought]', Seminario de la mujer, Universidad Autónoma de Madrid, 1988; 'Jornadas sobre la mujer [Conference on Women]', Seminario de la Mujer, Universidad de Granada, 1988.

14. Celia Amorós, *Hacia una crítica de la razón patriarcal* [Towards a Critique of Patriarchal Reasoning] (Barcelona: Anthropos, 1985); Amparo Moreno, *El arquetipo viril protagonista de la historia* [The Virile Archetype as the Protagonist of History] (Barcelona: La Sal, 1986); Mary Nash, 'Nuevas dimensiones'; Dominguez, Fagoaga, García Nieto et al., 'Interacción de pensamiento feminista'; Milagros Rivera Garretas, 'La historiografía de las mujeres en la Europa Medieval [Women's Historiography in Medieval Europe]', *Historia Social*, 4 (Spring-Summer 1989), pp. 137-47.

15. Rosa Maria Capel and Julio Iglesias de Ussel, *Mujer española y sociedad. Bibliografía (1900-1984)* [The Spanish Woman and Society: Bibliography (1900-1984)] (Madrid: Instituto de la Mujer, 1984); Díaz Sánchez and Dominguez Prats, *Las mujeres en la historia*.

16. MariCarmen Simón Palmer, 'La higiene y la medicina de la mujer española a través de los libros (siglos XVI-XIX) [Hygiene and Medicine of Spanish Women through books: Seventeenth to the Nineteenth Centuries]', *La mujer en la Historia de España. (Siglos XVI-XX)* [Women in the History of Spain (Sixteenth to the Twentieth Centuries] (Madrid: U.A.M., 1984) and 'La mujer en el s.XIX: notas bibliográficas [Women in the Nineteenth Century: Bibliographical Notes]', *Cuadernos Bibliográficos*, 21 (1974).

17. Montserrat Sebastià i Salat, *Thesaurus d'Història Social de la Dona* [A Thesaurus of the Social History of Women] (Barcelona: Generalitat de Catalunya, 1988).

18. Cristina Segura, 'Las mujeres en el medioevo hispano [Women in the Hispanic Middle Ages]', *Cuadernos de Investigación Medieval*, 2 (1984).

19. Adolfo Perinat and Maria Isabel Marrades, *Mujer, prensa y sociedad en España, 1800-1939* [Women, Press and Society in Spain, 1800-1939] (Madrid: Centro de Investigaciones Sociológicas, 1980); Mercedes Roig, *La mujer en la historia a través de la prensa. Francia, Italia, España. Siglos XVIII-XX* [Women in History through the Press: France, Italy, Spain: Eighteenth to Twentieth Centuries] (Madrid: Ministerio de Cultura, 1982); Isabel Segura and Marta Selva, *Revistes de dones, 1846-1935* [Women's Journals, 1846-1935] (Barcelona: Edhasa, 1984).

20. Mary Nash, 'Nuevas dimensiones'; Milagros Rivera, 'La historiografía'.

21. Mary Nash, 'Presencia y Protagonismo'; James Amelang and Mary Nash, *Historia y género. Las mujeres en la Europa Moderna y Contemporánea* [History and Gender: Women in Modern and Contemporary Europe] (Valencia: Edicions Instituto Alfons el Magnànim, 1990).

22. Isabel de Villena, *Protagonistes femenines a la Vita Christi* [Female Characters in Vita Christi], edited by Rosanna Cantavella and Lluïsa Parra (Barcelona: La Sal, 1987).

23. Duoda, comtessa de Barcelona i de Septimània, *De mare a fill escrits d'una dona del s.IX* [From Mother to Son: Writings of a Woman of the Nineteenth Century], prologue, transcription and notes by Mercedes Otero (Barcelona: La Sal, 1989).

24. Concepción Arenal, *La emancipación de la mujer en España* [The Emancipation of Women in Spain] (Madrid: Editorial Jucar, 1974); Emilia Pardo Bazán, *La mujer española y otros artículos feministas* [The Spanish Woman and Other Feminist Articles], selection and prologue by Leda Schiavo (Madrid: Editora Nacional, 1976).

25. Clara Campoamor, *El voto femenino y yo* [The Female Vote and Me], introduced by C. Fagoaga and P. Saavedra (Barcelona: La Sal, 1981).

26. Mary Nash, *Mujer, familia y trabajo en España, 1875-1936* [Women, Family and Work in Spain, 1875-1936] (Barcelona: Anthropos, 1983).

27. Mary Nash, *Mujeres Libres* (note 4 above).

28. Recently Spanish scholars have also developed studies on women in various cultures in ancient history with special emphasis on topics related to Roman law, family legislation, work, religion and the social condition of women. See, for example: *La dona en l'antiquetat* [Women of Antiquity] (Barcelona, 1977); *La mujer en el mundo antiguo* [Women in the Ancient World] (Madrid: U.A.M., 1986); Candida Martinez Lopez, 'Diosas, sacerdotisas y devotas en la Hispania meridional [Goddesses, Priestesses and Devotees in Southern Hispania]', *Actas del 1 Encuentro Interdisciplinar de estudios de la Mujer en Andalucía* (Granada: Universidad de Granada, forthcoming), and 'Virginidad – fecundidad en torno al suplicio de las Vestales [Virginity: Fertility around Vestal Torture]', *Studia Histórica*, 6 (1988), pp. 137-44; Alberto Prieto Arciniega and Maria Encarnación Sanahuja, 'El papel de la mujer en las Bacanales romanas [The Role of Women in Roman Bacchanals]', *Memorias de Historia Antigua, V-1981* (Oviedo, 1983); Fernando Wulff, 'Circe y

Odiseo, diosas y hombres [Circe and Odysseus, Goddesses and Men]', *Baetica*, 8 (1986).

29. S. Belmartino, 'Estructura de la familia y edades sociales en la aristocracia de León y Castilla según las fuentes literarias y historiográficas (siglos X-XIII) [Family Structures and Social Ages in the Aristocracy of León and Castille According to Literary and Historiographical Sources (Tenth to Thirteenth Centuries)]', *Cuadernos de Historia de España*, (1968), pp. 47-8.

30. Maria Luz Alonso, 'La dote en los documentos toledanos de los siglos XII-XV [The Dowry in Toledo Documents of the Twelfth to Fifteenth Centuries]', *Anuario de Historia del Derecho Español*, 48 (1978); Emma Montanos Ferrín, *La familia en la Alta Edad Media española* [The Family in the Spanish High Middle Ages] (Pamplona: 1980); Regina Sainz de la Maza, 'El monasterio santiaguista de San Pedro de la Piedra de Lérida [The Monastery of San Pedro de la Piedra (Military Order of Santiago) in Lerida]', *Anuario de Estudios Medievales*, 11 (1981).

31. Cristina Segura, 'Las mujeres' and *Las mujeres medievales y su ámbito jurídico* [Medieval Women and their Legal Environment] (Madrid: U.A.M. 1987); Medieval Section of the Conference held by the CIHD, 'De la casa a la fábrica. La mujer como elemento de transformación social', University of Barcelona, 1986; Miguel Angel Ladero Quesada, D. Ozanan, and Reyna Pastor (eds.), 'Coloquio hispano-francés', *La condición de la mujer en la Edad Media* [The Condition of Women in the Middle Ages] (Madrid: Casa de Velázquez-Universidad Complutense, 1986).

32. José Hinojosa Montalvo, 'La mujer en las ordenanzas municipales en el reino de Valencia durante la Edad Media [Women in Municipal Ordinances in the Kingdom of Valencia during the Middle Ages]', *Actas 3ª Jornadas de Investigación Interdisciplinar* (Madrid: U.A.M. 1984); Milagros Rivera Garretas, 'Dret i conflictivitat social entorn de les dones a la Catalunya pre-feudal i feudal [Law and Social Conflict around Women in Pre-Feudal and Feudal Catalonia]', in Mary Nash (ed.), *Més enllà del silenci. Les dones a la historia de Catalunya* [Beyond Silence: Women in the History of Catalonia] (Barcelona: Generalitat de Catalunya, 1988); Segura, 'Las mujeres'; S. Romeu Alfaro, 'La mujer en el Derecho Penal Valenciano [Women in Valencian Penal Law]', *Estudios dedicados a Joan Peset Aleixandre*, vol. 3 (Valencia: Universidad de Valencia, 1982).

33. M. Isabel Fierro, 'Mujeres hispano-árabes en sus repertorios biográficos [Hispano-Arab Women in Biographical Catalogues]', in *Las mujeres medievales*; M. Marín, 'Notas sobre onomástica y denominaciones femeninas en Al-Andalus (s. VIII-IX) [Notes on Names and Female Denominations, Eight to Ninth Centuries]', *Homenaje al Prof. Daño Catanelas*. (Granada: 1987).

34. Teresa Maria Vinyoles i Vidal, 'Dues vocacions femenines a les darreries de l'Edat Mitjana [Two Female Vocations in the High Middle Ages]', *III Coloqui d'Història del monaquisme català* (Barcelona, 1974); Montserrat Cabré, 'Formes de cultura femenina a la Catalunya medieval [Forms of Female Culture in Medieval Catalonia]', in Mary Nash (ed.), *Més enllà del silenci*.

35. Teresa Maria Vinyoles i Vidal, *La vida quotidiana a Barcelona vers 1400* [Everyday Life in Barcelona around 1400] (Barcelona: Fundació Salvador Vives Casajuana, 1985); 'Ajuts a donzelles pobres a maridar [Aids for Poor Maidens in Finding Husbands]', *La pobreza y la asistencia a los pobres en la Cataluña medieval*, vol. 1 [Poverty and Assistance for the Poor in Medieval Catalonia]

(Barcelona: CSIC, 1980); and 'L'esdevenir quotidià: treball i lleure de les dones medievals [Everyday Life: Work and Leisure of Medieval Women]', in Mary Nash (ed.), *Més enllà del silenci*.

36. Paulino Iradiel Murugarren, 'Familia y función económica de la Mujer en actividades no agrarias [Family and Economic Functions of Women in Non-agrarian Activities]', *La Condición de la Mujer en la Edad Media* (Madrid: Universidad Complutense, 1986); Reyna Pastor, 'Las mujeres en las explotaciones agrarias de la Edad Media [Women in Agrarian Exploitations in the Middle Ages]', *La condición de la mujer* and 'El trabajo de la mujer en la explotación campesina. Castilla y León, s.XI-XIV [Women's Work in Farming Exploitations: Castille and León, Eleventh to Fourteenth Centuries]', *Coloquio De la Casa a la fábrica, siglos V-XX* (Centre d'Investigació Històrica de la Dona, University of Barcelona, October 1986). *Papers de Treball del CIHD*. 1990, pp. 4-22; also, 'Reflexions sur l'etude du Prof. R. Smith et proposition sur le travail de la femme dans l'explotation rurale. Castille et León, siècles XI-XIV [Reflections on the Study by Prof. R. Smith and Proposal on Women's Work in an Agrarian Exploitation. Castilla and León, Eleventh to Fourteenth Centuries]', *Settimana 'La donna nell'economia, secc XII-XVIII'* (Instituto Internacionale di Storia economica Francesco Datini, Prato: April 1989, forthcoming); Milagros Rivera Garretas, 'Dret i conflictivitat social [Law and Social Conflict]'; Teresa Maria Vinyoles i Vidal, 'La condició social de les dones a la Catalunya de la Baixa Edat Mitjana [The Social Condition of Women in Catalonia in the Late Middle Ages]', *Perspectiva Social*, 26 (1988), pp. 21-32.

37. Duoda, comtessa de Barcelona i de septimània, *De mare a fill*; Manuel J. Pelaez. 'La mujer en la obra de Francesc Eiximenis. Un ejemplo de literatura antifeminista en la Baja Edad Media [Women in the Works of Francesc Eiximenis: An Example of Antifeminist Literature in the Late Middle Ages]', *Collectanea Franciscana*, 53 (Roma: 1983); Isabel de Villena, *Protagonistes femenines*.

38. Ladero Quesada, D. Ozanana and R. Pastor (eds.), *La condición de la mujer*; Rivera Garretas, 'La historiografía'.

39. Ellen G. Friedman, 'El estatus jurídico de la mujer castellana durante el Antiguo Régimen [The Legal Status of Castillian Women during the Old Regime]', in *Ordenamiento jurídico y realidad social de las mujeres. S.XVI-XX* (Madrid: U.A.M. 1986); Maria Victoria López Cordón, 'La situación de la mujer a finales del Antiguo Régimen [The Situation of Women at the End of the Old Regime]', in *Mujer y sociedad en España (1700-1975)* (Madrid: Ministerio de Cultura, 1982); Maria Victoria López Cordón and Valentina Fernández Vargas, 'Mujer y régimen jurídico en el antiguo régimen [Women and the Legal Regime in the Old Regime]', in *Ordenamiento jurídico*.

40. Maria Victoria López Cordón, 'La literatura religiosa y moral como conformadora de la mentalidad femenina (1760-1860) [Religious and Moral Literature Conforming the Female Mentality]', *La mujer en la historia de España*; Dolors Ricart, 'El model femení a la Catalunya del segle XVIII a través de les fonts eclesiàstiques [The Female Model in Catalonia in the Eighteenth Century through Ecclesiastical Resources]', *Actas del Primer Congrés d'Historia Moderna de Catalunya* (Barcelona: 1984); Anna Venancio i Castells and Dolors Ricart i Sampietro, 'Dona, cultura i experiència religiosa (s.XVI-s.XVIII) [Women, Culture and Religious Experience (Sixteenth-Eighteenth Centuries)]', in Mary Nash (ed.), *Més enllà del silenci*.

41. López-Cordón, 'La literatura religiosa'; Montserrat Carbonell i Esteller 'El treball de les dones a la Catalunya Moderna [Women's Work in Modern Catalonia]', in Mary Nash (ed.), *Més enllà del silenci*, and 'Les dones a la Catalunya dels segles XVI-XVIII [Women in Catalonia from the Sixteenth to the Eighteenth Centuries]', *Perspectiva Social*, 26 (1988), pp. 33-41.

42. Mariló Vigil, 'La vida cotidiana de las mujeres en el barroco [Daily Life of Women in the Baroque]', *Nuevas perspectivas sobre la mujer* [New Perspectives on Women] (Madrid: U.A.M., 1982), and *La vida de las mujeres en los siglos XVI y XVII* [The Life of Women in the Sixteenth and Seventeenth Centuries] (Madrid: Siglo XXI, 1986).

43. Maria Victoria López Cordón, 'La literatura religiosa'; Carmen Martin Gaite, *Usos amorosos del dieciocho en España* [Love Customs in Eighteenth-Century Spain] (Madrid: Siglo XXI, 1972); Elena Sánchez Ortega, 'La mujer en el Antiguo Régimen: tipos históricos y arquetipos literarios [Women in the Old Regime: Historical Types and Literary Archetypes], *Nuevas Perspectivas*; Vigil, *La vida de las mujeres*.

44. Conchita Gil Martín, 'Las relaciones paternofiliales en los libros de propagandística católica [Father-Child Relations in Catholic Propaganda Books]', *Actas del Primer Congreso de Historia Moderna de Catalunya* (Barcelona: Universidad de Barcelona, 1984); Elena Sánchez Ortega, 'La mujer, el amor y la religión en el Antiguo Régimen [Women, Love and Religion in the Old Regime]', *La mujer en la historia de España*; James Amelang, 'Los usos de la autobiografía: monjas y beatas en la Cataluña moderna [The Uses of Autobiography: Nuns and *Beatas* in Modern Catalonia]', in James Amelang and Mary Nash, *Historia y Género*.

45. Antonio Gil Ambrona, 'Entre el trabajo y la oración: las ocupaciones de las otras esposas: siglos XVI-XVII [Between Work and Prayer: The Occupations of the Other Wives: Sixteenth-Seventeenth Centuries]', *El trabajo de las mujeres* (Madrid: U.A.M., 1986); Elena Sánchez Ortega, 'La mujer en el Antiguo Régimen: tipos históricos y arquetipos literarios', *Nuevas Perspectivas*.

46. Rosa Rossi, 'Teresa de Jesús', *Mientras Tanto*, 14 (February 1983), pp. 63-81, and *Teresa de Avila* (Barcelona: Ed. Icaria, 1984).

47. Ignacio Atienza Hernández, 'Las mujeres nobles: clase dominante, grupo dominado. Familia y orden social en el Antiguo Régimen [Noble Women: Dominant Class, Dominated Group. Family and Social Order in the Old Regime]', *Ordenamiento jurídico*; Antonio Gil Ambrona and Ariadna Hernández, 'El fracàs conjugal durant la segona meitat del segle XVIII [Marriage Failure during the Second Half of the Eighteenth Century]', *L'Avenç*, 67 (January 1984), pp. 18-23.

48. López Cordón, 'La situación de la mujer'; Isabel Moll Blanes, 'Propietat i cicle vital de la dona [Property and Women's Life Cycle]', *Colloquio De la Casa a la Fábrica* (CIHD University of Barcelona, 1986).

49. Montserrat Carbonell i Esteller, 'La beneficiencia a finals del segle XVIII. La Casa de Misericordia de Barcelona [Charity at the End of the Eighteenth Century: The Casa de Misericordia in Barcelona]', *Actes del Primer Congrés d'Història Moderna de Catalunya* (Barcelona, 1984), and 'El treball de les dones a la Catalunya Moderna', in Mary Nash (ed.), *Més enllà del silenci*; Maria del Carmen Gómez García, 'Trabajo y actividades de las religiosas en los conventos malagueños (s.XVIII) [Work and the Activities of the Religious in the Convents of Malaga

(Eighteenth Century)]', *El trabajo de las mujeres*; Florentino López Iglesias, 'Oficios y actividades de las mujeres oretenses en el Antiguo Régimen [Trades and Activities of Women in Orense in the Old Regime]', *El trabajo de las mujeres*.

50. Siro Villas Tinoco, 'La mujer y la organización gremial malagueña en el Antiguo Régimen [Women and Guild Organisations in the Old Regime]', *Ordenamiento jurídico*.

51. Antonio Gil Ambrona, 'Entre el trabajo y la oración: las ocupaciones de las otras esposas: siglos XVI-XVII', *El trabajo de las mujeres* and 'Mujeres religiosas, mujeres heterodoxas [Religious Women, Heterodox Women]', *Historia 16*, 145, no. 13 (May 1988), pp. 59-63; MariCarmen Gómez García, *Instituciones religiosas femeninas malagueñas en la transición del siglo XVII al XVIII* [Female Religious Institutions in Malaga in the Transition from the Seventeenth to the Eighteenth Century] (Málaga: Diputación Provincial, 1986); Margarita Ortega, 'Casa o convento. La educación de la mujer en las edades Moderna y contemporánea [House or Convent: The Education of Women in the Modern and Contemporary Ages]', *Historia 16*, 145, no. 13 (May 1988), pp. 41-48.

52. M. Angeles Durán, 'El pensamiento económico de Fray Luis de León [The Economic Thought of Fray Luis de León]', *Nuevas Perspectivas*.

53. V. Graullera Sanz, 'Un grupo social marginado: las mujeres públicas. (El burdel de Valencia en los siglos XVI y XVII) [A Marginalised Social Group: Public Women. (The Brothel in Valencia in the Sixteenth and Seventeenth Centuries)]', *Actes du I Colloque sur le Pays Valencien a l'època Moderne*(Pau: 1980); Maria Teresa Lopez Beltrán, *La prostitución femenina en Malaga en tiempos de los Reyes Católicos* [Female Prostitution in Malaga in the times of the Catholic Kings] (Malaga: Servicios de Publicaciones de la Diputación, forthcoming); Angelina Puig and Nuria Tuset, 'La prostitución en Mallorca (s.XVI): ¿El Estado un alcahuete? [Prostitution in Majorca (Sixteenth Century): Is the State a Pimp?]', *Ordenamiento jurídico*, and 'Pas de la baixa edat mitjana a l'edat moderna. La prostitució i altres violències sexuals [Transition from the Late Middle Ages to the Modern Age: Prostitution and other Sexual Violence]', *Actas del Primer Congrés d'Història Moderna de Catalunya* (Barcelona, 1984).

54. Montserrat Carbonell i Esteller, 'La beneficiencia'; G. Precioso, *La mujer en la Casa de Beneficiencia de Valencia (finales del s.XVIII-principios del s.XIX)* [Women in the Casa de Beneficiencia in Valencia. (End of the Seventeenth Century to the beginning of the Nineteenth Century)] (Valencia: Universidad de Valencia, forthcoming).

55. Maria Palacios Alcalde, 'Formas marginales de trabajo femenino en la Andalucia Moderna [Marginal Forms of Women's Work in Modern Andalusia], *El trabajo de las mujeres*.

56. Montserrat Carbonell i Esteller, 'El treball de les dones'.

57. James Casey et al., *La familia en la España Mediterránea. (siglos XV-XX)* [The Family in Mediterranean Spain. (Fifteenth to Twentieth Centuries)] (Barcelona: Crítica, 1987); F. Chacon (ed.), *Familia y sociedad en el Mediterráneo occidental. Siglos XV-XIX* [Family and Society in the Western Mediterranean: Fifteenth to Nineteenth Centuries] (Murcia, Universidad de Murcia, 1987).

58. Anne J. Cruz, 'La prostitución legalizada como estrategia antifeminista en las novelas picarescas femeninas [Legalised Prostitution as an Antifeminist Strategy in Female Picaresque Novels]', *Actas de las 6ª Jornadas Interdisciplinarias*

(Madrid: U.A.M. 1986); José Antonio Maravall Casanoves, *El mundo social de la Celestina* [The Social World of the Celestine] (Madrid: Gredos, 1981).

59. Mary Nash, 'Treball, conflictivitat social i estratègies de resistència: la dona obrera a Catalunya Contemporània [Work, Social Conflict and Resistance Strategies: Working Women in Contemporary Catalonia]', *Més enllà del silenci*; Scanlon, *La polémica feminista*; Paloma de Villota, 'Los motines de Castilla la Vieja de 1856 y la participación de la mujer. Aproximación a su estudio [The Riots in Old Castille in 1856 and the Participation of Women]', *Nuevas perspectivas sobre la mujer*.

60. Cristina Dupláa, 'Les dones i el pensament conservador català contemporani [Women and Contemporary Catalan Conservative Thought]', in Mary Nash (ed.), *Més enllà del silenci*; Mary Nash, 'La mujer como objeto literario [Women as a Literary Object]', *Historia 16*, 145, no. 13 (May 1988), pp. 54-8; and M. Nash, *Mujer, familia y trabajo*; Scanlon, *La polémica feminista*.

61. Antonio Elorza, *El fourierismo en España* [Fourierism in Spain] (Madrid: Ediciones Revista de Trabajo, 1975).

62. Montserrat Duch i Planes, 'El papel de la dona en el nacionalismo burgués [The Role of Women in Bourgeois Nationalism]', *Estudios de Historia Social*, no. 20-29 (January-June 1984), pp. 301-309; Concha Fagoaga, *La voz y el voto de las mujeres. El sufragismo en España, 1877-1931* [Women's Voice and Vote: Suffragism in Spain, 1877-1931] (Barcelona: Icaria, 1985); Pilar Folguera (ed.), *El feminismo en España. Dos siglos de Historia* [Feminism in Spain: Two Centuries of History] (Madrid: Editorial Pablo Iglesias, 1988); Joana Luna and Elisenda Macià, 'L'associacionisme femení: catolicisme social, catalanisme i lleure [Female Associationism: Social Catholicism, Catalanism and Leisure]', in Mary Nash (ed.), *Més enllà del silenci*.

63. Mary Nash, 'Nuevas dimensiones'; Karen Offen, 'Defining Feminism: A Comparative Historical Approach', *Signs. Journal of Women in Culture and Society*, 14, 1 (1988), pp. 119-57.

64. Mary Nash, 'La dona moderna del s.XX: La Nova Dona a Catalunya [The Modern Woman of the Twentieth Century: The New Woman in Catalonia]', *L'Avenç* (February 1988), pp. 7-10.

65. Karen Offen, 'Defining feminism'; Perrot, *Une histoire des femmes est-elle possible?*; M. De Giorgio and Paola Di Cori, 'Politica e sentimenti. Le organizzazioni femminili cattoliche dall'età giolittiana al fascismo [Politics and Feelings: The Catholic Female Organisations from the Age of Giolitti to Fascism]', *Revista di Storia Contemporanea*, 3 (1980), pp. 337-71.

66. Rosa Maria Badillo Baena, 'Transformaciones ideológicas en la sociedad malagueña de principios de siglo: el pensamiento feminista de Suceso Luengo de la Figuera [Ideological Transformations of Malaga Society at the Beginning of the Century: the Feminist Thought of Suceso Luengo de la Figuera]', *Jábega*, 51 (1986); Patricia O'Connor, *Gregorio and María Martinez Sierra* (Boston: Twayne Publishers, 1977); M. Dolores Ramos, 'Belén Sarraga y la pervivencia de la ideá federal en Málaga, 1898-1933 [Belén Sarraga and the Perseverance of the Federal Idea in Malaga, 1898-1933]', *Jábega*, 53 (1986), pp. 63-70; Elizabeth Starcevic, *Carmen de Burgos. Defensora de la Mujer* [Carmen de Burgos: Defender of Women] (Almería: Editorial Cajal, 1976).

67. Xabier de Bursain, 'Emakume. La organización de la mujer en el nacionalismo vasco [Emakume: The Women's Organisation in Basque Nationalism]', preliminary note by Antonio Elorza, *Estudios de Historia Social* no. 2-3 (July 1972); Concha Fagoaga and Paloma Saavedra, *Clara Campoamor. La sufragista española* [Clara Campoamor: The Spanish Suffragist] (Madrid: Dirección General de Juventud y Promoción socio-cultural. Subdirección General de la Mujer, 1981).

68. Cristina Dupláa, 'Les dones i el pensament conservador'; Joana Luna and Macià, 'L'associacionisme femení'; M. Ugalde Solano, 'El hogar, la profesión y la actividad política en las agrupaciones de Emakume Abertzale Batza de Navara (1931-1936) [Home, Profession and political activity of the Emakume Abertzale Batza in Navarre (1931-1936)]', *Congres De la Casa a la fábrica* (CIHD, University of Barcelona, 1986); 'Las mujeres en el nacionalismo vasco durante la II República [Women in Basque Nationalism during the Second Republic]', *La Mujer en la Historia de España*.

69. Joana Luna, 'L'Esport. ¿Un miratge de l'alliberament? El club femení i d'esports, 1928-1936 [Sport: A Mirage of Liberation? The Female Sports Club, 1928-1936]', *L'Avenç*, 112 (February 1988), pp. 26-29; Elisenda Macià, 'L'Institut de Cultura: Un model de promoció cultural per a la dona catalana [L'Institut de Cultura: A Model of Cultural Promotion for Catalan Women]', *L'Avenç*, 112 (February 1988), pp. 18-20; Mary Nash, 'Aproximación al movimiento eugénico español: el primer curso eúgenico y la aportación del Dr. Sebastián Recasens [Approximation to the Spanish Eugenics Movement: The First Eugenical Course and the Contribution of Dr. Sebastián Recasens]', *Gimbernat. Revista Catalana d'Història de la Medicina i de la Ciencia*, 4 (1985), pp. 195-202.

70. Mary Nash, 'La presa de consciència de la discriminació de les dones en temps de la revolució industrial, especialment als països anglosaxons [The Awareness of Women's Discrimination at the time of the Industrial Revolution, especially in Anglo-Saxon Countries]', and 'La trajectòria del moviment feminista des de finals del segle XX fins al període de les dues guerres mundials [The Trajectory of the Feminist Movement from the End of the Twentieth Century to the Period of the Two World Wars]', *Perspectiva Social*, 26 (1988), pp. 43-58.

71. C. Fuiz de Almodovar, 'El enclaustramiento de la mujer en la sociedad islámica [The Cloistering of Women in Islamic Society]', *Cuadernos de Historia y Arqueologías medievales*, 4-6, (1985-1986); 'La posición de la mujer musulmana en el matrimonio: su desarrollo social a partir del testimonio coránico [The Position of Muslim Women in Marriage: Their Social Development from the Koran]', *Congreso Internacional de Al-Andalus: Tradición, Creatividad y Convivencia* Córdoba, 1987; *Historia del movimiento feminista egipcio* [History of the Egyptian Feminist Movement] (Granada: Universidad de Granada, 1986), (microfiche).

72. Mary Nash, 'Política, condició social i mobilització femenina: les dones a la Segona República i a la Guerra Civil [Politics, Social Condition and Female Mobilisation: Women in the Second Republic and the Civil War]', in *Més enllà del silenci*; Maria Gloria Nuñez Perez, *Trabajadoras en la Segunda República. Un estudio sobre la actividad económica extradoméstica. (1931-1936)* [Women Workers in the Second Republic: A Study of Extradomestic Economic Activity (1931-1936)] (Madrid: Ministerio de Trabajo y de Seguridad Social, 1989).

73. Lester Golden, 'Les dones com avantguarda: els rembomboris del pa del gener de 1918 [Women as a Vanguard: the Bread Riots in January 1918]', *L'Avenç*, 44 (December 1981), pp. 45-50; Temma Kaplan, 'Female Consciousness and Collective Action: The Case of Barcelona, 1910-1918', *Signs*, 7, 3 (Spring 1982), pp. 548-66; Mary Nash, *Mujer y movimiento obrero en España. 1931-1939* [Women and the Labour Movement in Spain: 1931-1939] (Barcelona: Fontamara, 1981), and 'Treball, conflictivitat social', *Més enllà del silenci*; Maria Dolores Ramos, 'Realidad social y conciencia de la realidad en la mujer: obreras malagueñas frente a la crisis de subsistencias (1918) [Social Reality and Awareness of the Reality of Women: Women Workers from Malaga and the Subsistence Crisis (1918)], *Ordenamiento jurídico*.

74. Marta Bizcarrondo, 'Los orígenes del feminismo socialista en España [The Origins of Socialist Feminism in Spain]', *La mujer en la Historia*; Mary Nash, *Mujeres Libres* and *Mujer y movimiento obrero*; Alvaro Soto Carmona, 'La participación de la mujer en la conflictividad laboral (1905-1921) [The Participation of Women in Labour Conflict (1905-1921)]', *Ordenamiento jurídico*.

75. Temma Kaplan, 'Other Scenarios: Women and Spanish Anarchism'; R. Bridenthal and C. Koonz, 'Becoming Visible', *Women in European History* (Boston: Houghton Mifflin, 1977), and 'Female Consciousness'; Mary Nash, *Mujeres Libres*, *Mujer y movimiento obrero*, and 'Treball, conflictivitat social'; Ramos, 'Realidad social y conciencia'; Paloma de Villota, 'Violencia y represión contra la mujer bajo Fernando VII, 1814-1833 [Violence and Repression against Women under Fernando VII, 1814-1833]', *Ordenamiento jurídico*; 'Los motines de Castilla la Vieja', *Nuevas perspectivas* and 'La mujer castellano-leonesa en los origenes del movimiento obrero (1855) [Castilla- Leonese Women and the Origens of the Labour Movement (1855)]', *La mujer en la historia*.

76. Albert Balcells, 'La mujer obrera en la industria catalana durante el primer cuarto del siglo XX [Working Women in Catalan Industry in the First Quarter of the Twentieth Century]', *Trabajo y organización obrera en la Cataluña contemporánea. (1900-1936)* [Work and Working-Class Organisation in Contemporary Catalonia (1900-1936)] (Barcelona: Laia, 1974), and 'Les dones obreres a Catalunya durant el primer quart del segle XX [Working Women in Catalonia during the First Quarter of the Twentieth Century]', *Perspectiva Social*, 26 (1988), pp. 65-74.

77. Mary Nash, 'Treball, conflictivitat social'.

78. Mary Nash, *Mujeres Libres* and *Mujer y movimiento obrero*.

79. Encarnación Barranquero Texeira, 'Los niños que hicieron la guerra [Children at War]', *Baética*, 10 (1987); Bizcarrondo, 'Los orígenes del feminismo socialista'; Mary Nash, *Women, Antifascist Resistance and Revolution: The Spanish Civil War* (Denver: Arden, forthcoming).

80. Carme Peñalver, 'Les dones i les associacions populars: una presència invisible [Women and Popular Associations: An Invisible Presence]', *L'Avenç*, 112 (February 1988), pp. 22-25.

81. Mary Nash, 'La reforma sexual en el anarquismo español [Sex Reform in Spanish Anarchism]', *Coloquio Internacional. Las tradiciones culturales del anarquismo español* (Internationaal Institut voor Sociales Geschiedenis, Amsterdam, Ruhr – Universitat Bochum and Université Toulouse-le-Mirail, June 1988, forthcoming).

82. Encarnación Barranquero Texeira, 'El trabajo de la mujer y la Nueva Sociedad [Women's Work and the New Society]', *El trabajo de las mujeres*; MariCarmen Garcia Nieto, 'Unión de Muchachas, un modelo metodológico' [Unión de Muchachas: A Methodological Model]', *La mujer en la historia*; Mary Nash, *Mujeres Libres* and *Mujer y movimiento obrero*. Also 'Le donne nella Guerra Civile [Women in the Civil War]', in Claudio Natoli and Leonardo Rapone (eds.), *A Cinquant'anni dall Guerra di Spagna* [Fifty Years since the Civil War] (Milan: Franco Angeli, 1987).

83. Mary Nash, 'Milicianas and Home Front Heroines: Images of Women in Revolutionary Spain (1936-1939)', paper presented at Turning Points in History, First International Conference of the International Society for the Study of European Ideas, Amsterdam, September 1988 (forthcoming *History of European Ideas*).

84. MariCarmen Garcia Nieto, 'El trabajo no-pagado de las mujeres madrileñas durante la Guerra Civil [Unpaid Work by Madrid Women during the Civil War]', *Coloquio – De la Casa a la fábrica* (CIHD, University of Barcelona, 1986); Mary Nash, *Las mujeres en la Guerra Civil* [Women in the Civil War], (Madrid: Ministerio de Cultura, 1989).

85. Elena Posa, 'Una dona portadora de valors eterns. La Sección Femenina 1934-1952 [A Woman – Bearer of Eternal Values]', *Taula de Canvi*, 5 (May-June 1977); Encarnación Jiménez, 'La mujer en el franquismo. Doctrina y acción de la Sección Femenina [Women under Franco: Doctrine and Action of the *Sección Femenina*]', *Tiempo de Historia*, 83 (October 1981), pp. 4-15; M. T. Gallego, *Mujer, Falange y Franquismo* [Women, *Falange* and Francoism] (Madrid: Taurus, 1983).

86. Alicia Alted Vigil, 'La mujer en las coordenadas educativas del régimen franquista [Women in the Educational Trends of the Franco regime]', *Ordenamiento jurídico*; Giuliana di Febo and Marina Saba, 'La condición de la mujer y el papel de la Iglesia en la Italia fascista y la España Franquista: ideología, leyes y asociaciones femeninas [The Condition of Women and the Role of the Church in Fascist Italy and Francoist Spain]', *Ordenamiento jurídico*; Giuliana di Febo, *La santa de la raza. Un culto barroco en la España franquista* [The Saint of the Race: A Baroque Cult in Franco's Spain] (Barcelona: Icaria, 1988).

87. Giuliana di Febo, *La Santa de la Raza*; Mary Nash, 'Pronatalism and Motherhood in Franco's Spain', in Gisela Bock and Pat Thane, *Maternity: Visions of Gender and the Rise of the Welfare State* (London: Routledge, forthcoming).

88. Mary Nash, 'Pronatalism and Motherhood'.

89. Tomasa Cuevas, *Mujeres de la resistencia* [Women of the Resistance] (Barcelona: Sirocco Books, 1986); Giuliana di Febo, *Resistencia y movimiento de mujeres en España 1936-1976* [Resistance and the Women's Movement in Spain 1936-1976] (Barcelona: Icaria, 1979).

90. Cristina Borderias, 'Identité femenine et changement sociale. Barcelone 1920-1980 [Female Identity and Social Change: Barcelona 1920-1980]', *V Coloqui d'Historia Oral* (Universidad de Barcelona, 1985); Rosa Maria Capel Martínez, *El trabajo y la educación de la mujer en España, 1900-1930* [Work and the Education of Women in Spain (1900-1930)] (Madrid: Ministerio de Cultura, 1982); Mary Nash, *Mujer, familia y trabajo*; Nuñez Perez, *Trabajadoras*; Alvaro Soto, 'La cuantificación de la mano de obra femenina en España [The Quantification of the Female Work-Force in Spain]', *La mujer en la Historia*; Gloria Nielfa Cristobol,

'Las mujeres en el comercio madrileño en el primer tercio del siglo XX [Women in Madrid Commerce in the First Third of the Twentieth Century]', in *Mujer y sociedad.*

91. Cristina Borderías, 'Discriminación femenina y segregación sexual del trabajo. Una aproximación microsocial: La Compañía Telefónica Nacional de España [Female Discrimination and the Sexual Segregation of Work: A Microsocial Aproximation. The Spanish Telephone Company]', *El trabajo de las mujeres*; Maria Gloria Nuñez Pérez, 'Metodología, fuentes y centros documentales para el estudio de la participación de las trabajadoras en el ámbito laboral nacional, (1931-1936) [Methodology, Sources and Documentary Centres for the Study of the Participation of Women Workers in the National Labour Context, 1931-1936]', *El trabajo de las mujeres.*

92. Mary Nash, 'Trabajadoras y estrategias de sobreviviencia económica: el caso del trabajo a domicilio durante la Primera Guerra Mundial [Women Workers and Strategies for Economic Survival: The Case of Homework During the First World War]', *El trabajo de las mujeres*, and 'Treball, conflictivitat social'.

93. Isabelle Bertaux-Wiame, Cristina Borderías and Adele Pesce, 'Trabajo e identidad femenina: una comparación internacional sobre la producción de la trayectoria social de las mujeres en España, Francia e Italia [Work and Female Identity: an International Comparison of the Social Trajectory of Women in Spain, France and Italy]', *Sociologia del Trabajo*, 3 (Spring 1988), pp. 71-90; Nielfa, 'Las dependientes'; Nash, 'Trabajadoras y estrategias de sobreviviencia económica'.

94. Cristina Borderías Mondéjar, 'Entre el trabajo asalariado y el trabajo doméstico: cultura, conciencia femenina y política [Between Wage Work and Domestic Work: Culture, Female Consciousness and Politics]', *Congres. De la casa a la fábrica* (CIHD, University of Barcelona, 1986); S. Narotsky, *Trabajar en familia. Mujeres, hogares y talleres* [Working in the Family: Women, Homes and Workshops] (Valencia: Edicions Alfons el Magnánim, 1988).

95. Narotsky, *Trabajar en familia*; Mary Nash, 'Trabajadoras y estrategias de sobreviviencia'; Enric Sanchis Gomez, *El treball a domicili* [Homework] (Valencia: Institució Alfons el Magnànim, 1986).

96. Pilar Pérez-Fuertes Hernández, 'Notas acerca del modelo vasco de industrialización: la división del trabajo entre hombres y mujeres. 1876-1913 [Notes on the Basque Model of Industrialisation: the Division of Work Between Men and Women, 1876-1913]', *Mujeres y hombres.*

97. Gloria Franco Rubio, *La incorporación de la mujer a la Administración del Estado, Municipios y Diputaciones: 1918-1936* [The Incorporation of Women to State Administration, Municipalites and *Diputaciones*: 1918-1936] (Madrid: Dirección General de la Juventud, 1981).

98. Rosa Maria Capel Martínez, 'Las cigarreras y el Reglamento para las fábricas de Tabaco de 1927 [Female Cigarette Makers and the Regulation of Tobacco Factories in 1927]', *Congres De la casa a la fábrica* (CIHD, University of Barcelona, 1986); Claude Morange, 'De "Manola" a obrera. (La revuelta de las cigarreras de Madrid en 1830. Notas sobre un conflicto de trabajo) [From "Manola" to Worker. (The Revolt of the Female Cigarette Makers in Madrid in 1830. Notes on a Labour Conflict.)]', *Estudios de Historia Social*, 12 & 13 (January-June 1980), pp. 307-20.

99. Ana Yetano Laguna, *La enseñanza religiosa en la España de la Restauración* [Religious Teaching in Spain under the Restoration] (Barcelona: Anthropos, 1988).

100. Maria Carmen Garcia Nieto, 'El trabajo no pagado'; Mary Nash, 'Women, Antifascist Resistance and Revolution'.

101. Maria del Carmen Gómez Garcia, 'Trabajo y actividades de las religiosas en los conventos malagueños (siglo XVIII) [Work and the Activities of Nuns in Malaga Convents (Eighteenth Century)]', *El trabajo de las mujeres*; Joana Luna and Elisenda Macià, 'L'associacionisme femení'.

102. Maria Teresa Chicote, 'El trabajo de las mujeres en el ámbito rural de la provincia de Madrid. 1930-1945 [Women's Work in a Rural Environment in the Province of Madrid, 1930-1945]', *El trabajo de las mujeres*; Carmen Sarasúa García, 'Lactancia y cuidado de los niños en el siglo XIX: de trabajo pagado a obligación natural de las mujeres [Wet-Nursing and the Care of Children in the Nineteenth Century: From Paid Work to the Natural Obligation of Women]', *Bulletin du Departement de recherches Hispaniques Pyrenaica* (Junio 1984).

103. Maria Antonia Ferrer i Bosch and Maria Jesus Villaverde, 'Economía y mujer campesina en la Cataluña del siglo XIX. Lectura de los protocolos notariales [Economy and Peasant Women in Catalonia in the Nineteenth Century: A Reading from the Notary Protocols]', *El trabajo de las mujeres*.

104. Juana Anadón and Antonia Fernández, 'El profesorado femenino en la Escuela Normal Central de Maestras de Madrid, 1859-1900 [Female Teachers at the Central Teacher Training College in Madrid, 1859-1900]', *El trabajo de las mujeres*; Esther Cortada, *Escuela mixta y coeducación en Cataluña durante la Segunda República* [Mixed Schools and Coeducation in Catalonia during the Second Republic] (Madrid: Ministerio de Asuntos Sociales, 1988); Geraldine Scanlon, 'Revolución burguesa e instrucción femenina [Bourgeois Revolution and Female Instruction]', *Nuevas perspectivas sobre la mujer*.

105. Giuliana di Febo, 'Orígenes del debate feminista en España. La escuela krausista y la Institución Libre de Enseñanza (1870-1890) [Origins of the Feminist Debate in Spain. The Krausist School and the Institución Libre de Enseñanza], *Sistema. Revista de Ciencias Sociales*, 12 (January 1976), pp. 49-82.

106. Alicia Alted Vigil, 'La mujer en las coordenadas educativas'; Maria Inmaculada Pastor Homs, *La educación femenina en la postguerra (1939-1945). El caso de Mallorca* [Female Education in the Postwar (1939-1945)] (Madrid: Ministerio de Cultura, 1984); Marina Subirats, 'L'Educació de les dones. Del franquisme a la transició [Women's Education: From Francoism to the Transition]', *Perspectiva Social*, 26 (1988), pp. 93-102.

107. Ana Maria Aguado Higón and Maria Carmen Romeo Mateo, *Educación y trabajo. La situación de la mujer en la sociedad valenciana (1780-1833)* [Education and Work: The Situation of Women in Valencia Society (1780-1833)] (Valencia: University of Valencia, forthcoming); G. Gomez-Ferrer, 'La imagen de la mujer en la novela de la Restauración: hacia el mundo del trabajo [The Image of Women in the Restoration Novel: Towards the World of Work]', in *Mujer y sociedad*.

108. Ester Cortada i Andreu and Montserrat Sebastià i Salat, 'La dona i la institucionalització de l'educació [Women and the Institutionalisation of the Education of Women]', in Mary Nash (ed.), *Més enllà del silenci*.

109. Teresa Ortiz, *Médicos en la Andalucía del siglo XX. Número, distribución, especialismo y participación profesional de la mujer* [Doctors in Andalusia in the Twentieth Century: Number, Distribution, Speciality and Professional Participation of Women] (Granada: Fundación Averroes, 1987).

110. Casey, *La familia*; Chacon, *Familia y sociedad*; Dolors Comas d'Argemir, 'El comparativismo y la generalización de los estudios sobre historia de la familia [Comparitivism and the Generalisation of Studies on the History of the Family]', *Historia Social*, 2 (Autumn 1988), pp. 135-43, and 'El cicle de vida familiar: condició social i imatges culturals sobre les dones [Family Life Cycle: Social Condition and Cultural Images of Women]', in Mary Nash (ed.), *Més enllà del silenci*; Mary Nash, 'El estudio del control de natalidad en España: ejemplos de metodologías diferentes [The Study of Birth Control in Spain: Examples of Different Methodologies]', *La Mujer en la Historia*.

111. Mary Nash, 'Les dones i la Segona República: La igualtat de drets i la desigualtat de fet [Women and the Second Republic: Equality of Rights and Inequality in Practice]', *Perspectiva Social*, 26 (1988), pp. 75-83, and 'Política, condició social i mobilització femenina: les dones a la Segona República i a la Guerra Civil [Politics, Social Condition and Female Mobilisation: Women in the Second Republic and in the Civil War]', *Més enllà del silenci*.

112. Carmen Aramburu, 'Separación matrimonial y divorcio (1932-1981) [Marriage Separations and Divorce (1932-1981)]', *Langaiak*, 2 (March 1983), pp. 72-77; Carles Gascón i Pous, 'El divorci a Barcelona, 1932-1938 [Divorce in Barcelona, 1932-1938]', *Congres De la Casa a la fábrica* (CIHD Universidad de Barcelona, 1986); R. Lezcano, *El divorcio en la II República* [Divorce under the Second Republic] (Madrid: Akal, 1979).

113. Pilar Folguera Crespo 'Política natalista y control de natalidad en España durante la década de los veinte [Natalist Policies and Birth Control in Spain during the Twenties]', *Ordenamiento jurídico*; Mary Nash, 'El neomaltusianismo anarquista y los conocimientos populares del control de natalidad en España [Anarchist Neomalthusianism and Popular Knowledge on Birth Control in Spain]', in Mary Nash (ed.), *Presencia y protagonismo* and 'L'avortament legal a Catalunya: una experiéncia fracassada [Legal Abortion in Catalonia: An Unsuccessful Experience]', *L'Avenç*, 58 (March 1983), pp. 20-26.

114. Mary Nash, 'Género, cambio social y la problemática del aborto [Gender, Social Change and the Problem of Abortion]', *Historia Social*, 2 (Autumn 1988), pp. 19-35, and 'Marginality and Social Change: Legal Abortion in Catalonia During the Civil War', *Seventeenth Annual Conference. Spanish and Portuguese Historical Association* (Minnesota: University of Minnesota, forthcoming).

115. Danièlle Bussy Genevois, 'El ideal jurídico republicano (1931-1933) y el Seguro de Maternidad [Ideal Republican Law (1931-1933) and Maternity Insurance]', *Ordenamiento jurídico*; Josefina Cuesta, 'Hacia el Seguro de Maternidad: la situación de la mujer obrera en los años veinte [Towards Maternity Insurance: The Situation of Working Women in the Twenties]', *Ordenamiento jurídico*; Maria Gloria Nuñez Pérez, 'La implantación y los resultados del Seguro de Maternidad en la II República [The Implementation and Results of Maternity Insurance in the Second Republic]', *Ordenamiento jurídico*.

116. Mary Nash, 'L'avortament legal a Catalunya' and 'Género, cambio social y la problemática del aborto'.

414 *Mary Nash*

117. Mary Nash, 'Ordenamiento jurídico y realidad social del aborto en España: Una aproximación histórica [Legal Ordinances and the Social Reality of Abortion in Spain: a Historical Approximation]', *Ordenamiento jurídico.*
118. Mary Nash, 'La reforma sexual en el anarquismo español'.
119. Matilde Cuevas de la Cruz and Luis Otero Carvajal, 'La prostitución y legislación en el siglo XIX. Aproximación a la consideración social de la prostituta [Prostitution and Legislation in the Nineteenth Century: Approximation to the Social Consideration of the Prostitute]', *Ordenamiento jurídico*; I. Muñoz Robledo, 'La prostitución en España. Andalucia siglos XV-XVI-XVII. Málaga en la prostitución [Prostitution in Spain: Andalusia Fifteenth, Sixteenth, Seventeenth Centuries. Malaga in Prostitution]'. *Primer Encuentro de Estudios Interdisciplinarios de la Mujer en Andalucia* (Granada: 1988).
120. Mary Nash, *Mujeres libres* and *Mujer y movimiento obrero.*
121. Comas d'Argemir, 'El cicle de vida familiar'; Pilar Folguera, *Vida cotidiana en Madrid. Primer tercio del siglo através de las fuentes orales* [Everyday Life in Madrid: The First Third of the Century through Oral Sources] (Madrid: Comunidad de Mardid, Consejería de Cultura y Deporte, 1987); Carmen Martín Gaite, *Usos amorosos de la postguerra española* [Love Customs in Postwar Spain] (Barcelona: Anagrama, 1987).
122. M. Alberto Robatto, *Rosalía de Castro y la condición femenina* [Rosalía de Castro and the Female Condition] (Madrid: Partenón, 1981); José M. Alegre, 'Las mujeres en el Lazarillo de Tormes [Women in the *Lazarillo de Tormes*]', *Arbor*, 117 (April 1984), p. 460; N. Alonso, *Partir, defender callar: tres posibilidades de conclusión en la novela española contemporánea* [Leave, Defend, Be Silent: Three Possible Conclusions in the Contemrpoary Spanish Novel] (Madrid: Atenea, 1983); Carmen Bravo Villasante, 'Vida y obra de Emilia Pardo Bazán [Life and Works of Emilia Pardo Bazán],]', *Revista de Occidente*, (1962); Sheley Steven, 'La apología feminista de Rosalía [The Feminist Defence of Rosalía]', *Congreso Internacional sobre Rosalía de Castro y su tiempo* Santiago de Compostela, 1985.
123. Alicia Fernández Pérez, 'La mujer trabajadora del Barroco a través de la picaresca [The Baroque Women Worker as seen through the Picaresque]', *El trabajo de las mujeres*; Paloma Fernández Quintanilla, *La mujer ilustrada en la España del s.XVIII* [The Enlightened Woman in Spain in the Eighteenth Century] (Madrid: Ministerio de Cultura, 1987); Paloma Villota, 'La Ilustración y la capacidad intelectual de la mujer [The Enlightenment and the Intellectual Capacity of Women]', *Septimas Jornadas Interdisciplinarias* (Madrid: U.A.M. 1989); *Realidad histórica e invención literaria en torno a la mujer* [Historical Reality and Literary Invention about Women] (Málaga: Servicio de publicaciones de la Diputación Provincial, 1987).
124. Guadalupe Gómez Ferrer, 'La imagen de la mujer en la novela de la Restauración: Ocio social y trabajo doméstico [The Image of Women in the Restoration Novel: Social Leisure and Domestic Work]', in *Mujer y sociedad.*
125. Cristina Peña-Marín, 'La femineidad, máscara e identidad [Femininity, Mask and Identity]', *Nuevas Perspectivas sobre la mujer.*
126. *La mujer en el mundo de habla inglesa: autora y protagonista* [Women in the World of Spoken English: Author and Character] (Málaga: Servicio de Publicaciones de la Diputación Provincial, 1987).

127. Maria José González Castillejo, 'Literatura femenina y mentalidad religiosa. El discurso de la sumisión en la II República [Female Literature and Religious Mentality: The Discourse of Submission in the Second Republic]', *Mujeres y Hombres*.

128. Cristina Dupláa and Guadalupe Gómez-Ferrer, Propuesta del Seminario de Estudios Historicos de las Mujeres, [Proposal Presented] Fundación Ortega y Gasset and Instituto de la Mujer 1988.

22

Women's History in Yugoslavia

Andrea Feldman

For decades several arguments with which Yugoslav feminists are concerned seem to have remained unchanged. It seems that right- and left-oriented critics of feminist efforts throughout this century have continually criticised their elitism, both sides characterising it as a drawback rather than an advantage.

Chairing the founding meeting on 19 May 1925 of one of the first feminist societies in Yugoslavia, Dr. Milica Bogdanović specified the need for an organisation that is 'going to educate and persuade women not to vote for a Hindenburg or a Mussolini'.[1] This was a bold statement when we bear in mind that the meeting was held at the Esplanade, a luxurious fin-de-siècle hotel in Zagreb, and was made before an audience consisting primarily of women intellectuals. But it met with harsh criticism from all sides. There was no possibility that conservative politicians, supported by nascent public opinion in the Kingdom of Yugoslavia (that semi-colonial and still quite young but already troubled country), would grant the demands for female suffrage and other equal rights that had emerged in the context of the inter-war women's movement.

On the other hand, the so-called 'proletarian' or communist movement recognised the potential of the women's movement and its demands, but was unable to deal with the women whom they called 'members of the bourgeoisie'. Nothing more than the pearl necklace of the chairperson of the meeting mentioned above was necessary to antagonise the ascetic revolutionaries, and to trigger an ideological reaction. The feminists were proclaimed 'agents of bourgeois influence', as members of an élite who did not care about working-class women and who by the limitations of their class origins and prejudices were unable to foresee the inevitability of socialist revolutionary change.

Amazingly enough, this kind of argumentation changed on the eve of the Second World War, when the Communist Party of Yugoslavia (CPY), the only political party banned at the time, was searching for various allies in order to gather strength and to win the revolution. So, as the late Lydia Sklevicky wrote in her pioneer work on women's history in Yugoslavia, 'the most consistent form of specific demands on women's behalf was produced in the programme of the CPY in 1940. They demanded the protection of reproductive rights (including abortion rights, equal rights for children born in and out of wedlock, social protection of unmarried mothers and their children, equal pay for equal work and protection against sexual harassment, admission to all professions and finally – universal suffrage and full political rights for women)'.[2]

But historians in post-war Yugoslavia continued the arguments of the pre-war revolutionaries. As conservative and highly ideological scholars, they served the régime as best they could according to the demands of strict marxist ideology. The only recognised historical writing was the one that justified the rule of the CPY, and the basic type of historical writing was political history.

The tendency in the Yugoslav post-revolutionary society was to push into oblivion all kinds of ideas, initiatives or activities that were incompatible with the mainstream ideology and that might eventually harm the image of the unified (and hence fortunate) Yugoslav peoples.[3]

In the late sixties and seventies, the winds of change began to blow in Yugoslavia (as elsewhere in Europe). As a direct result of the influence of the social movements in the West, an interest in modern feminism started to grow in Yugoslav centres – particularly Zagreb, Belgrade and Ljubljana.

In 1976 several young feminists met in Portorož while attending a typical marxist conference on 'The Social Position of Women and the Family in Self-managing Socialism', organised by the Marxist Centres of Slovenia and Croatia. It was the first time that a workshop had been convened to discuss the single topic of feminism. The women present at that meeting referred to various problems of modern feminism in Europe – from the typology of modern feminism, to feminist attitudes towards the family, and to the aims and methods of modern feminism and questions of equality and emancipation. The meeting in Portorož elicited no excessive reactions, either from the officials or from the public. The papers presented were published in a special volume and the matter seemed to be safely closed.[4] Nevertheless, for a few women this meeting was a turning point, an encouragement to further, more active theoretical and intellectual interest in feminism. The women who had participated exchanged experiences, read feminist literature, formed an informal network, and travelled to other European countries, becoming acquainted with activists in feminist movements.

In Autumn 1978 the international conference 'Drug-ca žena: the women's question – a new approach' was organised in the Student Cultural Centre in Belgrade. The organisers of this first full-fledged post-war feminist meeting, Dunja Blažević and Žarana Papić, planned different sections to deal with issues like women and revolution, modern feminist movements, sexuality and identity of women, and women and culture. But, as it turned out, all the women who were present grouped themselves around the first topic. They considered the theoretical and practical problems of the development of feminist movements in the west and compared them to the situation in Yugoslavia (which at that time still seemed to be the only successful socialist project in Europe, and as such did not yet bear a rigid communist stigma).

The experience of the discussions at this meeting were new and surprising for all the women participants from Yugoslavia; it was extremely inspiring. There was some reaction to this meeting in the Belgrade press, and on the radio and television.

Some of these attacks trivialised the meeting and reflected an obvious misunderstanding of what had happened during the conference, as well as of the feminist issues themselves.[5] The Yugoslav participants responded with detailed reports of the meeting in various newspapers. This was the beginning of a 'war of words' that has continued to the present.

The second line of attack came from official quarters. Several women politicians and members of the only official (and hence Party-controlled) women's organisation began to give interviews in the papers repeating the sophism that there was no 'women's question' apart from the class question and therefore feminism could not offer anything new with respect to methods for solving a problem that did not exist.[6] Their basic idea was that socialism resolves the question of class conflict, which includes the women's question (as well as the question of nationalism!) so that there was no need to consider the women's question separately.

Thereafter, several new feminist groups were formed, joined by women (and some by men, too) to articulate the problems they were facing either as women, or as feminists, or as homosexuals or lesbians, or in other ways. At the end of 1979 the group 'Women and Society' was formed in Zagreb under the auspices of the Sociological Association of Croatia. During the last decade this group has become the centre for research in women's studies, although without any kind of official or financial support. The women professionals started to work individually on different kinds of feminist and women's studies topics ranging from women's history and the anthropology of gender to discussions on marxist feminism and women's writing and art. The aims of this group were to encourage and organise debates, to offer perspectives on social change and to articulate the position of women in society as a relevant social and theoretical question. The women of this research centre developed interdisciplinary approaches to these projects, organised extra-curricular lectures and seminars for students in the social sciences and humanities, published the results of their work and contributed a great deal to what Lydia Sklevicky called 'the cultivated dialogue' of the Yugoslav academic as well as alternative scenes.[7] Out of this group there emerged several separate sub-groups of specific interests. One of these focused on women's history.

Upon Lydia Sklevicky's initiative, several women historians working in different posts in museums, archives and institutes gathered together in an extra-curricular postgraduate seminar in women's history in 1984/85. We produced papers on a variety of problems, including the definition of women's history and the treatment of women in school textbooks. Our efforts initiated certain changes in some of the new editions of the history textbooks, and our ambition is to continue working on what Gerda Lerner has called 'compensatory history' and 'contribution history'[8] for women in Yugoslavia and at the same time to ensure that women's voices will not be silenced. Consequently, our aim is to broaden our views and to challenge the common knowledge as well as to rewrite the history of women and feminist activities in this country.[9]

This is an ambitious project, to say the least, since our recently founded organisation (since 1989 a member of the IFRWH/FIRHF) has no university or any other institutional backing or source of funds. But it is our firm conviction that research in women's history will become a part of university history programmes in Yugoslavia in due course.

NOTES

This article is dedicated to the memory of my friend and colleague Lydia Sklevicky (1952-1990) who was the head of our National Committee for Research in Women's History.

1. Document, Archives of the Institute for the History of the Worker's Movement of Croatia, group IV/3537 (1925).
2. Lydia Sklevicky, 'Karakteristike organiziranog djelovanja žena u Jugoslaviji u razdoblju do drugog svjetskog rata [Characteristics of the Organized Activities of Women in Yugoslavia before the Second World War]', *Polja*, 309 (1984), pp. 454-6.

3. There is a link between the ways in which the communists in Yugoslavia tried to come to terms with national (ethnic) and women's problems – by actually not allowing them to be recognised until they emerged again during the major political and economic crises of the eighties.

4. *Društveni položaj žene i razvoj porodice u socijalističkom samoupravnom društvu* [The Social Position of Woman and the Development of the Family Within the Socialist Self-Managed Society] (Ljubljana: Komunist, 1979), published documents from an official conference in Portorož, 1976. See the summaries in English.

5. These attacks were published in 'Večernje novosti' [The Evening News] and 'Omladinske novine' [The Youth Paper] of Belgrade.

6. Rada Iveković, 'Yugoslav Neofeminism', in Robin Morgan (ed.), *Sisterhood is Global* (New York: Anchor Books, 1984), pp. 737-9.

7. Andrea Feldman, 'Eine alternative Frauengruppe in Zagreb,' [An Alternative Women's Group in Zagreb] in *Die ungeschriebene Geschichte* (Vienna: Wiener Frauenverlag, 1985), pp. 113-23.

8. Gerda Lerner, *The Majority Finds Its Past: Placing Women in History* (Oxford: Oxford University Press, 1979), pp. 145-7.

9. Lydia Sklevicky, 'More Horses than Women: On the Difficulties of Founding Women's History in Yugoslavia', *Gender & History*, 1, no. 1 (Spring 1989), pp. 68-75.

23

The 'History of Women' in Greece

Efi Avdela

It is commonly accepted today that the questions historians ask of the past are directly related to their concerns and inquiries about the present. The writing of history is not a neutral act, but has evident ideological and therefore political connotations. In this way, the development of the new field of history called 'the history of women', internationally, over the last twenty years, is directly linked to the growth of the feminist movement. Defining women's status as social and therefore reversible, contemporary feminists turned to the past in order to study the various forms of gender inequality, the mechanisms that maintained and reproduced it, the moments of resistance and suppression. What they did in fact was to bring women to the forefront of history, giving them a past or, in other words, a collective identity, and revealing gender relations as a driving force of history.

Conditions were favourable. The development of social anthropology opened new fields of knowledge to historical research, more related to the 'private domain' where the presence of women could not be easily ignored: family organisation, reproductive practices, sexual behaviour. The flourishing of social history and the focusing of the historian's interest on 'those who had no right to history', to quote Lucien Febvre, is part of a wider intellectual movement that has influenced social studies throughout Europe. Although women were not included among the new cognitive objects revealed by the New History, this omission made it all the more imperative to provide them with a history, in spite of everything. The result can be witnessed in the relevant international literature.

With the spreading of research and the accumulation of knowledge on women's history, internal differences stemming from different theoretical premises gradually became visible. As we move from seeing women as victims to viewing women as pillars of authority, and from the optic of female culture to that of gender relations, the image of the past is defined by different political views on the present oppression of women and the possibility of reversing this situation in the future. At the same time, however, although the study of women's history became increasingly academic, during a period when the feminist movement was at a low ebb, most women historians were confronted, in their professional environment, with the modern reflection of the relations they were studying in the past. Beyond the specificities of each national situation, the history of women remained for the 'established' academic community a subject viewed with indifference or suspicion, when it was not considered too important to be left in the hands of women. In point of fact, it became an area of conflict, raising methodological and theoretical questions about the conditions of possibility for the generation of historiographical knowledge. It is therefore not at all surprising that dialogue with male colleagues is always difficult and problematical, when it is not totally non-existent.

In Greece, as in many other countries, the first modern references to the history of women are directly connected to the development of the feminist movement after 1974.[1] The articles published on this question in the feminist journal *Skoupa* [Broom], between 1979-1981, and the related books of the Women's Publishing Group during that same period, reflect a common political practice whose aim was to reconstruct the collective memory of the political subject under formation, that is, the movement for women's liberation. It is no accident, therefore, that these first texts deal, almost exclusively, with the past of women's protest in Greece and elsewhere, with the history, that is, of the feminist movement as such. The discovery that the 'revolt started way back'[2] brought a new dimension to the present struggle, confirming the historic and therefore evolving and reversible character of women's oppression.

Beyond this common starting point with other countries, however, the history of women did not develop at the same rate in Greece. The constraints on its development, which were directly linked to the situation of historical studies and social studies in general as well as to the specificities of the women's movement in the country, can be observed at three levels. First, we must acknowledge the limited academic concern for the status of women in Greek society, which results in a lack of dialogue on potential methodological and theoretical options for the study of women's history. Second, we remark the absence of a significant number of feminist historians in universities, which made it impossible to create an appropriate environment that would generate and sustain interest in these issues. Finally, we note the limited and fragmented studies on women's history in Greece, produced by isolated women researchers who, in most cases, worked outside the established institutions for historical research and writing.

These last years, however, attest that increasing numbers of women historians are now focusing on the study of the various forms that have characterised gender relations in Greek history. Although we lack a systematic record of such information, some features can nevertheless be identified.

These features of gender relations in Greek history are the subject of a number of research projects undertaken as dissertations in Greek but more often than not at universities outside Greece. A few other studies are being undertaken by isolated researchers, who are not connected to any academic institution. Finally, some studies of women's and gender issues are included in the research programmes of Greek agencies that have expanded the established institutional framework for historical research (notably banks and the Youth Secretariat). Most of these research projects, however, are still in progress and their results have not yet been published.

Greek urban society, since the creation of the Greek state and during the first half of the twentieth century, remains the field of reference for the larger part of this research. Subjects include women's relation to the family, education, work, and politics, as these are recorded both in ideological terms and in concrete social reality.[3] Special emphasis is given to the study of organised women's protest and its past forms.[4]

It is quite clear that these choices of time and place are due equally to the need to analyse the mechanisms that have determined the present status of women in Greek society, and to the difficulties encountered in locating sources related to women's lives in earlier periods. With respect to the latter, the contribution of social anthropology is important since it can facilitate investigation into the characteristics of the rural areas in the remote past.[5] The gaps in the questions covered, however, will remain.

As the number of published studies on women's history in Greece is still limited, it is difficult to identify the preferred methodological options in approaches to the various issues. It would seem, however, that an effort is being made both to integrate each specific treatise into a wider context with reference to both genders and to look for new sources of evidence about women's lives in the past, thus expanding the circle of 'history's winners'.

The main problem facing women researchers who study the history of women in Greece, however, is their isolation, the lack of co-ordination for more effective information and exchange among themselves and between themselves and scholars in other countries. Of course, the great number of recent studies on nineteenth- and twentieth-century Greece represent valuable material for research on women; these will help to highlight any similarities or specific conditions between Greece and the findings of the relevant international historiography. This undertaking, however, is not yet a collective one. Nor do we find evidence of any real concern for widening its scope, thus promoting regular options for such study from the standpoint of other fields as well, and not just from the historian's point of view. Many questions remain: Inside or outside universities and research centres? Women's studies or a wider consideration of gender relations? Women's history as a separate field or the restitution to history of the forgotten half of humanity? Or again, what is the relation between academic study and political action? These are all questions which cannot easily be answered by individual exploration, as long as academic practice remains cut off from the political demand that bred it.

It is also a fact that contemporary Greek historical writing, which has been aspiring in these last few years to renew the subjects of and approaches to historical research, has not included women's history among its interests. This may not be strange considering that one of the characteristics of such recent historiography is to lay claim to an ideological and political character, denouncing history's presumed neutrality. It is quite possible that current Greek historians do discern the effects which the questions asked of the past regarding gender relations might have on the reading of the present. Because if the history of women is in fact the history of gender relations,[6] these relations are historically marked by inequality. And adherence to this view would not lead to the writing of women's history, or even history seen from the women's angle, but to the writing of another history altogether.

NOTES

This article was originally published in Greek in the journal *Synchrona Themata* [Contemporary Issues], in a special issue on 'Contemporary Trends in the Historiography of Modern Hellenism', nos. 35-36-37 (1988), pp. 171-173. This English version, translated by Myrto Atzitiri, is published here with permission.

1. Special reference should be made to the earlier work of women like Athena Tarsoulé, Koula Xiradaki and others, who although working in complete isolation succeeded in collecting valuable material on the presence of women in recent Greek history. See, among others, Athina Tarsouli, *Heleni Altamoura. He proti zographos stin Hellada meta to hikossiena* [Eleni Altamoura: The First Woman Painter in Greece after 1821] (Athens: 1934) and *Hellinides piitries, 1857-1940* [Greek Women Poets, 1857-1940] (Athens: 1951); Koula Xiradaki, *Apo ta Archia tou Elegtikou Sinedriou. Parthenagogia ke daskales tou hipodoulou Hellinismou* [From the Archives of the Court of the Auditors: Girls' Schools and Women Teachers in Greek Communities under Ottoman Occupation], vols. 1-2 (Athens:

1972-1973) and *Ginekes sti Philiki Heteria – Phanariotisses* [Women in the Philiki Heteria – Women from Pharani] (Athens: 1971).

2. From the anthology of texts with the same title *He exegersi archizi apo palia. Selides apo ta prota vimata tou ginekiou kinimatos* [The Revolt Started Way Back: Pages from the First Steps of the Women's Movement], edited, translated, and introduced by Eleni Varikas and Costoula Sklaveniti (Athens: Ekdotiki Homada Ginekon [Women's Publishing Group], 1981).

3. See the following books: Sidiroula Ziogou-Karastergiou, *He Messi Ekpedefsi ton koritsion stin Hellada (1830-1893)* [Girls' Secondary Education in Greece (1830-1893)] (Athens: Historiko Archio Hellinikis Neoleas – Geniki Gramatia Neas Genias [Historical Archives of Greek Youth – Youth Secretariat], 1986); Alexandra Bakalaki and Eleni Elegmitou, *He ekpedefsi 'is ta tou ekou' ke ta ginekia kathikonda. Apo tin idrisse tou hellinikou kratous eos tin ekpedeftiki metarithmissi tou 1929* [Education in Household and Female Duties: From the Foundation of the Greek State to 1929] (Athens: Historiko Archio Hellinikis Neoleas – Geniki Gramatia Neas Genias, 1987); Eleni Fournaraki, *Ekpedefsi ke agogi ton koritsion. Helliniki provlimatismi (1830-1910). Ena anthologhio* [The Education and Training of Girls. The Greek Situation (1830-1910): An Anthology] (Athens: Historikoi Archio Hellinikis Neoleas – Geniki Gramatia Neas Genias, 1987); Efi Avdela, *Dimossii hipallili genous thilikou. Katamerismos tis ergassias kata phila ston dimossio tomea stin Hellada (1908-1952)* [Civil Servants of Feminine Gender: the Sexual Division of Labour in the Greek Civil Services (1908-1952)] (Athens: Hidrima Erevnas ke Pedias tis Eborikis Trapezas tis Hellados [Foundation for Research and Culture of the Commercial Bank of Greece], forthcoming in 1990).

4. See Efi Avdela and Angelika Psarra, *Ho pheninismos stin Hellada tou Messopolemou. Mia anthologia* [Feminism in Inter-War Greece: An Anthology] (Athens: Gnossi Publications, 1985); Eleni Varikas, *Hi exegersi ton Kirioin. He genessi mias pheministikis sinidissis stin Hellada, 1833-1907* [The Ladies' Revolt: The Birth of Feminist Consciousness in Greece, 1833-1907] (Athens: Hidrima Erevnas ke Pedias tis Eborikis Trapezas tis Hellados [Foundation for Research and Culture of Commercial Bank of Greece], 1987. See also the special issue 'To helliniko pheministiko endipo [The Greek Feminist Press]' of the journal *Diavazo* [I Read], no. 198 (1988) as well as various articles on Greek women's history published in the feminist journal *Dini* [Whirl], nos. 1-5 (1986-1990).

5. See, on this question, the studies of Nora Skouter-Didaskalou, in particular her book, *Anthropologika gia to ginekio zitima (4 meletimata)* [The Women's Issue from an Anthropological Angle (4 Studies)] (Athens: O Politis, 1984).

6. See the interview with French historian Michelle Perrot, 'He historia ton ginekon ine he historia tis schessis ton philon [Women's history is the history of gender relations]', published in the Greek feminist journal *Dini*, 1 (1986), pp. 77-83.

24

Women's History in Ireland

Mary Cullen

Women's history in Ireland appears to be in the early stages of a period of significant growth. The volume of published work, while still very small, has been increasing steadily over the past few years. The same few years have seen the emergence for the first time of what can be called a community of historians of women. As yet we have not achieved an infrastructure in the sense of funding, resources and a secure base in academe, but the essential ingredient of enthusiasm is present and expanding. The status of women's history in the academy is still far from satisfactory. As yet no Irish university has a professorship or lectureship in women's history. Courses in women's history do not form part of the core or compulsory curriculum. Nor does the position of women academics hold out much promise for the immediate future. Women constitute only a small minority of the academic staff in the country's history departments and not one chair of history is occupied by a woman.

None of these few women staff members has herself been a student in a department where women's history is taught. All have been trained and have researched for their higher degrees in conventional male-centred history programmes. The few who did begin to research and write women's history did so largely from personal feminist commitment since it promised little in the way of career advancement. Until recently they worked for the most part in isolation. They rarely had colleagues with whom to discuss their own work or the field in general. Publications attracted little serious attention, favourable or otherwise, from other historians.

Nevertheless, over the past decade or so, and particularly the last five or six years, the picture has begun to change. A new generation of candidates for higher degrees is choosing topics in women's history. So far such candidates are unable, in any Irish university, to work with

429

supervisors who have themselves taken degrees in women's history, and often work with supervisors who have little familiarity with the field. Yet these young historians are beginning to emerge and to publish, and to create a pool from which trained historians of women can be appointed to academic positions.

The current economic climate and the conservative attitude of the history establishment in Ireland combine to prevent full advantage being taken of this emergence of specialists. New posts are seldom created and when they are, or when existing posts are filled, expertise in women's history is rarely sought. Many of Ireland's new historians of women have to look for jobs outside the country, a brain drain women's history here can ill afford.

On the positive side, some courses in women's history have begun to appear on the curriculum in many third-level institutions in recent years. While always optional in some sense and not part of the compulsory curriculum, they give new generations of students, women and men, the opportunity of attending women's history courses, and their presence on the curriculum gives the field a real, if somewhat ambiguous, establishment validation.

Another positive development is the emergence of the nucleus of a small but potentially important community of historians of women in Ireland. Three separate but interlinking projects can be noted.

The first is the Feminist History Forum set up in 1987. It meets monthly in Dublin and aims to provide time and space for information sharing and debate about issues in feminist history. It is a small group whose attendance varies between six and fourteen, and most of the members are young historians and postgraduate students. Already its meetings have led to the publication of one important contribution to women's history.[1]

The next development was the Society for the History of Women (SHOW). This was formed in 1988 by postgraduate students in University College, Dublin, the largest college in the National University of Ireland. The society has organised two conferences, the first in 1988 on the theme 'From Famine to Feminism' and the second in 1990 on 'Women, War and Peace'. Both attracted large attendances and papers were read by established historians from Ireland and other countries as well as by young Irish researchers. It is hoped that the collected papers from both conferences will be published in the near future.

The third project also dates from 1988 when the International Federation for Research in Women's History requested that an Irish national committee be set up to prepare for the 1990 Madrid conference. While the Irish national committee was an ad hoc group of women historians rather than of historians of women, it acted as the catalyst which sparked off a lot of heretofore latent interest. It led in turn to the foundation of the Irish Asssociation for Research in Women's History, whose executive and membership are drawn from Ireland north and south of the border, from Northern Ireland and the Irish Republic. Its first conference was held in Belfast in 1989 and the second in Dublin in 1990. The Association publishes a newsletter and is participating in the development of a women's history collection and archive.

In Ireland such developments enjoy both the benefits and disadvantages of a small population. On the credit side it is relatively easy to know personally most of the others working in the field, and for historians within and without the academy to meet and interact. There is an overlap of membership and mutually supportive interaction between organisations. The isolation of individuals working in women's history is becoming a thing of the past. On the other hand, the small numerical base means that the continued existence of groups such as those mentioned, and particularly the first two, is always precarious. Both are run by a few individuals on their own time and with no outside resources. If or when those involved are no longer in a position to continue, the future of the activity will be immediately in jeopardy.

Another positive feature of the Irish scene is the general interest in women's history among feminists and practitioners in women's studies. Many of the first publications in women's history written from a feminist perspective were produced by feminist rather than mainstream presses. In recent years post-graduate degree and diploma courses in women's studies have been introduced in a number of universities and in all of these women's history is an essential component. Women's studies conferences of all kinds seldom fail to include historical contributions. In turn women's history conferences attract participants from the feminist movement and other women outside the academy. Women's studies groups at local level outside the formal education system have been a distinctive feature of feminism in Ireland and these too almost invariably show a thirst for knowledge of women in the past. All these factors point to the potential for a mutually beneficial dialogue between women's history and Irish feminism.

When we turn to the actual writing of women's history in Ireland I see a basic need for more reflection and debate about what has been done and what needs to be done. Our lack of this sort of analysis is, I believe, linked to the way women's history has developed in Ireland. Many historians are coming to the field at a time when at a global level women's history has survived the difficult early stages and won acceptance as a legitimate, if peripheral, area. As a result some of those involved have little understanding of the feminist origins of the new women's history and their implications. Others believe that women's history has achieved legitimacy only by virtue of outgrowing those origins.

The new women's history grew from feminists' search of the past for the roots of the sexism they experienced in the present. This led to the identification of the invisibility of women in mainstream history as the product of sexist value-systems of the present. Feminist historians countered this by writing history from a woman-centred perspective. This history takes nothing about women's past for granted and treats the status quo at any period as something to be questioned and subjected to historical scrutiny. It substitutes for the patriarchal paradigm, that only men were active agents in history, a new paradigm that women too were active agents. By seeing women as a group with a history of continuity and change, and as a legitimate subject for historical research and analysis, it brings the relations between the sexes for the first time under the scrutiny of the historian. These new perspectives have proved their value for recovering women's past and raising radical questions about the writing of history in general.

Lack of understanding of these origins cuts historians off from much of the potential of women's history. It results in a wide variation in grasp of the significance of the vigorous debates in progress in the wider world of women's history on such methodological and theoretical questions as: the relationship of women's history to 'mainstream' history; whether women's history has or should have a political purpose; the uses and abuses of 'gender' as a tool of historical research and analysis; the problems in finding a definition or definitions of 'feminism'.

We need a wider awareness in Ireland of the origins of the new women's history and a wider familiarity with the debates flourishing in other countries. We also need to nurture a native Irish discourse and debate with the broadest possible participation of individuals and points of view. Relevant to this discussion is the fact that as yet there is no Irish periodical of women's history. Access to international debate is largely available only to those who have access to English and American journals. This is, of course, of immense benefit and will continue to be so if and when an Irish publication appears. But we need the latter also as a forum for analysis, discussion and constructive criticism in the Irish context.

We now need to develop a more critical approach to our work. Again, the small numbers involved in writing women's history have positive and negative consequences. We have tended to be uncritically approving of each other's work because we believed, correctly, that encouragement and confidence were priorities. We have reached a stage where I believe we will be best served by assessment that combines praise and support with constructive criticism and analysis.

The impact of the new women's history began to take effect in Ireland from the mid-1970s with the introduction of the concept of women as a distinct group for historical study.

One of the few areas of female activity to have previously attracted historians' attention was the political. However, the female political activity that had been 'visible' to mainstream historians was that of 'great' individual women within male-dominated politics. In Ireland, as elsewhere, one of the few areas of male-dominated politics where women had been able to achieve the necessary high profile had been that of revolutionary movements. Women's history has broadened the focus to include feminist movements.

In the late nineteenth and early twentieth centuries Ireland experienced a ferment of intertwined political and cultural activity, constitutional and revolutionary nationalism and unionism, pacifism, the rise of labour, feminism, the Gaelic and Anglo-Irish cultural renaissances. In all of these women were deeply involved, often in a number of areas at the same time. Tensions and conflicting loyalties posed painful dilemmas for many women, and the rich diversity and complexity of women's political involvement is emerging in the new work. The pioneering collection *Women in Irish Society: The Historical Dimension*, published in 1978, began the process of opening up these and other issues in women's history from the new perspectives.[2] Most attention has so far been given to the interaction of women's suffrage, nationalism and socialism, notably in the work of Margaret Ward,[3] Rosemary Cullen Owens,[4] and Cliona Murphy,[5] and a number of articles by other historians.[6] Anna Parnell's account of her involvement in the Ladies' Land League of the 1880s has recently been published with a useful feminist introduction.[7] A major need in this area is for more examination of the problems and experiences of unionist women.[8]

Women in the Irish Free State, which came into existence in 1922 and became the Republic of Ireland in 1949, achieved adult suffrage from the start, and there has been some examination of their activity in the public political sphere in the early decades of the new state.[9] While historians have not yet given much attention to the contemporary feminist movement there have been other contributions of value.[10]

Biographies of women political activists have always been a popular genre with the emphasis again on nationalist and socialist activity. The genre is flourishing today and the recent works give more attention to feminist issues, with which almost every political activist had some involvement or sympathy. Women whose primary commitment was to feminism are now beginning to find biographers.[11] The feminist publishers, Attic Press, have produced two slim volumes of brief biographies of a wide range of Irish women.[12] These are useful contributions in themselves and show how valuable a more detailed dictionary of women's biography would be.

Little has so far been published on aspects of feminist activity other than suffrage. An article by myself shows that Irish feminists were involved in all the major areas of nineteenth-century European feminism, including, in addition to suffrage, employment, education, married women's property rights and opposition to sexual double standards.[13] Of these, only education has received much scholarly attention.

This was a central feminist concern, with significance for employment, suffrage and other objectives. Eibhlin Breathnach has researched the feminist campaigns to gain access for women to university education,[14] and Anne V. O'Connor has examined influences on girls' secondary educaton.[15] These included the feminist campaigns to upgrade girls' education to the level of boys and the impact of these on convent schooling. The original campaigners were Protestant middle- and upper-class women but the Catholic middle classes were quick to take advantage of their success and to put pressure on the convent schools to provide the teaching required to prepare their daughters to avail themselves of new employment opportunities, and even to provide teaching for university examinations. The publication in book form of the theses on which Breathnach's and O'Connor's articles are based would be welcome.

An important aspect of nineteenth-century Irish feminism, on which little work has yet appeared, is its origins in the earlier interests and activities of Irish women. A pioneering contribution is a doctoral thesis on 'Women and Philanthropy in Nineteenth-Century Ireland' by Maria Luddy.[16] This is being prepared for publication at the time of writing, and Luddy has also published two articles based on this research.[17] The links between the roots of Irish feminism and the broader area of women's social and economic history will repay further investigation.

So far we do not know a great deal about the political activity, feminist or otherwise, of Irish women in earlier periods. There is a useful recent biography of Lady Morgan, best-selling novelist and nationalist (1776-1859).[18] Biographies of two Irish women prominent in political and leadership roles in the sixteenth century, one in Gaelic society and the other in the newer Anglo-Irish culture, show how women of the ruling families in both cultures could and did exercise considerable political power.[19] A number of the contributions to *Women in Irish Society: The Historical Dimension* throw light on some related aspects,[20] while the two volumes *Missing Pieces* also make a contribution.[21] The forthcoming publication of a collection of more in-depth studies of women in Irish society in the sixteenth, seventeenth and eighteenth centuries should further extend our knowledge.[22] Publication of papers read at the September 1990 conference of the Irish Association for Research on Women's History on Anna Wheeler, the early nineteenth-century feminist and socialist, and Isabella Todd, the Belfast woman who was one of the pioneers in most areas of feminist action from the 1870s to the 1890s, will also be welcome.[23]

In social and economic history the concept of women as a group as the subject of historical enquiry has given an impetus in a field where women had previously received little attention. The volume of work is still small and scattered over such a diverse range of topics that only limited comment is possible at present. It can be said, however, that it ranges from the essentially descriptive, which produces much useful information about the 'hows' and 'whats' of women's lives but not so much about the 'whys,' to work which, seeing women as self-determining rather than responding passively to outside influences, raises questions about the 'whys' and tends to see the limitations imposed on female activity as themselves the subject for historical investigation. Most of the writing in the field falls somewhere on a continuum between these two extremes. A recent collection of essays on marriage in Ireland throws light on various aspects of women's situations.[24] Some of the contributions to *Women in Irish Society: The Historical Dimension*, already mentioned in relation to women's political activity, are also relevant to women's socio-economic history.[25] These include broad survey essays on the position of women in early Irish society, in the middle ages, in the seventeenth and eighteenth centuries, and in the second half of the nineteenth century and the early decades of the twentieth. Since then most of the research has been on the nineteenth and twentieth centuries, though the forthcoming book on women in the sixteenth, seventeenth and eighteenth centuries mentioned above should fill some of the gaps and give pointers for future research.[26]

Most of the research on the nineteenth and twentieth centuries has concentrated on specific aspects of women's lives and work,[27] while there are also some useful overviews.[28] Women's involvement in trade unions has also received attention.[29] The approach which centres on women as active agents is used in *Women Surviving: Studies in Irish Women's History in the Nineteenth and Twentieth Centuries*, edited by Maria Luddy and Cliona Murphy.[30] The essays in this collection deal with prostitution, nuns and autonomy, women as breadwinners in labouring families, female paupers and their interaction with the workhouse system of poor relief, and domestic servants in Dublin.[31] This approach shows the women studied, while the victims of a double oppression as poor and as female, using initiative and resourcefulness in manipulating the system to their best advantage.

The same picture emerges when Irish emigration is studied from a woman-centred perspective. Emigration from Ireland in the late nineteenth and early twentieth centuries was unique in Europe in its high

proportion of young, single, female emigrants who travelled without
family or male protection and made new lives for themselves overseas.
The qualities of independence and self-reliance this pattern indicates
reappear – though seen from a rather different perspective – in the
reputation gained by those who became domestic servants in the United
States as impertinent and resistant to discipline.[32] Examination of the
conditions in Ireland which led so many young women to leave forever is
another woman-centred approach which shows great promise for deepening
our knowledge of Irish women's lives.[33]

Woman-centred definitions of 'work' have opened further
perspectives on Irish women as independent agents. Conventional male-
centred definitions of work are often irrelevant when applied to women's
work and can conceal or distort the reality of women's lives. Much of the
work done by women inside and outside the home was not remunerated,
but it had both economic and social value and is intrinsic to the patterns
of continuity and change in women's history. The philanthropic work of
middle-class women made a major contribution to the provision of social
services which were later taken over by the state and to the development
of thinking in the social science debates about the reform of society.[34] It
shows middle-class women acting with initiative and independence similar
to that shown by their poorer sisters. Despite the limited amount of work
done to date it is clear that attention to the interaction of gender and class,
combined with a woman-centred perspective, holds promise for the history
of Irish women.

The new women's social and economic history is taking a fresh
look at nuns. Nuns had not been completely invisible in mainstream
history. Religious congregations of women proliferated in Ireland from the
late eighteenth century, and the numbers of institutions and members grew
throughout the nineteenth and much of the twentieth centuries. They
provided an enormous range of services and institutions, including schools
for the poor and the wealthy, hospitals, orphanages, asylums for unmarried
mothers, female industries. The numbers of women religious overtook and
surpassed the numbers of male priests. Their activities were both highly
visible, important to society and, significantly for their visibility to
historians, posed no threat to paradigms of male authority since nuns were
in the final analysis subject to the control of their bishops.

The typical historiography of women religious was a biography of
one of the founding mothers of the religious orders, usually a woman of
strong character from a wealthy family. The biographies tended to be
hagiographical and, while recounting her achievements and those of her
nuns, raised few awkward questions about women's role and male
authority.

In a number of pioneering writings Caitriona Clear has examined religious life as a career option for middle-class women. She looks at the content and structure of that work, the social and economic background of the women who entered and the extent and limitation of their freedom of action within a male-controlled church.[35] Tony Fahey has shown how the nuns who educated poor children with the primary objective of giving their pupils a basic grounding in the Catholic religion were co-opted by the state to serve its agenda of using education to socialise docile and obedient future citizens.[36] Similar paradoxes emerge in the education of middle-class girls where Anne V. O'Connor and Eibhlin Breathnach show how nuns contributed to feminist developments in education under pressure from the demands of middle-class Catholic families that convent schools provide the new employment-oriented education for their daughters.[37]

Life in the convent offered middle-class Catholic women, as an alternative to marriage, a career which promised respectability, security and challenging work, a combination otherwise obtainable by few women in the nineteenth century. Did this defuse frustrations which otherwise might have fuelled feminist demands for women's admission to the professions and other lucrative careers reserved for men only? If so, does it follow that the most potentially feminist Catholic women entered religion? Or, can the example of nuns be seen as a model of work and status that pushed Catholic lay women towards assertion of women's claims?[38] Research that examines nuns' own perspectives on these and other issues is eagerly awaited.[39]

An overall summing up of the state of the art in women's history in Ireland today is difficult. The existing work is unevenly spread, and some important areas have received almost no attention. Sexuality and the different stages of the life cycle stand out here.[40] So do theory and analysis.[41] I have already said I believe we need more of both of these. The enthusiasm is there already and, as the volume of work grows, the dialogue may well develop. The present survey is a purely personal attempt at an overview and, if it provokes others to disagree and to put forward alternative views, it may help to get that dialogue under way.

NOTES

1. Maria Luddy and Cliona Murphy (eds.), *Women Surviving: Studies in Irish Women's History in the Nineteenth and Twentieth Centuries* (Dublin: Poolbeg, 1990).

2. Margaret MacCurtain and Donncha Ó Corráin (eds.), *Women in Irish Society: The Historical Dimension* (Dublin: Arlen House, 1978).

438

Mary Cullen

3. Margaret Ward, *Unmanageable Revolutionaries: Women in Irish Nationalism* (Dingle: Brandon, 1983); M. Ward, '"Suffrage First – Above All Else!" An Account of the Irish Suffrage Movement', *Feminist Review*, 9, no. 1 (1982), pp. 21-31.

4. Rosemary Cullen Owens, *Smashing Times: A History of the Irish Suffrage Movement* (Dublin: Attic Press 1984); R. C. Owens, '"Votes for Ladies, Votes for Women": Organised Labour and the Suffrage Movement', *Saothar*, 9 (1983), pp. 32-47.

5. Cliona Murphy, *The Women's Suffrage Movement and Irish Society in the Early Twentieth Century* (New York: Harvester Wheatsheaf, 1989); C. Murphy, '"The Tune of the Stars and Stripes": The American Influence on the Irish Suffrage Movement', in Luddy and Murphy (eds.), *Women Surviving*, pp. 180-205.

6. See Margaret MacCurtain, 'Women, the Vote and Revolution', in M. MacCurtain and D. Ó Corráin (eds.), *Women in Irish Society*, pp. 46-57; Beth McKillen, 'Irish Feminism and National Separatism, 1914-23', *Eire/Ireland*, 18, no. 3 (1981), pp. 72-90; Marie O'Neill, 'The Ladies' Land League', *Dublin Historical Record*, 25, no. 4 (1982), pp. 122-33; M. O'Neill, 'The Dublin Women's Suffrage Society and its Successors', *Dublin Historical Record*, 38 (1984-85), pp. 126-40; Ellen Hazelkorn, 'The Social and Political Views of Louie Bennett, 1860-1956', *Saothar*, 13 (1988), pp. 32-44.

7. Dana Hearne (ed.), *The Tale of a Great Sham* (Dublin: Arlen House, 1986).

8. Nationalist and unionist politics in Ireland in the nineteenth and early twentieth centuries centred on the Act of the Union of 1800 which created the United Kingdom of Great Britain and Ireland. Unionists wanted to maintain the union while nationalists wanted to replace it by some form of home rule or by a completely independent Irish state.

9. Maurice Manning, 'Women in Irish National and Local Politics 1922-77', in M. MacCurtain and D. Ó Corráin (eds.), *Women in Irish Society*, pp. 92-102; Mary Clancy, 'Aspects of Women's Contribution to the Oireachtas Debate in the Free State, 1922-37', in M. Luddy and C. Murphy (eds.), *Women Surviving*, pp. 206-32. See also, Yvonne Scannell, 'The Constitution and the Role of Women', in Brian Farrell (ed.), *De Valera's Constitution and Ours* (Dublin: Gill and Macmillan, 1988).

10. June Levine, *Sisters: The Personal Story of an Irish Feminist* (Dublin: Ward River Press, 1982); Ailbhe Smyth, 'The Contemporary Women's Movement in the Republic of Ireland', *Women's Studies International Forum*, 11, no. 4 (1988), pp. 331-41; *Irish Women into Focus: The Road to Equal Opportunity* (Dublin: Office of the Minister of State for Women's Affairs, n.d.).

11. These distinctions are difficult to make, but, for women whose primary commitment was to feminism, see Leah Levenson and Jerry H. Natterstad, *Hanna Sheehy-Skeffington: A Pioneering Irish Feminist* (Syracuse, N.Y.: Syracuse University Press, 1986); Margaret Mulvihill, *Charlotte Despard: A Biography* (London: Pandora, 1989). For other biographies, see Mary Rose Callaghan, *Kitty O'Shea: A Life of Katherine Parnell* (London: Pandora, 1989); Anne Haverty, *Constance Markievicz: An Independent Life* (London: Pandora, 1988); Gifford Lewis, *Eva Gore-Booth and Esther Roper: A Biography* (London: Pandora, 1988); Margaret Ward, *Maud Gonne, Ireland's Joan of Arc* (London: Pandora, 1990); Charlotte

Fallon, *Soul of Fire: A Biography of Mary MacSwiney* (Cork: Mercier, 1986); Samuel Levenson, *Maud Gonne* (London: Cassell, 1976); Nancy Cardozo, *Maud Gonne: Lucky Eyes and A High Heart* (London: Gollancz, 1979); Diana Norman, *Terrible Beauty: A Life of Constance Markievicz* (London: Hodder and Stoughton, 1987); Irene Ffrench-Eagar, *The Nun of Kenmare* (Cork: Mercier Press, 1970). See also Elizabeth Coxhead, *Daughters of Erin: Five Women of the Irish Renascence* (Gerrards Cross: Colin Smyth, 1979; first published 1965); and Mary McNeill, *The Life and Times of Mary Ann McCracken 1770-1866* (Belfast: Blackstaff Press, 1988; 1st pub. 1960).

    12. Irish Feminist Information, *Missing Pieces: Herstory of Irish Women* (Dublin: Attic Press, 1983); and *More Missing Pieces: Herstory of Irish Women* (Dublin: Attic Press, 1985).

    13. Mary Cullen, 'How Radical was Irish Feminism between 1860 and 1920?', in P. J. Corish (ed.), *Radicals, Rebels and Establishments* (Belfast: Appletree, 1985), pp. 185-201.

    14. Eibhlin Breathnach, 'Women and Higher Education in Ireland, 1879-1910', *Crane Bag*, 4, no. 1 (1980), pp. 47-54; and 'Charting New Waters: Women's Experience in Higher Education 1879-1908', in Mary Cullen (ed.), *Girls Don't Do Honours: Irish Women in Education in the Nineteenth and Twentieth Centuries* (Dublin: Women's Education Bureau, 1987), pp. 55-78.

    15. Anne V. O'Connor, 'Influences Affecting Girls' Secondary Education in Ireland 1860-1910', *Archivium Hibernicum*, 41 (1986), pp. 83-98; and 'The Revolution in Girls' Secondary Education 1860-1910', in Mary Cullen (ed.), *Girls Don't Do Honours*, pp. 31-54; Anne V. O'Connor and Susan M. Parkes, *Gladly Learn and Gladly Teach: A History of Alexandra College and School, Dublin 1866-1966* (Tallaght: Blackwater Press, 1983).

    16. Ph.D thesis, University College, Cork, 1989.

    17. See Maria Luddy, 'Women and Charitable Organisations in Nineteenth-Century Ireland', *Women's Studies International Forum*, 11, no. 4 (1988), pp. 301-5; and M. Luddy, 'Prostitution and Rescue Work in Nineteenth-Century Ireland', in M. Luddy and C. Murphy (eds.), *Women Surviving*, pp. 51-84.

    18. Mary Campbell, *Lady Morgan: The Life and Times of Sydney Owenson* (London: Pandora, 1988).

    19. Anne Chambers, *Granuaile: The Life and Times of Grace O'Malley c.1530-1603* (Dublin: Wolfhound, 1979); and *Eleanor, Countess of Desmond c.1545-1638* (Dublin: Wolfhound, 1987). See also A. Chambers, 'Granuaile: "A Most Famous Feminine Sea Captain"', *Études Irlandaises*, 6 (1981), pp. 101-7, and Maire MacNeill, *Maire Rua, Lady of Leameneh* (County Clare: Ballinakella, 1990).

    20. Donncha Ó Corráin, 'Women in early Irish Society', pp. 1-13; Katharine Simms, 'Women in Norman Ireland', pp. 14-25; Gearoid O Tuathaigh, 'The Role of Women Under the New English Order', pp. 26-36; Joseph Lee, 'Women and the Church since the Famine', pp. 37-45. See also, Katherine Simms, 'The Legal Position of Women in the Later Middle Ages', *Irish Jurist*, new series (1975), pp. 96-111; and Mary Condren, *The Serpent and the Goddess: Women, Religion and Power in Celtic Ireland* (San Francisco: Harper and Row, 1989).

    21. See note 9 above.

    22. Margaret MacCurtain and Mary O'Dowd (eds.), *Women in Early Modern Ireland 1500-1800* (Edinburgh: Edinburgh University Press, 1990).

23. By Dolores Dooley, University College, Cork, and Maria Luddy, University of Warwick, respectively.

24. Art Cosgrove, *Marriage in Ireland* (Dublin: College Press, 1985). Margaret MacCurtain's essay on 'Marriage in Tudor Ireland', pp. 51-66, is particularly informative on women.

25. See note 17 above.

26. See note 19 above.

27. See, for example, Joanna Bourke, 'Women and Poultry in Ireland', *Irish Historical Studies*, 15, no. 9 (May 1987), pp. 293-310; Clare Eager, 'Unequal Opportunity: Women, Employment and Protective Legislation, 1919-1939', *Retrospect* (1988), pp. 11-15; David Fitzpatrick, 'The Modernisation of the Irish Female', in P. O'Flanagan et al. (eds.), *Rural Ireland: Modernisation and Change 1600-1900* (Cork: Cork University Press, 1987), pp. 162-80; Mona Hearn, 'Life for Domestic Servants in Dublin 1880-1920', in M. Luddy and C. Murphy (eds.), *Women Surviving*, pp. 148-79; Betty Messenger, *Picking Up The Linen Threads: Life in Ulster's Mills* (Austin: University of Texas Press, 1978).

28. Jenny Beale, *Women in Ireland: Voices of Change* (Dublin: Gill and Macmillan, 1986); Mary E. Daly, 'Women in the Irish Workforce from Preindustrial to Modern Times', *Saothar*, 7 (1981), pp. 64-82. Imelda Brophy, 'Women in the Workforce', in David Dickson (ed.), *The Gorgeous Mask: Dublin 1700-1850* (Dublin: Trinity College, 1987), pp. 51-63.

29. Mary E. Daly, 'Women, Work and Trade Unionism', in M. MacCurtain and D. Ó Corráin (eds.), *Women in Irish Society*, pp. 71-81; Mary Jones, *'These Obstreporous Lassies': The History of the Irish Women Workers' Union* (Dublin: Gill and Macmillan, 1989); Francis Devine, 'Women in the Irish Trade Unions: A Note', *Oibre: Journal of the Irish Labour History Society*, 2 (July 1975); pp. 1-13; Emily Boyle, 'The Linen Strike of 1872', *Saothar*, 2 (1976), pp. 12-22.

30. See note 4 above.

31. Studies by Maria Luddy, Caitriona Clear, Mary Cullen, Dympna McLoughlin, Mona Hearn respectively.

32. Hasia R. Diner, *Erin's Daughters in America: Irish Immigrant Women in the Nineteenth Century* (Baltimore and London: Johns Hopkins, 1983).

33. See H. R. Diner, *Erin's Daughters*; R. E. Kennedy, *The Irish, Emigration, Marriage and Fertility* (Berkeley: University of California Press, 1973); David Fitzpatrick, 'A Share of the Honeycomb: Education, Emigration and Irishwomen', *Continuity and Change*, 1, no. 2 (1986), pp. 217-34; Pauline Jackson, 'Women in Nineteenth-Century Irish Emigration', *International Migration Review*, 18, no. 4 (1984), pp. 1004-20; M. J. R. O'Brien, 'Cork Women for Australia: Assisted Emigration 1830-1840', *Journal of the Cork Historical and Archaeological Society*, 93, no. 252, pp. 21-9; Joy Rudd, 'Invisible Exports – The Emigration of Women This Century', *Women's Studies International Forum*, 11, no. 4 (1988), pp. 307-311; Portia Robinson, 'From Colleen to Matilda – Irish Women Convicts in Australia 1788-1828', in Colm Kiernan (ed.), *Australia and Ireland: Bicentenary Essays 1788-1988* (Dublin: Gill and Macmillan, 1986), pp. 96-111; Janet A. Nolan, *Ourselves Alone: Women's Emigration from Ireland 1885-1920* (Lexington: Kentucky University Press, 1989); and Ide O'Carroll, *Models for Movers: Irish Women's Emigration to America* (Dublin: Attic Press, 1990). See also, Dympna McLoughlin,

Shovelling Out Paupers: Female Emigration from Irish Workhouses to North America 1840-70 (forthcoming).

34. See notes 13 and 14 above.

35. Caitriona Clear, *Nuns in Nineteenth-Century Ireland* (Dublin: Gill and Macmillan, 1987); 'Walls Within Walls: Nuns in Nineteenth-Century Ireland', in Chris Curtin, Pauline Jackson, and Barbara O'Connor (eds.) *Gender in Irish Society* (Galway: Galway University Press, 1987); 'The Limits of Female Autonomy', in M. Luddy and C. Murphy (eds.), *Women Surviving*, pp. 15-50. For nuns' work, see also, Evelyn Bolster, *The Sisters of Mercy in the Crimean War* (Cork: Mercier Press, 1964), and *The Correspondence of Catherine McAuley 1827-1841* (Cork: Mercier Press, 1989). Frank Hurley, 'Kinsale Nuns in the Crimea: 1854-56', *Kinsale Historical Journal* (1986), pp. 31-6. Irene Ffrench-Eagar, *The Nun of Kenmare*.

36. Tony Fahey, 'Nuns in the Catholic Church in Ireland in the Nineteenth Century', in Mary Cullen (ed.), *Girls Don't Do Honours*, pp. 7-30. For critical assessments of the influence of the Catholic Church on Irish women's lives, see J. Lee, 'Women and the Church since the Famine', and Liam O'Dowd, 'Church, State and Women: The Aftermath of Partition', in C. Curtin, P. Jackson, and B. O'Connor (eds.), *Gender in Irish Society*, pp. 3-36.

37. See notes 11 and 12 above.

38. T. Fahey, 'Nuns in the Catholic Church'.

39. For nuns' experience of spirituality, see Margaret MacCurtain, 'Towards an Appraisal of the Religious Life of Women', *The Crane Bag*, 4, no. 1 (1980), pp. 26-30; and for laywomen's experience, see 'Fulness of Life: Defining Female Spirituality in Twentieth-Century Ireland', in M. Luddy and C. Murphy (eds.), *Women Surviving*, pp. 233-63.

40. For some approaches to women's sexuality, see Jo Murphy-Lawless, 'The Silencing of Women in Childbirth or Let's Hear It For Bartholomew and the Boys', *Women's Studies International Forum*, 11, no. 4 (1988), pp. 293-98; Maria Luddy, 'Prostitution and Rescue Work in Nineteenth-Century Ireland', in M. Luddy and C. Murphy (eds.), *Women Surviving*, pp. 51-84, and Dympna McLoughlin, 'Workhouses and Female Paupers', pp. 117-47. See also, A. Cosgrove (ed.), *Marriage in Ireland*.

41. Mary Cullen, 'Women, History and Identity', *Maynooth Review* (May 1980), pp. 65-79; 'Invisible Women and their Contribution to Historical Studies', *Stáir* (1982), pp. 2-6; and 'Telling it Our Way: Feminist History', in Liz Steiner-Scott (ed.), *Personally Speaking: Women's Thoughts on Women's Issues* (Dublin: Attic Press, 1984); Maria Luddy and Cliona Murphy, '"Cherchez La Femme": The Elusive Woman in Irish History', in M. Luddy and C. Murphy (eds.), *Women Surviving*, pp. 1-14.

25

Women's History in Italy

Paola Di Cori

A brief summary of the main achievements of women's history over the last two decades would need to stress the following points: in a comparatively short space of time, we have succeeded in constructing a new historical subject; sexual difference has entered the previously undisputed territory of masculine historiography, so that the actors who form the objects of historical research have been identified according to their sex; above all, the sexual identity of those who 'make' history – of those who write it, study it, teach it – has been recognised as crucial. We women have dismantled the supposedly neutral viewpoint of historical research, and created a dual perspective where formerly there was only one: re-examining the past, women have affirmed their identity as historical subjects; in the present, women have affirmed themselves as sexed subjects who belong to the historical profession, thus introducing a completely new point of view into the discipline. In short, women's history has confronted historians of both sexes with the issue of their sexual identity, and the relationship between this and their methodology and decisions about what to study.

Feminist historians everywhere have shared common experiences of struggle to achieve these results; they have shared, too, the confrontation with a dominant history which has greeted their efforts with comparative indifference, with paternalism, or, in some cases, with outright hostility. My concern in focusing on the Italian situation will be to highlight those elements which, although not peculiar to Italy, have been decisive in determining a particular form of development for women's history there.[1] The first of these is the state of historical studies in Italy during the period in which women's history was just coming into being. Anyone attempting to do historical research on women in Italy in the early 1970s was faced with problems unknown to her counterparts in England,

444   *Paola Di Cori*

the United States, or France – problems arising out of the backwardness and provincialism which, with isolated exceptions, characterised the whole historical profession in Italy at that time.

The historian Ernesto Galli della Loggia has written a critique of Italian historiography which, although I would disagree with its overall argument, does offer some apt comments on the state of historical research here until quite recently:

> Anyone leafing through a historical journal published in Italy in the 1950s and 1960s, could not fail to be struck by the vagueness and the obviousness of the interpretative frameworks, by an approach which is at once dully academic and coldly ideological, by the disdain for any kind of comparative method – whether geographical or interdisciplinary, by the failure to profit from any other branches of knowledge, apart from a little economics.[2]

This is the situation feminist historians in Italy have inherited, which has inevitably affected the development of women's history in this country. The legacy and use of, as well as conflict with, different national historiographical traditions are always, in my opinion, essential factors in determining the varied characteristics of women's history in different contexts, as well as in deciding whether or not it can move forward.

The second aspect of the Italian situation which I would stress, is the importance traditionally attached to political participation in this country, and the very close relationship between politics, culture, and social commitment of any kind. This complex relationship is rooted in the family and social structures typical of a Mediterranean society like Italy, and has been the subject of numerous anthropological studies on the Mediterranean area.[3] The responsibility of intellectuals in public and political life is a very important theme in Italian history and Italian culture. Until the mid-1970s it would have been nonsense in Italy to consider culture and politics, intellectual work and political commitment as if they were two completely separate domains.

Besides the Gramscian idea of the organic intellectual, so important among Communists and leftists in general, intellectuals have traditionally enjoyed in Italy a high degree of respect and recognition in the public arena, and have been very influential in the media. Several widely known academics have acted as mayors in the 1970s. Massimo Cacciari – a famous philosopher – heads the 1990 election campaign of the Communist Party in Venice. It is very common – and has always been so – that the lead article on the front page of some major newspapers is written by a philosopher, a novelist or a literary critic. The most famous examples in the early 1970s were Pasolini's articles for the daily *Corriere della Sera*. Equally important have been those written on many occasions by Primo Levi, Italo Calvino or Umberto Eco.[4]

Lastly, I would underline the peculiar characteristics of the educational system in this country. For example, among the more industrialised nations, only Italy has not carried out a complete reorganisation of university education in the post-war period. Twenty years after the explosion of 1968, staff and student protests are still a regular occurrence in our universities. The major upheavals have been the student protests of 1977, and the occupations that began in most Italian universities in December 1989. Four aspects of the university system are of particular relevance to us here. There is, firstly, the absence of any organised university curriculum in the humanities, and the practice, instead, of arranging individual study programmes. We should note, too, the lack of any obligation to attend courses, so that students can complete their degrees without ever having attended a lecture or met a faculty member to discuss their work. Thirdly, there is no real disciplinary control over teaching staff, nor is there any control over the quality, quantity, and content of what they teach.[5] Lastly, as regards the power structure within Italian universities, we can cite the comments of an American anthropologist on the Italian academic system: 'The system is centralised and bureaucratised, but nevertheless functions in a personalistic fashion at the local level, with established chair holders (often referred to as barons) having exceptional power'.[6]

I will return later in this article to the various aspects of the Italian situation which I have described above. It is enough here to anticipate some of my points with a brief description of the relationship between these aspects and the situation of women's history in this country. The first aspect (the state of historical studies) is essential for an understanding of the phases of development of women's history in Italy: a first phase characterised mainly by traditional political history; a second phase dominated by a strong feminist ideology; and finally the growth of research in social history and in historical anthropology in the 1980s. The second aspect (the close links between politics and culture) is important for an understanding of how feminist historians (and also feminists doing historical research, which is not necessarily the same thing) were able to establish a research area that, especially at first, developed outside the formal institutions and yet had a relatively wide cultural impact. In fact, for many years, it was only the existence of feminist-run women's centres in all the major Italian cities that enabled us to hold seminars and conferences, publish books and journals, teach, and promote a fertile exchange of ideas about women's history – activities which were completely absent from the formal academic institutions. The third aspect which I described, the educational system, explains some of the more recent features of women's history in Italy: the proliferation of publications, seminars, conferences and courses on women's history inside the universities; the hundreds of theses on issues raised by feminism; and at the same time the total absence of official teaching posts in women's history (the only exception is in the private university Luis in Rome).

Keeping the above points in mind, we can begin to trace the pattern of development of women's history in Italy. It is worth noting that this development, which took place in the second half of the 1970s, coincided with the period of crisis and decline of the feminist consciousness-raising collectives. Although some short articles on historical topics were published in the more popular feminist magazines, such as *Effe*, from 1973 onwards, in contrast to developments in England or the United States, the initial stages of the Italian feminist upsurge of the 1970s were marked by a complete rejection of history, which was perceived as a denial of the female experience.[7] Deeply influenced by the experience of feminism, the earlier studies in women's history were concerned with stressing the ruptures, the periods of discontinuity and suffering, created in human history by the negation and exclusion of women. This approach marks the two most important works to appear in this period: *La Signora del gioco. Episodi della caccia alle streghe* [The Mistress of the Game: Episodes in the Witch Hunts], by Luisa Muraro, and *La Resistenza taciuta. Dodici vite di partigiane piemontesi* [The Hidden Resistance: The Lives of Twelve Piedmontese Women Partisans], edited by Annamaria Bruzzone and Rachele Farina – both published in 1976.[8]

These two books helped to construct what might be termed the 'acknowledgement phase' in women's history. This phase was characterised by three main elements: the identification of the research object; the viewing of this object as a mirror of the self; the affirmation of continuity with a past tradition and of gratitude towards that tradition. In a brief afterword to her book, Luisa Muraro offers a cogent summary of this approach:

> This book was written to honour the memories of women who were tried as witches. I began to study witch trials because I wanted to find answers to certain questions that were troubling me. I wanted to understand the relationship between a woman like me, or like the women I know, beginning with my mother, and everything that has been said about witches and for which witches were put to death. The historians whose books I had read offered no answers to my questions ... it seemed to me that ... [these women] ... through the records of their suffering, were

demanding acknowledgement. It was then that I decided
to write this book. But just as long as I identified with
these women, I was unable to write it. I was prevented by
an impossible desire for justice, and by an insistent,
paralysing, imaginative sympathy. I was able to write only
in moments of detachment; and I wrote for this reason,
too, to separate myself from them.[9]

Although very different from the two books described above, the works
of Franca Pieroni Bortolotti, the only professional historian of an earlier
generation who was to become passionately interested in the issue of
reconstructing a women's history, belong with them in the
'acknowledgement phase'. She published the second volume of her
historical study, *Socialismo e questione femminile in Italia* [Socialism and
the Woman Question in Italy] in 1974, and edited a collection of Anna
Maria Mozzoni's writings the following year. An Italian Communist Party
activist, Franca Pieroni was interested in women's public political
involvement, and her research describes the groups of women involved in
political activity from the second half of the nineteenth century.[10] Another
publication worthy of note in this period was a special edition of the
journal *Problemi del Socialismo*, which contained a collection of historico-
political articles on 'The Woman Question in Italy from the Nineteenth
Century to the Present', with one study of the fascist period written by a
male marxist historian, Enzo Santarelli.[11]

Two different interpretations of women's presence in the past
emerged in this period; each of them resting on and promoting very
different conceptions of 'woman'. They informed two distinct approaches
to women's history, which for a long time found no meeting points. On
one side, as in the cases of Muraro and Bruzzone-Farina, the central
purpose was to explore the difference, the otherness, the specificity of
women, while seeking to ensure that the affirmation of difference served
as more than just a confirmation of women's absence from, or fragmentary
presence within, the historical record, and did not simply perpetuate their
estrangement from it. On the other side, as in the works of Franca Pieroni,
the aim was to affirm and retrace the complex web of a continued female
presence in, and interaction with, the social and political sphere over the
centuries. A long process of combining and refining these two approaches
has provided us with tools of analysis which are now taken for granted
within feminist historiography; these approaches, then, must be credited
with having made current research possible.

Muraro's, Bruzzone-Farina's and, although less obviously,
Pieroni's works are all in some way, and for very different reasons,
'inimitable'. There is, in fact, no direct descent, no real thread running

from them to later feminist historical writing. Leaving aside the question of what we may owe them, this break is very significant because it almost allows us to pick out a date, the precise moment in which women's history in Italy came into being; and, as in any birth event, the crucial feature of this process is one of separation – a gradual distancing from the original matrix.

The years 1976 to 1979, which coincided with the demise of the feminist consciousness-raising collectives, were those in which women's history in Italy acquired a clear identity. This is a difficult process to analyse: its protagonists were still too uncertain in their movements and goals to translate theories and programmes into action, but nevertheless important developments took place that enabled women's history to move well beyond the two distinct approaches which I described earlier.

One fundamental change was in the women who were now entering the historical profession. From the mid-70s, many women of my generation became involved in the feminist movement just at the time they were completing post-graduate studies. We were also witnessing the deepening crisis of Italian historiography, and participating, from far too marginal a position, in the early attempts to bring fresh life into the discipline. We were, in fact, pursuing individual research in complete isolation, within a fragmented university structure where disorganisation contributed to a growing demoralisation.

In the early 1970s, we were teaching courses on general themes raised by feminism – counter-culture seminars in a certain sense. Only in the second half of the decade did we begin to bring together all the questions, issues, and analytical tools that are now a familiar part of historical research on women, and only now, some years later, are we able to gauge the significance of what was to prove a fundamental turning point: the beginning of the process of identification of woman-as-subject with woman-as-object. Within a very short space of time, this process demolished an old and deep-rooted research relationship, and the sexual identity of the historian was recognised as fundamental to the new historical methodology.

The main lines of research that would be developed in the 1980s began to emerge between 1976 and 1979. They involved a few dozen feminist historians, most of them born in the 1940s, who had become teachers in secondary schools or who held either lower-level posts in the universities or temporary research posts. Their research focused on women's political, religious and charitable associations, on oral history, on historical anthropology. Meanwhile, US and British publications on women's history had become more widely available.[12]

In the field of traditional historiography, and largely thanks to the journal *Quaderni Storici*, there was increasing interest in Italy in these years in research on the history of the family, on the relationship between writing and the spoken word, on proto-industrialisation, on popular religion, and so on. The works of E. P. Thompson, and journals like *History Workshop*, *Radical History Review*, and *Annales*, became essential reference points for anyone doing social and economic history in Italy at the end of the 1970s.[13]

In the area of national political debate, the period from 1976 to 1979 saw the dizzy growth and then decline of right- and left-wing terrorism and of the student revolts of 1977. These events, and in particular the assassination of Aldo Moro in 1978, produced a profound identity crisis among intellectuals and a significant change in their traditional relationship with the public sphere. There followed a period of reflection and of widespread disengagement from political activity.[14] This disengagement emerged clearly in the historical writings of the 1980s, characterised, according to a recent study, by a significant move away from the use of history for political ends, and towards a 'history of politics', and by a growing rejection of any ideological purpose in dealing with topics of immediate political relevance.[15]

This shift was mirrored within the feminist movement, in which there were important changes in the nature of women's organisations around the end of the 1970s. Women's history was no longer being produced within the feminist structures that typified the first half of the 1970s, but under very different conditions. As the consciousness-raising collectives declined, there was a growth in women's centres – often funded by local or regional government. These centres became spaces for theoretical elaboration, for cultural and political exchange, and for the transmission of historical knowledge. The first and most important of these centres, the Virginia Woolf Centre, was established in Rome in 1979, and the second in importance was set up in Bologna shortly afterwards; by 1985 there were already more than a hundred such centres in Italy.[16] Articles by feminist historians began to appear in academic historical journals, and seminars on women's history multiplied in the universities.

A whole series of important initiatives and research projects came into being in these years: the publication of *Memoria* – the first women's history journal; a new series of the feminist journal *DWF* (which had been publishing important foreign articles, in translation, since 1975) was produced; a special issue of *Quaderni Storici* on maternity and childbirth, edited entirely by women (another issue of *Quaderni Storici*, on popular religion, contained several contributions from feminists); numerous articles and booklets using oral sources and collecting women's life stories; the publication of at least two important books – Sylvia Franchini's study of Sylvia Pankhurst, and Rina Macrelli's study of the battle against state-regulated prostitution in Italy.[17] It was certainly no coincidence that most of these publications emerged at the same time – at the end of 1980 and the beginning of 1981.

Two conferences held in 1982 – one in Modena on the links between social and political history, biography and autobiography, and one in Bologna on oral history – provided the opportunity to assess the main achievements of women's history in Italy at that time.[18] However, both meetings were bedevilled by difficulties in communication and uncertainty about future plans. The main causes of these difficulties lay in the absence of any institutional legitimacy and the fragility of individual professional identities – a situation common to almost all feminist historians. But the need to find a theoretical and methodological direction was also becoming clearer and clearer, although it was not yet openly discussed.

Gianna Pomata's essay 'La storia delle donne. Una questione di confine [Women's History: A Question of Boundaries]', published at the end of 1983, was an important attempt to respond to these needs by proposing an extremely convincing theoretical model based largely on English feminist research in historical anthropology.[19] Pomata's essay was the first in Italy to offer a carefully constructed theoretical model for women's history, although its excessive reliance on English feminist anthropological scholarship – little known in this country – reduced the opportunity to stimulate a wider debate.[20] Another very positive aspect of Pomata's work was the insistence on interdisciplinarity as a prerequisite of any methodological proposal for women's history, a point which is still at the heart of current international debate on women's history, although from different perspectives, as the discussion around Joan Scott's article on gender has shown. Pomata's article, together with a monograph published in 1985 by Annarita Buttafuoco on the Asilo Mariuccia (an institution founded in the early twentieth century by a group of Milanese feminists to house homeless girls and prostitutes), set in motion a period of intense activity within women's history in Italy.[21] The period 1984 to 1987 saw a rapid growth in public meetings, seminars and collective research projects, as well as an intense renewal of feminist political debate following on the publication of a document produced by the Milan Women's Bookshop (without doubt the most influential feminist group in the country), and the change of leadership and strategy in the PCI Women's Committee.[22]

Another aspect of this growth lay in work on the history of Italian feminism. Following the route opened up by Franca Pieroni Bortolotti, several studies of the history of the Italian women's movement in the second half of the nineteenth and the first half of the twentieth centuries were published between 1985 and 1988, most focusing on the continuity between groups active in the 1870s and those of the decades following 1900.[23]

Once again, we should note that these developments took place on both the cultural and political levels. We could describe women's history in this country as 'amphibious': since the end of the last decade in particular, it has developed within quite distinct areas of work and theoretical elaboration, which sometimes intermingled and sometimes existed side by side. It has remained outside the main areas of feminist activity and debate, yet at the same time has operated within the feminist movement. For many years now, we have witnessed the parallel development of teaching and research programmes both within the universities and in the many women's centres active throughout the country. Women's history has existed both inside and outside the feminist publishing houses. Alongside the growth of publications by feminist presses, there has been an increase in the numbers of articles on women's history accepted in academic publications that until recently would have rejected any such contribution just because of its suspected connections with feminism.

The most exciting initiatives and achievements over the last ten years have undoubtedly occurred outside the formal institutions, and we are only now seeing the beginnings of some level of legitimacy within the universities. This situation does highlight the undeniable fragility of our relationship with the formal institutions, but at the same time it has enabled our historiography to avoid the excessive rigidity and academicism that have often characterised women's history in other countries.

The enormous vitality that this area of study undoubtedly possesses was demonstrated very clearly by the first Italian women's history conference held at Bologna University History Department in 1986; by the first feminist studies conference that took place at Modena University Department of Political Economy in March 1987; and by an exhibition in Siena, also in March 1987, of visual and written material on women's education in nineteenth-century Italy.[24] Even more recently, feminist historians have come to deal with the regional dimensions of women's history. In April 1989 a conference devoted to women in Lombardy was held in Milan.[25]

It was after these initiatives in particular, and after many later ones which have been important but have had less of an impact, that we can describe women's history and its protagonists in Italy as having reached intellectual and political maturity. I will add, finally, that a recent important step in this process of growth has been the creation, in February 1989, of the Italian Association of Women Historians, which has seventy-one founding members. The Association is based in Bologna and publishes the bulletin *Agenda*; in October 1989 it held a conference on 'Subjectivity, Research, Biography' in Florence.[26] Around 40 per cent of the Association's members are university lecturers; the rest are school teachers, librarians and students. As well as doing historical research, they are involved in organising summer courses on women's history and initiating proposals for change in the school history curriculum and for the introduction of women's history courses at the university level.[27]

Given the lack of academic power and influence, it would not be appropriate to feel a high degree of optimism for the future. Yet it would be equally inappropriate to be too pessimistic. The birth of the Association is a sign that in the last few years its members have acquired far greater professional confidence, and no longer feel torn between feminist and professional commitments, as historians devoted to women's history. In the past decade women's history in Italy has been able, in coming of age, to turn a true weakness within the academy into a relatively strong presence outside it. Yet, this achievement has also had some problematic side-effects. One of the most serious consequences of the academic weakness has been the difficulty feminist historians face in establishing a reciprocally stimulating dialogue with young students. Frozen into low-level and part-time university jobs, Italian women's historians of the 1970s generation have found it very hard to transmit the best of their own tradition to the younger generation.

It is hard to say which will be the more appropriate strategy for the 1990s. I would personally recommend, on the grounds of past experience, a greater degree of flexibility in politics, theory, and empirical research, and a more productive exchange between these three inextricably interrelated areas of feminist experience.

NOTES

This is an updated and partially revised version of the article: 'Prospettive e soggetti nella storia delle donne. Alla ricerca di radici comuni [Issues and Subjects in Women's History: In Search of our Roots]', published in Maria Cristina Marcuzzo and Anna Rossi-Doria (eds.), *La ricerca delle donne. Studi femministi in Italia* [Research by Women: Feminist Studies in Italy] (Turin: Rosenberg & Sellier, 1987). For this volume, the text has been translated from the Italian by Margaret Fraser.

1. The two journals *DWF* and *Memoria* provide the best sources of information on developments and debates within women's history in Italy. *DWF*, which first appeared in 1975, was published in four separate series; from 1976 to 1986 it was published under the name *Nuova DWF*, reverting to its old name with the most recent series in 1986. *Memoria*, subtitled *A Journal of Women's History*, was first published in 1981. The most relevant issues of *DWF* are: 3 (April-June 1977) 'Donna e ricerca storica [Women and Historical Research]'; 10-11 (January-June 1979), 'Solidarietà, amicizia, amore [Solidarity, Friendship, Love]'; 15 (Winter 1981), 'Il luogo delle ipotesi. Femminismo e conoscenze [A Space for Hypotheses:

Feminism and Knowledge]'; 21 (1982), 'Politica e cultura nella stampa emancipazionista (1861-1924) [Politics and Culture in the Feminist Press (1861-1924)]'. There are historical articles in every issue of *Memoria*; issue 9 (dated 1983 but only appearing in the autumn of 1984) was dedicated to feminist historiography and had the title 'Sulla storia delle donne. Dieci anni di miti ed esperienze [On Women's History: The Ideals and Experiences of the Past Ten Years]'. The following special issues of the journal *Quaderni Storici* are also important: 41 (1979), 'Religioni delle classi popolari [Popular Religion]'; 44 (1980), 'Parto e maternità. Momenti della biografia femminile [Childbirth and Maternity: Stages in Women's Life-Story]'; 53 (1983), 'Sistemi di carità [Charitable Institutions]'; 55 (1984), 'Calamità paure risposte [Attitudes and Responses to Disasters]'; 68 (1988), 'Servi e serve [Male and Female Servants]'.

For nineteenth and twentieth century women's history, see Paola Pirzio's survey articles: 'Donne nella politica e nella storia [Women in Politics and History]', *Italia Contemporanea*, 148 (September 1982) pp. 81-96, and *Rivista di storia contemporanea*, 1 (1985). There are useful bibliographies in Ginevra Conti Odorisio, *Storia dell'idea femminista in Italia* [A History of Feminist Thought] (Turin: ERI, 1980), and Marima Addis Saba et al. (eds.), *Storia delle donne una scienza possibile* [Is a Women's History Possible?] (Rome: Felina, 1986). Two recent articles are: Lucetta Scaraffia, 'Essere uomo, essere donna [Being a Man, Being a Woman]', in Piero Melograni (ed.), *La famiglia italiana dall'Ottocento a oggi* (Bari: Laterza, 1988), and Francesca Romana Koch, 'Le donne dal dopoguerra ad oggi [Women since the Second World War]', in *Storia della società italiana*, vol. 25 (Milan: Teti, forthcoming).

2. Ernesto Galli della Loggia, 'Una storiografia indifferente [Indifferent History]', *Il mulino*, 306 (July-August 1986), pp. 586-601.

3. See John Davis, *People of the Mediterranean* (London: Routledge, 1977); and Shmuel Noah Eisenstadt and Luis Roniger, *Patrons, Clients and Friends: Interpersonal Relations and the Structure of Trust in Society* (Cambridge: Cambridge University Press, 1984).

4. See especially: Norberto Bobbio, 'Intellettuali e vita politica in Italia [Intellectuals and Political Life in Italy]', in *Politica e Cultura* (Turin: Einaudi, 1955); Ernesto Galli della Loggia, 'Ideologie, classi e costume [Ideologies, Classes and Behaviour]', in Valerio Castronovo et al. (eds.), *L'Italia Contemporanea 1945-75* (Turin: Einaudi, 1976); Giulio Bollati, 'Peripezie italiane di politica e cultura [The Vicissitudes of Politics and Culture in Italy]', in *L'Italiano* (Turin: Einaudi, 1983); for a longer-term perspective, see the collection of articles in 'Intellettuali e potere [Intellectuals and Power]', *Storia d'Italia*, vol. 4 (Turin: Einaudi, 1981).

5. Roberto Moscati, *Università: fine o trasformazione del mito?* [The University: The Myth Transformed or Ended?], (Bologna: Il Mulino, 1983).

6. George R. Saunders, 'Contemporary Italian Cultural Anthropology', *Annual Review of Anthropology* (1984), pp. 447-465.

7. Two anthologies of sources are essential as introductions to these questions: Rosalba Spagnoletti (ed.), *I movimenti femministi* [The Feminist Movements] (Rome: Savelli, 1978), and Biancamaria Frabotta (ed.), *Femminismo e lotta di classe in Italia (1970-1973)* [Feminism and Class Struggle in Italy (1970-1973)]; see also the volumes of the *Lessico politico delle donne* [The Women's Political Dictionary] (Milan: Gulliver, 1979).

8. Luisa Muraro, *La Signora del gioco. Episodi della caccia alle streghe* [The Mistress of the Game: Episodes in the Witch Hunts] (Milan: Feltrinelli, 1976); Anna Maria Bruzzone and Rachele Farina (eds.), *La Resistenza taciuta. Dodici vite di partigiane piemontesi* [The Hidden Resistance: The Lives of Twelve Piedmontese Women Partisans] (Milan: La Pietra, 1976).

9. Muraro, *Signora del Gioco*, p. 237.

10. On Franca Pieroni, see Paola Di Cori, 'Franca Pieroni Bortolotti: una storia solitaria [Franca Pieroni Bortolotti: A Lonely History]', *Memoria*, 16 (1986), pp. 135-8, and my review of Pieroni's *Sul movimento politico delle donne. Scritti inediti* [On Women's Political Movements: Unpublished Writings] (Rome: Utopia, 1987), in *Gender & History*, 1, no. 2 (Summer 1989), pp. 234-6. Bortolotti's major works were: *Alle origini del movimento femminile in Italia, 1848-1892* [The Origins of the Women's Movement in Italy, 1848-1892] (Turin: Einaudi, 1963); *Socialismo e questione femminile in Italia, 1892-1922* [Socialism and the Woman Question in Italy, 1892-1922] (Milan: Mazzotta, 1974); an edited volume of writings by Anna Maria Mozzoni, *La liberazione della donna* [Women's Liberation] (Milan: Mazzotta, 1975); *Femminismo e partiti politici in Italia 1919-1926* [Feminism and Political Parties in Italy 1919-1926] (Rome: Edition Riuniti, 1978); *La donna, la pace, l'Europa. L'associazione internazionale delle donne dalle origini alla prima guerra mondiale* [Women, Peace, and Europe: International Association among Women from Its Origins to the First World War] (Milan: Franco Angeli, 1985).

11. Enzo Santarelli, 'Il fascismo e le ideologie antifemministe [Fascism and Anti-feminist Ideology]', *Problemi del socialismo*, special issue on 'La questione femminile in Italia dal '900 ad oggi [The Woman Question in Italy from 1900 to the Present]', 4 (October-December 1976), pp. 75-106, published separately in 1977 under the same title (Milan: Franco Angeli, 1977).

12. See especially the issues of *Nuova DWF* in this period.

13. See in particular Arnaldo Momigliano, 'Linee per una valutazione della storiografia nel quindecennio 1961-1976 [Towards an Evaluation of Historical Research: 1961-1976]', *Rivista storica italiana*, (September-December 1977), pp. 728-751; Ruggiero Romano, *La storiografia italiana oggi* [Italian Historiography Today] (Milan: Espresso-Strumenti, 1978); and the collection of articles in Pietro Rossi (ed.), *La storiografia contemporanea. Indirizzi e problemi* [Themes and Problems in Contemporary Italian Historiography] (Milan: Il Saggiatore, 1987).

14. I have dealt with the issue of the relationship between disengagement in politics, the birth of women's history, and the problem of the historian's subjectivity in Paola Di Cori, 'Soggetività e pratica storica [Subjectivity and Historical Practice]', *Movimento operaio e socialista*, 1-2 (1987), pp. 77-90.

See also Luigi Manconi, *Vivere con il terrorismo* [Living with Terrorism] (Milan: Mondadori, 1980); Gianfranco Pasquino (ed.), *Il sistema politico italiano* [The Italian Political System] (Bari: Laterza, 1985); and David Moss, *The Politics of Left-Wing Violence in Italy 1969-85* (Basingstoke: Macmillan, 1989). For the crisis within the left, see Ernesto Galli della Loggia et al. (eds.), *Il Trionfo del privato* [The Triumph of the Private] (Bari: Laterza, 1980), and the various contributions in *Il concetto di sinistra* [The Left as a Concept] (Milan: Bompiani, 1982).

15. See Piero Bevilacqua, 'Storia della politica o uso politico della storia? [The History of Politics, or the Political Uses of History?]', *Meridiana*, 3 (1988), pp. 165-82.

16. See *Le donne al Centro. Politica e cultura dei Centri delle donne negli anni '80* [Women at the Centre: The Politics and Culture of Women's Centres in the 1980s] (Rome: Utopia, 1988).

17. See references in notes 1, 2 and 18, and also Silvia Franchini, *Sylvia Pankhurst 1912-24: Dal suffragismo alla rivoluzione sociale* [Sylvia Pankhurst 1912-24: From Women's Suffrage to Social Revolution] (Pisa: Ets, 1980); and Rina Macrelli, *L'indegna schiavitù. Anna Maria Mozzoni e la lotta contro la prostituzione di Stato* [This Hateful Bondage: Anna Maria Mozzoni and the Battle Against State-Regulated Prostitution] (Rome: Editori Riuniti, 1981).

18. The conference papers have been published respectively in *Percorsi del femminismo e storia delle donne* [Developments in Feminism and Women's History], supplement to *Nuova DWF*, 22 (1983), and in *Fonti orali e politica delle donne: storia ricerca, racconto* [Oral Sources and Women's Politics: History, Research, Narratives] (Bologna: Centro di documentazione delle donne, 1983).

19. Gianna Pomata, 'La storia delle donne. Una questione di confine [Women's History: A Question of Boundaries]', in *Il mondo contemporaneo: Gli strumenti della ricerca. Questioni di metodo* [The Modern World: Research Tools and Methodological Issues], vol. 2, part 2 (Florence: La Nuova Italia, 1983).

20. See the debate on Pomata's essay, with contributions from Paola Di Cori, Giulia Calvi, Simonetta Piccone Stella, and Maria Arioti, published in *Memoria*, 9 (1984), pp. 50-61.

21. Annamaria Buttafuoco, *Le Mariuccine. Storia di un'istituzione laica. L'asilo Mariuccia* [The Mariuccia Girls: The History of a Lay Institution – the Mariuccia Refuge] (Milan: Angeli, 1985).

22. On the recent political debates within Italian feminism, see Yasmine Ergas, *Nelle maglie della politica* [Enmeshed in Politics] (Milan: Angeli, 1986); 'Il movimento femminista negli anni 70 [Feminism in the 1970s]', a special issue of *Memoria*, 19-20 (1988); see also the collective volume *Esperienza storica femminile nell'età moderna e contemporanea* [Women in Early Modern and Modern History], part 2 (Rome: Unione Donna Italiane-Circolo 'La Goccia' Roma, 1989). A recent paper by Teresa de Lauretis deals extensively with the theoretical and political issues raised in these debates. See her 'The Essence of the Triangle or, Taking the Risk of Essentialism Seriously: Feminist Theory in Italy, the U.S. and Britain', *Differences*, 1, no.2 (Summer 1989), pp. 3-37.

23. See Annarita Buttafuoco, *Cronache femminili. Temi e momenti della stampa emancipazionista in Italia dall' unità al fascismo* [Women's Reports: Issues in the Emancipation Press in Italy from the 1860s to Fascism] (Arezzo: Università degli studi di Siena, 1988), and two articles concerning the legislation on women's suffrage by Mariapia Bigaran, 'Progetti e dibattiti parlamentari sul suffragio femminile: da Peruzzzi a Giolitti [Parliamentary projects and debates on women's suffrage: from Peruzzi to Giolitti], *Rivista di storia contemporanea*, 1 (January 1985), pp. 50-82, and 'Il voto alle donne in Italia dal 1912 al fascismo [Women's suffrage in Italy from 1912 to fascism]', *Rivista di storia contemporanea*, 2 (April 1987), pp. 240-265. In an earlier article, I focused on Catholic organisations in the first decades of the twentieth century, arguing that the loss of memory of a strong first wave of feminism in Italian history is partly due to the strength and influence of powerful Catholic groups. They were in fact the only non-fascist organisations allowed to survive under the Mussolini regime. See Paola Di Cori, 'Storia,

sentimenti, solidarietà nelle organizzazioni femminili cattoliche dall'età giolittiana al fascismo [History, Sentiment, Solidarity in Female Catholic Organisations from the Giolitti Era to Fascism]', *Nuova DWF*, 10-11 (January-June 1979), pp. 80-124. See also, more recently, the collective volume, *Esperienza storica femminile*, cited above in note 22.

24. See Lucia Ferrante, Maura Palazzi, and Gianna Pomata (eds.), *Ragnatele di rapporti. Patronage e reti di relazione nella storia delle donne* [Patronage and Networks in Women's History] (Turin: Rosenberg & Sellier, 1988); contributions by Alain Boureau, Edoardo Grendi, and Sofia Boesch Gajano to *Quaderni Storici*, 3 (December 1989); Marcuzzo and Rossi-Doria (eds.), *La ricerca delle donne*; Silvia Franchini, 'L'istruzione femminile in Italia dopo l' Unità: percorsi di una ricerca sugli educandati pubblici di élite [Women's Education in Italy after Unification: A Research Project on the Elite Public Boarding Schools for Girls], *Passato e presente*, 10 (January-April 1986), pp. 53-94; and the various contributions on 'L'educazione delle donne all'indomani dell'Unità. Un problema a molte dimensioni [Women's Education after Unification: A Multi-Dimensional Issue], *Passato e presente*, 17 (May-August 1988), pp. 11-36.

For further information on these initiatives, see Paola Di Cori, 'Le dimensioni della memoria [Dimensions of Memory]', in Maria Rosa Cutrufelli (ed.), *Scritture, scrittrici* (Milan: Longanesi, 1988).

25. The conference was on 'Donna Lombarda. Un secolo di vita femminile [Lombard Woman. A Century in Women's Lives]'. See the catalogue of the exhibition with the same title (Milan: Electa, 1989), especially the two introductory articles by Annarita Buttafuoco, 'Uno specchio dotato di memoria. Note su fotografia e storia delle donne in margine alla mostra [A Mirror with Memory. Notes on Photography and Women's History]', and Roberta Valtorta, 'Figure di donne: una lettura [Female Figures: A Reading]. See also the catalogue of another Milan exhibition on women's historical experience in Italy and Europe, Rachele Farina (ed.), *Esistere come donna* [To exist as a woman] (Milan: Mazzotta, 1983); and the catalogue and articles accompanying an exhibition on Venetian female workers in the pearl industry, Anna Bellavitis, Nadia Maria Filippini, and Maria Teresa Sega (eds.), *Perle e impiraperle. Un lavoro di donne a Venezia tra '800 e '900* [Pearls and Pearl-threaders. A Woman's Occupation in Venice at the Turn of the Century] (Venice: Arsenale, 1990).

26. See the Società Italiana delle Storiche [Italian Association of Women Historians], *Agenda*, 0 (1989). The conference papers, including my own on 'Soggettività e storia delle donne [Subjectivity and Women's History]' have been published in Anna Scattigno and Maura Palazzi (eds.), *Discutendo di storia* [Debating History] (Turin: Rosenberg & Sellier, 1990),

27. See the proposal for a secondary school teaching unit in 'Le donne in Italia negli anni Cinquanta [Women in Italy in the 1950s]', in *I viaggi di Erodoto*, 9 (1989), pp. 180-92, edited by Gruppo di lavoro dell'IRSIFAR.

26

Women, Gender, and Family in the Soviet Union and Central/East Europe: A Preliminary Bibliography

Mary F. Zirin

Major contributions to this bibliography have been made by Irina Corten (Soviet and Russian entries), Rachel Mann (South Slavic sociology and folklore), and Andrea Feldman (Yugoslavia). Many of the citations first appeared in *Women: East – West,* a newsletter of Slavic women's studies sponsored by the Association for Women in Slavic Studies.

Table of Contents

General Background

Imperial Russia and the Soviet Union

457

458   *Mary F. Zirin*

V. Arts in Russia and the USSR

Central and East Europe

> General
> Bulgaria
> Czechoslovakia
> German Democratic Republic
> Hungary
> Poland
> Rumania
> Yugoslavia

Abbreviations Used:

MERSH	-	Modern Encyclopedia of Russian and Soviet History
MERSL	-	Modern Encyclopedia of Russian and Soviet Literature
MLA	-	Modern Language Association (annual bibliographies)
RLT	-	Russian Literature Triquarterly
SEEJ	-	Slavic and East European Journal
SEER	-	Slavonic and East European Review
SR	-	Slavic Review

General Background

Boxer, Marilyn J. and Jean H. Quataert (eds.). *Socialist Women: European Socialist Feminism in the Nineteenth and Early Twentieth Centuries.* New York: Elsevier, 1978.

Braun, Lily. *Selected Writings on Feminism and Socialism.* Alfred G. Meyer, tr. & ed. Bloomington: Indiana University Press, 1987. The selections are drawn from books and articles that Braun published between 1895 and 1912. Topics covered include women and work, women and politics, feminism, sexuality, family life.

Gimbutas, Marija. *The Goddesses and Gods of Old Europe, 6500-3500 B.C.: Myths and Cult Images.* Berkeley: University of California Press,

1982. Documentation of the prevalence of goddess worship and matrifocal culture in pre-Indo-European society.

Jančar, Barbara Wolfe. *Women Under Communism*. Baltimore, MD: John Hopkins Press, 1978.

Levin, Eve. *Sex and Society in the World of the Orthodox Slavs, 900-1700*. Ithaca, NY: Cornell University Press, 1989. '. . . Levin explores sexual behaviour among the peoples of Serbia, Bulgaria, and Russia from their conversion to Christianity in the ninth and tenth centuries until the end of the seventeenth century'.

Michaelson, Evalyn J. and Walter Goldschmidt. 'Female Roles and Male Dominance Among Peasants'. *Southwestern Journal of Anthropology*, 27 (1971), pp. 330-52.

Pruska-Carroll, Malgorzata. 'Women's Studies in the Slavic World'. *SEEJ*, 23, no. 2 (1979), pp. 325-7.

Rueschemeyer, Marilyn. *Professional Work and Marriage: An East-West Comparison*. New York: St. Martin's Press, 1986.

Women in the First and Second World Wars: A Checklist of the Holdings of the Hoover Institution on War, Revolution and Peace. Helena Wedborn, comp. Stanford, CA: Hoover Institution Press, 1988.

Imperial Russia and the Soviet Union

I.   *Bibliography and Reviews of the Literature.*

Engel, Barbara Alpern. 'Women in Russia and the Soviet Union', *Signs*, 12, no. 4 (Summer 1987), pp. 781-96. A review essay of recent work in the field.

Manning, Roberta F. 'Bibliography of Works in English on Women in Russia and the Soviet Union: A Guide for Students and Teachers'. *Slavic and European Education Review*, 1 (1979), pp. 31-62.

Women and Writing in Russia and the USSR. Diane Nemec-Ignashev and S. Krive comps. Northfield, NM: Carlton College, n.d. Particularly valuable in its breakdown of articles in journals, anthologies and collections. It is available from: Department of German/Russian, Carleton College, 1 North College, Northfield, MN 55057.

Women in Russia and the Soviet Union. Tova Yedlin and J. Wilman, comps. Institute of Soviet and East European Studies, Bibliography No. 3. Ottawa: Carleton University, 1985.

II. *History and Culture* (See also Autobiography, section IV below.)

Alexander, John T. *Catherine the Great: Life and Legend.* Oxford University Press, 1988.

Atkinson, Dorothy, Alexander Dallin and Gail Warshofsky Lapidus (eds.). *Women in Russia.* Stanford, CA: Stanford University Press, 1977. A wealth of valuable information, ranging from historical studies to the contemporary position of women in the professions and higher education, women and sex in Soviet law, and women in Soviet politics.

Bergman, Jay. *Vera Zasulich: A Biography.* Stanford: Stanford University Press, 1983. An analysis of this famous woman revolutionary's ideology and a compelling account of her life amidst the conflicts and tensions of revolutionary politics.

Bohac, Rodney. 'Russian Peasant Inheritance Strategies'. *Journal of Interdisciplinary History*, 16 (Summer 1985), pp. 23-42.

Bohachevsky-Chomiak, Martha. *Feminists Despite Themselves: Women in Ukrainian Community Life, 1884-1939.* Englewood CT.: Ukrainian Academic Press, 1987. 'The first history of the women's movement in the Ukraine. The book reveals that Ukrainian women, constrained by national and traditional issues, began to develop self-help organisations in their rural communities. It analyses a vast range of material, encompassing Ukrainian women in the Russian and Austrian Empires, the national liberation struggle, the interwar period, international feminism, and Ukrainian women in the Soviet Union'.

-----. 'Feminism in Ukrainian History'. *Journal of Ukrainian Studies*, 12 (Spring 1982), pp. 16-30.

Brennan, James F. *Enlightened Despotism in Russia: The Reign of Elisabeth, 1741-1762.* New York: Peter Lang, 1987.

Broido, Vera. *Apostles into Terrorists: Women and the Revolutionary Movement in the Russia of Alexander II*. London: Maurice Temple Smith, 1977.

Chernyshevsky, Nikolai. *What Is to Be Done?* Michael R. Katz, tr., William G. Wagner, annot., Michael Katz and William Wagner, intro. Ithaca, N.Y: Cornell University Press, 1989. At last teachers have an unbowdlerized edition in English from which to teach Chernyshevsky's peculiar recipe for re-making Russian woman.

Clements, Barbara Evans. 'The Enduring Kinship of the Baba and the Bolshevik Woman'. *Soviet Union*, 12, no. 2 (1985), pp. 161-84.

-----. 'The Birth of the New Soviet Woman'. *Bolshevik Culture: Experiment and Order in the Russian Revolution*. In Abbott Gleason, Peter Kenez, and Richard Stites, (eds.) *Bolshevik Culture: Experiment and Order in the Russian Revolution*. Bloomington: Indiana University Press, 1985, pp. 220-37.

-----. 'Working Class and Peasant Women in the Russian Revolution, 1919-1923'. *Signs*, 8, no. 2 (1982), pp. 215-35.

-----. 'Bolshevik Women: The First Generation'. In Yedlin (ed.). *Women in Eastern Europe and the Soviet Union*. See below, section III.

-----. *Bolshevik Feminist: The Life of Alexandra Kollontai*. Bloomington: Indiana University Press, 1979. Kollontai's ideas and the milieu in which she was operating are depicted clearly and objectively.

-----. 'Alexandra Kollontai: Libertine or Feminist?' In Carter Elwood (ed.). *Reconsiderations on the Russian Revolution*. Columbus OH: Slavica, 1976, pp. 242-55.

-----. 'Kollontai's Contribution to the Workers' Opposition'. *Russian History*, 2, no. 2 (1975), pp. 191-206.

-----. 'Emancipation through Communism: The Ideology of A. M. Kollontai'. *Slavic Review*, 32, no. 2 (June 1973), pp. 323-38.

----- and Colette Shulman. *Women of the Soviet Union*. Brunswick, NJ: Transaction Books, 1987.

Cottam, K. J. *Soviet Airwomen in Combat in World War II*. Manhattan KS: MA/AH Publishing, 1983. 'Cottam... shows respect for the reader by avoiding the cliches of cultural stereotyping that androcentric historiography imposes upon women in non-traditional roles.... All in all, [she] presents the reader with a military history that is also a valuable contribution to women's history' (From a review by N. J. Stewart-Smith, *Minerva*, (Summer 1984), pp. 77-79.)

-----. 'Soviet Women in Combat in World War II: The Rear Services, Resistance Behind Enemy Lines and Political Workers'. *International Journal of Women's Studies*, 5, no. 4 (September/October 1982), pp. 363-378.

-----. 'Soviet Women in Combat in World War II: The Ground Forces and the Navy'. *International Journal of Women's Studies*, 3, no. 4 (July/August 1980), pp. 345-55.

-----. 'Soviet Women in Combat in World War II: The Ground Air Defence Forces'. In Tova Yedlin (ed.). *Women in Eastern Europe and the Soviet Union*. See below, section III.

Coughlan, Robert. *Elizabeth and Catherine: Empresses of All the Russias*. New York: Putnam, 1974.

Curtiss, John S. 'Russian Sisters of Mercy in the Crimea, 1854-1855'. *SR*, 25, no. 1 (March 1966), pp. 84-100.

Dan, Lidia. *From the Archives of L. O. Dan: Selected, Annotated and with an Outline of Dan's Autobiography*. Boris Sapir, ed. Amsterdam: Stichting International Instituut voor Sociale Heschieden, 1988.

Donald, Moira. 'Bolshevik Activity Amongst the Working Women of Petrograd in 1917'. *International Review of Social History*, 27 (1982), pp. 129-60.

Dunn, Patrick P. '"That Enemy Is the Baby": Childhood in Imperial Russia'. In Lloyd deMause (ed.). *History of Childhood*. New York: Psychohistory Press, 1974, pp. 383-405.

Edmondson, Linda. *Feminism in Russia, 1900-1917*. Stanford University Press, 1984. The non-revolutionary feminists' campaign for women's rights from its beginnings in the late 19th century, through the movement's politicisation in 1905, to the Bolshevik triumph in 1917, which silenced the last bourgeois feminists.

-----. 'Russian Feminists and the First All-Russian Congress of Women'. *Russian History*, 3, no. 2 (1976), pp. 123-49.

Elnett, Elaine P. *Historic Origin and Social Development of Family Life in Russia*. New York: Columbia University Press, 1926. A survey of Russian family life and the role of women from prehistoric times through the second half of the 19th century.

Engel, Barbara Alpern. 'The Woman's Side: Male Out-Migration and the Family Economy in Kostroma Province'. *SR*, 45, no. 2 (Summer 1986), pp. 257-71.

-----. *Mothers and Daughters: Women of the Intelligentsia in Nineteenth-Century Russia*. Cambridge: Cambridge University Press, 1983. This well-researched study covers the period of Nicholas I to Alexander II, with particular emphasis on the 1860s and 1870s, focussing on the experiences of women involved in the Russian populist and terrorist movements.

-----. 'Mothers and Daughters: Family Patterns and the Female Intelligentsia'. In David L. Ransel (ed.). *The Family in Imperial Russia*. Champaign-Urbana: University of Illinois Press, 1978, pp. 44-59.

Engelstein, Laura. 'Morality and the Wooden Spoon: Russian Physicians View Syphilis, Social Class, and Sexual Behavior, 1890-1905'. *Representations*, 14 (1986), pp. 169-208. Reprinted in Catherine Gallagher and Thomas Laqueur (eds.). *The Making of the Modern Body: Sexuality and Society in the Nineteenth Century*. Berkeley: University of California Press, 1987.

Farnsworth, Beatrice. 'The Litigious Daughter-in-Law: Family Relations in Rural Russia in the Second Half of the Nineteenth Century'. *SR*, 45, no. 1 (Spring 1986), pp. 49-64.

-----. 'Village Women Experience the Revolution'. In Abbott Gleason, Peter Kenez, and Richard Stites (eds.). *Bolshevik Culture: Experiment and Order in the Russian Revolution*. Bloomington: Indiana University Press, 1985.

464	Mary F. Zirin

-----. *Aleksanda Kollontai. Socialism, Feminism, and the Bolshevik Revolution.* Stanford: Stanford University Press, 1980. A solid, well-written piece of scholarship. The author does an excellent job of relating Kollontai's political career to broader trends in the socialist and feminist movements of her day.

Fieseler, Beate. 'In a Female Voice: Good Morning, Russia! Eindrucke und Einsichten vom Kongress *Women in the History of the Russian Empire* [Impressions and Insights from the Conference *Women in the History of the Russian Empire*]', University of Akron and Kent State University, USA, August 1988. *IWK* [Internationale wissenschaftliche Korrespondez zur Geschichte der Arbeiterbewegung], 24, no. 4 (1988), pp. 539-51.

-----. 'Russische Sozialdemokratinnen 1890-1917 [Russian Social-Democrat Women 1890-1917]'. *IWK*, (September 1985), pp. 308-25.

-----. '"Dienst am Volk" oder revolutionäre Massenbewegung: Intelligencija-Frauen und Arbeiterinnen in städtischen Zirkeln Russlands, 1870-1900 ["Service to the People" or the Revolutionary Mass Movement: Women of the Intelligentsia and Working Women in Urban Circles of Russia, 1870-1900]'. *Archiv für die Geschichte des Widerstandes und der Arbeit*, 7 (1985), pp. 89-100.

Friedrich, Paul. 'Semantic Structure and Social Structure: An Instance from Russian'. In Ward Goodenough (ed.). *Explorations in Cultural Anthropology*. New York: McGraw-Hill, 1964. A rich article exploring traditional Russian culture through kinship terms.

Frierson, Cathy A., 'Razdel: The Peasant Family Divided'. *Russian Review*, 46, (1987), pp. 35-52.

Frumkin, Jacob, et al. *Russian Jewry 1860-1917.* Mirra Ginsburg, tr. New York: 1960.

Geiger, K. *The Family in Soviet Russia.* Cambridge MA: Harvard University Press, 1968.

Glickman, Rose L. *Russian Factory Women. Workplace and Society, 1880-1914.* Berkeley: University of California Press, 1984. An incisive, detailed account of the lives of Russian factory women during the formative years of Russian industrial capitalism.

Goldman, Wendy. 'Freedom and Its Consequences: The Debate on the Soviet Family Code of 1926'. *Russian History*, 11, no. 4 (1984), pp. 362-88.

Goldstein, Darra. *A la Russe: A Cookbook of Russian Hospitality*. New York: Random House, 1983. Materials on Russian food in culture and literature.

Haimson, Leopold, with Ziva Galili y Garcia and Richard Wortman. *The Making of Three Russian Revolutionaries: Voices from the Menshevik Past*. Cambridge: Cambridge University Press, 1987. Life histories, drawn from personal interviews, of three prominent Mensheviks, including Lydia Dan.

Halle, Fannina. *Women in Soviet Russia*. London: Routledge, 1933. The first three chapters are a historical survey of Russian women up to the Soviet period. The rest of the study is devoted to the revolutionary movement and the emancipation of women in the 1920s and early 1930s. The author is a feminist.

Heldt, Barbara. '*Rassvet (1859-1862) and the Woman Question*'. *SR*, 36, no. 1 (March 1977), pp. 76-85.

Hubbs, Joanna. *Mother Russia: The Feminine Myth in Russian Culture*. Bloomington: Indiana University Press, 1988. Hubbs shows 'that traditional Russian society was women-centered in its divinities, folklore, art, and social organization. She explores the masculine response to the feminine myth, and reveals how, as Russian society grew increasingly patriarchal, among the peasantry, pagan matrifocal beliefs persisted'.

-----. 'The Worship of Mother Earth in Russian Culture'. In James T. Preston (ed.). *Mother Worship: Themes and Variations*. Chapel Hill: University of North Carolina Press, 1982.

Hughes, Lindsey A. J. 'Sophia, "Autocrat of All the Russias": Titles, Ritual and Eulogy in the Regency of Sophia Alekseevna'. *Canadian Slavonic Papers*, 28, no. 3 (September 1986), 266-86.

-----. 'Sophia Alekseyevna and the Moscow Rebellion of 1682'. *Slavonic & East European Review*, 63, no. 4 (1985), pp. 518-39.

-----. 'Sophia, Regent of Russia'. *History Today*, 32 (July 1982), pp. 10-15.

-----. 'Sophia Alekseevna'. *MERSH*, 36 (1984), pp. 165-72.

Ingemanson, Birgitta. 'Letters from Aleksandra Kollontaj in Sweden'. *Russian Language Journal*, 41, no. 140 (1987), pp. 197-214.

Itsel, Leonid. *Aleksandra Kollontai – Diplomatka i kurtizanka: Grezy pchely trudovoi* [Aleksandra Kollontai – Diplomat and Courtesan: Dreams of a Worker Bee]'. Tel Aviv: Zerkalo, 1987. A 'popular, semifictionalized account' which, according to Beatrice Farnsworth, 'add[s] little to solid knowledge' of Kollontai's life (*SR*, 47 (Fall 1988), pp. 541-2).

Ivanits, Linda. *Russian Folk Belief*. Armonk, New York: M. E. Sharpe, 1989.

Jacobson, Esther. *Burial Ritual, Gender and Status in South Siberia in the Late Bronze-Early Iron Age*. Papers on Inner Asia 0893-1863, 7. Bloomington, IN: Indiana University Research Institute for Inner Asian Studies, 1987.

Johanson, Christine. *Women's Struggle for Higher Education in Russia, 1855-1900*. Kingston and Montreal: McGill-Queen's University Press, 1987.

-----. 'Autocratic Politics, Public Opinion, and Women's Medical Education During the Reign of Alexander II'. *SR*, 38, no. 3 (September 1979), pp. 427-43.

Kaiser, Daniel H. 'Symbol and Ritual in the Marriages of Ivan the Terrible'. *Russian History*, 14, nos. 1-4 (1987), pp. 247-62.

Kelly, Mary. *The Goddess Embroideries of Russia and the Ukraine*. Dryden, N.Y: Tompkins-Cortland Community College, Liberal Arts Division, 1983. See also Central and East Europe, below.

Kerblay, Basile (ed.). *L'Evolution des Modèles familiaux dans les Pays de l'Est européen et en U.R.S.S. Cultures et sociétés de l'Est*, 9. Paris: Institut d'études slaves, 1988.

Koblitz, Ann Hibner. *A Convergence of Lives. Sofia Kovalevskaia: Scientist, Writer, Revolutionary*. Boston: Birkhauser, 1983. A scholarly biography of the famous 19th-century mathematician whose life reads like a novel.

-----. 'Career and Home Life in the 1880s: The Choices of Sofia Kovalevskaia'. In Pnina Abir-Am and Dorinda Outram (eds.). *Uneasy Careers and Intimate Lives: Women in Science*. New Brunswick, NJ: Rutgers University Press, 1987, pp. 172-90.

-----. Entries on Sofia Kovalevskaia and Elizaveta Litvinova. In Louise Grinstein and Paul Campbell (eds.). *Women of Mathematics: A Bio-Bibliographic Sourcebook*. New York: Greenwood, 1987, pp. 103-13, 129-34.

-----. 'Changing Views of Sofia Kovalevskaia'. In Linda Keen (ed.). *The Legacy of Sonya Kovalevskaya*. Contemporary Mathematics 64. Providence: American Mathematical Society, 1987, pp. 53-76.

-----. 'The First Generation of Russian Women Scientists'. *Proceedings of the International Conference on the Role of Women in the History of Science, Technology and Medicine in the 19th and 20th Centuries*, 1. Budapest: MTESZ, 1983, pp. 99-103. A longer version appears in Spanish: *Universidades*, 98 (October-December 1984), pp. 175-83.

-----. 'Sofia Kovalevskaia and the Mathematical Community'. *The Mathematical Intelligencer*, 8, no. 1 (1983), pp. 20-9.

Kochina, Pelageya. *Love and Mathematics: Sofya Kovalevskaya*. Moscow: 1985. Translated into English. A biography by a scholar and mathematician, one of the few women members of the Soviet Academy of Sciences, who has studied Kovalevskaya's life and works for over thirty years.

Kollmann, Nancy Shields. *Kinship and Politics: The Making of the Muscovite Political System, 1345-1347*. Stanford: Stanford University Press, 1987.

-----. 'Ritual and Social Drama at the Muscovite Court'. *SR*, 45, no. 3 (Fall 1986), pp. 406-502.

-----. 'The Seclusion of Elite Muscovite Women'. *Russian History*, 10, no. 2 (1983), pp. 70-87.

Kollontai, Alexandra. *Selected Writings*. Elizabeth Waters, ed. London: Allison and Busby 1977. See also Clements, Farnsworth, Ingemanson, Itsel in this section and IV below.

Krupskaia, Nadezhda. *O Nadezhde Krupskoi: Vospominaniia, ocherki, stat'i sovremennikov* [About Nadeshda Krupskaia: Reminiscences, Essays, Articles by Contemporaries]. Moscow: 1988.

Levin, Eve. See also under Pushkareva below.

-----. *Sex and Society in the World of the Orthodox Slavs, 900-1700.* Ithaca, N. Y.: Cornell University Press, 1989.

-----. 'Infanticide in Pre-Petrine Russia'. *Jahrbücher für Geschichte Osteuropas,* 2 (1986), pp. 215-24.

-----. 'Women and Property in Medieval Novgorod: Dependence and Independence'. *Russian History,* 10. no. 2 (1983), pp. 154-69.

Lewitter, L. R. 'Women, Sainthood and Marriage in Muscovy'. *Journal of Russian Studies,* 37 (1979), pp. 3-11. A comparison of attitudes toward women expressed in the *Domostroy, The Life of St. Juliana Lazarevskaya* and Ivan Pososhkov's *Paternal Testament.*

Longworth, Phillip. *The Three Empresses: Catherine I, Anna and Elizabeth of Russia.* London: Constable, 1972.

Mamonova, Tatiana (ed.). *Russian Women's Studies: Essays on Sexism in Soviet Culture.* Oxford, Eng.: Pergamon, 1989. Mamonova's new book is a miscellaneous, sloppy, badly translated set of articles on topics ranging from writers to contemporary issues and a great disappointment to admirers of her courageous initiative in founding an underground feminist journal in the USSR in the late 1970s.

Massell, Gregory J. *The Surrogate Proletariat: Moslem Women and Revolutionary Strategies in Soviet Central Asia, 1919-1929.* Princeton University Press, 1974.

Mazour, Anatole. *Women in Exile.* Tallahassee, FL.: Diplomatic Press, 1975. A sketchy description of the odyssey of the Decembrist women.

McNeal, Robert H. *Bride of the Revolution: Krupskaya and Lenin.* Ann Arbor: University of Michigan Press, 1972.

-----. 'Women in the Russian Radical Movement'. *Journal of Social History,* 5, no. 2 (Winter 1971-72), pp. 143-63.

Meehan-Waters, Brenda. 'Popular Piety, Local Initiative, and the Founding of Women's Religious Communities in Russia, 1764-1907'. *Kennan Institute for Advanced Russian Studies*, Occasional Paper, 215 (1987).

Mikhnevich, Vl. *Russkaia zhenshchina XVIII stoletiia* [The Russian Woman of the Eighteenth Century]. Kiev: 1895.

Moyle, Natalie K. 'Mermaids (*Rusalki*) and Russian Beliefs About Women'. In Anna Lisa Crone and Catherine V. Chvany (eds.). *New Studies in Russian Language and Literature*. Columbus, OH: Slavica, 1987.

Nash, Carol. 'Educating New Mothers: Women and the Enlightenment in Russia'. *History of Education Quarterly*, 21 (Fall 1981), pp. 301-16.

Neumann, Daniela. *Studentinnen aus dem Russischen Reich in der Schweiz, 1867-1914* [Women Students from the Russian Empire in Switzerland, 1867-1914]. Zurich: Verlag Hans Rohr, 1987.

Noonan, Norma C. 'Marxism and Feminism in the USSR: Irreconcilable Differences?' *Women and Politics*, 8, no. 1 (1988), pp. 31-49.

Patin, Louise. *Journal d'une institutrice française en Russie pendant la révolution 1917-1919*. Paris: Editions de la Table ronde, 1987.

Pavliuchenko, E. A. *Zhenshchiny v russkom osvoboditel'noi dvizhenii: Ot Marii Volkonskoi do Very Figner* [Women in the Russian Freedom Movement: From Maria Volkonskaia to Vera Figner]. Moscow: 1988. As the author herself notes, the book is a set of brief sketches, an introduction to major figures in the history of Russian women's social and political activism in the 19th century.

Porter, Cathy. *Women in Revolutionary Russia*. Cambridge: Cambridge University Press, 1987. A 48-page pamphlet with maps and photographs.

Pushkareva, N. L. and Eve Levin. 'Zhenshchina v srednevekovom Novgorode XI-XV v'. *Vestnik Moskovskogo Universiteta, Seriia istorii*, (June 1983), pp. 78-89. Reprinted in English as: 'Women in Medieval Novgorod, Eleventh to Fifteenth Century', *Soviet Studies in History*, 23, no. 4 (Spring 1985), pp. 71-90.

Raeff, Marc (ed.). *Catherine the Great: A Profile*. New York: Hill & Wang, 1972. Collection of essays.

Ransel, David L. (ed.). *The Family in Imperial Russia*. Champaign-Urbana: University of Illinois Press, 1978. This collection of articles, which came out of a conference on 'Mother and Child in Russia', addresses basic women's issues in Russian history and still offers important data and theoretical contributions.

-----. *Mothers of Misery. Child Abandonment in Russia*. Princeton: Princeton University Press, 1988. 'Ransel explores the creation and management of [the Moscow and Petersburg foundling homes] and compares them to the European... programs on which they were modeled'. He 'examin[es] the foundling system as a point of contact between educated society and the village... He presents a wealth of archival and published data on the plight of peasants, especially peasant women'.

Rorlich, Azade-Ayse. 'The 'Ali Bayramov Club, the Journal *Sharg Gadini* and the Socialization of Azeri Women: 1920-30'. *Central Asian Survey*, no. 3/4 (1986), pp. 221-39. Rorlich's article sketches the progress made towards women's education and equality in Azerbaidzhan in the 1920s.

Selivanova, Nina. *Russia's Women*. New York: Dutton & Co., 1923. A general survey, outdated.

Shashkov, S. S. *Istoriia russkoi zhenshchiny* [History of the Russian Woman]. 2nd ed. St. Petersburg: 1879). An enlightened and provocative outline of the historical position of Russian women.

Shchepkina, E. '"Zhenskaia lichnost" v istorii Rossii [The Female Personality in Russian History]' *Istoricheskii viestnik* (July 1913), pp. 149-69.

Shinn, William T., Jr. *The Decline of the Russian Peasant Household*. Edward L. Keenan, fwd. Washington Papers, 124. New York: Praeger, 1987.

Stites, Richard. *The Women's Liberation Movement in Russia*. Princeton: Princeton University Press, 1978. A basic text for Russian women's studies.

Sutherland, Christine. *The Princess of Siberia: The Story of Maria Volkonsky and the Decembrist Exiles*. New York: Farrar, Straus, Giroux,

1984. Popular biography which draws on the Volkonsky family archives in Rome.

Tishkin, G. A. *Zhenskii vopros v Rossii, 50-60e gody XIX v* [The Woman Question in Russia, 1850s-1860s]. Leningrad: 1984.

Tuve, Jeanette. *The First Russian Women Physicians*. Newtonville, MA: Oriental Research Partners, 1984.

Varfolomeeva, T. B. *Severo-Belorusskaia svad'ba* [The Northern Belorussian Wedding]. Minsk: 1988. Materials on wedding rites and traditional songs.

Viola, Lynne. '*Bab'i bunty* and Peasant Women's Protest during Collectivization'. *Russian Review*, 45 (1986), pp. 23-42. The article documents the important role played by women in resistance against farm collectivization in the late 1920s and early 1930s.

Voilquin, Suzanne. *Mémoires d'une Saint-simonienne en Russie (1839-1846)*. Paris: Edition des Femmes, 1977.

Voltaire and Catherine the Great: Selected Correspondence. A. Lentin, ed., notes, and intro. Elisabeth Hill, intro.; reprinted, Cambridge, MA: Oriental Research Partners, 1974.

Waters, Elizabeth. *Women in Post-Revolutionary Russia*. London: Macmillan, 1988.

-----. 'Teaching Mothercraft in Post-Revolutionary Russia'. *Australian Slavonic and East European Studies*, 2 (1987), pp. 29-56.

Wilberger, Carolyn Hope. 'The View from Russia'. *French Women and the Age of Enlightenment*. Bloomington: Indiana University Press, 1984, pp. 380-94.

Winter, Ella. *Red Virtue. Human Relationships in the New Russia*. New York: Harcourt, Brace & Co., 1933. The classic on Soviet women of that period; not scholarly from a modern viewpoint but well worth reading.

Worobec, Christine D. 'Reflections on Customary Law and Post-Reform Peasant Russia'. *Russian Review*, 44, no. 1 (January 1985), pp. 21-5.

-----. 'Customary Law and Post-Reform Peasant Russia'. *Canadian Slavonic Papers*, 26, no. 2/3 (June-September 1984), pp. 220-34.

Zguta, Russell. 'The Ordeal by Water (Swimming of Witches) in the East Slavic World'. *SR*, 36, 2 (June 1977), pp. 220-30.

Zhirmunsky, V. M. 'The Theme of Heroic Courtship'. In Felix J. Oinas and Stephen Sudakoff (eds.). *The Study of Russian Folklore*. The Hague: Mouton, 1975.

III. *Contemporary Society*

Abramova, A. A. *Trud zhenshchiny* [Women's Labour]. 2nd ed. Moscow: 1987.

Atwood, Lynne. 'Gender and Soviet Pedagogy'. In George Avis (ed.). *The Making of the Soviet Citizen: Character Formation and Civic Training in Soviet Education*. London: Croom Helm, 1987, pp. 107-135.

Blekher, Feiga. *The Soviet Woman in the Family and in Society: A Sociological Study* New York: John Wiley, 1979. Bernice Madison, *Russian Review*, 40, no. 3 (1981), pp. 348-49, faulted it for handling too much material too sketchily (37 topics in four chapters), mainly 'via massive use of Soviet writings'. Madison wonders why the needed reforms in women's situation that have been so thoroughly identified in the USSR are so slow in coming; perhaps, she writes, 'they will continue at a slow and halting pace if Soviet women do not organize together for political power so that their needs do not get submerged in the endless problems that beset drives to reach general Party objectives'.

Bridger, Susan. *Women in the Soviet Countryside: Women's Roles in Rural Development in the Soviet Union*. Cambridge: Cambridge University Press, 1988. '...the first substantive Western treatment of the role of women in Soviet rural development. It analyses both the gains made and the problems still faced by rural women in a society where development policies have been accompanied by a formal commitment to sexual equality'.

Brown, Donald (ed.). *The Role and Status of Women in the Soviet Union*. New York: Teachers College Press, 1968.

Browning, Genia K. *Women and Politics in the USSR: Consciousness Raising and Soviet Women's Groups*. New York: St. Martin's Press, 1987.

Buckley, Mary (ed.). *Soviet Social Scientists Talking: An Official Debate about Women*. London: Macmillan, 1986.

Bushnell, John. 'Shifting Strata: Ethnicity, Gender and Work in Soviet Central Asia'. In Terry L. Thompson and Richard Sheldon (eds.). *Soviet Society and Culture: Essays in Honor of Vera S. Dunham*. Boulder, CO: Westview Press, 1988.

Bysiewicz, Shirley Raissi and Louise I. Shelley. "Women in the Soviet Economy: Proclamations and Practice". In Olimpiad S. Joffe and Mark W. Janis (eds.). *Soviet Law and Economy* Law in Eastern Europe 32. Dordrecht: Martinus Nijhoff Publishers, 1987, pp. 31-49.

Celmina, Helene. *Women in Soviet Prisons*. New York: Paragon, 1986. The author, a Latvian, was arrested in 1962 for 'anti-Soviet agitation' and spent five years in Soviet prisons and labor camps. Although her memoir contains some interesting material, it suffers from personal bitterness and a rather narrow perspective.

Dodge, Norton (ed.) *Women in the Soviet Economy*. Baltimore, MD: John Hopkins Press, 1966. A thorough but somewhat outdated study.

Dragadze, Tamara (ed). *Kinship and Marriage in the Soviet Union: Field Studies*. London: Routledge & Kegan Paul, 1984.

Ershova, E. N. and E. E. Novikova. *SSSR – SShA: Zhenshchina i obshchestvo. Opyt sravnitel'nogo analiza* [USSR – USA: Woman and Society]. Moscow: 1988. A Marxist analysis of the position of women in the two countries which reaches the conclusion that the socialist approach is superior.

Fisher, Wesley Andrew. *The Soviet Marriage Market: Mate-Selection in Russia and the USSR*. Studies of the Russian Institute Columbia University. New York: Praeger, 1980.

Fitzpatrick, Sheila. '"Middle-class Values" and Soviet Life in the 1930s'. In Thompson and Sheldon (eds.). *Soviet Society and Culture*. See under Bushnell above.

Frank, April. *Family Policy in the USSR Since 1944*. Palo Alto, CA: R & E Research Associates, 1979.

Good, Jane E. and David R. Jones. *Babushka: The Life of the Russian Revolutionary Ekaterina Breshko-Breshkovskaia (1844-1934)*. Newtonville, MA: Oriental Research Partners, 1989.

Gray, Francine du Plessix. *Soviet Women: Walking the Tightrope*. New York: Doubleday, 1990. Gray, a distinguished journalist, travelled throughout the Soviet Union in the late 1980s and assembled a collection of 'startlingly candid and outraged opinions' by and about Soviet women. The book is far from being as comprehensive as the title suggests: her sample is drawn mainly from the ranks of upper-class professionals and the problems she discusses are primarily those affecting private life; the workplace, the farm, and the broader environment barely appear.

Hansson, Carola and Karin Liden. *Moscow Women*. New York: Pantheon, 1983. Interviews with thirteen Soviet women of different backgrounds providing an interesting glimpse into their professional and personal lives.

Holland, Barbara (ed.). *Soviet Sisterhood*. Bloomington: Indiana University Press, 1985. An excellent, up-to-date source dealing with a variety of subjects, based on thorough research and first-hand observations of Soviet life. The authors of the articles in this volume are British women scholars.

Home, School and Leisure in the Soviet Union. Jenny Brine, Maureen Perrie, and Andrea Sutton, eds. London: Allen and Unwin, 1980.

Ispa, Jean M. 'Soviet Immigrant Mothers' Perceptions Regarding the First Childbearing Year: The 1950s and the 1970s'. *SR*, 47, no. 2 (Summer 1988), pp. 291-306.

Juviler, Peter H. 'Cell Mutation in Soviet Society: The Family'. In Terry L. Thompson and Richard Sheldon (eds.). *Soviet Society and Culture*. See under Bushnell above.

Lapidus, Gail Warshofsky. *Women in Soviet Society: Equality, Development, and Social Change*. Berkeley: University of California Press, 1978. A trenchant analysis of the impact of Soviet economic development on the status of women since the 1917 revolution.

----- (ed.). *Women, Work, and Family in the Soviet Union*. Armonk, NY.: M. E. Sharpe, 1982. A collection of recent Soviet sociological and demographic studies on women, with commentary. Good reference material.

-----. 'The Interaction of Women's Work and Family Roles in the USSR'. In Barbara Gutek, Laurie Larwood, and Ann Stromberg (eds.). *Women and Work: An Annual Review*, 3. Beverly Hills: Sage Publications, 1987.

Mace, David and Vera Mace. *The Soviet Family*. Garden City, NJ: Doubleday, 1963. Study written from the standpoint of leading marriage counselors.

Mamonova, Tatyana. *Women and Russia: Feminist Writings from the Soviet Union*. Boston: Beacon Press, 1984. Essays by twenty Soviet women, published and distributed covertly in the USSR and now translated into 11 languages; topics include mothering and health care, women in art and culture, women in the dissident and peace movements, and women in prisons. Mamonova was one of the founders of the unofficial feminist movement in the USSR. She was exiled from the USSR in 1980.

Mandel, William M. *Soviet Women*. New York: Anchor Press, 1975. A readable study, with a good bibliography, particularly of Soviet sources. The factual information is generally reliable, although the author's interpretations of it tend to idealise the situation of Soviet women.

McAuley, Alastair. *Women's Work and Wages in the Soviet Union*. Boston: Allen & Unwin, 1981. A 'creative and lucid' analysis of wage differences in the USSR over several decades, arguing that the lower wages paid women are due 'largely to a persisting occupational segregation' (*Russian Review* 41 (January 1982), pp. 83-84.).

Mickiewicz, Ellen. 'Regional Variation in Female Recruitment and Advancement in the Communist Party of the Soviet Union'. *SR*, 36, no. 3 (September 1977), pp. 441-54.

Millar, James R. (ed.). *Politics, Work, and Daily Life in the USSR: A Survey of Former Soviet Citizens*. Cambridge: Cambridge University Press, 1987.

Moses, Joel C. *The Politics of Women & Work in the Soviet Union & the United States: Alternative Work Schedules & Sex Discrimination*. Research Series, 50. Berkeley: Institute of International Studies, University of California, 1983.

Muzyria, A. A. et al. *Zhensovet: Opyt, problemy, perspektivy* [The Women's Council: Experience, Problems, Perspectives]. Moscow: 1989.

Rimashevskaia, N. 'Current Problems of the Status of Women'. *Soviet Sociology: A Journal of Translations*, 27, no. 1, pp. 58-71.

Sacks, Michael Paul. *Work and Equality in the Soviet Union: The Division of   Labor by Age, Gender and Nationality*. New York: Praeger, 1982.

-----. 'Shifting Strata: Ethnicity, Gender and Work in Soviet Central Asia'. In Terry Thompson and Sheldon (eds.). *Soviet Society and Culture*. See under Bushnell above.

Seton Watson, Mary. *Scenes from Soviet Life: Soviet Life through Official Literature*. London: BBC Publications, 1986. Seton-Watson's expanded version of radio talks includes a section on women in Soviet society as reflected in recent fiction.

Shlapentokh, Vladimir. *Love, Marriage, and Friendship in the Soviet Union: Ideals and Practices*. New York: Praeger, 1984.

Soviet Women. A special issue of *Canadian Woman's Studies/les cahiers de la femme* 10, no. 4 (Winter 1989). The members of the guest editorial board (Janet Hyer, Meg Luxton, Ester Reiter, Shelagh Wilkinson) spent two years exploring the lives of Soviet women, travelling twice to the USSR to gather materials and commission articles packed with information and features on topics grouped under the general headings of 'Perestroika, Glasnost and Women', '"The Woman Question" – Practice and Policy', 'Profiles', 'The Arts', and 'Education'. From its bright cover to the book reviews, this issue of CWS/cv is a great help in distinguishing women's voices amid the chaos of glasnost.

St. George, George. *Our Soviet Sister*. Washington, DC: Robert B. Luce, 1973. A rather superficial treatment of the subject. Appended to the text is an abridged translation of Natal'ia Baranskaia's celebrated story, 'A Week Like Any Other' (Nedelia kak nedelia); see also Baranskaia, section IV below.

Stuart, Robert C. 'Women in Soviet Rural Management'. *SR*, 38, no. 4 (December 1979), pp. 603-13.

Taubman, Jane and William. *Moscow Spring*. Summit Books, 1989. Material of interest to women's studies, particularly the chapter entitled 'Feminism?'.

Waters, Elizabeth. 'Domestic Labor and Soviet Society'. In Brine, Perrie, Sutton (eds.). *Home, School and Leisure in the Soviet Union*. See above under title.

Yedlin, Tova (ed.). *Women in Eastern Europe and the Soviet Union*. New York: Praeger, 1980. Includes bibliography.

IV. Russian and Soviet Literature

General:

Alekseev, A. A. 'Iazyk svetskikh dam i razvitie iazykovoi normy v XVIII v.' [The Language of Society Ladies and the Development of Language Norms in the 18th Century]'. In V. V. Zamkova (ed.). *Funktsional'nye i sotsial'nye raznovidnosti russkogo literaturnogo iazyka XVIII v.* Leningrad: 1984. Role played by upperclass women's writings and letters in the development of the literary language.

Andrew, Joe. 'The Lady Vanishes: A Feminist Reading of Turgenev's *Asya*'. *Irish Slavonic Studies*, no. 8 (1987), pp. 87-96.

-----. *Women in Russian Literature: 1780-1863*. New York: St. Martin's Press, 1988. This book seems curiously old-fashioned. It mixes formalist methodology and Marxist feminism of the British school to convict not just narrators or heroes, but also their authors (Radishchev, Karamzin, Pushkin, Gogol'. and Lermontov) of an ahistorical sexism. Female characters appear largely as victims until Turgenev's Elena, who gets passing marks, and Chernyshevsky's Vera Pavlovna, who receives quite different treatment than the earlier heroines.

Armstrong, Judith. *The Unsaid Anna Karenina*. London: Macmillan, 1988.

Astman, Marina. 'Obraz "infernal'noi" zhenshchiny v russkoi literature [The Image of the "Infernal Woman" in Russian Literature]'. In Vsevolod Setchkarev (ed.). *Otkliki: Sbornik statei pamiati Nikolaia Ivanovicha Ul'ianova (1904-1985)*. New Haven, CT: Yale University Press, 1986, pp. 83-96.

-----. 'Women Writers in Recent Soviet Literature: A Review Article'. *Ulbandus*, 5 (Fall 1987), pp. 164-68.

-----. 'Evoliutsiia zhenskikh obrazov v tvorchestve Pushkina [The Evolution of Female Images in Pushkin's Work]'. *Zapiski Russkoi akademicheskoi gruppy b SShA*, 20 (1987), pp. 57-69.

Awsienko, Nina. 'The Burdens of "Superfluous Talent"'. *Journal of Russian Studies*, 29 (1975), pp. 11-19.

Barker, Adele Marie. *The Mother Syndrome in the Russian Folk Imagination*. Columbus, OH: Slavica, 1986. '. . . a psychological investigation into the mother-son relationship in Russian folk and literary tradition from the *byliny* to Dostoevsky'.

-----. 'The Mother's Hold: Case Studies from Russian and Homeric Epic'. *American Contributions to the Tenth International Congress of Slavists, Sofia, September, 1988: Literature*. Columbus, OH: Slavica, 1988.

Behrendt, Patricia. 'The Russian Iconic Representation of the Christian Madonna: A Feminine Archetype in *Notes from the Underground*'. In Alexei Ugrinski et al. (eds.). *Dostoevski and the Human Condition After a Century*. Westwood, CT: Greenwood Press, 1986.

Beletskii, A. 'Turgenev i russkie pisatel'nitsy 30-kh – 60-kh godov' [Turgenev and Russian Women Writers of the 1830s – 1860s]'. *Tvorcheskii put' Turgeneva*. Petrograd: 1923.

Biriukov, Sergei. '"V mir prekrasnykh prevrashchenii": Fol'klornye motivy v sovremennoi poezii ["Into the World of Beautiful Transformations": Folkloric Motifs in Contemporary Poetry]'. *Literaturnoe obozrenie* (September 1984), pp. 20-5.

Clayton, J. Douglas. 'Towards a Feminist Reading of *Evgenii Onegin*'. *Canadian Slavonic Papers*, 29, no. 2/3 (1987), pp. 255-65. Clayton discusses the extent to which Pushkin identified with his famous heroine.

Clyman, Toby. 'Chekhov's Victimized Women'. *Russian Language Journal*, 28, no. 100 (Fall 1974), pp. 26-31.

Corten, Irina H. 'Feminism in Russian Literature'. *MERSL*, 7 (1984), pp. 176-93.

-----. 'Solženicyn's Matrena and Rasputin's Dar'ja: Two Studies in Russian Peasant Spirituality'. *Russian Language Journal*, 33, no. 114 (Winter 1979), pp. 85-96. Two literary characters as contemporary examples of traditional Russian spiritual values.

Derzhavets, Igor. 'Agaf'ia Rostislavna – Avtor *Slova o polku Igoreve*? [Agaf'ia Rostislavna – Author of *The Lay of Igor's Armament*?]'. *Pamir* (August 1979), pp. 84-94. Shades of Robert Graves! Derzhavets presents evidence that the classic Russian medieval epic was written by a woman.

Dunham, Vera Sandomirsky. 'The Strong-Woman Motif'. In Cyril Black (ed.). *The Transformation of Russian Society*. Cambridge, MA: Harvard University Press, 1967, pp. 459-83.

Fainshtein, Mikhail Sh. *Pisatel'nitsy pushkinskoi pory: Istoriko-literaturnye ocherki* [Women Writers of Pushkin's Time: Historico-literary sketches]. Leningrad: 1989. The book offers a series of balanced and sympathetic, if unscholarly, portraits of a number of women writers of the early 19th century.

Farris, June Pachuta. 'Selected Bibliography'. In Roberta Reeder (ed.). *Down Along the Mother Volga: An Anthology of Russian Folk Lyrics*. Philadelphia, PA: University of Pennsylvania Press, 1975, pp. 238-42.

Feinstein, Elaine. 'Poetry and Conscience: Russian Women Poets of the Twentieth Century'. In Mary Jacobus (ed.). *Women Writing and Writing about Women*. New York: Barnes and Noble, 1979. Brief biographical sketches (some from personal interviews) and translated excerpts of poetry by Akhmatova, Tsvetaeva, Morits, Aliger and Akhmadulina.

Fitzlyon, April. 'I. S. Turgenev and the "Woman" Question'. *New Zealand Slavonic Journal*, (1983), pp. 161-73.

Gasiorowska, Xenia. *Women in Soviet Fiction 1917-1964*. Madison, WI: University of Wisconsin Press, 1968. The only book-length study of the subject in English; thoroughly researched and engagingly written.

-----. 'Working Mothers in Recent Soviet Fiction'. *SEEJ*, 25, no. 2 (1981), pp. 56-63.

Gillespie, David. 'Women from Town and Village in Recent Soviet Russian Prose'. *Journal of Russian Studies*, 48 (1984), 36-43.

Glasse, Antonia. 'The Formidable Woman: Portrait and Original'. *RLT*, 9 (1974), pp. 433-53.

Greene, Diana. 'Male and Female in *The Snail on the Slope* by the Strugatsky Brothers'. *Modern Fiction Studies*, 32 (Spring 1986), pp. 97-108.

-----. 'Images of Women in Fedor Sologub'. *Proceedings of the Kentucky Foreign Language Conference 1986: Slavic Section*, 4, no. 1. Lexington, KY: Department of Russian and Eastern Studies, University of Kentucky, 1986, pp. 90-103. How Sologub's marriage to Chebotarevskaia influenced the images of women in his works.

-----. 'An Asteroid of One's Own: Women Soviet Science Fiction Writers'. *Irish Slavonic Studies*, no. 8 (1987), pp. 127-39.

Grossman, Joan Delaney. 'Feminine Images in Old Russian Literature and Art'. *California Slavic Studies*, 11 (1980), pp. 33-70.

Heldt, Barbara. 'Tolstoy's Path toward Feminism'. *American Contributions to the VIII International Congress of Slavists, Zagreb 1978*. Columbus, OH: Slavica, 1978, pp. 523-35.

-----. 'Russian Literature'. *Women in Print I: Women's Studies, Research in Language and Literature*. New York: MLA Publications, 1982, pp. 149-54.

-----. 'Chekhov (and Flaubert) on Female Devotion'. *Ulbandus Review*, 2, no. 2 (Fall 1982), pp. 166-74.

-----. *Terrible Perfection: Women and Russian Literature*. Bloomington: Indiana University Press, 1987. An important feminist reading of Russian literature (primarily 19th century) which argues that women found their voices in autobiography and poetry; in fiction male appropriation of female images exercised a repressive effect on women's self-expression.

Hermann, Lesley. '*Jacques* in Russia: A Program of Domestic Reform for Husbands'. *Studies in the Literary Imagination*, 23, no. 2 (Fall 1979), pp. 61-72.

Hughes, Ann. 'Sergei Zalygin and the "Zhenskiy Vopros"'. *Journal of Russian Studies*, 50 (1986), pp. 38-44.

Johanson, Christine. 'Turgenev's Heroines: A Historical Assessment'. *Canadian Slavonic Papers*, 26, no. 1 (1984), pp. 15-23.

Karp, Carole. 'George Sand and Turgenev: A Literary Relationship'. *Studies in the Literary Imagination*, 12, no. 2 (Fall 1979), pp. 73-81.

Kourova, O. I. 'Elizy, Klimeny, Filisy: Nabliudeniia nad uslovno-poeticheskimi imenami v russkoi literature XIX veka [Elizas, Climenes, Phylisas: Observations on Cliché Poetic Names in 19th Century Russian Literature]'. *Russkaia rech'* (April 1982), pp. 9-13. An onomastic approach to the use of women's names in literature.

Krasnova, O. K. 'Zhenskii vopros v romane P. D. Boborykina *Zhertva vecherniaia* [The Woman Question in P. D. Boborykin's Novel *Zhertva vecherniaia]'. Vestnik Leningradskogo Universiteta. Seriia Istorii, Iazyka i Literatury*, 14, no. 7 (1982), pp. 53-8.

Lauridsen, I. 'Beautiful Ladies in the Works of Vasily Aksenov'. *Vasily Pavlovich Aksenov: A Writer in Quest of Himself*. Columbus, OH: Slavica, 1986.

Lee, Nicholas. 'Manifestations of the Feminine in Solzhenitsyn's *August 1914'*. In Julian Connolly and Sonia Ketchian (eds.). *Studies in Honor of Vsevolod Setchkarev*. Columbus, OH: Slavica, 1987.

Little, T. E. 'Pushkin's Tatyana and Onegin: A Study in Irony'. *New Zealand Slavonic Journal*, 1 (1975), pp. 19-28. Little argues that we take the characters more seriously than Pushkin did.

de Maegd-Soep, Carolina. *Chekhov and Women: Women in the Life and Work of Chekhov*. Columbus, OH: Slavica, 1987.

-----. *The Emancipation of Women in Russian Literature and Society: a Contribution to the Knowledge of the Russian Society in the 1860s*. Ghent State University, 1978.

-----. 'George Sand et l'Emancipation de la Femme russe'. *Slavica Gandensia*, 3 (1976), pp. 7-30.

Manheim, Michael. 'Dialogue between Son and Mother in Chekhov's *The Sea Gull* and O'Neill's *Long Day's Journey into Night'. The Eugene O'Neill Newsletter*, 1 (1982), pp. 24-9.

Matich, Olga. 'The Idiot: A Feminist Reading'. In Alexei Ugrinski et al. (eds.). *Dostoevski and the Human Condition After a Century.* See Behrendt above.

-----. 'A Typology of Fallen Women in Nineteenth-Century Russian Literature'. In Paul Debreczeny (ed.). *American Contributions to the Ninth International Congress of Slavists, Kiev, September, 1983. II. Literature, Poetics, History.* Columbus, OH: Slavica, 1983, pp. 325-43.

-----. 'Androgyny and the Russian Silver Age'. *Pacific Coast Philology,* 14 (1979), pp. 42-50.

Møller, Peter Ulf. *Postlude to the Kreutzer Sonata.* John Kendal, tr. Leiden: E. J. Brill, 1988.

Morgan, Lyndall. 'Shukshin's Women: An Enduring Russian Stereotype'. *Australian Slavonic and East European Studies,* 1, no. 2 (1987), pp. 137-46.

Nikolskaya, Tanya. '"The Contemporary Woman" in Early Twentieth Century Russian Literature'. *Irish Slavonic Studies,* 8 (1987), pp. 107-13.

Ono, Michiko. 'Tolstoy's Views on Man and Woman in His Works and Life'. *Japanese Slavic and East European Studies,* 9 (1988), pp. 21-37.

Opitz, R. 'Turgenevs Elena und ihre Freier [Turgenev's Elena and Her Suitors]'. *Zeitschrift für Slawistik,* 29, no. 4 (1984), pp. 546-55.

Pachmuss, Temira. 'Women Writers in Russian Decadence'. *Journal of Contemporary History,* 17 (1982), pp. 111-36.

-----. 'Women Writers in Russian Modernism 1890-1910'. *Russian Literature and Criticism.* Evelyn Bristol, ed. and intro. Oakland, CA: Berkeley Slavic Specialties, 1982, pp. 144-57.

Peters, Jochen-Ulrich, 'Utopien vom "anderen Leben": Sowjetische Frauenliteratur zwischen Faktographie und Fiktion [Utopias from the "Other Life": Soviet Women's Literature Between Factography and Fiction]'. *Russische Sprache und Literatur der Gegenwart in Unterricht und Forschung: Materialen des Internationalen MAPRJAL-Symposiums Mainz, 5-8 Oktober 1981.* Hamburg: Buske, 1982.

Peterson, Dale E. 'From Russia with Love: Turgenev's Maidens and Howell's Heroines'. *Canadian Slavonic Papers*, 26, no. 1 (1984), pp. 24-34.

Pirog, Gerald. 'The City, the Madonna, and the Woman: Metaphoric Interference in Blok's *Ital'janskie stixi*'. *Forum at Iowa on Russian Literature*, 2 (1977), pp. 71-86.

Porter, Robert. 'The Mother Theme in Valentin Rasputin'. *Canadian Slavonic Papers*, 8, no. 3 (1986), pp. 287-303.

Proffer, Carl. *The Widows of Russia, and Other Writings*. Ann Arbor, MI: Ardis, 1987. Includes memoirs of Nadezhda Mandel'shtam, Lily Brik, Bulgakov's widows, and others; articles on the current literary scene.

Protopopov, Mikhail. 'Zhenskoe tvorchestvo' [Women's Writings]'. *Russkaia mysl'* (January, February and April 1982). An example of the prescriptive criticism that damned the 'passive' heroines of Russian classic and contemporary literature alike.

Rancour-LaFerriere, Daniel. 'Puškin's Still Unravished Bride: A Psychoanalytic Study of Tat'jana's Dream'. *Russian Literature*, 25 (1989), pp. 215-58. Rancour finds hints of Onegin's homosexuality in Tat'iana's dream.

Rosenholm, A. 'Kritik der Reproduktion imaginierter Weiblichkeit: Turgenevs Elena-Figur [A Critique of the Rendering of Imagined Femininity: Turgenev's Elena-Image]'. *Studia Slavica Finlandensis*, 4 (1987), pp. 166-93.

Rosenshield, Gary. 'Varen'ka Dobroselova: An Experiment in the Desentimentalization of the Sentimental Heroine in Dostoevskii's *Poor Folk*'. *SR*, 44, no. 3 (Fall 1985), pp. 525-33.

Russian Literature Triquarterly, 9 (Spring 1974). An entire issue of the Ardis journal devoted to Russian women writers.

Sandler, Stephanie. 'The Two Women of Bakchisarai'. *Canadian Slavonic Papers*, 29 no. 2/3 (1987), pp. 241-54.

Seeley, Frank Friedeberg. 'Dostoevsky's Women'. *SEER*, 39 (1960-1961), pp. 293-312.

484 *Mary F. Zirin*

Sheveleva, Irina. 'Materinskoe i zhenskoe [Maternal and Feminine]'. *Nash sovremennik* (March 1988), pp. 165-8. A review of contemporary poetry by Soviet women.

Shklovskii, Evg. 'Eta sil'naia slabaia zhenshchina? [That Strong Weak Woman?]'. *Literaturnaia gazeta*, (August 3, 1983), p. 5.

Sipovskii, V. V. 'Tat'iana, Onegin i Lenskii (K literaturnoi istorii Pushkinskikh "tipov") [Tat'iana, Onegin and Lenskii (Toward a Literary History of Pushkin's "Types")]'. *Russkaia starina* (May 1899), pp. 311-29.

Smirnyw, Walter. 'Turgenev's Emancipated Women'. *Modern Language Review*, 85, no. 1 (1985), pp. 97-105.

Syritsa, G. A. 'Iazykovye sredstva sozdaniia zhenskikh obrazov v romane L. Tolstogo *Voina i mir* [Linguistic Devices in the Creation of Women's Images in L. Tolstoy's Novel *War and Peace*]'. *Russkii iazyk v shkole*, no. 2 (1985), pp. 70-4.

Vysotskaia, Natal'ia. 'Tri monologa: Sushchestvuet li "zhenskaia poeziia"? [Three Monologues: Is There "Women's Poetry"?]'. *Literaturnaia gazeta* (March 16, 1983), p. 5.

Warner, Nicholas O. 'Character and Genre in *War and Peace*: The Case of Natasha'. *MLN*, 100, no. 5 (1985), pp. 1012-24.

Anthologies

Always a Woman: Stories by Soviet Women Writers. Nina Kupriyanova, ed. Moscow: 1987.

Balancing Acts: Contemporary Stories by Russian Women. Helena Goscilo, ed. Bloomington: Indiana University Press, 1989. 'A fine collection, which expresses poignantly the inner lives and arduous social problems of Soviet women' – Francine du Plessix Gray. The anthology includes stories by Natalia Baranskaia, Maia Ganina, Nina Katerli, Rimma Kazakova, Nadezhda Kozhevnikova, Elena Makarova, Anna Mass, Liudmila Petrushevskaia, Galina Shcherbatskaia, Viktoria Tokareva, Tatiana Tolstaia, Liudmila Uvarova, Inna Varlamova, and Irina Velembovskaia. Available in paperback.

The Image of Women in Contemporary Soviet Fiction. Sigrid McLaughlin, ed., transl. and intro. London: Macmillan, 1989. A selection of recent works by both men and women.

Rossiia glazami zhenshchin: Literaturnaia Antologiia [Russia Through the Eyes of Women: A Literary Anthology]. Marina Ledkovsky Astman, ed. and intro. Tenafly, NJ: Hermitage, 1989. Selections (1920-1980) by Akhmatova, Tsvetaeva, Evgeniia Ginzburg, I. Grekova, Baranskaia, Marina Rachko, Nadezhda Mandel'shtam, Ruf Zernova, Lidiia Chukovskaia, Liudmila Stern, Tat'iana Nikolaeva, Bella Akhmadulina and Irina Ratushinskaia with glossary and brief biographies at the end.

Russian and Polish Women's Fiction. Helena Goscilo, tr. and ed. Nashville: University of Tennessee Press, 1985. The works chosen are the translator's personal choices rather than an overview of the subject. Russian prose includes a tale by Evdokia Rostopchina (19th century), two sketches by Ol'ga Forsh, and stories by Vera Panova and Inna Varlamova. Polish authors include Eliza Orzeszkowa, Maria Konopnicka, Gabriela Zapolska, Maria Dąbrowska, Pola Gojawiczyńska, Maria Kuncewiczowa, and Zofia Nalkowska. The introduction and biographical material about the authors provide useful information.

Russkie poetessy XIX veka [Russian Women Poets of the 19th Century]. N. V. Bannikov (ed.). Moscow: 1979. The selection includes: 18th century songs by Zubova and Sandunova; poems by Bunina, Volkova, Z. Volkonskaia, E. P. Rostopchina, Gotovtsova, N. Teplova, Pavlova, Zhadovskaia, N. Khvoshchinskaia, Barykova, Figner, Chiumina, M. Lokhvitskaia, P. Solov'eva, Ejnerling-'Galina', and Shchepkina-Kupernik. Brief biographical essays on each author.

Uchenova, V. V. (ed.). *Dacha na Petergofskoi doroge: Proza russkikh pisatel'nits pervoi poloviny XIX veka* [A Summer House on the Peterhof Road: Prose by Russian Women Writers of the First Half of the 19th Century]. Moscow: 1986. Annotated edition of works by writers, including Zinaida Volkonskaia, Nadezhda Durova, Elena Gan, Elizaveta Kologrivova, Maria Zhukova, Iulia Zhadovskaia, Avdot'ia Panaeva, and Nadezhda Sokhanskaia.

----- (ed.). *Svidanie: Proza russkikh pisatel'nits 60-80kh godov XIX veka* [Rendezvous: Prose by Russian Women Writers of the 1860s -1880s]. Moscow: 1987. The second in a three-volume anthology of prose by and about prerevolutionary Russian women. The works included are: Maria Markovich (ps.: Marko Vovchok), Sof'ia Khvoshchinskaia (Iv. Vesen'ev),

Mar'ia Tsebrikova, Sof'ia Soboleva (V. Samoilovich), Nadezhda Khvoshinskaia (V. Krestovskii) and Sof'ia Kovalevskaia.

----- (ed.). *Tol'ko chas: Proza russkikh pisatel'nits kontsa XIX -- nachala XX veka* [Just One Hour: Prose by Russian Women Writers of the Late 19th - Early 20th Century]. Moscow: 1988. The third volume of Uchenova's anthology includes: Ol'ga Shapir, Maria Krestovskaia, Anastasia Krandievskaia, Valentina Dmitrieva, Tat'iana Shchepkina-Kupernik, Elizaveta Militsyna, Varvara Tsekhovskaia, Ariadna Tyrkova, Lidia Avilova, and Anastasia Tsvetaeva.

Women Writers in Russian Modernism. Temira Pachmuss, tr. and ed. Champaign-Urbana: University of Illinois Press, 1978. A well arranged, annotated anthology with an informative introduction. Currently out of print.

Individual writers:

Bella Akhmadulina (b. 1937)

Three Russian Poets: Margarita Aliger, Yunna Moritz, Bella Akhmadulina. Elaine Feinstein, tr. New York: Persea Books, 1979.

Condee, Nancy. 'Axmadulina's *Poemy:* Poems of Transformations and Origins'. *SEEJ*, 29, no. 2 (Summer 1985), pp. 176-87.

Ketchian, Sonia. 'Poetic Creation in Bella Axmadulina'. *SEEJ*, 28, no. 1 (Spring 1984), pp. 42-57.

-----. 'The Wonder of Nature and Art: Bella Axmadulina's "Secret"'. In Anna Lisa Crone and Catherine V. Chvany (eds.). *New Studies in Russian Language and Literature.* Columbus, OH: Slavica, 1987.

Anna Akhmatova (1889-1966). See also Roskina, Autobiography below.

Akhmatova, Anna. *Complete Poems.* 2 vols. Judith Hemsche, tr. with Roberta Reeder. Somerville, MA: Zephyr Press, 1990. Critical introduction, notes on the poems, historical chronology, photographs and drawings, bibliography.

-----. *Sochineniia* [Works]. 2 vols. Gleb Struve and Boris Filippov, ed., intro., and annot. Inter-Language Literary Associates, 1967-1968.

-----. *You Will Hear Thunder.* D. M. Thomas, tr. & intro. Athens: Ohio University Press, 1985.

-----. *Selected Poems.* Walter Arndt, ed. Walter Arndt, Robin Kendall, and Carl Proffer, trs. Ann Arbor, MI: Ardis, 1979.

-----. *Stikhotvoreniia i poemy* [Short Verse and Long Poems]. Leningrad: 1976.

Chukovskaia, Lidia. *Zapiski ob Anne Akhmatovoi* [Notes About Anna Akhmatovoi]. 2 vols. Paris: YMCA-Press, 1976-1980.

Driver, Sam. 'The Supernatural in the Poetry of Anna Akhmatova'. In Amy Mandelker and Roberta Reeder (eds.). *The Supernatural in Slavic and Baltic Literature: Essays in Honor of Victor Terras.* Columbus, OH: Slavica, 1989.

-----. *Anna Akhmatova.* New York: Twayne, 1972.

Haight, Amanda. *Anna Akhmatova: A Poetic Pilgrimage.* Oxford University Press, 1977.

Ketchian, Sonia. 'Metempsychosis in the Verse of Anna Axmatova'. *SEEJ*, 25, no. 1 (Spring 1981), pp. 44-60.

-----. *The Poetry of Anna Akhmatova: A Conquest of Time and Space.* Slavistische Beitrage, 196. Munich: Otto Sagner, 1986. Verse tr. by F. D. Reeve. 'An examination of Akhmatova's brilliant use of fire imagery, metempsychosis and intertextuality to honor her past masters and to expand the limits of her verse'.

-----. 'An inspiration for Anna Akhmatova's *Requiem*'. In Julian Connolly and Sonia Ketchian (eds.). *Studies in Honor of Vsevolod Setchkarev.* Columbus, OH: Slavica, 1987.

-----. 'A Source for Anna Axmatova's 'A String of Quatrains': Hovannes Tumanian's *Quatrains*'. *SEEJ*, 31, no. 4 (Winter 1987), pp. 520-32.

Leiter, Sharon. *Akhmatova's Petersburg.* Philadelphia: University of Pennsylvania Press, 1983. Leiter traces the theme of Petersburg-Petrograd-Leningrad as it developed throughout Akhmatova's life with generous, well-translated quotations from her works and fascinating photographic documentation.

488   *Mary F. Zirin*

.Rosslyn, Wendy. *The Prince, The Fool and the Nunnery: The Religious Theme in the Early Poetry of Anna Akhmatova.* Brookfield, VT: Gower Publishing, 1984.

Timencik, Roman. 'Axmatova's *Macbeth*'. *SEEJ*, 24, no. 4 (Winter 1980), pp. 362-68.

Toporov, V. N. *Akhmatova i Blok* [Akhmatova and Blok]. Oakland, CA: Berkeley Slavic Specialties, 1981.

Vilenkin, Vitalii. *V sto pervom zerkale: Anna Akhmatova* [In the 101st Mirror: Anna Akhmatova]. Moscow: 1987. For Sonia Ketchian's rave review, see *SEEJ*, 32, no. 4 (1988), pp. 664-65.

Margarita Aliger

Three Russian Poets: Margarita Aliger, Yunna Moritz, Bella Akhmadulina. Elaine Feinshtein, tr. New York: Persea Books, 1979.

Lidia Avilova (1865-1943)

Avilova, Lidia. 'The Puzzle'. Marian Schwartz, tr. *The Yale Review*, 72, no. 4 (July 1983), pp. 522-40.

Natal'ia Baranskaia (b. 1908)

Baranskaya, Natalya. *A Week Like Any Other.* Pieta Monks, tr. Seattle, WA: Seal Press, 1990. Baranskaia's twenty-year-old *Nedelia kak nedelia* is unfortunately even more relevant to American women today, when a larger percentage of them are working without adequate trade-offs in child-care and other help. The other stories in this collection show Baranskaia as a light chronicler of the problems and rewards of daily life in the Soviet Union.

-----. *Nedelia kak nedelia* [Just Another Week]. Lora Paperno, Natalie Roklina, and Richard Leeds, eds. Columbus, OH: Slavica, 1989. An accented glossed, annotated, and 'very slightly abridged' edition of Baranskaia's famous story for classroom use.

Kay, Susan. 'A Woman's Work'. *Irish Slavonic Studies*, 8 (1987), pp. 115-26. A retrospective look at Baranskaia's 'Nedelia kak nedelia' and other works.

Anna Barkova

Ageev, A. and L. Taganov, 'Anna Barkova'. *Ogonek*, no. 35 (1988), pp. 15-16. Brief article about early Soviet poet of proletarian origins.

Nina Berberova

Berberova, Nina. 'Sentence Commuted'. Marian Schwartz, tr. *The Literary Review*, 28 (Summer 1985), pp. 489-532. Winner of *TLR* Novella-in-Translation contest.

-----. *The Accompanist*. Marian Schwartz, tr. New York: Atheneum Press, 1988.

Barker, Murl. 'The Short Prose of Nina Berberova'. *RLT*, no. 22 (Winter 1988), pp. 489-532.

Ol'ga Berggol'ts

Berggol'ts, Ol'ga. *P'esy i stsenarii* [Plays and Scenarios]. Leningrad, 1988.

Ina Bliznetsova

Bliznetsova, Ina. *Dolina tenet: Stikhotvoreniia* [The Valley of Snares: Poems]. Tenafly, NJ: Hermitage, 1988.

Sof'ia Briullova (b. Kavelina, 1851-1877)

Zviguilsky, Tamara. 'A propos d'un centenaire: une correspondante de Tourgueniev, Sofia Kavelina (1851-1877)'. *Cahiers Ivan Tourgeniev, Pauline Viardot, Maria Malibran*, 1 (October 1977), pp. 30-36.

Lidia Chukovskaia (b. 1907). See also under Akhmatova above.

Chukovskaya, Lydia. *Sofia Petrovna*. Evanston, IL: Northwestern University Press, 1989. A translation, corrected and approved by the author, of Chukovskaia's unforgettable novel of the Stalin terror (*Opustelyi dom*, previously published in English as *The Deserted House*), as well as a chapter from her *Process of Expulsion*.

-----. *To the Memory of Childhood*. Eliza Kellogg Close, tr. Evanston, IL: Northwestern University Press, 1988. The book is both an affectionate memoir of a childhood under the magical aegis of her father, Kornei Chukovskii, and a 'pedagogical treatise without pedantry'.

Valentina Dmitrieva (1859-1947/8)

Dmitrieva, Valentina. *Povesti i rasskazy* [Novellas and Stories]. Moscow: 1976.

Anna Dostoevskaia

Belov, Sergei. *Zhena pisatelia. Posledniaia liubov' F. M. Dostoevskogo* [The Writer's Wife: F. M. Dostoevsky's Last Love]. Moscow: 1986.

Nadezhda Durova (1783-1866). See also: Anthologies above and Autobiography below.

Durova, N. A. *Izbrannye sochineniia Kavalerist-devitsy* [Selected Works of the Cavalry Maiden]. Vl. B Murav'ev, ed., intro., and notes. Moscow: 1988. The best selection of Durova's works yet published in the USSR. Murav'ev's footnotes are an improvement over recent Soviet editions, and his introduction assesses positively Durova's character and her striving for personal freedom.

Barbara Heldt. 'Nadezhda Durova: Russia's Cavalry Maid'. *History Today*, 33 (February 1983), pp. 24-28.

Elena Gan ('Zenaida R-va'. 1814-1842)

Nielsen, Marit Bjerkung. 'The Concept of Love and the Conflict of the Individual vs. Society in Elena A. Gan's *Sud sveta*'. *ScandoSlavica*, 24 (1978), pp. 125-38.

Lidia Ginzburg

Ginzburg, Lydia. 'The Poetics of Association'. *RLT*, 22 (Winter 1988), pp. 105-42.

Pratt, Sarah. 'Lidija Ginzburg's *O starom i novom* as Autobiography'. *SEEJ*, 30, no. 1 (1986), pp. 45-53. Useful article that defines 'autobiography' in the broadest sense and outlines Ginzburg's life in and as literature.

Zinaida Gippius (1869-1945)

Gippius, Zinaida. *Stikhotvoreniia* [Poems]. T. V. Pachmuss, comp. Paris: YMCA-Press, 1984.

Gove, Antonina Filonov. 'Gender as a Poetic Feature in the Verse of Zinaida Gippius'. *American Contributions to the Eighth International Congress of Slavists*, 1: Linguistics and Poetics (Zagreb and Ljubljana, 1978), pp. 379-407.

Matich, Olga. 'Zinaida Gippius and the Unisex of Heavenly Existence'. *Die Welt der Slaven*, 19/20 (1974-1975), pp. 98-104.

-----. *Paradox in the Religious Poetry of Zinaida Gippius*. Munich: Wilhelm Fink Verlag, 1972.

Pachmuss, Temira. *Zinaida Hippius: An Intellectual Profile*. Carbondale: Southern Illinois University Press, 1971. One of the best works on Hippius to date.

-----. 'Zinaida Hippius: A Modern Hypatia'. In S. D. Cioran, W. Smyrniw, and G. Thomas (eds.). *Studies in Honor of Louis Shein*. Hamilton, Ontario: McMaster University Printing Services, 1983.

Zlobin, Vladimir. *A Difficult Soul: Zinaida Gippius*. Simon Karlinksy, ed., intro. and notes. Berkeley: University of California Press, 1980.

'I. Grekova' See Venttsel below.

'Elena Guro' – See Notenberg.

Natalia Il'ina

Il'ina, Nataliia. *Belogorskaia krepost'* [The Belogorsk Fortress]. Moscow: 1989. A collection of her satirical prose from 1955-1985.

Vera Inber (1890-1972)

Inber, Vera. 'Nightingale and Rose' *North American Review*, 266 (March 1981), pp. 48-50.

Nadezhda Khvoshchinskaia ('V. Krestovskii'. 1824-1889)

Khvoshchinskaia, Nadezhda. *Povesti i rasskazy* [Novellas and Stories]. 2 eds. Moscow: 1963; Moscow: 1984.

Anna Kirpishchikova (1838-1927)

Kirpishchikova, Anna. *Izbrannye proizvedeniia* [Selected Works]. 2 eds. Molotov, 1951; Sverdlovsk, 1963.

Aleksandra Kollontai (1872-1952). See Russia section II above (Clements, Ingemanson, Itsel, Kollontai) and Autobiography.

Kollontai, Alexandra. *A Great Love.* New York: Pantheon, 1981. 'A Great Love'. 'Thirty-Two Pages', and 'Conversation Piece'.

Bammer, Angelika. 'Women and Revolution: Their Theories, Our Experience'. *Bucknell Review,* 27, no. 1 (1982), pp. 143-56. The article compares Kollontai's *Svobodnaia liubov'* to Christa Wolf's *Nachdenken über Christa T.* and Shih Ming's 'Fragment from a Lost Diary' from a feminist perspective.

Faure, Christine. 'The Utopia of the New Woman in the Work of Alexandra Kollontai and Its Impact on the French Feminist and Communist Press'. In Judith Friedlander et al. (eds.). *Women in Culture and Politics: A Century of Change.* Bloomington: Indiana University Press, 1986, pp. 376-89.

Ingemanson, Birgitta. 'The Political Function of Domestic Objects in the Fiction of Aleksandra Kollontai'. *SR,* 48, no. 1 (1989), pp. 71-82.

Anna Korvin-Krukovskaia (1843-1887) See Naginski below under Kovalevskaia.

Sofia Kovalevskaia (1850-1891). See Russia, section II above (Hibner, Kochina) and Autobiography below.

Naginski, Isabelle. 'A *Nigilistka* and a *Communarde*: Two Voices of the Nineteenth-Century Russian Intelligentka'. In Avriel H. Goldberger (ed.). *Woman as Mediatrix: Essays on Nineteenth-Century Women Writers. Prepared under the Auspices of Hofstra University.* Westport, CT: Greenwood, 1987, pp. 145-58. The article describes the fates of Kovalevskaia and her sister Anna Korvin-Krukovskaia.

Nadezhda Kozhevnikova.

Baigushev, A. 'Preodolenie: O proze Nadezhdy Kozhevnikovoi [Overcoming: The Prose of Nadezhda Kozhevnikova]'. *Molodaia gvardiia* (March 1984), pp. 265-75.

Egorova, E. 'Mirazh prisutsviia [The Mirage of Presence]'. *Oktiabr'* (August 1983), pp. 202-3. About Kozhevnikova's *Elena prekrasnaia* [Fair Helen].

Elizaveta Kuz'mina-Karavaeva

Gakkel', Sergei. *Mat' Mariia (1891-1945)* [Mother Maria (1891-1945)]. Paris: YMCA-Press, 1980.

Lavrov, A. V. and A. N. Shustov. 'Poema E. Iu. Kuz'minoi-Karavaevoi o Mel'mote skital'tse [E. Iu. Kuz'mina-Karavaeva's Narrative Poem about Melmoth the Wanderer]'. *Pamiatniki kul'tury*. Leningrad: 1986-1987, pp. 77-102.

Mikulina, Elena. *Mat' Mariia* [Mother Maria]. 2d ed., Moscow: 1988. Novel based on the life of the Russian poet and nun who died in a Nazi concentration camp.

Shustov, A. 'Doch' Rossii [A Daughter of Russia]'. *Belye nochi*. Leningrad: 1985, pp. 198-227.

Inna Lisnianskaia

Lisnianskaia, Inna. *Stikhotvoreniia: Na opushke sna* [Poems: On the Edge of Sleep]. Ann Arbor, MI: Ardis, 1984.

Nadezhda Lokhvitskaia ('Teffi', 1875-1952)

'Teffi', Nadezhda. *All About Love*. Darra Goldstein, tr. Ann Arbor, MI: Ardis, 1985.

Haber, Edythe C. 'Teffi's *Adventure Novel*'. In Julian Connolly and Sonia Ketchian (eds.). *Studies in Honor of Vsevolod Setchkarev*. Columbus, OH: Slavica, 1987.

Vera Lourie

Lourie, Vera. *Stichotvorenija – Poems*. Thomas R. Beyer, Jr., ed. and intro. Berlin: Berlin Verlag-Arno Spitz, 1987.

Maria Markovich ('Marko Vovchok', 1834-1907)

'Marko Vovchok'. *Sobranie sochinenii* [Collected Works]. 3 vols.
Moscow: 1957.

-----. *Ukrainian Folk Stories*. N. Pedan-Popil, tr. N. B. Timothy, ed.
Saskatoon: Western Producer Prairie Books, 1983.

-----. *Skazki i byl': Istoricheskie skazki i bytovye rasskazy* [Tales and Truth:
Historical Tales and Stories from Real Life]. Kiev: 1988. Stories in
Ukrainian and Russian.

Elizaveta Mnatsakanova (b. 1922)

Janecek, Gerald J. 'Paranomastic and Musical Techniques in
Mnacakanova's "Rekviem"'. *SEEJ*, 31, no. 2 (1987), pp. 202-21.
Introduction to avant-garde poet Elizaveta Arkad'evna Mnatsakanova
'notable for her application of musical forms to poetry and for her focus
on paronomasia as a dominant poetic technique'.

Yunna Moritz

Three Russian Poets: Margarita Aliger, Yunna Moritz, Bella Akhmadulina.
Elaine Feinstein, tr. New York: Persea Books, 1979.

Evdokia Nagrodskaia (1866-1930)

Dalton, Margaret. 'Istoricheskii roman E. A. Nagrodskoi *Reka vremen* [E.
A. Nagrodskaia's Historical Novel *The River of Time*]', *Novyi zhurnal*,
165 (December 1986), pp. 186-206.

-----. 'A Russian Best-Seller of the Early Twentieth Century: Evdokiya
Apollonovna Nagrodskaya's *The Wrath of Dionysus*'. In Connolly and
Ketchian (eds.). *Studies in Honor of Vsevolod Setchkarev*. See Haber
above.

-----. 'Evdokija Nagrodskajas Beziehungen zum russischen Symbolismus:
Liebe, Mystik und Feminismus [Evdokia Nagrodskaia's Ties to Russian
Symbolism: Love, Mysticism and Feminism]'. In V. Setschkareff, P.
Rehder and H. Schmid (eds.). *Ars Philologica Slavica: Festschrift für
Heinrich Kunstmann*. Munich: Verlag Otto Sagner, 1988, pp. 64-74.

Galina Nikolaeva (1914-1963)

Nikolaeva, Galina. *Gibel' komandarma i drugie rasskazy* [The Army Commander's Death and Other Stories]. Moscow: 1945.

Aleksandrova, A. 'Vsia zhizn' – bitva v put' [Life Is a Running Battle]'. *Znamia* (May 1984), pp. 217-33.

Chashchina, Liudmila, '"Otkrytaia nastezh' dusha cheloveka. . ." ["The Human Soul is Wide Open . . ."]'. *Neva* (June 1985), pp. 160-1. Biographical elements in Nikolaeva's poetry.

Strel'tsova, E., 'Preodolenie [Overcoming]'. *Literaturnoe obozrenie* (May 1985), pp. 62-4.

Eleonora Notenberg ('Elena Guro', 1877-1913)

Guro, Elena. *The Little Camels of the Sky*. Kevin O'Brien, tr. Ann Arbor, MI: Ardis, 1983.

-----. *Selected Prose and Poetry*. Anna Ljunggren and Nils Ake Nilsson, eds. Stockholm: Almqvist and Wiksell, 1988.

Banjanin, Milica. 'The Use of Metonymy in the Works of Elena Guro'. *Forum at Iowa on Russian Literature*, 1 (1976), pp. 70-82.

-----. 'Nature and the City in the Works of Elena Guro'. *SEEJ*, 30, no. 2 (Summer 1986), pp. 230-46.

-----. 'Looking Out, Looking In: Elena Guro's Windows'. Josip Matešić and Erwin Wedel (eds.) *Festschrift für Nikola R. Pribić'*. Neuried: Hieronymus, 1983, pp. 3-17.

Baschmakoff, Natalia. '"Nad krainei prizivnoi polosoi...": Mestnost' i prostranstvo v tvorchestve Eleny Guro ["Over the Farthest Calling Zone . . .": Locality and Space in Elana Guro's Works]'. *Studia Slavica Finlandensis*, 4 (1987), pp. 1-34.

Avdot'ia Panaeva (1819-1893)

Gregg, Richard. 'A Brackish Hippocrene: Nekrasov, Panaeva, and the "Prose of Love"'. *SR*, 34, no. 4 (December 1975), pp. 731-51.

Sofia Parnok

Parnok, Sovia. *Sobranie stikhotvorenii* [Collected Poems]. S. Poliakova, ed., intro., & annot. Ann Arbor, MI: Ardis, 1979.

Poliakova, S. *[Ne]zakatnye ony dni: Tsvetaeva i Parnok* [Days Without End: Tsvetaeva and Parnok]. Ann Arbor, MI: Ardis, 1983.

Karolina Pavlova (1807-1893)

Pavlova, Karolina. *Polnoe sobranie sochinenii* [Complete Works]. Moscow-Leningrad: 1939; 2nd ed., 1964.

-----. *A Double Life,* Barbara Heldt, tr. and intro. (Reprint: Oakland, CA: Barbary Coast Books, 1987).

Greene, Diana. 'Karolina Pavlova's "Tri dushi"': The Transfiguration of Biography'. *Proceedings of the Kentucky Foreign Language Conference 1984: Slavic Section*, 2, no. 1. Lexington, KY: Department of Russian and Eastern Studies, Univeristy of Kentucky, 1984. Greene identifies prototypes for the three women poets depicted as the American Lucretia Davidson, the French Delphine Gay, and Pavlova herself and discusses Pavlova's pessimism about the fate of women poets.

Irina Ratushinskaia (b. 1954)

Ratushinskaia, Irina. *Grey Is the Color of Hope.* Alyona Kojevnikov, tr. New York: Alfred A. Knopf, 1988. Gallant and affecting memoir of incarceration in a labor camp from 1983-1986 as a prisoner of conscience in the *gulag*.

------. *Pencil Letter.* New York: Alfred A. Knopf, 1988. These poems, written during Ratushinskaia's three years in a labor camp and immediately after her release, are ill-served by ten miscellaneous translators, but her spirit and sensitivity show through.

-----. *Skazka o trekh golovakh/A Tale of Three Heads. Short Stories in Russian and English.* Diane Nemec-Ignashev, tr., intro., and afterword. Tenafly, NJ: Hermitage, 1986.

-----. *Vne limita.* Frankfurt/M: Posev, 1986. In English as: *Beyond the Limit.* Frances Padorr Brent and Carol J. Avins, trs. Evanston, IL: Northwestern University, 1987.

Evdokia Rostopchina (1811-1858)

Rostopchina, Evdokiia. *Talisman.* Viktor Afanas'ev, ed. and intro. Moscow: 1987. A selection including poetry, Rostopchina's play 'Neliudimka [The Unsociable Woman]', and autobiographical materials.

-----. *Stikhotvoreniia. Prosa. Pis'ma* [Poems. Prose. Letters]. Moscow: 1986.

Pedrotti, Louis. 'The Scandal of Countess Rostopcina's Polish-Russian Allegory'. *SEEJ*, 30, no. 2 (Summer 1986), pp. 196-214. Rostopchina's 'Nasil'nyi brak' and its stormy reception.

Zinaida Shakovskaia

Beaujour, Elizabeth Klosty. *Alien Tongues: Bilingual Russian Writers of the 'First' Emigration.* Ithaca, NY: Cornell University Press, 1989. The work focuses on Vladimir Nabokov, Elsa Triolet, Vasily Yanovsky, and Zinaida Shakovskaia.

Lidia Seifullina (1889-1954)

Seifullina, Lidia. *Povesti i rasskazy* [Novellas and Stories]. Moscow: 1989.

Marietta Shaginian (1888-1982)

Shaginyan, Marietta. *Mess Mend – The Yankees in Petrograd* S. D. Cioran, tr. Ann Arbor, MI: Ardis, 1989.

'Teffi' – See N. Lokhvitskaia

Sofia Tolstaia

Smoluchowski, Louise. *Lev and Sonya: The Story of the Tolstoy Marriage.* New York: Putnam's, 1987. From the Russian sources Smoluchowski has written a credible, even-handed account of the Tolstoys' forty-eight years together, the moral of which seems to be that diaries are dangerous weapons best kept under lock and key.

Tat'iana Tolstaia

Tolstaia, Tat'iana. *Na zolotom krylt'se sideli*. Moscow: 1987. In English as: *On the Golden Porch*. Antonina W. Bouis, tr. New York: Alfred A. Knopf, 1989.

Goscilo, Helena. 'Tat'iana Tolstaia's "Dome of Many-Coloured Glass": The World Refracted through Multiple Perspectives'. *SR*, 47, no. 2 (Summer 1988), pp. 280-90.

'I. Grekova'. 'Rastochitel'nost' talanta [An Extravaganza of Talent]'. *Novyi mir* (January 1988), pp. 252-6. A somewhat bemused review of Tolstaia's *On the Golden Porch* .

Elsa Triolet. See Zinaida Shakovskaia, above.

Marina Tsvetaeva (1892-1941)

Tsvetaeva, Marina. *Poklonis' Moskve . . .: Poeziia. Proza. Dnevniki. Pis'ma* [Greetings to Moscow: Poems. Prose. Diaries. Letters]. A. A. Saakiants, comp., intro. & annot. Moscow: 1989.

-----. *Izbrannye proizvedeniia* [Selected Works]. Moscow-Leningrad, 1965.

-----. 'October in a Railway Car'. *RLT*, no. 22 (Winter 1988), pp. 55-64.

-----. *Selected Poems*. Elaine Feinstein, tr. & intro. New York: E. P. Dutton, 1987.

-----. 'The Devil'. Marian Schwartz, tr. *Yale Review*, 70 (Spring 1981), pp. 363-70.

-----. *A Captive Spirit: Selected Prose*. J. Marin King, ed. Ann Arbor, MI: Ardis, 1980.

Chvany, Catherine V. 'Translating One Poem from a Cycle: Cvetaeva's "Your Name is a Bird in My Hand" from "Poems to Blok"'. In Crone and Chvany (eds.). *New Studies in Russian Language and Literature*.

Faryno, Jerzy. *Mifologizm i teologizm Tsvetaevoi ('Magdalina' – Tsar'-devitsa – Pereulochki)* [Tsvetaeva's Mythologism and Theologism ('Magdalina' – Tsar-Maiden – Back Lanes)]. Vienna: Wiener Slawistischer Almanach, 1985. '. . . an ambitious and highly successful attempt at mapping a large area of Tsvetaeva's poetics' – *SR*, 46, no. 1 (Spring 1987), pp. 165-6.

Feinstein, Elaine. *A Captive Lion: The Life of Marina Tsvetaeva*. New York: E. P. Dutton, 1987. A good sketch of the poet's stormy character; short on knowledge of Russian sources.

Gove, Antonina Filonov. 'The Feminine Stereotype and Beyond: Role Conflict and Resolution in the Poetics of Marina Tsvetaeva'. *SR*, 36, no. 2 (June 1977), pp. 231-55.

Hasty, Olga Peters. 'Tsvetaeva's Onomastic Verse'. *SR*, 45, no. 2 (Summer 1986), pp. 245-56.

Heldt, Barbara. 'Two Poems by Marina Tsvetaeva from *Posle Rossii*', *Modern Language Review*, 77, no. 3 (1982), pp. 679-87.

Karlinsky, Simon. *Marina Tsvetaeva: The Woman, Her World and Her Poetry*. Cambridge: Cambridge University Press, 1985. A definitive portrait of the poet and her troubled times.

-----. 'Tsvetaeva's Turn'. *London Review of Books* (12 November 1987). A generous review of Feinstein's *A Captive Lion* and *Selected Poems*, which is in essence a concise guide to Tsvetaeva scholarship, including a 'magisterial' biography by Irma Kudrova completed in the early 1980s but not yet published in the USSR.

Proffer, Ellendea (ed.). *Marina Tsvetaeva. A Pictorial Biography*. 3rd ed. Ann Arbor, MI: Ardis, 1988.

Razumovsky, Maria. *Marina Tsvetaeva: Mif i Dejstvitel'nost* [Marina Tsvetaeva: Myth and Actuality]. E. N. Razumovskaja-Sajn-Witgenstejn, tr. London: Overseas Publications Interchange Ltd., 1983. This study, originally in German, covers Tsvetaeva's life primarily in historical context.

Saakiants, Anna. *Marina Tsvetaeva. Stranitsy zhizni i tvorchestva (1910-1922)* [Marina Tsvetaeva. Pages from Her Life and Work (1910-1922)]. Moscow: 1986.

Shveitser, Viktoria. *Byt i bytie Mariny Tsvetaevoi* [Marina Tsvetaeva's Way of Life and Her Being]. Fontenay-aux-Roses, France: Syntaxis, 1988.

Sloane, David A. '"Stikhi k Bloku": Cvetaeva's Poetic Dialogue with Blok'. In Crone and Chvany (eds.). *New Studies in Russian Language and Literature*. See Chvany above.

Taubman, Jane. *A Life Through Poetry: Marina Tsvetaeva's Lyric Diary*. Columbus, OH: Slavica, 1989.

Tavis, Anna. 'Lives and Myths of Marina Tsvetaeva'. *SR*, 47, no. 3 (Fall 1988), pp. 518-21.

Gertrude Vakar

Lee, Nicholas. 'Gertrude Vakar'. In Anna Lisa Crone and Catherine V. Chvany (eds.). *New Studies in Russian Language and Literature*. Columbus, OH: Slavica, 1987.

Inna Varlamova

Varlamova, Inna. *A Counterfeit Life*. Ann Arbor: Ardis 1989. 'A good presentation of the significance mastectomy can have in a woman's life, combined with a sober reassessment of the life of the intelligentsia in the 1960s' – Helena Goscilo.

Zinaida Vengerova (1867-1941)

Rosenthal, Charlotte. 'Zinaida Vengerova: Modernism and Women's Liberation'. *Irish Slavonic Studies*, 8 (1987), pp. 97-105.

Elena Sergeevna Venttsel ('I. Grekova'. b. 1907). See also under Tat'iana Tolstaia above.

Grekova, Irina. *Russian Women*. New York: Harcourt Brace Jovanovich, 1983. 'Ladies' Hairdresser' and 'The Hotel Manager'.

-----. *Ship of Widows*. New York: Doubleday, 1987; paperback, Topsfield, Mass.: Salem House, 1987.

'Marko Vovchok' -- See Markovich above.

Iulia Voznesenskaia

Voznesenskaya, Julia. *The Women's Decameron*. W. B. Linton, tr. New York: Atlantic Monthly Press, 1986.

-----. *The Star Chernobyl*. Alan Myers, tr. London: Quartet Books, 1987.

Lidia Zinov'eva-Annibal (d. 1907)

Nikol'skaia, T. D. *'Tvorcheskii put' L. D. Zinov'evoi-Annibal* [L. D. Zinov'eva-Annibal's Creative Path]'. *Blokovskii sbornik*, 8 (1988), pp. 123-137. 'The Soviet scholar... tentatively posits an alternative modernist female prose tradition that includes the writings of Gippius, Zinov'eva-Annibal, and Elena Guro'. – Charlotte Rosenthal.

Autobiography and memoirs.

General:

Engelstein, Laura. 'In A Female Voice (Review Essay)'. *SR*, 44, no. 1 (Spring 1985), pp. 104-107. A review of 'memoirs of women who lived through the Stalinist ordeal': Raisa Berg, Maria Ioffe, Irina Kichanova-Lifshits, Lidia Shatunovskaia, Nadezhda and Maia Ulanovskie, and Lidia Zhukova (see below for citations).

Anthologies:

Five Sisters Against the Tsar. Barbara Alpern Engel and Clifford Rosenthal, trans. & eds. Alix Kates Shulman, fwd. New York: Alfred A. Knopf, 1975. Re-issued: Winchester, MA: Allen & Unwin, 1987. Updated bibliography. Excerpted memoirs of the revolutionary movements of the 1870s-1880s by Vera Figner, Vera Zasulich, Praskovia Ivanovskaia, Olga Liubatovich, and Elizaveta Kovalskaia.

Individual:

Andreyev, Olga Chernov. *Cold Spring in Russia.* Arthur Miller, fwd. Michael Carlisle, tr. Ann Arbor, MI: Ardis, 1978. A memoir by the adopted daughter of Socialist Revolutionary Victor Chernov of a happy childhood in France and Italy and the repression and hardship the family endured in the new Soviet state.

Alexander, Tania. *Tania: Memories of a Lost World.* Bethesda, MD: Adler and Adler, 1988.

Berg, Raisa. *Sukhovei: Vospominaniia genetika* [Dry Hot Wind: A Geneticist's Reminiscences]. New York: Chalidze Publications, 1983.

Blok, Liubov'. 'Facts and Myths about Blok and Myself'. Lucy Vogel, tr. and ed. *Blok: An Anthology of Essays and Memoirs.* Ann Arbor, MI: Ardis, 1982.

Bonner, Elena. *Alone Together.* Alexander Cook, tr. New York: Alfred A. Knopf, 1986.

Dashkova, E. R., *Zapiski. Pis'ma sester Vil'mot iz Rossii* [Notes: The Wilmot Sisters' Letters from Russia]. Moscow: 1987. A combined edition of the memoirs of the famous 18th-century. Russian woman educator and intellectual (translated from French) and letters written by her English friends the Wilmots during their visits to Russia in the 1800s.

-----. *The Memoirs of Princess Dashkov.* Kyrill Fitzlyon, ed. & tr. London: J. Calder, 1958.

Natal'ia Dolgorukaia

Townsend, Charles E. *The Memoirs of Princess Natal'ja Borisovna Dolgorukaja.* Columbus, OH: Slavica, 1977. The text in Russian and English and extensive commentaries on background and language of the memoirs of the young princess (1714-1771) who followed her disgraced husband into exile.

Nakhimovsky, A. 'A Syntactic, Lexicological and Stylistic Commentary on the Memoirs of Princess Natalja Borisovna Dolgorukaja'. *Folia Slavica,* 8, nos. 2/3 (1987), pp. 272-301.

Durova, Nadezhda. *The Cavalry Maid.* David Lapeza and John Mersereau, tr. and intro. Ann Arbor, MI: Ardis 1988.

-----. *The Cavalry Maiden: Journals of a Russian Officer in the Napoleonic Wars.* Mary Fleming Zirin, tr., intro. & notes. Indiana University Press and Angel Books [London], 1988. Durova's journals of her nearly ten years in the tsarist cavalry offer an interesting mixture of cultural and military history and personal revelation (intended and inadvertent).

Ginzburg, Evgenia. *Journey into the Whirlwind.* Paul Stevenson and Max Hayward, trs. New York: Harcourt Brace Jovanovich, 1967.

-----. *Within the Whirlwind.* Ian Boland, tr. Heinrich Böll, intro. New York: Harcourt Brace Jovanovich, 1981. Two remarkable works of autobiography that testify to the resilience of the human spirit under imprisonment in the Gulag.

Ioffe, Maria. *Odna noch': Povest' o pravde* [One Night: A Tale about Truth]. New York: Chalidze Publications, 1978.

Kern, A. P. *Vospominaniia o Pushkine* [Reminiscences of Pushkin]. Moscow, 1987.

Kichanova-Lifshits, Irina. *Prosti menia za to, chto ia zhivu* [Forgive Me for Living]. New York: Chalidze Publications, 1982.

Kollontai, Alexandra. *The Autobiography of a Sexually Emancipated Communist*. New York: Herder and Herder, 1971. See also entries under Clements and Farnsworth, Pt. II and Individual Authors above.

Kosterina, Nina. *The Diary of Nina Kosterina*. Mirra Ginsburg, tr. New York: Crown Publishers, 1968. The teenage years from 1936-1941 of a girl who became a partisan in World War II.

Kovalevskaya, Sonya. *A Russian Childhood*. Beatrice Stillman, tr., ed., and intro. New York: Springer-Verlag, 1979. It also includes an analysis of Kovalevskaya's mathematics by P. Y. Kochina (see Pt. II above).

Krupskaia, Nadezhda. See Pt. II above.

Labzina, A. E. *Vospominaniia, 1763-1819* [Reminiscences, 1763-1819]. St. Petersburg: 1914; reprinted, Judith C. Zacek, intro. Cambridge, MA: Oriental Research Partners, 1974.

Mandelstam, Nadezhda. *Hope Against Hope*. Max Hayward, tr. New York: Atheneum, 1970.

-----. *Hope Abandoned*. Max Hayward, tr. New York: Atheneum, 1974.

-----. *Kniga tret'ia* [The Third Book]. Paris: YMCA-Press, 1987. Mandel'stam's three volumes of classic memoirs testify for her generation of destroyed writers.

Odoevtseva, Irina. 'Na beregakh Nevy [On the Banks of the Neva]'. *Zvezda* (February 1988), pp. 94-131. Odoevtseva's memoirs of the years 1918-1922, now published for the first time in the USSR.

Orlova, Raisa, *Vospominaniia o neproshedshem vremeni* [Reminiscences of Times Not Past]. Ann Arbor, MI: Ardis, 1983. In English as: *Memoirs,* S. D. Cioran, tr. New York: Random House, 1983.

Piatnitskaya, Julia. *Diary of a Bolshevik's Wife* (in Russian). Benson, VT: Chalidze Publications, 1987.

Pregel, Sofia Iul'evna. *Moe detstvo* [My Childhood]. 3 vols. Paris: Novosel'e, 1973-1975.

Roskina, Nataliia. *Chetyre glavy: Iz literaturnykh vospominanii* [Four Chapters: From Literary Reminiscences]. Paris: YMCA-Press, 1980.

Shatunovskaia, Lidia. *Zhizn' v Kremle* [Life in the Kremlin]. New York: Chalidze Publications, 1982.

Shtakenschneider, Elena A. *Dnevnik i zapiski, 1854-1866* [Diary and Notes, 1954-1966]. Moscow: 1934; reprinted, Barbara Engel, intro. Newtonville, MA: Oriental Research Partners, 1980.

Skariatina, Irina. *Little Era in Old Russia*. Indianapolis, IN: Bobbs-Merrill, 1934.

Tiutcheva, Anna Fedorovna. *Pri dvore dvukh imperatorov: Vospominaniia, dnevnik, 1853-1882* [At the Court of Two Emperors: Reminiscences, Diary, 1853-1882]. Moscow: 1928-1929; reprinted, A. J. Rieber, intro. Cambridge, MA: Oriental Research Partners, 1975).

Tsvetaeva, Anastasia. *Moi Sibir'* [My Siberia]. Moscow: 1988.

Ulanovskie, Nadezhda and Maia. *Istoriia odnoi sem'i* [The History of One Family]. New York: Chalidze Publications, 1982.

Vodovozova, E. N. *Na zare zhizni* [At the Dawn of Life]. 2 vols. E. S. Vilenskaia, ed., intro. & notes. Moscow: 1987. Memoirs, originally published in 1911, of childhood and institute years (1844-1862) by a prolific Russian writer of educational works for the young.

Zhemchuzhnaia, Zinaida. *Puti izgnaniia: Ural, Kuban', Moskva, Kharbin, Tian'tszin. Vospominaniia* [Paths of Exile: The Urals, Kuban, Moscow, Kharbin, Tian'tsin. Reminiscences]. Elena Iakobson, fwd & aftwd. Tenafly, NJ: Hermitage, 1987.

Zhigalova, Ol'ga. *Veter vetku klonit* [The Wind Bends the Branch]. Paris: 1948. In English as: *Across the Green Past*. Tatiana Balkoff Downe, tr. Chicago: Regnery, 1952.

Zhukova, Lidia. *Epilogi* [Epilogues]. New York: Chalidze Publications, 1983.

V. *The Arts in Russia and the USSR.*

Bannour, Wanda. 'Vierges et sorcières: Les Héroïnes d'opéra de Tschaikowsky'. *Littérature et opéra*. Grenoble: Presse universitaire de Grenoble, 1987.

Faleeva, V. A. 'Zhenskii personazh v russkoi narodnoi vyshivke [Women Characters in Russian Folk Embrodery]'. *Fol'klor i Etnografiia Russkogo Severa*. Leningrad: 1973, pp. 119-31.

Money, Keith. *Anna Pavlova: Her Life and Art*. New York: A. Knopf, 1982. A detailed, lively account of the life and career of the world's most renowned ballerina. Richly illustrated with photographs.

Mochalov, Lev. *The Female Portrait in Russian Art*. Leningrad: 1974. A beautifully illustrated edition. The introduction contains some astute observations on images of women in the Russian visual arts.

Mayne, Judith. *Kino and the Woman Question: Feminism and Soviet Silent Film*. Columbus, OH: Ohio State University Press, 1989. 'Using five specific films [Eisenstein's *Strike*, Pudovkin's *Mother*, Room's *Bed and Sofa*, Ermler's *Fragment of an Empire*, and Vertov's *Man with a Movie Camera*] Mayne demonstrates how the distinctive characteristics of emerging Soviet film – in particular, the theory and practice of montage – are informed simultaneously by a rigid sexual division of the universe and a complex view of the relationship between gender and class'.

Navailh, F. 'L'image de la femme dans les films de guerre'. *Essais sur le discours sovietique*. (Universite de Grenoble III), 6 (1986).

Tatyana Nazarenko. Album. Alexander Morozov, comp. & intro. John Crowfoot, tr. Leningrad: 1988. An album of reproductions by a contemporary Soviet artist.

Rosenberg, Karen. 'Shepitko'. *Sight & Sound: International Film Quarterly*, 56, no. 2 (Spring 1987), pp. 119-22. Rosenberg traces the slippery path between compromise and dissidence in the films of the prominent Soviet director Larisa Shepitko (d. 1979).

Rubinger, Krystyna (ed.). *Russian Women Artists of the Avantgarde. 1910-1930*. Cologne: Galerie Gmurzynska, 1979. Illustrations and text in English, German and French.

Central and East Europe

General

Bohachevsky-Chomiak, Martha. 'Socialism, Feminism and Nationalism: The First Stages of Women's Organizations in the Eastern Part of the Austrian Empire'. *Women in Eastern Europe and the Soviet Union*. New York: Praeger, 1980.

Brak u narodov tsentral'noi i iugo-vostochnoi Evropy [Marriage among the Peoples of Central and Southeast Europe]. Moscow: 1988. Collected articles published by the USSR AS Institute of Ethnography on marriage rites in Central and Southeast Europe Yugoslavia, Czechoslovakia, Poland, Bulgaria, Rumania, Albania, and Greece.

Braum, Charlotte. 'What Made Yetta Work? The Economic Role of Eastern European Women in the Family'. *Response. The Jewish Woman: An Anthology*, 18 (Summer 1973), pp. 32-38.

Denich, Bette S. 'Sex and Power in the Balkans'. In Michelle Z. Rosaldo and Louise Lamphere (eds.). *Woman, Culture and Society*. Stanford: Stanford University Press, 1974, pp. 243-62.

Erlich, Vera S. 'The Southern Slav Patriarchal Family'. *Sociological Review*, 32 (1940), pp. 224-41.

Goddesses and Their Offspring: 19th and 20th Century East European Embroideries (Roberson Center for the Arts & Sciences, 30 Front Street, Binghamton NY 13905). Lavishly illustrated catalog for exhibit held in the spring of 1987; it includes articles by Mary Kelly and Natalie Moyle.

Hammel, Eugene A. 'The Zadruga as Process'. In Peter Laslett (ed.). *Household and Family in Past Time*. Cambridge: Cambridge University Press, 1972.

Heitlinger, Alena. *Reproduction, Medicine and the Socialist State*. London: Macmillan, 1986; New York: St. Martin's Press, 1987. 'The book examines the social limits on the freedom whether, and in what manner, to reproduce in state socialist societies in Eastern Europe, especially Czechoslovakia'.

Jenson, J. H. 'The Changing Balkan Family'. *International Archives of Ethnography*, 51 (1968), pp. 20-48.

Kelly, Mary B. *Goddess Embroideries of Eastern Europe*. Winona, MN: Northland Press, 1989. One cavil: like so many books these days, this one did not get the editing it needed. That is minor, however, compared to the wealth of materials and information it contains. Kelly, an artist and Professor of Fine Arts, has done a fabulous job of research and comparison of goddess images throughout Eastern Europe and the European USSR, and her text combines facts, insights, and a charming personal narrative of her voyages of discovery. A detailed table of contents partially makes up for the lack of an index.

See Kerblay, section II above.

Kulisić, S. 'O postanku slovenske zadruge [On the Origin of the Slavic Zadruga]', *Bilten Instituta za Proučvanje Folklor,* Sarajevo, 3 (1955), pp. 43-7.

Moseley, P. E. 'The Distribution of the Zadruga within Southeastern Europe'. *The Joshua Starr Memorial Volume, Jewish Social Studies*, 5 (1953), pp. 219-30.

-----. 'The Peasant Family: The Zadruga of Communal Joint-Family in the Balkans and its Recent Evolution'. In Caroline F. Ware (ed.). *The Cultural Approach to History*. New York: Columbia University Press, 1940, pp. 95-108.

Reiter, Norbert (ed.). *Die Stellung der Frau auf dem Balkan: Beiträge zur Tagung vom 3.-7. September 1985 in Berlin* [The Position of Balkan Women: Contributions to the Conference of September 3-7, 1985, in Berlin]. Wiesbaden: Otto Harrasowitz, 1987.

Rihtman Auguštin, Dunja. 'Patriarchalismus heute [Patriarchy Today]'. In Pedro Ramet (ed.). *Yugoslav in the 1980s*. Boulder, CO: Westview Press, 1985.

Wolchik, Sharon and Alfred G. Meyer (eds.) *Women, State and Party in Eastern Europe*. Durham, NC: Duke University Press, 1985. Studies in women's history in East European countries, presented from a cross-cultural perspective. Richly diverse in topics, subjects, and data, the essays are coherently held together by consideration of common themes.

The concluding section examines views of women in literature, folklore, and research.

Yedlin. See Russia, section III above.

Bulgaria

Courtin, H. 'Les personnages masculin et feminin dans la chanson folklorique bulgare'. *Revue des études slaves*, 60, no. 2 (1988), pp. 439-44.

Dmitrova, Blaga. Poems in: *Poets of Bulgaria,* William Meredith, ed. Greensboro, NC: Unicorn Press, 1986.

Farkašová, Etela. 'Vera Mutafčievová: *Sedma vo dvojici'*. *Slovenské Pohl'ady na Literature a Umenie*, 98, no. 7 (1982), pp. 46-7. A discussion of women characters in the Slovak translation of Mutafchieva's novel.

Czechoslovakia

Born Unwanted: Developmental Effects of Denied Abortion. H. P. David, Z. Dytrych, Z. Matějček, and V. Schuller, eds. Prague: Avicena, 1988.

See Heitlinger, Central and East Europe, General above.

Hruby, Peter. 'Tři české čarodějky slov aneb sovětská polnice v živote a dile Marie Majerove, Marie Pujmanove a Jarmily Glazarove [Three Czech Sorceresses of Words or the Council Horn in the Life and Work of Maria Majerová, Maria Pujmanová and Jarmila Glazarová]'. *Zapad*, 9, no. 2 (April 1987), pp. 28-30.

Hykisch, Anton. 'Iva Hercíková: Stín spánku [Iva Hercikova: The Shadow of a Dream]'. *Slovenské Pohl'ady na Literature a Umenie*, 98, no. 9 (1982), p. 133. Images of women in the work of the Czech writer Iva Hercíková.

Lenčo, Ján. 'Miroslav Hanuš: Tři variace na lásku [Miroslav Hanuš: Three Variations on Love]'. *Slovenské Pohl'ady na Literature a Umenie*, 98, no. 10 (1982), pp. 121-24. Treatment of women in love.

Unterberger, Betty M. 'The Arrest of Alice Masaryk'. *SR*, 33, no. 1 (March 1974), pp. 91-106.

Winkler, Tomas. 'Eva Kováčová: Vážne vážne [Secret Passions]'. *Slovenské Pohl'ady na Literature a Umenie*, 98, no. 11 (1982), pp. 122-3.

Wolchik, Sharon L. 'The Status of Women in a Socialist Order: Czechoslovakia, 1948-1978'. *SR*, 38, no. 4 (Dec. 1979), pp. 583-602.

German Democratic Republic

History and Contemporary Society:

Dölling, Irene. *'Culture and Gender'*. In M. Rueschemeyer and C. Lemke (eds.). The Quality of Life in the German Democratic Republic: Change and Development in a State Socialist Society. Armonk, NY: M. E. Sharpe, 1989, pp. 27-47.

Altbach, Edith et al. (eds.). *German Feminism: Readings in Politics and Literature*. Albany: State University of New York Press, 1984.

Nickel, Hildegarde M. 'Sex-Role Socialization in Relationships as a Function of the Division of Labor: A Sociological Explanation for the Reproduction of Gender Differences'. In Rueschemeyer and Lemke (eds.). *The Quality of Life in the German Democratic Republic: Change and Development in a State Socialist Society*, pp. 48-58. See Dölling above.

Shaffer, Harry G. *Women in the Two Germanies: A Comparative Study of a Socialist and a Non-Socialist Society*. New York: Pergamon Press, 1981.

Literature:

Bossinade, Johanna. 'Haus und Front: Bilder des Faschismus in der Literatur von Exil- und Gegenwartsautorinnen: Am Beispiel Anna Seghers, Irmgard Keun, Christa Wolf und Gerlind Reinshagen [Home and Front: Depictions of Fascism in the Literature of Women Writers in Exile and on the Scene. The Example of Anna Seghers, Irmgard Keun, Christa Wolf and Gerline Reinshagen]'. *Neophil*, 70, no. 1 (1986), pp. 92-118.

Grobbel, Michaela. 'Kreativitat und Re-vision in den Werken Irmtraud Morgners von 1968 bis 1972 [Creativity and Re-vision in the Writings of

Irmtraud Morgner from 1968 to 1972]'. *New German Review*, 3 (1987), pp. 1-16.

Grunenberg, Antonia. 'Träumen und Fliegen: Neue Identitätsbilder in der Frauenliteratur der DDR [Dreaming and Flying: New Depictions of Identity in the Women's Literature of the DDR]'. *Probleme deutscher Identität: Zeitgenössische Autobiographien: Identitätssuche und Zivilisationskritik*. Bonn: Bouvier, 1983, pp. 157-84.

Hartinger, Walfried and Christel Hartinger. 'Does "Women's Literature" Deal Exclusively with Problems of Women?: Women's Liberation and the Relation of the Sexes in the GDR Literature of the 1970s'. *Journal of Popular Culture*, 18, no. 3 (1984), pp. 53-69.

Herminghouse, Patricia. 'Der Autor nämlich ist ein wichtiger Mensch': Zur Prosa ["The Writer Is of Course an Important Person": Prose]'. In Hiltrud Gnüg and Renate Möhrmann (eds.). *Frauen – Literatur – Geschichte: Schreibende Frauen vom Mittelalter bis zur Gegenwart*. Stuttgart: Metzler, 1985, pp. 338-53.

Heuenkamp, Ursula. 'Poetisches Subjekt und weibliche Perspektive: Zur Lyrik [Poetic Subject and the Feminine Perspective: Poetry]'. In Gnüg and Möhrmann (eds.). *Frauen – Literatur – Geschichte: Schreibende Frauen vom Mittelalter bis zur Gegenwart*, pp. 354-66. See Herminghouse above. East German women poets.

Hildebrandt, Irma. 'Emanzipation Ost: Frauenliteratur in der DDR' [Emancipation East: Women's Literature in the DDR]', *Deutsche Studien*, 24, no. 94 (June 1986), pp. 121-32.

Hilzinger, Sonja. 'Weibliches Schreiben als eine Aesthetik des Widerstands: Uber Christa Wolfs "Kassandra"-Projekt [Women's Writing as an Aesthetic of Resistance: Christa Wolf's "Kassandra" Project]'. *Neue Rundschau*, 96, no. 1 (1985), pp. 85-101. East German literature by women novelists.

Kaufmann, Eva. 'Die Frauenfrage in der Literatur der DDR [The Woman Question in the Literature of the DDR]'. *Zeitschrift für Germanistik*, no. 2 (May 1983), pp. 210-12.

Kuhn, Anna K. 'Peter Hacks' *Ein Gesprach in Hause Stein uber den abwesenden Herrn von Goethe*: A Feminist Reinterpretation of the *Geniebegriff*.' *Germanic Review*, 60, no. 3 (1985), pp. 91-97.

O'Brien, Mary-Elizabeth. 'The Divided Woman: Female Protagonists in Contemporary GDR Literature'. *New German Review*, 1 (1985), pp. 41-54.

Rosenberg, Dorothy. 'Another Perspective: Young Women Writers in the GDR'. *Studies in GDR Culture and Society, 4: Selected Papers from the Ninth New Hampshire Symposium on the German Democratic Republic.* Lanham, MD: University Press of America, 1984, pp. 187-98.

Christa Wolf

Cicora, Mary A. 'Language, Identity, and the Woman in *Nachdenken über Christa T.*: A Post-Structuralist Approach'. *Germanic Review*, 57, no. 1 (1982), pp. 16-22.

Dollenmayer, David, 'Generational Patterns in Christa Wolf's *Kindheitsmuster*'. *German Life and Letters*, 39, no. 3 (1986), pp. 229-34.

Gattens, Marie-Luise. 'Mädchenerziehung im Faschismus: Die Rekonstruktion der eigenen Geschichte in Christa Wolfs *Kindheitsmuster* [A Girl's Education in Fascism: The Reconstruction of One Person's Story in Christa Wolf's *Kindheitsmuster*]'. In Sylvia Wallinger and Monika Jonas (eds.). *Der Widerspenstigen Zahmung: Studien zur bezwungenen Weiblichkeit in der Literatur vom Mittelalter bis zur Gegenwart.* Innsbruck: Universität, 1986.

Jurgensen, Manfred (ed.). *Wolf: Darstellung, Deutung, Diskussion* [Wolf: Representation, Meaning, Discussion]. Berne: Francke, 1984.

Kuhn, Anna K. *Christa Wolf's Utopian Vision: From Marxism to Feminism.* Cambridge: Cambridge University Press, 1988.

Mauser, Wolfram (ed.) *Erinnerte Zukunft: 11 Studien zum Werk Christa Wolfs* [The Future Remembered: 11 Studies of the Writings of Christa Wolf]. Wurzburg: Koenighausen, 1985.

Pickle, Linda Schelbitzki, 'Christa Wolf's *Kassandra*: Parallels to Feminism in the West'. *Critique*, 28, no. 3 (Spring 1987), pp. 149-57.

512   *Mary F. Zirin*

Hungary

Volgyes, Ivan and Nancy Volgyes. *The Liberated Female: Life, Work, and Sex in Socialist Hungary*. Boulder, CO: Westview Press, 1977. A book with valuable data and bibliography, already outdated in its application of narrow Western feminist criteria to Hungarian society.

Poland

Ariadne's Thread: Polish Women Poets. Susan Bassett and Piotr Kuhiwczak, tr. Chingford, UK: Forest Books, 1988.

Baranowska, Magorzata. 'Pod czarną gwiazdą [Under a Black Star]'. *Twórczość*, no. 10 (October 1985), pp. 71-80.

Caldwell, Patrice. 'Earth Mothers or Male Memories: Wilhelm, Lem, and Future Women'. In Jane B. Weedman (ed.). *Women Worldwalkers: New Dimensions of Science Fiction and Fantasy*. Lubbock: Texas Tech Press, 1985.

Cottam, K. J. 'Veterans of Polish Women's Combat Battalion Hold Reunion'. *Minerva*, (Winter 1986), pp. 1-7.

Fink, Ida. *A Scrap of Time and Other Stories*. Madeline G. Levine with Francine Prose, tr. New York: Pantheon, 1987.

Gasiorowska, Xenia. 'Portrait of a Lady in Polish Positivist Fiction'. *SEEJ*, 20 (1976), pp. 261-72.

Goscilo. See Russia, section IV above.

Lorence-Kot, Bogna. *Child-Rearing and Reform: A Study of the Nobility in Eighteenth-Century Poland*. Westport, CT: Greenwood Press, 1985. '. . . an authentic, if harsh, description of the old Polish family based on memoir material' – *SR*, 45, no. 2 (Summer 1986), pp. 376-7.

Marzin, Florian F. 'Stanislaw Lem und die Frauen: Versuch der Erklärung einer Abwesenheit [Stanislaw Lem and Women: Attempt to Explain an Absence]'. In Florian Marzin (ed). *Stanislaw Lem: An den Grenzen der Science Fiction und daruber hinaus*. Meitingen: Corian, 1985, pp. 171-8.

Moskiewicz, H. *Inside the Gestapo: A Young Woman's Secret War*. London: Orbis Books, 1986.

Mrozowska, Jadwiga Toeplitz. *Stoneczne życie* [A Sunny Life]. Krakow: 1963. The travels of a Polish woman between the two world wars.

Peretz, Maya. 'Bondage and Freedom in the Voice of Polish Women Poets'. In Marilyn Gaddis Rose, (ed.). *Translation Perspectives III: Selected Papers, 1985-1986.* National Resource Center for Translation and Interpretation, SUNY-Binghamton, 1987.

Teczarowska, Danuta. *Deportation into the Unknown.* London: Merlin Books, 1985. The memoirs of a doctor who was deported from Poland to Siberia in WW II.

Romania

Bulgur, Raymonde A. 'Helen Vacaresco (1866-1947). *In the Gold of the Evening'. Journal of the American Romanian Academy of Arts and Sciences*, 10 (1987), pp. 202-12.

Moskoff, William. 'Sex Discrimination, Commuting, and the Role of Women in Rumanian Government'. *SR*, 37, no. 3 (September 1978), pp. 440-56.

Pakula, Hannah. *The Last Romantic: A Biography of Queen Marie of Roumania.* New York: Simon & Schuster, 1984. '. . . a solid piece of research that may be supplemented but will not be superceded for a long time' – Glen E. Torey, *SR*, 45, no. 2 (Summer 1986), pp. 390-1.

Yugoslavia

History and Contemporary Society:

Denich, Bette. 'Women, Work and Power in Modern Yugoslavia'. In Alice Schlegel (ed.). *Sexual Stratification: A Cross-Cultural View.* New York: Columbia University Press, 1977.

Despot, Blaženka. 'Women and Self-Management'. *Questions Actuelles du Socialisme.* Belgrade, 3 (1981).

Drakulić, Slavenka. 'Six Mortal Sins of Yugoslav Feminism'. In Robin Morgan (ed.). *Sisterhood is Global.* New York: Anchor Press/Doubleday, 1984.

Društveni položaj žene i razvoj porodice u socijalistickom samoupravnom društvu [Social Postition of Woman and Development of Family Within Socialist Self-Managed Society]. Ljubljana: Komunist, 1979.

Erlich, Vera S. *Family in Transition: A Study of Three Hundred Yugoslav Villages*. Princeton, NJ: Princeton University Press, 1966.

-----. 'Phases in the Evolution of Family Life in Jugoslavia'. *Sociological Review*, 37 (1945), pp. 50-64.

Feldman, Andrea. 'Der Verband universitätsgebildeter Frauen Jugoslawiens (1927-1939) [Association of University Women of Yugoslavia (1927-1939)'. In Jutta Dalhoff, Uschi Frey and Ingrid Schöll (eds.). *Frauenmacht in der Geschichte*. Dusseldorf: Schwann, 1986.

-----. 'Eine alternative Frauengruppe in Zagreb: Zwischen Aktivismus und Frauenforschung [An Alternative Women's Group in Zagreb; Between Activism and Women's Studies]'. In Wiener Historikerinnen (eds.). *Die ungeschriebene Geschichte*. Vienna: Wiener Frauenverlag, 1984.

First, Ruža. 'National Liberation Struggle and Women of Yugoslavia'. In Matia Mies and Rhoda Reddock (eds.). *National Liberation and Women's Liberation*. The Hague: Institute of Social Studies, 1982.

Halpern, Joel. *A Serbian Village*. New York: Columbia University Press, 1956.

Iveković, Rada. 'Yugoslav Neofeminism'. In Morgan (ed.). *Sisterhood is Global*. See Drakulic above.

Jančar, Barbara. 'New Feminism in Yugoslavia'. In Pedro Ramet (ed.). *Yugoslavia in the 1980s*'. Boulder, CO: Westview Press, 1985.

-----. 'Women in the Yugoslav National Liberation Movement: Overview'. *Studies in Comparative Communism*, nos. 2-3 (1981), pp. 143-64.

Karanović, M. 'Nekoliko velike porodične zadruge u Bosnia i Hercegovini [Several Large Family Zadrugas in Bosnia and Hercegovina]'. *Glasnik Zemaljskog Muzeja*, 41 (1929), pp. 63-80.

Moseley, P. E. 'Adaptation for Survival: The Varžić Zadruga'. *Slavonic and East European Review*, 21 (1943), pp. 147-73.

Pusić, E. 'The Family in the Process of Social Change in Yugoslavia'. *Sociological Review*, 5 (1957), pp. 207-24.

Simić, Andrei. 'Management of the Male Image in Yugoslavia'. *Anthropological Quarterly*, 42 (1969), pp. 89-101.

-----. 'Machismo and Cryptomatriarchy: Power, Affect and Authority in the Contemporary Yugoslav Family'. *Ethos*, 11, no. 1/2 (1983), pp. 66-86.

Sklevicky, Lydia. 'More Horses than Women: On the Difficulties of Founding Women's History in Yugoslavia'. *Gender & History*, 1, no. 1 (1989), pp. 68-75.

-----. 'Emancipated Integration or Integrated Emancipation: The Case of Post-Revolutionary Yugoslavia'. In Arina Angerman et al. (eds.). *Current Issues in Women's History*. London: Routledge, 1989.

-----. 'Der Utopie entgegen – Das Bild der "Neuen Frau" im Befreiungskrieg Jugoslawsiens 1941-1945 [Towards Utopia – The Image of the "New Woman" in the Yugoslav Liberation War 1941-1945]'. In Dalhoff, Frey and Schöll (eds.). *Frauenmacht in der Geschichte*. See Feldman above.

-----. 'Emanzipiatorische und integrative Tendenzen in der Frauenbewegung Jugoslawiens, 1918-1953 [Emancipatory and Integrational Tendencies in the Yugoslav Women's Movement, 1918-1953]'. In Wiener Historikerinnen (eds.) *Die ungeschriebene Geschichte*. See Feldman above.

Winner, Irene. *A Slovenian Village: Žerovnica*. Providence, RI: Brown University Press, 1971.

Literature:

Coote, Mary P. 'Women's Songs in Serbo Croatian', *Journal of American Folklore*, 90 (July 1977), pp. 331-38.

Juricić, Zelimir. 'All of Alija's Women: Andrić's Realization of *Ex Ponto* Visions'. In Evelyn Bristol (ed.). *East European Literature. Papers from the Second World Congress for Soviet and East European Studies*. Oakland, CA: Berkeley Slavic Studies, 1982, pp. 23-32.

Parun, Vesna. *Selected Poems*. Dasha Culic Nisula, ed. & tr. University Center, MI: Green River Press, 1985.

Šali, Severin (ed.). *Lirika slovenskih pesnic, 1849-1984* [Poetry by Slovenian Women Poets, 1849-1984]. Ljubljana: Mladinska knjiga, 1985.

Notes on Contributors

Efi Avdela (Ph.D., University of Paris VII, Jussieu) is a lecturer in Modern Greek Social History in the Department of Primary Education at the University of Thessaloniki [Salonika] in Greece. Her 1989 dissertation, 'Rapports salariaux et division sexuelle du travail: Les femmes fonctionnaires dans la première moitié du 20e siècle en Grèce [Salaried Relations and the Sexual Division of Labour: Women Civil Servants in Greece in the First Half of the 20th Century]', will be published in Greek in 1990. She is also the co-author, with Angelica Psarra, of *Ho pheminismos stin Hellada tou Messopolemou. Mia Anthologia* [Feminism in Greece between the Wars: An Anthology] (1985). She is a member of the editorial collective of the feminist journal *Dini*, and is currently investigating the tobacco industry and tobacco workers in Greece between the wars.

Bolanle Awe (D. Phil., Oxford University) has been Professor of History since 1976 and Director of the Institute of African Studies since 1983 at the University of Ibadan, Nigeria. She is also the co-ordinating chairperson of the Women's Research and Documentation Centre in that Institute. She served as a Member of the Cabinet and Commissioner for Education in her state government, 1975-1978. She has published widely on Nigerian history and is editing *Nigerian Women in Historical Perspective* (in press).

Aparna Basu (Ph.D., University of Cantab) is Professor of History, University of Delhi, India. Her publications include *Growth of Education and Political Development in India, 1898-1920* (1974); *Essays in the History of Indian Education* (1982); 'The Role of Women in India's Struggle for Freedom' (1976); and 'A Century's Journey: Women's Education in Western India: 1820-1920' (1988). She is on the editorial advisory boards of the *Indian Economic and Social History Review* and *Gender & History*.

Ida Blom (Ph.D., University of Bergen) is Professor of Women's History at the University of Bergen. She has published books on family planning (1980) and changes in obstetrics during the nineteenth and twentieth centuries (1988) as well as a substantial number of articles on Norwegian social, medical, and women's history. She is general editor of a five-volume Scandinavian 'Global History of Women', scheduled for publication in 1990-1991.

Gisela Bock (Dr. Phil., Free University of Berlin; Habilitation, Technical University of Berlin) is Professor of Women's and Gender History at the University of Bielefeld (West Germany) and external professor at the European University Institute (Florence). Her publications include *Thomas Campanella* (1974), *Die 'andere' Arbeiterbewegung in den USA, 1905-1922* (1976); *Zwangssterilisation im Nationalsozialismus: Studien zur Rassenpolitik und Frauenpolitik* (1986); *Il corpo delle donne* (1987); and a series of theoretical articles on women's and gender history in *Geschichte und Gesellschaft* and *Gender & History*.

Mary Cullen (M.A., University College, Dublin) teaches history at St. Patrick's College, Maynooth, County Kildare. Her main research interests lie in Irish women's history. She has published a range of articles, including 'Telling It Our Way: Feminist History', in Liz Steiner-Scott (ed.), *Personally Speaking* (1985). Her book, *Girls Don't Do Honours: Irish Women in Education in the Nineteenth and Twentieth Centuries*, appeared in 1987.

Nanna Damsholt (Dr. Phil., University of Copenhagen) is an Associate Professor at the Centre for Feminist Studies and Institute for History, University of Copenhagen, Denmark. She has published extensively on women and images of women in medieval Denmark. She has recently written on Danish medieval historiography (1000-1560) and is now working on her contribution to the all-Scandinavian Women's Global History.

Cécile Dauphin et al. The contributors to this jointly-authored article all participated in an ongoing interdisciplinary seminar concerning the problematics of 'masculine/feminine', held at the Centre de Recherches Historiques (CRH) of the Centre Nationale de la Recherche Scientifique (CNRS) in Paris, France. Their names and affiliations at the time of publication are listed below: *Cécile Dauphin* (CRH – CNRS); *Arlette Farge* (CRH – CNRS); *Geneviève Fraisse* (Philosophy – CNRS); *Christiane Klapisch-Zuber* (CRH – École des Hautes Études en Science Sociale [EHESS]); *Rose-Marie Lagrave* (Sociology – EHESS); *Michelle Perrot* (History – University of Paris VII); *Pierrette Pezerat* (CRH – EHESS); *Yannick Ripa* (History – INRP); *Pauline Schmitt-Pantel* (History – University of Paris VII); *Danièle Voldman* (Institute d'Histoire du Temps Present – CNRS).

Paula Di Cori (Dr. Phil., University of Rome) is a research associate and Lecturer in Contemporary History at the University of Urbino, Italy. She was a founding editor, in 1981, of <u>Memoria</u>, the first Italian women's history journal, and she has published many essays on twentieth-century Italian women's history and methodology. She was a visiting lecturer at the Harvard Divinity School (1982-83) and a visiting fellow at the Centre for European Studies, Harvard University (1983). Her present interests are in the field of feminist theory and the visual representations of men and women in nineteenth- and twentieth-century Italy.

Andrea Feldman (M.A., University of Zagreb, Yugoslavia) is an historian who was employed by the Institute for the History of the Workers' Movement in Zagreb. She is currently a doctoral candidate at Yale University in the Department of History. In the 1980s she was a co-ordinator of the first feminist group in Yugoslavia. As a founding member of the first women's history group in Zagreb, she has published articles on various feminist issues and has presented a number of scholarly papers at feminist conferences.

Ingeborg Fløystad (Dr. Phil, University of Bergen) is a senior university researcher in Bergen, Norway. Her main research has been in economic and social history, including living conditions of Norwegian workers in the eighteenth century, and the work of women and children 1870-1940.

Ute Frevert (Dr. Phil. and *Habilitation*, University of Bielefeld) was a fellow at the Institute for Advanced Study in Berlin, Federal Republic of Germany (1989-1990), and now holds the Chair in Women's History at the Free University of Berlin. Her publications include *Krankheit als politisches Problem 1770-1880* (1984), *Frauen-Geschichte* (1986), which has been translated as *Women in German History: From Bourgeois Emancipation to Sexual Liberation* (1989), (ed.) *Bürgerinnen und Bürger – Geschlechterverhältnisse im 19. Jahrhundert* (1988), and a series of articles on women's history in journals and edited volumes. **Heide Wunder** (Dr. Phil., University of Hamburg) is professor of early modern social and constitutional history at the University of Kassel. Her publications include *Siedlungs- und Bevölkerungsgeschichte der Komturei Christburg (13. – 16. Jahrundert)* (1968), *Die bäuerliche Gemeinde in Deutschland* (1986), and a series of articles on rural society in medieval and early modern Germany as well as on women's history. **Christina Vanja** (Dr. Phil, University of Kassel) is archivist of the Landeswohlfahrtsverband Hessen at Kassel, Germany. Her publications include *Herkunft, soziale Lage und Lebensweise der Frauen in den Zisterzienserinnenklöstern Caldern und Georgenberg und dem*

Prämonstratenserinnenstift Hachborn in Hessen im späten Mittelalter (1984), and a series of articles on women's history, especially on women's work in late medieval and early modern Germany.

Patricia Grimshaw (Ph.D., University of Melbourne) teaches women's studies and American history at the University of Melbourne, Australia. Her research has focused on women's lives in nineteenth-century Australia, New Zealand and the Pacific. She is the author of *Women's Suffrage in New Zealand* (1972, revised ed., 1987); co-author of *Colonial Frontiers and Family Fortunes* (1988); and co-editor of *Australian Women: Feminist Perspectives* (1981) and of *Families in Colonial Australia* (1985). Her new book, *Paths of Duty: American Missionary Wives in Nineteenth-Century Hawaii*, has just been published.

Francisca de Haan (M.A., University of Amsterdam) has a position as assistent-in-opleiding ('aio') at Maatschappij-geschiedenis, Eramus University Rotterdam. She expects to finish her Ph.D. thesis in 1991 on the feminisation of the office and the historical construction of the female office worker in the Netherlands. Her main fields of interest are the history of women's work, of the women's movement and of spinsters and lesbians.

Noriyo Hayakawa (M.A., Tokyo Metropolitan University) is currently teaching at the University of Chiba, Japan. She is completing a Ph.D. in German philosophy. She is co-editor of *Yoskikawa Kobunkan* [Women's History in Japan], of *Otuki Shoten* [Japanese Women in Showa Era], and edits a monthly review of history.

Anne-Lise Head-König (Docteur ès lettres, University of Geneva) is Professor of Economic History at the University of Geneva, Switzerland. Her research includes historical demography with special reference to inheritance patterns and marriage strategies, illegitimacy and forced marriage.

Yvonne Hirdman (Ph.D., University of Stockholm) is Professor of Women's History, at the University of Gothenberg, Sweden. She has published on the history of the Swedish Communist Party, the labour movement, housework, and maternity hospitals, and is now engaged in a reconsideration of the Swedish welfare state from the standpoint of the gender system. Her most recent article, on Alva Myrdal, appeared in *Kvinnovetenskaplig tidskrift* (1988).

Brigitte Mazohl-Wallnig (Ph.D. and *Habilitation*, University of Salzburg) is Assistant Professor of History at the Historical Institute, University of Salzburg, Austria, and has also taught at the University of Trento, Italy. She is a co-editor of the newly-founded journal (1990) *L'Homme: Zeitschrift für feministische Geschichtesswissenschaft.*

Mary Nash (Ph.D., Universidad de Barcelona) is Associate Professor of History in the Department of Contemporary History and Director of the Centre for Research on Women's History at the University of Barcelona, Spain. She is the author of several books and articles on women in the Spanish working-class movement and the Spanish Civil War. She has published historiographical essays and a series of articles on her present area of research: the politics of reproduction and eugenics in early twentieth-century Spain.

Maria Beatriz Nizza da Silva (Ph.D., University of São Paulo, Brazil) is Professor in the Department of History at the same University. She specialises in sociocultural history, and in family and women's history of colonial Brazil. Her recent published works include a study of the *System of Marriage in Colonial Brazil* (1984) and a series of articles on the historiography of women's history in Brazil.

Karen Offen (Ph.D., Stanford University) is an independent scholar, affiliated with the Institute for Research on Women and Gender, Stanford University (Stanford, California, USA). She has co-edited two documentaries, *Victorian Women: A Documentary Account of Women's Lives in Nineteenth-Century England, France, and the United States* (1981), and *Women, the Family, and Freedom: The Debate in Documents, 1750-1950* (2 vols., 1983) and is presently completing a book on the woman question in modern France. Her most recent publications focus on the comparative history of feminism and the historiography of women and the French Revolution.

Ruth Roach Pierson (Ph.D., Yale University) is Professor of Women's History and Feminist Studies at the Ontario Institute for Studies in Education, Toronto (Ontario), Canada, where she has served as Head of the Centre for Women's Studies in Education. She is the author of *'They're Still Women After All': The Second World War and Canadian Womanhood* (1986); editor of *Women and Peace: Theoretical, Historical and Practical Perspectives* (1987); and co-editor of *Delivering Motherhood: Maternal Ideologies and Practices in the Nineteenth and Twentieth Centuries* (1990), and of *No Easy Road: Women in Canada, 1920s to 1960s* (1990).

522

Petra Rantszch (Dr. Phil.) teaches history and German language at the 'Clara Zetkin' College of Education in Leipzig, and is member of the Research Centre 'Women in History' at this college. She has published *Helene Stöcker – Between Pacifism and Revolution* (1984) and has written on the history of the progressive bourgeois women's movement in Germany, especially from 1918 to 1933. She is now investigating the life and work of Bertha von Suttner. Erika Uitz earned her Ph.D. in 1957 and her Habilitation in 1965 at the Karl Marx University in Leipzig. Since 1969 she has been a Professor of History and was, until recently, at the Institute for Historical Research, Academy of Sciences of the former German Democratic Republic, Berlin. She has published on popular movements in the Middle Ages and on medieval urban history. Since 1977 she has worked almost exclusively on the role of women in the Middle Ages, publishing *Die Frau in der mittelalterlichen Stadt* (1988), forthcoming in English in 1990.

Jane Rendall (Ph.D., University of London) is Senior Lecturer in the History Department and the Centre for Women's Studies, University of York, England. Her interests lie in the history of feminism and women's history in eighteenth and nineteenth-century Britain. She has recently published *The Origins of Modern Feminism* (1985); edited *Equal or Different* (1987); and co-edited (with Susan Mendus), *Sexuality and Subordination* (1989). She is the book review editor for the journal *Gender & History*.

Phyllis Stock-Morton (Ph.D., Yale University) is Professor of French History and Women's History at Seton Hall University, New Jersey, USA. She is the author of *Better Than Rubies: A History of Women's Education* (1978); and *Moral Education for a Secular Society: The Development of Morale Laique in Nineteenth-Century France* (1988). During her presidency of the Conference Group on Women's History of the United States, she participated in the organising of the IFRWH/FIRHF.

Regina Wecker (Dr. Phil. I, University of Basel) studied at the Free University of Berlin, University of Aberdeen/Scotland, and at the University of Basel/Switzerland. She is now Lecturer on Modern History and Swiss History at the University of Basel and is doing research on the history of women's labour and on the history of divorce in Switzerland, preparing her *Habilitation*. She was co-organiser of the first meeting of Swiss women historians and co-editor of *Frauen. Zur Geschichte weiblicher Arbeits- und Lebensbedingungen in der Schweiz* (1984), and of *Auf den Spuren weiblicher Vergangenheit* (1985), both special issues of Swiss historical reviews devoted to women's history. Her other publications include *Frauen in der Schweiz. Von den Problemen einer Mehrheit* (1983), *Lasst hören aus neuer Zeit. Gesellschaft, Wirtschaft und Politik im Kanton Luzern seit dem Ersten Weltkrieg* (1986), and various articles on women's history in Switzerland.

Mary F. Zirin (Ph.D., University of California, Los Angeles) is an independent researcher who lives in Altadena, California, USA. Her current investigations focus on the lives and works of nineteenth-century Russian women writers. She is the founding editor of *Women East-West*, an English-language newsletter for Slavic and Central/East European women's studies, and has recently translated Nadezhda Durova's *The Calvary Maiden: The Journals of a Russian Officer in the Napoleonic Wars* (1988).

INDEX

Beth McAuley